# WE CANNOT REMAIN SILENT

**A book in the series**
*Radical Perspectives: A Radical History Review book series*

Series editors: Daniel J. Walkowitz, New York University
Barbara Weinstein, New York University

# WE CANNOT REMAIN SILENT

Opposition to the
Brazilian Military Dictatorship
in the United States

James N. Green

DUKE UNIVERSITY PRESS

DURHAM AND LONDON 2010

© 2010 Duke University Press

All rights reserved

Printed in the United States of America on acid-free paper ∞

Designed by Heather Hensley

Typeset in Quadraat by Tseng Information Systems, Inc.

Library of Congress Cataloging-in-Publication Data appear
on the last printed page of this book.

**Miriam D. Green**
*in memoriam*

**and to Suiá, Yama, Pablo, and Sonya,**
*the next generation*

# CONTENTS

## ABOUT THE SERIES

History, as radical historians have long observed, cannot be severed from authorial subjectivity, indeed from politics. Political concerns animate the questions we ask, the subjects on which we write. For over thirty years the *Radical History Review* has led in nurturing and advancing politically engaged historical research. Radical Perspectives seeks to further the journal's mission: any author wishing to be in the series makes a self-conscious decision to associate her or his work with a radical perspective. To be sure, many of us are currently struggling with the issue of what it means to be a radical historian in the early twenty-first century, and this series is intended to provide some signposts for what we would judge to be radical history. It will offer innovative ways of telling stories from multiple perspectives; comparative, transnational, and global histories that transcend conventional boundaries of region and nation; works that elaborate on the implications of the post-colonial move to "provincialize Europe"; studies of the public in and of the past, including those that consider the commodification of the past; histories that explore the intersection of identities such as gender, race, class and sexuality with an eye to their political implications and complications. Above all, this book series seeks to create an important intellectual space and discursive community to explore the very issue of what constitutes radical history. Within this context, some of the books published in the series may privilege alternative and oppositional political cultures, but all will be concerned with the way power is constituted, contested, used, and abused.

"Speaking truth to power" is a political strategy long celebrated by historians of radical and oppositional movements, and it is at the very heart of James N. Green's gripping study of opposition to the Brazilian military dictatorship, starting with the title: *We Cannot Remain Silent*. Chronicling the emergence of a hemispheric human-rights discourse and activism in response to illegal detentions and torture by the military regime that ruled Brazil from 1964 to 1985, Green gives particular attention to a diverse group of academics, clerics, and exiles based in the United States who sought to counteract press censorship in Brazil and media indifference in the United States by publicizing the way power was being used and abused by the Brazilian government. Not only does Green's research disclose an aspect of (U.S.-based) opposition to the regime that had previously gone largely unacknowledged, but it also demonstrates how a transnational approach to this history can reveal and reconstitute a series of narratives that are crucial for understanding the politics of this era.

We Cannot Remain Silent is an exemplary piece of radical historical research in its attention to multiple perspectives and innovative narrative strategies. Green is well aware that a conventional historical account dedicated to the activities—however admirable—of North American academics and clerics could be (mis)read as a tale of enlightened First World actors riding to the rescue of Third World victims. Thus, he repeatedly reminds his readers, in each chapter and its companion "capítulo," that these protests abroad cannot be understood apart from the activism of Brazilian opponents of the regime and apart from their relentless efforts to call attention to what was happening, sometimes to themselves, in the jail cells and interrogation chambers of the military dictatorship. Green's study offers us historical insights into everything from the articulation of a genuinely transnational human-rights discourse as a result of Latin America's multiplying, U.S.-backed military regimes, to the transformation of the field known as "area studies." And in an academic world where most historians now think beyond national borders, We Cannot Remain Silent prompts us to carefully consider the political implications of our increasingly transnational scholarship.

## ACKNOWLEDGMENTS

My personal relationship with Brazil is deeply embedded in this book. Soon after graduating from college, I moved to a working-class neighborhood in Philadelphia with seven other young radical Quakers to live in a commune and engage in a weekly Latin American study group. Each of us chose to report on a different country. For some reason, I selected Brazil. In gathering material for my report, I discovered the publications of the North American Congress on Latin America (NACLA) and an interview with the Brazilian student leader Jean Marc Van der Weid, published by the Chicago Area Group on Latin America. They captured my imagination and started me off on a quest to learn more about the country, its history, and its political situation during the military regime. I am very grateful to Pamela Haines, Alan Blood, Ellen Forsythe, Peter Blood, Ruth Reber, Shay Long, and Eli Hochstetler (who has since passed away) for that intense two-year experience. At some point, I sent a letter to the Committee against Repression in Brazil (CARIB). After receiving a response, I journeyed to Washington, D.C., where I met Marcos Arruda, a principal character in this book. Marcos was, at the time, a Brazilian political exile and one of the leaders of the antidictatorship movement in the United States. I was immediately struck by his charismatic and gentle nature, and he encouraged me to help out in the campaigns being organized about Brazil. He also introduced me to his sister, Martinha, who has become a lifelong friend.

I played a marginal role in working against the Brazilian military regime in the early 1970s. In gathering signatures to help obtain the release of the jailed activist Manoel da Conceição, I soon discovered how little people in the United States knew about Brazil. The coup d'état in Chile turned my attention toward that country, and between September 1973 and December 1975 I worked endless hours first in Philadelphia and then in the San Francisco Bay Area to educate the U.S. public about the military regime of Augusto Pinochet. Lisa Kokin and Lorraine Thiebaud have remained close friends from that period, and they helped inspire this work.

In January 1976, I embarked on a grand tour of Latin America with a bag slung over my shoulder and my life savings held snugly in a money belt. I traveled through Central America, spent six months in Colombia, and then journeyed down the Amazon River and through the Brazilian Northeast, learning the Portuguese language and absorbing Brazilian culture along the way. I ended up living in São Paulo, where I taught English. There, I was fortunate to stumble into a network of Brazilian organizing clandestinely and later openly against the military regime. Many of those friendships have lasted to this day. I will always be indebted to Hélio Goldsztejn for introducing me to that world. Some of the people with whom I worked in the 1970s were instrumental in helping me research this book three decades later. I want to thank Henrique Carneiro, Lauro Ávila Pereira, and especially Edméa Jafet, who has been a generous host for my many interludes in São Paulo. She is one of the most amazing women I know.

Ana Celeste Indolfo, Vera Lúcia Hess de Mello Lopes, Maria Luisa Falcão, and Sátiro Nunes at the National Archive and Cristiane Batista Santana and Larissa Rosa Correa at the State Arquive in São Paulo offered their invaluable assistance in uncovering material for this project. Fátima Neves and William Martins helped me trace references and locate crucial documents.

Over the years, I have had the immense pleasure of working with a broad array of fine Brazilian scholars who have supported this project with enthusiasm. In some cases, they have shared their research with me, helped me in archives, or introduced me to people who appear in this book. They have been universally generous with their warmth and time. They include Beatriz Kushnir, Carlos Fico, Celso Castro, Denise Rollemberg, Durval Muniz de Albuquerque, Fernando Henrique Cardoso, Helena Bocayuva, Isabel Lustosa, Jesse Jane Vieira de Sousa, João Roberto Martins, Filho, José Celso Castro Alves, Leôncio Martins Rodrigues, Lilia Moritz Schwarcz (my newest old friend), Luiz Raul Machado, Maria Paula Nascimento Araújo, and Tânia Pelligrini. Nadia Nogueira played a special role in helping me to finish the manuscript.

This project would not have been possible without initial funding from the American Council of Learned Societies. David M. Hays, the archivist for the Amnesty International Collection at the University of Colorado at Boulder Libraries, helped me find material on Brazilian political prisoners, while Emilio Bejel kindly hosted my stay in that city. Crueza Maciel generously shared the Brady Tyson archive with me. I am also deeply indebted to Sharon

Sievers, professor emerita at California State University, Long Beach, and the former chair of the history department, who supported this project and my academic career in so many ways. My thanks go out as well to Dorothy Abrahamse, who was the dean of the College of Liberal Arts at California State University, Long Beach, and the best academic administrator I have ever met. Joahana Villanueva and the interlibrary loan staff at California State University, Long Beach, also offered immeasurable support for my research. I am deeply grateful to my colleagues in the history department at Brown University.

One of the greatest pleasures in teaching at Brown has been working with amazingly talented students. Abigail Jones helped me shape the content of chapter 1, especially our joint research on Lincoln Gordon and U.S. support for the 1964 military coup d'état. Benjamin Brown and Natan Zeichner were superb research assistants who efficiently tracked down obscure references and hard-to-obtain newspaper and periodical references. Caroline Landau helped in the final phases of my research, kindly read the manuscript twice to make suggestions, and caught many typos and other errors. Writing this book while teaching and directing the Center for Latin American and Caribbean Studies at Brown University was a major challenge. Susan Hirsch has been a tireless and efficient program administrator, and I am appreciative of the support that Eliana Esteves, José Torrealba, Jennifer Lambe, and Christopher Hardy have provided the center to assist its growth over the last four years.

A number of colleagues who work on Brazil have been particularly munificent. I want to thank especially Barbara Weinstein, Jeffrey Lesser, Jeffrey Needell, Kenneth Serbin, Marshall Eakin, Paulo Sérgio Pinheiro, Sidney Chalhoub, Susan Quinlin, Timothy Power, and Zephyr Frank for their ongoing support of my academic career. One of the greatest honors of the last five years has been getting to know and work with Thomas E. and Felicity Skidmore. I want to thank Tom for reading the manuscript twice and making excellent suggestions for how to pare down the original 920 pages to a workable volume, and Felicity for being such a stalwart supporter of my enthusiastic and ambitious plans. I would also like to thank the anonymous readers at Duke University Press for their careful reading of the manuscript and the many detailed suggestions for how to improve the first version.

It would be impossible to acknowledge individually all of the book's protagonists who granted interviews, referred me to others, and shared their personal archives with me. They are all amazing people who have dedicated their lives to social justice. Each and every one of them has remained modest and humble about their own involvement in the multiple movements against the military regime. This is their story.

Finally, all my love and appreciation goes out to my extended Brazilian family, especially my three godchildren, to my dearest sister Marycarolyn G. France, who also carefully read the entire manuscript, to Karen Krahulik and Susan Allee, who trusted and believed in me, to my mother Miriam D. Green, who always supported me in each and every thing I have done in life and unfortunately did not live to see this book in print, and above all to my lifelong partner, Moshé Sluhovsky.

**Truth to tell,**

**we are all criminals**

**if we remain silent.**

———

Stefan Zweig (1881–1942),
letter to his wife, Friderike, 1918

Reenactment of "parrot's perch" interrogation method. Living Theater, *Seven Meditations on Political Sado-Masochism*.

# TROPICAL DELIGHTS AND TORTURE CHAMBERS, OR IMAGINING BRAZIL IN THE UNITED STATES

The rains grow heavier. Soon everything soaks through. The rivulets in the primeval forest fill up. The patter of rain is everywhere. We must be getting home.

Are these people cannibals? To us they are gentle friends. —**Harald Schultz, "Indians of the Amazon Darkness," National Geographic, May 1964**

For those Americans coming of age during World War II, Carmen Miranda personified Brazil. Her effervescent personality, ostentatious costumes, six-inch platform shoes, jangling jewelry, and ubiquitous headgear of turbans and fruit baskets projected a zany, carefree performer from an exotic tropical paradise. "Brazil's ambassador" to the United States represented the continent-sized country as a place filled with happy-go-lucky people who engaged in unending, ebullient Carnival celebrations set in a South American Eden. In the late 1950s, the Franco-Brazilian film production of *Black Orpheus* shifted international representations of Brazilian Carnival to the Rio de Janeiro's hillside slums. Carmen Miranda was white, originally hailing from Portugal, even though her American audiences may have read her as an exotic Latina who was somewhat racially and ethnically different. The cast of *Black Orpheus*, however, was unmistakably of African heritage and represented a different image of Brazil. Based on a romantic rendering of the Orpheus-Eurydice legend with the pulsating rhythms of Carnival festivities woven into the plot, *Black Orpheus* is arguably the film that most shaped international visions of Brazil in the twentieth century.[1] The breathtaking shots of Rio's Guanabara Bay captured from atop the surrounding hills and a magical soundtrack also introduced European and American audiences to bossa nova, a new musical style, and portrayed a country where racial tensions did not seem to underlie day-to-day interactions. In *Black Orpheus*, Rio de Janeiro (and by extension Brazil) is a lyrical land of amazing landscapes, majestic sunrises, and, yet again, fun-loving people.

In the early 1960s a middle-class beach beauty captured in the song "The Girl from Ipanema" joined Carmen Miranda and Rio's dark-skinned slum dwellers as an alluring presentation of an imagined tropical sexuality. For the U.S. audience for travelogues, *National Geographic* spreads and popular articles on Brazil, the ever-present backdrop of expansive Amazonian jungles, remote uncivilized Indians, and wild and lascivious Carnival celebrations framed notions of Brazil.[2] With a "tall, tanned, young and lovely" girl from Ipanema in the foreground slowly sambaing on Rio's sizzling sands, bossa nova offered a soundtrack to this fantasy that was smooth, syncopated, enticing, and inviting.

Seductive women and expansive Amazonian jungles were not the only images of Brazil cast onto the international landscape. Brazil was, indeed, a colorful country, but in the early 1960s U.S. Cold Warriors feared that it was ominously close to becoming "too red." The victory of the Cuban guerrilla movement in 1959 injected new energy and direction into Latin American nationalist and anti-imperialist movements. In Brazil, leaders of peasant leagues in the Northeast, sectors of the student movement, some junior officers and rank-and-file military, militant labor activists, and leftist intellectuals all found inspiration in the intransigence of the new Cuban regime that stood up to Washington's imperial arrogance in Latin America.[3]

To those in Brazil and abroad who favored the political, economic, and social status quo, a twist of political events in August 1961 caused particular alarm. President Jânio Quadros, the mercurial right-leaning politician, suddenly resigned after having served only seven months of his term. Next in line to succeed him was Vice President João Goulart, the leader of the Partido Trabalhista Brasileiro (Brazilian Labor Party, PTB), who had been elected to the second highest office in the land that year on a split ticket. Quadros's resignation stunned the nation and panicked right-wing civilians and generals alike, who attempted to block his left-leaning populist successor from assuming the presidency. Military maneuvers met resistance and collapsed. Goulart took office under a compromise agreement that limited his power as president.

The next two and a half years were a political and economic rollercoaster for Brazil. Goulart promoted a series of nationalist reforms, including a limit on foreign companies' profit remittances, and a modest land reform. Labor, peasants, students, and the left mobilized to demand radical social change. Goulart, himself a large landowner, was far from interested in leading a socialist revolution in Brazil, yet the Kennedy and Johnson administrations withdrew support from the leftward-moving federal government. At the same time, Washington funded the election of regional politicians opposed to the Goulart government and channeled foreign aid to governors sympathetic to U.S. interests.[4] Inflation soared, and conservative sectors of the middle class, backed by an equally conservative wing of the Catholic Church, mobilized against Goulart's rule. The increasingly polarized political situation provided the necessary conditions for the armed forces to stage a military coup on March 31, 1964. President Johnson was prepared to intervene directly to back the insurgent military leaders, but this proved unnecessary. Clandestine CIA and FBI operations, diplomatic overtures by U.S. ambassador Lincoln Gordon, and logistical backup by the Pentagon offered the required assurances that Washington would support the military's seizure of power. On April 2, 1964, at Gordon's insistence, Johnson recognized the interim government. Twenty-one years of military rule had begun.

The United States press gave near-unanimous support to the Johnson administration's lightning-speed recognition of the new military government and the coup leaders' anticommunist agenda. Reporters largely ignored the massive arrests of regime opponents, dubbing the change of power a "bloodless coup" that had avoided a civil war.[5] News from Brazil gave an uninformed U.S. public the impression that the new government had defended democracy from a communist assault. This notion merely reinforced the pervasive public sentiment in which 80 percent of U.S. citizens in 1964, an all-time high, feared communist threats when polled about foreign policy issues.[6] Very few in the United States protested the 1964 military coup. Even such outspoken senators as Wayne Morse of Oregon, who already questioned Johnson's Vietnam War policies, congratulated the president for his quick recognition of the new government, heralded the change in regime, dismissed any accusations of U.S. intervention, and denied that the military had installed a dictatorship.[7] News coverage of the political events in Brazil soon disappeared from the front pages of U.S. newspapers and magazines.

In the spring of 1974, ten years after the military seized power in Brazil, thousands crowded into New York City's Madison Square Garden for "An Evening with Dr. Salvador Allende" to protest the September 11, 1973, military coup d'état in Chile. The homage to the recently deposed socialist president featured the folk singer Phil Ochs and a cameo performance by Bob Dylan. The eclectic public of political activists and an array of music fans grew silent as fifteen members of the Living Theater Collective quietly walked on stage. Dressed in black, the actors formed a half circle, sat with their legs crossed in the semi-lotus position, and began to chant softly. As seconds slowly slid by, the sound of their individual tones merged into a collective drone that calmed the audience and focused their attention on the performance unfolding in a slow-motioned pantomime. Almost imperceptibly, one of the actors, of obvious African heritage, gradually rose and began to look fearfully to the left and right, his dreadlocks whipping in the air as his head moved slowly back and forth in apparent panic. At a snail's pace, two other actors menacingly approached. As if caught in a silent black-and-white movie running at half its normal speed, the two men gradually lunged at him, grabbed him by the arms, and dragged him across the stage. With Tai-chi precision, they struck him with make-believe blows until he offered no resistance. The assailants stripped off his clothes and bound his hands to his feet. Sliding a wooden pole between the cruxes of his tightly bound extremities, they lifted him off the floor and perched the pole on two wooden sawhorses, leaving him hanging upside down, naked and exposed. For the next several minutes, the audience witnessed the pantomimed infliction of electric shock to the youth's anus and genital area. Each surge of imaginary voltage produced by a simulated army field generator sent convulsions through the actor's body. Howls of pain punctuated each administration of electric current. After the tenth jolt, the youth's body hung limp and defeated.

Prominent anti–Vietnam War peace activists had organized that night's political and cultural event. The sweeping arrests of left-wing supporters of Allende, the mass detentions in Chile's national soccer stadium, and the reports of large numbers of executions of leftists had shocked international public opinion and generated hundreds of solidarity activities throughout the United States. Although that evening's dramatic symbolic reenactment of the torture of a political prisoner underlined a method employed by the new Chilean regime, the Living Theater had actually developed the dramatic scene to denounce the ongoing gross violation of human rights taking place in Brazil.

The Living Theater had arrived somewhat naively in Brazil in 1970 to perform their experimental productions. The following year, police arrested them on trumped-up marijuana possession charges and expelled the group from the country. When the troupe returned to the United States, they joined a nascent national movement to isolate the Brazilian military regime. While few criticized the Brazilian military when it came to power in 1964, by 1969 a cluster of academics, clergy, Brazilian exiles, and political activists had resolved to employ diverse means to educate the American public about the political situation in that distant land and to mobilize opposition to the dictatorship. As we will see, five years later they had been relatively successful. Furthermore, the strategies, tactics, and approaches they employed to raise the issue of human rights violations in Brazil served as the basis for all similar future work related to Latin America carried out in the United States. Many at Madison Square Garden may not have had a clear notion of Latin American geography or even details about political events unfolding to the far south as a wave of repressive regimes took power in the 1970s. Nonetheless, by 1974 most informed U.S. political activists, especially those involved in anti–Vietnam War protests, had developed at least a vague association between the Brazilian government and its torture chambers.

The events in Chile further expanded the sensibility about human rights violations in Latin America. Almost immediately after the 1973 coup, dozens of solidarity groups sprang up in most major U.S. cities. In subsequent years, tens of thousands of activists protested Pinochet's authoritarian measures. Revelations about the involvement of the White House, the CIA, and U.S. multinational corporations in the destabilization of the Allende government merely reinforced a growing cynicism that had mushroomed during the Vietnam War about the abusive powers of U.S. foreign policymakers. Other military takeovers in Uruguay and Argentina mobilized similar concerns about the decline of basic human rights in South America. Soon after Jimmy Carter entered the White House in 1977, the words "arrest," "torture," and "repression," which an informed public had previously associated with Brazil, became synonymous with the description of the military regimes that had assumed power throughout Latin America. By the late 1970s, human rights activists had imposed a new yardstick for measuring Washington's Latin American foreign policy. Over the next decade, national solidarity committees with hundreds of local affiliates supported the Sandinista revolution in Nicaragua and the Salvadoran and Guatemalan insurgencies. They organized massive demonstrations, direct-action sit-ins, and other protests against the Reagan administration's complicity with the counterrevolutionary forces in Central America. According to one analyst, "more than one hundred thousand U.S. citizens mobilized to contest the chief foreign policy initiative of the most popular U.S. president in decades."[8]

*We Cannot Remain Silent* developed out of a conversation at the Latin American Studies Association Conference in 1998. Between sessions, a young left-wing Brazilian historian shared his frustrations about how Brazilianists (as U.S. scholars who study Brazil are either affectionately or ironically labeled) had a rather superficial understanding of his country's history and culture. What's more, he added, they had done little to oppose the military dictatorship. This, I knew, was not the case, and so for the next hour we talked about some of the many activities that this book documents. This lack of knowledge about the international political campaigns conducted in the early 1970s concerning Brazil convinced me to write an article on the topic. After completing two research forays into the Brazilian Foreign Ministry (Itamaraty) archives in Brasília, I realized I had enough material for a book. As I presented portions of my research at Brazilian universities and at the Brazilian Historical Association, I also perceived a pervasive impression held by most Brazilian intellectuals about a supposed inaction of their U.S. counterparts in response to the military regime's repressive rule. There are several reasons why this notion is so widespread.

First, as international campaigns developed in the late 1960s and early 1970s, the dictatorship censored the Brazilian media. Scattered news did appear in the press, many times in the forms of chauvinistic editorials or nationalist diatribes that denounced "international communist conspiracies" to defame the country. Yet unless one was directly linked to an underground organization involved in disseminating abroad news about torture and repression, even the most informed person could only glean from the media a vague sense of the dimension of international campaigns against the regime. A second reason that Brazilians knew little about efforts in the United States against the military dictatorship rests on a long-standing and complex relationship with the giant to the north. Although traditionally the Brazilian elites looked to Europe and later to the United States for cultural affirmation, a strong anti-American (that is, anti–United States) current ran through the Brazilian academic world in the 1950s, 1960s, and 1970s, as nationalist, anti-imperialist, and Marxist perspectives framed geopolitical and macroeconomic analyses. Many, if not most, students who passed through Brazilian universities during this period considered the United States responsible for unequal and unjust international economic relations and Latin America's ongoing underdevelopment. Brazilian opponents of military rule argued that the U.S. government had been intimately involved in Goulart's overthrow years before scholars got access to classified U.S. documents to confirm this allegation.[9]

To left-wing opponents of the military regime, U.S. imperialism was the international enemy and loyal backer of the generals in power. In an atmosphere that disdained U.S. policies worldwide, most people assumed that citizens of that country agreed with the Washington establishment's overseas initiatives. Even though many Brazilian youth admired U.S. music and culture and the media covered stories of the social and political rebellions that rocked the country, politicized students and left-wing militants largely lumped together the U.S. government and its citizens as one unified entity that supported the Brazilian and Latin American status quo. Reflective of this thin appreciation for the subtleties of U.S. culture and society was the fact that the University of São Paulo, at the time the nation's leading institute of higher education, did not offer any courses on U.S. history. Although most left-leaning academics considered U.S. imperialism as the mainstay of the regime, few bothered to study seriously an international adversary that so loyally supported the dictatorship.

Clandestine operations by the CIA in Latin America did not help matters. A common assumption in the 1960s was that the U.S. foreign aid programs, such as the Alliance for Progress, were saturated with intelligence gatherers. Brazilianists, like other Americans in Brazil, were on the CIA's payroll, so it was commonly thought. That assumption made it difficult to imagine that U.S. scholars studying the country could share many of the political values or perspectives of their Brazilian colleagues.

Most U.S. scholars who have written about the importance of the Carter administration's human rights discourse in the late 1970s mention briefly the groundbreaking work by activists against torture in Brazil in the early 1970s but emphasize the flurry of organizing related to reports of torture and repression in Chile after the 1973 military takeover.[10] Thus, the political scientist Lars Schoultz rightly argues, "Human rights conditions in these nations [of Latin America], particularly Brazil and later Chile, were the first to attract the attention of U.S. human rights activists."[11] The human rights specialist David P. Forsythe concurs, emphasizing that "individuals associated with the National Council of Churches argued that it was their concern with torture in Brazil and American funding for foreign police training which, with the support of Senators Church, Abourezk, and others, had really started the renewed U.S. concern for human rights between 1969 and 1971."[12]

Following the lead of these scholars, *We Cannot Remain Silent* documents and analyzes in detail the activities of dedicated church and left-wing activists, exiled Brazilians, and Latin Americanist scholars who played a major role in introducing the issue of human rights in Latin America into the national political debate. In Europe, a parallel campaign against torture and human rights violations in Brazil (and, later, other countries of Latin America) developed during this same period, but that movement is beyond this work's scope. In both the United States and Europe, Brazilian political exiles, allied at times with left-wing sectors of the Catholic Church and other forces, waged a relentless campaign to isolate the Brazilian government.[13] The diverse clusters of activists that organized against the dictatorship in multiple ways formed in effect what the political scientists Margaret E. Keck and Kathryn Sikkink have termed "transnational advocacy networks." Given the clandestine nature of much of the domestic resistance to the Brazilian generals, especially after 1968, these linkages did not follow exactly along the lines of the "voluntary, reciprocal, and horizontal patterns of communication and exchange" outlined by Keck and Sikkink.[14] International contacts were at times precarious and information transmission often problematic, but the ability of activists to use the symbolism of the tortured body to elicit support and activate international political leverage proved at times to be a successful strategy.

The call for moral accountability of U.S. government policy also remained at the core of the campaigns that questioned Washington's complicity with the authoritarian regime. The tactics and strategies that activists working on Brazil employed to denounce torture and repression in Brazil developed and expanded, helping to shape people's responses to the political situation in Chile. These efforts initiated a gradual shift in U.S. official and public opinion and provided a basis for much broader campaigns against repression, torture, and disappearance in Latin America after the Chilean coup. Facing a hostile White House that overtly backed military regimes throughout Latin America during the Nixon-Ford years (1969–76), activists targeted Congress to enact measures limiting U.S. government support for repressive regimes abroad.[15] Early legislative victories included language in the Foreign Assistance Acts of 1973 and 1974 mandating the president to "deny any economic or military assistance to the government of any foreign country which practices the internment or imprisonment of that country's citizens for political purposes."[16] In 1975, the Harkin Amendment to the Foreign Assistance Act gave Congress the power to limit U.S. economic assistance to "any country which engages in a consistent pattern of gross violations of internationally recognized human rights."[17] The following year, Congress expanded this restriction to include military aid. After Jimmy Carter adopted and popularized human rights as a guiding criterion for U.S. foreign policy during the 1976 electoral campaign, what had once been a somewhat isolated political critique of U.S. foreign policy by leftists and certain liberals suddenly became part of national discussions about the direction of government policies abroad.

*We Cannot Remain Silent* also examines the genesis of what the historian Kenneth Cmiel has observed as the mainstreaming of human rights discourse regarding Latin America in the United States in the late 1970s.[18] As Lars Schoultz has pointed out, "The 'Brazilianists' taught the rest of the human rights cadre everything they needed to know to get started."[19] The building of a national network of activists with international connections, the documentation of systematic torture and repression, the public positioning of prominent figures against human rights abuses, and the patient building of contacts with congressional allies and the press all contributed to the forging of an image of Brazil under military rule as a land of torture and terror. They also underlined the sentiment that the U.S. government should not have supported the regime. Graphic tales of the treatment of political prisoners created powerful symbols for a discussion about political repression in Latin America under authoritarian military regimes backed by the U.S. government.

For readers unfamiliar with late-twentieth-century Brazilian history, understanding the nature and practice of the military dictatorship can be challenging. Throughout the book, I have offered brief synopses of political, economic, and social developments in Brazil that clarify the context in which activists in Brazil and the United States carried out their work. Several chapters also present somewhat detailed considerations of the debates and discussions within the U.S. and Brazilian governments about the internal Brazilian political situation, U.S.–Brazilian relations, and the international human rights campaign. Understanding how policymakers understood and responded to changes during the period enables the reader to comprehend the shifts in the approaches activists adopted. Because the U.S. media played a crucial role in shaping U.S. public opinion and in offering the uninformed reader news and information about Brazil, the book also considers how coverage changed over time and how activists attempted to influence the content of that coverage.

Finally, I have tried to humanize what could have been a somewhat sterile analysis of political campaigns and foreign policy shifts by revealing something of the lives of the nearly hundred people whom I interviewed for this book. Everyone I contacted immediately agreed to my request to be interviewed. Some seemed surprised, but were delighted, that someone was interested in telling their stories. Because many of the U.S. actors in this narrative had lived, studied, worked, or done research in Brazil, brief accounts of their interests or involvement in the country help to clarify why they became involved in political activism. Likewise, catching a glimpse of the life histories of those Brazilians who ended up as activists in the United States not only explains their commitment to the cause but also reveals how opposition to the military regime developed in Brazil. In deference to a long-standing Brazilian tradition, I have generally referred to Brazilians by their full or first names, while usually doing the opposite for the U.S. protagonists of this story.

No doubt many Brazilian readers will be pleasantly surprised to learn the extent to which some people in the United States attempted to raise awareness about the political situation in Brazil during the military regime. However, scholars of U.S. public opinion and foreign policy present a rather pessimistic portrait of the public's knowledge of or interest in Latin America.[20] Ignorance, indifference, arrogance about the innate superiority of the United

States, and even an abysmally low level of understanding about Latin America in Congress and at the State Department have all been obstacles for developing successful human rights campaigns in the United States. As one North American historian who has worked on Brazil for the last four decades commented after a presentation of my research, "I was in Brazil in the 1970s, and no one knew or even cared about Brazil."[21] There is a kernel of truth in that observation. For all of the efforts mobilized by academics, activists, and others concerning Brazil in the early 1970s, Chile after 1973, and Central America in the 1980s, those involved seemed to be battling against certain apathy about international affairs among the U.S. public, especially when a foreign country seemed remote and apparently had little impact on individuals' lives. To a great extent, the groundswell of opposition to the Vietnam War was directly related to the realization by millions that they or their loved ones might have to serve (and perhaps die) in Southeast Asia in an increasingly senseless war. In this respect, Brazil was and remains distant and indistinct to most Americans. Activists described in this volume had to develop campaigns in the context of a prevalent self-satisfied and chauvinist attitude that considered the United States the beacon of democracy worldwide. They chose to point to the contradictions. If the United States was the paradigm of freedom and justice, how could its government support a regime that tortured its citizens? Why, in the name of democracy, did the White House back a brutal military government? As the impact of virulent anticommunist discourse faded in the midst of the Vietnam War movement, it became easier to challenge aspects of U.S. policy, namely, support for a repressive regime that seemed out of sync with an idealized notion of the nation.

Those who teach Brazilian history and culture constantly face the fact that most people with whom we come into contact still think that Rio de Janeiro is the capital of Buenos Aires, that Brazilians speak Spanish as their first language, or that the country is largely populated by primitive aborigines and man-eating tropical fish, to mention only a few of the misconceptions we have encountered over the years. Carmen Miranda and the Girl from Ipanema have largely faded from the stable of stereotypes only to be replaced by other equally insipid images.

Likewise, some of my Brazilian friends and colleagues, especially those with a historic antipathy toward U.S. foreign policy, have often surprised me with naive and unilateral conceptions of the United States, even though on the whole Brazilian intellectuals are currently far more informed about the United States than their American counterparts are about Brazil. Such is the unequal and unbalanced international relationship of culture, power, and information. Yet if the United States remains culturally, politically, and economically hegemonic in the early twenty-first century, then all the more reason to understand historically how individuals living in the United States, yet motivated by the political situation in Brazil and the rest of Latin America, attempted to chip away at some of that endemic isolation.

## PRÓLOGO

---

## "Era um país subdesenvolvido"

It was an underdeveloped country

**Carlos Lyra and Francisco de Assis,**
**"Canção do subdesenvolvido," 1962**

Brazilian peasant mobilization, early 1960s. ACERVO ÚLTIMA HORA, ARQUIVO PÚBLICO DO ESTADO DE SÃO PAULO.

Martinha Arruda could not pinpoint the first time she heard a bossa nova tune, but it was sometime in junior high school in 1958 or 1959. Later, in high school, her best friend was a talented singer from a well-to-do family, whose circle of friends included many of the artists who would shape Brazilian music for the next decades. "My friend's house was a gathering place. She would invite everyone over, young people who were just beginning to sing and compose."[1] In that informal, bohemian atmosphere of Rio de Janeiro and in the mountainside vacation town of Petropolis, where her friend's family had a summer home, Martinha spent many leisurely hours learning new songs and joining in with others to render old favorites. There she met singers and musicians who were transforming Brazilian sound.

Martinha was descended on her mother's side from a distinguished family, but by the 1950s her family possessed only modest means. Moreover, her mother, Lina Penna Sattimini, a vivacious and independent woman, had separated from her husband and gotten a job working in the United States, entrusting her five children to the care of their father and the oversight of a rather strict, though loving, grandmother. Lacking a traditional middle-class home life and possessing a passion for performance, the retreat to her friend's house provided Martinha with an idyllic adolescence. As she conjured up those years, Martinha remembered her teens spent in endless hours of music and laughter as friends and acquaintances gathered to play the guitar, sing songs, read poetry, and discuss art, theater, dance, movies, and culture.

As scholars have pointed out, bossa nova's soft, soothing melodies and romantic lyrics in part captured the optimism of the late 1950s, when Juscelino Kubitschek, a confident and modernizing political leader, offered the nation a new capital city, Brasília, for a country that could be transformed by leaping fifty years forward in five.[2] Brazil had the potential to overcome backwardness and underdevelopment and fulfill its destiny. The uniqueness of the bossa nova sound and its immediate international success merely confirmed other possible conquests, as Kubitschek renovated the nationalism that former president Getúlio Vargas had so successfully channeled for his own political ends during the previous three decades. The "petróleo é nosso" (the oil is ours) campaign to nationalize foreign oil companies in the early 1950s, championed by students, the left, and an array of patriotic forces, led to other calls for state control over the country's resources in the late 1950s. If Brazil could only master its own wealth, it could actually become the country of the future that Stefan Zweig, the European Jewish writer who had moved in exile to Brazil in 1941, had envisioned for the nation a decade and a half before.[3]

Now a retired Presbyterian minister living in Cranston, Rhode Island, Jovelino Ramos also remembered the late 1950s as an exciting time. "1958 was a very political year," he recalled. "It was the year that Francisco Julião started the Ligas Camponeses [Peasant Leagues] in the Northeast. At the end of the year, Fidel Castro took power in Cuba. Pius XII died, and John XXIII was elected pope. Juscelino was president, and Brasília was being built . . . And it was the first time that Brazil was the World Cup champion."[4] In 1958, Jovelino, who hailed from the state of Minas Gerais, was studying at the Presbyterian Theological Seminary in Campinas, an hour or so from the growing industrial metropolis of São Paulo. "Before I finished the last year of the theological course, I went to work in a factory. It was the period of the worker-priests in France. As seminarians and Protestant pastors, we wanted to have that experience." After finishing his degree, Jovelino moved to Rio and became involved in the União Cristã de Estudantes do Brasil (Brazilian Student Christian Union), an ecumenical movement of Protestant students. "Many things were happening. The students were in the streets. . . . and Cuba began to dominate the political scene."

After completing his degree in theology, Jovelino was offered a scholarship to study at the Yale Divinity School. He spent the next two years there, where he met and married his first wife, Myra. "When I returned to Brazil in the middle of 1962, Brazil had changed entirely. Jânio Quadros had resigned the presidency, and the right did not want [vice president] João Goulart to take office. This was the period of the rise of [Leonel] Brizola,[5] who inspired part of the army that forced the opposition to respect the Constitution." Many other changes had taken place as well. Protest music had joined bossa nova as a popular musical genre among many students and middle-class youth. The Alliance for Progress, Kennedy's initiative to offer a U.S. government–sponsored Latin American development plan that also challenged the spread of communism, was entering Brazil in full force. In response, young engagé artists satirized the Alliance with the song "Canção do subdesenvolvido" (Song of the Underdeveloped). It became the unofficial anthem of Centro Popular de Cultura (People's Cultural Center), one of the left-leaning student movement's initiatives to link the university to the poor and dispossessed.[6] The tune parodied Washington's economic model for Brazil, criticized U.S. cultural influences, and ridiculed the paternalistic inferiority embedded in the notion of the Alliance for Progress's plan for Brazil.

Jovelino also noted that many Protestant students with whom he had worked before departing to the United States had become leftists. Some were in Ação Popular (Popular Action), others were in the pro-Soviet Communist Party, others in the pro-Chinese Communist Party of Brazil, but the majority was not linked to any political party. They participated in elections, supported left-wing governors, and passionately argued for a comprehensive agrarian reform. "There were lots of marches and rallies supporting agrarian reform," Jovelino remembered.

With a masters' degree from Yale in theology and social ethics, Jovelino accepted his local presbytery's invitation to lead the effort to organize a new church in Ipanema. "Many of the students who had been liberal when I went to the United States, and were now leftists, came to my church. On Saturday evenings they crowded into my house in Santa Teresa to socialize and sometimes to have planning meetings. Without choosing to, I became a kind of pastor for left-wing students." Pope John XXIII's encyclical *Pacem in Terris* (1963) quickly become a manifesto for those Catholics pushing for greater commitment to social change. "As engaged Protestants we welcomed it. It deepened our theological perspective to deal with social concerns and relate to the popular reform movement of time," Jovelino explained.

The pope's pronouncements for peace and social justice also inspired Marcos Arruda, Martinha's older brother. As the oldest of five children, he suffered the most with his parents' incessant fights and their emotion-laden separation. At the time, Marcos thought that the only way to reunite his parents would be to become a priest. Against his mother's wishes, he insisted on studying in a seminary. "My initial motivation was the separation of my parents," Marcos confessed many years later.[7] "It was a gesture to renounce everything that I loved in life, a kind of test. I spent two and a half years there, but I couldn't stand it. It was a militaristic life, yet I learned a lot. I studied, and I built a universe of friendships that has lasted to this day, but I suffered a lot." Marcos finally left the seminary and passed the university entrance exam in geology. "I started to work with the JUC, the Juventude Universitária Católica (Catholic University Youth). It was the turning point in my life. Through the JUC, I acquired a social conscience. I started to question my own position within [the field of] geology, so I studied the political and social aspects of geology. I tried to think of ways to enrich the country and change its social structure."

Jovelino and Marcos were not unique in the search to link their religious upbringing with a commitment to social justice. An ecumenical spirit, reinforced by Vatican II reforms and the convergence of sectors of the Catholic and Protestant churches with the nationalist, development-oriented move-ment, supported structural economic reforms to close the gap between the rich and the poor. The optimism of the time also produced a new political or-ganization, Ação Popular (Popular Action), that grew out of various Catholic youth and student organizations and moved toward Marxism, coalescing left-leaning Protestants along the way.[8] In the early 1960s, Ação Popular offered a progressive alternative to the pro-Soviet Communist Party, the Maoist Communist Party of Brazil, and various Trotskyist groupings. Many radical religious youth, as Jovelino noted, declined left-wing political party affiliation, identifying themselves as unattached leftists. Others, like Marcos, who rejected the moderation of the Communist Party, eventually joined Ação Popular.

As Marcos mapped out a political program demanding that, just like Bra-zil's oil, the country's mineral deposits should remain in national hands through state control, and Jovelino offered his apartment in the hillside neighborhood of Santa Teresa for Saturday meetings of radicalized youth, Brady Tyson, a young Methodist missionary from Texas, was setting up house with his wife and five children in São Paulo. Like Jovelino Ramos, he was a part of the progressive ecumenical movement that understood that the mes-sage of the Gospel to require active involvement in eliminating poverty and injustice. His mission in Brazil also grew out of a long commitment to fight for social and racial equality in the United States. Among the politicized Bra-zilian youth with whom Brady worked in the Methodist Church was Anivaldo Padilha, affectionately known as Niva. His family had migrated from Minas Gerais in the 1950s and found a new spiritual and social network in the Meth-odist Church.[9] Niva became active in the youth movement and eventually headed the national organization. When he was a student at the University of São Paulo, he, like Marcos Arruda, joined Ação Popular.[10]

In 1963, if one were to have plotted a chart of the interlocking networks that linked Martinha, Marcos, Jovelino, Brady, and Niva, one would have probably found one or two, rather than six, degrees of separation among them. (As Niva once commented to me, "It's not that this is a small world; it's just that the left travels in small circles.") A year before the military came to power, they all shared in the cultural, social, and political optimism about their country's future. Brazil, an "underdeveloped" giant, held great pos-sibilities for social and economic transformation. Development, however, needed to come with social justice. Certainly, at the time, none of them could have imagined that ten years later they would all find themselves in the United States participating in diverse ways in a decentralized and dispersed movement against the military dictatorship. In part, this book is the story of their paths toward activism in the United States. They and many other Brazilians and their allies in the United States will slip in and out of this narrative. In New York, Washington, Berkeley, and other cities across the United States, they joined a handful of clergy, academics, students, and activists to denounce the use of torture and the violation of human rights in Brazil (and later in other parts of Latin America). They employed creative tactics and invented new ways to educate the U.S. public and influence Washington politicians about the situation in Brazil. As a group, they remain to this day extremely unassuming about their successes as they took on a military regime supported by an ostensibly omnipotent world power. Yet their seemingly modest efforts eventually helped influence a shift (at least for a time) in U.S. foreign policy toward Latin America.

# 1

# REVOLUTION AND COUNTERREVOLUTION IN BRAZIL

We are meanwhile undertaking complementary measures with our available resources to help strengthen resistance forces. These include covert support for pro-democracy street rallies (next big one being April 2 here in Rio, and others being programmed), discreet passage of word that USG [United States Government] deeply concerned at events, and encouragement [of] democratic and anti-communist sentiment in Congress, Armed Forces, friendly labor and student groups, Church, and business. We may be requesting modest supplementary funds for other covert action programs in near future. — **Telegram from U.S. ambassador Lincoln Gordon to Washington, March 27, 1964**

The movement which overthrew President Goulart was a purely, 100 percent — not 99.44 — but 100 percent a purely Brazilian movement. Neither the American Embassy nor I personally played any part in the process whatsoever. — **Former U.S. ambassador to Brazil Lincoln Gordon, U.S. Senate hearings, February 7, 1966**

Ambassador Lincoln Gordon and President Lyndon B. Johnson, White House, March 1964. PHOTO BY YOICHI OKAMOTO. LYNDON B. JOHNSON LIBRARY.

Cândido Portinari, at the time considered "Brazil's most renowned artist," painted the portrait of President Jânio Quadros that graced the cover of the June 30, 1961, issue of *Time* magazine.[1] Brazil's chief executive, only five months in office, stares somberly at the readers of the nation's number one news weekly. His dark hair and mustache and matching black-rimmed glasses cast a foreboding shadow over the red-framed magazine. *Time*'s editors billed the inside story as "the most definitive report to date on the President of South America's greatest and most complex country."[2] The inside spread charted the politician's meteoric rise to power, discussed his independent foreign policy that refused to adapt to a bipolar Cold War paradigm, and compared him to the nation as a whole: "Jânio Quadros has burst on the world like Brazil itself—temperamental, bristling with independence, bursting with ambition, haunted by poverty, fighting to learn, greedy for greatness."[3]

As was true of most press coverage of Latin America at that time, the Cuban Revolution provided the backdrop for the feature article. "In the drive to rebuild U.S. prestige and influence after Cuba, an obvious place to start is Brazil, which most experts regard as the key nation in Latin America. A strong healthy Brazil does not guarantee democracy in Latin America, but it is certain that if Brazil does not make it, few other nations will."[4] *Time*'s notion of Brazil as a continental kingpin suggested the "domino theory" that had come to justify the U.S. intervention in Vietnam and in other places. Were that country to "fall" to communism, other nations would follow suit.

The day after Quadros took office, the Bureau of Inter-American Affairs drafted a secret memo recommending how the U.S. government should deal with the new administration. The document registered concern about "Quadros's inclination toward an independent foreign policy" and suggested that Washington should offer assistance in meeting Brazil's balance of payments deficit.[5] Policymakers also encouraged the administration "to help Brazil to meet the problem of its depressed Northeast territory through the new Social Development program."[6] In offering its background justification for this action, the memo argued: "Brazilian leaders believe that their country is destined to become one of great world powers. Brazil has been resentful in the past with being treated by the United States as if it were just another of the Latin American 'banana' republics. It has sought a special relationship . . . desiring to be consulted by the U.S. on matters affecting the hemisphere. Also, Brazil has led the demands that the United States embark on a large-scale aid program for Latin America on the same scale as the Marshall Plan. It feels the $500 million social development program proposed by the United

States is a step in the right direction although it is disappointed by the magnitude."[7] The memo's final sentence offered a dire warning: "A Governor of one of the economically depressed provinces of Northeast Brazil has recently requested U.S. assistance on an urgent basis to combat growing Communist influence in that poverty-stricken area through a rural land development program."[8] Notably, Cold War threats loomed prominently behind promises of poverty-alleviation programs.

Two months after *Time's* cover story about Brazil's mercurial and quixotic president, Quadros resigned from office, defeated by, in his own words, "terrible forces [that] came forward to fight me and to defame me."[9] At the time, left-leaning Vice President João Goulart was leading a trade mission to "Red" China. Goulart, a protégé of former president Getúlio Vargas, had served as his labor minister in 1953–54. He had run as the vice presidential candidate of the Partido Trabalhista Brasileiro (Brazilian Labor Party, PTB) in 1955, handily winning on a split ticket that elected centrist Juscelino Kubitschek as president. He continued in office in 1961 by outpolling other parties' vice presidential candidates and continuing as second in command under conservative-leaning Jânio Quadros.

Opposition to Goulart quickly coalesced among conservative, anti-Vargas, and anti-PTB forces. Commanders of the armed forces threatened to block his ascension to the presidency. Military leaders loyal to Goulart and the constitution, as well as Goulart's brother-in-law, Governor Leonel Brizola, countered with threats of a civil war. Eventually, the contending sides reached a compromise. Goulart would be sworn in as president, but with limited power, and Brazil would adopt a parliamentary system led by a prime minister.[10]

The stage was set and the actors in place. Goulart's term in office would last a mere thirty-three months, cut short on April 1, 1964, by the military takeover that marked the beginning of twenty-one years of authoritarian rule. Anti-Goulart forces declared victory, dubbing their power grab a "revolution" that had defeated, so they claimed, an imminent left-wing revolution. Appropriating and recasting the term "revolution" into its opposite was one of many ways the generals played with political reality. Rather than aborting a revolution, the military stepped in to overturn the moderate reforms put forth by Goulart in early 1964.[11] They pledged to weed out corruption in government, curtail inflation, and halt the country's alleged rush toward communism.[12]

Although the military had pushed Goulart from power, the coup makers argued that he had actually abandoned the presidential office and violated the constitution by leaving the country without congressional permission. It remained a minor detail that Goulart was still at his ranch on Brazilian territory. The generals' loyal congressional supporters swiftly voted Ranieri Mazzilli, the speaker of the house, as provisional president, and U.S. ambassador Lincoln Gordon urged the White House to recognize immediately the new government.[13] President Johnson promptly backed Mazzilli on April 2. The brief message issued from the Oval Office began: "Please accept my warmest good wishes on your installation as President of the United States of Brazil. The American people have watched with anxiety the political and economic difficulties through which your great nation has been passing, and have admired the resolute will of the Brazilian community to resolve these difficulties within a framework of constitutional democracy and without civil strife."[14]

The next day in a telephone exchange between Thomas Mann, assistant secretary of state for inter-American affairs, and President Johnson, Mann commented: "I hope you're as happy about Brazil as I am." To which the president replied, "I am." Mann continued, "I think that's the most important thing that's happened in the hemisphere in three years." Johnson concurred, "I hope they give us *some* credit, instead of hell."[15] Johnson got his wish. The new military government quickly aligned itself with Washington, and Brazilian nationalists and left-wing critics immediately credited the United States with having masterminded the coup.[16]

Following a constitutional provision requiring the Brazilian congress to select a new president within thirty days if the presidency and vice-presidency became vacant, a purged legislature "elected" General Humberto de Alencar Castelo Branco. Although he was not the initiator of the plot to oust Goulart, other officers called in Castelo Branco to lead the military conspiracy.[17] His long military career and close relationship to the United States positioned him as the perfect candidate for the country's top political post. He was a graduate of the Brazilian Military Academy (1921), the French École Superieur de Guerre (1938), and the U.S. Command and General Staff School in Fort Leavenworth, Kansas (1943). When Brazil joined the Allies in World War II, he served in the general staff of the Brazilian Expeditionary Force in Italy. After the war he was the commander of the Fourth Army in the Brazilian Northeast and was the Army chief of staff immediately before assuming the presidency. He held the U.S. Legion of Merit and a Bronze Star. In a report sent to Washington soon after Castelo Branco's ascension to the presidency, Ambassador Gordon assured the State Department that the general "admires and appreciates [the] role U.S. has played since World War II as a defender of freedom."[18]

On April 20, 1964, Gordon held his first private talk in Brasília with the new president. The ambassador congratulated the general and indicated that Washington "looked on [the] April Revolution as [a] possible turning point in affairs [of] Latin America and [the] World as well as Brazil, provided proper use [is] made of [the] opportunity."[19] After a warning to Castelo Branco that "revolutionary excesses," including the withdrawal of political rights from the internationally renowned economist Celso Furtado, had been "especially badly received," most of their conversation focused on the initiative to Latin America begun by Kennedy, renewed economic aid to Brazil, and the international political scene. Gordon reported that he "left the interview with the feeling that this was a most auspicious beginning." Latin America's greatest country, which had been on the road to chaos and communism, was now, according to Gordon, on the path to prosperity and democracy. Although in retrospect Gordon has argued that at the time of the coup he had assumed that the military would put Brazil in order and quickly retreat to the barracks, this proved not to be the case. Instead the armed forces clung to power for two more decades. This chapter examines the contentious events that led to the 1964 coup, the behind-the-scenes analyses and maneuvering from the White House and State Department, the response on the floor of Congress to the military takeover, and the U.S. media's portrayal of the "revolution" that seemingly was taking place in Brazil.

### Cold Warriors in Tropical Lands

Lincoln Gordon assumed his post as U.S. ambassador to Brazil in the immediate aftermath of the presidential succession crisis of August 1961. A thatch of gray hair, an ever-present pipe, and sophisticated public declarations offered the image of an Ivy League professor turned public servant. A summa cum laude Harvard graduate and a Rhodes Scholar who had earned a Ph.D. in economics at Oxford in 1936, Gordon had served the U.S. government in various capacities during and after World War II. Among many activities, he helped develop the Marshall Plan into a concrete program.[20] In 1955, he returned to Harvard with a chair in international economic relations, working in the business school and the Center for International Affairs, and dabbled in research about economic development in Brazil.[21] The Kennedy administration tapped him to join the team elaborating a new policy initiative toward Latin America that eventually became the Alliance for Progress.

Kennedy appointed Gordon ambassador to Brazil soon thereafter. In an oral history interview in 1964, Gordon speculated on why Kennedy chose him for the ambassadorial post: "I suppose the reasons were pretty clear in my case. This is the biggest country in the hemisphere, and the Alliance for Progress was the principal expression of the Kennedy administration's Latin American policy. I knew a good deal about Brazil, having worked here on a research project for a couple of years. I was already widely acquainted among Brazilians; I had a reading knowledge of Portuguese and at least a foundation for speaking knowledge; and I was much involved in the Alliance for Progress. Here was an opportunity to help its application in the largest country in Latin America."[22]

The historian Thomas E. Skidmore has assessed Gordon's appointment in slightly different terms: "Lincoln Gordon was clearly a real Cold Warrior whose mission, as he saw it, was to make sure that Brazil didn't go communist."[23] While at Oxford, Gordon had witnessed firsthand the escalating conditions that would lead to World War II. The Nazi experience hardened his resolve that threats to Western civilization needed to be annihilated, and so emerged his stance on communism after the Cold War consensus became pervasive. Like many of his peers, Gordon viewed the world in Manichaean terms: a country either was with the United States or had aligned itself with communism.[24]

Brazil was still in turmoil over the presidential succession when Gordon arrived in Rio on October 13, 1961, and presented his credentials to the newly sworn-in president. In Washington, policymakers were taking a wait-and-see attitude about Goulart: "Pending the clarification of U.S. orientation, we propose to deal with the new government on the assumption that there has been no break in the continuity of the traditionally close and cordial relation between the United States and Brazil. As for President Goulart, we are prepared to give him the reasonable benefit of the doubt, while trying to encourage him to believe cooperation with the United States is to his and Brazil's advantage."[25] Over the next three years, this policy would shift dramatically.

### The Grand Alliance

On September 15, 1961, former president Kubitschek visited President Kennedy in the White House. During their formal meeting, Kubitschek addressed the potential deterioration in relations between the two countries. He insisted that he knew Goulart extremely well, particularly since Goulart had been his vice president, and could say that he was "a careful man and not a Communist." He also predicted that "Brazil would remain a truly democratic country."[26] After their formal meeting, Kennedy and Kubitschek moved out onto the White House porch for an informal conversation. They spoke of many other issues during their meeting. According to a White House memo, the Brazilian politician reminded Kennedy that "in May of 1958, after the incident-marked journey of Mr. Nixon through Latin America, he had written to President Eisenhower urging a careful reappraisal of the situation in the Hemisphere and suggested that U.S. policies toward Latin American countries be reformulated."[27] Kubitschek proposed a comprehensive U.S.-sponsored Latin American development program, named Operation Pan America. Kubitschek explained that, although both Eisenhower and Secretary of State Dulles showed interest in his ideas, they never translated it into constructive action as he thought Kennedy was determined to do. The Brazilian politician lamented that their terms in office had not coincided "so that an active program could be carried out on foundations that were well understood by both parties." Kubitschek went on to explain that Kennedy's new initiative to assist Latin American economic development was particularly important for the Brazilian Northeast, where most of the twenty-five million residents lived in serious poverty.

Tad Szulc, the *New York Times* correspondent stationed in Rio de Janeiro at the time, could not have agreed more. In a front-page piece on October 23, 1960, Szulc had written an alarmist article titled "Northeast Brazil Poverty Breeds Threat of a Revolt." The lead sentence proclaimed, "The makings of a revolutionary situation are increasingly apparent across the vastness of the poverty-stricken and drought-plagued Brazilian Northeast."[28] In his two-part series, Szulc painted an ominous picture of the region and portrayed a direct linkage between poverty and communism: "Racked by chronic malnutrition and rampaging disease," the article reads, "they seldom live much beyond the age of thirty. The misery is exploited by the rising Leftist influences in the overcrowded cities. The Communist-infiltrated Peasant Leagues, organizing and indoctrinating, have become an important political factor in this area." Szulc's second article was even more disquieting. The headline proclaimed, "Marxists are Organizing Peasants in Brazil," followed by a subhead stating, Leftist League Aims at a Political Army 40 Million Strong."[29] A *Times* editorial, "The 'Fidelistas' of Brazil," followed Szulc's sensationalist and highly exaggerated reporting. It reiterated the journalist's arguments: poverty produced protest movements that in turn led to communist infiltration and influence. The editorial was straightforward: "Mr. Szulc's findings do suggest that, it is time, that the United States took a far more positive part in aiding our neighbors south of the Canal. We can fight the 'Fidelistas' everywhere in Latin America, not with armed force but with the kind of economic aid that proceeds from science and proper understanding."[30] The *Times* was endorsing an idea and a strategy that Kubitschek had floated in 1958 and the Kennedy administration had repackaged in 1961 as the Alliance for Progress.

In the interview in 1964, Lincoln Gordon admitted that Szulc's reporting injected the idea of the Brazilian Northeast into the U.S. public's imagination. "[The articles] talked about this area with its tradition of droughts, great poverty compared with the rest of the country, the development of peasant leagues, Recife as the so-called communist capital of Brazil, etc. The broad impression was an area with twenty odd million people in it with explosive political and economic and social conditions . . . I'm sure that most of the American public had never heard of the Brazilian Northeast until these *New York Times* articles appeared in 1960. But this had sensitized the people."[31]

The White House's embrace of the Alliance for Progress as the most efficient means to block communist influence also marked a policy shift from the previous administration. Eisenhower's approach had combined a confidence in private investment as a means of economic development, military aid as a tool for containing subversion, and frequent admonitions to Latin American leaders as a way of discouraging their developing closer ties with the Soviet Union.[32] Eisenhower's policymakers rejected Latin American proposals for massive foreign aid along the lines of the Marshall Plan's reconstruction of postwar Europe.[33] Pressure from Latin American leaders, including Kubitschek, coupled with Vice President Nixon's cold reception in Peru and Venezuela, led members of the Eisenhower administration to rethink their economic policies toward the region. The overthrow of the Cuban dictator Flugencio Batista in late 1958 by the Castro-led guerrilla army accelerated Eisenhower's responses to what seemed a growing rift between the United States and Latin America. At a meeting of ministers of the Organization of American States held in Colombia in September 1959, the gathered diplomats approved the "Act of Bogotá" that linked economic and social development. U.S. representatives conceded that private investment was insufficient to respond to pressing social and economic problems. Shifting its attitude to foreign aid, the Eisenhower administration pledged to establish a $500 million Social Progress Trust Fund to support low-cost housing, schools, and health services.[34]

These measures were not sufficient to diminish a growing preoccupation with the Cuban Revolution, and Latin America became a campaign issue during the 1960 presidential contest between Kennedy and Nixon, as the

Massachusetts senator blasted the Eisenhower administration for not having an adequate policy for the country's southern neighbors. Drawing on ideas from the Marshall Plan, as well as from East Coast intellectuals and policy advisers such as Lincoln Gordon, the newly elected Kennedy administration put together a transition period task force to create new policies for the region. Headed by Adolph Berle, who had implemented Franklin D. Roosevelt's Good Neighbor Policy for Latin America during World War II, the task force offered a program blueprint designed to highlight Kennedy's fresh approach to foreign policy.[35] The Alliance for Progress was to be "a great common effort to develop the resources of the entire hemisphere, strengthen forces of democracy, and widen vocational and educational opportunities of every person in all of the Americas."[36] Kennedy officially launched the Alliance at an elegant White House reception on March 13, 1961, surrounded by Latin American diplomats and members of Congress. His ten-point program for a ten-year plan promised a "decade of democratic progress."[37] The Alliance would be a "vast cooperative effort, unparalleled in magnitude and nobility of purpose."

To build broad-based support in Latin America for this initiative, the Kennedy administration requested that the Organization of American States convoke a special conference of ministers to discuss the proposal. The White House called in Gordon to coordinate U.S. efforts, and representatives from throughout the Americas met for twelve days in Punta del Este, Uruguay, to concretize the Alliance. Secretary of the Treasury C. Douglas Dillon pledged that the United States would guarantee $20 billion in private and public funds over the subsequent decade to make the Alliance a reality. It was a daring promise that the White House would fail to keep, and that Congress would fail to fully fund.[38]

### Volunteering Abroad—College Kids and Committed Catholics

On a cold October night on the steps of the University of Michigan Student Union building, John F. Kennedy gave what he called "the longest short speech I've ever made."[39] Three weeks remained in the presidential race. In his brief and somewhat incoherent remarks, Kennedy challenged his audience of students and loyal supporters to tackle social problems at home and abroad through a government-sponsored youth service corps.[40] The idea immediately became popular with campaign handlers and enthusiastic student supporters. Soon after his famous inaugural address to the nation on January 20, 1961, in which the president asked his fellow citizens to serve their country in new selfless ways, Kennedy signed Executive Order 10924 establishing the Peace Corps.[41] A $30 million congressional appropriation for the program's first year launched hundreds of U.S. youth on life-changing experiences across the globe. Communism would be routed, at least in part, by the can-do goodwill and the fervent idealism of the nation's youthful ambassadors offering assistance to "backward" countries on their path to modernization and development.[42]

The first group of forty-two U.S. citizens serving in Brazil arrived in Rio on March 23, 1962, for a two-year stint, after a brief month's training session in Washington, and four weeks "outbound" training in Puerto Rico.[43] An intensive language-training program gave them the basics of Portuguese, and then they embarked on their mission in nine states. Their efforts in tackling the rural poverty that Ted Szulc had identified to the *Times* readership two years earlier put them on the front lines of an ideological assault against the expanding influence of communism in northeastern Brazil and other parts of the country.

The enthusiasm of Kennedy liberals that created the Alliance for Progress also intersected with transformations in the U.S. Catholic Church, in large part because of a call in 1960 by Pontifical Commission in Rome for lay volunteers to work among Latin America's priestless millions. Many U.S. Catholic activists involved in civil rights and social justice made Latin America the destination of their missionary work. Genuine concern for the poor and needy abroad was layered over Catholic anticommunism and the fear that Godless socialism might conquer the U.S.'s "backyard." In 1961, at a conference of major U.S. religious orders, the Vatican proposed that each religious community of men or women send at least 10 percent of its members to Latin America by the end of the decade. In the same idealistic spirit of the Peace Corps, thousands of Catholics became "Papal Volunteers" and traveled to Latin America to work in community development, health, educational, and other social projects.

In early 1963, conservative-leaning Cardinal Cushing of Boston took up the rallying cry: "Go to Latin American; help others go."[44] The National Catholic Welfare Conference's Latin America Bureau produced the publication *Latin America Calls!* to help mobilize this effort.[45] Its title encapsulated the sentiment behind this new campaign. The poor and needy of Latin America beckoned; U.S. Catholics should heed their appeal. "Hungry Kids Make Hardy Rebels" announced a huge ad in every issue. "The poor—tens of millions of them in Latin America—are striving every day toward better ways of living," read the copy. "Good people in the Church in every country of Latin America ask aid to train sturdy leaders who will teach thousands of illiterates, both old and young, give them healthier ways, win them to God-liness, save them from joining the enemies of society." This bimonthly pro-nouncement came accompanied by a dramatic black-and-white photograph designed to motivate charity to the Latin American poor. The picture varied but the image was constant. Poorly dressed, hungry children with plaintive eyes stared into the camera, begging for assistance. "Help Latin America's Bishops, priests, Sisters, lay volunteers build Christian life through Chris-tian leadership!" pleaded the ad. In order to channel this charity, the U.S. Catholic Church hierarchy established the Bishops' Committee for Latin America, with Cardinal Cushing as its chairman, and created the Latin America Bureau to carry out the work of implementing the Papal Program for Latin America.[46] Recognizing that not every Catholic could go, the Catholic bishops of the United States, under the direction of Cardinal Cushing, set up the Latin American Victory Fund, driven by unabashed anticommunism. "This aid is especially needed currently in Northeast Brazil and other back-ward areas where Catholic life is jeopardized by powerful Communist orga-nizations."[47] Noting that "fifteen percent to forty-five percent of the ordinary people of Latin America are under the spell of the Red," the Victory Fund made a forceful appeal: "Wanted: Workers for the Victory of Christian Justice Over the Reds in Latin America!"[48]

In addition to the Victory Fund, the Latin American Bureau had another revenue source to finance its ambitious projects—the U.S. Bishops' National Annual Collection for Latin America. On a designated Sunday every year, parishes throughout the country turned over all contributions to the Latin American Bureau to finance its efforts.[49] It was a weighty sum. Ironically, as we will see, the apparatus and mechanisms constructed to halt communist encroachment in Latin America—whether through government or religious volunteer programs—created institutions and structures that would end up supporting progressive and left-wing movements throughout the continent.

### Aiding and Abetting

The Kennedy administration had adopted a wait-and-see attitude toward Goulart when he first assumed office. Eleven months later, Ambassador Gordon, Deputy Assistant Secretary of State for Inter-American Affairs Richard Goodwin, and President Kennedy had made up their minds about the new government. In a meeting at the White House on July 30, 1962, Gordon said, "I think one of our important jobs is to strengthen the spine of the military. To make clear, discreetly, that we are not necessarily hos-tile to any kind of military action whatsoever if it's clear that the reason for the military action is . . ." The president finished his sentence, "against the left." Gordon continued: "He [Goulart] is giving the damn country away to the . . ." Again, Kennedy finished, "communists." A few moments later Goodwin commented: "We may very well want them [the Brazilian military] to take over at the end of the year, if they can."[50]

Although Gordon, Goodwin, and Kennedy may have wished for Goulart's rapid demise, it would take longer than they anticipated for the Brazilian generals to coalesce into a coherent group capable of staging a successful coup. In the meantime, Washington pursued a policy to encourage anti-Goulart forces. Covert funding of the political opposition and overt signals to the right bolstered those favoring a military takeover. In addition, the Alliance for Progress offered a public gesture of U.S. generosity. Resources of the newly consolidated U.S. government program under the direction of the Agency for International Development, as well as a complex array of programs that supplied Brazil with assistance—ranging from the Peace Corps program and Food for Peace to the U.S. AID-sponsored American Institute for Free Labor Development (AIFLD) and funds for military and police training—formed a countervailing support wall to shore up the country against the supposed imminent fall of Brazil to communism.

Scholars have documented the ways covert funding channeled through the CIA supplied resources to conservative Brazilian forces with an anti-left-wing agenda.[51] The 1962 elections became one target in this campaign. Incomplete access to CIA and other national security documents allows researchers to identify only the overall approaches to the U.S. embassy's efforts to carry out a government destabilization plan backed by covert actions. In an interview in March 1977 with Gordon, the former ambassador guessed that the U.S. government spent up to $5 million on the 1962 elections to back anti-Goulart candidates.[52] Adjusted for inflation, that amount would be $33.7 million today, hardly a small sum in the battle to win the hearts and minds of Brazilian voters. Gordon defended the effort by arguing that it had not been enough to affect the outcome of the elections: "I won't deny that there was American money. But if you analyze it, it wasn't much per congressman. Basically, it was money to buy radio time, have posters printed, that type of thing."[53] As Ruth Leacock has documented, U.S. funds and other efforts to defeat left-wing or populist candidates had uneven results. Alliance for Progress monies for high-profile development projects in the Northeast that anti-Goulart politicians could take credit for failed to tip the balance in the crucial Pernambuco gubernatorial elections, and Miguel Arraes, the leftist mayor of the capital Recife, easily won at the polls against a candidate supported by State Department officials.[54]

The Kennedy administration's growing distrust of Goulart also led to a new aid policy elaborated on December 11, 1962, in a meeting of the National Security Council designed to bypass the Brazilian government through contracting aid assistance directly to state and local bodies. The policy, known as "islands of administrative sanity," violated provisions in the Brazilian constitution; yet it gave Washington the opportunity to channel significant resources to Carlos Lacerda, the conservative governor of the state of Guanabara (Rio de Janeiro), a presidential aspirant for the 1965 elections and Goulart's most outspoken civilian critic.[55]

The U.S. government employed other partnerships to achieve a dual foreign policy objective of promoting development and good will through aid efforts while undermining political forces considered hostile to U.S. interests. One vital vehicle that targeted the labor movement was the American Institute for Free Labor Development (AIFLD). U.S. involvement in Latin American unions was not new, but the AIFLD marked an invigorated attempt to influence labor unions with strong left-wing tendencies.[56] The AIFLD was founded in 1962 with the backing of the AFL-CIO, the nation's largest labor federation, and most major U.S. corporations doing business in Latin America. However, approximately 90 percent of AIFLD's funding came from USAID through government contracts.[57] Phillip Agee, a former CIA operative in Latin America, has claimed—with names and details—that undercover agents worked within the institute to promote State Department policy objectives.[58] The AIFLD promoted the ideology of "business unionism," or the harmony of interests between labor and capital. It also vehemently opposed the influence of communists, socialists, and nationalists within trade unions. The program covered all of Latin America, but AIFLD gave special attention to Brazil. Its main objective was to train labor leaders and promising young rank-and-file members in modern labor-management practices that included contract negotiations and collective bargaining agreements. The institute's curriculum emphasized anticommunism over militant trade unionism and accommodation over confrontation. Training in union practices, however, was the AIFLD's main mission.

In 1963, the Instituto Cultural do Trabalho (Cultural Institute of Labor), AIFLD's organizational base in São Paulo, sent thirty-three influential Brazilian trade union leaders to the United States for a three-month course.[59] According to the AIFLD's own admission, upon their return, many joined the conspiracy that overthrew the Goulart government in 1964. Several months after the military took power, the journalists Harry Conn and Tad Szulc quizzed William Doherty, at the time the AIFLD director of social projects, about his assessment of the efficacy of that organization's mission to educate Latin American unionists in the values of the U.S. labor movement. Doherty boasted of the institute's successful efforts: "Well, very frankly, within the limits placed upon them by the administration of João Goulart, when they returned to their respective countries, they were very active in organizing workers, and helping unions introduce systems of collective bargaining, and modern concepts of labor-management relations. As a matter of fact, some of them were so active that they became intimately involved in some of the clandestine operations of the revolution before it took place on April 1. What happened in Brazil did not just happen—it was planned—and planned months in advance. Many of the trade union leaders—some of whom were actually trained in our institute—were involved in the revolution, and in the overthrow of the Goulart regime."[60] In the aftermath of the coup, Doherty's declaration might merely have been bureaucratic boasting designed to inflate the AIFLD's importance to boost government funding.

It is difficult to access accurately the actual role the institute may have played in shaping policies of Brazilian labor leaders who actively backed the military takeover and then led the ouster of pro-Goulart and other left-wing forces. AFL-CIO papers on Latin American affairs offer few clues that might confirm or question Doherty's portentous pronouncement about AFL-CIO operations in Brazil in the early 1960s. Voluminous documentation, stored in files several inches thick, outlines AIFLD's day-to-day operations in Brazil between 1960 and 1963. It includes correspondence between Washington and the São Paulo office, memos describing internal squabbles among Brazilian unionists, and plans to organize AIFLD-sponsored "informational" trips to the States. Only *seven* single pages of innocuous content remain in the files for 1964. We may never know what was contained in these folders and what was purged. However, extensive documentation picks up again in 1965 and continues through the rest of the decade, revealing intensive activities by U.S. unionists on behalf of their brethren in Brazil.

Equally murky is the exact extent to which Washington's funds to support the Brazilian police in the same period ended up backing activities beyond the stated scope of their congressional appropriations. In *Political Policing: The United States and Latin America* Martha J. Huggins argues that U.S. foreign police assistance programs contributed to the creation of Latin American bureaucratic-authoritarian states that came to power in Brazil (1964),

Uruguay (1973), Chile (1973), and Argentina (1976). U.S. police training in Brazil began in 1957. After the Brazilian military coup of 1964, Office of Public Security police advisors worked with the new Department of Public Safety in Brasília, the National Institute of Identification, and the National Information Service, whose primary mission was "to collect and analyze information pertinent to [Brazilian] national security, to counter [mis]information, and to [gather] information on international subversive affairs."[61] The centralizing efforts promoted by U.S. police advisors to unify policing, surveillance, and intelligence-gathering activities against opponents of the military regime led, according to Huggins, to a complicity with the security apparatuses in Brazil that routinely employed torture as a means of extracting information.[62]

In spite of U.S. government reservations about Goulart, military aid—like AID projects, AIFLD training, and police advising—increased in the years between Quadros's resignation in 1961 and Castelo Branco's rise to power in 1964. In defending his tenure in Brazil, Gordon has argued that economic aid dropped and foreign loans stalled in the same period because of Goulart's irresponsible policies. Whether sanctioning erratic economic policies that failed to curb inflation by delaying foreign loans was a rational economic policy decision or was actually designed to weaken Goulart, there seemed to be no hesitation in continuing aid to the Brazilian military in the period building up to 1964. The United States and Brazil had forged a military alliance since the 1940s, and it did not falter during the Goulart years.[63]

### Connecting with Coup Makers

Assistance to the military and police were not the only ways that the U.S. government chose to influence the internal affairs of the armed forces. The critical situation that Washington policymakers had identified called for special attention. President Kennedy approved Ambassador Gordon's request that Washington assign Colonel Vernon Walters as the U.S. military attaché to serve as the liaison between the embassy and the Brazilian generals plotting Goulart's overthrow.[64] Walters was the perfect person for the position. He had served with the Brazilian Expeditionary Force that joined the Allies in Italy during World War II and spoke fluent Portuguese. In the immediate postwar period, he was the assistant military attaché at the American Embassy in Rio. The U.S. Army then assigned him to work with the Marshall Plan in Europe, and he later accompanied Richard Nixon on his 1958 visit to Venezuela. When Walters arrived in Rio in October 1962 as the new military attaché, thirteen Brazilian officers who had served with him in Italy greeted their American friend. The next morning he met with the ambassador. According to Walters, Gordon succinctly laid out his orders: "From you I want three things: First I want to know what is going on in the Armed Forces; second, I want to be able in some measure to influence it through you; and third, most of all, I never want to be surprised."[65] Walters dutifully obeyed.

In his memoir, *Silent Missions*, Walters recollects that when he arrived in Brazil the military officers who wanted to depose Goulart were organized in small plotting groups and were not yet in communication with one another. Walters explains that the military conspirators slowly developed a coherent organization and plan: "Early in 1964 from many friends I finally got the impression that some of the plotters were beginning to get in touch with one another on a coordinated national scale. Couriers began to travel. Contingency plans began to become more specific. Directives and think papers began to circulate. Through friends I was aware of this." At the time, Castelo Branco headed the Fourth Army in the Northeast but visited Walters on at least two occasions in Rio. Walters insisted that they never talked of internal Brazilian affairs. When Castelo Branco returned to Rio as the army chief of staff, he met Walters frequently. In his memoir, Walters makes a point of emphasizing repeatedly that, although he had many conversations, meetings, and informal social encounters with Castelo Branco during the period that the general led the coup conspiracy, the two never discussed politics.

Although the federal government has declassified most State Department documents about the 1964 coup, it has sanitized of them for national security reasons. Lines, paragraphs, and even pages are blacked out and inaccessible to researchers. Thus, only circumstantial evidence points to Walters as a key figure in advising and/or assisting in coup planning. It seems clear that, at the very least, he assured military conspirators that Washington would support their movement for a regime change. Walters also proudly boasted that he accurately predicted the date the military would seize government control. Framing the revolt in the coup planners' own terminology, he writes, "I had calculated for some time that the anti-leftists were running out of time. The revolution could not occur during the carnival or Lent, especially not during Holy Week, and it would fail if they tried it on April Fools' Day. Easter fell that year on March 30. It could only be on the thirty-first. I had so informed my superiors."[66] Walters had left no surprises for Gordon.

### Goulart's Last Year in Office

Jovelino Ramos, Marcos Arruda, and Niva Padilha all remembered Goulart's thirteen final months in power as a time of intense political mobilization, student activism in poor and working-class neighborhoods, agitation at the universities in favor of redirecting the nation's priorities toward development that benefited the society as a whole, and extreme polarization. Francisco Julião's Peasant Leagues in the Northeast, literacy campaigns, and the growth of new left-wing political groups that saw themselves as more radical than the Communist Party all fostered a sense among nationalists, socialists, and others that Brazil was in the process of significant transformation. A revolution seemed to be in the making.

In January 1963, Goulart won a national plebiscite restoring full presidential powers. Mounting inflation and a balance of payment deficit, however, had begun to paralyze the economy and foster resentment and opposition among the middle classes. Goulart responded with an economic stabilization plan that reduced government spending to control the deficit, curbed wages, and reduced credit. These measures lost him support among labor backers, yet they were not drastic enough to curb skyrocketing inflation that distanced him from the middle classes. In congress, Goulart faced another dilemma. His own political party, the PTB, did not have a majority, and an unstable electoral alliance with the Partido Social Democrático (Social Democratic Party), Kubitschek's centrist party, and a cluster of other smaller parties could not guarantee enough support to enact a successful legislative agenda. Nor did the right-wing União Democrática Nacional (National Democratic Union) have enough votes to impeach him.

By late 1963, Goulart turned to more nationalist postures to shore up his political support at home. In December he issued a decree ordering a review of all government concessions in the mining industry, raising the fear that the government might nationalize foreign interests, such as the U.S.-owned Hanna Mining Company. The next month, he finally issued the regulations that enacted the profit remittance law, a measure passed by the congress the previous year and designed to encourage reinvestment of profits from foreign companies in the Brazilian economy. The U.S. government stood firmly against the measure, and Ambassador Gordon argued that the law discriminated against foreign capital. Finally, at a massive rally on March 13, Goulart announced a set of measures, including a limited land reform and the expropriation of some foreign oil refineries. Banners and signs scattered throughout the crowd called for the legalization of the Communist Party. Leonel Brizola, Goulart's firebrand brother-in-law, gave a speech convoking the government's supporters to carry out a reform agenda. The tone of the rally also sent a signal to the diverse forces planning the coup and those willing to support one. Lincoln Gordon watched the public demonstration that afternoon on television, picking up the final speeches on the radio as he hurried to the airport for a flight back to Washington for a special meeting convened by Thomas Mann.[67] In the eyes of the U.S. ambassador, the situation in Brazil had reached crisis proportions.

Thomas Mann had been assistant secretary of state for economic affairs under Eisenhower and the ambassador to Mexico during the Kennedy administration. The three-day series of meetings that he convened included President Johnson, top administration officials, and all of the U.S. ambassadors and AID directors in Latin America. In these consultations Mann presented his foreign policy approach to the hemisphere. Someone leaked the essence of his policy, dubbed the Mann Doctrine, to the U.S. press. Foreign journalists picked up the story and published it in Brazil. Mann was quoted as suggesting that "the United States will not in the future take an *a priori* position against governments coming to power through military coup."[68] It was an obvious signal to the Brazilian military forces conspiring to overthrow Goulart.

The administration asked Gordon to stay in Washington after the Mann meetings for a full cabinet-level review of policy alternatives toward Brazil. The ambassador urged the acceleration of military planning for a U.S. naval operation to back the coup.[69] Secretary of State Dean Rusk requested that the ambassador review the Brazilian situation and prepare a report within a week. Gordon rushed back to Brazil, where the political climate continued to polarize. Sectors of the Catholic Church, middle-class organizations, and conservative political forces stepped up their street mobilizations to protest Goulart's policies. Significantly, the anti-Goulart forces turned out large support among middle-class women who brandished their rosaries to signify their rejection of the government's Godless drift and protested the inflation-fueled sharp spike in prices.[70] Subsequent rebellions at the end of the month among noncommissioned officers and rank-and-file members of the armed forces in favor of democratizing the military—which Goulart did not crush and seemed to support—further startled the opposition. On March 27, Gordon sent Washington a telegram urging the administration to "prepare without delay against the contingency of needed overt intervention at a second stage."[71] The U.S. government launched Operation "Brother Sam" four days later.

The military conspiracy that Vernon Walters had followed so closely finally took shape. On March 31, just as Walters predicted (or helped plan), rebellious generals in the state of Minas Gerais led a march on Rio. Goulart flew to Brasília, then to his country estate in the south. His armed forces support crumbled. Left-wing, union, and other backers did not lead a coordinated or effective resistance. The Brazilian congress declared that he had abandoned his office. Johnson quickly recognized a provisional government. Two days later Goulart slipped into Uruguay. The generals had come to power.

### A Return to the "Special Relation"

A month after the coup, the U.S. ambassador gave his fourth talk at the Escola Superior de Guerra (Higher War College). This institution, founded in 1949 and modeled after the U.S. National War College, provided a forum for military and civilian leaders to exchange ideas about Brazilian national problems and international issues. Lincoln Gordon's talk, "New Perspectives on Brazilian-North American Relations," offered an optimistic view of international politics, although he noted that in Asia, Africa, and Latin America "there has been no visible reduction in communist forces undermining democratic institutions nor visible modifications of the tactics that they employed."[72] Gordon pointed to four recent victories for the "cause of freedom" in the world: the growing Sino-Soviet split; large-scale purchases of U.S. wheat by the Soviet government, reflecting a weakening of its national economy; recent elections in Venezuela; and the "Brazilian Revolution."[73] In Gordon's assessment, the Brazilian Revolution stood side by side with "the Marshall Plan, the end of the Berlin blockade, the defeat of Communist aggression in Korea, and the solution of the missile crisis in Cuba as one of the critical moments in world history at the mid century."

The U.S. ambassador pointed out to his audience that, fortunately, press coverage in the United States about the recent Brazilian events had been relatively accurate, although he bemoaned the ignorance of the American public (as well as many journalists) about Latin America in general and Brazil in particular. Listing many long-standing stereotypes about the continent that persisted, in which people from outside the region confused languages, countries, and cultures, Gordon emphasized that it was still all too pervasive to imagine that Latin American societies were made up of a handful of "rich and irresponsible landowners who lived in lazy luxury through the exploitation of a large and non-differentiated mass of hungry and ignorant peasants."[74] For those people who maintained these views, he added, "any change of regime in Latin America with the participation of the Armed Forces must be, inevitably, a reactionary coup to protect the egoistic interests of landowners." After having lived in Brazil for two and a half years, Gordon had come to understand how to endear himself to his nationalistic audience. The ambassador argued that Brazilians had managed to create a great civilization in the tropics with international excellence "in architecture, literature, law, music, poetry, to say nothing of soccer." Moreover, Gordon insisted, Brazil had a strong middle class and social mobility—two factors that encouraged democracy and equal opportunity.

Gordon then reiterated a question often posed to him by foreigners (and presumably his compatriots): "How could there have been any real dictatorship of the communist or Peronist kind in Brazil if the revolution had been capable of sweeping away the threat in two days with virtually no bloodshed?" The answer was simple: unlike the United States, which was torn apart by a bloody four-year civil war that cost the lives of a million men, the special genius of Brazil was that the country could solve its most serious social and political problems nonviolently. Gordon then went on to assure his audience that President Johnson was committed to the Alliance for Progress and that Washington would double its efforts to support Brazil's economic and social development. "This will not be achieved from one day to the next," he admonished his audience. "But these are the kinds of structural changes produced by investment, education, technical advancement, organization, and competent administration." With the supposed communist threat abated, the United States was committed to offering this kind of collaboration.

The "special relation" between Brazil and the United States that had slowly developed during the early twentieth century and had become consolidated during World War II and in the 1950s had been reestablished. The years of an independent foreign policy of both Quadros and Goulart in which Brazil flirted with the socialist block had come to an end. The conflicts between the Goulart government and U.S. companies over nationalization threats and profit remittance laws had dissipated. Gordon, at least from his own point of view, had saved Brazil from the communist threat.

### Managing the Press

Around the same time that Gordon was reassuring Brazilian policy and opinion makers that Washington was firmly behind the new military government, Roberto Campos, Brazil's new minister of planning, appeared on the U.S. television news show *At Issue*. He admitted that some excesses had occurred during the initial phase of the movement that deposed João Goulart. Campos argued, however, that there had been less violence and bloodshed in Brazil than in the struggle of the civil rights movement in the United States.[75] Like Gordon, he insisted that the Brazilian military had overseen a change in government through pacific means. Many mainstream journalists in the United States echoed this perspective about the new regime's benign treatment of government opponents in the aftermath of the 1964 military take-over. *Life* magazine, for example, commented, "The revolt was accomplished against little resistance and with practically no bloodshed."[76] The weekly news magazine's reporting of events featured a picture of supporters of the coup burning books and leftist literature outside the smoking ruins of the National Union of Students' headquarters in Rio de Janeiro. The article did not question the antidemocratic nature of the bonfire and only mentioned in passing that the military government had begun a "roundup of leftists." *Business Week* reassured its readers that "military commanders had staged a re-bellion, carried it out bloodlessly, and started to redirect the country toward more middle-of-the-road reform goals."[77] The *Christian Science Monitor* echoed that assessment by heralding the "deft, quick, bloodless, and well-managed revolution."[78]

Perhaps the most blatantly pro-coup journalism that reached a large U.S. audience in the months after the coup was an article titled "The Country That Saved Itself" by Clarence W. Hall, a senior editor for *Reader's Digest* and former executive editor of the *Christian Herald*. The twenty-seven-page special feature article offered a readership of approximately fifteen million Ameri-cans an enthusiastic assessment of the "Brazilian Revolution."[79] Hall told the "inspiring story of how an aroused Brazilian people stopped the com-munists from taking over their nation."[80] It is no secret that the *Reader's Digest* was a right-wing news magazine.[81] Hall had also carried out a relentless campaign by conservative Protestants to clean up Hollywood in the 1950s.[82] Yet it is impossible to know whether this special issue of *Reader's Digest* was a piece planted by the CIA, as many left-wing opponents of the military regime have speculated over the years, or whether Hall was merely offering an en-thusiastic piece of journalism by a confirmed anticommunist. Read from the distance of forty or more years, the article seems almost a caricature of bad, early 1960s Cold War propaganda.

In his assessment of U.S. press coverage of the 1964 Brazilian coup, the historian W. Michael Weis has shown that U.S. government officials suc-cessfully "managed the news" in the three-month period immediately after the military takeover to "hide U.S. involvement in the coup and to present a skewed version of reality."[83] Most U.S. reporters ignored the massive ar-rests of government opponents and other excesses, dubbing the change of power a "bloodless coup" that had avoided a civil war. To their credit, some U.S. news sources commented on the widespread detention of opposition-ists immediately after the coup d'état. *Time* magazine, for example, informed its readers that "at one point last week, some 10,000 political prisoners had been rounded up—4,000 in Rio alone. In Guanabara Bay, a white luxury liner and grey navy transport were pressed into service as temporary jails."[84] The *Newsweek* correspondent wrote: "In every Brazilian city, soldiers or policemen invaded homes, clubs, and bars, and hauled off to jail at least 5,000 'Communists,' including Miguel Arraes, the governor of the state of Pernambuco. Some of the victims were clearly Communists, but some clearly were not. And none were allowed lawyers or appeals; in fact, they were not even charged with crimes."[85] The *New York Times* acknowledged a month after the coup that "since April 1 the revolution has jailed thousands of alleged subversives."[86] In an editorial about the "Brazilian Revolution" a week later, the *Times* pointed out some excesses of the new government (the purge of the civil service, universities, labor unions, and political parties). Nonetheless, it counseled caution in coming to a quick decision about the new regime: "Yet, it still needs to be stressed that President Castelo Branco inherited a desperate economic and financial situation. He has emphasized that he earnestly desires to correct the great social injustices that obtain in Brazil today. He deserves to be given every chance to do so. Revolutions are not made in a day or a month."[87]

Even though most stories were reluctant to condemn the new Brazilian government, nevertheless, the State Department was concerned. Analysts monitoring domestic and international news coverage noted the "adverse criticism in U.S. and abroad of U.S. posture *vis à vis* removal of Goulart from Presidency" and recommended to Ambassador Gordon that the embassy limit its comments on the recent change in government. Undersecretary of State George Ball concurred and sent a telegram to Rio de Janeiro stating that he "believe[d] it especially important that news on communism, subversion, etc., emanate from Brazilian sources and that U.S. activities [should be] so conducted that such news will not be attributable to the U.S."[88]

### Reports on Torture

Although U.S. journalists had offered some information about repressive measures that took place after the military takeover, they did not seem to have followed or taken seriously the daily reports written by their Brazilian colleagues detailing torture carried out by the Brazilian government in Recife and Rio de Janeiro in the three months after the coup. Many of these denunciations appeared in the *Correio da Manhã*, which had originally backed the military takeover but soon joined the ranks of those critical of the new regime. The *Correio da Manhã* correspondent in Recife first referred to torture in a dispatch on April 7, 1964. Additional news coverage appeared throughout the year. Márcio Moreira Alves, a young journalist from a prominent Rio de Janeiro family, spearheaded the campaign of denunciations. Alves's investigative reporting substantiated over eighty cases of torture. "Silence is complicity, something I abhore," he defiantly wrote.[89] The methods employed by the military and documented by Alves would become all too familiar to opponents of the regime over the following years: electric shock, the parrot's perch, dunking in foul water, sensory depravation, and clapping a prisoner's ears to destroy the eardrums.

Alves used the *Correio da Manhã* articles as a vehicle to demand that an independent commission investigate allegations of torture and death in order to punish those responsible. The flurry of denunciations that appeared in the press forced President Castelo Branco to send his chief military advisor (and future president) General Ernesto Geisel to the Northeast to investigate the allegations in September 1964. While no one was punished during his visit, it served to halt the torturing of political prisoners in Recife for nearly a year. As Elio Gaspari, journalist and historian of the military regime, has pointed out: "The Geisel Mission wanted to be a liberal commitment by the government, but it ended up being an agreement that instead of ending torture pardoned it. The conciliation of September 1964 damaged the conscience of the military leadership by offering the impression of having saved simultaneously the skin of most prisoners and the uniform of the torturers. It fed the legend cultivated by the Armed Forces according to which even while leading a repressive regime, it could maintain distance from the crimes committed by the regime."[90]

In 1966, Alves compiled many of the articles and reports that he had collected in 1964 and 1965 and published them under the title *Torturas e Torturados* (Tortures and Tortured). The Ministry of Justice ordered the seizure of most copies of the first edition under the pretext that the volume "offended the dignity of the Armed Forces." The move was also part of an attempt to invalidate Alves's candidacy for the Federal Congress on the opposition Movimento Democrático Brasileiro (Brazilian Democratic Movement, MDB) ticket. In November 1966, the Supreme Electoral Court ruled that publishing denunciations of torture was not "subversive" and permitted the journalist to run for office. He was easily elected. In June 1967, the Federal Appeals Court overruled the decision of the Ministry of Justice to seize the book, permitting Alves to publish a second edition.[91] In *Torturas e Torturados*, Alves admitted that the torture of political prisoners had, indeed, declined in the Northeast by August 1964. However, he documented an increase of incidents in Rio de Janeiro by the air force, army police, the intelligence center of the marines, and the political police.[92]

As the military regime consolidated its rule, news of torture decreased. In 1964, there were 20 reported deaths of political prisoners (among them nine "suicides") and 203 denunciations of torture of detainees while under custody that were registered in military courts. As Elio Gaspari has pointed out, these statistics do not reflect the actual number of cases, as hundreds of others were arrested, tortured, and then released without formal charges made against them, making it hard to trace the actual number of torture victims. Nevertheless, the number of reported torture cases declined to 84 in 1965 and to 66 the following year. While these figures may underestimate the actual number of victims, the declining trend probably reflects reality on the ground and in the prisons.[93] The issue of torture receded to the sidelines, as political questions and the defense of freedom of speech, press, and the right to assembly under the dictatorship took center stage. This, in part, explains why journalistic accounts of the political situation in Brazil published in the United States between 1965 and 1969, even those written by those harshly critical of the regime, condemned the arbitrary nature of military rule but did not mention torture as a systematic government policy.[94]

### Congressional Complicity

In tone and style typical of most congressional debates, Senator Wayne Morse of Oregon took to the floor of the U.S. Senate on April 3, 1964, offering his "high compliments to the President of the United States" for statements attributed to him and published in an Associated Press dispatch regarding the recent events in Brazil.[95] After asking unanimous consent of the body to have the article titled "L.B.J. Sends Warm Note to Mazzilli" read into the *Congressional Record*, the august senator continued praising the president. "Here again, President Johnson has acted with the same great care, calmness, and deliberation that have characterized his other actions; and he deserves our thanks for the note he sent to the new President of Brazil." Morse, of course, was referring to Johnson's quick recognition of the new Brazilian regime the day before.

Senator Morse then emphasized that the U.S. government had *not* been involved in the military takeover. "I wish to make very clear that I can testify, on the basis of such knowledge as I have — and I think the members of the Senate Foreign Relations Committee were kept thoroughly briefed on all details of the developments in Brazil — that the United States in no way intervened or was responsible in any way for the action which occurred in Brazil. I am convinced that the developments there were completely Brazilian; and they were long in the making." Confident that he had been properly briefed by the government, Morse proceeded to repeat the script provided by Gordon, the CIA, and State Department officials, adding his own interpretative touch to the events that had just taken place the preceding week. "The developments in Brazil did not result from action by a military junta or from a coup by a military junta. Instead, the overthrow of the presidency of Brazil resulted from developments in which the Congress of Brazil, acting under the Constitution of Brazil, was the guiding force, and was reinforced by a military group which backed up the preservation of the Brazilian constitutional system." Morse argued that Goulart could have remained in Brazil and stood trial in connection with charges that would have been made against him, but he insisted, "The Congress of Brazil and the governors and the people of Brazil could not be expected to stand idly by and see their government and its forces gradually, step by step, turned over to a Communist apparatus." The Senator from Oregon then offered his opinion that President Johnson had "very appropriately waited until the legal and constitutional system of Brazil had worked its course" and then sent a "warm message" to the new president of Brazil. Johnson's "beautiful statement," prudence, and leadership, Morse argued, merited his congratulations.

Morse then proceeded to read a lengthy speech expressing his opposition to "McNamara's war in South Vietnam." Earlier that year, he and Ernest Gruening of Alaska were the only two senators who had voted against President Johnson's Gulf of Tonkin resolution empowering the White House to escalate the war in Vietnam. Ironically, although Morse was willing to take a lone stand in challenging the administration's foreign policy in Southeast Asia, he stood behind the White House when it came to Brazil. In comments to his fellow senators later that year, Morse reiterated his conclusions: "Tonight no Senator can cite Brazil as an example of a military dictatorship, because it is not. Self-government on the part of the Brazilian people continues to proceed. If anyone thinks not, let them look at what is happening in Brazil with respect to an exchange of points of view in Parliament, in the press, and in many sources and forces of public opinion."[96] House members echoed the opinion of their colleague in the Senate.[97]

U.S. ambassador Gordon had been wise in counseling the importance of staging an apparent legitimacy in the transfer of power after the military forced Goulart from office on April 1, 1964. That veneer of legality and the ongoing attempts by the generals in power to control political dissent within the framework of a parliamentary regime during its first years of rule allayed the fears of most U.S. politicians. They were impressed by the formalities of democracy in Brazil and ignored the fact that the generals had used the arbitrary authority of the Institutional Acts to guarantee that the constantly changing rules of the game kept them in power. In the first four years of military rule in Brazil, there was general, almost unanimous, agreement in Congress that the United States should back the new regime.

## Top Secret Documents

The White House, State Department officials, and their representatives in Brazil, moreover, contributed to congressional, journalistic, and public misconceptions and misunderstandings about the events on the ground in Brazil. Ambassador Gordon, among others, actively collaborated in the campaign of misinformation and denial. At the time of the coup, Gordon insisted that the U.S. embassy had been an innocent bystander, rooting for the anti-Goulart forces yet remaining meticulously above the fray. In Gordon's 1966 Senate confirmation hearing when he was nominated to become the assistant secretary of state for inter-American affairs, he repeated this posture: "Neither I nor other officials of the U.S. Government, nor the Government in any way, shape, or manner was involved, aiding and abetting or participating [in the overthrow of Goulart]." [98] This denial, however, became untenable in 1977 when a young graduate student at the University of Texas innocently stumbled on declassified material that essentially proved that the former U.S. ambassador and nominee for undersecretary of state had perjured himself in testimony before Congress and deceived the public in statements about events surrounding the coup.

In 1974, Phyllis R. Parker began the master's program at the Lyndon B. Johnson School of Public Affairs at the University of Texas in Austin. "I had worked in government as a social worker and as an administrator in the Texas Social Workers' School. I was burned out, so I went to graduate school," she remembered thirty years later. [99] Her interests were in foreign policy and education, and she had to do an internship and write a master's thesis to complete the degree. At her husband's suggestion she visited the LBJ Presidential Library to see if it had any material that she might use. "I was interested in Chile (because my husband had grown up there), or Peru or Brazil. They said that there had been a change in government in Brazil, and there would be declassified documents available. I imagined economic and political papers with charts, which did not sound interesting, but I thought that I could do it. And they said, 'Come back tomorrow, and we'll let you know what we have.'"

She returned the next day and an archivist informed her that the library had a large cache of documents on Brazil that were classified. "I said, 'What does that mean?' They said that I had to request that they be opened. I asked if I could request that *all* of them be opened. They said yes, so I signed a few papers and then went off to D.C. to work with [Congresswoman] Barbara Jordan, which was much more interesting."

When Parker returned to Austin at the end of the summer, her advisor recommended that she read Thomas E. Skidmore's *Politics in Brazil* to learn background history about mid-twentieth-century Brazil. Then she began examining the declassified presidential documents. "I looked at the papers thinking that I would just add something to what Skidmore had written . . . As I read more and more documents, I kept on thinking, 'Why hadn't Skidmore put this information in his book.' I thought that he was saving it to the end. So I looked at John Dulles's book and realized halfway through that they didn't know about it."[100] "It" was Operation Brother Sam, designed by Gordon and the Joint Chiefs of Staff to offer military and logistical support for the anti-Goulart forces should a civil war break out. Since 1964, Brazilian leftists had maintained that the U.S. government had actively supported the armed forces that deposed the Goulart government. Phyllis Parker had discovered proof that the left had been right: U.S. government officials had lied about Washington's involvement in the events of 1964.

Realizing that she had found, as the historian Richard Graham pointed out to her, a "pot of gold," she traveled to Boston to verify her findings at the Kennedy Presidential Library. "I spent a few days there, got some papers, and then went to Washington to interview Lincoln Gordon at the Brookings Institute . . . When he saw the documents he thought that the story was out and that he needed to do the best spin on it. The truth is that the story was not out, and I didn't understand things. But he talked, and I got to understand the documents." Ironically, Gordon ended up explaining the State Department's coding and helped Parker untangle the abbreviations, references, and obscure bureaucratic language embedded in the material that she had collected. He then sent her off to the Central Intelligence Agency to talk to Associate Director Vernon Walters. "I was an innocent young twenty-seven-year-old. He [Walters] asked me what specific questions I wanted to ask. I didn't understand what documents I had, so I asked about covert actions. He said that we had them everywhere, that it was no big deal . . . I asked him about the naval task force that was coming down. 'Oh, that was just to show an American flag to help with stability, and it would be there to help take out Americans if something blew up at the time.' I didn't know at the time that at the bottom of the documents in acronyms it indicated that the task force had nuclear capability."

Phyllis Parker published her findings in *Brazil and the Quiet Intervention, 1964*. It is a slim monograph, a mere hundred pages long.[101] Yet it revealed an important, untold story. In the preface, Parker poses the contradiction between the values of justice, equality, and political freedom as defended by the country's founding fathers and Washington policymakers' practices abroad: "U.S. policies seem structured to benefit the United States politically, economically, and militarily with little apparent regard for the impact these efforts have on the integrity of other nations' institutions. In this setting, the rights claimed in the Declaration of Independence sound increasingly like principles that apply only to the United States and its citizens, often at the expense of those very rights for other peoples."[102]

"Operation Brother Sam," the military contingency plan developed by the Pentagon and the White House that Parker uncovered, went into motion on March 31, 1964. The aircraft carrier *Forrestal*, accompanied by six supporting destroyers and four petroleum tankers, sailed toward Brazilian waters and was scheduled to arrive on April 11. Additional attack oilers, ammunition ships, and provision ships joined the task force. At the same time, the Joint Chiefs of Staff ordered 250 twelve-gauge shotguns airlifted to Puerto Rico and sent 110 tons of small arms and ammunitions to McGuire Air Force Base, New Jersey, for airlifting to Brazil. In addition, the military prepared large amounts of motor gas, jet fuel, aviation gas, diesel, and kerosene for transportation to Brazil.[103] The contingency plan remained just that. The swiftness with which the Brazilian armed forces seized power and the weakness of the resistance ensured that the military consolidated its control over the country quickly. With an interim president chosen, a façade of legitimacy covering the Brazilian military's actions, warm wishes extended by President Johnson, and apparent calm throughout the country, the White House canceled the orders directing the task force to proceed to Brazil. The United States government and its defenders dismissed as left-wing and nationalist hysteria those rumors and speculations that circulated in Brazil alleging that Washington had been behind the military takeover. Gordon could comfortably claim that the coup had been 100 percent Brazilian. In one rather narrow and formal sense he was right. The internal political dynamics of Goulart's government engendered widespread opposition among significant sectors of Brazilian society at the same time that confidence in Goulart's ability to govern waned, even among his erstwhile supporters. Those factors played the essential role in determining the results of events in 1964. Nevertheless, the

Washington policymakers still chose to intervene behind the scenes, pushing the outcome in their desired direction through a myriad of means. The Brazilian armed forces took power without having to call on the U.S. military force for direct and overt support, but the clandestine assistance encouraged and emboldened the opposition to Goulart.

When the news broke in 1976 about the declassified documents revealing Operation Brother Sam, former ambassador Gordon issued a six-page statement insisting that the 1964 "revolution" had been, as the title of his declaration insisted, "Made in Brazil." Criticizing "revisionist historians" who were "opposed to the entire thrust of U. S. foreign policy during the cold war," Gordon defended the statement that he had made to the Senate in February 1966 that "the movement which overthrew President Goulart was a purely, 100 percent—not 99.44 percent—but 100 percent purely Brazilian movement." However, he failed to quote the next sentence in his Senate testimony: "Neither the American Embassy nor I personally played any part in the process whatsoever." In defense of the task force, Gordon argued that it was for a "limited form of American action in a particular hypothetical contingency, a civil war with Brazil divided on geographic lines, the forces evenly matched, and with one side recognized by us."[104] Were that hypothesis to have taken place, Gordon argued, the task force would have served three objectives: "(a) to provide logistical support, especially in petroleum products, to the side we believed to represent moderation and democracy; (b) to discourage the opposing side through the showing of the American flag on a power vessel; and (c) to assist if necessary in the evacuation of American citizens from regions involved in civil combat."[105] Gordon maintained this line of argument twenty-five years later when he published a special supplement to his book Brazil's Second Chance defending the actions he had taken and the arguments he had made watching over the 1964 military takeover.[106]

Although Gordon stated in "Made in Brazil" that he had been concerned with evacuating American citizens from Brazil, he never mentioned this preoccupation in any of the declassified cables or telegrams that crisscrossed the wires between the ambassador and the State Department in 1964. Moreover, if Washington had sent the naval task force to Brazil to rescue all the Americans in the country at the time, it could never have done so in an efficient manner given the limited number of boats and the enormous size of the country. In 2003, Gordon again reiterated this justification: "In [the event of civil war], I believed that a 'showing of the American flag' might serve two purposes: (a) to exert psychological pressure in favor of the anti-Goulart side and (b) to assist in the evacuation of the thousands of U.S. civilians living in or visiting all regions of Brazil."[107] By this time, the ambassador seemed to have convinced himself that in March 1964 he had been concerned for the lives of American citizens in Brazil. This seems plausible enough, though, again, he never mentioned it as a cause for concern in 1964, and it seems suspicious that it became a line of defense only after the American public got wind of the naval operation's existence more than a decade later.

Gordon's own admission, however, proves to be the undoing of this argument. In an interview in 2005, Gordon explained how his son spent the 1963–64 academic year teaching in Brazil between high school and college. Following this line of conversation, Gordon was asked to remember whether he was concerned for his son's safety in March 1964. He responded: "No. I don't think that question arose. There wasn't any sizable anti-American[ism] . . . I was fairly certain it wasn't like Iraq at the moment . . . I don't recall that ever entering my mind . . . We didn't really have a sense of that kind of civil disturbance."[108] Gordon went on to discuss the evacuation portion of the plan, had it become necessary: "We had a plan for showing the flag and also evacuating our civilians if it got to that situation, which would have been a big job. I think there were 15,000. It would have been a big operation. And obviously whether it developed into nastiness, we never had any sense . . . but [civil war] wasn't a political threat to the American community."

What *was* a threat, apparently, was a Brazilian government that remained outside the orbit of U.S. influence and geopolitical interests. In 1964, the U.S. public, as well as senators (who had allegedly been thoroughly briefed), embraced the logic presented by the Johnson administration, its representatives, and the media that it managed. The Cold War consensus remained pervasive, and only a small number of liberal and left-wing journalists questioned U.S. foreign policy for Latin America or the rest of the world. The Goulart government's ambiguous program, moreover, never clearly declared itself in favor of a radical restructuring of Brazil's economy and society. It did not offer a clear-cut model for change, nor did it manage to excite or capture the imagination of the new generation of youth that had become active in the civil rights movement and was slowly beginning to question Johnson's policies in Vietnam. Publicity about poverty in the Brazilian Northeast may have inspired a handful of Peace Corps or Papal Volunteers to dedicate two years of their lives to helping the poor in the "developing" world, but bridges had not been built between Brazil and liberal or left-wing forces in the United States that could have elicited more than a flurry of journalistic denunciations of the military takeover. Slowly, over time, that situation would change.

## CAPÍTULO I

## "A gente quer ter voz ativa"

*We want to have our own voice*
*In this fate of ours have a say,*
*But the spinning wheel comes along*
*To steal fate, to take it away.*

**Chico Buarque, "Roda viva," 1967**

Student demonstration, Rio de Janeiro, 1967. ACERVO ÚLTIMA HORA, ARQUIVO PÚBLICO DO ESTADO DE SÃO PAULO.

Marcos Arruda entered his fourth year as a geology student at the Federal University of Rio de Janeiro in 1964.[1] After graduating, he had planned to find a job that would allow him to advance both his political and professional goals. As the president of the Geology Students' National Executive Body, an association linked to the National Union of Students (União Nacional de Estudantes, UNE), Marcos had a clear political agenda: Brazil should extract its mineral deposits within the context of an economic model that favored national development over the interests of foreign mining companies.

When news reached Marcos of the March 31 military coup, he immediately went to UNE's national headquarters, housed in an old majestic building facing the Flamengo Beach. As he approached the edifice, he saw it in flames. Right-wing youth were tossing furniture out of the windows. Marcos decided to head downtown to the National Engineering School to join resistance forces he hoped might be gathering to defend the constitutionally elected Goulart government. There he found that students had blockaded themselves inside the building, preparing to resist, but had few arms and no real notion of what to do. They soon realized they were setting themselves up for massive arrests, so they decided to disperse. As Marcos once again passed by the UNE headquarters, smoke billowed out of the building and flames leaped from the windows. He remembers crying as he confronted the new political reality facing the Brazilian left and the country as a whole. At the end of the year, the university's administration cancelled the graduation ceremony because it might have turned into a political event protesting the new military government and told the members of Marcos's class, known for their socialist leanings, to claim their diplomas individually at a university office.

Over the next two years, Marcos got closer to Ação Popular (AP), the left-wing organization that had gained so much influence in the student movement. AP's leadership was beginning to orient its members to consider jobs in factories or in the countryside as part of a strategy to build a mass-based opposition to the military regime. Frustrated by the limitations of his work as a professional geologist, unable to find a job in Rio because he was blacklisted, and sought by the political police as the government coordinated a wave of arrests targeting cadre of Ação Popular, Marcos moved to São Paulo in early 1967. At the time, the long arm of the law did not reach him in São Paulo, and he managed to get a job teaching geological science in a high school, while working part time as an editorial assistant at *Realidade*, an investigative magazine. He also found time, as he had done in Rio, to volunteer in a literacy program for workers. Marcos remembers how gratifying it was to help functionally illiterate workers develop reading and writing skills that also enabled them to construct their own vision of reality and exercise power over knowledge. Convinced by Ação Popular's proposal to "integrate into production," as the new political orientation was called, Marcos started looking for an industrial job. Shortly before the government crackdown on civil society in 1968, he found a job as an unskilled worker in a foundry. As he prepared to labor side by side with the working class, his friend Jean Marc Von der Weid, a student leader who was also a member of Ação Popular, had become a target of the military regime.[2]

Jean Marc's mother, Dona Regina,[3] still lives not far from the UNE headquarters that was set ablaze in 1964. Her living room looks out onto a graceful curve of apartment buildings lining the Flamengo Beach. Dona Regina's elegant, ample dwelling is carefully decorated with relics of a wealthy past. Portraits of nineteenth-century relatives hang alongside gilded mirrors and Brazilian baroque religious carvings, suggesting that the family's ancestors might have been coffee planters and slave owners. "My grandparents were large landholders, the Azevedo Sodré family. Later my grandfather was the mayor of Rio de Janeiro," she recounted in an interview.[4] It was this political heritage that Dona Regina credits with motivating her in 1968 to organize the families of students who had been arrested during that rebellious year. "My father was a liberal, above all a democrat. The landowners began to do things that he didn't agree with, so he got involved in the revolutions of 1922, 1924, 1930 . . . Because [President] Gétulio [Vargas] promised a constitution but then didn't offer one, in 1932 he joined the revolution in São Paulo. In 1937, he was in the Lower House when Gétulio closed the Congress, and then there were the years of Vargas dictatorship."

Regina Von der Weid, like most people from her social class and lineage, grew up in a traditional Catholic family. She married a Swiss mineralogist whom she met while he was examining deposits on her family's lands. Before the 1964 coup, her entire family had supported Carlos Lacerda, the right-wing journalist, governor of the State of Guanabara, and virulent opponent of Getúlio Vargas and later João Goulart. It was only natural that she and many family members joined the hundreds of thousands who marched through downtown Rio on April 2, 1964, in the "Victory March" blessed by Cardinal Jaime Câmara. Planned by conservative Catholics before the coup as one of a series of protests designed to coalesce opposition to Goulart, it was transformed by the organizers into a celebration of regime change. It was the last right-wing demonstration in which she or other family members participated.

When her son Jean Marc got involved in the radical high school students movement in 1966, Dona Regina was aware of her son's political activities. "A mother is always a bit worried, but . . . no one imagined that it would turn into what it became." After entering the university, Jean Marc immersed himself in student politics, eventually becoming a member of Ação Popular. By 1968, he was elected president of the student organization representing the Federal University of Rio's School of Chemistry and had become an important leader in protest activities.[5] Dona Regina recalled those years: "We never stopped backing him, but we felt that it was getting dangerous. At that point, I got involved with a group of mothers that supported the students." The group first met in a private high school and then every week in a different person's house. "We always brought knitting as a cover, just in case the police came and asked what we were doing. The group gave backing and assistance to students who were in prison, denounced arrests, and helped those who were underground." During one particularly violent confrontation between students and the police, Jean Marc was arrested and charged with multiple violations of the National Security Law. "He was in jail, but we didn't know where he was. We hired a lawyer. At the time, the president of the Brazilian Bar Association was a friend of mine, and the association mobilized its forces until we found out where he was." When Jean Marc was finally released under the condition that he appear in court on his trial date, he decided to go underground. Dona Regina calmly explained, "He knew that he would be found guilty because it was obvious that he was part of the National Student Union." At the time, holding a leadership role in the illegal student organization could mean several years in prison. Then, in September 1969, the police discovered his whereabouts and arrested him again. By then torture was the norm, and Jean Marc was given no mercy.

Jovelino Ramos did not know Jean Marc or Marcos Arruda personally in those years, even though all three of them had links with Ação Popular. "I was not a militant," Jovelino explained, "but I provided connections between AP and the progressive Protestant church."[6] In 1966, Jovelino joined a group of Catholic and Protestant intellectuals to produce the publication Paz e Terra (Peace and Land), inspired by Pope John XIII's ecumenical message. "I wrote for the magazine and was on the editorial board."[7] Jovelino also got his congregation involved in social action. Jovelino's multiple political activities eventually led to his arrest. "In 1966, they raided my house. The police arrived at 5:00 a.m. My wife opened the door . . . They said that they were from the customs office and had a package that I had to sign for." Jovelino's wife, Myra, woke up her husband. Jovelino, who had anticipated that the police would eventually arrest him, quickly came up with a plan. He took off his pajamas and entered the living room in his underwear. "They asked me if I was Reverend Jovelino, and I said, 'Yes.' They said that I had to let them search the house. They wanted to look at my books to see if I had any subversive material and then I had to accompany them. I said, 'No problem, I just need to get dressed. You don't want me to go in my underwear.'" Jovelino went into the bathroom and turned on the water. His wife came in, aimed the showerhead at the plastic shower curtain to make a lot of noise, and then returned to the living room. Meanwhile the police waited, accepted a cup of coffee, grew impatient, and finally broke into the bathroom to discover that Jovelino had disappeared. The police then organized a systematic neighborhood search for the underwear-clad reverend. Meanwhile, Jovelino, who had hidden nearby, called his friend Lysâneas Maciel, a well-known lawyer in Rio de Janeiro, who happened to be a member of the Ipanema Church. Maciel, who later became a vocal congressional opponent of the military regime, promptly showed up. He advised Jovelino to dress in his fanciest clothes. Jovelino contacted his wife, who brought him a suit, tie, and dark glasses, and he and his lawyer walked right through the police blockade, engaged in a heated discussion about Rio's rival soccer teams. Jovelino remained hidden under the protection of the Ipanema Church (now called Comunidade Cristã de Ipanama).

Several weeks later, he presented himself to the police and was charged with subversion. The government presented vague, generic accusations that between 1965 and 1967 he and several others had tried "through writing, study, plans, meetings, and other actions . . . to organize or reorganize . . . the Brazilian Communist Party by reactivating a preexistent clandestine organization called Ação Popular."[8] The charges alleged he had encouraged people in the church to become involved in social action. Realizing that possibilities for open and public opposition to the regime had disappeared from him and aware that he had become a target of continuing surveillance and harassment by the political police, Jovelino moved to the United States in March 1968 with the advice and help of friends. His political friends had argued that Jovelino possessed vital international contacts through the World Student Christian Federation (WSCF), and they suggested he might be helpful to the opposition abroad. Jovelino thought it would be a temporary exile, assuming things would improve within a year or so.

In 1967, the year the government charged Jovelino with subversion, the popular young songwriter Chico Buarque composed the score for a musical that opened in Rio in January 1968. The name of the show, Roda Viva (Spinning Wheel), could also be roughly translated as "the rat race" or life's hustle and bustle. *Roda Viva* parodied the life of a rock star consumed by his own fame.[9] The experimental theater director José Celso Martinez Correa took Chico Buarque's skeletal script and created an audience-confrontation piece that became an overnight hit. After a controversial run in Rio, the show moved to São Paulo. On July 17, 1968, right-wing thugs disrupted the performance, attacked the cast, and destroyed the scenery. When the musical opened in Porto Alegre in October, paramilitary groups kidnapped two actors, and the police shut down the show. It was yet another ominous sign of a gathering storm.

The musical's title song captured the spirit of the time. Those who opposed the military regime were on a spinning wheel that circled faster and faster. Regina Von der Weid, her son Jean Marc, Marcos Arruda, Jovelino Ramos, and thousands of others clung to that whirling wheel that offered hope for an end to the dictatorship. In the eyes of the generals, however, the events that unfolded in 1968 only confirmed their fear that, even though they controlled the political system, suddenly Brazil was spiraling out of control.

# 2

# THE BIRTH OF
# A MOVEMENT

News of the seizure of dictatorial power by the Brazilian military junta marks a disastrous reversal for liberty in Latin America. What is even worse is the continuation of American financial backing of such a regime.

By doing so, we are rapidly transforming the Alliance for Progress into an alliance for progressive militarism in the western hemisphere. The semantics from Washington and from the Brazilian cabal, seeking to allay fears for democratic institutions in that great nation, will not fool any but those who want to be fooled. —**Senator Wayne Morse, October 29, 1965**

Lyndon B. Johnson, White House, 1964.
PHOTO BY YOICHI OKAMOTO. LYNDON B. JOHNSON LIBRARY.

In the months following the 1964 military takeover, the Brazilian generals consolidated their political power over the country. On April 9, the military issued an Institutional Act, the first of many, that significantly expanded executive power. The arrests of thousands of left-wing activists pushed the Brazilian Communist Party and other socialist and revolutionary organizations underground. The new political climate also paralyzed many of Goulart's outspoken partisans in the labor movement and in the Brazilian Labor Party. A purged congress and the suspension of political rights of the most vocal populist, nationalist, and left-wing leaders that had supported the Goulart government, as well as other prominent politicians, among them former president Kubitschek and many of his backers, also undermined immediate political challenges to the military's rule. To consolidate their hold on power, the generals and their civilian allies then turned to economic stabilization. Washington policymakers and international lending agencies authorized new loans to bail out the faltering economy. The U.S. Agency for International Development (AID) and other Alliance for Progress–related programs significantly stepped up their activities. The U.S. Congress had authorized $625 million in program-type loans to Brazil during the less than three and a half years of the Quadros and Goulart governments. Of that amount, the U.S. government disbursed $525 million only after the coup. Congress authorized an additional $625 million to the country between late 1964 and 1968.[1] AID director William Ellis defended this policy to the House Subcommittee on Inter-American Affairs by arguing that, although the U.S. government could not control the political situation in country, it could support those groups within Brazil that "share our common view."[2] Through economic and military aid as well as diplomatic means, the Johnson administration sent a series of clear signals to Brasília that it gave its unconditional support to the military regime.[3]

Unlike other moments during the course of the twentieth century when the Brazilian military intervened in the political process to remove a government and then quickly relinquished power, this time the generals decided to prolong their grip on the reins of the state. In July 1964, Castelo Branco approved a constitutional amendment extending his term in office until March 1967. It also postponed presidential elections for fourteen months until November 1966. The following year, in October gubernatorial races in nine states, the moderate opposition candidates in Rio de Janeiro and Minas Gerais beat out the military-backed politicians of the União Democrática Nacional (National Democratic Union, UDN), signaling that in those two key contests the generals didn't enjoy as much popular support as they had thought. Although Castelo Branco let the winners take office, he responded to the voters' "electoral mutiny" by promulgating Institutional Act No. 2 (IA-2). The decree abolished the existing political parties and replaced them with two parties: the progovernment Aliança Renovadora Nacional (National Renovating Alliance, ARENA) and an opposition party Movimento Democrático Brasileiro (Brazilian Democratic Movement, MDB). The new authoritarian measure also made the future election of the president, vice president, and all governors indirect.

Castelo Branco did not stop there. In his attempts to ensure continuity in consolidating the goals of the 1964 "revolution," he issued a series of other decrees, pieces of legislation, and a new constitution. In February 1966, the government announced Institutional Act No. 3 (IA-3). With this decree, state legislatures, which were packed with progovernment majorities and appointed the state governors, would now also appoint the mayors of state capitals and other designated "national security" cities. In essence, an indirect electoral process selected all-important executive positions in the country. Castelo Branco also had to deal with the presidential succession, and General Artur Costa e Silva, his former competitor for the position of chief executive in 1964 and the war minister, was now the leading contender to replace him. The opposition MDB announced that it would boycott the rigged election process, and promilitary forces duly voted for Costa e Silva on October 6, 1966. In congressional elections the next month, the progovernment ARENA party retained a large majority in both houses; however, a new generation of young opposition politicians won seats in the Chamber of Deputies. Over 20 percent of the electorate invalidated their own ballots or left them blank. In a final legislative push in January 1967, the congress approved a new constitution that incorporated the arbitrary provisions in the different executive decrees. The constitution codified the indirect election of the president, fortified the executive branch's control over federal expenditures, and gave the federal government sweeping powers to address national security threats. In addition a National Press Law and a National Security Law, signed only four days before Castelo Branco left office, legally consolidated the military's notions that internal security threats endangered the nation more than any external ones. The legislation empowered the central government to limit public opposition, prohibit strikes, and curtail civil liberties. Before leaving office, Castelo Branco, the allegedly moderate military leader of the "revolution" who had supposedly protected the nation against "hard-line" forces in the military, had consolidated and legitimized the authoritarian power of the regime.[4]

Castelo Branco established new political norms. Over the following twenty years, every time military rulers concluded that their power was threatened, they changed the rules of the game through executive decree. Democratic procedures became moving targets, constantly manipulated and modified to fit the will of the armed forces and the civilian politicians who supported the military. The establishment of ARENA and the MDB created a new two-party formula that offered an appearance of congressional normalcy. This enabled the regime to maintain the façade of democratic rule. However, every time it seemed that oppositionists might gain the upper hand, new decrees cancelled electoral officials' mandates, suspended citizens' political rights, censored the press, restricted political debate, changed electoral laws, and intimidated those who spoke out.

Yet, from afar, the Brazilian military regime seemed different from that of other countries in Latin America where the generals had taken over the state. Castelo Branco did not evoke the image of the personal dictator who might remain in power for decades. In fact, over the course of twenty-one years in power, the top brass carried out a closed-door presidential succession process that gave the appearance that they were following the electoral timetable established before 1964. Here again, political expediency outweighed constitutional provisions in the transition of two of the five generals who assumed the office of the president, as the military changed the rules to respond to political crises. Overall, the generals who ran the country and their civilian supporters craftily manipulated the political system to retain backing among sectors of the population. They successfully used the maimed democratic institutions that remained in place to legitimize their hold on power. Although Senator Morse, who had supported the 1964 takeover, may have become disillusioned with the Brazilian government when news of Institutional Act No. 2 reached his Washington office, to most unsophisticated observers, including many foreign journalists, the new regime seemed at times only mildly authoritarian. That illusion helped garner international endorsement and sustain the military's hold on the country for the first three years. In late 1967 and throughout 1968, however, a new generation of radicalized youth challenged the political status quo and demanded an end to the military rule.

Few politicized people in the United States gazed southward during the mid-1960s. Those who did, however, saw that U.S. foreign policy also seemed to be running amuck in lands other than Southeast Asia. For some, Vietnam was not just an aberration in Washington's foreign policy but rather seemed to exemplify a pattern. This chapter charts the uneven and gradual clustering of those who began to question U.S. government policies toward Latin America in the 1960s. Slowly, imperceptibly, a loose network of individuals, groups, collectives, and projects emerged to challenge Washington's policies in Cuba, the Dominican Republic, and then Brazil, as the Cold War consensus began to fall apart in America.

## U.S. Hands off Cuba

Most scholars that have analyzed the radical political mobilizations of the 1960s in the United States point to the interaction of the civil rights and anti–Vietnam war movements as two forces that broke the relative political stability of the previous decade. The post–War War II assault on the Communist Party and its orbit had placed all left-wing organizations in the United States on the defensive by the early 1950s. McCarthyism and disillusionment with the Soviet Union had chipped away at the progressive layers of Popular Front "fellow travelers" who had supported the socialist state and many other left-wing causes. Within the liberal and leftist milieu, few paid much attention to Latin America. To their credit, liberal and progressive magazines joined the weakened "Old Left" in denouncing the CIA-sponsored political coup in Guatemala in 1954. Relatively few people, however, took to the streets and mounted picket lines to protest Washington's backing of the overthrow of the nationalist government of Jacobo Árbenz Guzmán and the installation of a military regime.

Four years later, a band of bearded fighters in the Sierra Maestra Mountains of eastern Cuba altered the apparent public apathy to political events unfolding in Latin America and the Caribbean. As the historian Van Gosse has argued in his study of the early response to the Cuban revolution in the United States, youthful enthusiasm for Castro and his fellow guerrillas broke through the Cold War curtain of containment.[5] Soon after Castro took power, public opinion polls showed almost a third of those surveyed looked favorably on Fidel.[6] Liberals and leftists offered their joint support for the Cuban rebels with a cause in the initial phases of the revolution. Student leaders including Saul Landau and Staughton Lynd joined this movement as their first action in a long history of participation in organizations critical of U.S. foreign policy. African American activists and artists such as LeRoi Jones (later Imamu Amiri Baraka) wrote and spoke positively about the new Cuban government. Fidel Castro's decision to stay at the Hotel Theresa in Harlem during a meeting at the United Nations in 1960 sent a signal to many that the Caribbean-based revolution backed the fight against racial discrimination in the United States. Students and intellectuals, liberals and leftists, and emergent radicals (both black and white) offered their backing to the Cuban revolution. Gosse points to these solidarity efforts as a fundamental founding movement of the embryonic New Left that would flourish throughout the decade and beyond.[7]

An article in the Nation magazine on January 23, 1960, sparked the coalescing of these disparate forces into what became the Fair Play for Cuba Committee.[8] The committee's debut in a New York Times advertisement three months later suggested that the U.S. media had offered filtered and biased stories about the Cuban revolution.[9] The ad refuted reports from U.S. News and World Report, Newsweek, and other media sources about the nature of the Cuban revolution and called on readers to learn "more of the truth about revolutionary Cuba as it is today" by contacting the Fair Play for Cuba Committee in New York City. James Baldwin, Simone de Beauvoir, Truman Capote, Norman Mailer, and Jean-Paul Sartre were among the literati who sponsored the committee's public unveiling. According to Gosse, 1,500 wrote in asking about more information or requesting to join the committee.

Fair Play for Cuba chapters sprang up immediately on campuses throughout the country, paralleling the upsurge in support for the civil rights movement in the South, student challenges in San Francisco to the House Un-American Activities Committee, and the growth of the Student Peace Union nationally.[10] Campus groups organized debates and forums about the events unfolding in Cuba, and some students even found cheap ways to travel to the island that summer to learn more about the revolution.[11]

In spite of this public enthusiasm for Castro and his cause, tensions between the United States and Cuba mounted dramatically and diplomatic ties unraveled quickly throughout 1960. In March, President Eisenhower secretly authorized a plan for an exile invasion of the island. Two months later, Cuba and the Soviet Union established diplomatic relations. Soon thereafter, the Cuban government nationalized U.S.-owned oil refineries when they refused to refine Soviet oil. In retaliation, the U.S. government cut Cuba's guaranteed quota of sugar sales. By October, the new revolutionary government had nationalized all major enterprises in private hands, including 166 U.S.-owned businesses. In January 1961, Washington broke diplomatic relations and banned all travel to the island. On April 17, 1961, Cuban exiles, trained by the CIA in Guatemala, invaded the island and were promptly defeated by the Cuban militia at the Bay of Pigs.

Across the nation, Fair Play for Cuba Committee chapters organized picket lines and protest rallies about Washington's involvement in the attempt to overthrow the Castro regime. Why, then, did a "Fair Play for Brazil"

Committee not arise in 1963 to support the Goulart government or in 1964 to protest the military takeover? There are numerous possible explanations. Gosse argues that many male students and scattered intellectuals found a fascination for the Cuban rebels, and especially the figure of Fidel—both before the guerrillas came to power and in the first years of their revolutionary government—because the bearded fighters in their army fatigues represented a freewheeling spirit of youthful masculine revolt. Neither Quadros nor Goulart projected anything near that image. In April 1959, only months after taking power, Castro carried out a "truth operation" public relations and media campaign, touring New York and Washington and visiting Harvard and Princeton. His whirlwind visit, including his stay in Harlem, evoked curiosity and enthusiasm for the radical changes he proposed for the island nation. Goulart came to Washington three years later, in April 1962, on a goodwill mission that included a speech to a joint session of Congress and lengthy conversations with President Kennedy and other officials. He visited the White House dressed in a dark business suit and tie. He toasted his host with the assurance that "Brazil looks to the United States' participation in world affairs and to its enlightened government with great hopes and great expectations." The Brazilian president also heralded the Alliance for Progress "as a great contribution to making life in the Americas ever closer to the United States."[12] Goulart focused his visit on international loans and economic development and establishing a closer collaboration with the United States.[13] Neither his persona nor the purpose of his visit captured the imagination of idealistic or enthusiastic American youth. He was just another head of state. Nor did the Goulart administration project a sustained positive radical image abroad that might have won the sympathy of rebellious youth and anti–Cold War crusaders. Goulart defended a vague program for "basic reforms" that he only unfurled in the last months of his rule. Although grassroots activists were developing innovative literacy campaigns in the Brazilian Northeast, and Peasant Leagues pushed for land redistribution, news of these radical initiatives only filtered back to the United States in alarmist news articles.

The Kennedy and Johnson administrations also learned from the Bay of Pigs fiasco about the importance of covering up covert operations. The American public received news about the U.S. support for the Cuban exiles' invasion immediately after it took place. Three years later, the White House, State Department, and Pentagon carefully hid their logistical support for the Brazilian military and successfully managed the press. Thus, a small handful of liberals and emerging radicals who had developed a skeptical stance toward U.S. foreign policy wrote articles critical of the Brazilian military, but no constituency rallied around the defeated forces in Brazil. Moreover, for those who continued to back the Cuban revolution throughout the 1960s, Castro represented a positive challenge to U.S. hegemony. Brazil, for those who informed themselves about the matter, represented a defeat. In 1965 another island in the Caribbean, however, would spark renewed interested in Latin America among certain sectors in the United States.

### Invading Another Island

On April 28, 1965, five hundred U.S. Marines landed outside Santo Domingo, the capital of the Dominican Republic. Within two weeks, 22,000 additional members of the U.S. armed forces had occupied the island. Their objective, according to the Johnson administration, was to prevent another Cuba. In order to give the U.S. military action the appearance of being a multilateral effort instead of a return to "gunboat diplomacy," the United States requested that the Organization of American States (OAS) authorize the use of military force to support the U.S. invasion. The Johnson administration also attempted to get other countries to agree to send in troops after the occupation of the island had already taken place. To assist the Latin American lobbying effort, the State Department sent the veteran diplomat Averell Harriman to Brazil to get Castelo Branco's support for the invasion, and Walters and Gordon's influence with the new government likely played a key role in obtaining Brazil's commitment to the force. As part of Brazil's quid pro quo for agreeing to U.S. requests to join the Inter-American Armed Force, the United States permitted a Brazilian officer to become chief of the joint operation. On May 8, the council of the OAS supported the proposal for an Inter-American Armed Force to join U.S. troops in occupying the Dominican Republic. In a public relations gesture, the U.S. government later changed the contingent's name to the Inter-American Peace Force.[14]

Several weeks after the invasion, a group of U.S. academics, calling themselves the University Committee on the Dominican Republic, decided to protest the Johnson administration's actions. "We were astonished and utterly outraged that we had invaded," recalled Kenneth Erickson, who at the time was a graduate student in political science at Columbia.[15] Peter Eisenberg, who was working on his doctorate in Brazilian history at Columbia University, spearheaded the campaign. He called on the tightly knit cohort of Columbia graduate students in Latin American history, political science, and anthropology to assist him in drumming up support among their colleagues across the nation.[16] They drafted a statement titled "Letter of Latin American Specialists to President Johnson on the Dominican Crisis" and quickly got over a hundred signatures of scholars working on Latin America from Yale, Texas, Michigan, Berkeley, Stanford, and other universities. Michael Hall, who was a graduate student at Columbia at the time, remembered that one of the ways that they got signatures was by sending out a mailing to the members of the Conference on Latin American History to solicit support from scholars throughout the country.[17] The statement against the intervention appeared as an advertisement in the October 23, 1965, edition of the *New York Times*.[18] The academics backing the *Times* ad included some of the most prominent professors of Latin American studies in the country as well as junior scholars who would lead the field over the next thirty years.

There is no indication that the ad actually changed the minds of any officials in the Johnson administration who set policies for Latin America. Nevertheless, it registered a minority opinion that probably represented the views of the majority of experts on Latin America working in U.S. academia. Public opinion in the United States remained solidly behind the invasion, with as many as 76 percent of citizens polled favoring the military action.[19] Although Senator William Fulbright, the chair of the Senate Foreign Relations Committee, held hearings during the summer to register his opposition to Johnson's policy, he could not find consensus among his colleagues and his committee never produced a report. Moreover, in a vote in the House in September 1965, representatives backed the invasion 312 to 52.[20] The significance of the *New York Times* ad rested more in the fact that a substantial number of Latin Americanists had come out against a Democratic administration. The slowly escalating war in Vietnam had not yet created a campus consensus against Johnson's war policies in Southeast Asia. Still, opposition to the administration's policies regarding the civil war in the Dominican Republic reflected a shift in the way many intellectuals viewed United States foreign policy toward Latin America. The events surrounding the invasion of the Dominican Republic also had a profound effect on a cluster of radicalized missionaries and returned volunteers who had experienced United States intervention firsthand either on the Caribbean island or from another vantage point in Latin America. Many went on to become key leaders in the Latin American solidarity movement in the following years.[21] One such figure touched by the Dominican Republic invasion was the Methodist missionary Brady Tyson, who had remained in Brazil after the 1964 coup and had become ever more deeply involved in activities critical of the regime.

Four months after the U.S. Marines landed in Santo Domingo, the student association (Diretório Acadêmico) of the School of Philosophy, Social Sciences, and Literature in São José do Rio Preto, state of São Paulo, invited Brady Tyson to give a talk about the political situation in Latin America. The student organizers requested that he focus especially on the U.S. invasion of the Dominican Republic and Washington's relations with Cuba.[22] Although Tyson's speech criticized certain aspects of U.S. foreign policy, he, like the Latin Americanists who signed the *New York Times* statement about Johnson's intervention on the Caribbean island, still positioned his arguments within the context of the Democratic Party's liberal wing. At the same time, Tyson unapologetically identified himself as a leftist who believed in nonviolent direct action—a reflection of his involvement with the Fellowship of Reconciliation, a pacifist organization, and his support for the civil rights movement led by Martin Luther King Jr.

Tyson began his bouts with established authority as an outspoken critic of the status quo when he was a student at Rice Institute (later University) in Houston, Texas, where he served as the editor of *The Thresher*, the school newspaper. In 1948, he published an editorial calling on Rice to end segregationist policies that denied admission to Afro-American students. The statement caused a flurry of opposition from alumni, students, and school administrators.[23] His stance marked the beginning of his long-term relationship with the civil rights movement.

After graduating from Rice, getting a degree in theology, and serving as a Methodist pastor in several Texas congregations, Tyson earned a doctorate from the American University School of International Service. The Methodist Church then assigned him as a missionary to Brazil, where he was the pastor of three small churches, as well as the Methodist chaplain to the university community in São Paulo.[24] Tyson quickly became involved in the ecumenical student movement, working to build bridges between progressive Protestant and Catholic organizations in Brazil, exerting a lot of energy trying to establish closer relationships between the progressive leaning União Cristã de Estudantes do Brasil (Christian Union of Brazilian Students) and the more conservative Aliança Bíblica Universitária (University Biblical Alliance), to no avail.[25] In addition to his work in the Methodist Church's youth ministry, Tyson taught at the School of Sociology and Politics in São Paulo, placing him in the thick of the intellectual and political life of the city. His home became a central point for young U.S. scholars coming to Brazil to study, as well as for young progressive religious activists.[26]

On December 29, 1965, the Ministry of Justice ordered Brady to appear in its São Paulo offices and informed him that he had to leave the country immediately or the Brazilian government would expel him. The records in the political police (DEOPS) archives do not detail the "political offenses" that warranted his forced departure from the country, but the police noted the "extremist ideas" in his São José do Rio Preto speech.[27] Fearing that if he remained in Brazil and faced a trial his wife and five children would undergo severe hardship, Tyson negotiated three months leeway in order to put things in order in Brazil and then left the country in March 1966.[28] In a letter to their friends, relatives, and members of their church, Tyson and his wife Jean explained their decision to leave Brazil: "In the climate of suspicion and betrayal generated by systematic government repression, it was inevitable that we, like so many of our friends, should become the victims of intimidation. Brady's close association with the Brazilian university students and professors inevitably brought him under suspicion by the present military government."[29] Tyson found a job teaching political science at Southampton College of Long Island University.[30] The next year he joined the faculty of American University in Washington. His position at the university and his credentials as an academic permitted him to use his expert knowledge about Brazil against the military regime.

### Studying Latin America

The success of the Cuban revolution fueled the formation of the Alliance for Progress as a moderate and reformist measure to counter the Cuban call to revolution. It also focused U.S. government attention toward research universities that might train the experts who could shape U.S. foreign policy and implement assistance programs throughout the hemisphere. When Fidel Castro and his rag-tag army rolled into Havana on January 8, 1959, few major research universities had Latin American specialists or significant centers for the study of Latin America. Stanford University in California and Columbia University in New York, among a handful of other institutions, quickly attracted students interested in graduate training and became spawning grounds for a generation of young and enthusiastic scholars, many of whom would become leaders among their peers in providing a progressive critique of U.S. foreign policy.[31]

Like many other young graduate students pursuing a doctoral degree in the early 1960s, Ralph Della Cava accidentally ended up studying Brazil. During his first year in graduate school in 1960 at Columbia University, he had focused on sociology and then turned to Latin American history in 1961 when the historian Lewis Hanke, one of the foremost Latin American scholars of his generation, arrived. Della Cava had planned to examine Italian socialist immigrants to Argentina, but Charles Wagley, Columbia's eminent anthropologist specializing in Brazil, convinced him to write a seminar paper on Padre Cicero, a religious figure from the Northeast. It ended up becoming his dissertation topic and later a book.[32] Before traveling to Brazil in 1963 to do his doctoral research, Della Cava already had close links with the Catholic left in the United States, including young progressive priests such as Philip and Daniel Berrigan, who would later become leaders in radical Catholic wing of the anti–Vietnam War movement. "I went to the 1963 March on Washington with the Berrigans," he proudly remembered.[33]

His contacts with the Catholic left in the United States led Della Cava to make similar connections in Brazil. On March 31, 1964, Della Cava, his wife, and friends walked out of the cinema in downtown Rio de Janeiro and were greeted by machine gun fire by rebellious troops. The next day he closely followed radio reports about Goulart's resignation, and over the following months he received news of friends who had gone underground after the coup. "When I left Rio after having done all of my research at the National Archive, I stopped in Bahia, Recife, and Forteleza to visit the families of people hiding in Rio who were either part of Ação Popular [Popular Action], or the JUC [Juventude Universitária Católica—Catholic University Youth] and told them about their kids."[34] With deep connections among Brazilian oppositionists, over the next two decades Ralph Della Cava would play a crucial role in organizing political opposition the military dictatorship in the United States.

As leading graduate programs across the country recruited the best young students to study Latin America, other prestigious universities scrambled to train specialists who could quickly gain expert knowledge on Latin America in order to teach undergraduates and graduates interested in learning more about the changes taking place in the countries south of the Rio Grande. The case of a young Harvard scholar of German history exemplifies a trend. In 1960, Thomas E. Skidmore received his doctorate at Harvard. His specialty was modern European history with a focus on German and British history. Skidmore recalls, "I was just beginning my teaching career in the Harvard History Department as a German historian when the University offered me the chance to exchange teaching for three years of paid leave . . . [to] change my field." Harvard wanted specialists on Latin American history. The offer guaranteed him an assistant professorship when he returned to teaching in the fall of 1964, and if the change did not work, the university would allow him to return to teaching German history. "I had no hesitation in accepting, even though I was almost entirely ignorant of Latin America."[35] Skidmore admitted that he had not even known that the language spoken in Brazil is Portuguese until the previous year, when he had seen *Black Orpheus*. Armed with generous financial assistance, he chose Brazil and set off south to learn about the country. He returned with volumes of notes, clippings, and papers and turned them into the book *Politics in Brazil, 1930–1964: An Experiment in Democracy*, which became an instant classic.[36] He also joined other academics in speaking out against the military regime in Brazil.

Skidmore's switch from Germany to Brazil might have been a bit unusual, but the trend toward a marked increase in resources dedicated to the study of Latin America continued over the decade. The Ford Foundation stepped in to support the growth in the number of Latin American studies programs nationwide. The Social Science Research Council started directing significant monies toward young scholars interested in doing research in Latin America. The U.S. government offered National Defense Language Fellowships (NDLF) for students to learn Spanish and Portuguese as part of Washington's geopolitical concerns about the encroaching influence of communism in Latin America, and the Fulbright Foundation continued to offer financing for those interested in studying the region. Margaret (Meg) Crahan, a graduate student at Columbia University in the early 1960s, remembered how new resources poured into Latin American studies: "Everyone had money with increased fellowships. I had a Columbia fellowship, and I gave it up for an NDLF because essentially it was greater [money]. I was the only female [in Latin American studies] receiving a Columbia fellowship at the time, and they said, 'How can you give it up?' I replied, 'Because they pay summer as well.'"[37]

The growing number of academics working on Latin America also expanded the demand for regular interdisciplinary forums where researchers could share their findings, make new contacts, and socialize.[38] These disparate academic forces coalesced in 1966 with the creation of the Latin American Studies Association (LASA). In spite of significant financing for this new field from government and private foundations, LASA saw itself as an independent professional organization. According to one of its founding members, those at the first meeting "voiced the view that the Secretariat should not be closely identified with any part of the Executive branch of the

United States Government, or with any university, but rather that it should be in appearance and fact an independent entity."[39] In part, this call for "neutrality" vis-à-vis the government came from a reservation among a significant sector of Latin Americanists about Washington's foreign policy objectives in Latin America, especially after the invasion of the Dominican Republic. Revelations in 1965 about Project Camelot, a social science research project funded by the Department of the Army to study revolutionary warfare in Latin America, alarmed scholars. Many feared that the U.S. research might be linked to covert intelligence-gathering operations in the region.[40] The call for independence from Washington also reflected a desire to establish an organization that did not bend to the pressure of a given administration's programs or objectives for Latin America.[41]

Writing about the different factors that led to the formation of LASA in 1966, Howard F. Cline, the director of the Hispanic Foundation of the Library of Congress, noted that the Cuban revolution occasioned a burst of support for the effort to found the association: "At some point in its future career, that organization [LASA] might well erect a monument to Fidel Castro, a remote godfather. His actions in Cuba jarred complacency in official and university circles, dramatically revealing that all was not well in Latin America and that something must be done about it. Revived national concern with Latin America again created a climate in which serious programs could begin and even flourish."[42] The Latin American Studies Association became an umbrella interdisciplinary professional organization that brought together scholars from all political persuasions. Within the field, however, a radical current emerged that wanted to link scholarship to political action.[43]

### The North American Congress on Latin America

By 1966, interest in Latin America had widened beyond university campuses. In November of that year, a diverse coalition of individuals founded the North American Congress on Latin America (NACLA).[44] Initially, NACLA acted as an open forum to unite individuals who opposed U.S. intervention in Latin America and favored far-reaching social change throughout the continent. Brady Tyson attended a founding meeting of NACLA and wrote a report of the gathering for the new organization's newsletter. According to Tyson, the prime movers behind the formation of NACLA were members of the Students for a Democratic Society and University Christian Movement personnel. They joined with peace movement activists, left-wing Catholics, returned volunteers from the Peace Corps and other developmentalist or church-related programs in Latin America, graduate students, young university professors, and a few Latin Americans living in the United States.[45] Supporters of the NACLA project had widely divergent visions of the organization's mission, ranging from advocates of pacifist nonviolence to those supporting armed struggle in Latin America. Some saw the organization as a way to appeal to officials in order to change government policies, while others prioritized educating the American public as a means of creating a "radical alternative to present attitudes and policies."[46] Some saw their role as building alliances and supporting Latin American revolutionaries; others argued that "the Latin American revolution is largely contingent upon some form of revolution in the United States."[47]

NACLA's Brazil connection was not limited to the participation of Brady Tyson. Paulo Singer, a Brazilian sociologist who would be forcibly retired from the University of São Paulo by the military regime two years later, attended the meeting on February 11, 1967, of New York–East Coast supporters of NACLA. There he argued that North American scholars needed to develop a general theory about imperialism instead of "producing monographs dealing with specific and limited aspects of the overall problem."[48] The writer John Gerrassi, who had close personal and political links to Brazil, headed up the fundraising campaign to develop a magazine that would "encourage in-depth research and journalism conducive to analysis and action."[49] Timothy Harding, an expert on Brazilian labor history and assistant professor of Latin American history at California State University, Los Angeles, also attended the February 11 meeting, representing political activists on the West Coast who shared the goals of combining research and action related to Latin America.[50] NACLA's day-long conference closed with an evening talk by Dom Hélder Câmara, the archbishop of Recife, Brazil. The military had targeted him as an enemy of the new regime. The archbishop symbolized the growing influence of progressive ideas within the Latin American Catholic Church. Dom Hélder's allegiance to Brazil's poor also paralleled the initiatives of Maryknoll missionaries and other Catholic activists from the United States committed to working among the lower classes in Latin America and bringing back news of these social struggles to a broader North American audience.

The NACLA project, with support from newsletter sales and the United Methodist Church, the Presbyterian Church, the Division of Youth Ministries of the National Council of Churches, and the University Christian Movement, ended up focusing on research about Latin America.[51] The NACLA *Newsletter* quickly grew from a modest eight-page mimeographed bulletin to a publication that included in-depth articles about United States–owned multinational corporations with heavy investments in Latin America, military aid to the region, and national political processes throughout the continent. NACLA's importance as a national coalescing force of solidarity activists should not be underestimated. By providing a continual flow of information about the economic, political, and military relationships between the United States and Latin America, the NACLA *Newsletter* and the collective's other publications provided students and activists with comprehensive analyses of the mechanisms of U.S. imperial domination.[52]

### Returned Volunteers

Another factor that fueled a growing interest in Latin America was the return to the United States of thousands of people who had volunteered their services and dedicated their idealism and energy in an attempt to help alleviate poverty and encourage progress in a "developing" country. Living in Latin America as an "ambassador" of the United States had forced many of these young Americans to rethink their assumptions about their government's role in the world. The Peace Corps, as well as other service organizations, was aware of the negative reactions that the programs had in some foreign quarters, so they included training to prepare young volunteers for inevitable late-hour discussions with anti-American critics. Whether or not the overseas experience provoked U.S. citizens to question their government's foreign policy, strong links unavoidably developed between the volunteers and new friends, families, and colleagues in their host countries. Some fell in love and stayed in Latin America, while others came home with a Latin American husband or a wife. For many, returning to the United States proved to be just as difficult a cultural adjustment as their adaptation at the beginning of the program. The desire to retain links with Latin America remained strong.

Such was the case of Paul Silberstein. He was born into a family of leftists; his parents had moved to Fontana, California, to establish a farm cooperative and escape the tide of McCarthyism in the 1950s. Paul grew up in a progressive home within a hostile political environment.[53] As a student at the University of California, Riverside, he became involved in antiwar activities through the Students for a Democratic Society. He had a cousin in the Peace Corps, and he knew that he wanted to enroll in the program as soon as he graduated. He went to Brazil in 1966. When Paul finished his commitment to the Peace Corps, he enrolled in the new master's program in anthropology at the National Museum of Anthropology in Rio on a Ford Foundation fellowship. However, in 1969 his local draft board informed him that he had to return to the United States. Unwilling to go to Vietnam, he applied to a graduate program at Berkeley and received a student deferment. By chance, someone introduced him to a person working on a new publication, the *Brazilian Information Bulletin*. Before long, he was an active behind-the-scenes supporter of the newsletter. Paul's enchantment with Brazil, layered upon the progressive and critical upbringing he received from his left-wing parents and the unspoken knowledge that he had acquired as a child growing up in a such a household that it was wise to be discreet and not ask questions, led him to a six-year collaboration with the anti-dictatorial forces in Berkeley. His effort had national and international repercussions.

Paul had chosen the official U.S. government-sponsored path to traveling abroad, a move that changed his life. Yet there were many other volunteer organizations that offered young idealistic North Americans the opportunity to travel south to dig wells, work in *favelas* (slums), teach English to peasants, or organize rural cooperatives. Harry Strharsky is a case in point. By chance, he became involved in Latin America, and later, again by chance, he became a leading figure in the movement against the Brazilian dictatorship in Washington in the early 1970s. "I was in a seminary in Milwaukee, the Metropolitan Seminary for the state of Wisconsin. We had a couple of students from the Dominican Republic who I went to school with and befriended. One was a couple of years ahead of me and actually became ordained and went to the Dominican Republic. In 1968, he recruited people from Wisconsin, Panama, Nicaragua, Cuba, and a number of different countries in and about the Caribbean to assist him in setting up a social service organization in the rural areas of Santo Domingo, Santiago de los Caballeros in the northern part of the Dominican Republic."

The next summer, a larger group returned to the rural village, including two young women. One of them, Loretta Merkel, later married Harry Strharsky and joined him in playing a crucial role in the campaign against torture and repression in Brazil and other countries of Latin America. Reminiscing thirty years later about that summer, she commented, "I was surprised how well we could communicate with people with our limited Spanish, how fast I had learned Spanish, and . . . how people could communicate in ways that were either beyond language or that we made language do with what we had." After almost forty years together, Loretta and Harry talk in tandem, complementing shared memories and lived experiences. Harry recalled that the experience in the Dominican Republic brought together people "from two different cultures and two different backgrounds with completely different educations and lifestyles and work. They engrained in us a real appreciation of and a hunger to learn from other people, from other cultures." Loretta completed his comments: "We were able to relate to a real place that nobody in our neighborhood had ever heard of. They were real people. There was real learning going on for us because we were used to running water and clean houses, and we went to a place where there wasn't running water or inside plumbing." "But dirt floors," Harry added.

Soon after returning from the Dominican Republic, Harry left the seminary, and Loretta spent a year teaching language arts and social studies in a predominantly African American Catholic school in Holly Springs, Mississippi. The decision to travel south as a teacher flowed from her commitment to supporting the civil rights movement. In 1970, Harry and Loretta married and eventually raised three sons. For the next four decades, civil rights activities, the anti–Vietnam War movement, the campaign against repression and torture in Brazil, political organizing after the 1973 coup in Chile, Marxist study groups, a visit by Loretta to Cuba, and a series of community and grassroots efforts—all sprang from their identity as "good Christian people." The Dominican Republic had changed the course of their lives.

Not everyone became involved in Latin America through a stint in the Peace Corps, work in a summer camp, or missionary service. Allen Young, like Paul Silberstein a "red diaper" baby, that is, the child of left-wing parents, became interested in Latin America while an undergraduate at Columbia University. After finishing a degree in journalism and spending a summer traveling in Mexico and Central America, he earned a master's degree in Latin American studies at Stanford and then received a Fulbright scholarship to Brazil. He arrived in mid-1964 and worked as a freelance journalist, peddling articles to the Christian Science Monitor and other U.S. publications.[54] As a self-styled radical, Young penned a series of articles for the Monitor critical of the military regime that also offered news about the grassroots opposition to the dictatorship.[55] As in similar articles in the New York Times and other mainstream newspapers, he questioned the economic policies of the military government, its restrictive control over the press and free speech, and the ongoing campaigns against the opposition. The on-the-scene reporting by Young and James Nelson Goodsell of the Christian Science Monitor, Juan de Onis from the New York Times, and other correspondents stationed in Brazil provided those in the United States who wished to be informed about the political situation just enough critical insight to break through the Cold War rhetoric that shaped State Department and other official pronouncements. Their reporting also helped fuel a nascent opposition in Congress.

## Congressional Rumblings

In late October 1965, two days after Castelo Branco decreed Institutional Act No. 2 that dissolved existing political parties and made the future election of the president, vice president, and all governors indirect, Wayne Morse, the maverick Democratic senator from Oregon, released the reproachful press release cited at the beginning of this chapter. Like a prophet shouting in the wilderness, Morse denounced U.S. support for the military regime. His criticisms went unheeded by his peers in Congress and only merited a tiny five-line note on page ten of the New York Times.[56] Nonetheless, the Times did issue an editorial that warned about the danger of the move away from democracy. Times correspondent Juan de Onis also wrote a series of reports that pointed out the encroaching authoritarianism in the country.[57] Hélio Jaguaribe, a prominent Brazilian political scientist who was a visiting professor at Harvard at the time, entered the muted public debate in a letter to the New York Times that called on Brazilians living abroad to rally against the military regime. "Those who happen to be outside Brazil, in free countries, should form committees of democratic resistance, pooling their efforts and resources to help the organization within Brazil in a multiparty struggle against the military dictatorship."[58] His rallying cry for concerted action remained unheeded for several years.

While scattered criticisms of the Brazilian military circulated in the press, the State Department insisted that U.S. officials refrain from making any public comments pertaining to the Institutional Act or other "purely internal developments in Brazil," since they might be "open to serious misinterpretation in Brazil and elsewhere."[59] In behind-the-scenes debates, Washington policymakers discussed the implications of the new government measure.

Regarding the concern that the Institutional Act might spur on the opposition to the generals, CIA analysts argued that "the newly decreed powers will unify the military behind the president . . . [that] should be able to contain any major threat to political stability."[60] Ambassador Gordon weighed in against the suspension of U.S. aid. Although he conceded that the gesture might put the U.S. government "on record throughout the hemisphere in favor of democratic processes," Gordon insisted that curtailing support would "undermine all positive objectives of U.S. policy in Brazil, political as well as economic and security."[61]

After the promulgation of Institutional Act No. 2 in October 1965, Morse began to shift his thinking about Brazil. During the 1966 Senate Foreign Relations Committee hearings to consider the nomination of Lincoln Gordon as assistant secretary of state for Inter-American Affairs, Senator Morse and Senator Albert Gore Sr. of Tennessee raised numerous questions about U.S. involvement in the 1964 coup. Of particular concern to Morse was the U.S. aid package to Brazil. Gordon remained firm in his conviction that economic aid could serve the goal of strengthening democracy in the country. Others, including senators Frank Church of Idaho and Edward M. Kennedy of Massachusetts, seemed rather satisfied with Gordon's performance as ambassador in Brazil and enthusiastically endorsed his nomination to the top post for Latin America at the State Department.[62] Morse then voiced his objections to Gordon's confirmation on the Senate floor: "He talked himself out of my vote at the hearing, for I reluctantly came to the conclusion that here was another junta man, and here was a nominee who testified he favored the coup that took place in Brazil."[63] Before registering his dissenting vote, Morse made a prescient prediction: "I am satisfied that history will bear me out. I am satisfied that a great loss to American prestige will occur and possibly a great loss in terms of blood and revolution in Latin America. Our policy will be proved wrong again. Once again in Brazil, when the chips of freedom were down, the United States walked out on freedom."[64] Nevertheless, Morse remained relatively isolated in his assessment of the political situation in Brazil until 1968.

With Lincoln Gordon in command of Latin America at the State Department, the Johnson administration appointed John W. Tuthill as the new ambassador to Brazil. Unlike Gordon, Tuthill did not have close contacts with the inner circles of the Castelo Branco government, and he was less confident in unconditionally backing all of the authoritarian measures of the regime.[65] In 1967, Tuthill implemented a model project to downsize the U.S. diplomatic presence in Brazil, which had grown to 920 U.S. citizens and an additional thousand Brazilian employees working for the U.S. government. Known at "Operation Topsy," it sought to streamline U.S. operations in Brazil.[66] His effort also responded to the "nationalistic orientation of the new Costa e Silva regime," and the fact that "the ubiquitous American official had become a special irritant."[67] Tuthill's efforts also aligned with congressional sentiment that considered many of the Alliance for Progress programs to be bloated and inefficient. To a certain extent, Morse represented the extreme viewpoint of the cluster of senators who had expressed doubts about Washington's Latin American foreign policy since the late 1950s. The historian Steven C. Rabe summarized their perspective: "These mainly liberal Democrats did not question the basic tenets of U.S. policy: anticommunism, free trade and investment, and the hegemony of the United States in the Western Hemisphere. Their differences with the [Eisenhower] administration were over means. By supporting military dictators and denying economic assistance, the administration might be forcing desperate Latin Americans to turn to radical solutions."[68] The Alliance for Progress, Kennedy's response to the Cuban revolution and the potential for revolutionary insurrections throughout the continent, brought a marked increase in U.S. foreign aid to Latin America, including funds for military and counterinsurgency programs. Once again, in the mid-1960s, Morse stood alone in his objections to internal security programs that he feared would "produce a new wave of political repression and military dictatorships in Latin America."[69] As with his critique of Washington's policies in Vietnam, few initially supported Morse. Senator Gruening of Alaska backed Morse as he had in issues regarding Southeast Asia, and Senator Stephen Young of Ohio joined him in supporting a ban on military aid to Latin America.[70] Until 1968, their numbers would grow to no more than a handful of legislators who questioned Washington's policies in Latin America.

## CAPÍTULO II

---

# "Caminhando e cantando e seguindo a canção"

Marching and singing and
following the song . . .

**Geraldo Vandré, "Pra não dizer
que não falei de flores," 1968**

Funeral of Edson Luís, Rio de Janeiro, March 29, 1968. ACERVO ÚLTIMA HORA, ARQUIVO PÚBLICO DO ESTADO DE SÃO PAULO.

For many young people who lived through the 1960s in the United States, Europe, and much of Latin America, 1968 has become a particularly magical moment, so filled with memories and loaded with significances (many applied retrospectively) that it is hard to sort out nostalgic representations of the past from that year's complicated realities. Zuenir Ventura's lively chronicle about how many Brazilian youth lived through those dense twelve months records the energetic and optimistic rollercoaster ride with a dreary December denouement.[1] The intermingling of culture and politics promised momentous transformations, both in Brazil and abroad. Yet in Brazil, the year ended in a dismal disappointment for those who had thought that the dictatorship's days were numbered.

In Brazil, the singer and composer Geraldo Vandré encapsulated the sentiment of that year's hope, unity, and change in a politically engaged almost sacred song of a youthful opposition that proclaimed "We are all equal," marching together arms linked, singing, and chanting in massive mobilizations against the dictatorship. The imagery is reminiscent of "We Shall Overcome," the trademark anthem of the U.S. civil rights movement. In spite of their rather somber rhythms and tones, both movements' hymns offered uplifting optimism that portended victory. The close-up shot of the line of Brazil's top young artists participating in the March of 100,000 on June 26, 1968, represented the depth and breadth of opposition to the regime among intellectuals and icons of popular culture. Nonetheless, the hard-line dictatorial measures on December 13, 1968, with the promulgation of Institutional Act No. 5, quashed all dreams that Brazil might soon return to a democracy.

In the United States, 1968 was the year of campus sit-ins, anti–Vietnam War protests, and the emergence of the Black Power, Chicano, and women's rights movements. The cultural explosion of "sex, drugs, and rock and roll," hippie communes, and countercultural cooperatives blossomed nationwide as well. Protests and politics mixed freely in alternative newspapers, music, and nonconformist lifestyles. Similarly, student and left-wing dissent rocked Brazil. The political songs of Gerardo Vandré and others are examples of a flood of protest music that was popular among the under twenty-five crowd.

Some scholars point to a controversy at a music festival in São Paulo in September 1968 to argue that there was a clear-cut cultural divide within the sixties generation.[2] On one side were partisans of music imbued with overt political messages. On the other side were the partisans of the free-spirited internationally influenced tropicalismo of Caetano Veloso and Gilberto Gil that relied on "foreign" electric guitars and emphasized cultural and personal freedom. This chasm, so the argument goes, pitted the political against the

alienated, or, seen from the other side of the divide, the boring (*chato*) po-
liticos versus the free-spirited. Yet those who cheered the political content
of Vandré's songs while booing songwriters and performers such as Veloso
and Gil shared something with their supposed opposites. Similarly, those
who castigated the left as being hopelessly rigid, old-fashioned, and dreary
shared the same visceral desire for an end to the dictatorship and radical
change throughout the country, whether political, social, or cultural.

In many ways, the events that took place during 1968 in Brazil set the
stage for a crisis in the military regime that led to the increasingly repressive
measures employed over the next decade. (In the United States, those same
twelve months deepened the political awareness of a new generation, some
of whom would respond to calls to fight for human rights in Brazil and the
rest of Latin America.) Every generation imbues its youthful memories with
golden hues, since growing into adulthood parallels a discovery of romance
and sexuality, as well as distinct aspirations, opinions, and even politics that
differentiate one from parents and others of the previous generation. Institutional Act No. 5, however, was such a drastic political measure and drew such
a heavy curtain over the optimistic dramas that had unfolded in the previous
two years that it remains a monumental reference point, especially for those
from the middle class who came of age in the 1960s.[3]

Such is the case of Monica Arruda, the youngest of the five Arruda children and affectionately called Moni by friends and family. After her parents
had legally separated and her mother moved to the United States to work as
a freelance interpreter, Moni spent time with her in Washington. "I came
back from the U.S. at the end of 1964 . . . At first, I was not very political. I
was more following the flow of things. I was sixteen and somewhat alienated."[4] Still in high school, she began dating a university student who was
part of a political crowd led by Jean Marc Von der Weid, a dashing and charismatic leader of the proscribed National Student Union. "I became politicized by participating in a student theater group and attending meetings at
the university . . . I joined all of the marches in 1968, including the March of
100,000."

In the terminology of the time, Moni was a sympathizer of the organized
left. She joined street demonstrations that at times ended up in confronta-
tions with the police. When requested, she offered logistical assistance to
activists by hiding those who had gone underground and supporting relatives
and friends of political prisoners. During one demonstration, Moni ran into
a friend who had also joined the protest. A police baton had cracked open her
forehead. "She was running away from the tear gas bombs . . . and she got

dizzy. We took her to the João Caetano Theater, where we were rehearsing a play, put ice on her wound, and took care of her. We lived through many moments like that one." Institutional Act No. 5 (IA-5) ended all street protests and closed down most legal forms of redress against the military regime. Moni summed up the aftermath of IA-5 as simply "a nightmare."

Based on first impressions, one might assume that Martinha, Moni's older sister, was on the countercultural side of the alleged divide between politics and culture. While Moni joined demonstrations, Martinha was stage struck, spending her free time after work rehearsing. Her contacts with the world of musicians, poets, and artists had framed her adolescence. Even when she traveled to the United States with her younger sister, she found herself gravitating toward Latin American artists and intellectuals living in Washington. "I couldn't relate to the Americans I met," she remembered. "They seemed so square."[5] Martinha's mother had rather pragmatic and traditional notions of young women's career paths, even though she had herself been rather courageous and free-spirited in separating from her husband and moving abroad, a rare and scandalous act for a Brazilian middle-class woman in the 1950s.[6] Her mother insisted that Martinha enroll in a secretarial school so that she could get a job in Washington. Martinha quickly learned the skills that became her source of income when she returned to Rio in 1965 and decided to study at the National Theater Conservatory. She became a serious, hardworking secretary by day and a bohemian actor at night. Then 1968 came, and student protests escalated. Martinha found herself observing street demonstrations from the window of the tall office building where she worked, silently rooting for the students, while her conservative coworkers cheered the police. Looking back over those times, Martinha has a clear sense of what her role was in that tumultuous year. "I led a very normal life, doing theater at night and working at a conservative [careta] office during the day . . . I did not have the courage to confront the dictatorship, get arrested and be tortured . . . I thought I would reveal information with the first bit of pain. I did not have that internal ideological strength . . . I thought that it was my role to protect those who had the strength and courage." At the time, Martinha and Moni lived in an apartment with their boyfriends in Ipanema. It became one of many clandestine meeting places where student leaders who had gone underground gathered to plan demonstrations and build alliances across ideological divides while organizing resistance to the regime and maintaining cohesion, as they became increasing encircled by the government. "We knew that people were getting arrested, tortured, exiled every day, and our friends were involved. So we had to help them any way we could."

Martinha insists that her actions were representative of a generation. "There was a horrible dictatorship. We were in favor of freedom. Caetano Veloso, [Gilberto] Gil, everyone was singing for freedom. 'É prohibido prohibir' [It is forbidden to forbid]. Everyone doing cultural work, theater, music wanted to get rid of the dictatorship. Everyone knew who was being persecuted. We needed to liberate the country, so the entire generation went along with the movement."[7]

At the same time that Moni and Martinha, living in Rio, were lending their house to friends for secret meetings and allowing unknown people stay a night or two, no questions asked, their older brother Marcos toiled a twelve-hour day as a worker in a São Paulo factory and attended secret party meetings at night. His willingness to endure a grueling daily rhythm resulted from the complex mixture of a deeply religious upbringing and a political conviction that only a carefully executed collective endeavor could leverage change in a country living under harsh military rule. "The experience of Belgium and French worker-priests was inspiring," Marcos remembered in an essay about his time working in a factory. "In Brazil there were also priests living and laboring as workers or peasants. Jesus was a vibrant example for me, born poor, in a working-class family, and who chose to share his life as a simple worker, prioritizing 'the poor, prostitutes, and sinners.'"[8] However, work on the factory floor was grueling. "We had to be standing at our machine at 5:55 a.m. every day in a large room that held 150 workers, in a factory of 3,000 employees. We left at 6:00 p.m. when the factory siren went off. They answered protests against a twelve-hour workday this way: 'If you don't want to, you can quit. There are hundreds of other workers at the factory gates every day looking for a job.'"[9] Given his meager salary, Marcos could not make ends meet: "My friend João and I would embark on a long trek from our neighborhood to the factory the last week of every month, when we didn't have enough money to pay for the bus. That meant getting up an hour earlier!"[10] Fourteen hours spent working or getting to and from the factory left little time for political organizing among coworkers and neighborhood contacts. Yet Marcos managed to continue working and doing political activities until May 1970, when political police picked him up for allegedly belonging to an underground organization involved in armed struggle against the regime.

Not all paths to politicalization were products of a linear evolution in which a Brazilian protagonist moved from empathy and reflection about social injustice to radicalization and action, armed or otherwise. Nor did all Brazilians who became involved in international campaigns against the dictatorship do so on a simple movement to political activism. Individual life trajectories opened different doors to those who became involved in a series of rather decentralized and many times disorganized international campaigns against the dictatorship. For all of them, however, 1968 became an emblematic time marker. Although its causes and effects bled into the previous and posterior years, it was a symbolic turning point in their lives.

Maria Helena Moreira Alves is a case in point. She has a larger-than-life personality, full of energy, love, and passion. Her book *State and Opposition in Authoritarian Brazil* and Thomas E. Skidmore's pioneering work *The Politics of Military Rule in Brazil, 1964–85* remain the two classic English-language histories of the dictatorship.[11] For over three decades a left-wing activist in the United States, Brazil, and Chile, she does not shy away from admitting her family roots. "I come from an elite family. On my mother's side we came from coffee planters, the Visconde do Rio Preto . . . We were part of the Brazilian upper class."[12] Her brother Márcio Moreira Alves characterized the legacy of their mother's family succinctly: "The coffee wealth amassed by slave labor was sufficient to protect four generations of prolific males from politics and work."[13] While Márcio enjoyed male privileges of the wealthy, Maria Helena recalled that she and her sister Branca lived "a very sheltered life." Their programmed destiny was to find eligible men from their social class, marry, and have children. Nevertheless, Maria Helena wanted to study at the university. At first, her father objected. Why does a well-bred woman from an elite family need a university degree? After all, his wife had not gone beyond secondary school. Maria Helena finally convinced her father, and in 1962 she started studying psychology at the Catholic University in Rio de Janeiro. "It was there that I discovered the world. I used to come to classes with a chauffeur and a chaperone. He would drop me off and pick me up. So my freedom was when I was at the university." Sure enough, her father's worst nightmares came true. Maria Helena fell in love with a student leader, who was also a communist. "My family at that time supported the military, opposed Goulart, and was furious about my being with a student who was a communist and a leader of the [movement demanding the] nationalization of the electrical company. My father literally locked me in a room and sent me to the United States to a convent with an order written in the passport: Minor. Cannot return to Brazil without her father's permission."

Perhaps in rebellion or perhaps defeated, three months later Maria Helena met an Ivy League–educated professional, ten years her senior, and immediately married him. "He was an architect, Catholic, and American; my parents were delighted." They organized a formal wedding with 1,500 guests, and then Maria Helena settled into what she later remembered as middle-class boredom in Cambridge, Massachusetts. After Cristina, her first child, was born, she began working with a women's group that had formed an alternative day care center and quickly became involved in the women's movement. As the Vietnam War escalated, so did her involvement in the movement to end the conflagration in Southeast Asia. Although she had vaguely followed news from Brazil, including her older brother's career move from journalist to congressman, her native land seemed far away. She focused her political commitment in the United States. Then, in late December 1968, Maria Helena received a phone call from a reporter asking if she knew the whereabouts of her brother, Márcio Moreira Alves. "I simply hadn't been following the political situation in Brazil, and suddenly I discovered that my brother and father were in hiding and my mother under house arrest. You can imagine the panic that I was in."

March of 100,000, Rio de Janeiro, June 26, 1968. EVANDRO TEIXEIRA.

# 3

## THE WORLD TURNED UPSIDE DOWN

Brazilian students have a long tradition of protest. Their grievances are legitimate and pose a long-range threat to the maintenance of stability.

**— "Restless Youth," CIA report, September 1968**

Eight months after the generals seized power in 1964, a purged Congress passed a new educational reform bill. The Suplicy de Lacerda Law, known as the Lei Suplicy, attempted to control radicalized students by reformulating the representational structure of the National Union of Students and forbidding student organizations from engaging in politics. Designed to depoliticize the student movement, it had just the opposite effect. Throughout 1966 and 1967, many university students joined intellectuals, artists, journalists, and left-wing politicians as a leading force in the opposition to the military regime, mobilizing on campuses and in the streets. In a renewed effort to quash ongoing student organizing around political issues, the government amended the Suplicy Law in early 1967 and abolished all student organizations at the national and state levels, permitting associations only within individual colleges and universities. The measures also banned student strikes and political activities among high school students, who had become a significant contingent of the youthful opposition to the generals in power. Pushing student organizations underground, however, did not diminish their influence. They mobilized against a major overhaul of the university system proposed by a joint commission of the Ministry of Education and the U.S. AID mission in Brazil, protested the lack of slots for students who had successfully passed the university entrance exams but were not permitted to matriculate, and continued to demonstrate against the arbitrary actions of the military regime.[1]

Although the organized left had splintered into many different parties, organizations, factions, and groups in the aftermath of the 1964 military coup, these divergent tendencies brokered tactical agreements within the student movement locally, regionally, and nationally and ensured a semblance of unity within the context of operating clandestinely. The National Union of Students secretly held its 28th Congress in a Dominican convent in Belo Horizonte in July 1966 and continued to mobilize throughout 1967 against the new Costa e Silva government. Two major political currents emerged during this period among student activists. One, led by Ação Popular and other political groups, pushed for broadening student protests to address national and international issues, while at the same time focusing on legitimate educational complaints but eschewing talks with the military government. A more moderate grouping, led by supporters of the Brazilian Communist Party and people of other political tendencies, argued for limiting protests to student-related issues and favored an attempted dialogue with the regime as a means of "unmasking" it. At the same time that the majority current led by Ação Popular called for mass political mobilizations against "U.S. imperialism and the military dictatorship" and Communist Party supporters cautioned moderation, political sympathies with Cuban and Maoist Chinese urban and rural guerrilla strategies for revolutionary change in Latin America broadened among student activists.[2]

In 1966 and 1967, the Armed Forces had quickly eliminated several attempts at organizing rural guerrilla encampments that revolutionaries had hoped might have blossomed into popular insurrections or prolonged military confrontation with the regime. Yet the surge of student activism during the same period offered new recruits for groups advocating revolutionary violence to overturn the "revolution" of 1964. Actions designed to capture arms and obtain funds to sustain underground organizations slowly escalated in this period.[3]

The Johnson administration accurately predicted this potentially new development in revolutionary leftists' political strategy. The Country Analysis and Strategy Paper (CASP) for Brazil that circulated among State Department officials in January 1968 foresaw that "a shift by activist subversive groups to urban terrorist activities is likely."[4] The CASP also outlined, among other items, U.S. policy toward Brazil's internal political and security needs. The general objectives emphasized "progress toward a stable government responsive to the people and committed to rational policies," as well as growing popular participation in the political process at all levels, commensurate with greater political and civil sophistication."[5] However, the specific objectives combined support for the "development of responsible and reform-minded politicians capable of exercising effective civilian leadership in the 1970s" within the context of "representative political institutions" with increased training and education of Brazilian military leaders. The State Department's goals were to "(a) improve the capability of the Brazilian armed forces to react to subversive threats, (b) create a greater understanding of the role of the military in a popularly responsive government, and (c) indirectly, maintain the pro-American orientation of the armed forces."[6] This included supporting improvements in operational logistics and administrative capacity of the Brazilian armed forces, equipment modernization, improvement in training, organization and management procedures, riot control techniques, and public relations of the state and federal police forces. Recognizing that the State Department did not endorse all of the Costa e Silva government policies, the report recommended that the U.S. government try to alter "the present political system in Brazil by subtle pressure in favor of such matters as direct elections, partial amnesty, free collective bargaining, and a meaningful opposition party." At the same time, the report recommend retaining Washington's ability to "disassociate" from those Brazilian government policies considered "undesirable." In short, Washington policymakers recognized the importance of preserving the special relationship between Brazil and the United States but realized that tensions might arise within that long-term association.

As the year began, few Brazilians could have predicted what was in store for the country by that December's end.[7] Not even the State Department had a talent for prognostication. In January 1968, it certainly was not apparent that the Brazilian economy would take off at an average annual 10 percent growth rate in the following four years. Inflation had dropped from 34 percent in 1965 and 39 percent in 1966 to 25 percent by the end of 1967, but in 1968 economic growth remained flat and wages static.[8] In the political sphere, the military regime had remained in power for almost four years, and in spite of President Costa e Silva's promise for a return to democratic rule, the Armed Forces did not seem anxious to relinquish control to civilians. By early 1968, however, opposition politicians began taking the offensive. Carlos Lacerda, the right-wing journalist, former governor of the state of Guanabara that encompassed Rio de Janeiro, and virulent opponent of the Goulart government, attempted to outmaneuver the military's control over the two-party regime. Frustrated that the military had foiled his presidential aspirations, Carlos Lacerda lobbied hard to convince former presidents Kubitschek and Goulart to join his Frente Ampla (Broad Front) in an effort to unite disparate political forces against the regime.[9] Although Lacerda's initiative failed to sustain traction and the military outlawed the alliance in April 1968, the attempt to constitute a united front against the dictatorship dovetailed with an emboldened stand taken by politicians in the Brazilian Democratic Movement, the legal opposition party permitted by the military regime. As student mobilizations escalated throughout the year with growing support from broad sectors of the middle class, youthful and energetic politicians, among them Márcio Moreira Alves, became more and more outspoken in their repudiation of the military's repression of student protests and the curtailment of civil liberties.

Rather than recreating a detailed history of the intricate sequence of events that took place in Brazil during 1968, a subject amply documented by many scholars, this chapter examines how the U.S. government and media understood the political situation that unfolded that year and how Washington policymakers responded to the authoritarian measures imposed on the country at the year's end. Historians of Brazil generally concur that the promulgation of Institutional Act No. 5 (IA-5) on December 13, 1968, marked a qualitative change in the nature of the regime. The veneer of democratic governance dissolved as the Armed Forces shut down Congress, eliminated the writ of habeas corpus, and implemented a series of other totalitarian measures. Moreover, beginning in 1968 the regime systematically used torture to intimidate and silence its opposition while extracting information to dismantle organized radical resistance to its rule. As Elio Gaspari, journalist and expert on the military regime, has persuasively argued, the government's level of violence, especially its use of torture as a methodical means of muting or crushing oppositional forces, serves as an accurate barometer to measure the nature of the military regime at a given moment.[10] The issue of torture would eventually become an important focal point of international condemnation of the military regime. Thus, December 1968 not only became a symbolic dividing line for student activists and other opponents of the regime that distinguished between hopeful possibilities and dismal prospects but it also marked the moment after which many more voices in the United States began to register their opposition to the Brazilian military regime.

### Reporting Youthful Unrest

When students returned to classes after Carnival in early 1968, few would have thought that a demonstration against the poor quality of food at a student cafeteria in downtown Rio would spark national student protests that would threaten to destabilize the regime. Yet a complex chain of circumstances linked the events of March 28, when police killed a high school student named Édson Luís de Lima Souto during a public protest, to December 13, when President Costa e Silva enacted Institutional Act No. 5.

U.S. journalists were aware of the growing opposition to the military regime. Numerous news items reported that a sector of the Catholic Church, led by Archbishop Hélder Câmara, had registered its opposition to the Costa e Silva government.[11] On the other hand, even though the student movement had escalated in the previous year and a half, the events of early 1968 generally caught the U.S. news media by surprise. A brief Times article in late March reported that 20,000 people accompanied the body of Edson Luís de Lima Souto in a funeral cortege, which began at the State Assembly building, where students guarded it in a round-the-clock vigil and wake, and ended at the cemetery for a somber burial.[12] It was the largest demonstration in Brazil since hundreds of thousands had poured into the streets in 1964 to celebrate the overthrow of Goulart. This time, however, the protests were against the military and not in their favor. Newsweek, Time, and the Christian Science Monitor, among other newspapers and magazines, also ran short stories describing the student unrest that had rocked Rio in late March and early April.[13] Paul Montgomery, the *Times* correspondent assigned to Rio de Janeiro, ran a series of mostly small articles between April and May mentioning student protests in Rio de Janeiro without placing the movement within a larger context of the political contestation in full swing and the unraveling of the military's support among significant sectors of the middle class.[14] Montgomery also reported on the labor rally in São Paulo on May 1 that ended in a violent confrontation between workers and student protesters and the police.[15] Nonetheless, his stories and those of other foreign correspondents in Brazil during this same period offered only thumbnail sketches of these and other events.

Although U.S. student demonstrations had become front-page news throughout 1967 and 1968, perhaps the *Times* editors, as well as those of other news sources, offered scant coverage of the Brazilian protests because they didn't fully appreciate the implications of student upheavals abroad. French student protests followed by a general strike that shut down the country and the economy, however, seemed to signal that a worldwide revolt was taking place, and government officials in Washington closely monitored student unrest in Brazil and around the world. On September 18, 1968, CIA director Richard Helms addressed remarks to President Johnson and his cabinet in a meeting that discussed, among other matters, the global protest movement of students and other youth.[16] Helms based his comments on a CIA report that analyzed the subject in a bold, sweeping tone: "Youthful dissidence, involving students and non-students alike, is a worldwide phenomenon. It is shaped in every instance by local conditions, but nonetheless there are striking similarities, especially in the more advanced countries. As the under-developed countries progress, these similarities are likely to become even more widespread." The first section of the top-secret document outlined the underlying reasons for student unrest and presented a review of the complexities of activism around the globe. Although the paper focused mainly on Europe (both East and West), a few third world countries were featured. Argentina and Brazil represented Latin America.

The anonymous author of the Brazil section presented a succinct history of the student movement since 1964, focusing on the "radical" student activists linked to the National Union of Students. Using the language of the military regime, the report commented, "The revolution [of 1964] weakened but did not completely destroy the effectiveness of these groups," and acknowledged that student activists had successfully reorganized underground.[17] The CIA analyst estimated the level of support for mobilizations among students: "Although the majority of Brazilian students are apathetic and apolitical—only 10 to 20 percent ever participate in student politics—they share many attitudes in common with the activists. One of these is an inordinate faith in Brazil's destiny and a deep disappointment over present day reality—poverty and illiteracy, undeveloped natural resources, and the lack of opportunity."[18] The report also noted that police repression of student protests "has led to charges of brutality and has been responsible for a general increase in public support for the students' legitimate demands."[19] It ended by predicting that "student demonstrations, no matter how well organized and widespread, will not bring down the government."

### Collision Course

While U.S. media sources emanating from Brazil proved unreliable or inadequate, the State Department's daily accounts and weekly news summaries sent from Brazil to Washington must have served as valuable sources for the September CIA report on the state of student unrest worldwide.[20] The analyst who wrote the section on Brazil cogently commented in the section headed "Prospects" that "popular support for the students would not have crystallized had the government moved to implement needed reforms." The report continued by commenting that, although student demonstrations might not bring down the government, "they may cause divisions within the military over the handling of the continuing turmoil. Military dissatisfaction with the inept performance of President Costa e Silva and some of his key ministers is likely to increase in proportion to the disturbances." Presciently, the section ended with the comment, "Mounting student and military frustration with government inaction, however, does not bode well for even short-range stability in Brazil."[21]

On August 29, the military police invaded the University of Brasília. Many sons and daughters of congressional representatives and government employees attended the university, and the police's repressive tactics particularly outraged the residents of the country's capital.[22] Several days later, first-term congressman Márcio Moreira Alves delivered a speech that discouraged people from participating in the upcoming September 7 Independence Day celebrations. He further suggested that Brazilians should extend the idea of boycotting this patriotic event to "young girls who dance with cadets and go out with young officers" and characterized the military regime as a "nest of torturers."[23]

This off-handed remark about an improbable campaign to demoralize the military regime got only a small note in the *Folha de São Paulo*. However, the congressman's speech served as a pretext among military officers to mobilize sentiment within the Armed Forces against what seemed to be an opposition that was getting out of control. General Emílio Garrastazu Médici, at the time the head of the National Intelligence Service (and later to become Costa e Silva's successor as president), circulated the congressman's proposal within the military, provoking pressure on the government to respond to Alves's "seditious" speech.[24] The constitution, however, gave politicians immunity from prosecution for comments made in their capacity as legislators. Costa e Silva, therefore, directed his political allies in the ARENA party to lift this protection so that the government could punish the congressional representative for his "unjustified verbal aggression against the Military Institution."[25] When the majority of progovernment politicians on the Justice Committee balked at the move, Costa e Silva ordered them replaced with loyal supporters.

The regime's heavy-handedness backfired. Dozens of ARENA party members recoiled at the proposal to lift Alves's immunity, and a congressional majority voted to protect his right to speak out. This legislative insubordination had suddenly become a political mutiny. It was precisely the pretext that a sector of the military needed to push for harsher measures to silence opposition forces, end the political anarchy reigning throughout the country, and return the nation to its proper course of stability and order. The following day, December 13, the Minister of Justice read Institutional Act No. 5 over the radio and television to a shocked nation. The proclamation of Institutional Act No. 5 became a front-page story in newspapers throughout the United States, marking a sharp shift in journalistic discourse about the Brazilian government. Over subsequent weeks, hundreds of articles described and analyzed the indefinite closure of Congress, the suspension of the writ of habeas corpus, the increased press censorship, the detention of former president Kubitschek and former governor Carlos Lacerda, and the abrogation of the rights of politicians from ARENA, the military's party, and the oppositional MDB. William Montalbano, writing for the *Miami Herald*, called the Brazilian armed forces' measures the "convulsive overreaction of a revolution gone sour" and a "desperate gamble of a government that has lost the confidence of the people." The *Christian Science Monitor* opened an article on the crackdown by informing its readers, "Brazil's military leaders have imposed a stringent, dictatorial rule over Latin America's largest nation."[26] These comments summarized the general tone of the U.S. press in response to what many analysts have called "the coup within the coup," or the beginning of the military dictatorship's most repressive years.

## Washington's Dual Strategy

Institutional Act No. 5 and supplemental decrees issued over the next six months left no doubt that the Brazilian government would not tolerate dissent. The U.S. charge d'affaires, William Belton, who had taken over responsibilities in the embassy because the State Department had called Ambassador Tuthill back to Washington the previous week for consultations, quickly predicted that the new Institutional Act meant that "any real or imagined resistance to government can now be expected to be repressed vigorously."[27] The day after the government issued the decree, Belton outlined a preliminary assessment of the political situation. Institutional Act No. 5, he argued, "signals [the] bankruptcy of an effort by [the] Brazilian military to demonstrate that they [are] better able than civilian elements [to move] toward goals of development and political stability through democratic means."[28] Belton then mapped out a political posture that he recommended Washington policymakers adopt. He made several substantive suggestions, among them that Washington should issue a public statement at a high U.S. government level "deploring the setback in [the] development of Brazilian democracy" in order to "encourage friends of democracy in Brazil." Such statements should not "point a finger too accurately at the persons or groups responsible" since they are "fundamentally favorable to the U.S. and can be counted on to side with us either sentimentally or overtly in any East-West confrontation." In addition, it was "highly likely" that the military would continue to control Brazil "for a number of years to come." That being the case, Belton suggested that the U.S. government needed to "obtain cooperation in enterprises of mutual interest and through them . . . work to help Brazil emerge from the underdevelopment of which their own attitudes are one manifestation."[29] Belton also recommended that the State Department make a public comment during its daily press conference that would indicate Washington's reaction to the new governmental measures.[30] The script that he prepared for the press secretary provided overall guidelines for U.S. policy in response to these new developments. If asked, Belton suggested that the State Department spokesperson explain that the events taking place in Brazil were an internal matter. He also recommended that there should be no statement implying either the continuation or cessation of aid and any other cooperative assistance program.

At a State Department press conference on December 16, Robert J. McCloskey, the government's spokesperson, followed the general outline of the talking points that Belton had laid out in the scripted response to journalists' questions. However, he restricted his reservations about the political situation. "We are fully aware, as sincere friends of Brazil and its people, that the recent events there present serious potential problems as to individual freedom . . . and the rhythm of the country's development," he cautiously stated. During the briefing, one journalist asked whether the U.S. government intended to suspend diplomatic relations, since the Brazilian government had "suspended constitutional guarantees." The State Department representative answered in the negative, reiterating Belton's argument that it was not necessary to suspend diplomatic relations because a coup d'état had not deposed existing authorities in the country.[31]

State Department policy recommendations, circulated secretly to the embassy and consulates in Brazil, were circumspect about public pronouncements against the regime as they seriously considered the proposal to suspend aid temporarily to the country. One memo proposed that the five or six top U.S. government officials in Brazil should consider individually and privately approaching twenty to thirty influential Brazilians, indicating the off-the-record fact that Washington was "distressed" about developments in Brazil without "publicly shaking our finger at the GOB [Government of Brazil]." The memo recommended that embassy officials get out the same message to selected members of the U.S. and foreign press "on a background basis."[32]

The following day the State Department drafted a memorandum for Walter Rostow, special assistant to the president on national security affairs, recommending temporarily holding up two approved appropriations—the sale of Douglas A-4 jet aircraft to Brazil and the authorization to begin negotiations with Brazil for a $143 million economic assistance package for 1969. The memo reiterated the policy that the U.S. government should "quietly" express its regret at the reduction of human liberties taking place in Brazil while "simultaneously, without public criticism or admonition," slowing down or stopping those economic actions that might be thought of as evidence of U.S. approval for the Brazilian government's measures.[33]

Perhaps because he had received word that the U.S. government was considering placing its aid packages to Brazil under review, Brazilian finance minister Delfim Neto made a public declaration in São Paulo about the issue of a possible aid freeze. The finance minister, who had enthusiastically voted in favor of IA-5 in the National Security Council meeting on December 13, 1968, stated that he did not expect Washington to restrict aid as a result IA-5 "because they, as well as we, know the reasons which forced the government to adopt this measure."[34] The minister also voiced "optimism that foreign investments would not be affected because conditions of security, profit opportunities, and freedom of action would continue [to] make Brazil attractive for foreign capital." The president of the U.S. Chamber of Commerce in São Paulo echoed the minister of finance's confidence in the appropriateness of IA-5 and its relationship to U.S. investments in Brazil. He self-assuredly commented to the consul general that "American business in São Paulo is for the GOB [Government of Brazil] and feels IA-5 is [the] best thing that could have happened to the country."[35]

In late December 1968, State Department officials faced a dilemma. Editorials in major U.S. dailies had decried the Brazilian regime as an outright military dictatorship, pressuring the State Department to respond in some way. The day after Delfim Neto predicted that Washington would not suspend aid, a State Department representative indicated that U.S. aid programs to Brazil were "under review."[36] No public rebuke of the regime accompanied the announcement.

U.S. diplomats, it seems, calculated that the suspension of aid to Brazil would constitute just the right amount of pressure to exert on Costa e Silva so that he would change the course he had set for the country. Yet State Department officials continued to debate the exact approach to take when talking to Brazilian government officials.[37] The State Department's suggested "script" for embassy personal encouraged those in contact with Brazilian officials to appeal to the "Alliance within the Alliance." In conversations they should emphasize that "there is still time and good opportunity to avoid the congealing of public opinion in the U.S.A. along lines that would make it very difficult for any administration in this country to continue those degrees of cooperation and mutual assistance." The memo stressed that U.S. government officials should not tell the Brazilians how to conduct themselves, and the style of the approach should be "calm, friendly, and frank—no histrionics, no threats and not tutelary or directive nuance." The tightrope maneuvering that State Department officials recommended entailed discreetly trying to convince sectors of the Brazilian military to moderate their measures so that the political situation would not place the U.S. government in the position of having to distance itself from the regime. At the same time, despite the proposal by U.S. government policymakers in Washington to consider working with "disaffected groups in the country," the embassy apparently carried out no concerted effort other than meeting periodically with some prominent oppositional figures to get their appraisal of the ongoing political crisis.

### Editorial Dissent and Public Opinion

Until late December 1968, the mainstream U.S. press rarely characterized the Brazilian government as a military dictatorship or targeted the regime with sharp editorial comments.[38] Now the Costa e Silva government received harsh criticism on the editorial pages of the country's leading newspapers. The *Washington Post* called on the Nixon administration to distance itself from the regime.[39] The *New York Times* proclaimed, "Brazilian military leaders have again swept aside constitutional government and fastened a dictatorship on the country."[40] The *Christian Science Monitor* argued that Costa e Silva has installed "what looks like an outright military dictatorship."[41] U.S. news reporters complained to the embassy that the Brazilian government censored international phone conversations and cut off connections "when words 'arrest,' 'dictatorship,' etc. [were] mentioned."[42]

The extreme measures adopted by the Brazilian military shook U.S. diplomats as well. In a memo to the State Department, Ambassador Tuthill commented that the political situation in Brazil "cannot be viewed as a valid rationale for the drastic measures imposed by Institutional Act No. 5, particularly when one bears in mind the strong powers that the GOB [Government of Brazil] had in hand under the Constitution, the Press Law and the National Security Law." The ambassador's incredulous reaction to Brazilian officials' justification of their harsh measures is noteworthy. Geopolitical considerations—as determined by the State Department—required that the U.S. government retain a close relationship with Brazil, yet the subtext of Tuthill's remarks indicates that there was little confidence in the arguments employed by the defenders of IA-5.

In the aftermath of IA-5, the Brazilian government retained a hard-faced public stance that seemed to indicate that the generals cared little about international public opinion. Reports of meetings between U.S. government officials and the Brazilian top brass, however, prove that the military was quite concerned about the repercussions of their actions abroad. On December 20, the U.S. Army attaché met with General Orlando Geisel, the chief of the Armed Forces' General Staff, because the latter wanted to discuss the U.S. press's editorial comments on the Brazilian situation. Although Geisel, the brother of future president Ernesto Geisel, was a supporter of former president Castelo Branco and was not a part of the inner circles of the Costa e Silva government, he remained a powerful figure within the Brazilian military. According to the U.S. military attaché, when Geisel finished reading a file that contained the editorials from the *New York Times*, the *Wash-*

ington *Post*, and the *Christian Science Monitor*, his face "flushed with anger." Geisel then defended Costa e Silva's measures and questioned the editorials' references to democracy, stating, "Writers who refer to the democratic anxieties and aspirations of eighty million Brazilians are dreaming if they believe that most of our population even suspects what democracy in the U.S. sense is. Our people have not shown the slightest concern over recent measures. Most of them accept and want any measures that will allow them to work in peace without worrying about agitation and exploitation." Reporting on the meeting, Ambassador Tuthill commented to Washington officials that Geisel's reaction likely reflected the sentiment of a large segment of the Brazilian military, noting that the general was usually "calm, measured and low key" in approaches to crises.[43]

General Golbery do Couto e Silva, the former head of the National Intelligence Service and chief adviser to former president Castelo Branco, reported to a "reliable Embassy source" that the "only current restraints on immoderate military elements have been the ferocity of foreign press reaction, particularly American, to events since December 13 and the attitude of the Church."[44] In other words, U.S. editorials, *not* U.S. diplomatic conversations, had restrained the Brazilian military. However, Golbery cautioned embassy officials against strong international pressure, especially from the United States, because it might force the military to close ranks in support of extreme nationalism. Ambassador Tuthill trusted Golbery's assessment. He commented to the State Department that even though the former head of the National Intelligence Service was now on the "outside," he remained "one of the most balanced and intelligent figures around Castelo Branco and retains a number of military contacts, making his assessment reasonable in light of information available to [the] Embassy from other sources."

General Orlando Geisel was outraged at U.S. editorial comments about Brazil, and General Golbery de Couto e Silva indicated that international press coverage had restrained the heavy hand of the dictatorship. Yet the U.S. press's criticisms of the new authoritarian measures did not entirely reverse long-standing and commonplace analyses by the media about the nature of the Brazilian regime before IA-5. The December 18 *Times* editorial that added to Geisel's fury over U.S. press coverage read in part, "The military has a good case for overthrowing President Goulart's corrupt government in 1964, for Brazil was then wallowing in political anarchy and economic chaos. It can make no case for eliminating the limited democracy permitted under Mr. Costa e Silva to satisfy a clique of hypersensitive officers who claim a monopoly on patriotism and honesty."[45]

In response, Robert M. Levine, a young assistant professor at New York State University at Stony Brook, penned a critical response to the paper's assessment of the Goulart government. Levine's short letter to the editor represented the first of a string of public pronunciations by U.S.-based Brazil scholars against the military dictatorship in the aftermath of Institutional Act No. 5. It is worth quoting in its entirety.

> I wish to object to one statement in your editorial on Brazil (Dec. 18) which holds that the military had a "good case" for overthrowing the constitutionally elected Government of João Goulart in 1964.
>
> Since when does any nation's armed forces have such a right? What of the repression and cultural terror which followed the so-called revolution of April 1, 1964—the mass arrests, censorship and anti-intellectualism in the name of anti-Communism? Or of the new regime, allegedly opposed to corruption, maintaining some of the most corrupt politicians in Brazil in office because they backed the coup?
>
> We are reminded of the cartoon, which appeared in a Rio de Janeiro newspaper in mid-1964 showing work men building prisons. The revolution is now moving "from a destructive to a constructive" phase, the caption read. And finally, we are reminded of the breathless haste in which the Johnson Administration moved to recognize that regime. The Brazilian people deserve better than this.[46]

Levine's comments criticized the general trend in the U.S. media and among Washington politicians and policymakers since 1964 that offered a simple narrative to explain events in Brazil. A corrupt Goulart had brought the nation to the brink of economic and political chaos, and the military had been justified in shoving him aside in order to bring the nation back to normalcy. The Costa e Silva government, however, had exceeded the initial popular mandate to overthrow Goulart and bring order to the country by limiting democratic rule. It merited a stern rebuke. This traditional reading of the political situation in Brazil by the *Times'* editors was not unlike the response by the State Department to the military's new authoritarian measures. Levine and a growing number of academics, clerics, intellectuals, and activists would take the U.S. government to task for vacillating between reservations about the new political situation in Brazil and ongoing support for the regime.

### "Subversive" Catholics

While the lame duck Johnson administration fine-tuned its response to Institutional Act No. 5 and the U.S. media condemned the government's measures, the State Department had to deal with another diplomatic crisis. The military regime had arrested Darrell Rupiper and Peter Grams, two U.S.-born priests, who were members of the Oblates of Mary Immaculate Order and assigned to work in northeastern Brazil. On the evening of Sunday, December 15, 1968, just two days after the military seized total control over the government, fifty armed police surrounded their parish church in a poor neighborhood of Recife and arrested them, along with two parishioners. The Brazilian government accused them of "serious subversive activities" and violating the National Security Law because their parish newsletter had condemned Institutional Act No. 5.[47] The same day that the State Department confirmed that the AID program for Brazil was "under review," it announced the arrest of the two priests.[48] The incident added pressure on Washington to take firmer actions against the clampdown in Brazil.

Rupiper had come to Brazil in 1964. He had already held certain sympathies with the reform wing of the Catholic Church while in seminary. In Recife, Archbishop Hélder Câmara's leadership in articulating an ever-more intransigent critique of the government emboldened Rupiper and other missionaries to become more active in talking about the root causes of the dismal conditions the poor faced.[49]

Recalling the events of December 15, 1968, Rupiper commented that he had a premonition that he would be arrested. "That night, the last mass of the day, I was preaching . . . and all at once I felt really strange. In fact, so strange that I stopped, and I asked [myself], 'Darrell what is going on here?' Then I heard a voice. It said, 'This is the last time you'll be talking to my people.' You know it was God speaking to me for sure. It was so real I just started crying. I told myself, 'God, I still got this in me.' It took me a little time to pull myself together, and then I finished the homily. After the mass, a couple of friends came and asked what was going on, and I then told them that. We talked for about half an hour." As they left the church, they saw that fifty soldiers had surrounded the building. Eight plainclothes police officers arrested Rupiper and his fellow priest, as well as two active parishioners.

Although the police never physically abused them, perhaps because they were foreigners or because the U.S. consul eventually got involved in the case, the police held them in a section of the prison where torture was taking place. According to Rupiper, Peter Grams, three years younger than Rupiper and with much less experience in Brazil than his fellow priest, suffered greatly, because he could hear the screams of political prisoners brutalized during interrogations.

At one point during their ten-day incarceration, a general visited them and offered the priests two options: they could either leave the country quietly or face a military tribunal on charges of being communists and inciting people to revolution. The general advised them that, due to the backlog of cases, they might have to remain in jail for two years before a trial could take place. They acquiesced to the general's first proposal. It was only then that the Brazilian authorities permitted a representative from the Church to visit the priests. Although Archbishop Hélder Câmara had been trying to get word of their condition and see the Americans, the government had blocked his initiative. According to Rupiper, during the visit the archbishop stated that he had learned that Washington had sent a telegram to Brasília threatening to sever all military aid if the Brazilian government did not release the two Americans. On Christmas Day, the Brazilian government expelled them from the country. When interviewed by the press upon arrival in the United States, Grams explained why the Brazilian government detained them: "We were saying that there was starvation, sickness and lack of education, while huge amounts of money were being spent on the military establishment."[50] Both reported that they had witnessed serious abuse of political prisoners, "We could hear the screams of people being beaten," they reported to the press. Then the story faded away. Both the Brazilian and the U.S. governments had been saved from having to deal with a serious diplomatic crisis.

### Resuming Aid

As the new year approached and Richard M. Nixon prepared to assume the presidency, U.S. government officials continued to debate their policy on aid to Brazil. In late December, State Department Brazil specialist Jack Kubisch drafted a ten-point memo titled "Developments in Brazil: Significance of Institutional Act No. 5."[51] Suggesting a kind of Latin American exceptionalism, Kubisch argued, "Brazil's needs and performance cannot be measured against North American or northwest European standards of constitutional democracy, nor even easily expressed in Anglo-Saxon terms." He nevertheless recognized that human rights "as defined by minimum international standards, have already suffered to some extent and remain under serious threat." The State Department official conceded that IA-5 was "an important watershed in Brazil's political development," and was far more significant than the first institutional act of April 1964 or IA-2 of October 1965. Kubisch admitted, "In retrospect we believed we erred after [the] October '65 Act in not drawing back further from our close association and public identification with [the] Castelo Government." He continued by arguing that Brazil had been unable to succeed with an open democracy from 1945 to 1964 and now had lost its chance—at least for the present—to move ahead "even under [a] strongly guided semi-authoritarian democracy." This assessment, however, did not modify the conclusion that State Department officials had emphasized over the previous two weeks in the flurry of telegrams exchanged between Rio de Janeiro and Washington, namely, "U.S. interests and objectives in Brazil are virtually [the] same now as they were eleven days ago."

In fact, while the State Department placed aid under "review" as a means of signaling displeasure with IA-5 and distancing itself symbolically from the regime, its overall relationship to the military regime had not changed. Brazilian military leaders, at least, seemed to read it that way, as reported to the consul general in São Paulo by multiple sources. At an Inter-American Military Conference held in Rio de Janeiro, Brazilian military officers emphasized the fact that the U.S. military "fully supports extraordinary action." Another source within the Brazilian army reported to the consulate that "Brazilian military men [are] confident of U.S. understanding and support despite any public statements by U.S. 'civilians.'"[52] The report noted that "hard line" civilians were taking a similar attitude. The reporting diplomat did not anticipate any significant change in the attitude of key military leaders "as word of [the] U.S. position gets around."

In the week before Nixon's inauguration in Washington on January 20, the State Department began to elaborate its policy regarding loan resumptions. Belton recommended that the U.S. government maintain "fundamentally friendly relations" without condoning antidemocratic excesses, given the fact that some form of workable democracy would be an "extremely long-term process on which the U.S. can have only indirect and marginal influence."[53]

## Nixon's New Policies

Vice President Nixon's 1958 Latin American tour had ended in embarrassment and had pushed the Eisenhower administration to rethink its policy in that region of the world. Therefore, it came as a surprise when Nixon did not even mention Latin America in his Inaugural Address on January 20, 1969. In Washington's diplomatic circles, representatives from diverse Latin American countries complained about Nixon's silence. In response, presidential aides hastily scheduled a rather disorganized official visit by Galo Plaza Lasso, the secretary general of the Organization of American States, to the White House several days later.[54] Press officials spun the fact that it was the first official visit to the new president as a sign that Nixon was interested in Latin America. At the secretary general's suggestion, Nixon invited

New York governor Nelson Rockefeller to tour the continent in a series of brief "listening" trips. Rockefeller had served as President Roosevelt's coordinator for inter-American affairs from 1940 to 1944 and as assistant secretary of state for American republic affairs from 1944 to 1945.[55] Some observers speculated that Nixon's choice of Rockefeller was a cynical way of dismissing a political rival by sending him off on a thankless mission to an area of the world where he had some previous experience.[56] The governor of New York nevertheless took up the assignment with energy and enthusiasm, organizing whirlwind visits to countries throughout the continent, squeezed in between gubernatorial obligations. The announcement of Rockefeller's tour of Latin America suggested that the new administration would adopt a new policy for the region, perhaps replacing the Alliance for Progress altogether with a new approach to its neighbors to the south.

By mid-March, the decision to renew aid to Brazil was on President Nixon's desk for his signature. Some administration officials argued that the U.S. government needed to resume assistance before Rockefeller visited Brazil. That same month, Charles Elbrick replaced Tuthill as the new U.S. ambassador to Brazil. Following a custom established by his predecessor, Elbrick met informally with Foreign Minister Magalhães Pinto to discuss the pending aid question, among other issues. Elbrick explained that the Nixon administration faced a serious "problem" with "Congressional opinion," placing at stake "not just assistance to Brazil, but Congressional attitude toward [the] entire foreign aid program" since many U.S. congressional representatives believed that "economic assistance should be closely related to [the] political orientation of [the] receiving government."[57] According to Elbrick, Magalhães Pinto seemed to understand the State Department's "problems" with Congress, but he pushed for the release of $50 million as a "sign of confidence" in order to prevent the development of anti-American attitudes among the Brazilian military. Elbrick then emphasized that it continued to be "of utmost importance" for the Brazilian government to "provide us with openings which would help us to proceed with other facets of our program." The constant appearance of lists of people losing their political rights and the continued denial of human rights, the U.S. ambassador argued, was a source of serious criticism of the Brazilian government in the United States. Elbrick also emphasized that, should the U.S. government release the $50 million, it was essential that the Brazilian government not use this fact "as evidence of support by U.S. for the current state of affairs in Brazil."

The Brazilian government, however, did not provide the opening requested by the State Department that would act as a cover for the resumption of U.S. aid. In late April, President Costa e Silva ordered the summary retirement of sixty-eight university professors and cancelled the political rights of fifty-nine state legislators and twenty-four assorted politicians for ten years. The military also removed from office a number of Foreign Ministry officials and various state and federal bureaucrats. The Nixon administration, nonetheless, simply lifted its aid restrictions on Brazil in May 1969. At the end of the day, the Nixon administration, like the State Department officials who pushed for placing the aid program "under review" as a means of "quietly" convincing the Brazilian military to ease up on its violations of human rights, prioritized what they considered the "long-term" goals of U.S.-Brazilian relations. In their day-to-day communications, government officials rarely reiterated in detail the strategic objectives laid out in that year's Country Analysis and Strategy Papers. Yet government officials embedded that strategic vision in their analyses as they drafted memos, wrote reports, and sent telegrams to Washington. U.S.-owned companies had over $1.6 billion invested in the country, no small amount for the time.[58] The military regime warmly welcomed U.S. capital, which was one of the reasons that the U.S. Chamber of Commerce in Brazil applauded Institutional Act No. 5. Moreover, the Brazilian Armed Forces' virulent anticommunism made the country a firm ally in global geopolitical conflicts.

Ultimately, State Department officials in Washington and Brazil failed to heed the most cogent information provided by one of their sources. General Golbery de Couto e Silva, an architect of the 1964 coup, chief adviser to President Castelo Branco, founding director of the National Intelligence Service, and subsequently one of the masterminds behind the military's controlled liberalization at the end of the 1970s, offered the U.S. embassy what seems to have been disinterested advice. U.S. editorials, rather than signals about displeasure through the suspension of U.S. aid, had prevented the military from taking more extreme measures, Golbery argued. Yet, had the State Department adamantly echoed the editorials of the *Washington Post*, *New York Times*, and *Christian Science Monitor*, to cite only three examples, their diplomatic gestures might have had more effect on the political climate in Brazil.

State Department Brazil expert Jack Kubisch pointed out in passing that the United States had missed an opportunity in not distancing itself from the Castelo Branco government in 1965 after the enactment of Institutional Act No. 2. Yet he failed to follow up on his own comment with a different policy approach three years later. In spite of attempts to portray its policy as one that distanced Washington from the extremes of the Costa e Silva government, the United States continued to appear as a close ally of the Brazilian military dictatorship. At least in the eyes of most observers, in the spring of 1969 the "special relationship" between Brazil and the United States seemed firmly in place. Even after Rockefeller's three-day jaunt to Brazil in June 1969, when the governor made public gestures indicating that he was "listening" to the opposition, and even after he publicly communicated concerns about the internal political situation, the U.S. government seemed firmly aligned with the Brazilian military.

### Protected from the People

Because Nelson Rockefeller had a busy schedule as governor of New York, he divided his "listening" tour of Latin America into four quick trips. During his second swift visit to the region, he met with significant student protest in Ecuador, in which ten people died in clashes between protesters and police. As a result, the Venezuelan government, fearful of student unrest that would have been reminiscent of Nixon's 1958 visit to the country, revoked its invitation. Subsequently, the State Department cancelled visits to Peru and Chile. Concerned that Rockefeller's stopover in Brazil on his fourth journey south of the Rio Grande might incur more bad publicity at home and abroad for the government, Costa e Silva took numerous precautions. The military government issued orders to all news editors to screen out any articles that might have an adverse effect on Rockefeller's stay in the country and divulge only favorable news about his fact-finding trip to Latin America.[59]

Immediately before Rockefeller's arrival, the government also initiated operations in which hundreds of "subversives" were arrested in an effort to discourage any organized protests during the official visit. Among those sought by the police was Jean Marc Von der Weid, the president of the National Student Union, who was directing the underground student organization's national protests of the visit.[60] During the three days Rockefeller spent in Brazil, security was extremely tight. The *Times* journalist reported that a man standing in a small crowd outside the São Paulo airport to see Rockefeller walked away in disgust after police herded the group far from the airport gates. "When Robert Kennedy came here three years ago, I was able to shake his hand at the airport. Now, I can't even see Rockefeller," he said.[61]

The governor insisted on his role as an emissary who came to promote dialogue and understanding.[62] Instead, Rockefeller spent an hour with the vice president and a delegation of ARENA politicians in the halls of the closed Congress.[63] That same day, in meetings with President Costa e Silva, however, Rockefeller raised questions of press censorship, student arrests, and political and academic freedom. At the end of their meeting, Foreign Minister Magalhães Pinto held a news conference reassuring the foreign press that Costa e Silva had promised the governor that he planned to reconvene the Congress shortly.[64]

As part of the governor's itinerary, the U.S. embassy in Rio de Janeiro arranged a meeting with seven students, who emphasized to Rockefeller and the press that they were not student leaders, "The student leaders are all in jail or are in hiding," said Maurício Camargo, one of the participants in the meeting.[65] Rockefeller assured them that he had raised the issues of student arrests and academic freedom in his meeting with the president, but gave the students no indication of Costa e Silva's response. One can read the governor's decision to meet with students as a diplomatic signal from the Nixon administration to register its dissatisfaction with some of the military government's policies. However, it is just as likely that Rockefeller's staff organized the event as an attempt to reframe the images emanating from the Latin American trips since they had been getting bad press at home.[66] Under controlled conditions in Brazil, Rockefeller could meet with students without fearing that the encounter might be yet another embarrassment for the "listening tour."[67]

The political situation in Brazil proved unsettling for at least one aide who accompanied the governor on the trip. Joseph E. Persico, one of Rockefeller's speechwriters, recounted in his memoirs that while the entourage was in Rio de Janeiro, he had dinner with Brazilian friends he had known when he was stationed in Brazil as a United States Information Agency foreign officer. "The husband was a businessman, his wife a high-level, longtime employee of the American embassy. Hardly bomb tossers, they were roughly the equivalent of middle-of-the-road Republicans."[68] According to Persico, they recounted "harrowing cases of friends who had been tortured or jailed without explanation or had simply disappeared." Urged by his friends to include something in the speech he was preparing for Rockefeller's stopover in Brazil, Persico included the point in his draft remarks. When Rockefeller saw them he was reportedly furious: "Don't you understand? That's exactly what these people resent, our sticking our noses in their business, Americans trying to tell them how to run their internal affairs." According to Rockefeller's speechwriter, the governor of New York struck the passages supporting a return to democracy from the text.

On the surface, the overall impression left from the Rockefeller visit, as projected in the United States, was that despite some disagreements the two countries remained on good terms. Several months after returning from his last sojourn south, Rockefeller issued his report. It emphasized the traditional Republican formula for Latin America—trade over economic aid. On the other hand, the Nixon administration endorsed Rockefeller's recommendation that Washington increase military aid to friendly governments in Latin America.[69]

On May 29, 1969, several weeks before Rockefeller's three-day visit to Brazil, a group of American professors, advisors, and administrators engaged in educational work in the cities of Rio de Janeiro and São Paulo visited the U.S. embassy in Rio de Janeiro. The purpose of their meeting was to present a letter and an accompanying report addressed to Nelson Rockefeller to call his attention to "recent governmental measures [in Brazil] that are particularly prejudicial to higher education."[70] Focusing on the forced retirement of professors from Brazil's public universities, they explained, "Our letter and report are not written in the spirit of a broad indictment of all measures since 1964 that are inconsistent with American notions of democratic government and personal rights and freedoms. Rather, we have limited our comments to a field within our competence, and made a specific indictment of policies detrimental to education and thus to Brazilian development." Arguing that censorship "backed by repressive police controls" had limited open criticism by Brazilians, the authors of the letter called on Rockefeller to meet with representatives of those who had signed the missive in order discuss the report with him. They also informed the embassy that that some 200 distinguished American professors were planning to send a signed telegram to President Costa e Silva "protesting the forced retirement of some 65 well known Brazilian educators." This effort marked the first concerted campaign among U.S. academics and others to speak out against the military regime.

# CAPÍTULO III

---

## "Agora falando sério"

Now seriously speaking
I want to not lie . . .

**Chico Buarque, "Agora falando sério," 1969**

Father Antônio Henrique Pereira Neto spent the day of May 26, 1969, with a group of parents and children in a suburb of Recife, the northeastern city where fathers Darrell Rupiper and Frank Ganns had worked among the poor until they were expelled on Christmas Day 1968. For the previous three and a half years, the recently ordained priest had served as an assistant to Archbishop Hélder Câmara, dedicating his ministry to students in conjunction with Juventude Universitária Católica (University Catholic Youth, JUC).[1] Padre Henrique was also an outspoken critic of the regime. In late March 1968 he had delivered an impassioned message at a mass memorializing Edson Luís, the high school student whose death had sparked the nationwide wave of student protests. Because of his progressive positions and visibility, he had received death threats from the Comando de Caçar aos Comunistas (the Commando to Hunt Communists), a right-wing paramilitary death squad linked to the police and military that executed regime opponents and those they considered marginais (criminals).[2]

According to eyewitnesses, as Padre Henrique left the meeting around 10:30 p.m., three armed men approached him and whisked him away in a car. The next day, someone discovered the young priest dead in a wooded area of the Recife University campus. His hands had been tied up, and his body was covered with bruises and signs of torture. His face was almost unrecognizable. Three bullets had pierced his body.[3] Death came from two wounds in the back of the head.[4]

Dom Hélder Câmara immediately issued a statement condemning the crime, noting that it had been "only one in a series of premeditated acts that included threats and admonitions."[5] Over previous months, unknown assailants had fired shots at the archbishop's residence and at the church's administrative offices. The prelate concluded his brief public statement affirming, "We believe it is our right and duty to raise our voices in protest so that at least the sinister work of this new Death Squad cannot continue." He also announced that Padre Henrique's name was "on a list of 32 persons marked for death."[6]

U.S. Embassy official William Belton wrote several reports to the State Department about the priest's death.[7] In one memorandum, he suggested, "Serious further strain on Church-State relations [is] anticipated in [the] region, quite possibly with national repercussions."[8] Belton's comment was a confirmation of his previous prediction, in the immediate aftermath of IA-5, of a growing breach between the Catholic Church and the military.[9]

About 5,000 people accompanied the funeral procession, confronting police squads who wanted mourners to remove banners considered subversive. Dom Aloísio Lorscheider, the general secretary of the National Conference of Brazilian Bishops, flew to Recife to offer his condolences to the murdered priest's relatives and show solidarity with the archbishop and the Catholic Church's progressive wing.[10] On June 3, the archbishop received a message from Pope Paul VI noting "the sad news of the tragic death of Padre Henrique Pereira Neto."[11]

A month after the Padre Henrique's murder, Dom Hélder celebrated a thirty-day mass in his honor. The U.S. consul reported that Dom Hélder, "speaking in the name of the slain priest," indicated that "the current situation creates a climate favorable to arbitrary decisions, abuses, and crimes."[12] The archbishop reportedly added, "The present situation leads those more impatient individuals to clandestine activity, radicalism and violence."

On the same day that Dom Hélder used the pulpit to lambaste the military regime, U.S. Catholic priests, lay activists, and their allies in the peace movement organized a picket line in front of the Brazilian consulate in Chicago. The Coordinating Committee on Latin America, one of many newly formed left-wing groups with an international focus that had emerged within the context of a growing anti–Vietnam War and anti-imperialist sentiment, organized the protest. Sidney Lens, the national chairperson of the group, claimed in a press release announcing the picket line that it was part of a nationwide protest. Lens, a freewheeling radical, former union activist, and leader of the antiwar movement, indicated his committee had planned similar demonstrations on the same day in New York, Boston, Washington, and Los Angeles.[13] The communiqué reiterated the information disseminated by the global network of progressive Catholic priests and activists who had mobilized in support of the Brazilian Church's stand against the military regime and had organized similar protests in Europe after the death of Padre Henrique.[14] The press release emphatically stated, "This murder was committed by the Communist Hunt Commandos, a rightist group with considerable army influence. It would not have taken place without the silent assent of the government, since the Army is the ruling force in Brazil."[15] Lens then linked Washington policymakers to the developments in Brazil. "The incident casts a stigma on the United States, since our government supports and has given mammoth aid to this military dictatorship ever since it came into being in April 1964."

The picket line protest took the Brazilian consular officers in Chicago entirely by surprise, but they allowed three representatives to enter the building.

Outside demonstrators distributed the statement "Why We Picket the Brazilian Consulate" to passers-by. "In Brazil," the leaflet proclaimed, there is "no freedom, no democracy, no Presidential elections." The statement also drew a connection between the death of the slain priest and the campaign of intimidation against Dom Hélder Câmara, "the famous Archbishop of Recife," and an "advocate of nonviolent change." The pamphlet announced, "We North Americans cannot stand idly by while such things happen in Brazil, for the absence of social justice can very well lead to another Vietnam." As in the press release, the protesters denounced the fact that the Brazilian government had received "more than a billion in aid from the U.S. since it became a dictatorship" while the "real minimum wages of workers was only 54 percent of what they were in 1963." The statement called on people to wire or write the Brazilian ambassador in Washington demanding the release of all political prisoners, the reintroduction of free speech, assembly, and press, and the end to harassment of the opposition.

The delegation that met with the consul general personified 1960s grassroots religious activism. Father William Hogan had marched in civil rights demonstrations with Martin Luther King Jr. and served in predominantly African American parishes on Chicago's South Side. Many referred to him as a "rebel with a collar."[16] Another member of the group, Carl Zeitlow, was a long-time Quaker activist and pacifist involved in the Chicago antiwar movement. At the time, he was the staffperson for the Nonviolent Training and Action Center that actively supported regional political demonstrations.[17] According to the consul general, the delegation politely presented the press release and pamphlet and left without further incident.

Although Lens claimed in his press release that the Latin American Coordinating Committee had organized a national protest about Padre Henrique's murder, it is not clear that activists replicated the Chicago picket line of no more than a dozen people in other cities. There was no coverage of the event in Chicago's mainstream press or in newspapers in other planned locations. Brazilian ambassador Mário Gibson Alves Barboza forwarded the consul's report to Brasília with no indication that a similar event had taken place in Washington. In 1969, picket lines and protest actions had become common occurrences across the country. The focus was usually Vietnam or national issues and certainly not Brazil. In fact, this modest protest might have gone unrecorded in the historical record had the Brazilian consul not dutifully collected the protest statement and press release and forwarded them to the Brazilian embassy in Washington, where a clerk filed them in the Foreign Ministry archives.

## "No Peace in Latin America without Justice"

U.S. Catholic activists working in Latin America or supporting the Church's missionary efforts made significant use of the symbolism surrounding the death of one of Dom Hélder Câmara's religious lieutenants. By 1969, Dom Hélder had become an iconic representative of those forces in the Latin American Catholic Church dedicated to the poor and oppressed. News coverage featuring his public persona as a belligerent opponent of the military government gained international notice that turned him into the public face of Catholic Brazil abroad.

Padre Henrique's death highlighted both the risks and the dedication of people of faith committed to social justice. *Latin American Calls!*, the monthly missionary newspaper, gave news of his assassination front-page headline coverage.[18] The photograph of a rustic wooden figure of Christ—with its arms bound together and its body apparently bleeding—accompanied the story. The caption read, "A Brazilian Martyr." A double-paged inside spread also reported extensively on the situation in Brazil.[19] Father Rupiper wrote a passionate article telling the story of his recent expulsion from Brazil and the parting words of Dom Hélder: "We all thank you. Your fight for justice is only beginning. Go back and convert the American people. Unless their attitude changes, there can be no hope for progress here in Brazil."[20] Other articles denounced death squad activities in Rio and reported that many more Brazilian reformers were on the right-wing "terrorist death list."[21]

When the Latin American bureau of the National Catholic Welfare Conference began publishing *Latin America Calls!* in 1963, the newsletter had combined its campaigns against illiteracy and poverty and in favor of land reform with its vigilant combat against Marxism. As Catholics throughout the region embraced the gospel of social justice and political change in the wake of Vatican II, transformations in the Latin American Church were reflected in the pages of the U.S. publication. By 1969, the language of *Latin America Calls!* emphasized "conscientization" or political consciousness-raising rather than anticommunism. A prominent appeal showing the half-built gothic arches of a church proclaimed, "We've Stopped Building Cathedrals and Started Building the Church."[22] It replaced the standard one-page promotional theme "A Hungry Kid Makes a Hardy Rebel" that the editors had repeated in every issue since March 1965. The text explained, "The partially constructed cathedral shown above symbolizes the dynamic challenge now being faced and gradually overcome by the Church in Latin America. Cardinal Sales of Salvador, Bahia, Brazil, halted construction of that cathedral several years ago because a Christian response to the social-economic priorities of that area demanded that the money be spent on integral human development. Cardinal Sales's decision was to build the Church rather than a cathedral."

Political transformations in significant sectors of the Latin American Catholic Church had echoes in other venues designed to encourage a dialogue between North and South America. Liberal Catholics sought ways to reshape the balance of power between the Church in the United States and Latin America. In 1964, Latin American bishops had pressed for new forms of international dialogue with the U.S. church through the Catholic Inter-American Cooperation Program (CICOP). Its annual conferences held in the United States offered new opportunities for face-to-face conversations among bishops and Church leaders involved with Latin America. Marina Bandeira, a Brazilian church activist who attended the yearly CICOP conference in the 1960s, recalled how the annual meetings served as informal opportunities for progressive bishops and Church leaders to exchange ideas and, in the case of Brazil, mobilize support against the military regime, especially around the issue of torture.[23] The emphasis on social justice in resolutions issued at the Second General Assembly of Latin American Bishops (CELAM) held in Medellín, Colombia, in 1968 merely reinforced this new progressive thrust among U.S. Catholics involved in Latin America.

### Reverend Abernathy and the Archbishop

In the late 1960s, a very small sector of the radicalizing Catholic Church in Brazil and other parts of Latin America looked favorably on armed struggle as a means for social change. The overwhelming majority of the progressive wing of the Brazilian Church, including Dom Hélder Câmara, rejected this strategy. In the midst of the polarized political situation of 1968, the archbishop had declared that he had great respect for those who sacrificed their lives by choosing the way of violent revolution. Yet in that same year he began to place greater emphasis on his own personal commitment to nonviolence by forming the Action, Justice and Peace Movement.[24] Silenced by press censorship in Brazil after December 1968, Dom Hélder increased his use of the global stage to denounce the escalating levels of political repression. International pacifist organizations such as the Fellowship of Reconciliation served as one of the many vehicles for spreading his message abroad.

Vatican II's ecumenical thrust also encouraged greater contact with the progressive wing of Protestant churches. In the case of the United States, this meant deepening connections with those involved in the civil rights movement, especially the wing led by Dr. Martin Luther King Jr. and, after his assassination in April 1968, by his successor, Dr. Ralph Abernathy. Brady Tyson, the Methodist missionary forced out of Brazil in early 1966, was a long-time member of the Fellowship of Reconciliation. He served as an important intermediary between Brazil and the United States by creating a bridge between the archbishop and the reverend.[25] In late 1969, Tyson discreetly began negotiating a visit to Brazil by Reverend Abernathy. Arriving before Ralph and Juanita Abernathy, Tyson prepared a joint statement for the archbishop's signature calling for a "worldwide campaign to awaken the conscience of all people of the world to the great human cost of poverty, racism, and war."[26] The two leaders met behind closed doors for five hours and then issued the Declaration of Recife, expressing their mutual hope that "non-violent social protest can be an effective means of stimulating social justice throughout the world."[27]

Latin America Calls! reported on the event, but the meeting did not get much press coverage in the United States or Brazil. Nor did a revitalized international nonviolent movement connecting Brazil to the United States emerge from the encounter. The results were more modest, but still significant. Tyson, the Methodist minister, activist, and academic had helped strengthen a bond between the progressive wing of the Catholic Church in Latin America and an important leader of the U.S. civil rights movement. That link would be lasting.

In the cause of decency and the defense of the natural right of all men to voice their opinion without fear of imprisonment, we, members of the international community of scholars, protest this act on the part of a military tribunal while simultaneously deploring the inhuman treatment of political dissidents.

We doubt that ever in the history of Brazil has there occurred more systematic, more widespread, and more inhuman treatment of political dissidents.

RICHARD MORSE
THOMAS SKIDMORE
STANLEY STEIN
CHARLES WAGLEY
New York, Feb. 23, 1970

*The signers are from Yale, Wisconsin, Princeton and Columbia, respectively, and are specialists on Brazil.*

Letter to the editor, *New York Times*, February 23, 1970.

# 4

# DEFENDING ARTISTIC AND ACADEMIC FREEDOM

To those who would forget me, aquele abraço [that embrace]. — **To all Brazilian people, aquele abraço. Gilberto Gil, "Aquele abraço"**

Gilberto Gil's gentle lyrics sending a warm embrace to his audience ended an emotional farewell concert. His song also offered a last adieu from one of the most innovative singers and songwriters of his generation to his fans, as he prepared to board a plane on July 28, 1969, that would fly him to London and forced exile. Gilberto Gil and his friend and collaborator Caetano Veloso, both natives of the northeastern state of Bahia, had revolutionized Brazilian pop music in the 1960s with tropicalism (*tropicália*), an early postmodernist pastiche of rock and roll, traditional Brazilian sounds, and concrete poetry.[1] On December 27, 1968, they were pulled into the undertow of IA-5. They were arrested in São Paulo and kept in prison without any explanation from the government for fifty-seven days. The military finally released the two young pop singers under orders that they remain within the borders of Bahia State. Four months later government officials "invited" them to leave the country. As Caetano Veloso explained in his autobiography, *Verdade Tropical* (Tropical Truth), "Exile, imposed with the same rude informality that had characterized our arrest, seemed an intelligent solution to them."[2]

To this day, no one is exactly certain of the reasons for Veloso's and Gil's detention. In covering their farewell concert in Salvador, Bahia, the Brazilian press made elliptical references to their incarceration. Readers undoubtedly understood the allusions, which were obscure or inoffensive enough to pass the censor's red pen.[3] When Joseph Novitski, the *New York Times* journalist stationed in Brazil at the time, asked a representative of the First Army why the officials had imprisoned the two popular musicians, the colonel refused to let his name be published or to give a clear explanation: "You may say that they were detained for investigation by the Brazilian Army. The investigation is complete and has been laid before the military courts for trial."[4] In an interview before leaving the country, Veloso timidly speculated, "I guess they don't like what we do. They just don't seem to be able to stand anything open-ended . . . Anything that they can't force and control." Gilberto Gil added, "We have not yet understood why we were arrested. They never really told us."[5] No trial ever took place.

Throughout early 1969, the government slowly and meticulously applied the powers invested in it through Institutional Act No. 5 to intimidate and silence the opposition. Ultimately, the most dramatic manifestation of the military's excessive measures—the systematic torture of political prisoners—evoked a strong international repudiation of the military dictatorship. Yet, as we will see in following chapters, reports of such brutal treatment of oppositionists reached international media outlets only gradually. More immediately, the forced exile of top musical performers, the censorship of literature and art, and the persecution of prominent writers and academics managed to strike a cord among intellectuals internationally and provoke organized protests against the regime in first half of 1969. Only later would the issue of torture dominate the discourse against the Brazilian government.

### Artistic Protests: Boycotting the 1969 São Paulo Bienal

The same *New York Times* article that informed readers about the fate of Veloso and Gil also commented that a protest boycott of foreign artists, including those from the United States, France, the Netherlands, and Sweden, threatened to cripple the X São Paulo Bienal.[6] This exhibition, Brazil's most important international art event, was scheduled to open in September 1969. The São Paulo Bienal, founded in 1951 by São Paulo industrialists, intellectuals, and artists, rotated in off years with the Venice International Art Exhibition. By the late 1960s, these two expositions had become the most prominent forums for presenting the latest in innovative art.

The U.S. government had a long tradition of supporting international art exhibitions dating back to the mid-1940s, when the State Department administered United States exhibition activities overseas. In 1954, the United States Information Agency (USIA) assumed responsibility for organizing and circulating art exhibitions abroad. In 1965 the Smithsonian Institution took over that task, working especially with the Venice and São Paulo biennals. In the context of the Cold War and a world seen divided between the "democratic and freedom-loving West" and a "totalitarian" East, U.S. government participation in these events served several geopolitical interests. In countries such as Italy, where the left remained strong in the post–World War II period, the support of art exhibitions, literary production, and other cultural events was a battlefront in the war to win the hearts and minds of the local population, or at least its intellectual leaders.[7] In Latin America, Washington's backing of U.S.–produced culture had earlier roots in the Good Neighbor Policy that was designed to woo the countries "south of the border" to the Allies' side in World War II.[8] As in Europe during the 1950s and 1960s, Latin America became contested territory in the war against communism. Government-endorsed representation in the São Paulo Bienal was yet another way of affirming North America's talents for innovation, progressiveness, and creativity. Though discursively the State Department emphasized that it promoted freedom and democracy by supporting cultural production originating in the United States, Washington policymakers, as we will see, seemed to perceive no contradiction in allying with military regimes that limited cultural freedom.

A copy of the *New York Times* article reporting Gil's and Veloso's departure from Brazil can be found in the files of Lois Bingham at the Smithsonian Institution in Washington. At the time, Bingham was the chief of the International Art Program of the Smithsonian's National Collection of Fine Arts, the U.S. government–sponsored institution responsible for coordinating the participation of official American entries in international art exhibitions.[9] Apparently, someone had hastily ripped the article out of the newspaper and underlined the reference to the São Paulo Bienal boycott with a red pen. That same person had tagged another paragraph in the *Times* piece that summed up the climate in Brazil: "They [Veloso and Gil] left behind, as other musicians, artists and writers now in voluntary exile have left behind, a growing impression of a disjointed, almost unconscious government policy that is approaching cultural repression in Latin America's largest nation." Another inked underlining noted that police had arrested Veloso and Gil in São Paulo. This bit of marginalia registered a link between political repression in Brazil and U.S. participation in the São Paulo Bienal. It is also the only indication in the available archival records about the boycott that any U.S. government official, or representative of a sponsored agency, actually pondered the issue of the limitation of artistic freedom in relationship to U.S. foreign policy toward Brazil.

Earlier that spring, the Smithsonian Institution had proudly announced in a press release that it would collaborate with the Massachusetts Institute of Technology in producing and exhibiting the official United States entry in the São Paulo Bienal. "Gyorgy Kepes, Director of M.I.T's Center for Advanced Visual Studies, will direct the design and construction of what is expected to be a trend-setting American entry," the release affirmed.[10] The two-part exhibition involved the innovative use of lighting and technology in art works. In an alluringly ambiguous way, Kepes described one section of the U.S. exhibition as a "'community or society' of objects ranging from simple to more complex forms which will interact with each other and produce 'a sort of fabric.'" The other section, displayed in the same large space, was essentially a multimedia production with films, slides, and video tapes showing aspects of the American art scene.

The initiative to boycott the Bienal had come from two sources. In Brazil, the art critic Mário Pedrosa called for artists to withdraw from the exhibition. The French art critic Pierre Restany joined him in organizing European artists to refuse to participate in that year's event, and nine artists chosen by the French government decided to decline their invitations. In June 1969, after a tumultuous meeting at the Museum of Modern Art in Paris, 321 artists and intellectuals signed the statement "Non à la Biennalle" and called on their colleagues around the world to join them in protesting artistic censorship and repression in Brazil.[11] Hans Haake, who had been selected to participate in the American entry, led eight other artists to adhere to the boycott.[12]

Reporting on the protest in the *New York Times*, Grace Glueck indicated that European artists and intellectuals had contacted their American counterparts and informed them of a proposal initiated by Brazilians to demonstrate international opposition to the crackdown in Brazil by organizing an international boycott of the Bienal. The arrest of intellectuals, artists, and others opposed to the military, the Europeans argued, had created a climate unfavorable to artistic production. They pointed to the "burning of three erotic works and the seizure of 16 others at a recent exhibition in Bahia, plus imprisonment of the show's organizers and some artist participants, . . . the circulation of a letter by Bienal officials to foreign commissions, asking them not to send 'immoral' or 'subversive works' . . . [and] the regime's crackdown on civil liberties, kicked off by a decree last December 13 in which Congress was suspended and more than 2000 artists, intellectuals and political suspects were arrested."[13] Because of the call of Brazilian exiles and artists, the directors of the Swedish Modena Museet and the Dutch Stedelijk Museum withdrew their national entries, and the original French delegation pulled out, as did the second group chosen to replace it.[14]

In light of these protests, Kepes faced a major dilemma. On July 1, 1969, he drafted a memo to the artists participating in the U.S. exhibition at the Bienal. "I am enclosing a statement I wrote," he informed his colleagues, "which I hope expresses your own stand regarding our participation in the São Paulo Exhibition."[15] Kepes, an artist extremely committed to encouraging collective artist endeavors, echoed the growing politicization of many artists in the 1960s. "Our new scale of interest moves us away from isolated creative acts toward interdependent creative actions, aiming to bring greater integrity and quality to our manmade landscape and to our social-cultural behavior." Linking artists' work as a confirmation of "the integrity and quality of life" to a rejection of "any acts of power that distort or suppress life," the statement then spoke of the situation in Brazil. "The artists who are against all that stifles liberty, and thus creative growth, learned with increasing concern about the plight of our fellow artists and other intellectuals in Brazil, caused by the curtailment of democratic liberties." Kepes also obliquely criticized Washington's support of the Brazilian regime. "The artists from the United States are not unmindful either that the misplaced weight of our super-wealth and power is not unrelated to the tragic fate that our fellow artists face in Brazil." He then proffered two alternatives: a boycott of the Bienal because "international participation could be exploited by the present rulers to hide the absence of cultural liberty in their country" or "communication" with other artists and intellectuals by attending the event. Kepes opted for the latter, arguing that by not boycotting the event they had the opportunity to exchange "vital, progressive ideas." Citing the old Chinese saying that it is better to light a single candle than to curse the darkness, he concluded the statement by choosing the former.

Those artists who preferred to "curse at darkness" answered by informing Kepes of their decision to withdraw from participation in the Bienal. John Goodyear, a sculptor, wrote to both Kepes and the Smithsonian Institution that "enough evidence has reached me in the last few days to convince me that the hoped-for dialogue with Brazilian intellectuals will not materialize."[16]

Goodyear was one of six artists to initiate the boycott of the Bienal; three other artists soon followed suit. The *New York Times* broke the story on July 6, publishing excerpts from the statements explaining their decisions. The reasons that they offered for the boycott reflected the profound disillusionment with U.S. foreign policy by a segment of American society, as the Vietnam War escalated and many critics began to see the conflict as more than an isolated aberration in Washington's initiatives overseas.[17] Hans Haake, who, Goodyear recalled, was the force behind organizing the protest, wrote a blistering manifesto criticizing U.S. foreign policy: "The American Government pursues an immoral war in Vietnam and vigorously supports fascist regimes in Brazil and in other areas of the world . . . All expositions of the American Government are made to promote the image and the politics of this government . . . The energy of artists is channeled to serve a politics that these same artists scorn with good reason."[18]

### Washington Steps In

With this news of a possible boycott by the U.S. entry circulating in the press, the Smithsonian, State Department, and Brazilian government officials scrambled to prevent the collective endeavor from falling apart altogether. Charles Meyer, the assistant secretary of state for inter-American affairs, and Brazil specialist Jack Kubisch met with Brazilian ambassador Mário Gibson Alves Barboza to discuss a strategy for shoring up Kepes's collective work. Barboza reported to his superiors in Brasília that both Meyer and Kubisch offered to contact those responsible for the decision to convince them to reconsider. According to Barboza, they had explained that neither the State

Department nor any other government agency could interfere officially in the matter.[19] U.S. government officials' behind-the-scenes efforts, nonetheless, constituted a concerted attempt to patch up the problem and assure that this political protest did not damage the friendly relations between Washington and Brasília.

The United States Information Agency (USIA) also became involved in damage control. U.S. Information Services official Al Cohen telephoned Bingham to convince her to delay a public announcement about the artists' proposed boycott "so that perhaps some other countries would cancel first, [and the] U.S. wouldn't be seen as the bad boy."[20] With pressure from Kepes to go public with an announcement, Bingham indicated that she thought a lengthy delay improbable.

Concerned that the United States would end up unrepresented at the São Paulo Bienal, the State Department also prepared a contingency plan. Melvyn Levitsky, who worked at the Brazil desk, also contacted Bingham to guarantee that the Smithsonian Institution would send a U.S. "specialist" to attend a symposium that took place during the Bienal to debate issues of art and international exhibitions. Bingham scribbled a note to herself that Levitsky, in pitching the idea, emphasized the "importance that Brazil attached to B[ienal]; their inevitable disappointment at no U.S. rep[resentative]"; and the fact that the State Department "wants specialist there so [we] can make clear that the decision was not an official reflection of disapproval of Brazilian policies."[21] The protesting artists remained firm.[22]

On July 14, 1969, Kepes publicly announced in a joint press release with the Smithsonian Institution that "of the twenty-three artists who originally agreed to participate in our common enterprise, nine have recently withdrawn" from the "community exhibition," making it an unviable project. "Most have chosen to boycott as their way of registering a protest against lack of democratic process and consequent mistreatment of artists and intellectuals in Brazil." Although the remaining fourteen artists had originally intended to go, Kepes added: "I do not see justification for presenting at Brazil an incomplete exhibition. It would be misleading."[23]

## Alternative Exhibitions

Brazilian officials began emphasizing alternative measures to assure an official U.S. presence at the 1969 International Art Exhibition. Initially, they instructed their Washington representative to invite Gyorgy Kepes to participate in the symposium that took place at the same time as the Bienal. Working closely with the Bienal organizers, the Foreign Ministry informed

Barboza, "The Directors of the São Paulo Bienal consider Kepes's presence in the symposium that runs parallel to the Bienal to be of great use."[24] However, after Kepes's lukewarm responses to the ambassador's initiatives, including the fact that he had declined a luncheon invitation, the embassy, with the approval of Brasília, temporarily tabled that idea.[25]

Ambassador Barboza also continued to pressure the Smithsonian Institution to find another U.S. entry to send to São Paulo, although Lois Bingham seemed to balk at the idea. Her reservations may have been a passive acquiescence to the arguments of the boycotters, but a more straightforward reading of her memos indicates that she privileged mundane bureaucratic and professional considerations over moral or political questions. Bingham argued that the cataloging, shipping, mounting, and guarding of art exhibits displayed abroad required meticulous forethought and supervision. "It is by careful advance planning and preparation and the scrupulous observance of procedures such as I have described that this program has painstakingly built, over the past fifteen years, individual and institutional confidence in its competence and reliability."[26] She also expressed fear that a hastily mounted alternative art exhibit "would inevitably open to question the Smithsonian's commitment to the highest possible professional standards and goals." Acknowledging that the São Paulo Bienal is "one of the world's great international exhibitions of art," she argued, "The United States should not be represented by a second-choice exhibition, put together under hazardous conditions" because "neither top quality nor integrity could be maintained in the short time remaining to us."

While Bingham seemed to drag her heels about finding a replacement entry, the Brazilian ambassador and United State Information Agency continued to seek a substitute show. The USIA made inquiries through Smithsonian contacts in the New York office of Governor Rockefeller and in the Museum of Modern Art about exhibiting a part of the Rockefeller collection, but representatives turned down their request.[27] With direct negotiations between the Smithsonian and the Brazilian government to find a replacement show seeming to lead nowhere, the exhibition opening fast approaching, and the possibilities of official artistic representation in São Paulo apparently fading, Bienal organizers took matters into their own hands. Dr. Humbert Affonseca, a wealthy São Paulo businessman who worked with the Bienal and happened to be in the United States at that moment, shuttled between New York and Washington to round up work by American artists.[28] With the assistance of the Brazilian consul general in New York, Affonseca convinced the Leo Castelli Gallery to loan thirty-three engravings by Roy Lichtenstein and Jasper Johns to the Bienal. U.S. officials in Brazil backed the proposal and informed the Smithsonian that although the Bienal was "willing [to] pick up tab if necessary, [the] Bienal wonders if SI [Smithsonian Institution] cares [to] pay crating transport expenses, therefore officializing fait accompli of U.S. participation."[29] Lois Bingham, ever cognizant of the long-term implications of a last-minute endeavor for her own ongoing efforts to organize international exhibitions, wryly jotted a note to herself wondering how paying for the crating made the exhibition official. A week later the plan to send the Lichtenstein and Jasper prints also fell through, leaving the São Paulo Bienal without an "official" entry from the United States.[30]

### Present without a Presence

U.S. news coverage of the Bienal in the United States was generally unfavorable. The *New York Times* art critic Frederick Tuten gave a low grade to the international art exposition, commenting that he had returned from the Bienal "dazed by uncompromising banality."[31] Citing a scant turnout at the exhibition's inauguration, "consisting mostly of journalists, functionaries and their wives," he reported that the Bienal had been "beset with problems almost from the start, when the United States delegation withdrew its art and technology show as a protest against Brazilian censorship of a painting exhibition in Bahia, which the authorities considered to be pornographic." In reporting on the boycott, he noted, "By the time the Bienal opened, France, Holland, Sweden and Denmark had withdrawn their delegations. Mexico was reported to have made a substitution for its original contingent, and on the day of the inaugural, Venezuela cabled a request that its exhibition be removed. Many of Brazil's foremost artists had either been unwilling or unable to participate, or had not been invited to do so." He concluded, "Overall, whether or not because of the gaps produced by the dropouts, the Bienal was a lackluster affair—an exhibition of stunning derivativeness and of a mediocrity informed, in the case of certain artists, by the pace-setting art magazines."

Hurting from the results of the 1969 exhibition and anticipating another boycott in 1971, the Bienal founder and foundation president Francisco Matarazzo Sobrinho visited Washington in late 1970 to discuss with government officials the best means to guarantee a U.S. entry. American officials in Brazil enthusiastically backed this initiative. Anticipating a political controversy, John W. Mowinckel, the country public affairs officer, suggested that the Smithsonian avoid a collective exhibition and consider a "one-man exhibition of an outstanding American artist who is being enthusiastically received in American art circles at the present time." He emphasized that the "Embassy places the greatest importance in American participation in the art section of the next Bienal." Recognizing the fallout from the 1969 boycott, Mowinckel concluded, "Our failure to produce a major art exhibition in 1969 is still a subject of frequent conversation and a source of embarrassment."

The *New York Times* writer Grace Glueck, who had broken the boycott story in the press two years previously, was also the first journalist to announce the U.S. government decision not to participate in the 1971 São Paulo Bienal. Glueck reported that two letters were already circulating that encouraged artists in the United States and abroad to boycott the Bienal. In part, the statement declared, "We refuse to participate in cultural acts . . . that give an illusion of dignity to a Government which steps on its people by the bloodiest repressive tortures in our hemisphere."[32]

The successful disruption of the 1969 American entry and the threat of continued campaigns against U.S. government policy may not have been the overriding consideration in shifting U.S. policy vis-à-vis official sponsorship of international exhibitions, but it undoubtedly played a part. The nine artists who took a political stand in 1969 (even though, as John Goodyear pointed out, doing so may have slowed their careers) and the many others who signed a statement in 1971 anticipating a boycott joined a slowly mounting, largely uncoordinated campaign to tarnish the generals' image abroad. Gyorgy Kepes, who had initiated the original collective show, had been profoundly committed to building a community of artists. He designed his group exhibit to be a performance registering the viability of collaborative work among creative spirits working in diverse media. His vision was a collective one. So was the response by the artists in 1969 and 1971 to the increasing number of reports about the limitations on cultural freedom in Brazil. The absence of their presence in São Paulo seemed to have left its mark. In 1969, they were not the only U.S. intellectuals to speak about against the Brazilian military regime.

### Academics to Academics: Protesting Arrests and Dismissals

As Carnival concluded in late February 1969 and summer vacations for students ended, the Costa e Silva government prepared a series of measures to prevent renewed campus protests when classes began in March. On February 25, the military issued Decree 477. It provided procedures for the suspension of students for three years and professors for five years if, after a summary investigation carried out by the school's director, they were found to have engaged in "subversive activities." These included inciting or participating in strikes or attempted strikes, organizing protest parades or unauthorized meetings, and using areas of a school for "subversive" purposes or for acts "contrary to morals or public order." A U.S. official in Rio de Janeiro commented on the diktat in a cable to Washington. He noted that the "extremely broad sweep of [the] decree is [an] obvious GOB [government of Brazil] effort to maintain complete calm on volatile student front as schools reopen next week. Actions prohibited cover almost any student or teacher against whom authorities might want to move. If GOB wishes to effect wholesale 'cleaning' of educational system, it now has an additional vehicle."[33] As the report to the State Department predicted, the Costa e Silva government soon began its cleansing process in academic and intellectual circles.

In March 1969, the military initiated punitive actions on campuses throughout the country. In the northeastern state of Pernambuco, for example, the Fourth Army requested that the Catholic University draw up a list of "subversives" who could be purged from the campus under Decree 477. Father Geraldo de Freitas, the Jesuit rector of the university, refused to turn over names.[34] Two hundred students could not register for classes through "the selective refusal of scholarship aid on political grounds."[35] That same month, the Federal University of Pernambuco suspended twenty students for three years under the terms of Decree 477. Moreover, according to U.S. officials reporting on the situation, "during the week of March 24, a series of preventative arrests of student activists was made in anticipation of the protest activity during the ceremonies commemorating the anniversary of the 1964 revolution."[36] The patterns of control were similar throughout the country. In the first semester of 1969 alone, administrators used the decree to threaten or expel an estimated one thousand students.[37]

Students were not the only targets of the Costa e Silva government's measures to silence the opposition in the wake of the political upheavals of the previous year. Academics and intellectuals also faced persecution in the aftermath of Institutional Act No. 5 and other complementary government decrees. One such target was Caio Prado Júnior. On March 20, 1969, the Second Military Court of São Paulo indicted him for "incitement to subversion." Prado, who came from one of the most prominent elite families in São Paulo, was a "historian, philosopher and political figure of international stature."[38] In the early 1930s, he joined the Brazilian Communist Party. He was elected to the state legislature on the CP ticket in the 1946 elections, only to have his mandate invalidated in 1947 because of new anticommunist legislation. He authored numerous works that emphasized economic factors in analyzing Brazilian history and founded the *Revista Brasiliense* in 1955, as well as a publishing house. Both provided forums for left-wing intellectuals.

In 1967, students from the University of São Paulo interviewed the eminent historian for a campus newspaper. They queried him on Marxist theory, the current political situation, and his assessment of armed struggle as a valid strategy for the working class.[39] Prado offered guarded and moderate responses to the students, although he did not rule out the theoretical possibility that the proletariat might take up arms at some time in the future, if conditions were favorable. Two years later, the military used the interview, which had appeared in a modest student publication, to justify charges that one of the nation's most prominent Marxist historians had engaged in an incitement to subversion. It was an ominous sign for Brazilian intellectuals.

Sure enough, a month later, the government escalated its campaign against those university professors that it considered subversive. On April 25, 1969, forty-two federal civil servants in the field of education, most of them prominent university professors, were forcibly retired.[40] The initial list of those purged included well-known left-wing opponents of the regime such as Florestan Fernandes, a professor of sociology at the University of São Paulo, and José Leite Lopez, a professor of physics at the University of Rio de Janeiro. As a State Department aerogram noted, "No criteria for applying retirements are discernible. Some of professors punished, such as Jose Leite Lopes and his wife and Florestan Fernandes, are well known for leftist sentiments, others . . . are conservative in [their] political views."[41] The forced retirement of the three professors on the list from the University of São Paulo provoked an immediate protest from Professor Hélio Lourenço de Oliveira, the vice-rector and acting rector of the university. Less than a week later, he and twenty-three professors from the University of São Paulo appeared on a second list, announcing that the government had ordered their removal from their university positions.[42]

By coincidence, Philippe Schmitter, a young political scientist at the University of Chicago who had taught in Rio de Janeiro earlier in the 1960s, happened to be passing through Brazil on his way to Argentina for a research trip.[43] He delayed the next leg of his journey to write an urgent report to "Officials of the Latin American Studies Association and other Scholars Interested in Brazil" to inform Latin Americanists about the plight of Brazilian scholars. It painted a dismal portrait of the situation in Brazil. In describing the government's measures, Schmitter reported, "A subsequent regulation of the decree gave a more prominent role in the initiation of accusations to the

Division of Security and Information of the Ministry of Education, a quasi-military, secret police union within the Ministry. It also invited 'any other authority or person!' to file complaints! All investigations are to pass through this Division which will exercise, in conjunction with the Minister, ultimate authority over judgment and sentencing." He then explained that a second list appeared four days later that included twenty-four professors at the University of São Paulo, among them the institution's most eminent social scientists, as well as prominent scholars in the physical sciences and medicine. "In neither case were any specific accusations levied against the dismissed professors and researchers, nor were they given the slightest opportunity to defend themselves before or after 'sentencing.' The decisions came abruptly and arbitrarily—without warning to those involved and without explanation to the public at large."[44]

The reasons for these measures were complex. Conservative forces within the Costa e Silva government wanted to remove some of the more visible Marxist and left-wing scholars from the nation's most prominent higher educational institutions. Some officials also wanted to prevent certain professors from participating in major university reforms that the Costa e Silva administration had proposed in 1967 in conjunction with a Ministry of Education–U.S. AID agreement.[45] The military placed other faculty members' names on the purge lists for reasons of internal university politics, rivalries, and jealousies that had little to do with broader political issues.[46] James Nelson Goodsell, the Latin American correspondent for the *Christian Science Monitor*, reported, "Most of the retired professors could not in any way be regarded as political activists, and only a small portion, perhaps 20, could be considered mildly leftist. Some are known conservatives."[47] Schmitter speculated that these university expulsions were only the tip of the iceberg for more repressive measures yet to come. "The future of academic freedom and original research in Brazil is grim. Whether they come as part of a careful plan or as the result of vengeful, isolated initiatives, everyone anticipates further 're-tirements' of university personnel."[48]

With Schmitter's report in hand and other news reaching the United States from colleagues in Brazil, academics soon organized a collective response to these limitations on academic freedom in Brazil. In late May, seventy-eight specialists in Latin American studies signed and sent a cable to President Costa e Silva protesting the forced retirements. Heading the telegram was John Johnson of Stanford University, the president of the Latin American Studies Association, and Charles Wagley, an anthropologist and Brazil specialist at Columbia University. At the same time, another 283 scholars signed another cable urging Costa e Silva "immediately to remove restrictions your government has imposed upon scholars and permit them to return to their institutions and to work in a free and open intellectual environment." [49] Notice of the petition campaign in a *New York Times* article ensured that news of the protest reached a broader audience than simply the head of the Brazilian state.

Among the signatories of the first petition was former U.S. ambassador to Brazil Lincoln Gordon, who had been an adamant defender of the generals' seizure of power in March 1964. As described in chapter 1, Gordon had worked diligently to have the Johnson administration immediately recognize the new government. He also closely collaborated with the newly installed president, Marshall Castelo Branco. In late 1966, Gordon left his post in Brazil to become the assistant secretary of state for inter-American affairs, but by the end of 1968 he had retired from government service to become the president of Johns Hopkins University. Gordon explained his reasons for criticizing the regime he had once wholeheartedly supported to a *New York Times* reporter: "My objection to the removal of the professors is part of my general feeling of grave concern over the arbitrary use of power in Brazil since December." [50] The signature of the former ambassador who had so loyally backed the military in power was yet another indication that the measures of the Costa e Silva government had not won unconditional support from Washington's Alliance for Progress cold warriors.

The Brazilian officials in the Foreign Ministry who analyzed the impact of the *New York Times* article that had reported news of the protest petitions noted, "The signature of Lincoln Gordon on one of the two telegrams as well as his comments to the newspaper are not surprising, since the ex-ambassador in Rio de Janeiro was several times accused of undue interference in the internal affairs of Brazil." [51] For the military government, Gordon, who had once been a favorite of the Brazilian generals, had fallen into the camp of outside agitators. In the aftermath of the coup d'état of March 31, 1964, left-wing nationalists and anti-imperialists had criticized Gordon's actions in supporting the overthrow of the Goulart regime. Now that he was announcing a shift in his allegiances, right-wing nationalist forces within the Brazilian government turned the left-wing anti–U.S. government rhetoric around and distanced themselves from the former U.S. ambassador to Brazil. Gordon's displeasure with the new course of events since Institutional Act No. 5 merited news in the United States, but the Brazilian press, censored as it was, did not publish accounts of the protest statement. Nor did it give much coverage to internal opposition to forced retirements, even though students and faculty in Brazil protested the measures, organizing strikes at the University of São Paulo and the Catholic University and other actions throughout the country. With extended powers through IA-5, the military was soon able to deflate the actions in support of the academic community within Brazil. However, government officials seemed concerned about this visible internal and international protest. C. Burke Elbrick, the U.S. ambassador to Brazil, reported to the State Department that, according to "one reliable source," further purges had temporarily halted for a number of reasons, including "the Government's surprise at the extent of the reaction both within and outside Brazil to the Rio and São Paulo purges."[52]

### Ford Foundation Assistance

Several days after the Brazilian government first announced the forced retirement of university professors, U.S. officials reported that the Chilean and Argentine ambassadors had met with Professor Cândido Mendes de Almeida and Raul Prebisch, the former director of the Economic Commission on Latin America, to discuss a "possible rescue operation for Brazilian professors being summarily retired . . . and forbidden to practice their professions."[53] The telegram informed Washington that the Ford Foundation was exploring feasible initiatives to aid these academics. The following day, the embassy notified the State Department that the local Ford Foundation representative had sent a report to New York recommending that the institution make funds available for American universities to utilize retired professors in research projects, both in the United States and Brazil. Three days later, on May 3, 1969, twenty-seven academics founded CEBRAP (Centro Brasileiro de Análise e Planejamento—the Brazilian Center for Analysis and Planning), as a São Paulo–based research haven for those scholars punished by the military regime. The Ford Foundation offered $100,000 in startup funds for the center.

The possibility of financial backing from an institution that some leftist academics considered linked to overall U.S. foreign policy interests provoked an internal debate among those planning the center. After all, the Ford Foundation had recently been involved in a scandal in Europe because it had funded the Congress for Cultural Freedom, "an international association of intellectuals and academics" that also received support from the Central Intelligence Agency.[54] Florestan Fernandes, at the time Brazil's most eminent sociologist, declined to join this new São Paulo–based think tank because of the Ford Foundation's funding, and Otávio Ianni, another prominent scholar, delayed coming aboard for a year because of the issue.[55] In the process of negotiations about its financial assistance, Ford made it clear that it would not link funding to control over the content of research that the institute might choose to conduct. As established in 1969, CEBRAP brought together some of the leading and most creative scholars in the country. The initiative also prevented a brain drain because it set up an institution where many victims of the dictatorship's arbitrary measures could continue to work within the country.

Peter Bell, a Ford Foundation staffperson stationed in Brazil since 1964, played a crucial role in convincing the largest philanthropic institution in the United States to support CEBRAP.[56] Bell believed that Ford should encourage empirically based social science in Brazil, including political science, sociology, and social anthropology at a graduate level, so he began exploring possibilities of aiding university programs moving in that direction. One such initiative was at the Federal University of Minas Gerais in Belo Horizonte. An incident that occurred in that city while he was helping develop an assistance program at the university in the mid-1960s proved to be a turning point in his and Ford Foundation's relationship to Brazilian academics.

A goal of the Ford Foundation's program in Brazil was to identify and support young talented scholars who wanted to do graduate training abroad. One such student was Bolívar Lamounier. Bell met Lamounier at a conference at the Federal University of Minas Gerais as that institution was gearing up to launch a new graduate program in social science drawing from the college of philosophy, economic sciences, and law. Lamounier, a young political scientist, had applied for a visa to study in the United States, but consular officials denied his request without explanation. Taking advantage of Bell's presence at the conference, Lamounier asked the Ford Foundation staff member to accompany him to the U.S. consulate in Belo Horizonte to appeal the decision. Bell agreed. Lamounier, however, came out of the interview crestfallen. The consul then called Bell into his office and informed him that the U.S. government had turned down Lamounier's visa application because he was "the real thing," namely, "Bolívar is deep red." The consul also told Bell not to bother to help Lamounier anymore. Dejected, the two left the building. As they came out of the elevator, the Brazilian secret police, which had been waiting for Lamounier, pushed him into a truck and drove away. Bell tried to intervene, but police officers shoved him aside. Desperate, he returned to the consulate, but the U.S. representative was indifferent to the news about Lamounier's arrest. Of course, one can only surmise that the U.S. consul collaborated with the arrest of the young political scientist, as there is no direct evidence to substantiate that supposition. Receiving no assistance from the consulate, Bell returned to the conference. The event was a high-powered international gathering attended by some of the most prominent social scientists from Europe and the United States. One of the participants, who had a doctorate in political science from the Sorbonne, was also a government official close to President Castelo Branco. He used his connections to help Bell locate Lamounier. A group of conference attendees then decided to take a bus to the place where the police were holding him, although they were not able to talk to Lamounier. When Bell got back to Rio, the Ford Foundation's acting representative informed him that he had cabled Harry Wilhelm, the Latin American program director at the Ford Foundation headquarters in New York, to report Bell's "un-foundation like behavior." Rather than reprimanding Bell, however, Wilhelm sent him a cable congratulating him for what he had done.

Lamounier remained incarcerated for two months. Conference attendees organized an international campaign to get him released, and Justice William O. Douglas of the U.S. Supreme Court, who had visited Brazil around that time, even wrote a letter on his behalf. The Brazilian government freed Lamounier without ever filing charges against him. Bell's actions won the Ford Foundation's respect among many left-leaning scholars who had distrusted the philanthropic institution's intentions in Brazil. It also led to discussions between Brazil scholars and the foundation about supporting the project for setting up CEBRAP.

Even before the Institutional Act No. 5, Brazilian academics linked to the University of São Paulo (USP) had discussed the viability of establishing an independent research center, given the climate against academic freedom in the wake of the 1964 military takeover. When Fernando Henrique Cardoso was in Chile in 1966 and 1967, he talked with Brazilian scholars working there about the possibility of setting up a new research center within USP. In 1968, a group of academics at USP held a series of meetings to discuss the founding of such an institute. The repressive measures of early 1969 accelerated this process and expanded the number of professors who would be invited to join the center. Fernando Henrique Cardoso contacted Bell to see if the Ford Foundation would back the effort. William Carmichael, the Ford Foundation representative in Brazil, gave Bell permission to pitch the idea to New York. A reviewer in the New York headquarters, however, blocked the initial memorandum to support CEBRAP because he thought that the proposal was too controversial. As Bell remembers it, there were questions, for example, about Paulo Singer, who worked on demographic issues. The New York staffperson examining the memo had reservations about the idea because, to name one objection, Singer was against U.S.–sponsored population control programs. Without suggesting the elimination of Singer or other controversial scholars from participating in the plan to back CEBRAP, Bell and Frank Bonilla, a U.S. sociologist who was collaborating with him on the project, reworked the proposal. When top administrators looked at the final document, it got a green light from the headquarters in New York.

The final approval at Ford came from Harry Wilhelm, the same official who had congratulated Bell when he came to the defense of Bolívar Lamounier. (Ironically, Lamounier was among those pushed into retirement by the decrees in 1969, even though he wasn't even affiliated with a Brazilian university at the time.) In the 1970s, CEBRAP became a center of academic excellence. Because it allowed many professors to remain in the country rather than seek employment abroad, CEBRAP also served as a symbolic center of scholarly resistance to the military regime.[57]

In spite of the Ford Foundation's assistance in founding CEBRAP, some Brazilian social scientists who opposed the military dictatorship have been critical of how it shapes research priorities and graduate programs in Brazil. Sérgio Miceli, a leading social scientist who has written extensively on the history of the field's development in Brazil, acknowledges the Ford Foundation's humanitarian initiatives.[58] However, he has argued that the foundation unduly molded the agenda and priorities of social science research in Brazil through directed distribution of resources to certain institutions, programs, and individual scholars. One of the underlying arguments made by Miceli is that the unequal relationship of power and resources has privileged U.S. interests abroad. Nonetheless, Miceli has also noted how the repressive political situation in Brazil reshaped the operations and viewpoint of the staff that worked in the country. "The Foundation's local representatives did not allow themselves to be intimidated by the truculent behavior of the military regime nor by the distempers of American diplomatic status. The experience of living with the dictatorship, in the end, defined for the Foundation's directors their option in favor of association with intellectuals of the opposition; it is perhaps from this time that 'human rights' are incorporated as a central area for involvement, concern, and investment in Brazil."[59]

Ultimately, the Ford Foundation and the U.S. government had quite different approaches to the crisis in Brazilian education brought on by the military's intervention in the country's top universities. Talented scholars found themselves without income or employment. Some might have left the country had CEBRAP, with the Ford Foundation's assistance, not offered an alternative means of support. U.S. government officials in Brazil closely followed the plight of Brazilian academics, but there is little evidence that they intervened to assist them. Indeed, at least some State Department officials seemed hostile to efforts to come to the assistance of left-wing scholars who wanted to remain in Brazil.

### In Defense of a Marxist Scholar

As 1969 rolled on, so did the repressive apparatus designed to quell any opposition to the generals. The forced retirement of renowned scholars was followed by a series of measures designed not only to silence prominent critics of the regime but also to intimidate others into acquiescence. At the same time that the government forced singers like Caetano Veloso, Gilberto Gil, and Chico Buarque into exile, it brought others to trial on charges of subversion. Among them was Caio Prado Júnior, who still faced accusations of inciting subversive acts for the interview he had granted to students at the University of São Paulo.

In early 1970, Caio Prado Júnior's daughter, Yolanda, visited New York to seek international support for her father as his trial date approached. There she made contact with Ralph Della Cava, by then a young professor of Brazilian history at City University of New York, Queens, who had been collaborating in the coordination of a campaign to publish accounts of torture in different liberal publications, as well as preparing a dossier, Terror in Brazil, that documented ongoing human rights violations in the country. Yolanda also got in touch with Ivan Morris, who was a noted Japanese literature scholar at Columbia University with links to Amnesty International. His involvement brought that human rights organization into the case.[60]

At the same time, four prominent U.S. experts on Brazil, three historians and an anthropologist, sent a letter to the editor of the New York Times protesting Prado's imminent trial. The Times published the communication on Sunday, March 8, 1970, assuring a wide audience. The signers of this protest message were among the most well-known U.S. specialists on Brazil. All of them taught at top-ranking research universities.

A brief communication written by these eminent scholars was a blistering indictment of the military regime:

> Since the overthrow of the legally elected Government of Brazil in 1964, scholars abroad dedicated to the study of Brazil have watched with indignation successive encroachments upon the civil liberties of the Brazilian people. In the past months, we have been shocked to learn of systematic

efforts to muzzle the press, to silence public criticism at all levels, and to jail or exile those who protest against torture, imprisonment without cause, and suppression of civil rights.[61]

The statement then went on to denounce Prado's trial before a military tribunal and to deplore the "inhuman treatment of political dissidents." The four academics closed their epistle with a bold declaration: "We doubt that ever in the history of Brazil has there occurred more systematic, more widespread, and more inhuman treatment of political dissidents." Coming from such noted experts on Brazil, this was a harsh indictment of the military regime.

Over the following months another ninety-seven Latin Americanists from universities throughout the country signed on to a statement titled "A Protest to the Brazilian Government." The list was a Who's Who in Latin American studies in the United States. This was a significant show of support for Caio Prado Júnior, considering that at one time he had been a prominent member of the Brazilian Communist Party. Although he had broken with the Party by the 1960s and criticized its policies, all sectors of the left considered him a leading Marxist scholar.[62] The academics signing the statement reflected a broad range of scholars with different political allegiances. Some, like Peter Eisenberg and Kenneth Erickson, had worked hard as graduate students and young assistant professors to gather signatures for the 1966 statement against U.S. involvement in the Dominican Republic. Many senior scholars joined the protest even though they held more conservative political perspectives. The statement in support of Caio Prado Júnior indicated a widely held repudiation of the military regime and its measures against left-wing opponents. As we will see, it also alarmed the Brazilian government.

Soon after the protest letter appeared in the *New York Times*, the Brazilian government sentenced Caio Prado, at the time sixty-three years old, to a four-and-a-half-year prison term. Amnesty International U.S.A. adopted the "well-known historian and writer" as a prisoner of conscience and began a letter-writing campaign on his behalf. Ivan Morris, the Columbia professor who had responded to Caio Prado's plea for assistance, called in some Brazil activists for support. Ralph Della Cava helped organize a demonstration outside of the Brazilian consulate on June 13, where Latin Americanists and Amnesty International activists distributed leaflets "calling the attention of the American public to the treatment of prisoners of conscience in Brazil and, in particular, to the widespread use of torture in Brazilian prisons."[63]

Another letter to the editor published in the Sunday June 14, 1970, edition of the *New York Times* and signed by Henry J. Steiner, a professor of the Harvard Law School, and David M. Trubek, a professor of Yale Law School, criticized the recent sentencing of Prado. In part it stated, "The imprisonment of so distinguished a scholar stirs deep alarm and regret among many Americans who are concerned with Brazil. It stands as a symbol of a more repressive policy towards Brazilian intellectual life in general—and at a time when the Brazilian Government appears anxious to refute charges from varied sources of extreme, repressive conduct."[64]

Amnesty International's letter-writing effort, as well as the significant number of prominent scholars who had backed the campaign to release Prado, reached Senator William J. Fulbright, the chairman of the Senate Foreign Relations Committee. He in turn requested that the State Department supply more information on the case and about the general political scene in Brazil. The State Department Office of Congressional Relations responded to the senator's inquiries with a letter lifted from a State Department memo of May 5 about the conviction and imprisonment of Prado.[65] The staffperson then added the Nixon administration's position about the case: "We do not believe it would be helpful to our relations with the Brazilian Government, or to the outcome of Dr. Prado's appeal, to approach the Brazilian Government officially on behalf of one of its citizens. Such an inquiry clearly would be an intervention in Brazil's internal affairs, as well as an intrusion into the incomplete legal proceedings." The aide also suggested that Fulbright meet for an oral briefing with Robert W. Dean at the State Department's Office of Brazilian Affairs about the general political scene in Brazil, "as this is a complex situation." No available records indicate whether Senator Fulbright had a follow-up meeting with the State Department on Brazil.

In September 1970, the Supreme Military Tribunal reduced Prado's sentence to one and a half years of imprisonment. A year later, the Federal Supreme Court overturned his conviction. The government released him after he had served one year and five months of his sentence. In reporting on the case, U.S. ambassador William M. Rountree commented, "There have been repeated national security cases during the past year in which the STF [Federal Supreme Court] and the Supreme Military Tribunal have demonstrated a relatively more lenient attitude towards the defendants than the lower courts by reversing convictions or reducing sentences imposed by these courts which are more subject to the local pressures of the anti-terrorist effort."[66] The political scientist Antony W. Pereira, who has studied political cases that were appealed to the Supreme Military Tribunal during this period, concurs with this overall assessment.[67] In this case, Caio Prado Júnior's standing as an eminent scholar, international pressure, and the argument by attorney Heleno Cláudio Fragoso that Prado's declarations in a student publication hardly constituted a incitement to subversion seem to have convinced the civil court.[68]

In spite of the fact that the Supreme Military Court and the Federal Supreme Court ultimately reduced the sentences of some political prisoners, by 1970 it had become clear that international campaigns against the military regime required efforts that went beyond the denunciation of limitations to artistic and academic freedom. Since mid-1969, Brazilian oppositionists had managed to smuggle out of Brazil more and more reports that those arrested by the military regime were undergoing systematic torture as part of their interrogation. In late 1969, activists in the United States geared up to educate the American public about this barbaric physical violence that had become so pervasive in Brazil's police stations, clandestine jails, and official prisons.

## CAPÍTULO IV

_____

## "Acorda amor"

*Wake up my love.*
*I just had a nightmare.*
*I dreamt that someone was outside*
*Knocking at the door.*

**Leonel Paiva, Julinho de Adelaida**

**(Chico Buarque), "Acorda amor"**

Cover of *Veja* magazine, December 10, 1969.

M aria Teresa Porciuncula de Moraes, known as Tetê Moraes, is a documentary filmmaker based in Rio. She lived in the United States in the
early 1970s and collaborated with other female exiles in producing the book
*Memórias das mulheres no exílio* (Memories of Women in Exile). While relating
her experiences about living abroad, she revealed another story embedded in
her recollections about those trying years.[1]

> I finished my law degree in 1966, but I found out that I did not want to be
> a lawyer. I went to law school, which was fine because I was exposed to
> politics and the student movement and all of those questions about na-
> tional politics: Was the dictatorship going to end in a year, in two years, or
> in five? No one thought it would last so long. I began to participate more
> because the experience woke me up to the need to understand what was
> happening.[2]

Extended military rule had broadened the ranks of those who joined the
opposition to the dictatorship to include youthful members of Rio's middle
class. Their conservative parents may have celebrated the overthrow of
João Goulart in 1964, participated in the March of the Family with God for
Freedom, and supported Carlos Lacerda and the right-wing União Democrática Nacional (National Democratic Union) and later ARENA, but the generation that came to early adulthood in the mid-to-late-1960s saw the military
regime as an obstacle to their freedom.

Tetê's adolescence mirrored Rio's middle-class ideal: "I lived in Copacabana and went out a lot to have fun. I enjoyed the beach, parties . . . We played
the guitar. It was the time of bossa nova, of cultural discovery." Her university experience brought Tetê closer to politicized students, "After the coup
. . . I participated more in the resistance movement at the university." After
getting her law degree, Tetê passed an exam to enter the Brazilian Foreign
Service. She also began writing for an alternative newspaper, *O Sol* (The Sun).
"*O Sol* first came out as an insert in a sports paper, but it was so successful
that, within a month or two, it came out on its own. The idea was to produce
a daily that was creative, free-thinking, independent, and critical about what
was happening in Brazil and the world."[3] Although *O Sol* did not last, ending
in early 1968, Tetê realized that she wanted to be a professional journalist.
Over the next two years, she worked for the news magazine *Visão*, and then
the newspaper *Correio da Manhã*, balancing her morning job at the Chancel-
lery of the Brazilian Foreign Service with her afternoons and evenings as a
reporter and editor.

Tetê recalled that, after the government crackdown at the end of 1968, reports of the torture of political prisoners increased. "We received a lot of information at the newspaper that we couldn't publish, including reports from mothers looking for their children and telling horrible stories. I continued to have contacts with friends who had decided to join underground organizations. The police arrested and tortured some; others remained in hiding. We would receive information from them, and a group of friends realized that we had to do something to get this news out, so we set up a system to send information abroad to the *New York Times*, the *Washington Post*, *Le Monde*, Amnesty International, the *Monthly Review*, and a Brazilian correspondent with contacts in the United States."

Among the people in the group were Mário Pedrosa, the prominent art critic and former Trotskyist leader, his niece Maria Regina Pedrosa, and her husband Carlos Eduardo de Senna Figueiredo. "We would gather information, check its accuracy, and prepare reports. Two members of the group, Angela Xavier de Brito and Jader Cunha Neves, were sociologists linked to an underground organization. Also in the group was Rosica Darcy de Oliveira, who had been a friend since childhood, and her husband, Miguel Darcy de Oliveira, a diplomat." Sérgio Rocha, Tetê's boyfriend at the time and a journalistic photographer, was also a member of the group. Tetê recalled how their network operated: "We would send reports by mail or through foreign news agencies, with foreign correspondents, or with people traveling abroad who would carry out envelopes addressed to the *Washington Post* or the *New York Times*."

According to Tetê, in January 1970, authorities arrested and tortured Angela Xavier de Brito and Jader Cunha Neves. Soon thereafter, they went looking for Tetê, Sérgio, and the rest of the members of the group. "I was kidnapped," Tetê recalled. "I was living with my parents in Copacabana at the time. I had gone to the movies and was just getting home. I entered the garage in my car around one in the morning. When I parked the car, one of those big police vehicles drove in and blocked it. Two or three guys got out with machine guns and revolvers and forced me to drive my car to the DOI-CODI center on Barão de Mesquita Street." Tetê had read enough reports to know what was in store for her. "Two of the men got in the back seat and another sat in the front with a revolver. Another police car was behind us. Everyone was undercover in plain clothes . . . At one point, I thought of crashing my car and killing us all, but then I thought that I might have a chance of surviving. If I crashed the car, I wouldn't have a chance."

Throughout this period, Tetê and hundreds, if not thousands, of others, like Martinha and Mônica Arruda, hid friends or friends of friends who had gone underground or who were wanted by the political police. Many were simply involved in the student movement that the dictatorship had declared subversive. From 1967 to 1969, increasing numbers of students and break-away segments of the pro-Soviet Brazilian Communist Party embraced the idea of armed struggle. Some organizations inspired by the Cuban revolution argued that a vanguard Marxist-Leninist Party was no longer necessary and that the path toward a democratic government of national liberation was through militaristic means. Other political currents saw taking up arms as a way of both toppling the military regime and installing a socialist state. Most groups operated in urban areas, planning bank robberies and the seizure of arms, munitions, cars, and other support material. Their strategic goal was to establish rural guerrilla bases that would serve as the foci of a concerted popular war to overthrow the military. From 1968 on, a wave of bank robberies placed urban guerrilla actions on the political map. The government also stepped up the measures to dismantle the clandestine organizations and those who in some way or other supported such actions. Torture became the privileged means to extract information in order to contain the armed opposition.

The afternoon of the day that the police arrested Tetê, she had gone to the beach with her boyfriend Sérgio and then had arranged to take Chico Nélson, one of the people she was helping to hide, to the movies with his girlfriend. She had then dropped off Chico at the place where he was living secretly and had left her boyfriend at his parent's house. It was quite late at night when she arrived at home and the police apprehended her.

As it turned out, Chico was not just any ordinary young radical hiding from the police. Unwittingly, he had become entangled in a much larger drama that affected the entire military regime. In late August 1969, the military dictatorship faced a serious internal crisis. On August 29, President Costa e Silva suffered a stroke that left his right side paralyzed. His closest advisors and the Military High Command realized that he was temporarily (and perhaps permanently) unable to continue to rule the country. The group around Costa e Silva refused to adhere to the constitutional provision, which required that civilian vice president Pedro Aleixo assume the office of the president until the chief executive had recovered enough to resume his role as head of state. Since Aleixo had balked at removing Márcio Moreira Alves's congressional immunity and had opposed Institutional Act No. 5, the military regime had isolated him from the inner circles of power and considered him too unreliable to take over, even temporarily, the reins of state. Nor were the top brass willing to reopen Congress to permit the president of the Chamber of Deputies, the president of the Senate, or the president of the Supreme Court to follow the vice president in the constitutionally mandated line of succession, should the president become unable to exercise his official responsibilities. So, following the patterns established in 1964, they simply ignored all legal provisions, changed the rules of the game, and formed a "Triple Regency" composed of the three military ministers who would govern in the name of the president while remaining in their ministerial posts.[4]

Meanwhile, two revolutionary organizations had been planning to kidnap U.S. ambassador Charles Elbrick and demand the release of political prisoners who lingered in custody and suffered ongoing torture. On September 4, 1969, they carried out their plan. After four days of tense negotiations, the government gave in to their demands, ordering the release of fifteen political prisoners in exchange for Ambassador Elbrick. They also agreed to permit the publication of a manifesto drafted by the two revolutionary organizations that condemned the dictatorship. They did so for several reasons. First, the triumvirate that had come to power on the eve of the sequester due to President Costa e Silva's paralyzing stroke had neither the political cohesion nor the necessary will to risk creating a scenario in which the U.S. envoy might be assassinated, as his revolutionary captors had threatened, should their demands be rejected. Second, the Nixon administration placed extreme pressure on the Brazilian military to pursue any means necessary to avoid harm to the ambassador.[5] So Elbrick was released on September 7, Brazilian Independence Day, with a wound to his head, inflicted when he was grabbed by his kidnappers. Otherwise, he had been unharmed. This was not the fate of those who had detained him. The police and military carried out a systematic hunt to round up those involved in the action and interrogated them brutally after government officials captured them. As the dragnet swept through Rio, Tetê's friend Chico Nélson realized that he had become an indirect accomplice to the revolutionary plot to capture Elbrick.

Tetê recalled, "Chico Nélson, who has since passed away, was a journalist and a very good friend of my boyfriend Sérgio Rocha. Both worked at the O Cruzeiro magazine." Chico was also friends with members of one of the groups that kidnapped the ambassador and had let his colleagues use his car for underground action. He didn't know, however, that it would be used to kidnap the U.S. ambassador.[6] As Tetê remembers the incident, "When Chico reported to work on Monday, he was given the assignment to cover the site where the kidnappers had held the ambassador. He was a reporter, so he went. He walked through the house and, when he got to the garage, he saw his van. It still had his license plates on it. He discreetly walked out of the place and, in a state of shock, called Sérgio from a public telephone to ask him what to do." Eventually, Sérgio, Tetê, and their network of friends hid Chico in different houses.

After four months on the lam, Chico was getting stir-crazy. Because he could have cautious and careful contact with the outside world, Sérgio and Tetê had agreed to take him and his girlfriend to a late Sunday movie in the neighborhood of Flamengo. Few people whom they might know would attend that cinema, and so they thought it would be a safe excursion, with few risks. After enjoying a day at the beach, Tetê and Sérgio picked up Chico and his girlfriend, and they went to see *Macunaíma*, which, ironically, included a satirical scene about urban guerillas.

Many hours later, when Tetê arrived at the police station, she realized that she still had her address book in the straw beach purse that she carried with her. "It was early in the morning, and the guys who were going to interrogate me hadn't gotten there yet or were drinking coffee. As soon as I arrived, they took down my name and asked for my Identification Card. I told them I had to go to the bathroom. I tore up my address book, but I still wasn't sure why they had arrested me." Tetê assumed that it was because she had been hiding someone linked to the kidnapping of the U.S. ambassador, and she was prepared for the worst.

**5**

# THE CAMPAIGN AGAINST TORTURE

There is no surer way for the regime to swell its opposition and even make subversives and revolutionaries out of ordinary citizens than to make terror and torture virtually a way of life in Brazil.
— *New York Times* editorial, April 29, 1970

What the Berrigans Mean; Games Corporations Play; Stage — Buchwald and Feiffer on Broadway

Volume XCII No. 6    April 24, 1970    40 cents

# commonweal

ONE OF THE FIVE POLITICAL PRISONERS RELEASED BY THE BRAZILIAN MILITARY REGIME AND FLOWN IN EARLY MARCH INTO MEXICAN EXILE (IN EXCHANGE FOR THE SAFETY OF A KIDNAPPED JAPANESE DIPLOMAT) WAS A ROMAN CATHOLIC NUN, SISTER MAURINA BORGES DA SILVEIRA. ARRESTED IN OCTOBER, 1969, SISTER MAURINA, THE MOTHER SUPERIOR OF THE SAINT ANNE'S HOME IN RIBEIRAO-PRETO, SAO PAULO STATE, WAS SUSPECTED OF PROTECTING ALLEGED STUDENT "TERRORISTS" OPPOSED TO THE PRESENT MILITARY GOVERNMENT. DURING THE 19 DAYS SHE WAS HELD INCOMMUNICADO, RUMORS BEGAN TO CIRCULATE THAT SHE WAS BEING TORTURED BY THE CITY'S TWO HIGHEST POLICE OFFICIALS. THEN, IN MID-NOVEMBER, THE METROPOLITAN ARCHBISHOP OF RIBEIRAO-PRETO, DOM FELICIO DA CUNHA VASCONCELOS, REPORTEDLY OBTAINED INCONTROVERTIBLE EVIDENCE THAT SISTER MAURINA HAD BEEN SUBJECTED TO ELECTRIC SHOCKS AMONG OTHER CRUELTIES. WITH THE SUPPORT OF SEVENTY DIOCESAN PRIESTS, THE ARCHBISHOP IMMEDIATELY AND PUBLICLY ORDERED THE EXCOMMUNICATION OF THE CITY'S POLICE CHIEF AND HIS ASSISTANT.

IT SEEMS INCREDIBLE THAT TORTURE SHOULD HAVE BEEN INFLICTED UPON A RELIGIOUS IN THE LARGEST (CONTINUED ON PAGE 135)

# TORTURE IN BRAZIL

Cover of *Commonweal*, April 24, 1970. COPYRIGHT 1970 COMMONWEAL FOUNDATION, REPRINTED WITH PERMISSION.

Most people associate Amnesty International (AI) with the global campaign against torture. However, Amnesty International was silent about the human rights abuses in Brazil in the first years of military rule, in part because it was a new organization. Founded in London in 1961, Amnesty International based its operating philosophy on Articles 18 and 19 of the Universal Declaration of Human Rights, written in 1948, which state that it is the right of every citizen to be free to hold his or her own political and religious opinions and to express them.[1] From its inception the organization attempted to skirt Cold War geopolitical polarity by focusing concurrently on the violation of human rights in the "three main ideological regions of the world: communist, capitalist and the newly emergent nations of Africa and Asia."[2] Its attention toward the continents involved in decolonization from European rule reflected the main international preoccupation of British liberals and leftists at the time. Brazil and the rest of Latin America (with the exception of Cuba) were noticeably absent from the organization's initial activities and literature, although AI's first annual report noted that it had preliminary contacts in Mexico and supporters in Argentina. Political "neutrality," that is, balancing campaigns in favor of prisoners held in the socialist countries with those in advanced capitalist countries and the third world, remained a guiding principle of the organization. Political prisoners from national liberation struggles that employed violence or revolutionary organizations involved in armed struggle, however, did not qualify as candidates for "prisoner of conscience" status.

Amnesty International's approach to the release of political prisoners in time became the model for the human rights movement. Letter writing to political detainees and to government officials who held them was, from the founding of the organization, its main line of action. "Even if the letter is confiscated and never reaches him [sic], it will be opened by the government or prison authorities. Realization that the man or woman concerned is not forgotten has often resulted in the prisoner receiving better treatment and an improvement in his condition."[3]

In 1964 and 1965, the London office of AI did not report about the arrest of political prisoners in Brazil, and the U.S. branch of the organization was barely functioning. Perhaps this was because the nascent organization had few contacts in Brazil, and few Brazilian oppositionists, in turn, knew about the organization. Activities on behalf of Brazilian detainees, however, escalated in 1966 and 1967, as noted in that year's annual report: "Brazil continued to be the country in Latin America where Amnesty is most active, and nearly 100 prisoners have been adopted. Hundreds of people, including trade union leaders and members of the Communist Party have been sentenced by military courts since the coup d'état of April 1964. Some have been able to go into hiding or exile, but many more are serving heavy sentences or have been effectively deprived of their livelihood by the loss of their civil rights. A number of Amnesty Groups have heard from adopted prisoners who are in this predicament."[4]

In the same report, Amnesty International also mentioned the issue of the torture of political prisoners for the first time when it announced a new policy to "cooperate with the International Committee of the Red Cross to establish the right to investigate alleged cases of torture." The report directed national sections to "give the problem of torture special attention."[5] The right-wing military takeover in Greece in May 1967 offered Amnesty International the opportunity to implement this new policy almost immediately, as the generals in that country arrested thousands of political prisoners and subjected hundreds to violent interrogation.[6] The impact of this campaign forced Greece to withdraw from the Council of Europe in December 1969, under threat of expulsion. Because the U.S. government backed the Greek military regime, prodemocracy activists in the United States, along with the Greek actress Melina Mercouri, emphasized the issue of torture as a way to mount opposition to Washington's policies.[7]

By 1970, Brazil and Greece were the two leading symbols of human rights violations. Mainstream weeklies and news dailies of national and international impact joined progressive religious and secular magazines such as *Christianity and Crisis*, *Christian Century*, *Commonweal*, *Christianity Today*, and the *Nation* in reporting sophisticated excesses in human sadism employed by the Brazilian military regime. To a certain extent, Brazil had become associated in the public mind with torture and repression.[8] This chapter examines how that process took place.

### Andean Exile

As the majority of Brazil's congressional representatives sang the Brazilian national anthem on December 12, 1968, in celebration of their defiance of the generals' attempts to gag the legal opposition, Márcio Moreira Alves slipped out a side door and went underground. After using a network of friends and relatives to hide for several weeks, he left Brazil.[9] Alves managed to call his sister, Maria Helena, in Boston from somewhere in Argentina. Then he crossed the Andes and celebrated the New Year in Santiago, Chile.

At a press conference in Santiago, Alves announced he intended to remain in Chile for a week before proceeding to exile in Europe, but he soon changed his plans: "When I left Brazil on the last day of December 1968, my idea was to go to France, where I had a doctoral fellowship to study at the Sorbonne. When I got to Chile, Paulo de Tarso Santos, who had been Minister of Education and Culture in the Jango [João Goulart] government, said something very convincing to me. He said, 'You know nothing about Latin America. If you stay a year or so you will learn about Latin America, and then you can go to Europe. Is there a way to postpone your fellowship?' So I did what I needed to do, was convinced about the importance of Hispanic America, and I stayed in Chile a year and a half." [10]

Because of Alves's eminence as a public figure who had denounced torture in 1964, had written a book about the practice in 1966, and had confronted the military in 1968, he quickly became an ex-officio ambassador for the opposition in exile. Articulate, fluent in English and French, from an elite background, and with a Brazilian coffee baron's pedigree, Alves moved comfortably among the complex web of families, friends, and connections that constituted the fabric of Brazil's ruling civilian circles. Moreover, his mother, Branca Moreira Alves, had become a prominent lay leader in the Brazilian Catholic Church. The persecution of her son, as well as many priests, nuns, and Catholic activists, had moved the devout patrician into opposition circles. From Santiago, Márcio became a part of a network that emanated from Brazil with a simple goal—to collect reports of documented repression and disseminate them abroad. Thirty-five years later, Alves remembers: "Almost immediately I began to organize the Frente Brasileña de Informaciones to distribute information to the media in the United States and Europe about repression and torture in Brazil."

The activities of Márcio Moreira Alves and others in Chile were loosely coordinated with attempts by deposed Pernambuco governor Miguel Arraes and other exiles from the generation of 1964 to carry out similar work in Europe. Alves recalled, "We received information from all over Brazil through the different clandestine organizations. We never received false information. No one ever sent fabricated statements." Alves's reminiscences conjure up images of complex underground networks, with coded messages and clandestine couriers. The documentation on torture and repression, however, usually arrived in more modest ways, "We received a lot of denunciations through the mail," he recalled. "We had a post office box in Santiago and a lot came there . . . Many also came via the Catholic Church. My mother was a member of the Vatican's World Council of Laypersons that was a part of the Roman Curate. She would give something to a priest who was going to Santiago, who would deliver it to us."

Among the supporters of this effort was Jean Callado, the wife of the literary critic and writer Antônio Callado. "Jean Callado spent several months with us in Santiago. She was British and . . . wrote marvelously well, so much so that when we received the testimony of Frei Tito about the torture that he had suffered, she translated it for us. We sent it to *Look* magazine, which published it with a note saying that it had been smuggled out of Brazil."[11] Indeed, the special report in *Look* magazine was one of several dozen articles and dossiers that blanketed the U.S. printed media in 1970. The title said it all—"Brazil: Government by Torture."

Alves recalled the precarious nature of the work that he and others carried out in Chile in 1969 and early 1970. "When we created the Brazilian Front it was very rudimentary. We would reproduce texts with a mimeograph machine. It was simple; if we think of computers today, it was very primitive. There I realized that it was important to influence U.S. public opinion, so I began to seek contacts among academics abroad." Márcio traveled to the United States in June 1969, much to the dismay of Brazilian consular personnel in New York and Washington, who fretted over how he had managed to get a U.S. visa with a diplomatic passport that had been invalidated by the Brazilian government. At the invitation of American University professor Brady Tyson, Alves visited Washington, where he met with Senate majority leader Mike Mansfield and Senator Edward Kennedy to talk about the political situation in Brazil and elicit their support for a campaign to isolate the military regime internationally.[12] At the end of that year, another initiative from Brazil would make that campaign a reality.

### Presidential Succession and Torture Denunciations

In September 1969, soon after negotiating the release of fifteen political prisoners in exchange for the U.S. ambassador, the Military High Command had to address the issue of who would permanently succeed Costa e Silva, who had become disabled due to his stroke. On October 8 and 9, the High Command met and chose four-star general Emílio Garrastazú Médici as Costa e Silva's successor and Admiral Augusto Rademaker as vice president. Médici had served as the military attaché in Washington under the Castelo Branco presidency and then became the chief of the National Information Service. In 1969, he became the commander of the Third Army, which had jurisdiction over southern Brazil. In the presidential succession battle, he had the firm backing of the hardliners within the military.[13] Concerned with presenting a veneer of legality to cover this unusual act of succession, the Military High Command convened the Congress, which the government had closed since the issuance of Institutional Act No. 5 in December 1968, in order to ratify their choices for president and vice president. Before authorizing a convocation of the purged legislative body, however, the country's top generals promulgated a new constitution that further strengthened the power of the executive, reduced the number of representatives in Congress and state legislators, and limited the scope of congressional immunity. The military leaders also decreed Institutional Act No. 16 declaring the presidency vacant, ending the new presidential term on March 15, 1974, and laying down the rules for the "election" of the next president and vice president. Immediately after the defanged and virtually powerless Congress began its sessions, ARENA, the military's party, duly elected Médici and Rademaker to office. In protest, the opposition party MDB abstained from the process. Médici's rise to the political pinnacle of power portended an ominous future for both the legal and underground opposition to the military regime.[14]

By 1969, rumors circulated widely that torture had become common practice for anyone detained by the military. When the fifteen political prisoners arrived in Mexico after having been freed from prison in exchange for the release of the kidnapped U.S. ambassador in September 1969, they denounced the use of torture by their Brazilian captors. The *New York Times* and other international news sources quoted their accusations without giving them the credence of fact, and news censorship after Institutional Act No. 5 kept that part of the story out of Brazilian newspapers.[15] On December 2, 1969, Minister of Justice Alfredo Buzaid, in his first press conference, responded to a question about reports of alleged torture of political prisoners, stating that the president, as well as the Ministry of Justice, was keeping a close watch on human rights. "I don't intend to allow acts of torture to be practiced in this country that is seeking democratic paths." U.S. ambassador Charles Elbrick, who reported on this development to the State Department, indicated that initial public reaction to Buzaid's speech had been "overwhelmingly favorable" and that "presidential sources are reported to have confirmed rumors that the president passed down the order to security organizations some two weeks ago to cease torturing prisoners."[16] The ambassador also assessed that "the Médici government has become sufficiently alarmed at the rash of bad publicity here and abroad on the torture of political prisoners to take action to stop this practice." He concluded, "It is reasonable to assume that for the interim, at least, security organizations will take more care in their manner of interrogating prisoners."

Brazilian journalists interpreted the statement by the Ministry of Justice as a signal that government censorship about torture had loosened up. Perhaps, as U.S. officials speculated, the new Médici government would actually respond to domestic and foreign criticism and order a halt to violent interrogations. Brazilian newspapers and magazines began to report on the subject.

*Veja* magazine featured two cover stories about torture. The first issue broke the story about the government's alleged new position regarding violence with a bold red cover and a large font headline announcing: "The President will not allow torture." Walking a tightrope between criticizing the dictatorship and avoiding reprisals, the inside story stated that Médici considered that the guerrilla threat was under control and then proceeded to list the measures employed by the police to extract information from detainees. "The most common services that have been published in the European press—and which profoundly irritate the president of the Republic, who is informed of them through the SNI [National Intelligence Service] are the application of electric shocks on different parts of the body, including the genital organs and even the tongue."[17] It was the most public and bold indictment of the regime in the largest-circulating magazine in the country.

The following issue was even more audacious. The cover contained a single image that seemed to be an ancient lithograph shaded in tones of brown. The single word "Torture" bannered over the illustration announced that week's feature story. The scene on the front page depicted a cluster of figures in a dungeon-like space with huge stone walls, an arching ceiling, and a large wooden door. Friars and other figures stretched one man on a rack. Another figure pulled on a rope attached to a pulley that had hoisted a man high into the air. Heavy weights tied to his feet stretched him downward. A third person was bound upside down on an apparatus obviously designed to inflict pain. A scribe sat at a desk, seemingly taking down confessions. The message was clear. The Brazilian government was engaged in horrific medieval techniques of information extraction comparable to those employed during the Inquisition. The inside story gave substance to the image on the cover.[18] Detailed cases of detention, torture, and disappearance left no doubt that these were not excesses of a few exuberant government employees. In spite of official declarations insisting that the practice was under control and diminishing, torture was widespread in Brazilian prisons.

Two weeks was too much for the military regime. The government stepped in and ended any public discussion of the question through the national media. However, in this short window of opportunity, political prisoners and their supporters decided that the political moment was propitious for a more aggressive campaign against torture in Brazil and outside the country.

## Seeking Support Abroad

In late December 1969, Jether Pereira Ramalho and his wife Lucília traveled to New York. Jether, a lay leader in the Brazilian Congregational Church, had recently begun teaching sociology at the Federal University of Rio de Janeiro, and the couple was on a summer vacation. When they arrived in the city, they went directly to meet William Wipfler, at the time the assistant director of the Latin American Department of the National Council of Churches. Jovelino Ramos, the Presbyterian minister from Rio de Janeiro, who had left Brazil in 1968 after having been indicted for alleged subversive activities, affectionately greeted them.[19] Also present was an old friend, Rubem César Fernandes, who had fled Brazil for exile in the mid-1960s and had recently come to Columbia University to complete his doctorate in the history of social thought.[20] Domício Pereira, a Presbyterian minister from Rio de Janeiro who had journeyed to New York on a different flight and on a different day with the ostensible purpose of taking a course at the Union Theological Seminary, was also present at the meeting. The warmth of fond embraces and the jovial atmosphere so common when old friends reunite, however, were muted by a more serious undertone. Discreetly, Jether Ramalho and Domício Pereira had brought with them to the United States, nestled in their luggage and on their persons, a collection of documents detailing the fate of hundreds of Brazilian political prisoners. They turned over the material that they had carefully concealed to Wipfler so that he could examine it. Many years later, the Episcopal cleric recalled looking at the denunciations for the first time: "Several were scrawled on scraps of filthy paper, paper bags or wrinkled envelopes, and were difficult to decipher. Another was transcribed in minute lettering on a single square of toilet paper; reading it required a magnifying glass."[21] Wipfler remembered: "I knew things were bad in Brazil, but I hadn't seen anything in writing, any texts. They brought with them individual and group testimonies."[22] Among the materials that Pereira and Ramalho had smuggled out of Brazil was a statement drafted earlier that month by sixteen female political prisoners being held in a detention center in the Rio de Janeiro harbor. The document boldly declared, "We have written this letter from where we are imprisoned on the Ilha das Flores [Isle of Flowers] in Rio de Janeiro. Only now is information starting to trickle out about the atrocities that have been committed against political prisoners in our country; thus, the Brazilian public may still doubt that these criminal acts are really taking place. We can assure everyone that TORTURE DOES EXIST IN BRAZIL . . . Up to now, threats of more torture and even death have kept us silent. Recent statements, however, both by the president of the Republic and the minister of justice, as well as reports in the domestic and international press, lead us to believe that we have some protection against reprisals."[23] Shaken by what he had read and determined to help, Wipfler immediately invited the four Brazilians to set up operations in a vacated office at the National Council of Churches. For the next two months, they organized the material, indexing the denunciations and preparing a complete dossier that they could publish in English and distribute widely in the United States.[24] Wipfler also put the group in contact with Ralph Della Cava, who was the perfect academic-activist to join this new, broad-based effort to denounce the military regime.

### Clandestine Reporting Abroad

Unknown to the Protestant progressives who visited the National Council of Churches in late 1969, other groups in Brazil were devising discreet methods to disseminate information about torture and repression to an international audience. Miguel Darcy de Oliveira, the young Brazilian diplomat who was involved with Tetê Moraes, Sérgio Rocha, and others in circulating information abroad, remembered: "In the environment [of IA-5], intellectuals, militants of underground organizations, and people linked to the Church, all discovered torture in the first semester of 1969 when it was really employed. One of the few things that they could do was to denounce it. It was one of the few available alternatives to counterattack, other than the radical option of armed struggle."[25]

The group of friends that met intermittently to discuss the political situation and plan the dissemination of denunciations abroad used several avenues to achieve their goals. In 1969, Carlos Senna traveled to England to study at the London School of Economics. At the same time Miguel Darcy de Oliveira had been transferred to Geneva as part of the Brazilian diplomatic corps, accompanied by his wife, Rosica, who was Tetê's childhood friend. From Europe, they received documented reports prepared by Tetê, Sérgio, Jader, Angela, and Mário Pedrosa, translated them, and passed them on to journalists, Amnesty International, and other human rights organizations.[26] They sent other material directly to addresses of sympathetic politicians, public figures, and news organizations. Tetê Moraes remembered, for example, that she dispatched packages through the Brazilian mail to Senator Edward Kennedy's office in Washington. "I simply put a fake return address on the envelope and sent it through the regular mail service."[27]

In late January 1970, while Tetê de Moraes ripped up her address book in the bathroom at the torture center on Barão de Mesquita Street, she was sure that authorities had detained her for having hidden Chico Nélson. She had managed to catch a glimpse of Sérgio, her boyfriend, and realized that they had arrested him as well. Because revolutionaries had used Chico Nélson's van in the kidnapping of the U.S. ambassador, she knew that the government would also accuse her of being a member of one of the two organizations involved in the action. She imagined that she would also be tortured until she furnished the police with some lead or information about that organization and the kidnapping. "The interrogation began a little later. It was close to daybreak when the two or three torturers, who worked there, begin interrogating me. I tried to keep quiet and observe the kind of questions that they asked me. Then I realized it had nothing to do with Chico. They did not know anything about Chico. It was about our denunciation of torture."

Tetê later pieced together what had happened. Angela and Jader, who had joined one of the underground revolutionary organizations while continuing to work with Tetê, Sérgio, and others in the group, were picked up for hiding two young women who had been on the police's most wanted list. When the police ransacked their apartment, they found one of the reports about torture. Authorities arrested Tetê and Sérgio soon thereafter. The seventy-year-old Mário Pedroso escaped arrest because at the time he happened to be in Búzios, a beach resort near Rio. The other four members of the group were safely abroad. Tetê recalled, "They [the police] were only interested in the report about torture. Who had done it? At first, they [Angela and Jared] claimed that they were the only ones who put it together. However, the police insisted that it could not be the two alone. There was too much information. There was too much organization. The material was getting abroad, and it was discrediting Brazil. It was being published all over the place."

The irony of the situation, of course, was that the Brazilian government publicly denied that it tortured political prisoners, while the police proceeded to torture those who were denouncing such actions on the part of the military regime. That night, police beat Tetê and administered electric shocks. "I'm convinced that I was not hurt more because I was an employee of Itamaraty [Foreign Service], and they didn't know yet what kind of network we had. They must have thought, 'If we kill this woman there will be hell to pay.' They said this among themselves, and I overheard their conversations." The night watchman at Tetê's apartment building had witnessed her kidnapping and immediately alerted her parents. They mobilized family connections to determine her whereabouts and finally located her at the DOI-CODI center. Miguel and his wife Rosiska were in Geneva at the time. Miguel responded to an order by Itamaraty to return to Brazil. Officials arrested him at the airport.

The National Intelligence Service, the federal intelligence agency set up by the military regime, intervened directly in the case, and two investigations were initiated. One was for violation of the National Security Act and was directed by the Navy. The other was an internal Ministry of Foreign Services inquiry alleging that Tetê and Miguel had used the diplomatic mail pouches to send their reports about Brazil abroad. Angela and Jader remained in prison because they had other charges pending against them, but Sérgio, Tetê, and Miguel were released after three month's incarceration, largely due to considerable pressure. Miguel immediately left the country into exile. When authorities issued a new arrest order for members of the group, Mário Pedrosa sought sanctuary in the Chilean Embassy and requested political asylum. Tetê and Miguel obtained false documents and slipped out of the country to Chile, where they collaborated with the Popular Unity government of Salvador Allende. Their friend Chico Nélson remained clandestine in Brazil. The police never caught him. He eventually ended up in exile in Chile.

The Brazilian government publicly denied that it tortured oppositionists and presented the image that it ignored the international campaign to isolate the regime. Yet the arrest of the group of intellectuals that was distributing news of the internal political situation to the foreign press reveals how sensitive the regime was to international public opinion. "Subversion" emanating from its own Foreign Service apparatus must have particularly infuriated the generals in power, as they quickly moved to break up this informal network. Miguel reflected over thirty years later, "The repression thought that it was an orchestrated campaign. The image is a good one: an orchestra with a conductor that organizes everything. It wasn't that way. It was very spontaneous and disorganized." Moreover, it took many such decentralized initiatives to get out the word.

### Frustrated Effort

Not all attempts to collect and disseminate reports of torture during this period met with success. Sometime in 1969, while operating underground, Jean Marc Von der Weid, president of the outlawed National Union of Students, asked student activist Antônio Rangel Bandeira to put together a report of denunciations.[28] The plan entailed collecting documentation of torture and circulating it among sympathetic Brazilian journalists and other intellectuals. In the aftermath of the political mobilizations in 1967 and 1968, the government indicted Rangel on three separate counts of subversion for his student activities at the Rio de Janeiro Law School. Rather than face prison and inevitable torture, he went underground. Living clandestinely, moving from safe house to safe house, constantly on the run, did not offer ideal conditions to carry out such work. Nevertheless, it broke the boredom of living anonymously, and it was a way to respond to the constant news of the arrest and torture of friends, comrades, and members of other organizations.

In his memoirs about that period, Rangel wrote, "The material arrived in my hands through different revolutionary organizations, from relatives of the prisoners, and from human rights groups. I dove into a nightmare. Some of the statements came directly from the torture chambers . . . stained with blood."[29] During interminable days underground, Rangel labored to decipher the texts: "I would receive the information poorly written, sometimes illegible," he recalled. "I put it in journalistic format, and when I had finished we had forty pages of testimonies. It was the first document that contained such complete information. We printed it—at the time, we used a small clandestine press—and the National Union of Students began to distribute it among sympathetic journalists, lawyers. The idea was to disseminate the information in Brazil and abroad."[30]

But the plan backfired. "The facts that we related were so startling, so revealing of how horrible things actually were, not only for revolutionaries, but also for other critics of the government's policies or even relatives of activists, that the report had a boomerang effect." As Rangel recalled, "People read the report, were indignant, but also terrorized. They didn't want to continue offering logistical or other support. They became afraid of any action in support of democratizing the country. They understood that the efficient repressive machine, financed by some businessmen, didn't differentiate between revolutionaries and citizens discontented with the government. As the military itself said, first we torture, then we ask questions."[31] The planned campaign had to be suspended, and the report stopped circulating inside the country.

### Dossiers of Denunciations

If at least one attempt to mobilize support against torture ended up provoking fear among supporters of the opposition within Brazil, the relatively uncoordinated international campaigns seemed to hold greater hope. One channel was through the Catholic Church. Since 1968, a growing schism had been developing between many Catholic leaders and the military regime, in part due to an upswing in human rights abuses that at times targeted activists within the Church.[32] On December 16, 1969, a group of sixty-one prominent Belgian, French, and Italian Roman Catholics presented a lengthy dossier titled "Terror and Torture in Brazil" to the Pontifical Commission on Justice and Peace with the request that it be transmitted urgently to Pope Paul VI. The report, prepared by the general secretariat of Christian Student Youth in Paris, included a forty-eight-page background statement and a thirty-six-page compilation of first-hand accounts of killings and torture in Brazil. The endorsement called on the commission and its president, Maurice Cardinal Roy of Quebec, to denounce the tortures and thus reaffirm the Church's commitment to universal justice. "Knowing of these things," the letter said, "to keep silent would be to join those who kill." A preface to the dossier by the French Jesuit philosopher and intellectual Michel de Certeau reported that the documentation was only an outline of widespread political violence.[33]

The report was published in the December 1969 issue of the Paris monthly *Croissance de Jeunes Nations* under the title "Livre Noir: Terreur et Torture au Brésil (Black Book: Terror and Torture in Brazil). The dossier contained eleven separate documents. Two concerned the murder in May 1969 of Father Antônio Henrique Pereira Neto. A second document registered the public protest issued by thirty-eight priests from Belo Horizonte in July 1969 against the "physical and moral outrages" continuously committed against imprisoned priests and laymen since December 1968. Others listed violence inflicted on students, peasant leaders, and foreign priests. Three additional documents, signed by Archbishop Hélder Câmera of Recife and Olinda, spoke about the growing number of Catholic priests, nuns, and laypeople caught up in the government's repressive dragnet.[34] Several weeks later, the Pontifical Commission on Justice and Peace transmitted the dossier directly to Paul VI. The president of the commission stated in a letter to the group of intellectuals who had presented the report to the Vatican the previous month that the Pontiff was "following watchfully the situation of the Church in Brazil, and has kept himself constantly informed about it by the apostolic nuncio as well as by direct contacts with bishops."[35]

Five days after the report reached Paul VI, Archbishop Hélder Câmera met with the Pontiff in Rome. At the end of his audience, the Brazilian prelate indicated that the Vatican was concerned about events in Brazil: "Our conversation was a great comfort to my soul as a bishop, and I return from it with even redoubled courage," he commented to the press after his meeting.[36] The Brazilian archbishop also reported that the Paul VI had declared, "We have read the documentation that you have sent Us concerning torture in Brazil . . . The Church will tolerate no longer the commission of atrocities and tortures in a country that calls itself Christian."[37] In late March, Paul VI sent another signal abroad. While not uttering the words "Brazil" and "torture" in the same phrase, during an Easter week speech in St. Peter's Basilica deploring a wide range of contemporary evils from war to racism to drug trafficking, the Pontiff made a "duty-bound intervention" on behalf of political prisoners being tortured in Latin America.[38] Alarmed by the Pope's statement, President Emílio Garrastazu Médici sent Colonel Manso Neto to the Vatican after José Jobim, Brazil's ambassador to the Holy See, spent the last week in March conferring with the president and his advisers.[39] The cleavage that had developed between Brazilian bishops and the government over human rights had gone public and international.

### American Committee for Information on Brazil

Around the same time that the military regime was dismantling the group of intellectuals in Rio de Janeiro with contacts in Europe and the United States and the Vatican was considering the dossier presented by leading Catholic figures, the Brazilian emissaries at the National Council of Churches set in motion a series of efforts in the United States that would meet with success. A small cluster of experienced veterans in social change took up the task with determination. In a whirlwind of activities, Bill Wipfler, Ralph Della Cava, Brady Tyson, and others moved into action. For this core group of activists, several questions remained unanswered. What was the best way to disseminate the material provided by the Brazilian opposition? How could the group build broad support in the United States in order to pressure the Brazilian government to stop its violent treatment of political prisoners? Who might serve as their allies in this effort? How could they get the media to pay attention to Brazil?

No one seems to have taken notes or recorded the minutes of the meetings that the Brazilians and their American allies held over the next several months to plan an effective strategy. One incident, however, lingered in Della Cava's mind after all these years. In early 1970, he and Columbia University professor Charles Wagley experienced a rude awakening when they met with the foreign affairs editor of the *New York Times* to deliver a dossier of the material brought from Brazil documenting torture of political prisoners. Della Cava had hoped that the *New York Times* would come out with a strong editorial condemning torture in Brazil, and he encouraged the *Times* editor to take a stand. Della Cava reiterated this proposal in the cover article of the April 24, 1970, issue of *Commonweal* titled "Torture in Brazil." He wrote: "The American press should break its editorial silence about torture in Brazil. The Brazilian regime tends to be more sensitive to the *New York Times'* criticism than to *Le Monde's.*"[40] Della Cava was disappointed, however, with the editor's response to the material that they presented to him. "He basically said, if you didn't see the people tortured, we're not interested in the story."[41] Della Cava and his colleagues realized that the mainstream press would not shift its editorial stance about the violation of human rights in Brazil unless they created a climate that legitimized the authenticity of their sources and the documents that they had received. Therefore, the group decided to develop a multifaceted campaign to circumvent the major media's apparent reluctance to take an editorial position against torture in Brazil. One element in their plan consisted of attempting to place articles with the documentation that they had received from Brazil in several progressive and religious publications, with the expectation that the major newspapers, magazines, and news outlets would then pick up the story. They also identified four target groups—scholars working on Latin America, religious leaders, progressive activists, and politicians.

In order to give a legal and public face to their efforts, in February 1970 the group formed the American Committee for Information on. This anonymous public persona seemed designed, in part, to hide the participation of Brazilians in the group's efforts, since some feared that if their political activities were made public, they might face problems with either the U.S. or Brazilian government. Likewise, some of the American collaborators in the effort wanted to avoid difficulties in travels to Brazil. The group probably modeled the idea of the committee after ones that had been established by Brazilian exiles in Algiers, Paris, and Santiago by 1970.[42]

A major portion of the efforts of the newly Brazilian Information Front went into preparing an English-language pamphlet titled *Terror in Brazil: A Dossier*, based on the material brought from Brazil. The eighteen-page document presented a chronology of events in Brazil since the 1964 coup d'état, published the statement of female political prisoners held at Ilha das Flores, Rio de Janeiro, and highlighted the Brazilian Catholic Church's opposition to the regime's policies. Prominently placed on the second page was a statement titled "We Cannot Remain Silent." Religious leaders and leading academics signed the manifesto. The declaration stated in part, "We cannot remain silent in the face of the overwhelming evidence of the flagrant denial of human rights and dignity coming to us from Brazil . . . To do so would make us accomplices of those who are the authors and perpetrators of this repression."[43] The brief manifesto explained that several of the documents had been written by Brazilians and "smuggled out of Brazil at great risk to those involved." It closed by calling on readers of the dossier "to raise their voices in protest with us."

Operating out of the National Council of Churches, Bill Wipfler coordinated the collection of signatures for the "We Cannot Remain Silent" statement among leading religious figures. They included John Bennett, the president of the Union Theological Seminary, Irene Jones of the American Baptist Foreign Mission Society, Tracey K. Jones Jr., the general secretary of the Board of Missions of the United Methodist Church, and John Coventry Smith, the general secretary of the Commission on Ecumenical Missions and Relations of the United Presbyterian Church. The names of important figures from mainline Protestant churches attached to the dossier offered a tone of legitimacy to the claims made in the rest of the pamphlet, as did the support of Louis C. Colonnese, the director for the Division for Latin America of the United States Catholic Conference, which represented Catholic bishops.

As Wipfler collected the support of prominent religious figures, Della Cava approached leading Latin Americanists who soon thereafter would lend their support to the petition calling for the release of Caio Prado Júnior, mentioned in a previous chapter. The adherence of Richard Morse of Yale, Charles Wagley of Columbia, Stanley Stein of Princeton, and Thomas Skidmore of Wisconsin added to the impact of the statement. Speaking out against the government had its consequences, as Skidmore would learn later that year when the Brazilian government denied him a visa to conduct research and lead a seminar there. Although the names Wagley, Morse, Stein, and Skidmore carried weight among academics who studied Brazil and Latin America, equally important was the inclusion of prominent civil rights leaders such as Ralph Abernathy and Andrew Young. As president and executive vice president, respectively, of the Southern Christian Leadership Conference, they represented the legacy of Martin Luther King Jr. Through their close connection to Brady Tyson, these leading African Americans began to take political positions on issues related to Latin America. This, in turn, set a precedent for the more widespread response by civil rights leaders to the military coup d'état in Chile three years later and opposition to U.S. intervention in Central America in the 1980s. Rounding out the list of endorsees were figures such as the artist Hans Haake, who had boycotted the São Paulo Bienal the previous year, and Representative Benjamin S. Rosenthal, member of the Interamerican Affairs Subcommittee of the House Foreign Affairs Committee.

### Speaking Truth to Power

One of the first successes of the group was a two-page piece signed by the Brazilian Information Front (presumably from the group in Chile) that appeared in the February 26 issue of the New York Review of Books. A letter titled "Torture in Brazil" drew a comparison between the Council of Europe's decision to exclude the Greek military regime for murdering and torturing political prisoners and the silence about the similar situation in Brazil. "The European community took this step after a long and concerted effort to inform public opinion was made by writers, reporters, editors, and publishers throughout the Western Hemisphere."[44] The Brazilian Information Front open letter called on people in the United States to respond in a similar way: "Are the murder and torture against a Brazilian a lesser crime than against a Greek, a French, or an American citizen?"[45] A detailed description of the interrogation and torture of political prisoners held at the São Paulo headquarters of Operação Bandeirantes, the special unit dedicated to political repression, followed.[46]

The New York Review of Books material offered a bleak picture of the situation in Brazil for arrested oppositionists. Providing detailed descriptions of the prisoners with their names, ages, political affiliations, and the circumstances surrounding their arrests lent credibility to the allegations. Highlighting the inhumane treatment of female prisoners pointed to the excessively brutal nature of the regime, as if unacceptable torture was even more so when it involved women's bodies. The denunciations also seemed to be a significant factor in triggering an editorial response from one of the nation's top dailies.

The Washington Post led the way. An editorial appearing on February 28, 1970, written immediately after the New York Review of Books report on torture hit the newsstand, strongly castigated the military regime.[47] "Too many reports by too many reliable witnesses have been appearing about the torturing of 'subversives" for anyone to doubt that it goes on," the editorial declared. "These horrible facts are shocking but not surprising. Brazil's military masters, led by a slow-minded general named Médici, want their own way, and anyone who criticizes or questions that way is an automatic enemy of the state." The editorial argued that if a free election were to be held in Brazil, "the man who was most vocally anti-government would win hands down." The Post explained the rise in antigovernment terrorism in the country's urban areas. "Since the generals know only the language of brutality and force, many of those seeking to fight Brazil's immense poverty and injustice are learning the language of violence as well." The Washington Post opinion piece also predicted that a "nasty showdown" was approaching between the generals practicing political oppression and "the hopes for social justice expressed by many Brazilian students, intellectuals, and priests." The editorial ended with a stab at U.S. foreign policy. "The United States, as so often before in its foreign relations, is in danger of getting itself caught up on the side of the oppressors, forced to choose wrong."

Several elements are noteworthy in this editorial. First, the editorial board of the *Washington Post* was unequivocal in its assessment that torture had become a widespread practice in Brazil, official Brazilian government denials notwithstanding. Second, the newspaper understood the activities of the guerrilla movement (terrorists, in their terms) as a *response* to the repressive measures of the regime, rather than as the other way around, as the military claimed. The *Post* also linked motivations of the armed resistance to a desire to eliminate poverty and achieve social justice, rather than characterizing the guerrilla movement as merely made up of an irresponsible band of misguided youth. The message was strong and hard-hitting, and it provoked, as one could imagine, an indignant response from the Brazilian government.

As soon as Brazilian foreign minister Mário Gibson Barboza received a copy of the *Washington Post* editorial in Rio de Janeiro, he summoned the U.S. ambassador, Charles Elbrick, to Itamaraty. According to Elbrick's account of their meeting, Barboza apologized to the U.S. ambassador for calling him at such a late hour to discuss "an extremely unpleasant subject."[48] The Brazilian diplomat then characterized the content of the *Post* editorial as a "scurrilous, vicious, virulent, and insulting attack on Brazilian government" that also offended the president. He asserted that the editorial would provoke an "unfortunate and unpleasant reaction here in the Brazil," because people might interpret it as an expression of majority opinion in the United States. Significantly, and again according to Elbrick's account of the meeting, the Brazilian Foreign Ministry feared that the editorial about police brutality and torture might have a snowballing effect in the United States. Barboza even expressed his consternation about how to respond to the charges. It seems that the U.S. ambassador did not provide the minister of foreign relations any concrete suggestions for how to proceed. However, in a memo drafted after the meeting, Elbrick did offer the State Department some ideas about how to deal with the incident. "While appreciating difficulties created by widely publicized stories of police torture, where [sic] in some cases may be exaggerated and inaccurate, continuation of this type of article will doubtless result in increasing hostility on part of government here." Elbrick then gave the State Department advice about how to handle the charges about torture: "Possibly, Department in its public utterances and press briefings, could manage to put this matter in perspective. There is no doubt that a state of limited insurgency exists in Brazil and that a government feels obliged to take necessary measures to defend itself. This may or may not involve torture, systematic or otherwise, but it should also be remembered that terrorists are resorting to violence, murder, kidnapping, and assaults on persons and institutions which government can hardly condone." Elbrick presented a balanced equation. Torture, though its frequency and extent may be exaggerated, existed. However, one had to place the practice within the context of the actions of certain oppositionists who had taken up arms against the regime and engaged in violence to achieve their goal of toppling the government. In the interest of Brazilian national security, the military's excesses were relative.

As promised in his meeting with Elbrick, the Brazilian Foreign Ministry responded to the *Washington Post* editorial in a letter from Mozart Gurgel Valente, the Brazilian ambassador to the United States, published in the *Post* on March 5, 1970. The communication registered "shock" at the "unwarranted and disparaging personal attack on the president of Brazil" and indicated that the newspaper's stance could impair good relations between the two countries. Insisting that the Brazilian federal and state governments had registered their "condemnation of any violation whatsoever of human rights in treatment of political prisoners," the ambassador argued that, as reported in the world press, the fifteen individuals exchanged for the release of Elbrick arrived in Mexico "in perfect physical and mental condition, without showing any signs of violence or mistreatment."[49]

While the Brazilian government criticized the *Post* editorial, Richard S. Winslow Jr., a Foreign Service reserve officer with the Agency for International Development (AID), wrote a letter to the editor backing the newspaper's positions. He pointed out that during the fiscal year 1970, AID spent $451,000 on its "public safety" program in Brazil and "is now paying for 13 U.S. police specialists residing in Brazil and helping to train thousands of Brazilian police in 'criminal investigations,' 'counter-insurgency,' and the use of the most modern police equipment." He also alerted readers to the fact that in the fiscal year 1968, 16,000 Brazilian police were trained under this program, with the number increasing with each successive year.

This time the State Department scrambled to engage in damage control, crafting answers to anticipated press queries about U.S. government assistance to the Brazilian police. In response to a question about the purpose of the AID program, the State Department offered a prepared response: "The mission of the public safety program is to assist the Brazilian Federal Police headquartered at Brasília, to train police of the several Brazilian states in such subjects as: humane methods of crowd control, the development of country-wide crime-laboratory services, and maintenance of records."[50] The canned answer failed to mention counterinsurgency training that constituted a key component of the U.S. training of Brazilian police.

### Kennedy Speaks Out

Missoula, Montana seems an unlikely place to deliver a significant policy statement about Latin America, especially one that would provoke sharp reactions among defenders of the military regime in the Brazilian Congress. Yet on April 17, 1970, Senator Edward M. Kennedy offered a scathing critique of the U.S. foreign policy regarding Latin America over the previous decade.[51] After providing an extremely negative assessment of the Bay of Pigs invasion of Cuba (carried out under his older brother's watch in 1961) and the invasion of the Dominican Republic (while his middle brother was still attorney general), Kennedy lambasted the political failures of the Alliance for Progress. "In spite of our strong democratic traditions, the United States continues to support regimes in Latin America that deny basic human rights. We remain silent when political prisoners are tortured in Brazil. Students, priests, and nuns whose only crime was to know someone suspected of being a revolutionary suffer cruel punishment."[52] Kennedy went on to cite much of the information that had been published in the different articles, pamphlets, and materials distributed about human rights violations in Brazil. He then launched an attack on past and current U.S. policy toward Brazil. It is worth quoting at length from the speech:

> There is a shocking contrast between the political reality of the current Brazilian government and the political ideals of the Alliance. We should condemn that repression. It is a flagrant violation of our own ideals to be identified with it. Although the United States of America did not initiate the change in government in Brazil, we helped the Military Junta come to power. The Junta overthrew a constitutional government at a time when inflation warped the country's economy and observers feared increasing communist influence. Thirty days prior to the coup, we said that the United States would not automatically oppose the seizure of power by the military. Within hours, we recognized the Junta. Three months later we gave a $50 million dollar loan to the new regime. Last year, in spite of continuous reports about terror and oppression, we gave $19 million in military aid to the Generals' regime. The Council of Europe condemned the Greek military dictatorship for political oppression and torture of political prisoners. The Organization of American States can do no less.[53]

On April 21, in response to a question by a reporter about the Kennedy's University of Montana speech, a press officer for the State Department, Carl Bartch, declared that in recent weeks the department had "repeatedly expressed its concern to the Brazilian Government over the alleged torture of political prisoners in Brazil."[54] He added that "although assurances had been received from high Brazilian officials that the Brazil government does not condone this [torture]," the U.S. government was "not necessarily accepting the Brazilian government's policy statement as fully representative of what was taking place." Bartch went on to add that, contrary to Kennedy's statement, "the United States did not play any role in the Revolution that took place in Brazil in 1964."[55] The State Department spokesperson's comment caused alarm among Brazilian diplomats, and Kennedy's speech ignited a firestorm in the Brazilian Congress, as members of the MDB paired off against adamant defenders of the Médici presidency.

It seems quite evident that the U.S. government had been closely following the allegations of torture in Brazil for some time without making any public statements that might harm its special relationship with the Brazilian government. State Department officials in Brazil noted that in early December 1969 "the Médici government has become sufficiently alarmed at the rash of bad publicity here and abroad on the torture of political prisoners to take action to stop this practice."[56] In February 1970, U.S. government officials held conversations with Professor Cândido Mendes de Almeida, a Catholic human rights activist, and Heleno Claudio Fragoso, a lawyer for many political prisoners, to assess the situation of torture in the country. The government's report on these meetings stated: "Both sources expressed the view that torture—i.e., the physical abuse of prisoners in order to elicit information—is routinely used now in Brazil in interrogating suspected terrorists."

Faced with the mounting international campaign documenting widespread human rights violations in Brazil, the Nixon administration seemed to take a twofold approach to the issue. The State Department agreed with the Brazilian foreign minister that "continued U.S. press and Congressional criticism of [the] GOB [Government of Brazil] could have [an] adverse effect on U.S.–Brazil relations," so they quietly pressured the generals to distance themselves from the practice. Forced by the Kennedy speech to respond to allegations of torture, the State Department spokesman gave a public nudge to the Brazilian government, indicating reservations about the veracity of its claims, while privately assuring the Brazilians that their statement in no way meant a breach in an otherwise friendly relationship. This was reinforced in subsequent official statements on the matter. In the spring of 1970, when several U.S. congressional representatives pressed the State Department to clarify the human rights situation in Brazil, the assistant secretary for congressional relations responded with formulaic letters that gave the Brazilian government the benefit of the doubt. "High ranking members of the Brazilian Government have told us that the use of torture is not condoned by the Government and that such instances as may have occurred are unsanctioned, isolated, individual actions."[57] Then, following the line of defense suggested by Ambassador Elbrick several months previously, the form letters stated, "They [members of the Brazilian Government] have pointed out that the resolution of the problem is complicated by the ruthlessness of the terrorists themselves, whose methods of achieving their political ends routinely include assassination, bombing, arson, kidnapping and armed robbery, and whose victims are often innocent bystanders totally removed from the Brazilian political scene." The letter ended by reassuring the member of Congress that "reports of incidents of torture, which rose during the latter half of 1969, have fallen sharply since last December."

In an effort to close off debate on the subject, on May 8 the Brazilian government categorically denied the charges of torture. The official statement insisted that the frequent reports are "promoted by international agents of subversion and harbored by a morbid and sensationalist sector of the foreign press."[58] Those in prison, the statement continued, are "terrorists, detained while undergoing regular trial for crimes they committed assaulting defenseless persons, holding up banks and individuals, and kidnapping diplomats to negotiate their exchange for prisoners." This line of argument was remarkably similar to the one used by the State Department assistant secretary for congressional relations.

The declaration was too little, too late, for those who had been following the story. On April 29, even before the Médici government had released its public disclaimer, the New York Times finally came out emphatically against the military regime. In an editorial titled "Brazil: Terror and Torture" the newspaper declared, "There is something distinctly un-Brazilian about the regime's systematic and widespread employment of sadistic torture and terror against its opponents. Officials say such tactics, reminiscent of those followed by the present rulers of Greece, are necessary to combat growing Communist subversion . . . It is no longer possible, however, to discount the accumulating evidenced that a great many innocents—including wives and even children of suspected subversives—have suffered horribly."[59]

The Times editorial reflected the flood of articles that appeared in newspapers and magazines throughout the spring and summer of 1970 documenting and denouncing torture in Brazil.[60] On June 26, the Library of Congress Legislative Reference Service published a fifty-three-page report,

"Repression of Civil Liberties and Human Rights in Brazil since the Revolution of 1964," that ended with a section titled "Reports of Tortures: Catholic Church Condemnations."[61] A month later, on July 27, *Time* magazine joined the chorus of journalists reporting on the gross violation of human rights in Brazil. In a full-page article under the heading "Brazil" and titled "From the Parrot's Perch," the weekly news magazine drew heavily from the "Terror in Brazil" dossier prepared by the American Committee for Information on Brazil.[62] The article detailed the various methods devised by the Brazilian military police to extract information and quoted Catholic Church officials who had condemned torture. Also in July, *Look* magazine published a two-page special report titled "Brazil: Government by Torture" that had been diligently translated by Jean Callado and sent abroad by Márcio Moreira Alves and the Frente Brasileña de Informaciones. The article featured the first-person account of the torture of Tito de Alencar Lima, a Dominican brother training to be a priest. Leonard Gross, *Look*'s veteran correspondent in Brazil, who in 1965 had written, "What is remarkable about the Brazilian revolution is not that there were excesses, but that there were so few," had now come to a different conclusion. Gross wrote, in an introduction to the statement by Brother Tito about his torture, "Five years ago, LOOK warned repression would vitalize the extreme left. Exactly this has happened. Says one disgusted former supporter of the regime: 'Terrorism is the only means of protest.' Had the military held legitimate elections immediately after the coup, the gentle Brazilian majority would have spoken for democratic change. Today, it is too petrified to speak."[63]

At this point, Lincoln Gordon jumped into the debate, writing a letter to the editor of *Commonweal* to criticize Della Cava's April 24 article on torture in Brazil. Gordon objected to Della Cava's charge that he had been the "'architect' of an alleged U.S. Government policy of complicity with torture and fascist militarization in Brazil."[64] Gordon, at the time president of Johns Hopkins University in Baltimore, Maryland, insisted that the first Institutional Act was a "monstrous departure from basic democratic principle" and claimed that he even "gave some thought to symbolic withdrawal to Washington." Gordon explained, however, that since he considered that Castelo Branco would likely be elected president and he considered the general to be "moderate and constitutionalist," he rejected the idea. At the same time, he argued, "There were several candidates who openly spoke of themselves as would-be 'Fidel Castros' of Brazil," raising the risk that, given Brazil's size and location, "such a course of events—evidently hypothetical, but not implausible—might have made all of South America an area of left-wing totalitarian regimes." The former ambassador ducked any responsibility for the Pandora's box that he had helped open that led to the gross violations of human rights by 1969.

In his response to Gordon's letter, Ralph Della Cava, at the time a professor of Latin American history at City University of New York in Queens, pointed out that torture had occurred in Brazil under Gordon's watch and that then and in 1969, the ambassador still refused to speak out against the practice. Pointing out that in 1964 newspapers already covered stories of torture practiced against opponents of the new regime. Della Cava argued, "It is inconceivable that these public and official reports did not reach the ambassador or his staff."[65] He went on to ask, "On what basis then *did* the Rio Embassy formulate U.S. policy in respect to torture, to say nothing of the decisions that led to monumental increases in U.S. aid to Brazil in 1964, 1965, and 1966?" Della Cava then listed a litany of violations of constitutional and political rights that took place in Brazil while Gordon was ambassador and later undersecretary of state for inter-American affairs. He concluded by asserting, "Dr. Gordon's letter should be read as a model of what ails U.S. foreign policy."[66]

Márcio Moreira Alves, Tetê de Moraes, Miguel Darcy de Oliveira, Jether Ramalho, and their allies had been successful. If censorship, repression, and imprisonment silenced many Brazilian opponents of the regime in the country, their message had managed to circulate around the world. Lincoln Gordon was on the defensive. Even the military regime was on the defensive.

# CAPÍTULO V

---

## "Vai meu irmão"

Go my brother
Catch the plane
You're right
To run away from the cold.

**Vinicius de Moraes, Toquinho,
Chico Buarque, "Samba de Orly," 1970**

Approximately a week after the generals closed Congress in December 1968 and decreed Institutional Act No. 5, officers carted off the singer and songwriter Chico Buarque to the Ministry of the Army for questioning. He later captured that moment in the tender and ironic song "Wake Up, My Love," cited in capítulo IV, in which the person being arrested called out for a thief rather than a cop to save him. Chico's interrogators were fixated on his musical Roda Viva, and his detention seemed designed not only to intimidate him but to send a signal to other artists that they could be arrested at a moment's notice, as was the case a week later for Caetano Veloso and Gilberto Gil. Chico had already booked tickets to attend a Phonograph Industry fair in Cannes, France, and then had planned to go on to participate in a record release in Rome. He and his wife Marieta got permission to leave the country for fourteen days. They ended up staying in Italy for fourteen months. In a documentary filmed in Rome about those times, Chico recalled the climate in which he lived: "We were here [in Italy] and receiving news about what was happening in Brazil, and stranger and stranger things were happening in Brazil. I was advised not to return. At a given moment I had to make a decision . . . There was no security in returning to Brazil . . . We didn't know how long the arbitrary regime, the dictatorship, would last in Brazil and how long the terror would go on."[1]

As was the experience of many other exiles, cultural adaptation and economic survival, to say nothing of the longing for friends and family, made his time abroad particularly difficult.[2] Chico convinced his musical partner Toquinho to join him, and the duo opened shows for the aging diva Josephine Baker, who was touring Italy that year. They also managed to get a few gigs playing on their own, but they simply could not survive on their music in Italy.[3] Frustrated, Toquinho decided to return to Brazil. When he came to Chico's apartment to inform him that he was leaving that day, he played the music to a samba that he had just composed. Chico wrote the refrain on the spot and finished the lyrics to the "Samba de Orly" with the help of his close friend and collaborator Vinicius de Moraes. The painful lament of the songster registers the sad farewell to someone who can return to Brazil when he cannot.

Soon after Toquinho left, Chico himself decided to return to Brazil, where he continued to compose poetic lyrics that managed to maintain their political potency while circumventing the censor. When Chico left Brazil for exile, he was not a member of a political group that the military regime had outlawed and declared subversive. Nor did he face charges linked to accusations that would have assured him prison time and possible torture. His self-exile was a preventative act taken in the immediate aftermath of Institutional Act No. 5 designed to avoid what seemed to be the almost inevitable fate of artistic and intellectual opponents of the regime: escalating government persecution, closer personal scrutiny, and vigilant censorship of their work. The stifling atmosphere that restrained and restricted the creativity of artists, intellectuals, and academics had become so claustrophobic that Caetano Veloso, Gilberto Gil, and many lesser-known personalities had simply left the country, if only for a time.

Chico's prominence and popularity shielded him from the worst forms of retaliation for outspoken opposition to the regime. Before and after his exile, he was constantly harassed and intimidated but never physically harmed. That was not the case for those on the left who had chosen to join organizations and movements considered subversive by the regime. Even friends and supporters who eschewed clandestine activities but remained, in diverse ways, a part of the opposition ran the risk that the government might arrest them. The military regime could charge them as accomplices for any act that might have linked them to a secret meeting of the student movement, the distribution of a leaflet, the spray painting on a wall of a slogan against the dictatorship, or some other minor act of resistance to the regime. Moreover, the repressive apparatus constructed by the dictatorship often determined clumsily and many times wrongly who was an actual perpetrator of "subversion" or exactly what kind of underground activities someone was involved in when they apprehended, detained, and tortured activists. Such was the case of Marcos Arruda.

In early May 1970, Marcos received word that someone in another underground revolutionary organization needed help. Since 1968, Marcos had been working in a factory in São Paulo in concurrence with Ação Popular's political philosophy that called upon many of its cadre to "integrate into production," that is, live and labor with industrial workers. This was part of the organization's strategy for building a mass movement against the military regime. While Marcos was engaged in this intensive clandestine political work, he learned of a young woman, who was a member of Resistência Democrática (Democratic Resistance, REDE), a small group that favored armed struggle. She wanted to leave the organization, which was crumbling around her, and she needed a place to hide. Marcos had a first furtive meeting with her in which he agreed to find a safe house where she could stay, and they scheduled to meet again several days later. One of Marcos's comrades in Ação Popular warned him not to show up for the second meeting. "I had to," Marcos remembered. "She was in danger and had nowhere to go."[4] It was a near fatal mistake. The police picked her up soon after her first meeting with Marcos. Not wanting to reveal too many details about her own organization, she finally confessed under torture that she had scheduled a *ponto* with Marcos. The police escorted her to the prearranged meeting place; and when Marcos showed up, they arrested him. Government officials assumed he was a member of REDE, and the more he denied the fact, the more he suffered on the parrot's perch. He nearly died while imprisoned. Marcos's entire family mobilized to locate his whereabouts and get him out of prison. After a nine-month ordeal, documented in the book by his mother, Lina Penna Sattamini, *A Mother's Cry: A Memoir of Politics, Prison, and Torture under the Brazilian Military Dictatorship*, Marcos was released.[5] When he received news that he was on a government list to be rearrested, his family got him out of the country. Because his mother was a freelance interpreter working in Washington, he moved to the United States and began an eight-year exile abroad.

The act of exile, moving to a foreign land, and the challenges of adapting to a new country, language, and culture can be a traumatic experience. It can also open new possibilities for political work, personal growth, and professional development. None of the handful of Brazilians who traveled to the United States in the late 1960s or the early 1970s, including Jovelino Ramos, Marcos Arruda, and Niva Padilha, came officially as political exiles with the right to asylum. U.S. government policy supported the military regime, and the Nixon administration did not think the left-wing activists that the government had persecuted, arrested, and tortured merited that legal status. The White House and Congress reserved political asylum for those fleeing socialist or communist regimes, such as the Soviet Union, Eastern Europe, or Cuba, which they considered to be enemy states. Brazil was a loyal ally. Thus, those Brazilians who ended up in the United States did not arrive as political exiles and had to rely on informal support networks that could provide them with jobs, money, or places to live. They had to use a myriad of maneuvers to circumvent legal restrictions on immigration or to get student or special work visas that would allow them to come to the country and stay.

For Brazilians who had supported the Goulart regime or stood to its left, the process of international exile symbolically began immediately after the military coup d'état in 1964, when the president crossed over the Uruguayan border on April 4, two days *after* he had been deposed for allegedly having abandoned his office and the country. Many of his supporters followed him to Uruguay, but Chile and later Europe became the privileged destination for most exiles—either those fleeing immediate danger, those fearful that they might become entangled in a police sweep that would lead to their imprisonment, or those unwilling to continue living under a military government.

Probably the first post-coup political exile to the United States was the prominent economist Celso Furtado, who lost his political rights on April 9, 1964, with the declaration of Institution Act No. 1.[6] In 1959, he helped establish the Superindentência de Desenvolvimento do Nordeste (Agency for Northeast Development, SUDENE), a government agency designed to address the ongoing impoverishment of the region. During the Goulart government he was the country's first minister of planning. Soon after the military seized power, he fled to Chile. Furtado spent the 1964–65 academic year as a visiting scholar at Yale University. He then moved to France, where he assumed the chair in economic development at the University of Paris.[7]

In 1964, Fernando Henrique Cardoso, a promising young sociologist from the University of São Paulo, also left Brazil for exile in Chile, where he taught the sociology of development in various institutions in that country and then at the University of Paris-Nanterre, France, from 1967 to 1968. Returning to Brazil during the tumultuous year of 1968, he became a full professor at the University of São Paulo, only to be forcibly retired in April 1969. Although Cardoso played a crucial role in founding CEBRAP, the research institute that sustained and retained in the country many punished Brazilian academics, he also traveled extensively abroad as a visiting professor during the darkest years of the military regime. He spent time in Mexico City and Geneva, Switzerland, a year as a visiting research professor at Stanford University and a one-year tenure at Cambridge University in England, and some time at both the University of Paris and the École des Hautes Études en Sciences Sociales, among other prestigious academic institutions.[8] The publication of his work *Dependencia e desarrollo en América Latina* (Dependency and Development in Latin America), coauthored with Enzo Falletto and published in a half-dozen languages, catapulted him to international prominence for the elaboration of a series of ideas and arguments that became known as dependency theory.[9]

Cardoso and Furtado spent only limited periods of time in the United States and therefore played only minor roles in antidictatorship activities there in conjunction with the efforts of other political exiles and their allies.[10] However, the fact that the military regime had forced eminent scholars out of Brazilian universities with draconian measures reinforced the image that the generals were arbitrary, brutish, and anti-intellectual. The presence of Furtado, Cardoso, and others scholars circulating among intellectuals at the world's most prestigious universities merely affirmed negative portrayals of the military regime.

In a report in 1969 to Latin Americanists about the restrictions on academic freedom in Brazil, Philippe Schmitter appealed to his colleagues to support those scholars who might need employment abroad.[11] There is no precise accounting of professors who left Brazil and ended up in the United States, but at least four political exiles had a sustained presence in U.S. academia and left their mark in different ways. Emília Viotti da Costa was a rising star in Brazilian history at the University of São Paulo when the military forced her into compulsory retirement in April 1969 and barred her from employment in any government-related institute. She had been an important leader at the University of São Paulo in the debates concerning the joint agreement by the Brazilian Ministério de Educação e Cultura (Ministry of Education and Culture, MEC) and the U.S. Agency for International Development, known as the MEC-USAID accord, to restructure higher education in Brazil. Her criticisms of the proposed measures made her a lightning rod among right-wing colleagues who supported the military. Conservative faculty and progovernment administrators targeted her for retaliation because of her outspoken opposition to the university reforms proposed by the regime.[12] With a young family to support and no immediate employment options in Brazil, she accepted an invitation from Michael Hall to spend a semester in the United States as a visiting professor. Hall, a young professor of Brazilian history at Tulane University, had been one of the former Columbia University graduate students who had organized the petition campaign against the U.S. invasion of the Dominican Republic.[13] She returned the next year by invitation of the historian Joseph Love for another visiting professorship at the University of Illinois.[14] After a stint at Smith College, Emília Viotti da Costa moved to Yale, where she became a tenured professor. In New Haven, she focused on raising her family, and at Yale she confronted the challenges of adapting to a new language, culture, and academic system and continuing her teaching and research.[15] She was responsible for educating several generations of some of the most talented and prominent historians of Latin America while teaching at Yale.[16]

Eulália Maria Lahmeyer Lobo, an economic historian at the University of Rio de Janeiro, also lost her right to teach in Brazilian public universities in April 1969. During the early 1960s, she had been active in the university reform movement, and later, under the military dictatorship, she led the forces at her university who were critical of the MEC-USAID agreement.[17] After being forcibly retired, again by the same combination of denunciations by conservative colleagues and a reactionary university administration, Lobo received an invitation to teach at the University of South Carolina. She ended up working a semester each year in the United States and spending the other half of the year in Brazil, in order to continue her research and writing. Isolated in South Carolina and, like other Brazilian academics, concerned about her immigrant status in the United States, she remained only indirectly involved in antidictatorship activities in the United States.[18]

Abdias do Nascimento's route to the United States was somewhat different from those of Emília Viotti da Costa and Eulália Maria Lahmeyer Lobo. The Afro-Brazilian actor, artist, and intellectual began his lifelong career as a political activist and public intellectual in the 1930s as a member of the Frente Negra Brasileira (Brazilian Black Front) in São Paulo.[19] Imprisoned numerous times for protesting racial discrimination in the 1930s and 1940s, he went on to found the Teatro Experimental do Negro (Black Experimental Theater) in 1944. During the 1950s and 1960s, he actively organized and promoted conferences that challenged hegemonic notions that Brazil was a "racial democracy" and that Afro-Brazilians did not suffer discrimination. In 1968, he founded the Museum of Black Art in Rio de Janeiro. That year, facing several military government investigations for his political and cultural activities, he accepted a Fairfield Foundation fellowship to give a series of lectures in the United States. After the enactment of Institutional Act No. 5, he realized that it was not a propitious time to return to Brazil. The School of Dramatic Arts at Yale offered him a fellowship as a visiting scholar, and he then spent a year at the Humanities Center at Wesleyan University. In 1970, the State University of New York in Buffalo offered him a chair in African cultures in the New World at the Center for Puerto Rican Studies, where he remained until 1981. While in the United States, Abdias do Nascimento expanded on his theories about race in Brazil and helped frame the debate on racism and racial identity in Brazil. He was extremely influential in the formation of the Movimento Negro Unificado (Black United Movement) in the late 1970s and 1980s.[20]

Pedro Celso Uchôa Cavalcanti also ended up teaching in the United States. Active in a project to produce a series of books for a wide audience that offered a critical consideration of Brazilian history, Pedro fled the country after the coup in 1964. He ended up getting a doctorate in Poland and then secured a job at Washington University in St. Louis, Missouri. He was isolated from the cluster of Brazilians, clerics, and other activists in New York in the early 1970s that developed various campaigns against the military dictatorship. However, in 1974 he lent his name and his academic credentials to the effort to collect interviews from political exiles as part of a campaign to promote the idea of a general amnesty.[21]

Many other Brazilians who were a part of or supported the opposition to the military regime passed through the United States in the 1960s and 1970s. Bela Feldman-Bianco, Clóvis Brigagão, Evelina D'Agnino, Jovelino Ramos, Marcos Arruda, and Ruben César Fernandes, to mention only a few, entered graduate programs while carrying out political activities discreetly to avoid trouble with the Immigration and Naturalization Service, retaliation against family and friends in Brazil, or the problems that would ensue if they were to return to their native country.[22] They remained a minority among a much larger group of Brazilian graduate students, numbering in the hundreds, if not thousands, who came to the United States in this period through Brazilian government sponsorship and generous scholarships as a part of the military regime's investment in higher education and the training of a new class of academics and technocrats abroad.

In those cities and towns with clusters of politically engaged Brazilian exiles, such as Berkeley and New York, a core group of Brazilian activists met inconspicuously to engage in political discussions and to plan protest activities, while circulating in a larger community of Brazilian students living in the United States that would inevitably gather for various social events. Robert Stam, a professor of film studies at New York University, was a graduate student at Berkeley in the early 1970s and linked to the group of Brazilian activists there. "We would have regular meetings in which we would discuss the ongoing political situation in Brazil, study documents from the opposition, or plan a political event. Almost everyone in the group was a Brazilian or someone closely linked to Brazil."[23] The Brazilians were prudent, cautious, and discreet, and therefore they formed no public organization to give their activities a national profile as the Iranian students did through the Iranian Students' Association in the United States at the same time.[24] They feared potential infiltration of their groups by agents of the Brazilian government, and most planned to return to their home country after they finished their studies in the United States.[25]

Other Brazilians, who had come to the United States to avoid the stifling situation after Institutional Act No. 5, found odd jobs and other means to sustain themselves while living abroad. Martinha Arruda decided to join her mother in Washington, in the aftermath of the events surrounding her brother's traumatic arrest and torture and the severe repression facing Brazilian theater at the time. Although she did not work as an actor in the United States, she eventually moved to Berkeley, where she became close to members of the San Francisco Mime Troupe, a radical theater collective, and took courses in photography.[26] João Silvério Trevisan, who would later become a founding leader of the Brazilian gay rights movement and a prize-winning author, left his country after the military regime banned from distribution an experimental film that he had directed. While living in Berkeley, he established close contacts with the emergent gay and lesbian rights movement in the San Francisco Bay Area, an experience that reinforced his determination to found an organization in Brazil upon his return.[27] Maria Helena Moreira Alves, who had been "exiled" by her family to the United States before the coup d'état because she had fallen in love with a communist, became intimately involved in antidictatorship activities on the East Coast in the 1970s while she was at the Massachusetts Institute of Technology, writing her doctoral dissertation on the military regime.[28] Tetê de Moraes, who had escaped from a second arrest to exile in Chile, moved to the United States immediately before the 1973 coup d'état and studied in Washington, while quietly supporting efforts of local activists.[29] Judith Patarra, who was in New York as a correspondent for *Veja* magazine, also played an important behind-the-scenes role among activists on the East Coast. As a talented journalist who was also committed to the cause, she disseminated information about the situation in Brazil to those working against the dictatorship, while pushing the limits about what she could write for the Brazilian press through her coverage of events in the United States.[30]

Jovelino Ramos, Marcos Arruda, and Anivaldo Padilha had left Brazil because the government had filed charges of subversion against them that might have led to imprisonment. Marcos and Anivaldo left Brazil, as well, to avoid the possibility that another arrest would take them once again to the torture chambers. They dared step foot on Brazilian soil again only in 1979 when the government had declared amnesty, and the practice of torture against political prisoners had ended.

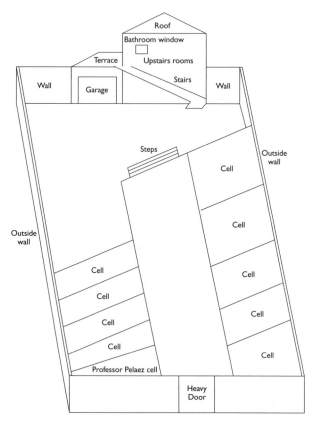

Drawing of place where Werner Baer, Riordan Roett, and Carlos Peláez were detained, June 1970. ACERVO DEOPS, ARQUIVO PÚBLICO DO ESTADO DE SÃO PAULO.

# LATIN AMERICANISTS
# TAKE A STAND

We request that you send us all possible information about the "American Committee for Information on Brazil," whose address is Post Office Box
1091, New York, NY 10027. — **Telegram from Ministry of
Foreign Affairs, Brasília, to the Brazilian Embassy, Washington,
July 27, 1970**

The campaigns to denounce the forced retirement of Brazilian academics in 1969 and to protest the trial of Caio Prado Júnior on charges of subversion broadened concern and interest about the Brazilian political situation among U.S. Latin Americanists. The growing number of newspaper and journal articles that appeared in the press in the late winter and early spring of 1970 reporting the systematic torture of political prisoners, however, sent a shock wave through the academic world. Outspoken opposition to the military regime among experts on Latin America coalesced during the Second National Conference of the Latin American Studies Association (LASA) that was held April 16 to 18, 1970, in Washington. Organizing around that event marked a watershed in the campaign against the military regime. After the second LASA conference, one could argue, the overwhelming majority of U.S. scholars working on Latin America positioned themselves against the Brazilian military regime. This chapter explores the dynamics that led to that transformation.

### Academics and Politics

The radicalization on university campuses in the late 1960s and growing opposition to the Vietnam War also affected Latin Americanists. A new generation of graduate students and young assistant professors set the tone for the LASA meeting in the nation's capital in April 1970. Many who attended the Washington conference considered their research in Latin America linked inextricably to the political upheavals taking place throughout the continent. Margaret Crahan, who had finished her doctoral dissertation on colonial Peru in 1967 and had landed a teaching position at Hunter College in the Bronx, recalled the tone of the times and the esprit de corps that was developing among her academic peers: "At the LASA meeting, there was a sense of being the younger generation. Many people had just recently finished [their dissertations], and a substantial delegation came from the West Coast. For a lot of us, we had not had a face-to-face [contact] before, and we felt a lot of commonality."[1] The shared approach to Latin America involved a commitment to supporting the political and social movements in Latin America that favored social justice; it also reflected the broader shift to the left in academic circles in the late 1960s, especially among graduate students and junior faculty.

In founding LASA, many senior scholars had distanced themselves from aligning with official U.S. government policies toward Latin America in a posture of apparent neutrality. Now a significant number of younger Latin Americanists insisted on taking political stands. Crahan remembered that many of the old guard opposed political resolutions: "This was an academic association, and [they thought] it was inappropriate. That was their attitude. On the other hand, the numbers were on our side . . . You were not just academics. If you worked on Latin America, you became directly involved in a whole series of issues."[2]

## Motions and Oppositional Oratory

No one seems to remember who initiated the idea of using the 1970 LASA conference as a forum for launching a national campaign against the military regime, but Brady Tyson, Ralph Della Cava, and other participants in the American Committee for Information on Brazil realized that the event was an optimal place to mobilize Latin Americanists nationwide. They brought hundreds of copies of the eighteen-page publication Brazil: A Report on Terror to the meeting and distributed it in a packet containing reprints from the articles published in Commonweal, Christianity and Crisis, and Christian Century, as well as newspaper articles about torture and repression in Brazil. They dispersed every packet.[3]

The group also arranged for the presence of Márcio Moreira Alves in the United States, so that he could attend the conference and then tour college and university campuses to reach the American public with information about the political situation in Brazil. Ralph Della Cava recalled how financially precarious their plan had been. "We literally brought him up [from exile in Chile] on money from a ticket that we had bought on a credit card or something. I helped organize talks in all of the universities where he spoke. I remember that when he spoke at the Brazil seminar at Columbia University, there must have been over a hundred people. They were hanging from the rafters."[4] As one of the two congressmen sanctioned by the dictatorship in 1968 for criticizing the military that had led to a showdown in Congress and the promulgation of Institutional Act No. 5 in December of that year, Alves was a living example of the arbitrary and undemocratic nature of the dictatorship. Moreover, his impeccable English and superb oratorical skills made him an optimal and "authentic" Brazilian voice of the opposition. His address to a packed audience at the LASA convention helped to consolidate support for a resolution against the military dictatorship.

Della Cava, Tyson, and the other activist scholars who attended the LASA meeting approached Thomas Skidmore, already one of the most eminent scholars of Brazilian political history in the United States, to request that he sponsor a resolution at the LASA business meeting that criticized the Brazilian government's human rights abuses.[5] Skidmore, who was a member of LASA's executive committee and the chair of the association's Government Relations Committee, agreed. During the Saturday afternoon business meeting, he presented a strongly worded resolution on Brazil to the membership for their ratification. The resolution read, in part:

> As members of LASA, we vigorously protest the violations of academic freedom and civil rights of professors, students and intellectuals now taking place in Brazil.
>
> We are even more disturbed about the frequent accounts of systematic torture being practiced on intellectuals and other individuals held prisoner by Brazilian authorities. Documented description of such inhuman behavior has already been submitted to Pope Paul VI by sixty-one leading European intellectuals and religious spokesmen. Courageous Brazilians have spoken out against the purges, repression and torture. American friends of Brazil can do no less.[6]

The resolution continued by calling for an end to academic purges, arbitrary arrests, and torture and a return to a respect of human rights. It also mandated that LASA's Government Relations Committee prepare a report for members of the association presenting the details of the situation of academics in Brazil and authorized the committee to send a mission to Brazil to prepare the report, if they thought it necessary.

In the floor debate, members of the Radical Caucus, a cluster of left-wing and Marxist scholars working on Latin America, proposed an amendment to the resolution denouncing the "documented role played by the United States A.I.D. program in the training of more than 16,000 Brazilian police in 'criminal investigation' and counter-insurgency since 1968." Reports of this training had circulated among leftists in Latin America and the United States, although the U.S. government systematically denied any involvement with police instruction related to torture, repression, or counterinsurgency measures. Many years later, Martha K. Huggins would document and analyze U.S. involvement in such police training in her book *Political Policing: The United States and Latin America*.[7] At the time, however, some still regarded these allegations as mere suppositions. Those reservations notwithstanding, as a Brazilian government official who attended the LASA conference and observed the resolution process noted, the plenary body had no objection to this addition. The proponent of the resolution immediately incorporated the amendment into the motion.[8]

The participation of the Radical Caucus in the resolution process represented a significant political shift in the composition of active Latin Americanists, as Meg Crahan noted. During the LASA conference, scholars with a radical critique of U.S. involvement in Latin America, as well as sympathy for revolutionary processes developing throughout the continent, were highly visible. Scholars with left-wing leanings, such as James Petras, Donald Bray, Karen Spaulding, Joel Edelstein, and David Epstein, chaired, presented papers, or were panel discussants.[9] The Radical Caucus also successfully pushed through a resolution permitting graduate students to vote at the plenary meeting. They also backed another "condemning the funding and control of Latin American research by corporate interests and military/political elites." In addition, the assembly supported two resolutions against the U.S. blockade of Cuba, and a fifth resolution calling for a "committee to be established to investigate cases of discrimination against women in the academic profession," and for LASA "to promote the establishment of child day care centers to facilitate women's participation in research and teaching." The meeting adjourned before the membership could consider another resolution condemning U.S. intervention in Latin America.[10]

The next day, former congressman Alves, with Professors Della Cava, Tyson, and Skidmore by his side, held a press conference attended by the *Washington Post, New York Times, Baltimore Sun*, and other major newspapers. In his initial statement, Alves presented details about incidents of torture. He accused the U.S. government of backing the "regime of terror" through U.S. AID programs. He also alleged that Washington had financed the training of 16,000 Brazilian police since 1968. According to the *Washington Post*, Alves also argued, "Neither external criticism nor a cutoff of U.S. military aid could topple the military regime." Alves insisted, however, "Only international public opinion could restrain the generals from 'routine' torturing of political prisoners."[11] At the end of the press conference, a representative of the Union of Radical Latin Americanists—as the Radical Caucus had reconstituted itself the previous day—read the resolution condemning the violation of individual rights in Brazil approved at the plenary session.[12]

None of the participants in the LASA convention who granted interviews for this book could recall many details of events as they took place in April 1970. They all agreed, however, that the LASA resolution marked a turning point in their efforts to broaden interest among their colleagues in order to mobilize against the escalating violence in Brazil.[13] Alves's declaration at the Saturday press conference that "only international public opinion could restrain the generals from 'routine' torturing of political prisoners" also became the overarching strategy for activists over the next two years. Moreover, as Alves reminded the press, U.S. citizens might actually make a difference.

### Tracking Opinions and Opponents

If the recollections of the participants in LASA meeting have faded after three decades, an on-site report prepared by the Brazilian Embassy offers a more permanent record of this historic moment for antidictatorship activists in the United States. The government official who surreptitiously attended the meeting noted that other floor resolutions had polarized the debate between radical and conservative currents within the association. The eyewitness estimated that the "radicals" had a slight edge over the conservatives among the 146 participates who voted on different resolutions. However, the Brazil resolution had provoked no opposition from the body and was passed unanimously, with the abovementioned amendment of U.S. involvement in police training incorporated into motion without objection.[14] The Brazilian observer emphasized the importance of LASA to the Brazilian Ministry of Foreign Affairs because the association brought together "the most renowned North American specialists about Latin America," and then he duly listed the names of prominent academics in the field who had attended the conference.[15]

Ever since LASA president John Johnson and the anthropologist Charles Wagley headed the list of scholars protesting the restrictions of academic freedom in Brazil in the spring of 1969, the Brazilian Embassy had been following Latin Americanists in the United States. Sometime in late 1969, the Ministry of Foreign Affairs obtained a copy of Schmitter's report about the forced retirement of Brazilian academics. Itamaraty requested that the Brazilian Embassy in Washington pursue intelligence gathering about Schmitter and Latin Americanists who had positioned themselves against the government.[16] In a report dated December 17, 1969, about LASA sent to Minister of Foreign Relations Mário Gibson Barboza by the Brazilian Embassy in Washington, Celso Diniz reported, "The Latin American Studies Association does not have a definite political orientation. Professors from almost all ideological positions participate in it; however, there is virtual unanimity about a preference for the North American model of government. This does not prevent the association from taking political positions, if they judge that academic freedom is threatened, as they understand it in this country."[17] The observation seemed to explain the cables sent in May 1969 by the Latin

American Studies Association to protest the forced retirement of university professors.

The Brazilian government official also attempted to locate U.S. academics along a political continuum, although it is not quite clear how he reached his conclusions. Skidmore was grouped with the professors from the "liberal wing," whereas Charles Wagley from Columbia was considered a part of the "conservative wing," a characterization that puzzled his family, friends, and former students.[18] As might be expected, the Ministry of Foreign Relations then passed on its information to the Brazilian intelligence services. Among those agencies that received copies of materials collected about those in the United States who opposed the dictatorship was the Departmento de Ordem Política e Social (DEOPS). Found in its São Paulo files is a translated copy of the public declaration, "We Shall Not Remain Silent" that was included in the pamphlet "Brazil: A Report on Terror" and distributed in a folder with other documents at the LASA meeting. By the name of each signatory of the manifesto, a clerk within the intelligence services had marked a crisscrossed circle in red pencil, indicating that a government official had made a file for each of those persons whose name was on the petition.[19]

This effort seems to have been part of a systematic attempt to track the political positions of U.S. scholars and others concerned about the situation in Brazil. A memo dated June 1, 1970, requested that the Brazilian Embassy send a second LASA membership list directly to the Departamento de Segurança e Informações, presumably to aid in identifying recalcitrant Latin Americanists.[20] When the Ministry of Foreign Relations pressed the Brazilian Embassy in Washington for more information on "professors or researchers dedicated to Brazilian or Latin American studies," the ambassador responded that the embassy had access only to the academic work of these scholars. He went on to comment in an "urgent secret" telegram to the minister: "In general, it would be extremely difficult for the embassy to obtain through any normally open channels of the diplomatic missions, accurate information about the ideological background of any U.S. citizen. Therefore, it would be necessary to open a channel of communication with a local security agency, possibly the FBI. I am consulting with your Excellency about the opportunity and the interest in proceeding in that manner."[21]

We do not know whether the Brazilian government pursued the channel suggested by the embassy and contacted the FBI or another U.S. government intelligence agency to get background information on U.S. scholars who had signed petitions against the Brazilian dictatorship. If they did attempt to open such a means of communication, we also do not know whether the FBI cooperated with this effort. It is clear from the documentation uncovered, however, that the Brazilian Ministry of Foreign Relations was concerned that the protests by U.S. academics contributed to the "negative image" of Brazil abroad. Moreover, as we will see, internal security forces in Brazil did not hesitate to follow closely at least some U.S. scholars while they were doing research in Brazil.

### Touring Campuses

Soon after the LASA conference, students in campuses across the nation rose up almost in unison in response to the Nixon administration's invasion of Cambodia. With contacts and speaking engagements lined up during the LASA convention, the exiled Brazilian congressman and Crahan toured the East Coast and the Midwest during these two tumultuous months, talking about the Brazilian political situation and linking it to the war in Southeast Asia and U.S. foreign policy. Márcio Moreira Alves's masterful command of the English language and his rhetorical flair for debate served him well during the tour.

According to Crahan, the power of Márcio Moreira Alves's presentations on that spring tour was that he embodied the concrete results of the U.S. government's support for the Brazilian military regime. The U.S. government had backed the military takeover in 1964. Four years later, the generals that Washington had supported had closed down Congress and purged hundreds of politicians to sustain their rule. Torture had become a common vehicle to extract information from oppositionists. Alves's personal history as a journalist made him a larger-than-life figure for students and scholars interested in understanding the impact of U.S. foreign policy on countries beyond Southeast Asia. He had investigated incidents of torture in the Northeast in 1964. As a congressman, he had denounced the regime in 1968. The dictatorship had stripped him of his political rights. Moreover, Márcio knew how to affect his public. Crahan recollected, "He was able to tie the situation in Brazil to types of things that in the United States people would take for granted . . . He was able to present a sustained analysis and yet offer the human element . . . He was able to balance it particularly for an academic audience. He wouldn't lose them because it wasn't just a spiel appealing to the emotions. He was able to integrate the intellectual and the emotional into an analysis with incredible clarity, internal logic, and coherence. He answered the questions in the same way."[22]

The former congressman himself reminisced that the number of people who attended his talks wasn't very large. "But they were impressed with what I had to say. I had the advantage of speaking English fluently and Crahan said that I had an old-fashioned oratorical style that was an asset. I guess they thought that someone who spoke English that well couldn't be lying." When asked if he got discouraged when he visited a university and few people attended his lecture, he responded, "I was carrying out an important task and starting anything was good. It there had been two people in the room, it would have been good—in general there were many more—because the movement could influence [the situation] in Brazil and interfere with Brazilian diplomatic efforts. Who knows, maybe something would slip into the Brazilian media in spite of the censorship, creating some kind of movement of hope in U.S. public opinion against the Brazilian government, against the Brazilian dictatorship?"[23]

Among the many stops on Márcio's swing through the campuses of major universities on the East Coast was a visit organized by Brady Tyson to Johns Hopkins University in Baltimore. At the time, the former ambassador Lincoln Gordon was the president of Johns Hopkins. Scheduling a lecture at Johns Hopkins was a clever move. Márcio's presence on the campus had the potential of sparking a sharp debate between one of the leading public figures opposing the Brazilian government and Gordon, considered by most Brazilian leftists an architect of the 1964 military coup.

Márcio Moreira Alves and Brady Tyson understood the potential polemic that could have surrounded a campus event about Brazil, and in late April 1970 the former congressman shaped his talk accordingly. No written copy of his lecture can be located, most likely because Márcio composed his speech extemporaneously. However, the local press covered the event and summarized his main arguments. According to the *Baltimore Sun*, "Dr. Lincoln Gordon, president of Johns Hopkins University, was sharply criticized yesterday by a former Brazilian congressman for his alleged role in the ouster of Brazilian President João Goulart in 1964, while Dr. Gordon was ambassador to Brazil."[24] Characterizing the current Brazilian government as "terrorist and repressive," Alves charged, "American Embassy officials met with conspirators of the coup several days before the takeover and were quick to assure them that the United States would support their government." He also leveled the accusation against Gordon that the former ambassador had not attempted to warn the Goulart government of the planned military takeover. Alves's more vehement charges against Gordon, however, involved his silence about torture in Brazil after the military had come to power. According to the *Sun* reporter who covered the event, Alves claimed that "Dr. Gordon had

ample opportunities to denounce the torture in Brazil" but had not done so."
Alves pointed out that seventeen months after the coup, Gordon had stated
that "this government represents the ideal government in view of the Alliance for Progress," a statement that Alves considered "ludicrous in light of
the obvious oppressive tactics of the regime." The newspaper also reported
that a table had been set up in the lecture hall with two chairs and micro-
phones "in the hope that Dr. Gordon would come and debate" with Alves. If
one can rely on the journalist's reporting, "Dr. Gordon was offered an invitation to the talk on several occasions, and had stated several times that he
would discuss the Brazilian issue at any time, but he did not show up."

The U.S. invasion of Cambodia a week after Alves's visit to Hopkins provoked a nationwide student strike. Hopkins, like most institutions of higher
education, shut down and the semester ended abruptly, in part to avoid further campus-based protests. While Crahan, Della Cava, and others involved
in Alves's speaking tour in spring 1970 all agreed that the effort had been
worthwhile in introducing the situation in Brazil to students throughout the
country, the concrete results of the effort are hard to measure. The tour seems
to have helped solidify a national network of students, professors, clergy, and
activists interested in solidarity with progressive struggles in Latin America.
Although it may have laid the basis for future work on Brazil and later campaigns after the military takeover in Chile on September 11, 1973, it was still
a modest beginning.

### Kidnapping Scholars

As Márcio Moreira Alves was wrapping up his tour of U.S. campuses in the
spring of 1970, three U.S. scholars doing research in Brazil had a run-in with
the repressive apparatus of the Brazilian state. On June 12, 1970, Werner
Baer, a professor at Vanderbilt University, returned to Rio de Janeiro from a
meeting in São Paulo. He had traveled there with Rudolph Blitz, a colleague
from Vanderbilt who was spending the month of June in Brazil as a visiting
professor under a U.S. AID contract. Baer was a young, energetic economist,
rising in the profession. That afternoon, he stopped by the Ford Foundation
offices, left Blitz at his hotel, and then went back to the apartment in Copacabana that he was sharing with Riordan Roett, another colleague from Vanderbilt. He parked his car outside the building, picked up his bags, and took the
back stairs up to the apartment. Just as he reached for the doorknob, the door
burst open. Three armed men grabbed him and pushed him into the apartment. Four others, also bearing weapons, waited inside. Baer's distraught
maid sat terrorized in the living room.[25]

When Baer asked what was going on, they told him shut up. The men then pushed him to one side of the room, ordered him to sit down, and began an interrogation session. His captors were dressed in sports clothes, and all seemed to be in their twenties or early thirties, except for their leader, a dark-haired, middle-sized man in his forties, who wore thick glasses. The other men addressed him as "Major," and he led the interrogation. The major asked Baer his name, what he was doing in Brazil, how long he had lived in the apartment, and if he knew a man named "Carlos." He then questioned the noticeably shaken professor about the Vietnam War, the Kennedy administration, and the student movement in the United States. He even solicited Baer's opinion about whether he thought Oswald had actually shot President Kennedy. Noting that Baer spoke excellent Portuguese, the major asked why that was so. The economist explained that he had been coming to Brazil for quite a few years. This provoked another line of questioning about the Goulart government. Baer ducked the potentially controversial subject by answering that he was an economist with no political involvements.

The leader of this armed squad refused to let Baer call the U.S. Embassy or the Ford Foundation. Nor would he identify himself or the others, only revealing that he was obeying his superiors' orders. Baer's interrogator then continued his inquiry about politics, pressing Baer about his opinion on the recent kidnapping of the German ambassador by revolutionaries to demand that the government free political prisoners. As he later reported in a deposition about the incident, Baer tried to answer the questions succinctly and in a conventional manner, but was perplexed about how to respond when the major wandered far afield from politics. Perhaps to play the role of "good cop" and put Baer at ease, the armed squad leader struck up a curious conversation. Did he think that Jacqueline Kennedy was pretty? Was she prettier than Maria Teresa, Goulart's wife and Brazil's former first lady? Diligence in one's mission, it seems, did not preclude a brief foray into the exotic to ask an American with knowledge of Brazil (and therefore presumably an expert in comparative aesthetic assessments) about the glamorous wives of prominent politicians of the past, if that was, indeed, the major's real intent.

After forty-five minutes of grilling, Riordan Roett arrived at the apartment. Roett, a political scientist, was also in Brazil on a Ford Foundation grant. The arresting officers rudely interrogated him, as they had Baer. "I came home from my Portuguese verb class," Roett recalled, "and found all of these thugs in my apartment. I remember one of the guys asked me if I knew someone named Carlos."[26] Roett and Baer explained that they knew a Carlos Peláez, a Cuban American professor from Vanderbilt who was also on the same AID-financed research trip in Brazil. One of the unidentified men ransacked Roett's bedroom until he found his address book, pocketing valuable items in the process. Carlos Peláez's address in Roett's book seemed to match something scribbled on a piece of paper that the major already held in his hand. The commander of the operation then confiscated the keys to Baer's car. Dividing into two teams and holding guns to Baer's and Roett's backs, the men escorted them in separate cars to Peláez's apartment in Ipanema. On route, the men detaining Baer casually stopped for coffee at a street-side stand. There, they chatted among themselves and mentioned to other customers, whom they seemed to know, that they could not go to a judo tournament because they were "on duty." All the while, their captors held Baer and Roett in the car at gunpoint, as they carried out their assignment with casualness. This seemingly contradictory comportment did not allay their fears about what might come next.

When the two cars arrived at Peláez's apartment, Baer was detained below, while several men accompanied Roett to the Cuban American's door. With a gun shoved into his back, Roett nervously rang the doorbell. Mrs. Peláez answered, let him in, and then realized that the men with him were armed. After a brief interrogation, when Peláez explained that he was in Brazil on a U.S. government contract, the men ordered him to dress and forcibly ushered him out of the apartment. Panic-stricken, his wife immediately called the American Embassy.

The two cars drove around the southern zone of Rio for twenty minutes or so and then the cars proceeded to the city's northern neighborhoods. At this point, the three captives were blindfolded. While heading toward their destination, the men holding Roett questioned him at length about his knowledge of the "terrorist and revolutionary groups" operating in Brazil and Latin America. Roett's familiarity with the subject seemed to whet their appetite for information, and they pushed him further to explain what he knew. The three sequestered scholars finally arrived at an interrogation center. To this day, Roett remembers this moment: "It was winter, and it was cold. They took us out of the jeep. We were blindfolded. They were guiding us; they weren't pushing us. And, I thought: 'This is it, we're going up against the wall and they are going to mow us down.' I truly believed that. But then that soon passed."[27] The armed "thugs," as Roett refers to them, led the three scholars through a courtyard, up a set of stairs, and into a small room where the blindfolds were removed.

For the next several hours, the unidentified men interrogated Baer, Roett, and Peláez separately about the political situation in Brazil, all the time under the explicit threat of violence if they refused to cooperate. Their captors wanted to know their opinions about the Brazilian left's strengths and chances of success, the use of terror and violence in politics, political kidnappings, and the influence of communism. Each of the three U.S. academics used slightly different tactics to deflect the probing questions about his political views. Peláez maintained that he was apolitical and considered himself conservative. Baer also claimed not to be interested in politics. When questioned about the kidnapping of the German ambassador, Roett insisted that his own political convictions were not leftist in nature. To back up this statement, he pointed out that he had refused to sign a petition initiated by North American professors criticizing the arrest of Professor Caio Prado Júnior and condemning tactics of the incumbent military regime. Indeed, Roett had not signed the statement that circulated in the United States with a hundred names of leading Latin Americanists, although he had received a copy in the mail after he had arrived in Rio. His captors, who for some reason knew this, pressed Roett about the petition. His reply: he had read it and destroyed it. This did not seem to satisfy his interrogators, who spent a great deal of time asking him about its content, even ordering him to write down the text from memory.[28]

At some point in the early morning, all three academics noticed a change in the kidnappers' attitude toward them. The man in charge of their detention suddenly became affable and jocular, simply asking them to write down their names, professions, and addresses before being released. Once again, their captors blindfolded them, drove them to downtown Rio, patted them on the back, and let them go. Before departing, their captors explained to the three that their superiors had ordered their detention, but now all was well. They returned the keys to Baer's car and disappeared into the night.

After reaching home, the three men contacted Stanley Nicholson, the acting director of the Ford Foundation in Rio. They also telephoned U.S. Embassy officials who had been attempting to locate the three scholars since Peláez's wife called hours before in desperation. Later, they wrote statements about the incident, documented the sacking of Roett's and Baer's apartment, and made an official complaint to the Brazilian police.

Who had detained the three scholars? What did they want from them? Why did the unidentified armed men dwell so much in their interrogations on Roett's alleged support of the petition that had circulated among Latin Americanists early in the year? Why did the men who had held them threaten violence yet not physically harm them? What effect would the incident have on U.S.–Brazil relations?

On behalf of the Ford Foundation, Nicholson wrote a strongly worded letter to the secretary of public security of the state of Guanabara, trying to discover who had been involved in detaining the three scholars. The correspondence briefly summarized the incident:

> In their own words, these professors related their experience: invasion of a private home by unidentified and heavily armed men, destruction and theft of property, forced submission to interrogation under implicit and explicit threat of violence, moved blindfolded to a building in a remote place, further interrogations and threats in a charged atmosphere, and release approximately seven hours after they were initially detained.[29]

Nicholson then emphasized the seriousness of what had happened, pointing out that the Ford Foundation, as a nongovernmental organization, had given US$25 million in aid to Brazil over the previous ten years. "We have assisted private, public, and governmental institutions in graduate instruction and research to help the preparation of Brazilian professors and technicians in the fields of agriculture, science, education, democracy and social science." Nicholson asserted that the "incident that took place on June 12 might affect the ability of the Ford Foundation to carry out work involving the technical assistance of Brazilian and foreign specialists." The letter threatened no action but clearly indicated that the foundation was extremely disturbed about the events that had taken place.

The U.S. ambassador to Brazil also sent the Ministry of Foreign Relations an aide-mémoir that backed Nicholson's letter. The official diplomatic memorandum did not insist that the three scholars' depositions (attached to the document) were veridical, but it did express concern about the actions described by them. "The Embassy, in bringing this matter to the attention of the Ministry of Foreign Affairs, hopes that appropriate investigation will be made for the purpose of providing information and an explanation concerning this occurrence."[30]

Three days after the incident, the U.S. Embassy staff in Rio de Janeiro already had a notion of who had been involved in the *arrests*, as they termed the detentions. A telegram from the American Embassy in Rio to the State Department noted that the three professors "were picked up by Brazilian security agents, presumably DOPS" (Departamento de Ordem Política e Social), the Brazilian government's political police.[31] The embassy added, "At no time would the agents identify themselves, and the prisoners were blindfolded to and from what we suspect to be the 31st Guanabara Police Precinct where they were questioned." Apparently the U.S. government did not communicate this suspicion to the three scholars, and to this day Werner Baer does not know exactly where he, Roett, and Peláez had been taken, in spite of the fact that the Cuban American had provided three detailed diagrams of the floor plan of the building where they were held and interrogated.[32]

On June 17, Ford Foundation representative Nicholson and the U.S. consul met with General Faustino, the chief of the staff of the Guanabara State Security Secretariat, to discuss the affair. According to the U.S. reporting officer, "Faustino seemed fully prepared [to] accept [the] assumption that [the] incident was [the] work of police," justifying the security forces actions by explaining that "after the kidnapping of an ambassador, police must undertake [the] widest possible search for clues."[33] There was no suggestion on the part of the Brazilian security officer that blindfolding a detained suspect or preventing him from knowing where he was being interrogated was an unusual procedure. Apparently, in the campaign against "subversion" any methods were justified, any police practice was acceptable, even if it ruffled diplomatic feathers and potentially caused an international incident.

As promised, the Brazilian Foreign Ministry official in charge of American affairs looked into the "incident." He requested that the National Intelligence Service investigate the matter. The Centro da Informação do Exército (Army Intelligence Center, CIE) also wrote a report on the affair. It offered two observations. "(1) The inconvenience of Professors ROETT, BAER, and PELÁEZ remaining in Brazil; (2) The inadmissibility of the interference of the private organization, the 'FORD FOUNDATION' in Brazilian government issues, in an aggressive tone, with threats and pressures typical of capitalist groups, boasting the advantages of their activities for Brazil, as if this lack of ethics might make our government or the Brazilian people afraid."

The report also reveals that the Brazilian intelligence agencies had initiated their surveillance of the U.S. academics before the kidnapping of the German ambassador in early June 1970. It also seems that Riordan Roett was the prime target during the secret arrest of the three U.S. scholars on June 12. The report characterized him in these terms: "In the USA Prof. ROETT is considered a man of the left, a leader in the academic world, capable, and intelligent."[34]

Of course, one must read internal documents of the army intelligence with great care. There is no guarantee that the information is accurate, and many times the reports are driven by ideological viewpoints aimed at pressuring a given position within the Armed Forces, the government bureaucracy, or among policymakers.[35] Nevertheless, the report's language and the Brazilian intelligence community's concerns permit one to understand some aspects of the internal logic embedded in the thinking of different sectors of the Armed Forces under the military dictatorship. In this case, it seems clear that the army intelligence service was particularly concerned about the links of U.S. academics to the international campaign against the military regime. In spite of the fact that Roett did not sign the petition in defense of Caio Prado Júnior, as he stated under interrogation, the military insisted that he and other U.S. academics were involved in efforts in Brazil to reproduce the statement in a paid advertisement that would be published in a Brazilian newspaper. In the climate of early 1970, with heavy press censorship and the broad powers of IA-5 in the hands of the government, that endeavor, as valiant as it might have been (if indeed there ever had been such an effort), would have most likely been doomed to failure. Nevertheless, the Brazilian military either had news of such a plan or imagined it possible. In either case, the possibility of such a denunciation of the regime fed into their fears that international campaigns were damaging Brazil's image abroad.

The linkage between Roett, his colleagues, and the petition campaign built the arguments in favor of the next recommendation in the army's intelligence report: "The integration of this group of facts indicates that for these elements to remain in Brazil, notably Drs. RIORDON ROETT and Dr. CARLOS MANOEL PELÁEZ, would hurt Internal Security." The report then issued a final warning, using the materials collected on the three academics to generalize about leftist infiltration:

> To complement the events mentioned, in addition to attesting to the inconvenience of these professors remaining in the country, it serves as a warning to authorities against the infiltration of leftist elements and allies of the subversives in our cultural milieu, through private foreign foundations who attempt to interfere in our internal affairs, permitting and covering for the presence of elements that come here with definite missions within the plans of the international communist movement.

The Brazilian government did not expel Baer, Roett, and Peláez from the country. Over the years, as Baer returned to Brazil to do research, he noticed that his name kept appearing in computers that security officials used to screen people entering the country, until he used connections in the government to have his name removed from the list.[36] Roett speculated that a combination of factors led to their detentions:

I was writing the first edition of this book on Brazilian politics, *Brazil: Politics in a Patrimonial Society*. The first edition had a section on guerrillas and guerrilla movements, based on newspaper sources. I had sent the manuscript back to Vanderbilt through the mail, and someone was obviously going through my mail. It was right after the kidnapping of the German ambassador, and they found in my briefcase a map of Santa Teresa opened to the quadrant where they thought the ambassador was being held, where old and dear friends of mine lived and still live. So it was all a coincidence, my writing about the guerrillas, someone at the Fundação Getúlio Vargas going through my desk or the mail, and my having the map, having friends in Santa Teresa. I suppose that if I were a law officer or a security agent I might have thought, hey, this is suspicious in the context of the Cold War and their own war. To this day, I do not know if I was the reason that Peláez and Baer got picked up, or if they had just decided to do a sweep of the Ford Foundation people. I have no idea why we were pulled into the same net.[37]

Roett's knowledge of the Brazilian guerrilla movement, as he pointed out in his deposition, and in his recollections three decades later derived from his general interest in the current political situation in Brazil.

The kidnapping was a one-time incident that did not seem to represent an official policy. Other U.S. scholars doing research in Brazil did not have similar experiences yet the incident reinforced the concerns of many U.S. experts on Brazil about the repressive political situation in the country. June Hahner, a historian working on a book in Rio de Janeiro, recalls a level of fear and worry about their Brazilian colleagues. "We interacted with Brazilian academics. We knew what was going on. We avoided discussing politics in order not to cause anyone any problems."[38] Angus Wright, who was doing doctoral research at the time in Salvador, Bahia, also remembered the tense political climate.[39] Although he had been active in the anti–Vietnam War movement in the United States, he rarely struck up a political conversation with Brazilian students, fearing that such speech could create a compromising situation for the Brazilians he met.

Although most U.S. scholars doing research in Brazil were cognizant of the repressive political situation and the precarious status of visiting researchers, the State Department apparently did not pursue the case of the temporary kidnappings of Baer, Roett, and Peláez beyond the end of the year. As far as Washington diplomats and policymakers were concerned, the affair was closed. During the early 1970s, the Nixon administration retained a cozy relationship with the military regime, and it seems that the State Department officials chose to downplay any conflicts between the two countries. The harassment of U.S. scholars, however, continued.

### Vetoing Visas

As Baer, Roett, and Peláez recovered from their frightening ordeal with the Brazilian political police, Thomas Skidmore, a LASA executive committee member and historian, prepared for a summer trip to Brazil. News of the detention and interrogation of his colleagues disturbed him, so he decided to request a face-to-face meeting with the Brazilian Embassy's cultural attaché in Washington. The three scholars had been secretly arrested on June 12, and Skidmore visited the embassy just eighteen days later. During their conversations, he informed the Brazilian official that Paulo Sérgio Pinheiro of the University of Campinas in the state of São Paulo had invited him to teach a course in August on the history of Brazilian social thought between 1870 and 1930, as well as another seminar on the political history of Brazil from 1930 to 1964. The meeting was in part a courtesy call; it was also an opportunity to test the political waters in Brazil.

Speaking of this incident in 2002, Skidmore admitted that he could not remember the details of the conversation with the Brazilian cultural attaché over the matter.[40] Nor had he saved his correspondence with the Brazilian government. The Brazilian Embassy, however, sent a string of telegrams to Brasília requesting advice on the subject. These diplomatic correspondences offer partial documentation about Skidmore's interactions with the Brazilian government. They also reveal how much certain representatives of the military regime were annoyed, if not threatened, by the campaign of United States scholars against torture, repression, and the limitations on academic freedom in Brazil.

According to the cultural attaché, Skidmore asked the advice of the Brazilian official about the wisdom of his traveling to Brazil, given his recent activities at the LASA conference. He was concerned about whether the strongly worded statements criticizing the Brazilian government that he had signed might jeopardize his status in Brazil. Skidmore explained that he wanted the Brazilian government to know about his travel plans because "he intended to operate openly as a university professor in the country." The response from Brasília was unequivocal: "Given Professor Thomas Skidmore's background, you should refuse to give him a visa."[41]

Brazilian diplomatic officials appeared quite disturbed by the growing international campaign to isolate the country that associated its government—and not the guerrilla movement—with "terror." Based on available documentation, it seems that defenders of the regime were poorly equipped to engage in damage control. They floundered to figure out exactly who made up the foreign opposition to their policies and how to silence them effectively. After barring Skidmore from the country in 1970 and noting no repercussions, someone in the government, it seems, backtracked and apparently tried to make amends for actions of other officials in punishing the historian for his political position. The following year, the government allowed him to return to Brazil. The harassment of Skidmore in 1970 may have prevented a follow-up report by LASA about conditions in Brazil that year, but a change in policy the next year did nothing to reverse the ever more pervasive notion that the Brazilian government sanctioned torture and repression. Likewise, the arrests of Roett, Baer, and Peláez did not silence opponents in the United States. As the year 1970 came to a close, denunciation of the Brazilian government by a handful of artists, academics, activists, and clergy had grown into the beginnings of a national campaign against the military regime. In the following year, Senate hearings would highlight the role of the U.S. government in training Brazilian police and would question Washington's foreign policy toward Brazil. At the same time, the modest efforts of figures such as Della Cava, Wipfler, Quigley, and Tyson would expand into broader activities to isolate the regime through initiatives by activists throughout the country.

## CAPÍTULO VI

### "Pode me prender, pode me bater"

*You can arrest me, you can hit me . . .*
but I won't change my opinion.

**Zé Keti, "Opinião," 1964**

Olavo Hansen, May 1, 1970. ACERVO DEOPS, ARQUIVO PÚBLICO DO ESTADO DE SÃO PAULO.

Dulce Muniz had a long day ahead of her and was a bit tired as she prepared coffee a little before six in the morning. She and friends had stayed up late the night before making banners and bundling leaflets for the May Day celebration organized by thirteen São Paulo trade unions, which was scheduled to take place at the Vila Maria Zélia Stadium in a working-class neighborhood on May 1, 1970. But before going there, she and fellow comrades of the Partido Operário Revolucionário (Trotskista) — Revolutionary Workers Party (Trotskyist), or POR(T), as it was known — had planned an additional activity for International Workers' Day.

"I was born in a small town in the state of São Paulo," Dulce recounted about her early years. "I came to the city of São Paulo to study when I was twenty. I turned twenty-one during the glorious year 1968. I wanted to study philosophy and social science at the University of São Paulo, but almost immediately got involved in theater." As she was preparing for the university entrance exam, Dulce, who had already become politically active in her hometown, joined the burst of demonstrations that took place in São Paulo in 1967 and 1968. "The first demonstration I went to was in front of the Municipal Theater. I met a theater group there and immediately joined it." That day, she met Hélio Muniz, her future husband. "He was a bank worker, and he did theater. He also belonged to a cell of the POR(T)."[1]

It was a long bus ride to the distant working-class suburbs of greater São Paulo. In the early morning, a dozen or so militants of the Trotskyist group converged on the neighborhood. Dulce reflected ironically: "Here we were, May Day, the Médici dictatorship at its height, and we were painting slogans on walls and distributing leaflets door-to-door. Afterward, we gathered in a small square. Our fists raised, we sang the *Internationale* and shouted 'Long Live the Fourth International! Long Live Socialism!" Then we went to the Maria Zélia Stadium."

When Dulce and Hélio arrived at the stadium, festivities were already underway. The POR(T) militants had planned to distribute political leaflets among those attending the day's events. "A group of us were standing around in a circle, among them comrade Alfredo. At the time, I didn't know who he was, only that he was a leader in the organization. He asked me what I did, and I told him that I worked in theater. While we talked, he kept on looking behind me, and then he said: 'Let's leave through the back entrance. This place is surrounded.' And so we moved toward the back of the stadium."

Their attempted escape was foiled, and seventeen people were arrested that day for distributing "subversive" leaflets.[2] A half-page mimeographed flier, "Long Live May First," that they distributed to the crowd is attached to their records in the São Paulo political police (DEOPS) archives. Penned in a thick revolutionary style directed to the "people and the workers of the world," it conveyed an optimistic message about possibilities for social transformation in Brazil.[3] The modest, typewritten political tract ended by calling for an increase in the minimum wage, the development of a workers' party based in the unions, support for agrarian reform, and the building of a united anti-imperialist front. The text probably went over the heads of most workers gathered that day in the stadium, and it seems that few people actually had the opportunity to read the "subversive" material before the police roundup.

When Dulce, Hélio, Alfredo, and the other members and supporters of the POR(T) got to the police headquarters, an official asked who among those detained had been previously arrested. It was then that Dulce learned that comrade Alfredo's real name was Olavo Hansen. "Olavo, I think, tried to a call attention to himself to protect us in some way, and said that he had [previous arrests]."[4] Indeed, according to police records, Hansen had been arrested in 1963 for distributing pamphlets about the Cuban revolution and again in 1965 for investigations about his relationship to the Trotskyist movement. In 1970, at age thirty-two, he worked as a computer programmer in a company that produced fertilizers in the city of Santo André, part of the industrial belt surrounding São Paulo. He was also active in the labor movement.[5]

Dulce considers that her training as an actress prepared her for the ordeal. During the police questioning of why she was at the stadium, she explained that she was a primary school teacher, seeking employment in São Paulo, who had accompanied her husband, a bank worker, to the May Day events. She demurely denied having noticed anyone distributing leaflets.[6] "After we were all interrogated, they put us on a small bus, and we were finally taken to DEOPS where we remained until we were freed."[7]

On May 5, 1970, a delegation of trade union leaders met with President Médici. It was the first summit between the head of state and labor officials since the general had assumed the presidency. After presenting a twenty-seven-page document containing a series of requests and demands, the workers' representatives denounced the arrest of seventeen people attending the May Day celebrations. The president indicated that he would "take appropriate measures."[8] That same day, Olavo, who had been identified as a leader of the group arrested on May 1, spent six hours under torture. When he returned to his cell, he recounted his treatment to fellow prisoners: burning of his skin with cigarettes, electric shock from a television picture tube, beatings on the soles of his feet and the palms of his hands, and the inevitable parrot's perch.[9] Dulce speculated that Olavo had been tortured so that he would tell them the location of the POR(T)'s printing press. "Since he wouldn't reveal the information, they doubled the bad treatment, and his suffering increased daily."[10]

The political police transported Olavo Hansen to Second Army's Military Hospital on May 8, the very day that the government issued a press release: "There is no torture in our prison, nor do we have people confined merely because of their political beliefs. In Brazil, no one is deprived of liberty simply for diverging from the democratic orientation defended by the Government." Those in prison, the statement continued, are "terrorists, detained while undergoing regular trial for crimes they committed assaulting defenseless persons, holding up banks and individuals and kidnapping diplomats to negotiate their exchange for prisoners."[11]

On May 9, 1970, Olavo Hansen died of kidney failure. According to police records, an officially sanctioned postmortem found that his death was due to poisoning by parathion, an extremely toxic chemical "used in the making of fertilizers and insecticides, in fact, a product used by the industry where he worked until April 30, 1970, a day before he was in the custody of DEOPS."[12] The conclusion of the police investigation: suicide.

Less than a week later, nineteen São Paulo leaders of unions representing a million workers sent telegrams to President Médici and the leaders of ARENA and MDB, demanding clarification about the death of Olavo Hansen while detained.[13] As outrage about Hansen's death grew, the São Paulo Metalworkers Union convoked a special meeting on May 19. The membership unanimously voted to conduct a thirtieth-day mass for his soul and closed the assembly with a minute of silence in his honor. An undercover police infiltrator attending the meeting concluded in his report: "During the assembly, it was clearly noted that the majority present were convinced that Olavo Hansen had been killed by elements of DEOPS."[14]

# 7

# HUMAN RIGHTS AND
# THE ORGANIZATION OF
# AMERICAN STATES

Up until recently, by virtue of the censorship, the
Brazilian public has been largely unaware of the
volume of critical stories being circulated in the
international press . . . Now, however, the public is
generally aware of what is being said about Brazil
in foreign countries, and Brazil's image abroad has
become a factor of domestic political significance.
This new element may lead the GOB [Government
of Brazil] to take the problem more seriously.
— **U.S. Department of State memo, November 3, 1970**

Reverend William Wipfler, Father Frederick McGuire, and Luiz Reque, Washington, June 1970.
*LATIN AMERICA CALLS!*, U.S. CONFERENCE OF CATHOLIC BISHOPS ARCHIVE.

By the spring of 1970, the veracity of reporting about the gross violation of human rights by the Brazilian military regime was beyond question. Editorials in the *Washington Post* and the *New York Times* indicated that these two public opinion makers no longer had any doubts that torture of oppositionists had become a common practice in Brazilian jails, equivocations by the U.S. Department of State in letters to congressional representatives notwithstanding. Activists had widely disseminated the documentation presented by Jether Ramalho and Domínico Pereira to Reverend Wipfler at the National Council of Churches (NCC) in late 1969. Fresh reports coming from Brazil reinforced the dossier's conclusions. Noted U.S. clergy, academics, and civil rights leaders had spoken out and signed petitions. In Brazil, at a meeting of bishops in Brasília on May 27, 1970, the body issued a document calling for government investigation of torture charges.[1] The statement in part declared, "It is a well known fact, in spite of all denials, that there exists among our own peoples, as well as among other peoples throughout the world, the firm conviction that there are repeated cases of torture in Brazil."[2] The time was ripe for a broader, more concerted campaign to pressure the Brazilian government to end human rights abuses.

With a president in the White House unwilling to curtail his cozy relationship with the Brazilian military regime, activists turned to allies in the U.S. Congress, as well as the Inter-American Commission on Human Rights (IACHR) of the Organization of American States (OAS). In both cases, it took over three years and long, laborious, and circuitous routes before these institutions took a stand against human rights abuses in Brazil. Throughout the entire process, Brazilian international representatives adamantly denied that security agencies routinely used torture on political prisoners. Moreover, they insisted that virtually all oppositionists arrested were not political prisoners but terrorists and therefore common criminals. Even when a significant international campaign had tarnished Brazil's image abroad, the military regime managed only clumsy responses, largely relying on bureaucratic stalling, bold-faced lies, and ineffective Cold War rhetoric to quell critics. By 1974, however, the Brazilian government was entirely on the defensive. The IACHR had found that gross human rights violations had occurred in Brazil. That same year, the U.S. Congress passed legislation limiting foreign aid to countries with governments that tortured their citizens. Seen in retrospective, the campaigns waged on behalf of Brazilian political prisoners served as a foundation for movements that addressed the flood of human rights violations that took place in Uruguay, Chile, and Argentina, as military regimes took over in those countries between 1973 and 1976. They also laid some of the groundwork for President Jimmy Carter's human rights policy in the late 1970s. Initially modest measures eventually reaped colossal results.

## An Ecumenical Initiative

On May 26, 1970, the International Affairs Committee of the U.S. Catholic Conference (USCC) issued a statement on Brazil. The date was symbolic, as it marked the first anniversary of the murder in Recife of Father Henrique Pereira Neto by right-wing elements. The statement linked the priest's death to a "wider picture of systematic terror" against the Brazilian Catholic Church. The declaration called upon "the appropriate international agencies, whether of the United Nations or the Organization of American States, to conduct a thorough on-site investigation into the charges of systematic terror and torture." It also urged "the immediate cessation of all U.S. assistance, private as well as public, to the government of Brazil should these grave allegations be substantiated."[3]

The driving force behind the pronouncement was Reverend Louis M. Colonnese, at the time the dynamic and dedicated director of the conference's Latin American Bureau. In a personal declaration attached to the official statement, Colonnese expressed his frustrations about how little action had taken place to curb the violence in Brazil: "My deep love for the people of Brazil compels me to ask whether such Church statements could become meaningless rituals with almost no pragmatic potential." He recounted that he had visited the pope in 1969 and presented him with a document about Brazil, and that since then the Holy See had received collaborating information that Brazilian bishops, priests, and religious and lay leaders were being unjustly imprisoned, tortured, and in some cases even murdered. Although Colonnese acknowledged that Pope Paul VI had expressed his "interest and concern," he pressed for further action, suggesting that the U.S. Catholic Church consider forwarding a recommendation to the Vatican that it sever all relations with the Brazilian government.

The Latin American Department of the National Council of Churches of Christ in the U.S.A. (NCC) issued a similar statement the following week. In a preface that outlined the complex U.S. involvement in Latin America, the pronouncement pointed out that Brazil was the third largest recipient of U.S. aid in the world, that some 600 U.S. industries operated in Brazil, and that almost 3,000 American Protestant and Catholic missionaries worked in the country. "In spite of the vast range of this involvement," the statement continued, "the people of the United States have not been apprised of the extensive information regarding the repression, terror, and torture by which Brazil is governed today."[4] Commenting that the Brazilian government frequently denied news of torture, the NCC statement countered that "the reports have been too numerous, too widely documented and recognized by too many reliable sources to be discounted." After expressing its solidarity with the USCC's pronouncement on Brazil, the NCC Latin America Department made a series of action proposals. They included a call upon the U.S. Congress to hold a hearing on the effects of U.S. government policy in Brazil and the suggestion that the Vatican, the IACHR, and the UN Commission on Human Rights investigate human rights abuses. The NCC and the USCC statements had set the agenda for pressuring governmental entities into action.

### International Appeals

Meanwhile, in Brazil, family, friends, and trade union activists attended a thirtieth-day mass for the soul of Olavo Hansen, ironically celebrated at the Igreja da Boa Morte (Church of the Good Death) located across the street from the São Paulo Metalworkers Union's headquarters. That same day, June 8, 1970, the general secretary of the Latin American Christian Trade Union Confederation, headquartered in Venezuela, sent a letter to the IACHR requesting that the entity investigate the arbitrary arrest, torture, and death of Hansen.[5] The communication related details about Hansen's death that had circulated in Brazil at the time. It was to the point:

> We wish to denounce the Government of Brazil for the assassination of the labor leader OLAVO HANSEN, leader of the São Paulo textile workers.
>
> The labor leader was arrested with 16 other comrades who were taking part in a peaceful May Day observance on May 1, 1970, in the sports arena known by the name of Maria Zélia and located in São Paulo. He was taken to DEOPS (headquarters of the regime's political and labor police). During the night he was subjected to prolonged questioning, returning to his cell in pitiful physical condition, unable even to stand. For several days he remained in his bunk, unable to get to his feet, with[out] speaking, and unable to urinate.
>
> Several days later, his body was discovered near the Ipiranga Museum, covered with contusions and hematomas, as the result of the brutal torture to which he had been subjected. His death was officially recorded on May 9, but his family was not notified until May 13, the date on which his body was found in the place mentioned.[6]

Some of the specifics of the petition to the IACHR turned out to be wrong.[7] Olavo was a member of the São Paulo Metalworkers and not the Textile Workers Union. He was taken to the Central Hospital of the Second Army in Cambuci and was not discovered near the Ipiranga Museum. However, four days did indeed lapse between his death on May 9 and May 13, when an employee of the Medical Legal Institute discreetly warned the family that if they didn't come to pick up his body, it would be buried in a pauper's grave, despite the fact that the police knew his identity and had his address on file.[8] Still, the unions' denunciation contained the basic facts.[9]

Olavo's parents did not believe that their son had committed suicide, and those who had received first-hand accounts about his condition after torture sessions knew that he had died as a result of torture. Nineteen São Paulo trade unions, five union federations, prominent figures in the Catholic Church, intellectuals, opposition politicians, and left-wing activists clamored for further investigation.[10] A State Department telegram titled "Murder of São Paulo Unionists Becomes 'Cause Celebre'" revealed that at least one U.S. government career diplomat discounted the official version that Hansen had committed suicide.[11] Another brief to the State Department addressed continued pressure by the opposition political party about the trade unionist's death. It concluded, "The government is placed in the uncomfortable position of either taking action in the Hansen case with all its potential for provoking difficulties for itself in military and police circles or allowing the MDB to keep revealing publicly the highly damaging details which it has developed concerning the events leading up to the death of Hansen and perhaps other cases of abuse of prisoners."[12] The petitioners and their supporters hoped that presenting the case to an international body adjudicating on human rights would force the Brazilian government to respond to charges rather than simply ignore the legal opposition and sweep the case under the rug.

Soon after Latin American union leaders filed their petition on behalf of Olavo Hansen, religious leaders in the United States used the same forum to denounce widespread use of torture on Brazilian political prisoners. On June 25, 1970, a month after the USCC released its statement about the situation in Brazil, Louis M. Colonnese directed a letter to Dr. Gabin Fraga, the president of the IACHR. The correspondence explained how the Latin American Department of the NCC and the USCC were jointly requesting that the commission "conduct a thorough on-site investigation of the charges of torture and repression in Brazil."[13] Unlike the petition by Latin American trade unionists that requested an inquiry into the death of a single individual, this second appeal was much broader in scope. Accompanying documentation supplied the names of dozens of political prisoners who had been beaten or tortured and included the names and ranks of people in the police and military involved in administering the pain. The material submitted along with the petition also included the documents "Dossier on Brazil" presented to the Pontifical Commission for Justice and Peace in Rome, "Terror in Brazil: A Dossier," distributed at the LASA conference in April 1970, "Terreur et Torture au Brésil," an article that had circulated in Europe, as well as numerous articles that had appeared in the United States, Brazil, and Germany.[14] Bill Wipfler recalled the initial reaction when he contacted the IACHR:

> I went down to Washington to talk with Luiz Reque, the secretary to the commission. Up until that point, they had only dealt with cases in the Dominican Republic, Cuba, and Haiti. When I talked about human rights violations in Brazil, Reque got nervous. Brazil was the biggest country in South America. He was not sure we knew what we were doing. When Father McGuire, Tom Quigley, and I later presented the documentation in thick-ringed binders, he was stunned. We had original documents, signed depositions, printed material, and all of it had been meticulously cross-indexed to show that there were multiple sources denouncing specific cases. It was all very organized. Here were representatives from the largest Catholic and Protestant organizations in the United States bringing in evidence and presenting a formal denunciation. He couldn't turn us away.[15]

The dossier became Case No. 1684. Over the next three and a half years, the Brazilian Foreign Ministry would expend considerable effort in denying the accusations presented by the Latin American trade unionists, the U.S. Catholic Conference, and the National Council of Churches.

Until the two petitions against Brazil were filed in June 1970, the IACHR had dealt with Brazil in only one other case. Just before leaving office in March 1967, President Castelo Branco pushed a new Press Law through Congress "to regulate freedom of thought and information." In October, the IACHR received a request to consider whether the new legislation violated human rights in Brazil. In early 1968, Dr. Gonzalo Escudero, the appointed rapporteur for the case, reported to the commission that it should consider the advisability of asking the Brazilian government "to adopt progressive measures in its present Press Law, in accordance with the power of the commission to make recommendations to the governments of member states of the OAS."[16] At that session, the commission requested a copy of the Press Law from the Brazil government and background information on the issue.

The Brazilian Ministry of Foreign Affairs ignored the request, and so the rapporteur raised the issue again at the commission's twentieth session held in Washington in December 1968. After deliberating on the case, the commission ruled that the petition was "inadmissible as an individual case, in view of the fact that it did not refer to specific events or situations that bear a relation to a disregard of human rights by the government against which the complaint is directed."[17] Ironically, the commission ruled on the case on the eve of the promulgation of Institutional Act No. 5. The day after the IACHR adjourned, the Costa e Silva government closed the Congress, expanded censorship, and initiated the harshest period in the dictatorship's rule.

The hard evidence submitted a year an a half later by representatives of two leading U.S. religious bodies and nonleftist trade unions created the possibility that an international body with the weight and prestige of the OAS might declare the Brazilian government culpable of gross violation of human rights. At the time, these appeals to the IACHR seemed to be one of the few avenues open to those trying to find new ways to wage an effective campaign to denounce the military regime.

The IACHR's deliberative process, however, is a slow one. Its procedures require that the country in question provide a response to the petition or complaint of human rights violations. The country accused generally has 180 days to turn over material. As the documentation reveals, the Brazilian Foreign Ministry instructed the Brazilian member of the commission to tie up the investigation with delayed responses and appeals of all commission findings, as both petitions gradually worked their way through the IACHR investigative process.[18]

On July 17, 1970, the commission duly requested that the government of Brazil supply pertinent information on Hansen's death. In its 24th Session held in October 1970, the body appointed Durward V. Sandifer, the U.S. member of the commission, to act as rapporteur for the Brazilian cases. The IACHR also sent a letter to the Brazilian government requesting consent so that Sandifer, accompanied by the executive secretary of the commission, might visit the country in order to gather information necessary to the performance of its duties. A month later, the Brazilian government publicly announced it would not permit the IACHR to conduct an investigation in Brazil because it would constitute interference in its internal affairs.[19] During the following two years, the military regime used the rules of the commission as a stalling tactic to postpone a final decision of the cases, usually only responding to inquiries a week before the 180-day time limit and then appealing the commission's request to gain another half year.

## Dossiers of Denunciation

As the IACHR moved slowly and deliberately, international pressure on the Brazilian government about torture continued to mount. On July 22, 1970, the International Commission of Jurists (ICJ) issued a ten-page report titled "Police Repression and Tortures Inflicted upon Political Opponents and Prisoners in Brazil." It was another blistering indictment of the military regime's excesses. The ICJ, a nongovernmental organization headquartered in Geneva with consultative status at the United Nations Economic and Social Council (UNESCO), based much of its report on denunciations presented to the group by the forty political prisoners released in exchange for the return of the kidnapped German ambassador Hollenben in June 1970. The document concluded, "It appears that torture is today a systematic and scientifically developed practice of the organs charged with maintaining the existing order . . . But, torture relies on silent complicity, the discretion of witnesses, and an illusion of normality. Public opinion in civilized countries has today by repeated and detailed accusations a very real chance of putting a stop to the inhuman practices suffered by so many men and women in Brazil."[20] The formula "silence equals complicity" had become the privileged metaphor in appeals to action.

Significantly, the report argued that the practice of the premeditated infliction of pain was "systematic and scientific." The document detailed how medical practitioners had collaborated in this effort: "By administering medicines and injections, they deprive the prisoner of the benefit of unconsciousness and allow the torturers to go on for several consecutive hours. On the other hand, the doctors ensure that the captive, who at a later stage may appear before a military or even civil judge, does not receive wounds which are too apparent."[21] As had become standard litany in all similar denunciations, the report listed the various torture techniques employed by the repressive apparatus. The document also accused the United States of having collaborated in training military personnel in counterinsurgency. "Brazilian officers have learned such methods from American experts and theoreticians who they meet in great number either in their own military schools in Brazil or during regular training courses in the Panama Canal Zone."[22]

U.S. State Department observers in Brazil evaluated the ICJ's document as a "slanderous report on torture of political prisoners in Brazil."[23] Likewise, in a message to the U.S. representative in The Hague, the State Department commented that the report was "highly overdrawn" but admitted that "torture has been selectively practiced on a small number of prisoners."[24]

The State Department totally rejected other sections of the report. During a press briefing the day after the ICJ issued the report, a journalist asked State Department spokesperson Carl Bartch about the accusation that Brazilians had learned procedures of torture and training from the United States. He flatly denied the charge.[25] (This allegation would resurface the following year during the Senate Hearings of Program Aid to Brazil led by Senator Frank Church.) Even ignoring the "exaggerations" in the document, U.S. government observers in Brazil considered the report to have been "one of the hardest blows against Brazil's foreign image in recent months."[26]

### Médici's "White Book"

The response presented by the Brazilian government to refute the claims that it engaged in gross violations of human rights was a report with the awkward official title "Information of the Brazilian Government to Clarify Supposed Violations of Human Rights Related in Communications Transmitted to the 'Inter-American Commission of Human Rights of the Organization of American States." One might suppose that its unofficial designation as the "White Book" reflected an attempt to offset the impact of the "Livre Noir" or "Black Book" that had circulated in Europe in 1969 itemizing abuses of the military regime. In classical Manichaean terms, the entire work was an exposition of the pure goodness of the Brazilian government in its battle against communism, terrorism, and international deceptions.[27] The dossier presented a series of objectives that it intended to prove in the report. They constituted the outline of the government's entire international counteroffensive: There were no "political prisoners" in Brazil. Those imprisoned were more interested in conducting terrorist criminal acts—which they carried out in a barbarous fashion—than in achieving any possible political objectives. The government handled all prisoners humanely. The "terrorists," in fact, received better treatment (due to their social origins and own resources) than other prisoners. There was no torture in Brazil.

The report also attacked the "campaign of defamations against Brazil." Its origins and the sources of the denunciations were "spurious, illegal, and clandestine." The effort was part of a psychological war of the International Communist Movement. International organizations aligned with the terrorist groups supported the campaign. The report then analyzed specific cases of alleged torture. They included the murder in 1969 of Father Antônio Henrique Pereira da Silva Neto, the death of Olavo Hansen the following year, as well as the mistreatment of others accused of being members of the groups engaged in armed actions to overthrow the government. The response ended by offering examples of Brazilian legislation, including the "Magna Carta of Brazil, one of the most perfect constitutions in the world," as proof that the country operated within the confines of law. Although the "White Book" was shrill and defensive in tone, it remained behind closed doors as part of the internal deliberations of the Department of Security and Information of the Brazilian Ministry of Justice. Nevertheless, the voluminous document repeated arguments that Brazilian government officials presented in public to defeat its treatment of political prisoners.

## Public Relations Abroad

On November 25, 1970, Colonel Octávio Pereira da Costa, President Médici's chief public relations advisor, made a lengthy but articulate and forceful speech at the monthly American Chamber of Commerce luncheon. According to a U.S. official attached to the São Paulo consul who attended the event, he received acclamation reserved for few such speakers.[28] In his presentation, Colonel Costa explained that in the past his office and the Brazilian government in general had been too preoccupied about internal public relations to worry much about the country's international image. The domestic situation, however, was now favorable, and the government could point to progress on various fronts. What's more, the people identified with the president. Given the distorted Brazilian image abroad, the government would now look outward. Costa explained four causes for Brazil's bad publicity abroad. First, those who believed that the country could only advance through socialism were systematically attempting to thwart the "free enterprise democratic path" chosen by Brazil. Second, disaffected Brazilian politicians and others living abroad wanted to discredit the government. Third, the foreign media preferred to emphasize negative rather than positive aspects of the country. Finally, many people disliked military governments without valuing the true nature of such governments and their leaders.

Analyzing this new public relations initiative, a Department of State political officer stationed in Brazil described the problem that the military regime confronted directly. "During the last year or two, Brazil's international public standing has suffered from highly critical, often exaggerated, articles appearing in the foreign media, especially in Europe and to a lesser extent in the U.S., which portrayed an image of Brazil as a suffering nation where an authoritarian military dictatorship reigns through the widespread repression of its opposition."[29] The officer noted that "the sadistic torture of innocents, the unwarranted cassation of public office-holders, the toleration of large-scale massacres of Indian tribes, etc." were among the major themes covered in these news articles. The Brazilian government's response was, in the words of the State Department official, "a new solution which is both financially feasible and designed to lend credibility to favorable publicity about Brazil."

U.S. State Department officials stationed in Brasília closely followed the Brazilian government's efforts to reshape its image around the world. They noted that the attempt to found a government news service to distribute favorable news stories abroad eventually fell by the wayside. One U.S. Embassy expert speculated that the government had discarded the idea "possibly on the basis of a conclusion that no foreign journal would publish such government handouts."[30] Another State Department document explained that the government in the end had rejected the proposal to set up a foreign information service "due to bureaucratic squabbling over which ministry would have ultimate jurisdiction over the proposed agency as well as because of the unacceptable high costs involved."[31]

Of the different strategies outlined, including, in June 1970, an internal government document titled "Promoting Brazil Abroad" and those mentioned later that year by Colonel Costa at the American Chamber of Commerce luncheon, the government settled on three items. It developed close collaboration with foreign correspondence stationed in Brazil. It encouraged progovernment Brazilians to travel abroad to brief editors of important publications about Brazil. Finally, it invited important foreign editors and journalists to visit the country. As one U.S. Foreign Service officer explained to the secretary of state, "The expectation is that these correspondents will be favorably impressed with Brazil's undeniable economic growth and development and that their resulting articles will serve as a counterweight to the derogatory campaign waged by the country's opponents."[32] Although at first some Brazilian officials denied that the government was seeking out foreign correspondents, news of the campaign leaked to the press. The deputy director of the Special Advisory Office for Public Relations confided to a political analyst in the American Embassy that the Brazilian government officially sponsored the initiative.

In part, the strategy of wining and dining journalists from abroad who normally did not cover the country was an effort to skirt the ill will between the military regime and many news writers stationed in Brazil, as tensions over press censorship and the control of foreign correspondents' reporting escalated. The editors of *Time* magazine had confronted the government in late 1968, when it removed the December 20 issue of the weekly from circulation in the country because it carried a story critical of Institutional Act

No. 5.[33] Throughout the late 1960s and 1970s, the Inter-American Press Association denounced the ongoing arrests of Brazilian journalists and government media censorship.[34] On various occasions, federal police detained foreign correspondents because of their political reporting on the situation in the country. The military regime's expulsion of journalists who they considered had violated the National Security Act caused further outrage among the international press assigned to Brazil.[35]

Most U.S. journalists living in Brazil and working for the mainstream media remained somewhat aloof from the government because of the lack of freedom of the press. Many also circulated among Brazilian intellectuals, who in general opposed the dictatorship. The Brazilian Embassy in Washington, which closely monitored press coverage about Brazil in the United States, characterized journalists such as Lewis Duiguid and Dan Griffin of the *Washington Post*, Joseph Novitski of the *New York Times*, William Carley of the *Wall Street Journal*, and Robert Erlandson of the *Baltimore Sun*, as outright hostile to the military regime.[36] Thus, the strategy designed by Itamaraty and the Special Advisory Office for Public Relations entailed reaching over the heads of these journalists to relatively inexperienced outsiders who easily might be impressed by a quick, controlled visit to the country. To facilitate this campaign, a representative of the Special Advisory Office for Public Relations met the journalists at the airport, arranged schedules and appointments with prominent Brazilians, and picked up many of the in-country expenses and sometimes the foreign airfare as well. Ultimately, the government hoped to offset the criticisms about the military regime contained in the columns penned by foreign journalists living in Brazil and published in European and U.S. newspapers and magazines.

### Influencing Foreign Journalists

Managing the news of reporters visiting Brazil for a brief period, therefore, seemed to be a much more modest and potentially more successful approach to reshaping Brazil's image abroad. Among the first foreign journalists to come to Brazil under this plan was a group of ten Britons associated with publications prominent in the fields of economics and finance. Officially, the Hambros Bank of London claimed responsibility for the trip, but according to U.S. State Department officials, the Brazilian Embassy in Great Britain actually organized and sponsored the all-expenses-paid visit. The nine-day tour took the journalists to "showcase" development projects to emphasize the country's expanding economic prowess, gave them access to key government officials, and organized ostentatious gatherings with the captains of Brazilian industry. A U.S. government official who received information about the managed tour through contacts at the British Embassy commented in a report to Washington, "There was no opportunity to visit the poorer areas of the country other than a quick jaunt to Salvador for a look at a state-owned offshore drilling rig in action."[37] Tours of journalists from other European countries followed the pattern set by the British visit.

It seems that the Brazilian government had much less luck with the Americans than the Europeans. In May 1970, the minister of foreign affairs authorized the Brazilian Embassy in Washington to spend $10,000 to pay expenses of visits by journalists and other foreign personalities, a considerable sum at the time. Itamaraty instructed the embassy to itemize the cost of the trip as "a visit of foreign personalities to Brazil for commercial promotion" and indicated that the receipt would show it as an expenditure for 1969.[38]

One of the U.S. journalists who came to Brazil on Itamaraty's tab was Selden Rodman, a freelance writer and poet working for the conservative newsmagazine National Review.[39] Celso Diniz, the Brazilian diplomat who encouraged the idea of inviting Rodman to Brazil, sent Itamaraty a telegram informing the Foreign Ministry that the journalist was willing to interview government officials, especially members of the Armed Forces, so as to "disseminate the real message of the Brazilian revolution."[40] Diniz noted that the National Review, under the direction of the conservative editor William Buckley Jr., was still a "modest" publication with a readership of 130,000; nevertheless, Buckley was an advisor to the White House, serving on the Vice President's Advisory Commission on Information. Although Diniz recognized that Buckley was a controversial figure, he pointed out that his column was the second most widely read in the country, implying that Rodman's trip might influence Buckley's own coverage of Brazil. Itamaraty picked up all of the journalist's expenses, and Rodman complied with his side of the bargain by publishing an enthusiastic portrayal of Brazil in the National Review.

Rodman's article, "Don't Underestimate Brazil," opened with an editorial lead-in that summed up the entire government press strategy: "Mention Brazil and most Americans think: political prisoners, torture. Nowhere, says Mr. Rodman, do you read of the accomplishments of the last three governments, of Brazil's extraordinary financial boom and economic advances."[41] In the article, Rodman offered a quick summary of Brazil's recent past. It combined unique interpretations of the military takeover with a standard conservative spin about Brazilian politics. According to Rodman, "Brazil has never had a 'democratic' government, though it has had several that were freely elected by that segment of the literate population which considered it worthwhile to vote." In the late 1950s, President Kubitschek, who believed in giving labor and the emerging middle class a share of the GNP, built Brasília, but he was corrupt and drove the country to bankruptcy. Quadros, his successor, was a demagogue, who suddenly resigned, "leaving his still more demagogic Vice President [João Goulart] (at the moment on a junket in Red China) to succeed him." (The trip was actually a commercial delegation to negotiate a trade deal with China.) Curiously, Rodman argued that the military "reluctantly" took power in 1964 to save Brazil from inflation. In this respect, he shifted away from standard interpretation that Brazil was on the verge of a communist revolution and the generals had rescued the country just in time. Rodman reported that President Castelo Branco, who was widely respected at home and abroad, was followed by the "desultory and arbitrarily paternalistic rule of his successor, Costa e Silva." The new president Emílio Garrastazu Médici was portrayed as hard-working, patriotic, and incorruptible, overseeing a tremendous economic boom that would eventually trickle down beyond the middle class to that 50 percent of the population that was still illiterate and poor. Nowhere in the piece did the author mention that he received an all-expenses-paid trip to Brazil in exchange for his favorable account of the country.

The tone of Rodman's article fell right in line with the approach that Colonel Costa had mapped out for his own domestic public relations campaigns. As the historian Carlos Fico has argued in his book *Reinventando o otimismo* (Reinventing Optimism), Costa's objective as the head of the Special Advisory Public Relations Office of President Médici from 1969 to 1974 was to shape government propaganda in order to create a positive and optimistic attitude to the country under military rule.[42] Although many of the films and domestic advertising campaigns presented a utopian Brazil that appears to be depoliticized, the Brazilian military had a very clear vision of Brazilian society and its people, whom they saw as "backward, unsophisticated, and therefore, made up of people who should be 'educated.'"[43] Costa probably thought the same about Brazil's international audience. After all, the International Communist Movement had easily manipulated world opinion to believe that torture took place in Brazil's prisons.

Rodman interviewed Costa for his *National Review* article. In response to Rodman's question about whether the government was concerned about stories of repression that created a bad image abroad, Colonel Costa commented, "We are very concerned, but we are calm about it. We want the truth to be known. But our major preoccupation is with the image we want to project among our own people: the image of a serious government concerned about social justice and creating confidence in its authority." Twenty years after stepping down as the head of the Special Office of Public Relations, Costa elaborated more fully on his approach to "promoting Brazil" in comments about the tension between the authoritarian regime and the propaganda that he had created for the Médici government in the early 1970s. "I didn't think that repression was the only path. I was convinced that a publicity [comunicação] campaign that would substitute the values of violence with values of understanding, love of the country, disarming spirits, could contribute, even on a small scale to normalizing the situation."[44]

Rodman had easy access to two members of President Médici's cabinet. Jarbas Passarinho, the minister of education, offered a buoyant picture of Brazil's expanding public school system, which Rodman uncritically reported. He also presented the generals as having laid the groundwork "for a prosperous and democratic society." Yet, in spite of the seemingly one-sided upbeat take on the socioeconomic and political situation in Brazil, Rodman's report did mention that Brazil was strong on economic growth but weak on democracy.

The National Review article also provided an interesting insight into how some foreigners viewed Brazil. In Rodman's discussions with Foreign Minister Mário Gibson Barboza, the Brazilian diplomat bemoaned the fact that after having lived in Washington for six years, he was well aware of the stereotypes that Americans had about Brazil—the tropical climate, the tons of coffee, and the wild animals and primitive people in the Amazon jungle. Rodman (reportedly with a smile) added the issue of torture to the list and noted that it might have become the newest newspaper cliché. In Rodman's eyes, so it seems, one could dismiss human rights violations as another naive and unilateral exotic image of the country. The journalist's cynical approach to the subject notwithstanding, he had touched on an important element in the reconfiguration of foreign notions of Brazil that was taking place at the same time that men and women of good will were mobilizing against inhumanity committed in Brazilian prisons.

Of course, the National Review was not Time magazine, the New York Times, the Christian Science Monitor, or the Washington Post, all of which by late 1970 had published numerous articles presenting a very negative image of the military regime for its U.S. readers. The Brazilian representatives in Washington had been extremely concerned about these publications' coverage. In the wake of Institutional Act No. 5, Ambassador Mário Gibson Barboza paid special attention to the Washington Post, attempting to convince owner Katharine Graham and the senior editors of the "errors and mistakes of assessment that the important newspaper had made about our country and the motives and proposals of the Revolution."[45] However, after six months of intensive interactions with leading newspapers in the country, he had come to the conclusion that the ideological positions of the *Post*, the *Times*, and the *Christian Science Monitor* led them to hostile reporting on Brazil in spite of his "tireless actions in clarifying [misleading reporting] to influential people in these journals, with no results." Barboza informed the foreign minister: "My evaluation is that this is not a problem of clarifications and persistence but an ideological position that is difficult to alter."[46]

The syndicated columnist Joseph Kraft also received a warm welcome from the special advisor on public relations in Rio de Janeiro, who met him at the airport, set up interviews with five government ministers, and then arranged a special meeting with the president during Kraft's five-day visit in late 1970.[47] Kraft confessed that he had originally planned to examine three issues in Brazil—"the military government," the relationship between the Church and the government, and terrorism. However, after his tour he realized that the big story was Brazil's economic growth.[48] Immediately after returning to the United States, Kraft penned two columns about the "driving push toward economic development" and the impressive 9 percent growth rate that year. He did balance his praise for the government's economic success with a final thought that "the one thing that could compromise Brazil's big bet on economic development is a policy of stiffer repression which would make martyrs of the terrorists and draw the Catholic Church into active opposition."[49]

Kraft's coverage of Brazil was precisely what the Brazilian government had had in mind. Brazil's World Cup soccer victory in 1970 boosted Médici's (and the regime's) popularity at home, but it meant very little to most Americans. The increase in the GNP, however, made good copy, as Kraft, Rodman, and others quickly noted. Was the increased reporting on Brazil's economic expansion (dubbed the "Brazilian Economic Miracle") a case of the journalist following a story or the government shaping a news agenda? As we will see in a subsequent chapter, even the most intransigent opponents of the dictatorship acknowledged the country's remarkable fast-paced growth during the Médici years, preferring instead to question the government's priorities and the impact of the "Miracle" on the poor and working class. The focus on the economy and development, however, served to shift attention away from the question of torture, censorship, and the undemocratic nature of the regime, if only by adding an upbeat angle to stories about Brazil. Nevertheless, many foreign journalists continued to report to their readership about the unsavory side of the military government, much to the dismay of Médici and his ministers.

## Redefining Terror

At the same time that the public relations projects of the government were hosting journalists, and Itamaraty officials were preparing the "White Book" as a guideline for countering the bad press abroad about torture and repression, as well as the charges under consideration at the IACHR, the Ministry of Foreign Relations waged another preemptive campaign. The Brazilian government did not intend to allow the IACHR to inspect its jails and evaluate its treatment of political prisoners. That would be a direct interference in internal affairs. The generals felt justified in doing what it took to crush the left. So, in the international public arena they pushed the OAS to take a radical stand against left-wing violence. It was a backhanded way of vindicating the domestic measures employed to stamp out the internal opposition, whether from the guerrilla movement or other sectors that belligerently challenged military rule. Arguing as they had in their responses to the IACHR that the alleged political prisoners mentioned in the international defamation conspiracy were mostly terrorists who should be considered common criminals, the Brazilian representative to the OAS, backing an Argentine resolution, led a battle to adopt new, more rigorous antiterrorist measures in that international body.

The kidnapping of U.S. ambassador Elbrick in 1969, followed the next year by the sequester of the Japanese consul, the German ambassador, and finally the Swiss ambassador, represented a desperate countermove by three of the left-wing groups that had take up arms against the military to get imprisoned comrades released from the torture chambers and safely out of Brazil. In an effort to proclaim a nonsectarian posture at a time when the Brazilian left was dismally divided, the organizations that conducted the kidnappings formulated lists of prisoners to be released that included student activists, Communist Party leaders, even priests and nuns who did not necessarily support the strategy of armed struggle. Even so, all 140 political prisoners released and transported abroad immediately lost their Brazilian citizenship, and the government banned them from returning to the country. By 1970, the terms "terrorist" and "terrorist sympathizer" had become catchall words employed by the Brazilian military dictatorship to include virtually any persons detained under the National Security Act or other similar legislation. Presumably, those accused of involvement in "subversive acts" had supported or were actively involved in terrorism of some sort or another.

Although the initial point on the OAS's agenda was to discuss the "actions and policies of the organization regarding acts of terrorism, and especially the kidnapping of people and extortion related to this crime," an Argentine proposal backed by the Brazilian delegation sought to broaden sanctions beyond those imposed on militants involved in the sequestering of diplomats.[50] Brazilian foreign minister Mário Gibson Alves Barboza was emphatic on this point in an address that he made to other OAS representatives in June 1970:

> The decision adopted by the Permanent Council of the OAS to include this question in the agenda of the Assembly, whose greatest merit is that it has simply been mentioned, is a response to the demands of the people of the Americas who are facing a need that cannot be postponed, [namely] to take urgent measures against the wave of violence that devastates our continent: assassinations, robberies of public and private property, kidnapping of diplomatic representatives, and acts of air piracy that are taking place on a sinister scale and in proportions that transcend our own national borders.[51]

The intention of the Brazilian government was to declare all of these acts, as well as any other actions directly or indirectly related to them, as common crimes rather than political deeds. This denied their perpetrators the right to request political asylum in another country and gave the country where the actions had occurred the right to extradite those who had fled or had been released in an exchange and flown abroad.[52] In a memo to President Médici about the discussions on the issue, Foreign Minister Barboza proudly boasted that Brazil had been "the undisputed leadership of the debate."[53] Throughout the second half of 1970, Brazilian diplomatic officials diligently worked behind the scenes to line up votes for the proposal.

In spite of intense intergovernment negotiations, OAS delegates could not reach a compromise agreement. A majority of the OAS representatives backed the U.S. proposal that limited the proposed convention to measures aimed at protecting diplomats and other officials on international missions from kidnapping. In response, Barboza led a six-nation walkout in protest.[54] Argentina, Ecuador, Paraguay, Haiti, and Guatemala followed Brazil's lead in leaving the session.[55]

The next day, with sixteen of the twenty-three member states present, the foreign ministers adopted the resolution by a vote of thirteen to one, with three abstentions. The resolution required inter-American cooperation in the apprehension, extradition, and trial of persons who committed criminal acts against diplomats. Chile, which had became a safe haven for Brazilian political exiles, voted against the measure, arguing that it limited the long-standing tradition of political asylum in Latin America.

In an editorial analyzing the vote, the *Washington Post* pointed out that the resolution had very little bite since "the member state which is most likely to provide asylum or safe transit for terrorists, Chile, voted against the draft." Noting that the six-member walkout had been unprecedented, the *Post* quoted the Brazilian foreign minister's lament that the OAS approach had not dealt with "terrorism as a whole." The editorial then went on to offer a pointed critique of the Brazilian government:

> Political terror has different roots in different places, but unquestionably the most fertile soil for its growth is found in those countries where the possibilities of peaceable and legal change within the system appear to be blocked. Surely it is no accident that in Brazil, with a military government which has shown itself particularly unready to put restraints on its police, terrorism is regarded as a particularly menacing problem. It is deplorable and unfair that innocent diplomats are kidnapped by terrorists who then use the diplomats as hostages to secure the liberty of their comrades already under government arrest. But the problem should be seen for what it is: not as a failure in cooperation between the police forces of the various hemispheric states, but as a failure of individual governments to cope adequately with their own elements of change and unrest.[56]

Once again, the Brazilian government seemed to have lost the battle of public perception, at least in the pages of a leading U.S. journal that had particular influence on Washington policymakers. Instead of making a case that it had been engaging in a justifiable war against left-wing extremists that required measures that might be messy at times but were essential in carrying the war to a successful conclusion, Brazilian diplomats were unable to show that they had broad international support for their policies among the nations of Latin America. As the *Miami Herald* concluded directly: "We find it no coincidence that the six—Haiti, Brazil, Ecuador, Paraguay, Guatemala and Argentina—themselves are either dictatorships or governments strongly influenced by the military."[57]

### Losing the Propaganda War

In December 1970, after two years of constant official denials that torture had taken place among prisoners under detention, the Brazilian minister of education, Jarbas Passarinho, made a major admission on television: "To say that there is no torture would be to avoid the truth. However, to say torture is a systematic policy of the government would not only be avoiding the truth, it would be infamy." Once again, the Brazilian government was on the defensive. Although conceding that the practice took place, Passarinho attempted to mitigate the impact of his statement with a counterattack. Brazil was no worse than accuser countries, an apparent reference to Edward Kennedy's United States and Le Livre Noir's France. Nonetheless, Passarinho had finally acknowledged what the State Department spokesperson had alluded to in the April 1970 press conference in response to the swell of denunciations surfacing in the United States and Europe. Yet the minister of education's admission was not far afield from the State Department's official line about torture in Brazil. Although such practices existed, they were neither government sanctioned nor systematic.

It was simply too little too late. The Brazilian government would drag out consideration of accusations of human rights abuses in the IACHR for another two years, but the damage to Brazil's image had been done. Refusing to let observers conduct on-site investigations, delaying responses to requests for more information until the last minute, and coming up with specious legal objections merely postponed the inevitable. In the Hansen case and in the case presented by the USCC and the NCC, the commission laid blame at the feet of the Brazilian generals. The report to the OAS General Assembly regarding the torture of dozens of political prisoners stated that "the evidence gathered in case 1684 leads to the persuasive presumption that in Brazil serious cases of torture, abuse, and maltreatment have occurred of persons of both sexes while they were deprived of their liberty."[58] The IACHR resolution also castigated the Brazilian government for refusing to "adopt the measures recommended by the commission, directed toward determining whether acts of torture, abuse, or maltreatment have been carried against persons detained in the establishments indicated; toward verifying whether the military and police authorities whose names are indicated have or have not participated in these acts; and, if so, toward making possible the punishment of those responsible."[59]

In one respect, however, the military regime had been successful. Its stalling tactics took advantage of the ample time allotted to respond to accusations, and numerous appeals had stretched out the final resolution of the investigation for almost four years. Médici left office before the IACHR managed to make its final recommendations to the OAS General Assembly in April 1974. That body simply received and filed them. By that time, international attention about torture and human rights abuses had turned away from Brazil to focus on the mass round-ups and executions of leftists in Chile after the military took over in that country on September 11, 1973. The Brazilian generals were no longer Latin America's number one pariahs.

Just a month before the OAS General Assembly received and filed the cases on Brazil, General Ernesto Geisel assumed the presidency in Brasília and hinted that he would pursue a gradual and controlled liberalization policy. A *New York Times* editorial reminded readers that the last two presidents had promised a similar return to democracy at the beginning of their terms and then reneged on their pledges.[60] A week after Geisel's inauguration, the *Miami Herald*, the *New York Times*, and the *Washington Post* all lamented the fact that the new government had continued censoring the press.[61] In these journalists' assessment, democratization, if it were indeed to come, would be slow in the making.

After the IACHR presented its report to the OAS General Assembly, it took no further action in the two cases. The U.S. ambassador to the OAS followed the Nixon administration's ongoing approach to Latin America by blocking any criticism of the authoritarian regime. Unlike Sandifer, the U.S. representative to the IACHR, who had remained nonpartisan as the rapporteur for the Brazil cases, the U.S. ambassador declined to push for a consideration of the reports on Brazil in the OAS General Assembly as a follow-up to the commission's findings. As a result, the IACHR sealed the comprehensive report, issuing only summaries of the denunciations and the Brazilian government's responses. The public received only a smattering of journalistic accounts of the OAS's investigation and results. One might ask whether the efforts of filing petitions, drafting responses, countering reports, and issuing press releases had any real effect on the political prisoners in Brazil.

Tom J. Farer, who served on the IACHR from 1976 to 1983, tackled this question after he completed his term on the commission, although he posed it in broader terms. "Governments still do not admit delinquencies. If individuals are freed, their liberation, if it is advertised at all, is presented as an act of official grace. It also is difficult to measure achievement outside the paper world of reports and communications because the commission has no absolute right of access to the prisoners, detention camps, and interrogation centers where hope is crushed and identity extinguished."[62] Obviously, no paper trail leads one from commission reports to Brazilian cellblocks to measure whether or not torturers used less electrical current on prisoners or executed fewer physical beatings of detainees because of the petitions filed in Washington in June 1970. In April 1974, it might have appeared that the effect of the final IACHR report was merely another slap on the wrist of a regime that simply ignored such reprimands and forged ahead with its day-to-day business of authoritarian rule. Yet the scattered documents found in the Itamaraty archives indicate a diplomatic corps particularly unnerved by what seemed to be an ever increasingly successful effort to isolate the country abroad. Essentially, the commission's findings had condemned the military regime, albeit in diplomatic terms. Even though the OAS failed to follow up by publishing a report or pushing for further actions against the military regime, the IACHR's conclusions became another in the long string of denunciations of abhorrent practices committed under the generals' watch. The cumulative effect ultimately reached a crescendo in the mid-1970s, forcing the military regime to realize that they were paying too high a price in permitting gross human rights violations to take place.[63]

Even if we can draw no immediate and direct causality between the denunciations examined by the IACHR and the end to torture in Brazil, the cases filed on behalf of hundreds of political prisoners offered a precedent that reached beyond the country's borders. As the commission ended its final deliberations on cases 1863 and 1864, sharply rebuked the government for its lack of cooperation, and found prima facie evidence of gross violations of human rights, activists submitted hundreds and then thousands of petitions to the IACHR regarding Uruguayan, Chilean, and Argentine political prisoners. Although Brazilian representative Dunshee de Abranches may have kept up a familiar diplomatic façade in consistently proclaiming the innocence of his government, this defense must have worn quite thin among other commissioners. The nearly unanimous decision of the commission (Brazil's vote aside) to rule that Brazil had committed gross human rights violations emphasized that its members were unconvinced by Dunshee de Abranches's feeble denials and delays.

Brazil's apparent success in diluting the impact of the commission's work probably influenced the Chilean dictator Augusto Pinochet's decision to outmaneuver the IACHR by actually allowing them to hold a session in the country and investigate alleged violations. His plan backfired. Unlike the Brazil cases, the commission's investigations and subsequent reports about Chile reached the General Assembly and produced a string of stinging indictment of the Chilean dictatorship.[64] Later investigations about Argentina also brought significant international attention to the plight of thousands of political prisoners.[65] Although those suffering in Brazilian jails may not have seen their pain lessened by the commission's investigation, the documentation of torture served to show that it was, in fact, systematic, widespread, and state sanctioned. Brazil's example made it more difficult for other governments to fall back on the "isolated incidents" defense.

Had the activists at the NCC and the USCC, along with scholars and Brazilian exiles, relied solely on this single avenue to respond to the urgent requests of their Brazilian friends, one might even conclude that their efforts were only partially successful. However, the petition to the IACHR was merely one of numerous campaigns that continued throughout the 1970s to isolate the Brazilian dictatorship abroad. On another front, in the congressional arena, a liberal Democratic senator from Idaho and a dedicated staff member on the Senate Foreign Relations Committee proved invaluable allies.

# CAPÍTULO VII

## Fado tropical

At some point this country is going to fulfill its destiny.

**Chico Buarque, Ruy Guerra, "Fado tropical," 1972–73**

Anivaldo Padilha, Berkeley, California, 1975. COURTESY OF ANIVALDO PADILHA.

Niva Padilha knew his Saturday was going to be hectic, so he got up early. First, he had to pick up a package left in the house of a friend's uncle and pass it on to another person. Then he had to attend the National Meeting of the Methodist Youth taking place in São Paulo that weekend. In 1970, Niva was thirty years old and an up-and-coming lay leader in the Methodist Church. He was director of the Methodist Church of Brazil Youth Department and represented the Methodists in the Latin American Union of Protestant Youth, which was supported by the World Council of Churches. Since 1967, he had also been a member of Ação Popular (AP), having joined the left-wing organization while studying at the University of São Paulo. In one of several interviews, Niva explained, "Ação Popular was formed basically from groups that emerged out of Ação Católica, those that came out of Juventude Universitária Católica [Catholic University Youth, JUC], and Juventude Estudantil Católica [Catholic Student Youth, JEC] that were high school students . . . I was a part of a movement called Movimento Estudantil Cristão [Student Christian Movement] that was Protestant, and there were conversations among them." As student groups reorganized in the aftermath of the 1964 coup, many activists moved to the left, including Niva. He continued his work in the Methodist Church as he became closer to the positions of Ação Popular. "My work in the Church was linked to cultural action, working mostly with youth to help the Church understand the political situation . . . and participate more in political action." Niva saw few contradictions regarding his left-wing militancy and his activism in the Methodist Church: "My work with AP and the Church were part of the same struggle against repression . . . The work in the Church was to get it to take a firm position against the dictatorship and fight for democratic and human rights."[1]

After 1968, the government systematically targeted militant left-wing organizations in order to annihilate them. Political work of all sorts became more difficult. Niva was used to operating discreetly, and that Saturday he had a simple task to carry out. Eliana, a member of AP, had contacted Niva several weeks before requesting that he help her hide a suitcase that contained financial records of the organization. She had recently fled to São Paulo to avoid arrest and had left the material with a supporter of AP for safekeeping. Niva planned to meet Eliana around eight o'clock, stop by the house of the uncle of another AP member, who was also active in the Methodist Church, to pick up the material, and then pass on to Eliana the package with documents that she needed to hide in a more secure place.

As the two turned the corner to walk down a narrow street to the house where the material was being stored temporarily, Niva suddenly had a sinking sensation. "I said to Eliana, 'I have a feeling we're going to get arrested.' She answered, 'Don't be ridiculous.'" Recalling the scene thirty years later, Niva described what happened next: "There was no sign the police were in the street. Nothing. I pushed the doorbell and a young man opened the peephole. I said that I had come to pick up a package . . . When I entered—Eliana was waiting downstairs at the entrance—I only saw machine guns pointed at me." Turned in by his friend's uncle who was a police informant, Niva, Eliana, and soon thereafter the uncle's two nephews were taken to Operação Bandeirante where they, like so many others, were tortured until they revealed information about Ação Popular. Throughout the interrogation sessions, Niva managed to hold onto the same story, namely, that he was a member of the Methodist Church's liberal wing and merely interested in learning more about the country's political reality. When the court temporarily released him before another trial, Niva quickly slipped across the southern border to Uruguay, using a church network that secretly assisted political fugitives to flee the country.

On June 18, 1998, Niva Padilha met me at the Metro Station near the São Paulo State Archive that houses the political police (DEOPS) records. As we walked to the archive, we talked about his experiences doing clandestine work. He explained that discipline was indispensable for an organization's survival. One also had to shroud a group in a tightly bound veil of secrecy. Maintaining a clandestine organization required strictly limiting information you knew about other militants. Hiding real names, house addresses, work locations, or other clues to the whereabouts and the identity of others was essential to protecting individuals, should someone be arrested, tortured, and forced to pass on information to the police. So "pontos," rapid meetings in public places rather than in private homes, kept knowledge compartmentalized and an organization intact. Missing an appointment could mean losing contact with the organization. Not showing up for a scheduled encounter could mean that a person had been arrested. Strict security measures required that if that person knew where you lived or worked, you needed to abandon your home or your job immediately, or risk being picked up yourself.

When we arrived at the State Archive, we moved to a small room to examine the police records related to Niva's arrest on February 28, 1970, and his interrogation over the subsequent two weeks. As the military regime's control weakened in the early 1980s, and gubernatorial elections brought opposition political parties to power in most major states, executive decrees ordered that the military turn DEOPS's archives over to civil powers so that the victims of state repression could have access to the regime's documents. Million of pieces of paper held in these state archives register, or seem to register, the history of repression. Yet, as historians know, the written word can hide as much as it reveals.

As Niva and I read the documents, with a tape recorder by our side, we faced a series of lies and deceptions folded into official-looking papers, on which modern-day scribes carefully noted statements that an officer in charge of the investigation duly signed. Screams of pain from electric shocks coursing through a prisoner's body do not show up in the police record. Indeed, a superficial reading of these papers might suggest that police officials had rather courteous and polite interactions with those detained, clarifying questions in subsequent interviews until they could piece together a definitive, coherent story and decide whether to press or drop charges. Some reports seem so blasé that one could imagine that an officer might even have been offering a cup of coffee before a sixth or seventh hour-long interrogation session at the end of which a prisoner "confirmed previous statements and had nothing more to declare." In short, officials have erased all signs of torture. These documents, however, also record other deceptions, for the task of any detained prisoner, indeed, her or his moral duty was to play a careful cat-and-mouse game with the interrogator to conceal information and divert questioning in a direction that would prevent further arrests. As Niva and I huddled over the police file, we noted the spaces between the lies.

The documents indicate that the police picked up Niva and Eliana at 9:00 a.m. on Saturday, February 28. Niva remembers that they pushed Eliana and him into the back seat of a vw bug and took them to Operação Bandeirantes, where torturers reigned with unrestrained power. In one of our interviews before the archival visit, Niva related that while in the car, Eliana had cast off her wedding ring to discourage a line of questioning about her husband. At the same time, Niva had torn up the piece of paper that contained his planned weekly ritual of *pontos*, his clandestine meetings with other AP militants. He also had managed to shove the bits of paper into a hole in the seat upholstery. In a miscalculation by the arresting officers, the police had left Niva and Eliana alone for a few minutes when they arrived at the police headquarters. The two quickly fabricated a story that would explain how they knew each other.

As the political police documents duly record, "preliminary interrogation

A-2" began at 10:00 a.m. and ended at 12:15.[2] "The first day they only hit me in the stomach and the chest and used the *palmatoria*, a medieval method of slapping you with a wooden paddle that hurt tremendously and destroyed the blood circulation," Niva recalled. The initial story that Niva spun, and that a recorder carefully noted in the report, emphasized that he was an active member of the Methodist Church who had raised a concern with other members about the fact that the youth were leaving the church. So, he explained to his interrogators that he had arranged to get reading material and organize a discussion group with a few people to talk over this problem. Niva confided to me in our conversations while we examined the files that he spun this tale to justify the left-wing material in the package that he and Eliana had intended to pick up that morning. During his "preliminary interrogation," Niva also told the police that he had met Eliana, quite by chance, at the bus station the week before. They had had a long conversation about politics. Again by chance, they ran into each other on the street that morning when he was on the way to pick up the package. It was a weak attempt at trying to cover up rather incriminating circumstantial evidence. The story did not hold up very long.

The police then interrogated Eliana. According to the written record, as taken down in longhand and then carefully typed as an official report, Eliana maintained a similar story. However, the other two members of the group, whose uncle had turned them in, broke down during their first interrogation session and revealed information that discredited Niva's and Eliana's version of events. "They were very young and inexperienced about this sort of thing," reflected Niva, registering no resentment about the fact that their quick confessions led to harsher interrogatory methods by the police. Having obtained contradictory stories, the police dragged all four of them back into the same room to confront them on the different accounts of how they knew each other and the nature of their political activities. That night came the Dragon's Chair. Niva was strapped to a metal covered chair with an electrical current applied to his body that provoked violent convulsions designed to extract "the truth." Niva's session lasted until early Sunday morning. As we leafed through the pages of the file, Niva recounted, "They would ask questions, and if you didn't answer in a way that they expected, they would torture you."

Our conversation moved to an assessment of the Bruno Barreto movie *O que é isso, companheiro?*, known in English as *Four Days in September*, about the kidnapping in September 1969 of the U.S. ambassador by Brazilian revolutionaries. Many on the left had criticized the film for portraying one of the torturers as a person who felt ambivalent about his work.³ My comments led Niva to recall his own principal nemesis during those days of confinement.

> Captain Albernaz was one of the people who tortured me. He tortured me a lot. Suddenly, the telephone rang, and the person who answered said it was his daughter. He stopped torturing me, picked up the telephone, and said, "Oh, my darling, how are you, my dear? No, don't worry; your father will get home in time to celebrate your birthday." He hung up the telephone and started yelling at me: "Talk! You better hurry up because I'm in a rush and have to go because my daughter is waiting." I realized that I was in front of a crazy man and a schizophrenic. I think that [film director Bruno] Barreto did not get it exactly right. Many people said that the torturer [in the film] was a nice guy. I do not think he was a nice guy in this sense, but we forget they had the other side of their lives.

After his first torture session, Niva fell into a deep depression. "I was desperate and wanted to commit suicide. It was the pain and the fear that I would not be able to maintain a lucid state . . . I knew that in spite of the torture, it was essential that I maintain control of the situation . . . I thought that the only way out was suicide, but I did not have a way to do it. I did not have a belt. They took away my glasses . . . I had to confront this."

As Niva recalls, he could not sleep for hours, and he started to experience a series of flashbacks about his life. "I thought, 'I'm not here by accident. I'm here because of a commitment I took on many years ago to fight for justice and freedom in this county.'" Niva remembered that during the torture sessions, one of the members of the "interrogation" team shouted at him: "Tell us everything because the war is over for you." That night in his cell, in flashbacks and introspection, he concluded that prison was also one front in the struggle. "The war is not over," he remembers thinking. "For me it will only be over when I die . . . Let them take on the responsibility for my death, not me. I even thought that my death could be helpful to draw attention and raise consciousness of many people in Brazil."

As these ideas raced through his mind, he turned the psychological tables on his adversaries.

> I thought, "Why are they torturing me? They are much stronger than me. They are not isolated. They have the entire Brazilian Armed Forces supporting them." At this point I was really tripping [viajando], thinking that they even had the U.S. Armed Forces, the most powerful nation in the world, backing them. With all of this strength and power, they still need

to torture me because they are weaker, morally they are weaker. You can call this rationalization or whatever, but the fact of the matter is that it worked for me. From the moment I thought in this way and thought that my death would not be in vain, I became much more relaxed. I was afraid, but I was more tranquil. I overcame that initial crisis.

Of course, no one registered this internal dialogue in the records of Niva's arrest. An invisible backdrop, it explains how Niva managed to foil his captors and maintain a consistent story. His recounting of the tale four decades later could also just as easily be a re-elaboration of those dreadful days to explain to himself how he managed to survive those horrific moments rather than a precise or accurate reflection of his thought processes as he confronted on-going torture. Nonetheless, as Niva's explanations to his interrogators unraveled, he finally admitted that he had had some peripheral connection to Ação Popular, but he continued to frame his involvement within the context of being a partisan of the liberal wing of the Methodist Church who sought to understand contemporary Brazilian problems.

As coincidence would have it, a young draftee and a member of the Methodist Church was assigned to guard duty at the OBAN headquarters. When he saw Niva in the prison, he was at first petrified, but at the end of his shift, he managed to carry out a rapid, furtive conversation with him. Niva told him to inform his family and members of the church. By this time, Niva's mother and sister had already realized that authorities had arrested Niva and were seeking him at different army and police facilities throughout the city. Church bishops also came to his assistance, attempting to visit him at the São Paulo torture center. Impudent officers, who had constructed a world vision in which anyone who sought out or supported those arrested must themselves be communists, rudely rebuffed the clerics.

After his release from prison, and facing the possibility of being re-arrested, Niva used what he later termed the "underground railroad," an ecumenical network of progressive religious people to get to Uruguay, where he stayed for a few days. He then passed through Argentina on his way to Chile, where he remained for a time. "I knew that a coup was a matter of time. The Chileans didn't believe it, but the Brazilians knew that it was only a matter of time." Because of his previous international work with the Methodist Church through its youth ministry, Niva had contacts with the National Council of Churches and a sister living in Washington. When he arrived in the nation's capital, Brady Tyson and a Methodist minister helped him get a scholarship at an English-language school that allowed him to extend his visa.

There he met Marcos Arruda, who had arrived in the city at around the same time. Both had been members of Ação Popular, but the clandestine nature of the organization and its compartmentalization meant that they had never met in São Paulo, although Niva heard about Marcos's treatment while he was in prison. They ended up staying in a house that was owned by the Presbyterian Church while Niva studied English. Their shared political affinities and perhaps their religious backgrounds provided perfect conditions for immediate political collaboration.

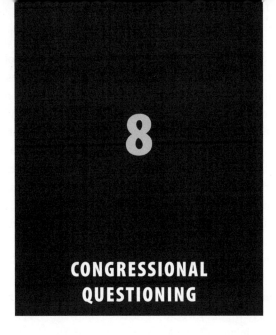

# 8

## CONGRESSIONAL QUESTIONING

It is far better for the United States to be on the side of the Brazilian people than on the side of a few generals who rule Brazil today by force and terror. — **Congressman Ron Dellums, August 3, 1971**

Senator Frank Church. FRANK CHURCH COLLECTION, BOISE STATE UNIVERSITY LIBRARY.

By the late 1960s, skepticism about Washington's foreign policy in Southeast Asia had moved gradually from campuses to Congress. Increasing numbers of liberal politicians began to rethink U.S. relations with Latin America as well. Senator William J. Fulbright of Arkansas and other members of Congress had had serious doubts about President Johnson's intervention in the Dominican Republic. Conservative Democrats and Republicans alike wondered whether the foreign aid to Latin America through the Alliance for Progress was actually meeting its stated objectives, namely, promoting reforms to head off revolution. As 1968 ended, the excessive measures of Institutional Act No. 5 focused certain attention on Brazil. Although the State Department's "review" of economic and military aid programs in the first semester of 1969 created the illusion that the new Nixon administration might sever close collaboration between the two governments, the decision in March 1969 to continue sending U.S. funds to Brazil diminished any hope that a new policy would come from the White House.

With former senator Wayne Morse no longer in the U.S. Congress, other august politicians slowly started to take his place, passing judgment publicly on the Brazilian government's policies and questioning further U.S. economic, military, and technical assistance to the military regime. In February 1969, Senator Charles Goodell, a liberal Republican from New York who had replaced Robert Kennedy in the Senate after he was assassinated in 1968, spoke out against the escalating repression in Brazil. Goodell had joined the growing minority of senators opposing the war in Vietnam, and his statement on Brazil read into the *Congressional Record*, like Morse's press release in 1965, registered outrage at the undemocratic measures and increasing deception of U.S. policy toward the country. In late 1966, as a member of the House of Representatives, Goodell had traveled to Brazil on an investigative tour. During his visit, he met with President-elect Costa e Silva, the right-wing politician Carlos Lacerda, Archbishop Hélder Câmara, labor leaders, U.S. AID technicians, and dozens of other Brazilians and U.S. citizens living there.[1] When Goodell reported on his tour of Brazil to his colleagues on the House floor in June 1967, he offered an optimistic appraisal of the situation in the country: "Mr. Costa e Silva expresses a strong belief in free government. He said there would be no further limitations of political rights after his inauguration. He flatly assured me that there would be political freedom."[2] The New York congressman also entered a detailed fifty-four-page report of his trip into the *Congressional Record* that assessed foreign military and economic aid to the country.

More than a year later, the new political situation in Brazil after the promulgation of Institutional Act No. 5 on December 13, 1968, alarmed Goodell. In a new statement read into the *Congressional Record*, the senator criticized the fact that the military had censored dispatches from *New York Times* reporting on events in Brazil. He lambasted the new measures depriving politicians of political rights for ten years, and he deplored the increased censorship of the Brazilian press. Questioning the democratizing effects of the Alliance for Progress, he noted: "The frequency of military coups throughout Latin America has been a disturbing feature of the history of that part of the world. Since 1961, there have been 16 coups in Latin America, resulting either in replacement of governments or suspensions of constitutions."[3] Goodell then called for a reconsideration of U.S. aid to Brazil. "When regression from the goals of the Alliance takes place in any place, as happened in Brazil, a careful reassessment of aid is in order to determine whether our aid in fact supports repression and whether termination or modification of aid would be efficacious in inducing a return to principles of the Alliance."[4] Goodell stopped short of proposing legislation to limit U.S. funding to Brazil. Instead, he expressed hope that Costa e Silva would change his ways and that the U.S. government would quickly appoint a new ambassador who "should go to his post with clear instructions to convey the disappointment of the government of the United States about Brazil's drift away from the basic practices of democracy and to work to influence a different direction for the future."

Mild as his proposals were, Goodell's statement marked the first time since the new authoritarian measures had gone into effect in Brazil that a member of the U.S. Congress had publicly criticized the regime and called for a possible reconsideration of normal aid funding. His statement, made in February 1969, provoked a sharp reaction from Foreign Minister Magalhães Pinto, who rejected such criticism of his country emanating from the U.S. Senate. "Brazil will not accept intervention in its internal affairs . . . criticisms by men who have only passed through our country will not alter our viewpoints or concern us."[5] The Brazilian military seized the *Jornal da Tarde* issue that had reprinted Goodell's statement. As U.S. State Department observers noted: "The For[eign] Min[ister]'s reaction to Goodell speech again demonstrates [the] extent of Brazilian sensitivity to foreign criticism and [the] fact that the speech had [a] real impact."[6] As the situation worsened in Brazil, more and more Congressional voices spoke out.[7]

### U.S. Aid to Latin America

After Morse's electoral defeat in 1968, Frank Church of Idaho assumed the chair of the Senate Foreign Relations Subcommittee on the Western Hemisphere. He took up this new assignment with gravity and dedication. In August 1969, he joined Charles Goodell, his Republican colleague from New York, in criticizing the military regime on the Senate floor, and he went much further than Goodell in his disapproval by characterizing the government as a military dictatorship: "This is no ordinary Latin American military junta. The military officers who are today running Brazil clearly intend to stay in power indefinitely and to impose their own kind of discipline on the country."[8] This was Church's first speech on the Senate floor denouncing the dictatorship, and it foreshadowed the approach he would take two years later when he would hold hearings about U.S. aid to the Brazilian government. The senator from Idaho pointed out that the Agency for International Development proposed furnishing $187 million in foreign assistance for the 1970 fiscal year, or 31 percent of all proposed assistance for the Alliance for Progress program. "[When] we furnish aid on a bilateral basis, we are inevitably closely identified with the government in power. We have not only furnished substantial economic assistance to the Costa e Silva government—and apparently intend to furnish even more—but worse, we have also supplied military training to its armed forces which are used in suppressing opposition to the regime."

Church worried that continued military assistance to Brazil could not only turn the opponents of that government against the United States but also alienate many Americans, especially the nation's youth. Stopping short of calling for a severance of relations with the country, Church nonetheless argued that Washington should "avoid identification as the political friend and economic prop of the present Brazilian regime." He concluded: "At the very least, of course, we should stop military assistance and withdraw our military missions."

Although Church offered a categorical condemnation of the U.S. government's backing of the regime led by Costa e Silva, the senator was by no means a radical. Among the early congressional doves, he remained a moderate voice within the flock. Because he represented the largely rural and traditionalist state of Idaho, Church had to walk a fine line between his criticisms of the Vietnam War, which dated back to 1965, and ensuring that he would not lose the support of his constituency. In his 1968 Senate reelection bid, a rabidly right-wing Republican challenged him. Nixon carried the state with 165,000 votes to Hubert Humphrey's 89,000. Yet in the senatorial race Church garnered 61 percent of the ballots cast.[9] It enabled him to continue his "independent" course in criticizing U.S. foreign policy in Southeast Asia and become more outspoken against Washington's policies in Latin America.

Church articulated his new approach to Latin America more explicitly soon after the kidnapping of Charles Elbrick, the U.S. ambassador to Brazil, in September 1969. In the closing speech at a conference of leading U.S. and Latin American development experts, Church called for a "drastic revision" of U.S. government policy on Latin America.[10] "The precipitous slide toward militarism in Latin America certainly underscores the failures of the political objectives of the Alliance of promoting democratic governments," Church declared. Arguing that "except for a handful of countries the Alliance funds have been used not to change the existing order but to benefit the existing elites," the Idaho Senator labeled President Kennedy's project for Latin America a "failure." Moreover, he insisted, current policies contributed "to the hostile and distorted image of the United States that now seems to be gaining such circulation in Latin America." As in his approach to Southeast Asia, Church suggested a withdrawal of the U.S. military presence and the replacement of bilateral economic aid with multilateral assistance. Church's remarks about Brazil and the rest of Latin America probably went unnoticed by his Idaho constituents. However, his comments annoyed conservative politicians and newspapers in Brazil. In São Paulo, U.S. consular officials, who maintained a complex web of connections among the economic and political elites of the city, reported that "conservative Paulistas" reacted negatively, and some even "furiously," to Church's statements on Brazil. They also considered his views about U.S. foreign policy as "'masochistic' and tantamount to 'national suicide.'"[11]

In April 1970, Church fine-tuned his views on Latin America in a major policy statement titled "Toward a New Policy for Latin America." Church called for more equitable trade agreements, an end to any future Dominican Republic–style military interventions, the development of multilateral aid assistance, and the cessation of military aid. Cognizant of the erosion of the faith among youth in the noble aims of American foreign policy, Church ended his speech by posing a central question regarding U.S. foreign aid. "When we pour our money into budgetary support for a notoriously authoritarian government, when we supply it with riot guns, tear gas, and mace, intelligent young Americans who still want to believe in our professed ideals, begin to ask elemental questions: 'If we are not *against* such dictatorships, then what is it we are *for* that really matters?'"[12]

### Kennedy Speaks Out

Church may have annoyed Brazilian politicians for the statements he made in 1969 and early 1970, but Senator Edward M. Kennedy's speech delivered at the University of Montana a week after Church's policy statement on Latin America provoked a fury in Brazil. As mentioned briefly in chapter 5, Mem de Azambuja Sá, a senator from the southern state of Rio Grande do Sul and a member of the pro-military government ARENA party, blasted Kennedy on the Senate floor in Brasília. He insisted that although "sadistic" elements may have infiltrated law enforcement agencies, the president, ministers, and governors had condemned the practice. The Brazilian Embassy in Washington prominently placed a transcript of Mem de Sá's speech on the first page of the bulletin that it circulated in the United States.[13] Obviously, the embassy wished to endorse the conservative Brazilian senator's closing words in his speech: "I emphasize what I have said precisely to state and guarantee that Mr. Kennedy doesn't speak for North America nor does he transmit the feeling of his people. Rather he implicates them unjustly."

Immediately following the transcription of Mem de Sá's speech, the embassy bulletin reported a statement made by U.S. commerce secretary Maurice Stans. The Nixon cabinet member visited the Ministry of Foreign Relations in Brasília the day after the State Department had held a press conference in which the spokesperson responded to questions about Kennedy's speech and outlined its position on reports of torture in Brazil. The Brazilian Embassy news brief reported that Stans "stated publicly that the government of President Nixon absolutely did not endorse the 'gross and unjust' criticisms that Kennedy had made against the Brazilian government." He added that the White House "valued the success achieved by the Brazilian authorities regarding political stability and economic progress." The slogan of "order and progress" that had been Brazil's motto since it was embossed on the Republican flag in 1889 was not only the mantra of the military regime; it had also become the justification for its support by its American allies to the north.

Even though Kennedy had presented his biting evaluation of the results of the Alliance for Progress and registered his sharp opposition to the support for authoritarian regimes in Latin America, he was in no position to assume a frontal assault on Brazil given the personal scandal about the Chappaquiddick incident that was rocking his career. Moreover, he was not a member of the Western Hemisphere Subcommittee that would have had direct jurisdiction over any Senate investigations about U.S. government policy in Brazil. Senator Frank Church proved a more likely candidate to take up the issue of Brazil. On June 25, 1970, the same day that the U.S. Catholic Conference and the National Council of Churches petitioned the Inter-American Commission on Human Rights to investigate abuses in Brazil, the NCC also sent a letter to Senator Church. Quoting the June 5, 1970 NCC statement denouncing torture in Brazil, the letter stated: "We call upon [the] Congress of the United States to schedule a Congressional Hearing on [the] effects of U.S. Government policy in Brazil, examining especially the nature and dimension of U.S. aid to determine to what extent public funds are used to support political repression in Brazil."[14]

Accompanying the letter and the NCC resolution on Brazil were copies of the articles that the loose network of clergy and scholars that had constituted the American Friends of Brazil had just published. They included William Wipfler's piece in *Christianity and Crisis*, Brady Tyson's feature article in the *Washington Post*, Ralph Della Cava's cover story in *Commonweal*, and Philippe Schmitter's critique of the punishment of Brazil academics published in PS, the newsletter of the American Political Science Association. These reprints offered abundant facts about the political and human rights situation in Brazil. The authors' academic and religious posts also underlined the legitimacy and mainstream nature of the accusations contained in the material and no doubt helped convince Senator Church and Pat Holt, the senior staff person on the Senate Foreign Relations Committee, to go ahead with the idea of holding a hearing about Brazil.

In a response to the NCC's letter, Senator Church wrote that he had been "much concerned by the reports of torture and political repression in Brazil" and thought that the idea of a hearing was a good one. However, he warned, "The full Foreign Relations Committee is so preoccupied with the situation in Southeast Asia that the prospects seem none too good."[15] He was a bit more optimistic in a memo to Holt, who was the Senate Foreign Relations Committee's expert on Latin America: "I think a hearing on the impact of the aid program in Brazil . . . is a good thing to do."

### The Church Hearings on Brazil

Pat Holt worked on the Senate Foreign Relations Committee staff from 1950 until his retirement in 1977. Soon after Richard M. Nixon's ill-fated tour of Latin America in 1950, Senator Wayne Morse, who chaired the Subcommittee on Latin America at the time, assigned Holt to work on the area. As Holt remembers it, Morse commented to him: "We're in trouble in Latin America. We've got to make an in-depth investigation to find out why and what to do about it."[16] During the 1971 hearing on U.S. policies and programs in Brazil, Holt was the staff person responsible for pulling the proceedings together. From the few documents in the archives of the Senate Foreign Relations Committee that deal with the 1971 Senate hearings, it is apparent that Brady Tyson also quietly worked behind the scenes to ensure that the Senate investigation would be as complete and in-depth as possible. From his office at American University, Tyson sent a series of notes to Holt, whom he addressed on an informal, first-name basis, offering reasons why the hearings should take place as soon as possible. Tyson pointed out, for example, that *Commonweal* planned to publish a response by Lincoln Gordon to Ralph Della Cava's strong critique of the former ambassador's involvement in the 1964 coup. "It's a good and very enlightening exchange. At long last, and at least, Gordon has become defensive about his role in 1964," he added. Tyson also suggested two of the "most significant people" who might testify at the hearing. One was Alfred Stepan, a professor of political science at Yale, who until 1969 had worked for the Rand Corporation and as an advisor to the National Security Council on the Interdepartmental Survey of U.S. Brazilian Relations. He was also a specialist on the Brazilian military. The other was Edward Hamlin, formerly of the CIA, who, according to Brady, was "appalled with U.S. support of Brazilian military fascism."[17]

In September 1970, Church leaked news of the plans to hold the hearing to Washington insider Jack Anderson, who published an announcement about the senator's intentions in his syndicated column.[18] "The United States has pumped almost $1.5 billion into the Brazilian military dictatorship, a regime that officially countenances the grisliest kinds of torture, sadism, and slow death. Even women and priests have been horribly, inhumanly abused. Their tormentors allegedly include Brazilian officers who have received military or police training in the U.S."[19] By suggesting that the U.S. government might have taught torture techniques to Brazilian security forces, Anderson was noticing allegations included in the International Commission of Jurists report of July 1970. Anderson reported that Church had requested that his staff draw up a "confidential detailed plan for hearings in January and February." Anderson added, "Nervous officials at the State Department, however, have begged Church not to give his findings a public airing. While they don't deny that torture has been permitted in Brazil, they claim the junta has become more moderate lately." The Washington muckraker concluded his column with a detailed description of the ordeal of Gisela Maria Cocenza Avelar, a Brazilian social worker tortured while in custody. The columnist explained that Church intended to determine if any of the officers identified in her mistreatment had received training in the United States. He also emphasized what would become a polemical element in the planning of hearings, namely, that Church's "purpose isn't to poke into Brazil's internal affairs but to find out whether U.S. funds help to subsidize the torturing."

Church made an official announcement of his intentions several days later. He then instructed his staff to prepare the groundwork for the hearings. Holt's original proposal to Church entailed an ambitious six-day schedule.[20] Holt recommended to Church that he focus on examining U.S. national interest in Brazil and "whether current U.S. policies are well-designed to protect and promote that interest." This meant engaging in a detailed examination of U.S. programs in the country. When news of the prospective Church hearings reached Brazil, the U.S. business community there immediately showed its displeasure. According to a State Department telegram, J. Irwin Miller, the chairman of the board of Cummins Engine, and other U.S. business leaders with interests in Brazil met with U.S. consular officials in São Paulo. They informed the State Department that "there was a strong consensus [among] U.S. business representatives—General Electric, Dow Chemical, Phillips Petroleum, J. Walter Thompson, Morgan Guaranty, Celanese Union Carbide, Cummins—that such investigation at this juncture could be extremely damaging to relations."[21] Apparently, Cummins, in the name of this group of U.S. investors in Brazil, wanted to persuade Senator Church that the investigation should be "closed and discreet."

As might have been expected, Brazilian government representatives in Washington were quite worried about the impact of the Church hearings on the public image of Brazil as well. As rumors of the proposed hearings spread through Washington, Brazilian Embassy officials speculated on the focus of the senatorial investigation. One Brazilian Foreign Service official informed Brasília that several congressional representatives were collecting data about alleged torture. He also expected that the hearing would investigate the case of the detained Vanderbilt professors the previous year and predicted that the incident would come out in the press.[22] In early January 1971, another senior Brazilian official in Washington explained to Brasília that in the previous year the embassy had spent considerable time countering the negative image of Brazil in the public arena and mass media in the wake of the activities of religious and academic associations and individuals. Efforts had been successful, the diplomat reported, largely due to the "spectacular economic growth that is well known here" and "the moderation with which the Brazil government treated the delicate question of the rescue of foreign diplomats kidnapped by terrorists." However, the Church hearings threatened to re-ignite the "anti-Brazilian" campaign.[23] To head off any possible damage, the Brazilian diplomat met with Pat Holt and Robert Dean, who was in charge of the Brazil desk at the State Department. In the meeting, Holt assured the Brazilians that they would not discuss internal Brazilian affairs but rather focus on U.S. programs in Brazil. Holt also let the Brazilian government know that he intended to visit the country on a brief fact-finding tour before holding the hearings.

## Gathering Evidence

Brady Tyson spent a considerable amount of time and energy offering back-channel advice to Pat Holt about the best ways to conduct the hearings. In a confidential memo to Holt, he suggested holding investigations that would answer the following questions:

1. Have U.S. AID Programs contributed significantly to the social and political development of Brazil?
2. Has the Public Safety Program been used, intentionally or unintentionally, to strengthen political repression in Brazil, including torture?
3. Have U.S. military aid and consultation and training programs contributed in any way to the rise of the Brazilian army to a dominant role in the Brazilian government?
4. Has the foreign policy of the United States, as manifested by its diplomatic representatives, tended to encourage the Brazilian government in its tendency to authoritarian and anti-democratic postures?
5. What should be U.S. diplomatic, military, and trade policy towards rightist military dictatorships in Latin America?[24]

In short, Tyson offered a comprehensive roadmap for how to conduct an investigation that would address all of the key issues raised by opponents of the military regime.

Over the course of several months, Holt and Tyson exchanged memos. The American University professor expanded his initial suggestions for possible witnesses and offered a long list of scholars, former diplomats, U.S. AID officials, and church leaders who had deep connections with Brazil and could testify about the current situation there. His intent seemed clear. If Senator Church called a broad range of experts on Brazil from the nation's leading universities, as well as government officials who had distanced themselves from current U.S. policies in Brazil and who in no way could be considered leftists, the investigation could act as significant pressure on the Brazilian government to change it policies toward internal dissent.

Among the names proposed by Tyson was John W. Tuthill, the former U.S. ambassador to Brazil who had replaced Gordon in 1966. Brady noted in his memo that "private information indicates that he is very eager to come back (from Italy) to testify, if it can be used to discuss what went wrong with

U.S. AID, and why the mil[itary] groups are too large." Pat Holt followed up on Tyson's suggestion and contacted the former ambassador to see if they could meet "whether on or off the record" about the period when Tuthill had been in Brazil.[25] Márcio Moreira Alves, Tyson's private source about Tuthill's willingness to talk, also contacted Holt about the matter. The former Brazilian congressional representative, who was then living in exile in Paris, had held informal discussions with Tuthill in Europe. Holt and Alves had met in Washington, when Alves had visited the Capitol to lobby against the military regime. As suggested by the warm personal tone of the letter, they had apparently developed a friendship. In a letter in March 1971 to Holt, Alves suggested that Tuthill would be an excellent witness. "He is the only high official I know of who has doubts about current policies towards Brazil. Moreover, he is definitely not a radical, which could produce a balanced statement and influence some of the less concerned Senators."[26]

Even though at the end the committee did not summon nongovernment witnesses to testify, several U.S. citizens who read about the proposed hearings, presumably in Jack Anderson's nationally syndicated column, voluntarily came forward to offer their testimony on the situation in Brazil. Catholic missionaries from Detroit who had worked with Archbishop Hélder Câmara in Recife offered to relate their understanding of "the reality of Brazil's military dictatorship" as well as "the part that the United States has played" in the country.[27] Rev. Darrell Rupiper, the American priest who had been arrested, charged with subversion, and then expelled from Brazil in December 1968, also indicated his willingness to be present.[28]

To prepare for the hearings, Pat Holt and Robert Dockery, another member of the Senate Foreign Relations Committee staff, spent two weeks in Brazil in mid-March 1971 gathering on-site information.[29] The U.S. Catholic Conference provided them with an extensive list of religious figures, mostly bishops and archbishops who had joined the opposition to the military regime.[30] During their trip, Holt and Dockery met primarily with U.S. Embassy officials and those attached to the U.S. AID, the United States Information Service, and the CIA.[31] Among Brazilian critics of the regime, they visited Professor Cândido Mendes, who worked with the Catholic Church's Peace and Justice Commission and had received Robert Kennedy when he toured Brazil in 1966.[32] Holt and Dockery also met with several U.S. journalists stationed in Brazil, including Joseph Novitsky of the *New York Times* and Kay Huff of *Time* magazine. After meetings in Brasília, Rio de Janeiro, and São Paulo, Holt went on to Porto Alegre in the south and Dockery flew to the Northeast before traveling back to the United States. During the hearings, Church gave the two staff members ample leeway to interview the witnesses, and it is obvious from the interrogations that the visit to Brazil had been a crash course informing them about the latest developments in the government's repressive campaign against the opposition. While Church asked the big questions, Holt and Dockerty engaged in detailed follow-up queries to State Department and Pentagon officials about U.S. government operations in Brazil.

When Holt and Dockery returned from their fact-finding mission to Brazil in April 1971, they began to put the finishing touches on preparations for the hearings. The committee asked witnesses to prepare responses to two main questions: "What is your view of the U.S. national interest in Brazil? What U.S. policies would best promote that interest?"[33] Because the hearings might address sensitive intelligence questions, the senator conducted them behind closed doors. Although the Senate released a sanitized transcript of the hearings in July 1971 with the title "United States Policies and Programs in Brazil," responses to some of the more provocative questions remain classified.[34]

### Police Training

Kicking off the first session held on May 4, Church emphasized the question of nonintervention in domestic issues. "How Brazilians organize their own affairs and how they treat each other are no proper concern of the U.S. Senate," Church insisted.[35] He then called on Theodore D. Brown, the chief of the AID public safety program in Brazil, and initiated a line of questioning designed to determine what, if any, role the United States had in training the Brazilian police in techniques that were in turn used to repress or torture Brazilian oppositionists.

After Brown gave a general overview of the program, Church got to the point—why was the United States training Brazilian police? Brown explained that the Office of Public Safety Program was designed to teach "modern techniques in the handling of people, whether it be crowd control or whether it be investigations" and that the program had been especially helpful in teaching "the minimum use of force" and "humane methods." Church immediately rebutted, "In light of the many reports that we hear of torture in Brazil, do you think you have been successful in inculcating humane methods in restraint?" Brown insisted that the United States had been successful in that regard. Church then pressed the chief public safety adviser about whether he had heard reports about the torture of prisoners by the Brazilian police. Brown admitted that he had discussed the issue with the director general of the Brazilian police, who had assured him that the Brazilian government did not condone such actions. Not satisfied with Brown's answer, Church retorted, "If you have been concerned about it and have had many discussions with Brazilian authorities, then what is the basis for your statement that you think the training program has been successful in inculcating methods of humane treatment?"

Even though the give-and-take between U.S. government officials and the senator and his staff continued for several hours, the two sides reached a standoff. Brown insisted that he had no direct knowledge of torture. Every time Church or Holt pushed him on the U.S. government's participation in "internal security" matters, Brown skirted the questions. He stated he knew nothing about DOI-CODI, the government's antisubversion operations. When Church raised the question of why police were using riot control gas masks with U.S. government insignias on them to control student protests at the University of Brasília in 1968, the State Department supplied a surrealistic answer: The Brazilian army had loaned the equipment to the military police without the U.S. government's knowledge. When the press reported that the police had been using U.S. supplies to repress student demonstrations, the U.S. AID Public Safety advisors discussed the issue with the secretary of Public Safety for the Federal District. Rather than returning the equipment to the army, they merely painted over the U.S. markings with black paint. In short, the U.S. police advisers had not seen human rights abuses, knew nothing about the police organizations that coordinated antiguerrilla activities, and were merely advising the police on nonpolitical operations.

Martha K. Huggins has argued convincingly in Political Policing that rather than making the Brazilian police more humane and respectful of citizen's rights, U.S. foreign police assistance programs did just the opposite: "'Modernization' and 'professionalization' have unintended (or sometimes intended) consequences that contradict the assumption that these processes always lead to greater constraint on police toward legality and justice." [36] According to Huggins's analysis of declassified sections of the 1971 Church hearings, the Central Intelligence Agency recommended "that the commanders of Brazil's four armies assume full responsibility for and control of all security elements—and that all-out war be declared on terrorists immediately." [37] Subsequently, the military established the DOI-CODI that organized police and military security forces into a coordinated national network to combat "subversion." DOI-CODI became one of the prime operational units for torture in Brazil. Although Church and Holt pounded Brown and CIA director Richard Helms about these issues, both officials ducked responsibility for any direct U.S. involvement in the torture of political prisoners by Brazilian police or paramilitary death squads.

### Why Such AID?

Another major part of the Church hearings focused on the U.S. Agency for International Development Program (USAID), at the time the third-largest foreign assistance program after support given to South Vietnam and India. Here Church represented two divergent views on foreign aid—that of a liberal Democrat who questioned providing assistance to a repressive regime and that of a senator from a conservative state who questioned the efficacy of spending taxpayers' dollars to help foreign countries. William A. Ellis, the director of USAID Brazil, defended the $2.1 billion in U.S. economic assistance received by Brazil during the fiscal years 1962–70, 60 percent of which came in the form of AID grants and loans with low interest rates and long grace amortization periods.[38] As discussed in chapter 1, before the military takeover in 1964, the Alliance for Progress used some of its aid to support conservative governors in election bids against pro-Goulart forces.[39] After the military came to power, they also released significant loans to help stabilize the new regime, and other aid programs expanded accordingly.

During the questioning Church pushed Ellis to articulate the U.S. national interests in providing such large amounts of support for a military government. Ellis explained that American aid had helped to stabilize the Brazilian economy, thus creating a favorable climate for U.S. private investment. Assistance oriented toward social and economic development also promoted political stability, which furthered U.S. security interests. Finally, humanitarian aid acted as a gesture to strengthen the close relationship between the two countries.[40] In testimony on the final day of hearings, U.S. ambassador Rountree reiterated Ellis's arguments.[41]

### Ripple Effects

Two months after Senator Church had concluded the hearings, he released a statement to the press along with published transcripts of the three-day investigation, with the CIA director's testimony and other responses sanitized from the text. The press release addressed the immediate issue related to the investigation—whether the U.S. military or police programs were linked to the repression of domestic opposition. Church declared that the subcommittee had found no direct connection. "However, the hearings do reveal what, in my personal judgment, is an altogether too close identification of the United States with the current Brazilian Government, and they raise a serious question about the wisdom of assistance to the Brazilian police and military."[42] Church criticized what he considered the lack of control by U.S. aid officials on the ultimate use of the training and equipment provided the Brazilian military and police. The statement also questioned the reasons for such close collaboration between the two nations, wondering what positive effect it had achieved other than to assure a safe business climate in Brazil for U.S. investors. Moreover, Church pointed out, the Brazilian government disagreed with many of Washington's international policies, refused to sign the Non-Proliferation Treaty, and had recently walked out of the OAS meeting that was discussing a new antiterrorist agreement. Finally, Church called attention to economic relations between the two countries. "We spent $2 billion of public money, among other purposes, to contribute to a favorable climate for investment of $1.7 billion in private money. Furthermore, the net effect of this private investment has been to take more money out of Brazil in the form of profits than has been put into Brazil in the form of new capital." In answers to questions from the press, the senator emphasized that he favored multilateral aid and an end to military aid that did not serve U.S. global strategy but rather controlled domestic dissidents.

Brazilian ambassador Araújo Castro had already prepared a statement criticizing the hearing results before their official release. "Senator Church's remarks as they have been reported to me certainly do not reflect either an accurate knowledge or a valid interpretation of the real situation of my country and certainly do not help in the cause of promoting understanding between friendly nations."[43] The declaration denounced any interference in internal Brazilian affairs.[44] The State Department also distanced itself from the Church hearings' findings. Spokesperson Charles Bray defended long-term U.S.-sponsored activities in Brazil: "A constant in our relations with Brazil over the years has been our programs of technical and economic cooperation designed to assist that country in its economic and social development and in the improvement of the quality of life of its people."[45]

Although several Brazilian accounts of the hearings mentioned the fact that accusations of torture were a subject of inquiry, the thrust of the criticisms was against an alleged interference in internal Brazilian affairs. The mainstream press, still predominantly prodictatorship in spite of certain conflicts over press censorship, sided with a nationalistic defense that turned the Brazilian government into the victim rather than the perpetrator. Moreover, the Brazilian press largely ignored Church's economic criticism of U.S.-Brazilian relations, which pointed out that U.S.-based companies took out more profits than they invested in the country. This was a standard complaint of Brazilian nationalists from the 1950s and 1960s that Church's statement seemed to echo.

In some ways, one could argue that the Church hearings contributed to the reconfiguration of relations between the two countries. Nationalistic posturing as a means of repelling international denunciations of human rights abuses combined with a shift in U.S. foreign policy priorities in the 1970s. A strengthened Brazilian economy and the acquisition of ample military training and hardware had enabled the military regime to begin to distance itself from such a close reliance on Washington. Pat M. Holt considered that the Church hearings "laid the basis for a movement which developed and which eventually led to the abolition of public safety program by law."[46] As momentum mounted to limit U.S. support for the dictatorship, the generals had already reached a threshold of economic development and military independence that offset the negative impact of such legislative measures. Nevertheless, the question of whether the United States government should provide economic and military assistance to Brazil had become a moral issue related to contested views about the future of U.S. foreign policy.

### Attempting to Slash Aid: The Dellums Amendment

The Church hearings did not provide conclusive evidence of the direct link between Office of Public Safety funds and the training of torturers by U.S. officials. Nonetheless, the close linkage between U.S. economic and military aid to Brazil and the perception that this translated into political support for the regime provided ample arguments for cutting off Washington's aid to the country. Representative Ron Dellums, the progressive African American Democrat from Oakland, California, who also represented liberal and radical Berkeley constituents, took the legislative initiative. Dellums used the Organization of American States' Human Rights Commission investigations as the basis for trying to limit executive leeway in arms sales to the military regime. With the support of Minnesota congressman Donald Fraser, Dellums presented an amendment to the Foreign Assistance Act of 1972 that stated: "No assistance shall be furnished under this or any other Act, and no sales shall be made under the Foreign Military Sales Act, to Brazil until such time as the President reports to the Congress that the Inter-American Commission on Human Rights has determined that the Government of Brazil is not engaging in the torture of political prisoners."[47]

Unlike Church, Dellums did not have to worry that his constituency might object to his political views. Since his arrival in the House of Representatives in early 1971 he had positioned himself as a leading voice for numerous progressive causes.[48] His defense of the proposal to cut off aid to Brazil until the U.S. government could clarify question of human rights violations presented a powerful argument:

> Someday the military will go back to their barracks, and the Brazilian people will have the right to ask, "Who supported this oppressive government, that tortured our young people, that censored our press, that circled our Congress building with troops and tanks because one Congressman dared to criticize the army during a session, and Congress—quite correctly—refused to accede to military pressures and stripped that Congressman of his congressional immunity so he could be tried in a military court?"[49]

The California representative also proposed a procedure that Congress would adopt several years later, namely, the cessation of aid until a report on the status of human rights in the country assured the body that the U.S. government was not supporting a repressive regime.

Dante Fascell, the chairman of the House Foreign Affairs Subcommittee of Inter-American Affairs, then rose to speak against the amendment. Fascell, a Florida Democrat who generally supported liberal issues in Congress, was much more conservative when it came to Latin America. He was also the House expert on the countries to the south of the United States, fluent in Spanish, and a powerful politician.[50] His line of defense against cutting off aid to Brazil followed the standard arguments articulated at times by the State Department and other times by Brazilian supporters of the military regime, and sometimes by both. "The government of President Médici is a popular one. It is riding a wave of rapid economic growth—nine percent annually over the past three years. It has demonstrated its concern for social as well as economic development. It has embarked upon popular programs to improve living conditions and develop Brazil's drought-stricken northeast area and its vast Amazon basin—including programs for land reform and agricultural colonization."[51] While torture had taken place in Brazil on occasion, the Brazilian government was attempting to curb it. The Brazilian and international media amply aired this issue, and the United States government had spoken to high-ranking officials expressing their concern. Moreover, the Brazilian government was preparing a response to allegations made to the Inter-American Commission on Human Rights. "Certainly there have been police excesses just as there have been police excesses right here in the United States. But let's put this in perspective."[52] Fascell concluded by stating: "None of us condones or justifies the abuses which have occurred but we must recognize the distinction between the deliberate programs of torture and individual overreactions, as reprehensible as they are, to acts of robbery and terror." The House defeated the proposal by a voice vote.

### Back in the Senate

As the anti–Vietnam war mood deepened in Congress, a growing number of doves took up other issues that reinforced their opposition to the Nixon administration's foreign policy. Although Dellums's amendment got nowhere in the 1971 Congress, the next year members of both houses introduced amendments to Foreign Assistance Acts to limit all funding to Brazil as long as the practice of torture continued. Liberal California Democrat John Tunney took the initiative in the Senate and followed the language Dellums proffered the year before in the House.[53] Most of the leading "peace" politicians in the Senate cosponsored the amendment.

As Tunney defended the amendment, he laid out the main principle behind all future similar human rights legislation: "I would think that it would be a universal proposition that the United States should not support with military assistance any government which is using torture as an instrument of national policy."[54] Tunney went on to argue clearly and concisely why Congress should limit aid to Brazil: "I can think of nothing in tradition which would justify our providing military assistance to a regime which tortures its own citizens. I cannot understand the rationale which would support the contention that torture should be overlooked by American policymakers; that the United States should continue to provide military support to a government which, using the excuse of anticommunism, abuses, mistreats, and represses its own citizens."

Compelling as their arguments may have been, the liberal Democrats in the Senate did not have a majority. Rather than voting the amendment down, and therefore registering an all-out defeat, those in favor of cutting off military aid to Brazil allowed a procedure that tabled the motion. All told, approximately, one-third of the Senate favored severing military aid to Brazil. This was a significant vote even though the amendment was defeated. Liberal Democrats had coalesced around the cause of human rights in Latin America in numbers that were not unlike those of the core coalition opposed to the Vietnam War. They seemed immune to Cold War anticommunist rhetoric that insisted on the support of authoritarian regimes as the first line of defense against subversion and terrorism. Those most concerned with this issue were building a base of support as a first significant step toward cutting military ties with the dictatorship.

On the other hand, the Nixon administration continued to characterize such Senate proposals as "interference in Brazil's domestic affairs." Supporters of military aid to Brazil considered that counterinsurgency and police riot control training programs were legitimate and "neutral" requests, whereas opponents saw this aid as crass collaboration with the maintenance of a repressive police apparatus that included torture among its arsenal of weapons to contain opponents. Moreover, this issue pitted the legislative and the executive bodies against each other precisely at a moment when Congress was trying to wrest power away from the White House over foreign policy. Thus, the Department of State insisted that the "Senate vote is not [an] appropriate vehicle for expression of U.S. concern over continuation of [the] mistreatment [of] political prisoners."[55] While declaring that they shared the Senate's concern on the matter, State Department officials indicated that they would "continue efforts to defeat expression of public criticism through Senate vote." They also emphasized in internal communications that "it [is] particularly important [that the] GOB [Government of Brazil] not misunderstand our position." In other words, quiet diplomacy would pressure the Brazilian government to change its ways and limit the incidents of torture.

### A Second Try in the House

Tunney managed to muster a third of his colleagues to back his amendment in the Senate. Dellums had not built a similarly sized contingent in the House willing to limit U.S. aid to Brazil. Nonetheless, in his second attempt to pass an amendment to the foreign aid bill, Dellums defended the measure directly. "When I offered the amendment last year, we were assured that the brutal repressive policies in Brazil were merely local overreactions to difficult problems . . . It would be difficult to deny that recourse to torture is systematic policy on the part of the Brazilian Government. I have newspaper articles here dated June 1972, which tell of torture, censorship, and repression. We simply can no longer fool ourselves that the regime is merely going through growing pains."[56]

As in the previous year, Representative Dante Fascell of Florida rose to defend continued aid to the military regime, arguing against Dellums's amendment with curious moral, pragmatic, and diplomatic objections. First, he insisted, torture and violence were part of human life. Second, given the rapid economic growth of Brazil, the effect of terminating U.S. aid would have "relatively marginal importance." Cutting aid, Fascell pointed out, would harm the people of Brazil who received benefits from U.S. foreign assistance programs. Finally, singling out Brazil would be politically and diplomatically unwise since "it might actually rally a great many Brazilians with a sense of nationalism to the defense of the present government and then have a result opposite to that which the gentleman from California is seeking." In response, Dellums reminded the congressional representative from Florida that the House had successfully passed a bill cutting off aid to Greece in spite of the similar arguments presented against taking that step. After a few minutes of further similar debate, the Dellums amendment was defeated by a resounding 325 votes to 65, with 42 not voting.[57] Clearly, the overwhelming majority of House members did not yet buy the arguments presented by Dellums. Perhaps, in part, this was due to the fact that the messenger was thought by many of his colleagues to be a radical African American activist whose far-left proposals and unorthodox comportment had no place within the halls of Congress. Despite Dellums's failure, the tide was turning. Congress would soon pass its first law limiting foreign aid based on human rights considerations.

### Toward Human Rights Legislation

A week after the military coup in Chile on September 11, 1973, Representative Donald M. Fraser from Minnesota introduced H.R. 10455 to establish a Bureau of Humanitarian Affairs within the State Department. The bill proposed the creation of a new assistant secretary of state for humanitarian affairs directed to advise the department on all matters having significant human rights implications. The resolution also called for the termination of "all military assistance and sales to any government committing serious violations of human rights" and the suspension of "any economic assistance directly supportive of the government committing such violation."[58] Throughout the fall of 1973, Fraser, the chair of the Subcommittee on International Organizations and Movements of the House Committee on Foreign Affairs, conducted fifteen days of hearings with forty-five witnesses on the international protection of human rights throughout the globe. Prominent among the countries examined were Brazil and Chile.[59]

According to the political scientist Lars Schoultz, scholars credit the Fraser hearings with firmly establishing the congressional concerns for human rights. During the subsequent 94th Congress (1975–76), Fraser held forty other hearings related to eighteen countries. Schoultz argues that these investigations catapulted Fraser into a leadership position on the question of human rights in the House of Representatives. The detailed, thorough, and authoritative manner in which Congressman Fraser and his staff assistant John Salzberg conducted the hearings made him the human rights expert in the House. This served to offset the power and influence of Dante Fascell, the Latin American specialist who had opposed Dellums's amendments in 1971 and 1972. Fraser's acquired legitimacy strengthened his position in the House Committee on Foreign Affairs negotiations about aid authorization. Furthermore, with the White House continuing to drag its feet in responding to growing popular interest in using the issue of human rights as a yardstick in foreign policy matters, Fraser's subcommittee hearings offered an important forum for the investigation of human rights violations.[60] Among those experts testifying during the 1973 hearings was Tom Quigley of the Latin American Bureau of the U.S. Catholic Conference. He emphasized the experiences that he and others had had following the cases that they had presented to the Inter-American Commission on Human Rights. Quigley's testimony served to emphasize the fact that despite claims by the Brazilian government and its supporters abroad, the incidence of torture and human rights violations had not declined in Brazil.[61]

Like Dellums's amendments to the Foreign Assistance Act of 1971 and 1972, Fraser's proposal for a Bureau of Humanitarian Affairs in the Department of State failed to win serious support in the House.[62] In 1975, a coalition of liberal congressional representatives and isolationists opposed to any U.S. foreign aid pushed through the first significant legislation that halted economic aid to countries engaged in gross violations of human rights. Presented by liberal Democrat congressman Tom Harkin of Iowa, the amendment to the International Development and Food Assistance Act of 1975 garnered the support of conservative House representatives who argued that, as long as Congress was unwilling to slash foreign aid altogether, it should at least limit aid to repressive regimes. In the Senate, liberal senators George McGovern and James Abourezk of South Dakota offered a similar amendment to the Senate foreign aid authorization bill during the floor debate. It passed by a voice vote.[63] Human rights activists finally had a legal leverage with which to hold Congress and the White House accountable.

Admittedly, most of the impetus for this new legislation did not come directly from the campaigns of the early 1970s about Brazil. The scope of interest in human rights had broadened considerably since Márcio Moreira Alves and Brady Tyson meandered through the corridors of Congress in 1969 seeking sympathetic senators to hear their case. Even though activists working on Brazil had managed to influence the news media enough that they consistently reported on and condemned the ongoing violation of human rights in Brazil, developments in Chile created a new political moment for those working on Latin America. The crisis of confidence in the U.S. government provoked by the Vietnam War and the Watergate scandal that surfaced in 1973 offered new possibilities for human rights activists. The standard State Department justifications for backing repressive regimes no longer held up so successfully. The anticommunist discourse of the early 1960s that had been the driving rationale for the Alliance for Progress was waning. By the mid-1970s, a new agenda emphasizing human rights had entered the political arena.

# CAPÍTULO VIII

## "While my eyes go looking for flying saucers in the sky"

I'm wandering round and round nowhere to go.
I'm lonely in London, London is lovely so.

**Caetano Veloso, "London, London," 1970**

Anti–Vietnam War demonstration, Washington. PHOTO BY FRANK WOLFE. LYNDON B. JOHNSON LIBRARY.

In April 1970, U.S. forces invaded Cambodia. Although the Pentagon had been operating secretly in both Laos and Cambodia, President Nixon's public announcement acknowledged the expansion of the conflict from Vietnam to neighboring Southeast Asian countries. Almost immediately, protests erupted on campuses everywhere. After the slaying of four students by nervous, trigger-happy National Guard units on Ohio's Kent State University campus, students nationwide walked out of classrooms and professors cancelled classes in what became a general strike of colleges and universities against the war. Millions mobilized demanding the withdrawal of U.S. troops from Southeast Asia, but the White House seemed indifferent to public protests.

Anti–Vietnam War sentiment, however, increased over the next year throughout the country. In the spring of 1971, pacifist, left-wing, and other political forces forged a shaky alliance that produced the largest mass protests to that date. On April 24, a million people marched on the Capitol demanding an end to the war. The following week, escalating civil disobedience actions in front of the White House and diverse government agencies designed to "shut down business as usual" brought tens of thousands of arrests. Washington, D.C. jails overflowed with anti-war protesters.[1]

During these tumultuous times, Loretta Merkel and Harry Strharsky, who had been involved in civil rights and antiwar activities before and after their work in the Dominican Republic, independently reflected about the future. They arrived at a similar conclusion. The conservative, hierarchical, and authoritarian nature of the Roman Catholic Church made it an unsuitable environment for their growing desire to address, as Harry articulated, "the injustices that we perceived in society, the gulf between the rich and the poor, the less-than-desirable distribution of wealth, the poverty in the cities, and racism." Both decided to leave the Church, and they talked of marriage. A chance encounter gave their lives a new direction and became what Harry described as a "second fork in the road." Father Louis Colonnese, the director of the Latin American Bureau of the U.S. Catholic Conference, passed through Milwaukee on a speaking tour. "I liked the things that he said because it was very different from what Church leaders said in the community in which I had grown up."[2] Harry went up to speak to Father Colonnese after his talk and asked if he could join the priest's call for participating in his social justice activities related to Latin America. Colonnese invited him to Washington to interview for a job as director of the library and research with the Latin American Bureau. "I jumped at it and went out in May of 1971 when they were having the biggest [anti-war] demonstration and were rounding up people in

RFK Stadium. . . . I had to fight my way to get to the place, running from the cops to get to the interview. They offered me the job, so I went to Washington, D.C." Loretta and Harry had recently married, and they made the joint decision to embark on this new adventure. "We didn't have any commitments, and so this was a great opportunity," Loretta recalled.

When the Brazilian government forced Brazilian singer/songwriter Caetano Veloso to leave his country for exile in London in 1969, he, too, found himself in a nation's capital that seemed to him at times as surrealistic as Harry Strharsky's visit to Washington, although for quite different reasons.[3] The lyrics of the first two songs he wrote after leaving Brazil, "A Little More Blue" and "London, London," capture the melancholic bewilderment he experienced meandering through the crowds of his new, albeit temporary, home, as he attempted to adapt to new people and their culture, which, while somewhat familiar, also seemed distant from what he had known. Accustomed to Brazil's repressive atmosphere, he was overwhelmed at times by his newfound sense of freedom. In one line of his mellifluous snapshot of someone "lonely in London without fear," he noticed the strangeness of seeing a group of people approach a policemen, who "seems so pleased to please them," that it left him lost, transfixed, and searching for "flying saucers in the sky."

For Harry, coming to Washington also provoked a kind of dizziness, similarly linked to the excitement of being in an almost magical new environment. He remembered his first day on the job. "I went to lunch with Louis Michael Colonnese, who had hired me, with Mary Lou Suhor, who subsequently ran the Cuban Resource Center in New York, with Marcos [Arruda] — it was his first day in the United States — and Margarita [Marjorie] Melville who had just gotten out of prison for the Catonsville 9." It was a cast of characters that represented the different strains in the Catholic left in the early 1970s. Colonnese had taken the Latin American Bureau in a radically different direction from the days in the early 1960s when it had backed an anticommunist crusade in Latin America. Marjorie Melville, a Maryknoll missionary, had heeded the call and gone to Guatemala to minister to the poor. She ended up supporting the guerrilla forces there. As a result, the government expelled her from the country. She returned to the United States, where she joined eight other radical Catholics in publicly destroying draft board records in Catonsville, Maryland, in protest of the war in Vietnam. No doubt, that day, as she enjoyed freedom after having served a two-year prison sentence, she was as euphoric and disoriented as Harry remembers he was.[4]

Marcos Arruda cannot recall the details of that lunch when he met Harry on the first day that he was in the United States. He had left Brazil against his will, simply to avoid being arrested again and risking further torture. His mother had insisted that it would be better for him to be in the United States, where he would be safe and could receive medical treatment. Marcos, however, felt tremendously guilty because he was suddenly living in a country of such wealth and abundance while his friends and comrades still languished in Brazil's prisons.[5]

Harry's and Marcos's first encounter that day marked the beginning of a remarkable friendship. Over the years, they built a bond of brotherhood that has lasted to this day. No one can remember exactly when it happened, but some time after that lunch on Harry's first day at the Latin American Bureau of the U.S. Conference of Bishops and Marcos's first day in the United States, they, Loretta, and others began planning activities to protest Brazilian president Médici's visit to the White House, scheduled to take place later that year. At some point in the summer or fall of 1971, Marcos, Harry, Loretta, and a handful of people also founded the Committee against Repression in Brazil—CARIB.

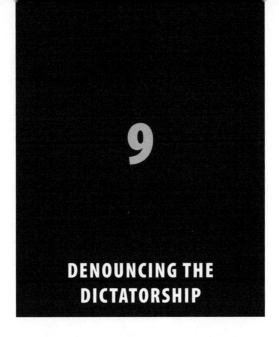

# 9

# DENOUNCING THE DICTATORSHIP

We didn't care whether we could make an impact; at least this was my idea. We just wanted someone to listen to us . . . We didn't have any hope of changing anything, but for my conscience, I couldn't stand by and let no one know that these things were happening. —**Paul Silberstein, collaborator,** *Brazilian Information Bulletin*

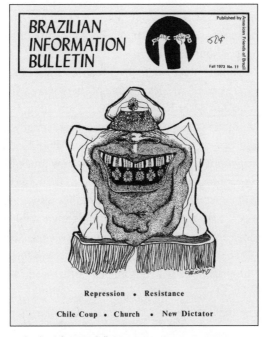

*Brazilian Information Bulletin.* REPRINTED BY PERMISSION OF THE COMMITTEE AGAINST REPRESSION IN BRAZIL (CARIB), HARRY AND LORETTA STRHARSKY.

In December 1970, militants of a guerrilla organization kidnapped the Swiss ambassador Giovanni Enrico Bucher, demanding the release of seventy political prisoners, the publication of a revolutionary manifesto, the freezing of prices for ninety days, and the suspension of fares on the Rio de Janeiro commuter trains to the poor and working-class suburbs. After a long period of negotiations, the military regime met their first demand but ignored the rest. Seventy revolutionaries and their families boarded a Brazilian airplane and were flown to Chile in January 1971. In Chile, they joined hundreds of compatriots who had left or fled the country in the aftermath of the 1964 coup. The same month that the Brazilian exiles and their families landed in Santiago, Saul Landau and Haskell Wexler were in Chile filming a documentary titled *Conversation with Allende* about the new democratically elected socialist president. By chance, while in Chile they also made a documentary about Brazil. Almost thirty-five years later, Landau recalled how they decided to make the film: "We read in the newspaper that seventy Brazilians had been flown to Santiago from Brazil in exchange for the Swiss ambassador, and so Haskell said, 'Why don't we check it out?' So, we went down to the place where the Chilean government had housed the newly arrived Brazilians. We told them who we were and that we wanted to make a film for the United States about what had happened to them in Brazil."[1] All of the Brazilians had been tortured, and the two filmmakers wanted to tell their story. "I think that the main purpose in doing the film was to bring to the attention of the American public the fact that torture had become a routine and systematic procedure in Brazil and that the U.S. government was backing a regime that was engaging in this kind of activity." As it turns out, *Brazil: A Report on Torture* was the first documentary film ever to record testimony about the use of torture on Latin American political prisoners.[2]

In the film, Landau interviewed seventeen of the released Brazilians. "Some of them were unable to speak; some of them were still in a traumatic state, literally unable to describe anything or say anything, but others in the film I think were quite articulate. It turns out that it really was a film not so much about torture as it was about heroism and political courage." Reflecting on the experience, Landau was struck by how much his participants wanted to show graphically what had happened to them in prison. "We had to restrain them in the recreation of the torture. They wanted to go in a much more realistic way . . . They wanted to show how truly terrible it was, and we said, 'Take it easy. People can imagine' . . . There was one scene which they insisted on—we were a little queasy, Haskell and I—where a rope is tied around one of the prisoner's testicles and the prisoner has to remain in a forty-five-degree angle propped up on his hands because if he lets go, he literally castrates himself because the rope is hanging from the ceiling. And we said, 'OK, that's enough,' and he said, 'No, no, you can tighten it, get in close.' They really wanted people to see the incredible brutality of it, and we said [that] people have good imaginations."

The final version of the documentary is a series of intimate interactions between the director and cameraman and the Brazilian revolutionaries who relate and then reenact the kinds of torture they had endured. As a given former political prisoner demonstrates the treatment that she or he received, others intervene with comments of what happens to the victim while the display of torture techniques takes place. One man strips to his underwear and then his comrades bind his hands to his feet, place a metal pole through the crux, and recreate the parrot's perch. A young woman is gagged and hung by her legs while others simulate a beating and demand half seriously that she turn her comrades in. A man reveals a scarred back, while another demonstrates with an unlighted cigarette how burns were inflicted on him to reveal information. The chaotic nature of the former political prisoners' demonstrations and the almost matter-of-fact way in which they relate what had happened to them while in prison lends authenticity to their denunciations. There is no doubt in the minds of the viewing audience that they are telling the truth.

One can assume that the almost lighthearted joking that accompanies their demonstrations served to deflect the emotional and physical traumas they had experienced while imprisoned and possibly relived as they recounted their stories. One notices personal anxieties as some relay what had taken place in jail. When Frei Tito (Tito de Alencar Lima), a young Dominican friar, retells the story of his arrest and torture, his eyes focus downward, as if he cannot face the camera and the pain of reliving those moments. On the other hand, Maria Auxiliadora Lara Barcellos, a self-proclaimed member of a revolutionary organization, speaks calmly as she gazes directly into the camera and describes the physical and sexual abuse that some female political prisoners received while incarcerated. She tranquilly explains why she decided to take up arms and defend herself when surrounded by the police.

Jean Marc Von der Weid, who had been elected the president of the UNE while the national student organization operated underground and had been charged by the government with various crimes, including coordinating nationwide demonstrations against Nelson Rockefeller's visit to Brazil in 1969, offers a passionate and articulate denunciation of the dictatorship. In another moving scene, Luís Alberto Sanz describes the situation of a childhood friend, who at the time was still imprisoned in Brazil. "Marcos [Arruda] was a trained geologist, one of the brightest students in his class, and an ex-seminarian who almost became a priest . . . After a long struggle in Brazil, Marcos came to feel that his profession as a geologist made no sense in a country like ours. It made no sense because the ones who control research are the American companies, and they don't really want people to do mining or oil research, so Marcos became a worker, a machinist in São Paulo."[3] In a rare moment in the film, in which one of the interviewees allows himself to express deep emotions and break through a calm and serious façade, Luís Alberto goes on to describe Marcos's arrest and torture. His throat tightens in an apparent attempt to hold back tears as he declares, "Marcos's situation today is that his left leg is paralyzed, and he can't say even one whole word—he stammers very badly when he talks. The only thing Marcos is guilty of is giving up being a geologist and becoming a machinist."[4]

Although many of those interviewed explain in general terms the reasons why they were fighting against the dictatorship, they offer little political context for their stories. Contrary to Laudau's intentions, the film relies more on an emotional connection between the viewer and the revolutionary protagonists than on an intellectual exposition about what was going on in Brazil at the time. Yet the audience is drawn into the drama, and the cast of characters seemingly comprises sincere, "good people." Their humanity permeates the film. Maria Auxiliadora, who becomes the featured personality in the documentary, captures the empathy of viewers with her youthful beauty, revolutionary dedication, and calm determination.

After Wexler and Landau had edited the film, they tried to screen it on public television. "It got very little play," Landau recalled. Nationwide, public television stations refused to air the documentary. "No arguments. Just said, 'Sorry, not interested.'" During the summer of 1971, activists organized a public showing of the film in Washington. An official of the Brazilian Embassy discreetly attended the event and reported on its content to his or her superiors. Upon receiving information about the documentary, the Brazilian minister of foreign affairs ordered the Ministry of Justice to deny visas to Landau or Wexler, should they attempt to enter Brazil.[5]

New York public television finally aired the film. By that time, Marcos Arruda was safely out of Brazil and living in Washington. He had undergone physical therapy to improve his health. He had also founded the Committee against Repression in Brazil. Around the same time, Paul Silberstein, who had returned from his stint as a Peace Corps volunteer and as a master's student in Rio de Janeiro, was living in Berkeley, where he saw a leaflet announcing the showing of a documentary about torture in Brazil. He went to see the film and met a Brazilian couple who since January 1971 had put out three issues of a modest publication, *Brazil Information Bulletin*. He immediately volunteered to help them with the project. As Paul watched the deposition of the Brazilian political prisoners on the wide screen, he couldn't have imagined that he would help organize a national tour for Marc Von der Weid, the outlawed student leader, who would travel across the United States repeating the denunciations recorded in the documentary. Nor could he have expected that Marcos Arruda would organize a White House protest against President Médici, and that Paul would edit an article about the event and publish it in the *Bulletin*. Yet as he recalled those years working quietly behind the scenes in Berkeley, he explained modestly, "We thought we were doing something for our conscience; we didn't think that we were going to change the world."

### Newsletters and Action Groups

The founding of the North American Congress on Latin America (NACLA) in 1967 had been important for encouraging political activism. The monthly newsletter containing analytical articles about the economic, political, and social conditions in Latin America had helped solidify an informal national network of returned volunteers, former missionaries, academics studying the continent, and Latin Americans living in the United States. The move by some members of the NACLA staff to Berkeley in 1970 offered greater access to West Coast activists, and the publication served as an especially important resource for Latin American solidarity groups in the Bay Area.[6] NACLA did not organize national gatherings of the several thousand people that subscribed to its monthly newsletter. Nor did it provide any concrete means for those who received the publication to communicate among themselves. Instead, NACLA's *Report of Latin America and the Empire* served as a reference point for people who held a critical view of U.S. foreign policy and favored social change in Latin America. The publication, however, put those who had contacted its offices in New York or Berkeley in touch with one of a number of small action-oriented working groups that had formed in this period in different parts of the country. In the late 1960s, leftists formed two other organizations with somewhat divergent political perspectives on Latin America— the U.S. Committee for Justice for Latin American Political Prisoners (USLA) and the Tri-Continental Information Center. Representatives of both groups had attended the founding meeting of NACLA, and both organizations also brought together people interested in Latin America.

The appearance of these organizations reflected a broader trend. Between 1970 and 1972, more than a dozen additional groups formed that shared the initial impulses of the original founders of NACLA, namely, political action and education.[7] They tended to be composed of the same disparate coalition of returned volunteers, radicalized students, Latin Americans residing in the United States, left-wing graduate students, and young professors at universities with Latin American studies programs. Some focused on a specific country, such as American Friends of Guatemala, the Committee against Repression in Brazil, the Cuban Resource Center, Friends of Haiti, and the Peru Information Group. Most other groups raised issues about Latin America as a whole. They usually had limited resources, with no more than a few dozen active members at a given time, modest rented office space, and if they were lucky, a few part- or full-time staff people earning "movement," that is, subsistence wages. Most operated collectively and produced a simple newsletter that linked issues of Latin America to contemporary political or labor struggles in the United States, as well as the ongoing war in Vietnam.

The National Council of Churches, through the United Ministries of Higher Education, supported several of these initiatives designed for outreach about Latin America to students on college campuses, providing the seed money and ongoing assistance at several universities. In Madison, Wisconsin, professors, students, and activists formed the Community Action in Latin America (CALA), which supported a small office, a newsletter, and an organizer, largely with this outside funding.[8] The radical student climate of Madison offered a welcoming environment for work on Latin America. Similarly, NCC funds supported the Latin American Policy Alternative Group (LAPAG) at the University of Texas, Austin, another campus that had a large cluster of radical student activists. LAPAG's activities included sponsoring left-wing speakers from Latin America who spoke on contemporary topics; a Latin American film series, which at the time was a novelty; and a radio program that focused on Latin America and was syndicated nationally.[9] Another group, the Committee on U.S.–Latin American Relations (CUSLAR) formed at Cornell in 1965, carried out similar work. Many of these small organizations formed in cities and towns with universities that had received federal funds to support academic programs on Latin America for the purpose of training experts who could implement U.S. government goals in the region. The political activists who participated in these committees or collectives on or near campus could appeal to Latin American centers to provide resources to fund speaking tours, sponsor film series, and organize conferences. These Latin America–focused education and action collectives such as

CALA, CUSLAR, and LAPAG were composed of an array of scholars, students, and activists and generally offered a left-wing political approach to studying and understanding Latin America. They relied on university space, sponsorship, and support for their events but maintained their autonomy from official university programs. Other groups, such as the Los Angeles Area Group for Latin American Solidarity (LAGLAS), brought together scholars of Latin America, a handful of Latin Americans, and political activists from various universities and acted as a clearinghouse to coordinate regionally.[10] Taken as a whole, the groups that focused on Latin America provided the foundation upon which the Brazilian work was built.

### Brazilian Information Bulletin

The campaign that the American Friends of Brazil had conducted at the meeting of the Latin American Studies Association in April 1970 had been extremely effective in getting the word out to specialists about the human rights situation in Brazil. After the LASA meeting and a speaking tour by Márcio Moreira Alves, the founders of American Friends of Brazil—Wipfler, Della Cava, Tyson, and others—decided to send the funds that had been raised through the sale of the dossier *Terror in Brazil*, as well as monies donated to the cause, to finance a new publication in Berkeley.[11]

The *Brazilian Information Bulletin* (BIB) came about as the result of an auspicious convergence of happenstance and political will. Sometime in 1970, a politically active Brazilian student, whom I will call Mário, was arrested in São Paulo.[12] After he was released, his Protestant family used its religious connections to get Mário out of the country. He first went to Chile with his partner, whom I will call Ana Maria, and then, through NCC connections, he came to the United States. Once again, through church networks, Fred Goff, who had moved to the West Coast to establish the NACLA offices in Berkeley, invited him to come to the Bay Area. There, Mário and Ana Maria started the *Brazilian Information Bulletin*. The first issue appeared in February 1971.[13]

The bulletin opened with a front-page headline declaring, "What Is Happening in Brazil." The lead article focused on what would become the principal line of denunciation during the first years of its publication—news of the torture of political prisoners and repressive measures against the regime's opponents. "Estimates of the number of political prisoners held in Brazilian jails run as high as 12,000," the *Bulletin* affirmed.[14] "These people are denied the right of *habeas corpus*, are often tortured and are held incommunicado for long periods. Scores have died from the tortures and beatings; others have been permanently maimed and handicapped."[15] This statement, as well as much of the information in the first issue of the journal, came from information collected by the American Committee for Information on Brazil and published in the dossier *Terror in Brazil*.

Three interwoven themes appeared consistently throughout the following five years of the *Bulletin*'s existence: (1) the growing gap between the rich and the poor as a side effect of the state's economic policies; (2) the unregulated extraction of the nation's natural resources in alliance with multinational corporations that reaped excessive profits from a cozy relationship with the generals in power; and (3) the negative impact of the Médici government's new $500 million road-building project in the Amazon basin "with the ostensible purpose of 'integrating' the nation, improving national security, providing land for the landless peasants of the Northeast, and opening up the vast wilderness for colonization and exploration."[16] The publication portrayed the new highway project that entailed "the construction of two roads cutting through more than 2,000 miles of jungle" as a means of opening the area to easy access for foreign companies interested in Brazil's natural resources. "The extent of the resources that will be opened for exploitation by these roads is not known exactly, though newspaper reports liken the whole operation to the California gold rush of the 1800s and the 'opening of the Western frontier' in the United States. The objects of desire were iron, manganese, tin, gold, diamonds, and timber."[17] In subsequent issues of the *Bulletin*, two additional themes would complement these dire warnings about the economic impact of the military regime's development plans: the environmental destruction of the Amazonian river basin because of the construction of the Trans-Amazonian Highway and the genocide of indigenous people in the region.

The premier issue's article on the Trans-Amazonian Highway followed the editorial and journalistic choices used when citing news of torture and repression, relying heavily on mainstream news sources to back up the allegations made in the *Bulletin*'s articles. The editors carefully footnoted information with citations from the nation's leading publications. Leafing through an issue of the *Bulletin*, Paul Silberstein remembered how the group who put the newsletter together constructed its legitimacy. "We relied on information that was printed in the press, and we relied on, I wouldn't call it underground information, but people would suggest stories that could be followed up on. And, if you look, there were citations given. Here is a case with an article on the Trans-Amazonian Highway where they quote *O Estado de São Paulo* and the *Christian Science Monitor*. So there was an effort to be scholarly and credible."[18]

The *Bulletin* also depended heavily on U.S. government publications, congressional hearings, and State Department documents to make their case.

A second major article in the newsletter's first issue exposed U.S. government training of Brazilian police at the International Police Academy in Washington and tied this form of foreign aid to repression against opposition to the military regime. Tables charted U.S. aid to Brazilian police, offered comparisons with foreign military support given to other Latin American countries, and listed the U.S. public safety advisors in Brazil, as well as the names of the Brazilian police trained in the United States. A note at the end of the article explained that the list of 110 Brazilian police officers represented only a portion of the 455 who had taken part in training sessions in the United States between 1961 and 1969. The editors of the *Bulletin* then called on its readership to help them collect more data: "We hope readers will let us know additional information abut these men and also any new names which should be added . . . We hope to soon publish a list of the known torturers in Brazil and see how this list matches with the U.S. trained officers." [19] The notion that the *Bulletin*'s readership could play an active role in conducting the research of the publication reflected the same spirit that characterized NACLA, as well as other small collectives and research groups that had sprung up in the 1960s to offer a radical reading of U.S. government policies at home and abroad. They espoused the idea that ordinary citizens should collaborate in building alternative knowledge about U.S. imperial designs and influence. Moreover, the call to collect data derived from an ongoing accusation that the U.S. government covertly trained the Brazilian police and military in torture techniques. U.S. citizens had a moral responsibility to uncover this fact, and the scholars, returned volunteers, missionaries, and others interested in Brazil were capable of creating an unofficial intelligence-gathering network that might locate the links between torture in Brazil and the U.S. government agencies that backed the military regime.

Between February 1971 and the winter of 1975, the American Friends of Brazil published sixteen issues of the *Bulletin*, as well as a joint publication titled *Supysáua: A Documentary Report on the Conditions of the Indian Peoples of Brazil*, produced in collaboration with Indigena Inc., an indigenous rights advocacy group also located in Berkeley. According to Paul Silberstein, the group that published the bulletin sold about 1,000 copies of each issue to libraries or to individuals who subscribed to the publication. They sold another 500 copies individually at political events and at other activities that focused on Brazil. [20] Given the size of the anti–Vietnam War movement in the early 1970s that mobilized millions in different actions, the thousand or so readers of the *Bulletin* represented a small audience. Nevertheless, issues of the publication ended up on the desks of congressional aides and U.S. journalists who used the newsletter as background information for stories that criticized the Brazilian military regime. According to those close to him, Dan Griffin, who wrote a series of hard-hitting articles in the *Washington Post* against President Médici's visit to the White House in December 1971, used data from the *Bulletin* to frame his articles.[21] Although it is impossible to measure the direct impact of the publication on policy and opinion makers, the *Bulletin* provided an alternative voice that legitimized criticisms of the Brazilian military regime and opposition to the State Department's policy of supporting the generals.

At the same time that the United Ministries of Higher Education of the National Council of Churches offered modest support to a handful of education and action collections linked to several selected universities, the NCC provided support for another program—Frontier Internship in Mission—that helped finance the emergent activities related to Brazil. The Frontier Internship in Mission program actually reversed the usual flow of volunteers from the United States and Europe to the southern hemisphere by supporting people from around the world to come to the United States and develop religious or missionary work. The program supported Mário and Ana Maria working on the *Brazilian Information Bulletin*. When the couple decided to leave the area, John Moyer, the campus minister at the Unitas House at the University of California, Berkeley, invited Niva Padilha to come to Berkeley to develop work on Latin America. From Washington, Arruda and Padilha agreed that Niva should move to the West Coast to develop political work about Brazil, while Marcos would continue efforts on the East Coast. Both the *Bulletin* and the West Coast staff of NACLA offered resources to develop a sustained national educational campaign about the political situation under the dictatorship.

By the time the fourth issue of the *Bulletin* began circulating in July 1971, the Brazilian government had received copies of the newsletter and ordered the embassy in Washington to learn more about the publication. The lead story of the fifth issue of the *Bulletin*, published in September 1971, opened with the headline "Tortures Continue Unabated."[22] It included a report on the arrest and release of Julian Beck, Judith Malina, and the Living Theater.[23] The month-long detention of the internationally renowned theater troupe provoked a global outcry and bolstered the image that Brazil had become the land of torture and repression.

## The Living Theater Imprisoned

In 1970, Julian Beck and Judith Malina and their avant-garde theater troupe accepted an invitation to visit Brazil and work with the São Paulo–based Teatro Oficina, led by José Celso Corrêa Martinez, one of the country's leading experimental playwrights and directors.[24] Their collaborative plans ran into rough times, so the anarchist-libertarian Living Theater moved to the picturesque Baroque former mining town of Ouro Preto in the state of Minas Gerais. They settled into a large house and began staging a new production, *The Legacy of Cain*. The troupe planned to perform the street spectacle that included 150 separate plays in different areas of Ouro Preto over a three-week period. The presence of a band of long-haired, free-wheeling Europeans and Americans, along with some Latin Americans and Brazilians who had joined their group, however, proved to be unsettling for at least some of the town's residents, as well as the Brazilian police.

On July 1, officials from the Department of Political and Social Police arrested most of the members of the troupe, charging them with the possession of a stash of marijuana.[25] Although members of the group freely smoked in their house, it is plausible that the police planted a large quantity on the premises to justify taking them into custody.[26] The police detained two other members of the group but did not charge them. They and a third member of the troupe, who had escaped arrest, returned to New York and mounted an international campaign for the release of Beck, Malina, and the rest of the Living Theater. The first news that circulated among left-wing, pacifist, and intellectual circles in the United States about their arrest indicated that the troupe had been tortured and forced to sign confessions.[27] The organizers of the Paradise Defense Fund, an ad-hoc committee put together to collect money for their legal defense, quickly corrected this misinformation by stating that "one Brazilian member of Living Theater [had been] beaten and tortured with electroshock to genitals, one Peruvian electric cattle-prodded. On July 2, to prevent co-workers further torment, Becks signed a blank paper 'confession.'"[28] Throughout their two-month-long detention and trial, the other members of the theater group were not roughed up by the police although they shared precarious living conditions with political prisoners and people detained for other alleged violations of the law.[29]

The U.S. and European press quickly picked up the story. An international campaign led by Allen Ginsberg with support from Leonard Bernstein, Marlon Brando, Bob Dylan, Jane Fonda, Mick Jagger, John Lennon,

Shirley McLaine, Yoko Ono, Andy Warhol, Tennessee Williams, and a host of other artists, intellectuals, and celebrities signed a petition demanding "the release of a group of artists with an international reputation, whose imprisonment deprives the world of a fount of high art."[30] Among the many news articles about the Living Theater's arrest, the *New York Times* ran a feature story reviewing the event, summarizing the experimental nature of their theater performances, and explaining the content of their latest creation. The *Times* also reproduced a striking image that originally had appeared in *Manchete*, Brazil's most widely circulated picture news magazine. Malina and Beck stare soulfully at the camera through a barred prison window.[31] *Newsweek* printed a similar image of Judith Malina standing alone behind prison bars, her hands grasping them as she glances upward to a distant camera. In the accompanying news article, the journalist commented, "Whatever the truth of the marijuana charge, the Living Theater's real crime has been to shake the very underpinnings of contemporary Brazilian life. The government is not likely to suffer such a challenge kindly, and as an unhindered dictatorship, the puritanical military regime can well afford to ignore international public opinion."[32] Living Theater supporters organized picket lines in front of the Brazilian Consulate in New York City and got several senators and the New York City mayor John Lindsay to send telegrams on behalf of the imprisoned troupe.[33] Brazilian artists, intellectuals, and opposition politicians joined the campaign.[34] The Brazilian press amply covered the arrest and investigation, which at first seemed to be simply a news story about a group of avant-garde artists from the United States whom the police had arrested for drug possession. The glamour surrounding the international celebrities who had weighed in on the case offered good copy and the seemingly nonpolitical nature of the arrests permitted journalists to skirt the censors at a time when the military regime tried to prevent the press from publishing articles that indicated domestic or international opposition to the dictatorship. After the artists had been incarcerated for more than two months, the Brazilian government caved in to international pressure and issued a decree ordering the expulsion of the European and U.S. members of the group from the country.

In 1970, a handful of academics and exiles had gathered several dozen signatures of religious figures and prominent scholars to denounce torture in Brazil. The arrest of the Living Theater troupe the next year had garnered the support of limousine liberals, Hollywood glitterati, left-wing intellectuals, and liberal politicians. Although the police did not harm Beck and Malina while they were in prison, the international campaign linked their situation to that of others incarcerated in Brazilian prisons. When they returned to the

United States, they fulfilled a promise to the political prisoners to spread the word about the situation in the country. During the next several years, they granted interviews in which they denounced the repressive nature of the Brazilian government.[35] They also supported the efforts of the *Brazilian Information Bulletin* and the other groups in decrying political repression in Brazil.

### Protests in the Nation's Capital

Harry and Loretta Strharsky were pleased that they had made the move to Washington from Milwaukee, Wisconsin, in the summer of 1971. The antiwar movement was at its height, and the flurry of political activities in the city was "exhilarating." For Harry, the details of those years remain blurred. "I'm surprised that we ever got any sleep because we were so busy," he recalled.[36] Strharsky worked during the day for the Latin America Bureau, and the couple set up a little apartment in Hyattsville, Maryland. Slowly, they developed friendships with others working at the USCC headquarters, including Tom Quigley, who at the time was assistant director of the Division for Latin America, and Mary Lou Suhor, who also worked for the division. Throughout the summer and early fall, the cluster of friends that was forming around Marcos Arruda discussed ways to increase awareness about the situation in Brazil and to emphasize Washington's role in supporting the military dictatorship.

In September, Dan Griffin, the assistant foreign editor for the *Washington Post* who had spent three years in Brazil working for the Catholic bishop in the northeastern city of Natal, met Marcos Arruda through contacts at the USCC. He conducted a feature-length interview with the exiled activist that appeared in the Sunday edition of the newspaper.[37] The article presented a thumbnail sketch of Arruda's journey from seminarian to geologist to factory worker and then described his arrest and prison ordeal in minute detail. A prominently placed photo of Arruda, his piercing eyes calmly directed at the camera, offered the reader an appealing image of the story's protagonist. The article laid the responsibility for Marcos's torture squarely on the shoulders of the Brazilian government, and Griffin made a point of noting that the Brazilian Embassy in Washington declined to comment on the piece that he was writing, stating that it "lacked any direct knowledge of the case." Griffin explained: "Representatives of the Brazilian government have admitted publicly that torture occurs in Brazil. However, the official explanation goes, torture is not a government policy but rather an isolated phenomenon, the result of individual excesses such as may occur in the back rooms of police states anywhere in the world." However, Griffin then gave voice to Marcos who commented, "Look, before he became president, Gen. Médici was head of SNI, Brazil's national intelligence agency." To press the point home, he added, "How can such things continue without President Médici, the former head of an anti-subversion agency, knowing about them?"

The following Sunday, the Post published an editorial that presented potent arguments that still seem relevant. "Torture is bad for governments that inflict it," the editorial began. "The damage to them may not be as visible as the injuries to their victims, but it is profound and cumulative. Once learning to depend on physical pain to coerce its dissidents, a government begins to forget the other means of commanding respect. The massive evidence of widespread and systematic torture in Brazil is an evil portent for any prospect of prosperous stability." The editorial continued by citing impartial and credible denunciations. "In some cases newspapers have been able to question at length the survivors of torture. This newspaper's interview with Marcos Arruda, published last Sunday, is an example. The pattern is, unfortunately, beyond argument." The lengthy editorial concluded with the following affirmation: "By invoking torture, a government reveals its doubts of its own competence. It signals that abandonment of any hope of the peaceful and voluntary reconciliation that is the reward of successful politicians. No outsider could render as scathing a judgment on the present Brazilian leadership as the judgment that, by resorting to torture, they have pronounced upon themselves." [38]

In late October, the group learned that the Nixon administration had set a date for President Médici to visit the White House. They realized that they had a political opportunity, and they began planning a public demonstration. Loretta remembered that when they started organizing the effort to protest Médici's visit, they came up with the name Committee against Repression in Brazil (CARIB) to formalize their activities. Harry recalled, "We actually gave ourselves a name so that we would have some way for people to contact us and for someone to take responsibility for what we were doing and to rally other people and interest around a state visit . . . Being in Washington and knowing what AID and U.S. government monies and interests were doing in propping up the dictatorship and [offering] U.S. police training . . . Our idea was to shock people into the knowledge that the monies that were given for liberal purposes for development and aid for Latin America were complicit with torture and police training." [39]

The group also decided to create photographic reenactments of torture scenes to display at their planned protest. Like Landau's and Wexler's film documentary that had demonstrated this violent treatment of political prisoners as a way to emphasize to the viewer that she or he was not gazing on an actual documented moment, Harry, Lorreta, and others also decided to simulate reality. They set up a small studio in their apartment to recreate the experiences Marcos had described to them. To the thoughtful viewer these visual statements—a headshot of a woman screaming in pain and the doubled-over figure of a man hung on the parrot's perch, among others— obviously revealed simulacra representations of reality and not clandestine shots registering moments of extreme physical torment. To this day, they remain hard to view, suggesting that when the group displayed them, at a time when the media had less effect on stunning the public's sensibilities, they likely had a powerful impact on the beholder.

Subsequently, supporters of CARIB integrated these images into an educational slideshow alternatively titled Brazil, 1972 A.D." and Brazil: Miracle for Whom? that opened with a photograph of Loretta Strharsky on the parrot's perch.[40] A close-up depicting a shocking recreation of this torture was punctuated with the statement "The victim does not always survive." Once again, activists chose to use the stark image of the tortured body to reach their audience. Although the slideshow continued by analyzing the political, social, and economic situation in Brazil under the military regime, the message of torture framed the presentation's central message. Ending with another image of Marcos undergoing simulated brutality, the slideshow script quoted from a speech delivered by Senator Frank Church on October 29, 1971: "While experience has shown that the U.S. aid programs have little if any relevance to the deterrence of communism or the encouragement of democracy, they have been effective in certain instances in keeping unpopular regimes in power. They have certainly contributed to that end in the case of the Greek colonels, the West Pakistani generals and the Brazilian junta. All of these regimes are dictatorships, but they are anticommunist dictatorships and therefore pass our eligibility test for membership in the 'free world.'"[41] The slide show concluded with "Apesar de você," a song by Chico Buarque that offered the hopeful refrain, "In spite of you, tomorrow will be another day." As the accompanying script explained, the military had banned the song's lyrics because they rendered a direct criticism of the regime's authoritarian and arbitrary rule.

As CARIB prepared for Médici's trip to the United States, the Nixon administration and the Brazilian government spent considerable time negotiating the details of the state visit. The original itinerary proposed by the Brazilians included two days in Washington, followed by a stopover to New York to meet with Governor Rockefeller, and then a tour of Tennessee Valley Authority sites, presumably to emphasize the fact that the Brazilian government was also involved in large-scale public works projects. In their conversations with the State Department, Brazilian diplomats also wanted to ensure that the U.S. government afforded Médici all the ceremonies due a head of state representing an emergent world power. The Brazilian ambassador in Washington pushed hard with the officers in the State Department in charge of protocol, insisting that Nixon greet Médici at the airport, that the Brazilian president address a joint session of Congress, and that the Brazilian government offer a dinner in the U.S. president's honor to reciprocate the state banquet at the White House.

Although the two sides ironed out their differences about where Nixon would greet Médici and who would attend a second banquet, the head of the Brazil desk at the State Department was wary of a proposed speech before Congress. "Are we sure Médici and FonMin [Brazilian Foreign Minister] want to risk (which we believe is high) refusal or a boycott of session or other action by U.S. congressmen known to be critical of Brazil, of existing limitations on the role of Brazil's Congress and of our relations with that country?"[42] In State Department briefings to the president and vice president in preparation for the state visit, officials offered an optimistic spin on the repressive nature of the Brazilian government. "Although authoritarian, the regime has made some concessions to constitutional procedures by reopening all legislative bodies and permitted (under controls) direct congressional and municipal elections in which the opposition won about 20 percent of the seats."[43] Nevertheless, as State Department officials admitted behind the scenes, the potential bad press resulting from an address to a joint session of Congress caused considerable alarm. A memorandum prepared for Secretary of State Henry Kissinger for press briefings warned that U.S. officials should avoid "controversial questions" that are "essentially Brazilian internal problems, i.e. the authoritarian nature of the government, and charges of repression and torture." The State Department strongly recommended that officials refer those who had questions to U.S. ambassador Rountree's initial statement in his testimony before the Senate Subcommittee on Western Hemisphere Affairs on May 11, 1971, "which stresses the value the U.S. Government places on our longstanding friendly relations with Brazil."[44] This had become the White House's standard way of deflecting criticism about torture in Brazil. The adjournment of Congress immediately before the visit provided a convenient deus ex machina that avoided a potentially uncomfortable moment for the Brazilian head of state and the U.S. administration that backed the military regime.[45]

If the State Department was worried about Médici being embarrassed in a congressional appearance, the Brazilian Foreign Ministry focused its anxieties on U.S. press coverage of the Brazilian president's U.S. stay. Foreign Minister Gibson Barboza asked the U.S. government to "use its influence to prevent excessively adverse press treatment of President Medici and GOB [Government of Brazil] during [the] Medici visit."[46] According to the U.S. consul stationed in Rio, Brazil's foreign minister Barboza stated that he "understood the concept of freedom of press in the United States and that the U.S. government had no control," but he added, "He knew of instances in which the government had successfully used its influence in specific cases." Barboza was reported to have emphasized that "he was not seeking to influence the news content on Brazil over the long run, but was only asking a 'cease fire' for the two days [of] the visit" and indicated that "the New York Times and the Washington Post are the main problems from the Brazilian viewpoint."[47]

Barboza also expressed concern that a "film presentation on torture in Brazil," presumably Landau and Wexler's film Brazil: A Report on Torture, was scheduled in New York to coincide with the Médici visit. According to the Brazilian government's sources, the film showing was to be sponsored "by [an] office for help to Brazilian victims of torture, an organization recently founded by Dr. Charles Wagley," the prominent anthropologist from Columbia University who worked on Brazil. State Department officials reported that Foreign Minister Barboza had asked if there was "anything that could be done to discourage the presentation of this film during the visit." The Washington official reportedly countered that "the exercise of U.S. government influence in cases like this can backfire and draw more attention to the event than it would have had to begin with."[48] Likewise, the suggestion that the U.S. government might simply prohibit the showing of Landau and Haskell's film while President Médici was in New York revealed how much official censorship and the silencing of the opposition had become commonplace in Brazil. As the public learned from the Watergate scandal, the Nixon administration was not against carrying out "dirty tricks" against its opponents, but the State Department understood that overt censorship could actually end up publicizing a film showing that might otherwise go unnoticed in the media. As it turned out, the Brazilian government cancelled the visit to New York, allegedly because the United Nations secretary general was ill. Foreign Minister Barboza felt no restraint in expressing "relief that [the] likelihood of demonstrations and security problems [are] greatly diminished thereby."[49] The U.S. press covering the events speculated that it was to avoid bad publicity. On the eve of Médici's arrival, the Brazilian government announced that he would not speak before the National Press Club or participate in any press conferences. The mainstream newspaper, O Estado de São Paulo, reported, "This attitude is being interpreted as a means of avoiding a focus on themes such as repression in Brazil."[50] The Washington Post journalist Dan Griffin echoed the reports that surfaced in the Brazilian press.[51]

Anticipating the Brazilian government's fear that news of ongoing torture of political opponents might tarnish its image abroad, the Committee against Repression in Brazil chose to organize a two-day demonstration in front of the White House to highlight the government's treatment of political prisoners. Rain poured down on the day that the Brazilian president arrived at the White House north portico in direct view of a ten-foot-high and thirty-foot-long banner that protesters had erected across the street. The banner read "Stop US $ Complicity with Brazilian Torture." Harry Strharsky, who later wrote a report titled "Grass-root Response to the Medici-Nixon State Visit" that was circulated to activists nationally, described the scene. "After the Brazilian and U.S. national anthems were played, Medici and Nixon were ushered into the White House and Secret Service officials promptly erected a number of large green room dividers on the porch in front of the doors and windows blocking any view that either Nixon or Medici had of the demonstrations across the street." While a band played the Brazilian national anthem on the White House porch, protesters paraded in front of the White House gate with Brazilian flags tied across their mouths "symbolizing the repression of freedom and political dissent in Brazil."[52] Immediately afterward, a Secret Service agent approached the demonstrators and told them to move their banner and poster display or else his men would do it for them. Rather than let the agents destroy the banner, they took it down and moved it back 500 feet. As they were disassembling the display, the agent radioed the police on the White House porch, who then removed the green blinders.[53]

That evening at the state banquet, President Nixon toasted Médici and described Brazil in glowing terms: "As I recall, Brazil is described there as a great sleeping giant lying eternally in a magnificent cradle. That was true of Brazil 150 years ago when it had its independence, and the United States was the first country in the world to recognize its independence. It was true of Brazil 100 years ago, 50 years ago, maybe even 25 years ago, or 10 years ago. But it is not true today." The president continued by asserting, "The giant is awakened. The people of Brazil know it. The people of the world are discovering it, and the visit of the president of Brazil to this country will tell this message to our people and tell it better, also, to the people of the world. This great giant is now awake—100 million people, unlimited natural resources, developing now not only on the coast, the beautiful cities that we all know, but developing, due to the leadership of our guest of honor tonight and those who have worked with him, developing the heartland of the country through highways and cities and exploration such as was only dreamed of before, but now is being actually done." The optimism of Nixon's toast mirrored the nationalist campaigns that emphasized the country's recent dramatic economic growth and large-scale construction projects. Brazil was a country on the move, and the White House recognized this fact. Brazil, according to Nixon, had finally achieved "its promise that people have dreamed about through the years." For Nixon the heart of the country's success was its willingness to encourage domestic and foreign ventures. "And I think the greatest tribute that I can pay to our distinguished guest tonight is that in the brief time that he has been President of Brazil there has been more progress than in any comparable time in the whole history of that country."[54] Emphasizing the ties that bound the United States to Brazil and praising the country's economic progress, Nixon concluded his toast by affirming, "We know that as Brazil goes, so goes the rest of the Latin American continent." Although Nixon was undoubtedly referring to Brazil's economic success that relied heavily on its open-door policy to U.S. investment, the president's comments left observers throughout Latin America perplexed or dismayed.[55] Was the fact that Brazil was a military dictatorship a sign that the country represented a precursor to other authoritarian regimes in Latin America?

Concurrently with the two-day protest activities, thirty-three prominent U.S. clergy and lay officials, including Reverend Ralph D. Abernathy and Reverend Andrew Young, chairman of the Martin Luther King Institute for Non-Violent Study, greeted Médici with a letter protesting "the high incidence of arrest, imprisonment and most inhuman torture . . . in the great nation of Brazil."[56] The letter said that the signatories were "deeply and increasingly troubled by what we have heard and read about the suppression of human rights, the campaign of defamation against certain of our fellow Christians and the high incidence of arrest, imprisonment and most inhuman torture perpetrated against supposed political offenders."

The Brazilian military also got a battering in the *Post*. Dan Griffin wrote a feature article that posed three "awkward points that will probably not be asked of Médici." They included the negative effects of the near double-digit annual GNP growth over the previous three years on the poor and the working class, the country's continuing lack of democracy, and the excessive concentration of power in the hands of the presidency.[57] Médici also received another unwelcome criticism during his speech to the Organization of American States when Peter Kami, a Brazilian student living in the United States, interrupted the address by shouting "Viva o Brasil livre" (Long live Free Brazil) and "Down with torture in Brazil" in Portuguese and English. Secret Service agents immediately jostled aside the youth, detained him, and later let him go. The news media broadcast the scene live in Brazil but in subsequent showings of the ceremony edited out clips of the speech that included the protest. Much to the chagrin of Brazilian officials, *Brazil: A Report on Torture* was also shown on New York public television and a panel of experts on Latin America then discussed the current situation in Brazil. Marcos Arruda, who had left Washington while the demonstration took place to avoid any problems with his visa status, participated in an event on Brazil at the University of Wisconsin in Madison attended by 250 to 300 people who viewed the Landau and Wexler film and heard his testimony about how he had been tortured the pervious year.

### Going National and International

The February 1972 issue of the BIB announced a new international forum— the Bertrand Russell Tribunal on Repression in Brazil—designed to denounce the ongoing political situation in the country.[58] Several months previously, a group of Brazilian exiles in Santiago, Chile, had met with Lelio Basso, at the time a deputy in the Italian Congress and leader of the Italian Socialist Party for Proletarian Unity. Basso had been a prominent figure in the antifascist resistance in Italy during World War II and a participant in the Russell Tribunal on Vietnam that had condemned alleged U.S. war crimes in Vietnam. The Brazilian exiles, representing twelve left-wing organizations, asked him to investigate the possibility of convening a second tribunal to try the crimes committed by the military regime since 1964. He agreed to their proposal and asked the Bertrand Russell Peace Foundation to organize the tribunal with the understanding that it would be more broadly constituted than the first tribunal and "open to the participation of the Communist, Christian, and Social Democratic trends that were not represented in the first Tribunal."[59] Jean Paul Sartre and Vladimir Dedijer, the chairman and the president of the sessions of the first tribunal and a Yugoslavian partisan leader during World War II, agreed to join Lelio Basso in organizing the tribunal, along with the Russell Peace Foundation. Throughout 1972 and 1973, CARIB attempted to develop support for the tribunal in the United States.

In mid-1972, Marcos Arruda invited Jean Marc Von der Weid, the former student leader and a fellow member of Ação Popular, to come to the United

States to work for the human rights campaign about Brazil. Von der Weid spent a month in Washington, where, among other activities, he indirectly lobbied Congress. Traveling on a Swiss passport, he managed to enter the United States under the radar of the State Department. Jean Marc had become a linchpin of international solidarity activities after the Brazilian government arranged for him and sixty-nine other prisoners to fly to Chile in exchange for the release of the kidnapped Swiss ambassador in January 1971.[60] Recalling his 1972 visit to the United States, as well as a second tour of the country the following year to generate support for the campaigns against the dictatorship, Von der Weid remembered that he had decided to travel to the United States because it was "the center of power." Although one could pressure European countries to do something about the situation in Brazil, he reflected, "The real forceful repercussions came from the United States. The Brazilian government took much more into account that which came from the United States."[61]

While in Washington, the radical student leader worked with contacts that Tyson and Arruda had established in Congress to lobby for an end to U.S. aid to Brazil. Von der Weid remembered that they did not try to pass a resolution condemning the Brazilian government. "We were inspired by something that had been done in relationship to Greece, and we did the same thing, namely, conditioning military aid on the verification that there had been no violation of human rights." As described in chapter 8, John Tunney's amendment to the Foreign Assistance Act introduced in the Senate in 1972 and a comparable proposal presented by Ron Dellums in the House mandated a cessation of U.S. funding to Brazil as long as the practice of torture continued. "We spent an entire month sending letters to everyone, all kinds of organizations, so that they would bombard the senators asking for their support. There was a very positive response." When Tunney presented the amendment on the floor of the Senate, his staff invited Von der Weid to Capitol Hill. "The Senator called me to Congress because he had a meeting with a representative of the Brazilian Embassy that was there to protest [the amendment], or speak against it, or clarify the situation, offer his opinion, and so on." Tunney's staff placed Von der Weid in one room and the Brazilian representative in the other, and the senator's aides moved back and forth between the two. "They brought me his arguments and they asked for countervailing information." According to Von der Weid, as related by Tunney's staff, the Brazilian envoy insisted that the news about Brazil was a lie. The country was democratic, there were elections, the Congress functioned properly, justice ruled, and they were in a state of war with the terrorists. "We answered all of his arguments one by one . . . The representative from the Embassy became more and more embarrassed and finally suspended the meeting and left. It was an interesting debate through an intermediary."

Although Von der Weid's congressional lobbying efforts failed to get legislation cutting off U.S. aid to Brazil, by 1972 one could note a decided shift in the printed media's coverage of Brazil. In 1964, the *Reader's Digest* had offered a straightforward apology for the military coup d'état. Dedicated religious women and determined politicians had saved Brazil from communism. Eight years later, the conservative monthly offered a more complicated story in its fiftieth anniversary issue. The change in coverage reflected a distinct modification in how journalists, writers, and intellectuals understood the situation in the country. The denunciations of repression, state violence, and torture had become so convincing that the *Reader's Digest* ended up providing the reader with two short articles that offered two different versions about what was happening in the country "long famous for coffee, Amazon jungles, carnival glamour and runaway inflation."[62]

A short introduction set up the tale of two Brazils. "Nowhere in the Western Hemisphere is there an economic success story to match that of this South American giant," the *Digest* article began. "Paralleling that story is another, far less happy one—of leftist terrorism and resultant police-state repression that have muzzled Brazilians' most precious freedoms."[63] The logic behind this assertion implicitly blamed authoritarian rule on guerrilla actions, as if the Institutional Acts, the closure of Congress, press censorship, and the elimination of habeas corpus had all come as a direct response to bank robberies, car-jackings, and kidnappings. The opening article featured the "boom extraordinary" and praised the soaring gross national product, increased per capita income, and the foreign investments pouring into the country. This "miracle," according to the article, manifested itself in increased production in almost every basic industry, an expansion in school construction, the development of the Amazon Basin, and a reduction in poverty. "Today, Rio's slum population is down to 550,000, and authorities plan to destroy the last *favela* by the end of 1973," the authors of the article reported.[64] "Slum clearance has been going on in all major cities as fast as cheap new housing can be built." The short piece ends with the positive promotion of Brazil's development in its vast hinterland. "Army engineers have built roads through jungles where no wheel ever turned before, to link remote areas with each other and with the coastal cities."[65] In short, Brazil was on the way to becoming an economic world power.

The second *Digest* article, however, offered a sobering story of the "other face" of Brazil.[66] Niva Padilha recalled that Brady Tyson had been in contact with Trevor Armbrister, a staff writer for the magazine in Washington, and provided him with information for the story. "I remember that I helped Brady prepare all of the background material for the article, and there was a long period of negotiations with Reader's Digest before they published it."[67] Neither Armbrister nor Tyson is still alive to confirm whether the magazine's bureau writer actually penned the piece or whether Brady Tyson served as his ghost-writer, but the details echoed the arguments made by opponents of the military regime. "In the past seven years the generals who direct the government have arrested more than 40,000 of their countrymen, often without warrants or formal charges. Constitutional guarantees suspended 'temporarily' are still suspended. Today Brazil has no independent legislature or judiciary. Universities have been purged, the press censored, labor-union activities restricted."[68] The author emphasized that Brazilian leaders claimed that these measures were designed to defeat "communist guerrillas" who wanted to turn the country into "another Cuba" but added, "Official repression is aimed at anyone who questions the regime." The author then presented a thumbnail history of the period from 1964 to the present, mentioning cases of legislators, priests, and journalists who were not communists or guerrilla fighters but suffered arbitrary imprisonment. Citing the Catholic Church as "the most organized aboveground opposition to the regime's methods," the article pointed to torture as an everyday weapon of social control. Although acknowledging that "most Brazilians seemed resigned to ignoring 'politics' and concentrating on prosperity," the piece ended with the warning that "by muffling legitimate dissent they [the generals] have made violence the main recourse for their opponents."[69]

### Dangers to Indigenous Peoples

The question of the arrest and torture of political opponents of the military regime constituted the principal focus of the campaigns against the Brazilian dictatorship, but, as mentioned previously, the Brazilian Information Bulletin's reporting on the development of the Trans-Amazonian Highway and the concomitant effect on the nation's indigenous population became important complementary themes. In the seventh issue of the bulletin, the editors republished a short article that had appeared in the San Francisco Chronicle, reporting, "One of Brazil's top Indian specialists has resigned because he says he's tired of being a gravedigger for Brazil's present policy."[70] In the article, Antônio Cotrim, who had spent more than ten years on Indian protection work in Brazil's forests, charged that "Brazil's government-controlled National Indian Foundation [Fundação Nacional do Índio, FUNAI] is nothing more than an organization to manipulate public opinion."[71] The piece went on to claim that FUNAI had not adequately protected the indigenous peoples of Brazil against land developers moving into their territory. Two issues later, a second article, this time drafted for the Bulletin, offered an overview of official policy toward the indigenous peoples. It focused on the period after 1967 when a government report detailed the role that the Indian Protection Service had played in being involved "directly and indirectly in the widespread destruction of the native Brazilian Indians with whose welfare it had been entrusted."[72] The article then described the Trans-Amazonian highway system's effects on the indigenous reserves. "It is clear," the article asserted, "that FUNAI is on the side of the land speculators and 'developers' when their interests clash with the Indians' interests." At the end of the piece, a bibliography directed Bulletin readers to other sources on the "contemporary situation of Indians in Brazil." In subsequent issues of the BIB, the status of encroachments on the indigenous population was a featured focus. The main argument was simple: rapid development, heralded by the military as an "economic miracle" that was contingent on the expansion and settlement into the Amazon River Basin, endangered the diminishing indigenous population.

The person largely responsible for documenting the Brazilian government's indigenous policy and disseminating it first through the pages of the Brazilian Information Bulletin and later in the quarterly journal Indigena was Shelton H. Davis. The young anthropologist had conducted two years of ethnographic fieldwork in Guatemala for his doctorate at Harvard. He then had become interested in the issue of the treatment of Brazilian indigenous peoples when he began a two-year stint as a visiting instructor at the National Museum in Rio de Janeiro. There he met Noel Nutels, a doctor who had provided medical assistance to indigenous peoples and had served briefly as the director of the Indian Protection Service during the last months of the João Goulart government.[73] "Nutels was very concerned that anthropologists weren't speaking up when they began announcing the construction of the Trans-Amazonian Highway in 1970," Davis recalled. "I met with Noel on several occasions, and he made it clear that something would have to be done internationally because it was very difficult for Brazilian academics and intellectuals to speak out at all because of the dictatorship."[74]

Davis returned to Harvard to teach and do more research on the situation of the indigenous peoples of Brazil. He began a close collaboration with Kenneth Brecher of the Institute of Social Anthropology at Oxford University and Patrick Menget, an instructor at the University of Nanterre in France. Both anthropologists had spent time with indigenous groups in the Xingu Park in Brazil. He also met Marie-Hélène Laraque, who was mobilizing support for the cause of Brazilian Indians among Native American leaders in Canada and the United States. Moving to Berkeley in 1973, Davis and Laraque founded Indigena Inc., a documentation and information center that published a quarterly magazine about the indigenous peoples of the Amazon Basin and organized "reciprocal exchanges of information between native peoples and organizations across the American continent."[75] During subsequent years, "Indigena Reports" on the ongoing development of the Trans-Amazonian Highway and its effects on native peoples of Brazil appeared in the *Bulletin*, as well as *Akwesasne News*, a publication of the North American Native American movement, and other progressive and left-wing newspapers. Reports of the deaths of indigenous peoples of the Amazon due to disease, hunger, displacement, and land invasions shaped an overall impression that the Brazilian government was involved in systematic campaigns to see the decimation of the indigenous population if it stood in the way of progress. This notion became imprinted as yet another of the crimes that the Brazilian generals had committed against the country's people.

### The Nature of the Regime

In February 1972, Information Brazil, the public face of the Berkeley group that produced the *Brazilian Information Bulletin*, sent out a "Brazil Bibliography" of suggested readings for people interested in learning more about Brazil. Interested readers were directed to Thomas E. Skidmore's *Politics in Brazil, 1930–1964*, which focused on the period before the military coup d'état; Ronald M. Schneider's *The Political System of Brazil: Emergence of a "Modernizing Authoritarian Regime, 1964–1970*; and Alfred Stepan's *The Military in Politics: Changing Patterns in Brazil*.[76] Information Brazil recommended several reports on torture and repression as well.

The bibliography also included two books on the Brazilian guerrilla movement: João Quartim's *Dictatorship and Armed Struggle in Brazil* and Carlos Marighella's volume *For the Liberation of Brazil*.[77] Although the military regime was in the process of decimating the guerrilla movement in Brazil, many U.S. leftists, reading from afar, still imagined armed struggle as an effective way of defeating the dictatorship. New Left and countercultural "underground" publications such as the *Berkeley Tribe*, *Black Panther*, *Great Fusil*, *Monthly Review*, *National Guardian*, *Old Mole*, *Ramparts*, and *Tricontinental* published reports about the Brazilian guerrilla movement, the kidnapping of militants, and the torture of political prisoners.[78] *Direct from Cuba* also supplied articles and interviews with Brazilian revolutionaries in exile on the island that promulgated support for guerrilla strategy. The alternative press in the United States picked up these stories and published them. Although the mainstream press occasionally portrayed Brazilian revolutionaries in a positive light, articles in the alternative press tended to lag behind the political events and paint overly optimistic possibilities for political insurgents.[79] These publications' public constituted a significant segment of the anti–Vietnam War and left-wing political movements of the early 1970s throughout the nation, but their readership received rather unilateral and simplistic images of Brazil that portrayed the country exploding with revolutionary fervor while facing fascist repression. Leslie H. Damasceno, who lived in the San Francisco Bay Area in the early 1970s, remembers the romanticized notion that her left-wing friends had about Latin America and the fact that people were reading the Brazilian guerrilla leader Carlos Marighella's *For the Liberation of Brazil* in a study group, as a practical manual for armed struggle.[80] During those heady days in radical Berkeley, some activists in the "movement" even went into the surrounding hills and practiced shooting. "The idea was to learn how to shoot a rifle because you actually thought you might become an urban guerrilla."[81] Filtered news about the revolutionary situation in Brazil reinforced an optimistic vision that the struggle in that country was linked to a potential revolution in the United States. The reading of a guerrilla manual might have created sympathy for left-wing opponents of the Brazilian military dictatorship among a small layer of leftists. Yet, like so many other images of Brazil, the portrayal of the country as a nation on the verge of a revolution likely left a one-sided and distorted representation in the minds of most who paid attention.

While sectors of the U.S. left rooted for the guerrillas, scholars engaged in a lively debate about the exact nature of the Brazilian regime and its future perspectives. In April 1971, historians and social scientists from the United States, Europe, and Brazil converged on Yale University for a workshop organized by Alfred Stepan to "unravel the significance of what was occurring in Brazil."[82] The workshop included the country's leading "Brazilianists," as well as academics who had played an activist role in opposing the dictatorship. In the introduction to an edited collection of the papers presented at the workshop, *Authoritarian Brazil: Origins, Policies, and Future*, Stepan acknowledged that the authoritarian regime had guided the nation toward record economic growth while maintaining regressive income distribution. He also pointed out that, while the military had carried out torture and repression, it also managed to garner support among certain sectors of the population. In their essays, Thomas Skidmore and Philippe Schmitter offered historical analyses of the legacy of previous authoritarian governments on the military regime. The exiled sociologist Fernando Henrique Cardoso argued that the nature of Brazil's "associated-dependent" development created an alliance between the military and international business. Contributors debated the relationship between economic growth and the repressive nature of the regime. They also considered the nature and possible longevity of the regime. Juan Linz, a sociologist and the only nonexpert on Brazil, argued that the country was going through an "authoritarian situation" rather than constructing an institutionalized and permanent authoritarian regime. Although in the long run Linz's analysis proved accurate, it took another fourteen years for the generals to relinquish power.

## Amnesty Internationals' Indictment

When the Yale University Press published *Authoritarian Brazil* in 1973, the country's image had been significantly tarnished abroad and the prediction that the military would not remain in power indefinitely did not seem very realistic. News items originating from the Catholic Church both inside the country and throughout the world had transmitted horrific stories about the military regime's techniques of extracting information from its opponents. The refusal of the Brazilian government to permit the IACHR to enter the country had left the enduring impression that the generals had something reprehensible to hide. The mainstream press started to publish systematic stories to confirm tales told about the treatment of political prisoners. In September 1972, Amnesty International issued a blistering report that "included the names of 1,081 alleged victims of torture." A second report that appeared shortly thereafter contained the names of alleged torturers. The continued silence on the part of the Brazilian government provoked Amnesty International to compile an extensive dossier titled *Report on Allegations on Torture in Brazil*. The group sent it "to all United States senators and congressmen and to a hundred and thirty-two United Nations delegations."[83] The thirty-page document circulated widely in the United States and Europe and surreptitiously in Brazil. It left no doubt in the reader's mind that the Brazilian government practiced and condoned the systematic torture of its citizens.

Sean MacBride, the chairman of Amnesty International's International Executive Committee, penned a foreword that condemned the Brazilian government for its lack of assistance to his organization in collecting data for the report. "As the Amnesty inquiry received no cooperation from the authorities, its sources of information were necessarily one-sided," McBride wrote, offering once again the opportunity for the Brazilian government to counter the conclusions drawn from the document. The report then detailed the Brazilian judicial system, pointing out, "The legal procedure is never adhered to since there are thousands of political prisoners in Brazil who have been awaiting trial for almost three years."[84] Laws, the report summarized, "are often contradictory and inconsistent, while institutional acts and secret decrees have abrogated provisions in the Constitution which were intended to protect human rights."[85] The report then presented accounts of the arrest and torture of several dozen political prisoners, offering corroborative evidence from statements provided by eyewitnesses, many of whom had been released and were in exile in Europe. Its conclusions about the effects of torture on silencing opposition were blistering: "But the actual psychological reason which leads governments to employ torture is doubtless found in the fact that torture has an immense capacity for intimidation which often succeeds in controlling the thoughts and will of people."[86] The report ended by offering "A Petition from Amnesty International to the Brazilian Government." The document reiterated the request for an international commission of inquiry to investigate the situation in Brazilian prisons and release all persons held in violation of Articles 9, 18, and 19 of the Universal Declaration of Human Rights on the 150th Anniversary of the Independence of Brazil, September 7, 1972.[87] The Brazilian government ignored the appeal. Nevertheless, in the 1972–73 *Annual Report*, AI assessed that the document had had an impact in Brazil and abroad: "The report had been well received overall and had been widely circulated in Brazil. Subsequent correspondence and case material arriving from entirely new areas in Brazil appear to be a direct result of greater knowledge of Amnesty International in that country. Amnesty International reprinted the report several times, and it became a standard reference work regarding torture in Brazil. It is expected to play a significant role in Amnesty's current campaign against torture."[88]

The *Report on Allegations of Torture in Brazil* relied on international public pressure and publicity to obligate governments to cease mistreating prisoners or to release them. There were, however, dangers in this approach, and AI was well aware of this. The organization's annual report for 1968–69 warned, "The publication of criticism always produces retaliation. Criticism does not always need to be public and great care is taken to avoid publicity if reasonable progress seems possible without it. But, publicity is one of the few weapons in the armory of a human rights non-governmental organization and from time to time is bound to be used. The extent of the publicity depends of course not on Amnesty but on the press and television."[89]

Another vital organizing tool was local chapters scattered throughout Europe, the United States, and later, as Amnesty International grew in prestige, especially after winning the Nobel Peace Prize in 1974, in other parts of the world. Small groups met regularly to organize letter-writing campaigns on behalf of "adopted" political prisoners. AI selected some individuals nationally or internationally as "prisoners of the month" or "prisoners of the year" when the organization wanted to mobilize significant support on their behalf. Lini Sattamini Penna remembers how crucial the Philadelphia AI group was in pressuring the Brazilian military to release her son.[90] Many times denunciations arrived at the AI offices in London after the Brazilian police and military had already extensively tortured a prisoner, and authorities had already turned over a torture victim to military tribunals for trial and sentencing. In these cases, Amnesty International groups closely followed the treatment of political prisoners, many times building close personal ties with the prisoner and her or his family over the course of many years of incarceration. Such was the case, for example, of Amnesty International Group No. 44 based in San Francisco that took up the case of the Teodor Ghercov, the Brazilian communist leader arrested in 1975 and held for three years.[91]

During the period when the Brazilian military government was in power, Amnesty International groups "adopted" several hundred cases.[92] Although scholars still debate the efficacy of AI and other international human rights organizations in preventing or reducing torture and ameliorating the prison conditions of those incarcerated, to this day Ivan Seixas has no doubt about the matter.[93] Ivan and his father, Joaquim Alencar de Seixas, were members of the Movimento Revolucionário Tiradentes (Tiradentes Revolutionary Movement, MRT), one of the guerrilla organizations seeking to overthrow the military regime. Authorities arrested Ivan and his father at the same time; Ivan was sixteen. Both were brutally tortured while Ivan's mother and aunt, detained in nearby cells, heard their screams. Joaquim Alencar de Seixas died almost immediately.[94] While in prison, Ivan was not aware that Amnesty International Group No. 68 in Stockton, California, had adopted his case. "I am absolutely certain that I survived because of international solidarity because that [Brazilian] press was impotent, and Church hemmed in and couldn't do much. There was no opposition, and the only thing that was left was international solidarity."[95]

When Ivan was finally released from prison, the prison officials turned over to him hundreds of letters written on his behalf, including one that he still prizes from Joan Baez, the politically engagé folk singer. In our interview, he particularly remembered Joyce Battilana, one of his staunchest supporters and letter writers. After the courts finally released Ivan from prison, his sister visited the group in Stockton to thank them personally for their efforts and asked Joyce Battilana why she had been so supportive of someone who had been a guerrilla fighter. As Ivan tells the story, "My sister asked, 'You know why Ivan was arrested?' 'Yes, I know, but it was unjust; that is it. I'm against it.' There's a tremendous richness there that gives one a lot of confidence in human beings, and I think that this should be remembered."

### Continued Campaigning

On Labor Day weekend, 1973, a group of twenty or so Brazilians and Americans from around the United States gathered in New York City to plan further nationwide actions on Brazil. A position statement that they drafted outlined goals designed to isolate the Brazilian dictatorship politically and economically while linking up with political struggles of people in the United States.[96] Marcos Arruda, one of the organizers of the meeting, offered an analysis about recent developments. Seeming apathy and lack of resistance in Brazil to the military regime was deceptive, he explained. Compared to the pre-1964 political situation, opposition was growing and getting more sophisticated. People were repressed but not unaware. Arruda outlined the presidential succession process and Médici's nomination of General Ernesto Geisel, the head of Petrobras, the state-owned oil company, as the next chief of state. He was pessimistic about possibilities that the Geisel administration would lead to political openings, as liberalization, so he argued, would likely lead to popular mobilization and subsequent hard-line policies. Arruda reminded his attentive audience that Costa e Silva, too, had come to power promising liberalization of the regime, and just the opposite had occurred. On the other hand, Marcos pointed out, there were pockets of resistance in the country. News had reached Brazilians abroad that guerrilla forces in the Amazon still resisted a campaign by the Armed Forces to shut it down. There were many important tasks at hand: preparations for the Bertrand Russell Tribunal on Repression in Brazil, an upcoming conference on Brazil at the University of Wisconsin at Madison and sponsored by Community Action on Latin America, and a proposal to raise the question of human rights violations on December 10, the United Nation's Human Rights Day.

A week later, no more than three dozen people gathered in Washington across the street from the Brazilian Embassy to denounce ongoing human rights violations. The banner that had been used in the 1971 protest in front of the White House directed the attention of motorists on Massachusetts Avenue to the assertion that the U.S. government was complicit with the torture of Brazilian political prisoners. Activists carried picket signs that read "Stop Brazilian Repression Now," "Free Brazilian Leaders Now," "Factories Run to Brazil and Leave U.S. Workers Jobless," "'Economic Miracle'? Not for Brazil's Poor," and "Stop U.S. Aid to Brazil's Dictatorship." A half-dozen motorcycle police monitored the protest. It was a modest, symbolic stance against the regime, not unlike hundreds of others held in front of the embassies of South Africa, the Philippines, South Korea, or Iran, protesting U.S. support for dictatorial regimes across the globe.

Four days later, people woke up to the news that Chilean socialist president Salvador Allende had been killed in a coup d'état, the military had ordered a state of siege, and thousands of leftists, including many foreigners, were being arrested. For people working on Brazil, September 11, 1973, changed everything.

(RIO 1) RIO DE JANEIRO, Aug. 15 —
MISSING — Stuart A. Jones, who has
been missing in Brazil for an undetermined period. He is the son of
Norman A. Jones, a U. S. citizen,
and Zuleika A. Jones, a Brazilian
fashion designer known internationally as Zuzu Angel. This picture
was taken two years ago, when Jones was 24. (APWIrephoto ) (BH)
1971 PPD - VEDADA PARA O BRASIL.

# CAPÍTULO IX

## "Navegar é preciso"

It's necessary to navigate.
It's not necessary to live.

**Caetano Veloso, "Os Argonautas," 1969**

Stuart Angel Jones, 1971, newswire release. FUNCAÇÃO GÉTULIO VARGAS,
CENTRO DA PESQUISA DE DOUMENTAÇÃO DA HISTÓRIA (CPDOC).

In 1971, Brazilian jails and torture centers were still overflowing.[1] Although it will be impossible to ever know the exact number of people arrested and tortured during the military regime, the statistical analysis of a large sample of cases by the *Brasil: Nunca Mais* (Brazil: Never Again) project gives an indication of the trend upward after 1968. Documented torture victims jumped from 85 in 1968 to 1,026 the following year, increasing to 1,206 in 1970, and then dropping to 788 in 1971, while the number of disappearances increased steadily in the early 1970s from 4 in 1971 to 41 in 1973. Detention meant torture and possible death.[2]

One such arrest took place on May 14, 1971, in Rio de Janeiro. At approximately 9:00 a.m., Air Force intelligence agents picked up Stuart Edgar Angel Jones, a twenty-six-year-old former student turned guerrilla fighter.[3] Stuart was a leader of the Movimento Revolucionário 8 de Octubro (MR-8) that had participated in the kidnapping of the U.S. ambassador in September 1969.[4] He had joined the group while an economics student at the Federal University of Rio de Janeiro. He went underground along with his wife, Sonia Maria de Moraes, in 1969.[5] Stuart Angel was the son of Norman Angel Jones, an American citizen, and Zuleika Angel Jones, an internationally recognized fashion designer known professionally as Zuzu Angel.

The morning he was arrested, Stuart had gone to a scheduled meeting with Alex Polari de Alverga, a member of another guerrilla organization, as a routine part of the procedure for sustaining contacts between the two groups.[6] Unbeknown to Stuart, the military had arrested Alex several days previously. While being tortured he had admitted to the appointment.

Revolutionary norms demanded that jailed leftists resist revealing information for twenty-four hours if not longer, so that others who were vulnerable to arrest had time to change hideouts or alter their routines to avoid capture. After a day of brutal grilling, revolutionary organizations expected their members to pass on just enough information so that the violence to oneself would ease up temporarily as the police verified the details that the person had revealed.[7] According to Alex, after two days of electroshock, he misinformed the police about the rendezvous, mentioned a slightly different place and time, and hoped that this would alert Stuart, who could then escape.

The tactic failed. Just as the police was closing down their stakeout, Stuart Angel drove up in a green vw bug. The plainclothes military quickly whisked him away to "Paradise," as political prisoners cynically called the interrogation center of the Air Force Intelligence Services, located at the Galeão Air Force Base in Rio de Janeiro. Stuart had disappeared.

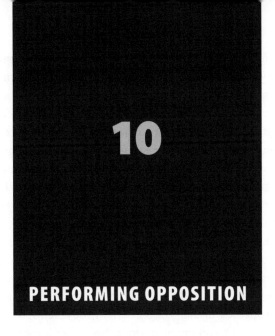

# 10

# PERFORMING OPPOSITION

The campaign against the dictatorship had a good effect internally. The prisoners felt supported and the dictatorship was afraid. If they [the military] did what they did, everyone remained silent, and there had been no international repercussions, then they would have continued. — **Augusto Boal**

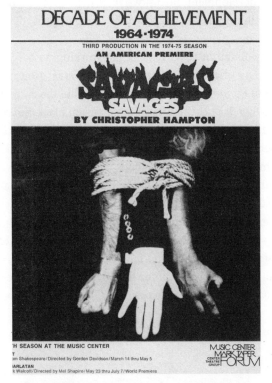

Program for *Savages*, 1974. REPRINTED BY PERMISSION OF MARK TAPER FORUM.

Sometime in late February 1971, Joanne Pottlitzer received an envelope at her Broadway theater district office. Pottlitzer was the founder and director of Theater of Latin America (TOLA), a New York–based major nonprofit arts organization that pioneered artistic exchange between the United States and Latin America. Writing about the incident many years later, she recalled, "The envelope had no return address. Inside was a tiny piece of paper that had been torn from a larger sheet with a note scrawled in pencil in hurried handwriting, 'I'm in prison. No one knows where I am. Contact Richard Schechner. Contact anyone you can think of. Help!!! Help!!!' It was from Augusto Boal."[1]

At the time, Augusto Boal, a Brazilian playwright and theater director, had achieved international prominence for his experimental theater productions. He would later become famous for his writings about and productions of the Theater of the Oppressed and the Invisible Theater. A graduate in chemical engineering from the University of Brazil in Rio de Janeiro, Boal had traveled to New York in 1953 to do graduate work. His father insisted that he study industrial chemistry at Columbia University, but Boal preferred pursuing his passion for drama. While learning about plastics to please his father, he also wrote plays and studied theater at Columbia with John Gassner, a noted professor who had worked with Arthur Miller and Tennessee Williams. Because Boal was the only Latin American student studying with Gassner at the time, the drama professor carefully read his works and acted as a mentor to guide his intellectual development. Boal's two years in New York had a deep impact on him, especially because they exposed the young playwright to theater from around the world.[2]

Returning to Brazil in 1955, Boal began working with Teatro de Arena, where he became a prime mover behind the innovative group that had introduced theater in the round to Brazilian audiences in the early 1950s.[3] Teatro de Arena's hit They Don't Use Tuxedos (Eles não usam black-tie) revolutionized Brazilian theater by presenting a drama of heroic working-class struggle, stripped of pervasive stereotypes of the lower classes. Swept up in the nationalist artistic movement of the early 1960s that attempted to wed the arts to popular culture and bring theater to the povo (people), Boal and other artists of Teatro de Arena presented dramas and politicized musical shows that combined engagé lyrics and prose denouncing social inequality and injustice.

Just as They Don't Use Tuxedos became an overnight hit in 1958, the musical production Arena conta Zumbi (Arena Tells the Story of Zumbi), co-written by Augusto Boal, became a political musical drama success after the military takeover in 1964. Arena conta Zumbi premiered in 1965. The show dramatized the struggle of Afro-Brazilian resistance to slavery led by the leader Zumbi. Retelling the historically based story of the late-seventeenth-century clash between residents of the Palmares, a runaway slave community in the hinterlands of the Brazilian Northeast, and the Portuguese colonial government, the musical play also offered a metaphor about opposition to and rebellion against the current military regime. The show portrayed the violence and torture inflicted on slaves but also glorified their resistance. The script intertwined the historical narrative with references to contemporary Brazil. For example, in one scene depicting the Portuguese invasion of Palmares, Boal inserted a speech by then-president Castelo Branco. Mirroring the new policies of the Brazilian dictatorship that had recently come to power, the Portuguese military leader in the play explained that instead of protecting the country's borders from foreign invaders, it was necessary to turn the army inward to defeat internal threats.[4]

Boal also borrowed Brechtian techniques in staging the production.[5] The cast performed as an ensemble, the actors shifting from one character to another.[6] By today's standards, the fact that most actors were descendants of Europeans but played the roles of enslaved Africans might be disconcerting to audiences and critics alike. However, the rebellious message of the piece captivated the mostly white, middle-class Brazilian audiences who held the notion that Brazil, unlike the United States, was a racial democracy, blind to differences in skin color. The play's comparisons of slave resistance in the late seventeenth century to contemporary opposition to the military also implied that the Brazilian underclasses, o povo, largely African-descended, were linked to middle-class critics of the regime.[7] In the 1960s, Brazilian intellectual circles generally adhered to a reductive Marxist perspective in which class contradictions (in this case the slaves and their allies) were considered more significant than race in revolutionary matters. Zumbi romantically symbolized a timeless unity of the Brazilian populace against exploitation and oppression, overcoming racial differences in the process.

### Zumbi in New York

In 1969, Joanne Pottlitzer, then in her third year as director of the Theater of Latin America (TOLA), invited Boal to bring the production of Zumbi to New York. "TOLA always operated on very little money," recalled Pottlitzer, "but we received a grant from the Rockefeller Brothers' Fund and were able to bring the production to New York in August 1969."[8] The musical played for three weeks at the St. Clement's Episcopal Church in Manhattan to capacity crowds.[9] The New York Times critic described the show: "The two-act musical was performed on the converted bare stage without even the help of multi-media aides, so popular in Off-Broadway productions these days. Instead the cast relied on natural grace and refreshing vitality to dramatize the story of Zumbi through songs, dance, and pantomime." The Times writer also emphasized the political content of the show: "The object of the political satire is to suggest the analogy between the colonial empire's suppression of the slaves in 1695, and the military junta's stiff controls on Brazil's freedom of expression 270 years later."[10] He closed the review by pointing out that, just as Arena conta Zumbi began its initial two-week run in New York, literary critics were giving rave reviews to one of the Brazilian writer Jorge Amado's novels, recently translated into English. "Together, the two events may help whittle down what Augusto Federico Schmidt, Brazil's foremost modern lyrical poet, described as the 'wall of silence' that has kept the United States from learning more about his country's culture and psychology."[11]

Initially, the show's audience was composed largely of Brazilians living in the New York area who could follow the Portuguese text. After the Times critic gave the work a glowing review, the play drew a broader, mixed-language audience. Arena conta Zumbi was so popular that the Theater of Latin America extended the show's run, as the show's themes about slave rebellion and African resistance struck a chord among liberal and leftist New York audiences.[12]

According to documents in the Brazilian Foreign Ministry archives, someone allegedly representing the group approached the Brazilian Embassy about possible financial backing.[13] That person requested that the Brazilian government pay for the transportation of the twelve-member troupe from New York to Washington, for a week-long engagement being negotiated with a local theater. At first, Brazilian authorities vacillated in their response to the request. In order not to "demonstrate a hostile attitude toward Brazilian vanguard theater," the New York consul general initially granted the group "symbolic assistance."[14] "When first exhibited in Brazil, 'Arena conta Zumbi' didn't have political connotations, only social ones, and was permitted by the censor," the Brazilian Foreign Ministry noted in one of numerous communications between Brazil and the United States.[15] However, the Brazilian Foreign Ministry drew back from the idea upon learning that Boal supposedly intended to present Arena conta Zumbi at the United Nations headquarters with the possible presence of the secretary general.[16]

In fact, the text of Arena conta Zumbi had not significantly changed since its debut in 1965. Rather, the political context in Brazil had shifted, and the repressive measures unleashed by the military in December 1968 had begun to provoke an international response. In the aftermath of government crack-downs, the political poignancy of the production hit too close to home. The subtleties of the political message contained in the musical drama may have been lost on many of the English-speaking members of the audience, but the concept of freedom against oppression sang out in the play's program and in the production itself. The first act included a litany of dramatizations of the violence against Brazilian slaves, from their forced captivity through their transportation to the New World, to the whippings, violence, and torture that they had to endure. Plays about slavery became popular during the late 1960s, when the civil rights movement sparked an interest in the history of African Americans. Although *Arena conta Zumbi* addressed chattel servitude, if viewed literally, it was preeminently about the limitations on personal and social freedoms experienced by Brazilians under military rule. The metaphorical connection with contemporary reality fueled its popularity in São Paulo as well as in New York.

As telegrams zipped across the wires between Brasília, Washington, and New York about whether or not to authorize assistance to the New York pro-duction, the *New York Times* critic's endorsement of the show caused the Bra-zilian Ministry of Foreign Affairs to make a definitive decision against any financial backing of the theatrical enterprise.[17] Although Boal's troupe never presented the play to the secretary general of the United Nations, as the Bra-zilian government feared that it might, officials still refused to support the production in any way.

Staging the suffering of the Brazilian people through vivid enactments of the torture of slaves marked, perhaps, the first time that a theater group por-trayed to U.S. audiences this type of violence occurring in Brazilian society. Moreover, the show premiered in New York and then toured in Washington precisely at the moment when Brazilian leftist guerrillas had stepped up their attacks on the military regime, kidnapping the U.S. ambassador to Brazil in Rio de Janeiro on September 4, 1969. *Arena conta Zumbi* featured the resistance of slaves, but the connection to the current reality in Brazil, and especially the call to fight back, would have been obvious to anyone attending a perfor-mance and conversant with international news.

Teatro de Arena's efforts to educate the American public about the po-litical situation in Brazil probably had little impact beyond the few thou-sand theatergoers in New York and Washington and the tens of thousands of readers who may have perused the reviews of the play, the Brazilian gov-ernment's worries about the country's image abroad notwithstanding. How-ever, Boal's arrest in São Paulo in February 1971 on charges of subversion had international repercussions and added to the growing opposition by U.S. artists and intellectuals to the military regime.

### Imprisonment and International Protests

On February 10, Boal had just finished a rehearsal of a new production at the Arena Theater in downtown São Paulo. The rain poured down heavily as he headed home for a quick evening meal before returning to the theater to observe an evening performance. His mind was preoccupied with plans for the future. Organizers of the International Theater Festival in Nancy, France, had invited the troupe to present their new production, as well as *Arena conta Zumbi*. Boal planned to travel to Europe in two weeks to negotiate details of the tour. They would also perform a new experience that they called *teatro-jornal* (newspaper theater) that involved "simple techniques and ways of transforming items in the newspaper into scenes that would allow anyone to do theater, regaining this art form for the people."[18] Suddenly a plainclothes policeman stopped him and asked if he were Augusto Boal. The director acknowledged his identity, and the officer arrested him. He was taken to a police station, where officials assured him that they would merely detain him for a few hours, just enough time to clear up a few questions.

During his first interrogation, the police insisted that Boal had acted as a courier for "subversive" groups, smuggling articles out of the country that denounced the military regime. He was also accused of having returned theatrical prizes awarded him and his theater group by *O Estado de São Paulo*, one of the nation's leading papers. In doing so, they claimed, he had denigrated the military regime. In addition, authorities alleged that he had acted as a go-between to arrange arms shipments to leftist revolutionaries in Brazil. Eventually, the Brazilian government charged Boal with being a member of the Ação Libertadora Nacional (ALN), one of the two revolutionary organizations that had participated in the kidnapping of the U.S. ambassador in 1969. By 1971, special antiterrorist unions were dismantling the ALN cell by cell.[19] Authorities arrested Boal because of his alleged links to members and supporters of that organization. The government based all the charges against Boal on confessions extracted from other political prisoners under torture. He remained incommunicado for ten days in solitary confinement. Several days after the police picked up Boal, he faced interrogations laced with electric shocks.

Boal's account of his arrest and torture is both shocking and mundane, for it bears close similarity to countless other testimonies about the sadistic excesses of the military regime. According to his version of events, during the torture session, a surrealistic exchange took place between Boal and his captors. His interrogator kept insisting that he had defamed Brazil abroad, and that this was a crime. But how? Boal retorted, hanging helplessly and vulnerable. The reply: "You defame [Brazil] when you go abroad and say that there is torture in Brazil." At this remark, Boal burst into laughter, which apparently annoyed and frustrated his torturer.[20] Unable to extract a confession from him, on March 12, authorities moved him to a state prison facility, where political prisoners, held in preventive detention, awaited formal charges and trial.

After Joanne Pottlitzer opened up the envelope that contained Boal's frantic plea for help, she unconsciously crumpled it up and threw it into a wastepaper basket. She then attempted to plow through her daily duties while at the same time trying to decide what to do, all the time frightened about "being directly implicated in such a volatile political situation."[21] At the end of the day, she retrieved the message and went to work.

Fifteen leading figures in the New York City theater community, including Richard Schechner, Joseph Papp, Joe Chaikin, Robert Anderson, Alan Schneider, Harold Prince, and Arthur Miller, signed a protest letter demanding Boal's release. The carefully worded statement was published in the letters to the editor section of the *New York Times*, although the newspaper only printed five of the fifteen names. The short missive denounced Boal's arrest by the Department of Political and Social Order, described as "the nonmilitary federal agency in Brazil in charge of political investigations."[22] The letter forcefully declared, "As members of New York's artistic community and as United States citizens, we are deeply concerned about suppression of distinguished artists in Brazil or any country." The letter pointed out that the Brazilian government had refused to grant the "International Red Cross and Amnesty International permission to carry out impartial investigations of the reported torture of political prisoners in that country's jails and prisons." The protest statement acknowledged, "The general climate of cultural repression in Brazil has been reported by the *Times* and other responsible news agencies" but noted that these news stories were the exception to the rule. "Perhaps the most alarming aspect of this situation in Brazil is the minimal coverage it receives in this country from our press. The public must be informed. And we urge it to stand with us in our concern for Augusto Boal and for the reinstatement of human rights in Brazil."

Arthur Miller was at the time the president of PEN International, an organization that defends the rights of writers around the world. Miller mobilized the association to send letters and cables to the Brazilian government on Boal's behalf.[23] Senator Frank Church also sent an inquiry to the State Department about Boal's incarceration.[24] A successful international campaign generated messages to the Brazilian government from the four corners of the globe, even from theater groups that did not really even know who Boal was.[25]

Reflecting on the impact of such international campaigns some thirty years later, Boal insisted that the protest letters were crucial on several fronts. First, they had a direct impact on easing his situation while in prison: "The jailer came up to me and said, 'Shit, you're an important person. We are getting all of these telegrams about you from I don't know where.' And he didn't really know where they were from, or who Arthur Miller or Jean Paul Sartre were." These messages also broke the isolation that political prisoners felt at times.

The campaign's ripple effect finally reached the Brazilian press. The *Jornal do Brasil* published a paraphrased version of the New York protest letter under the headline "Arthur Miller Defends Augusto Boal," two days after it appeared in the *Times*.[26] According to Boal, "a large dossier filled with letters people had written on his behalf was presented at the hearing."[27] On April 26, authorities brought Boal and six other prisoners before the Second Military Hearing Committee that released Boal and another of the other six prisoners with the status of "conditional liberty," due no doubt in large part to the international campaign on Boal's behalf. Concerned that the publicity surrounding the case had cast the Brazilian government in a negative light, the Ministry of Foreign Affairs instructed its Washington personnel to let the U.S. press know that the court had released Boal "so as to stop the exploitation that has taken place surrounding this episode."[28] In late June, the Second War Court of the Military Justice of São Paulo absolved Boal due to lack of proof of any involvement "in the subversive Aliança [sic] Libertadora Nacional."[29] Boal then chose exile rather than the possibility of another incarceration.

One of Boal's first visits abroad was to New York, where he met with Arthur Miller to thank him for his support and discuss his new project of "newspaper theater," described by a *Times* reporter as "a form of revolutionary satire gaining wide popularity in Latin America as a means of outwitting Government censorship."[30] Drawing parallels between the political situation in Boal's country of origin and another nation under military rule, Miller commented to the press, "The situation in Brazil is much like that of Greece. They are using the theater as a means of keeping alive some spark of freedom." Miller's analogy was rather appropriate since, as noted in chapter 5, the first successful international campaign against torture, spearheaded by Amnesty

International, focused on Greece and soon served as model for similar activities against human rights violations in Brazil. The *Times* piece also featured a friendly photo of Boal and Miller on the streets of New York. In the article, Boal announced he planned to return to New York to present a new play, *Torquemada*, a musical history of the Inquisition that he began writing while imprisoned in Brazil and had finished while exiled in Argentina.

### Fashion Shows and Missing Bodies

In May 1971, four months after Augusto Boal's arrest, Stuart Angel Jones vanished.[31] As was true of so many other mothers from middle-class families whose sons and daughters were swept up in the military's relentless dragnet against the left, the search for her son transformed Zuzu Angel. "I used to think only about work and earning money to give the best to my children," she sighed in her unfinished memoir, *My Way of Death*, the English title she gave to the collection of ruminations that documented her search and the endless frustration about not knowing her son's fate. "Now I have to enter into politics and become a militant . . . I became completely involved in searching for my son and then the children of others. Just when my fashion designs were successful."[32]

At some point over the next few days, an anonymous caller phoned Stuart's mother and told her that she should find a lawyer to defend her son because he had been arrested.[33] Thus began what some families of political prisoners and those who "disappeared" have referred to as their personal Calvary, a painful Via Dolorosa that took them from police station to army barracks, to military hospitals, to high-ranking officers, pleading, begging, cajoling, and bribing anyone and everyone to find news of a loved one. Almost immediately after receiving the news of Stuart's arrest, Zuzu Angel contracted the human rights lawyer Heleno Claudio Fragoso to assist her in finding her son.[34] Fragoso had defended many prominent oppositionists since the military took power in 1964. He had a reputation for being a courageous and dedicated lawyer. In November 1970, unidentified men kidnapped him and two other human rights lawyers to intimidate them into abandoning their defense of political prisoners. As Fragoso reflected in his memoirs, "I am convinced that they merely intended to terrorize and demoralize us. How could we defend others if we ourselves suffered violence? Our imprisonment did not discourage us. Rather, it constituted clear proof of what we had alleged: government agents were acting like common criminals."[35]

Although Zuzu had separated from her husband, she also mobilized his relatives in the United States to help her track down the whereabouts of her only male child. On May 25, Stuart's uncle, a U.S. citizen, sent a telegram to the U.S. Embassy in Rio de Janeiro requesting assistance in providing information about his nephew. Two weeks later, the American consul, James W. Reardon, responded that the Rio police had been unable to locate any arrest record for a Stuart Edgar Angel Jones. However, he informed the family, "They did take into custody a Stuart Edgar Angel *Gomes*, who was wanted for four separate accounts of burglary. Mr. Gomes escaped, however, and his whereabouts are unknown at present. Given the fact that the three given names are identical and that Gomes is a likely corruption of Jones, I believe it most likely that the police report concerns your nephew."[36] The news that a political prisoner had been arrested and then escaped was an ominous sign. It usually signaled that the person had died under interrogation.

After several months of persistence in seeking information about her son, news of Zuzu's ordeal reached the U.S. press. An AP story headlined "Brazilian Tortured to Death?" reported that a Brazilian congressional representative had demanded the investigation into "the disappearance of the 26-year-old son of an American and an internationally known women's fashion designer. There is reported to be evidence that the missing man, Stuart Jones, was tortured to death in prison."[37] The article caught the attention of U.S. government officials. The same day that the AP story hit the wires of the news service, the State Department sent the U.S. Embassy in Brazil a request for details of the case. The telegram noted, "Press and T.V. here are carrying stories about alleged torture and killing by Brazilian Air Force personnel in Rio last May of one Stuart Jones." The State Department requested more information, including the nationality of Jones, who "reportedly is son of a naturalized American citizen."[38]

Embassy officials in Brazil informed Washington about the inquiries they had made concerning Jones in late May and early June, as well as the particulars of a follow-up meeting with Heleno Fragoso. "In discussion with Jones' family lawyer, Heleno Fragoso, Emboff [Embassy Official] was shown original of Consul's letter in lawyer's file. In likely event that GOB [government of Brazil] security forces continue to deny any knowledge of arrest of Jones, it [is] quite possible that Fragoso and Jones' family will attempt [to] make public contents [of] letter which [is] their only 'proof' Jones taken into custody. Such situation could put Embassy in embarrassing position of contradicting GOB statement relating to Brazilian Internal Affairs."[39] According to the telegram, the U.S. government had received the information as a "result of a routine query to Guanabara State Police . . . [that] provided this information to regional security office's police contact." Fearful of a rift between Brazil and the United States if Zuzu or her attorney went public with the information obtained by U.S. government sources, the U.S. ambassador, William Rountree, informed Washington that "because of above circumstance, Embassy does not rpt [repeat] not plan at this time to disclose [the] source of [its] information to the Jones' family."

Stonewalled by the Brazilian and U.S. governments, Zuzu continued to follow innumerable leads, all of which proved to be false, until she learned through various sources about the probable fate of her son. After having been arrested, Stuart was tortured very badly, and it appeared that he revealed little if no information in the process. Alex Polari, whose revelation to the military under torture had resulted in Stuart's arrest and who was "interrogated" in same room with him later that day, wrote:

> On the same day, the interrogations continued with comings and goings from the torture room. Before that, during the afternoon, I heard for a long time a loud commotion in the patio of the CISA. There was the noise of cars being turned on, acceleration, shouts, questions and a constant choking that I noticed happened after the acceleration. With great effort, given my physical situation, I managed to look through the window that was about two meters off the ground, and I saw something that is difficult to forget. Together with many torturers, soldiers, and officers, was Stuart with his skin already semi-stripped off, being dragged from one side to the other of the patio, tied up to a vehicle; and, from time to time, with his mouth almost sealed to the car's exhaust pipe, he was forced to inhale the toxic gases being expelled.[40]

Polari also reported that his jailers had made cynical comments that Stuart would be "more food for the fish at the shoal." This comment referenced the widespread rumor that bodies of those political prisoners who died under torture "were taken by military helicopter to a military zone near the Marambaia shoal off the coast and from there thrown into the deep sea."[41]

In August 1971, Zuzu's lawyer submitted a version of Polari's eyewitness account of Stuart's death to the government-controlled Brazilian Human Rights Commission. Congressman Pedroso Horta, the House minority leader of the opposition political party, Movimento Democrático Brasileiro (MDB), also formally asked Justice Minister Alfredo Buzaid to investigate Fragoso's charges. Even though growing evidence indicated that authorities had indeed killed her son under interrogation, Zuzu kept up hope that he might miraculously turn up alive. Yet despite all her desperate attempts to locate her son (or his body), she kept running into dead ends.

## Fashion Turned Political

Starting with modest resources but boundless energy and optimism, Zuzu had built her career, beginning as a dressmaker in a tiny workshop in her home in Belo Horizonte and rising to become a trendy fashion designer with a chic boutique in the upper-class beachfront neighborhood of Leblon, Rio de Janeiro. In the 1960s, Zuzu Angel clothed the tanned bodies of Carioca beauties with long flowing dresses, flowery prints, and lacy frills from the Brazilian Northeast. Brazilian first lady Dona Yolanda Costa e Silva wore one of her creations when Queen Elizabeth II visited Brazil in 1968. The next year the National Council of Women honored her as Woman of the Year. Joan Crawford introduced her to the New York fashion scene in 1968;[42] and Bergdorf Goodman, one of the New York City's major department stores at the time, bought her entire 1970 collection.[43] Kim Novak, Margot Fonteyn, Liza Minnelli, Faye Dunaway, and Joan Crawford all wore her designer clothes.

In an international market that relied on long-standing stereotypes about Brazil, Zuzu's first U.S. fashion show in 1970 invoked Carmen Miranda, featuring bare midriffs and baiana turbans (headware used by Afro-Brazilian women from Salvador, Bahia) designed for casual summer party wear. Zuzu readily acknowledged the reference. "Carmen—she lived in Rio de Janeiro as I do—dressed in style of Bahia, because it is our own native style. Of course, she exaggerated."[44] Zuzu herself exaggerated when she borrowed other Brazilian folkloric images. For the same show, she created a fashionable Maria Bonita dressed in a yellow, purple, and turquoise silk print gaucho turnout with a large stylish *cangaceiro* hat.[45] The designer used the semiprecious stones of Minas Gerais to add sparkle to her costumed model. In a borrowing from Brazilian folkcraft, Zuzu decorated her bridal gowns with the delicate lace of the northeastern *rendeiras* or lace makers.[46] Her new creations covered the female body with references to Brazilian nature and its exotic culture. According to U.S. fashion critics, the recurrent theme throughout her collection was "the tropical bird, embroidered birds, storybook birds, and masses of colorful jungle birds."[47]

Her fashion show at the consul general of Brazil's residence in New York (Mr. and Mrs. Soutello Alves) on September 13, 1971, however, proved to offer quite a different vision of Brazil. The day of the show Zuzu spoke to Thomas Dine, an administrative assistant to Senator Frank Church. The fashion designer had sought support among U.S. congressional figures in her efforts to pressure the Brazilian government to locate her son, whom she hoped was not dead but had somehow miraculously survived and was detained somewhere. She then wrote a rushed letter to Dine explaining how the search for her son had affected her work. "Four months ago, when I began to think about it [the show], I was inspired by my country's colorful flowers and the beautiful birds. But, then, suddenly this nightmare entered my life and the flowers lost their color and the birds went crazy and I produced a collection with a political theme. It is the first time in the entire history of fashion where this has happened. So, I hope that this evening I will manage to make them think of the subject with this Collection. I apologize for this long letter, for this great Latin American tragedy that I am bringing to you."[48]

Zuzu's daughter, Ana Cristina, who was studying at Columbia University at the time, remembers that soon after her mother received an invitation for the show at the Brazilian Consulate, she decided to use the event to make a public statement about her recently disappeared son.[49] The Associated Press covered the story of this politicized fashion show, sending it over their wire service so that it appeared in papers throughout the United States and Canada.[50] Bill Cunningham, who wrote about the event for the *Chicago Tribune*, however, was disdainful of its political content: "Protests thru fashion are quite rare and seldom successful. The craft of fashion speaks clearest with joy."[51] Nevertheless, he offered a description absent from the Associate Press story: "The designer, herself, appeared in a long all-black gown with a dramatic scarf and belt made from 100 tiny silver crucifixes. A white porcelain angel hung around her neck." Several of the models also wore black armbands, a sign of mourning, over their checkered cotton dresses. Cunningham reported that instead of Zuzu's usual colorful prints of tropical images, "she embroidered cages over the birds, depicted cannon balls shooting 'angels,' and sewed on military caps and scrawny-looking children with black doves."

At the end of the show, Ana Cristina gently sang the song "Tristeza" (Sadness), a upbeat Carnival tune from 1966 that is undercut by sweetly melancholic lyrics.

Tristeza por favor vai embora . . .
Sadness, please go away.
My crying soul
Is seeing the end of me.
You made my heart
Your dwelling place.
Now my pain is just too much.
I want my happy life back.
I want to sing again.[52]

The silent audience seemed stunned at the impact of Zuzu's fashion statement.

More than three decades later, Ana Cristina remembered the event: "The reaction? They stood around without knowing how to react. They were shocked. There was very reserved applause. At the beginning [of the show] people didn't notice. It was something that increased little by little. At any rate, everyone was normal toward her. Lots of smiles and kisses. People in American fashion who knew my mother were very supportive. They already knew her suffering. Everyone knew about my mother's suffering, only Brazil didn't know."[53] After the event, Zuzu Angel declared to the press, "I shall continue to knock on all doors to let the world know—through my fashions, if necessary."[54] The photo of Zuzu that appeared over the Associated Press wire service revealed a woman who stared at the camera with a haunted, exhausted gaze.

The impact of her U.S. fashion show on a broader American audience must have been fleeting at best, as the article flashed across the wire service and appeared in a scattering selection of women's sections in local dailies through the country. However, in 1971 the news coverage about systematic torture in Brazil appeared more and more consistently in the press, and Zuzu Angel's continued campaign in Brazil remained a thorn in the side of the military. On August 15, 1971, the Associated Press ran a photo of Stuart over the wire service with the following caption: "Missing—Stuart A. Jones, who has been missing in Brazil for an undetermined period. He is the son of Norman A. Jones and Zuleika A. Jones, a Brazilian fashion designer, known internationally as Zuzu Angel. This picture was taken two years ago, when Jones was 24." Following, in block letters, was the warning: "VEDADA PARA O BRAZIL," or "PROHIBITED IN BRAZIL." Zuzu had managed to convince the international news agency to run the picture. This simple black-and-white head shot captured the charm of a dashing young man. It also referenced the disappearance of oppositionists, in this case the son of a Brazilian celebrity. The Brazilian generals clearly did not want the fate of Zuzu's beloved son to become a cause célebre.

### Latin American Fair of Opinion

In early March 1972, Boal premiered *Torquemada*, his latest drama in a production performed by New York University students. The play's prologue was also included in the Latin American Fair of Opinion, a month-long cultural event produced by the Theater of Latin America, directed by Boal, and staged at the St. Clement's Theater. It featured a "kaleidoscopic vision of Latin America through songs, poems, and plays" designed to educate, entertain, and politicize. The event was so popular, innovative, and successful that the Theater of Latin America won a *Village Voice*–sponsored Obie award for this Off-Broadway production.[55]

In a *Christian Science Monitor* interview Boal described how he began writing the script for *Torquemada* while still under preventive detention and in solitary confinement in Brazil. "I saw through the small window in my cell that every day a guard who had tortured a young woman was helping her to walk. He was going again to torture her . . . So I made drawings of scenes—the blocking out of my play—and told them that they were pictures for my little boy, who was then six."[56] Moved to Tiradentes Prison, Boal continued working on *Torquemada* by pretending that he was teaching himself French. Boal would write something innocuous in Portuguese on one side of the page and the script in French on the other side, since the guards could not read the foreign language. When the authorities finally released him, prison officials let Boal take the papers out with him because they thought there were simply language lessons.

Boal designed *Torquemada* as a play within a play. The drama juxtaposes the life of a group of political prisoners in a barracks-like cell with the story of Father Tomás de Torquemada, the Grand Inquisitor of Spain. The prisoners decide to present a play about the fifteenth-century inquisitor. As in *Zumbi*, Boal intertwined historical events with contemporary issues. Unlike his other productions, music and song do not underscore the raw reality of torture, past and present, portrayed in the drama. During the Latin American Fair of Opinion, Boal staged the prologue to the play, which reenacted his own torture experience, in the downstairs entrance of the theater space. The audience then went upstairs, where they could view four other short plays, presented simultaneously and continuously in different spaces in the theater.[57] The power of the performance was the raw emotion experienced by spectators as they watched an actor hanging upside down on the parrot's perch receive simulated electric shocks. Although the performance incorporated Brechtian techniques of creating a distance between the audience and the production in order to encourage reflection, Boal also relied on "empathy with the characters . . . to intensify the spectator's horror of this kind of violence."[58]

On March 22, 1972, João Augusto de Araújo Castro, the Brazilian ambassador to the United States, placed a phone call to Stephen Low at the Brazil desk in the State Department. After mentioning a number of subjects rapidly, the ambassador said that the Foreign Ministry had requested that he contact

U.S. government officials to inform them about the Latin American Fair of Opinion "at which a number of opponents of the present Brazilian government would speak, including Márcio Moreira Alves." The Brazilian ambassador had asked whether "anything could be done" but seemed doubtful that the U.S. government would intervene in matter like this, since the State Department "could not even handle Jack Anderson," referring to the syndicated columnist who had been systematically denouncing the military government in the *Washington Post* and hundreds of newspapers around the country.[59] Brazilian consular authorities in New York also sent observers to the fair to report on "the topics most directly related to Brazil." The six-page summary of the event included a short description of Boal's new work: "*Torquemada* by Augusto Boal: prologue of a longer play, presents a scene in which a youth is tortured on the 'parrot's perch' with electric shock and water [thrown] on his face to get him to confess his connection to subversive elements. No mention of the locality where the scene takes place."[60]

Like *Arena conta Zumbi* in 1969, the Latin American Fair of Opinion may have actually only been attended by several thousand New Yorkers, but the impact of these theater experiences far exceeded the numbers who attended the plays, art exhibits, films, and panel discussions. Boal, through his artistry and his own personal drama, had transmitted both the energy of resistance and a mechanism employed to discourage it. The echoes of his messages transcended the stage to reach journalists, editors, intellectuals, artists, theater critics, and others. Boal admitted that most of the people who attended his performances were already critical of U.S. foreign policy, including Washington's support of the Brazilian dictatorship, but he insisted that his work still had an impact. "We reinforced the idea that people were fighting, that they were in the struggle. If I had been released from prison, remained silent, and said nothing, it would have appeared that I had given up. But if you get out and speak out, even if you are preaching to the converted, the converted become stronger."[61] The shift in the tone of newspaper editorials in the United States about Brazil after 1968, as documented in chapter 5, suggests a symbiosis between oppositional cultural representation of Brazil and the political analyses presented by public opinion makers.

### The Living Theater

After the successful international campaign in the fall of 1971 that pressured the Brazilian government to deport the Living Theater members instead of prosecuting them for the possession of marijuana, the troupe regrouped in New York City. Over the next year and a half, Julian Beck and Judith Malina spent much of their time lecturing on campuses across the country in order to raise funds to sustain the group while they readjusted to the changing political situation in the United States.[62] In 1973 and 1974, the Living Theater toured the United States with a new presentation that, in part, denounced the torture and treatment of political prisoners in Brazil.[63] Almost thirty years after the first performance, Judith Malina recalled the origins of the play: "When we left the jail, we asked the prisoners who were left behind, 'What can we do for you? We are a poor theater group; we cannot send you money. That would be the first thing, of course, but since we can't send you money, what can we do?' All of them said, 'Tell people how it is. Show them what they do to us.' And so we evolved a piece called *Seven Meditations on Political Sado-Masochism* in which one scene was a reenactment of police torture very common in that prison where I was kept and in many others in Brazil at the time."[64]

Although none of the U.S. and European members of the theater group had suffered physical violence while imprisoned, Ivanildo Silvino de Araújo, a Brazilian member of the troupe, reportedly had received electric shock on the *pau de arara* (parrot's perch).[65] He eventually joined the Living Theater in the United States and performed the role of persecuted political prisoner in one of the scenes in this collective creation titled "A Meditation on Violence with a Text on Police Repression." The performance of *Seven Meditations* on campuses and at other venues across the country combined the enactment of torture with an indictment of the U.S. government's support for the Brazilian regime. As the actors representing the repressive Brazilian police apparatus administered increasingly intensive surges of simulated electric currents, Julian Beck read statements from Senator Frank Church's 1971 Senate Foreign Relations Hearings on U.S.-sponsored police programs in Brazil.

What was it about this stylized performance of torture that was so palpably upsetting and politically motivating? Of course, we have no real means of measuring the thoughts and emotional reactions of the audiences who observed the Living Theater, nor do we know exactly what impact it had on their lives. The power of the scene stemmed from more than the sight of the brutal and sadistic persecution of an innocent victim performed in painstakingly precise slow motion. A constellation of symbols and meanings permeated the performance. To a generation of activists coming of age in the late 1960s, the popularized image of Che Guevara with his long-flowing hair, unkempt beard, and red-starred black beret personified revolutionary masculinity. As has been well documented, in 1965 Che left his post as the Cuban minister of industry to support the revolutionary movement in the Congo.

When that endeavor failed, he relocated to Bolivia, where he was killed on October 8, 1967, while attempting to build a revolutionary base in the backlands, an area strategically located near Argentina and Brazil but totally inhospitable to guerrilla warfare. His tragic death in late 1967 positioned him to be the emblematic and ubiquitous figure of the international youth and student mobilizations of 1968—from Paris to Berkeley, Rio de Janeiro, and Mexico City. Che's sacrifice for the cause wed him to a generation that was rejecting capitalist materialism and saw the struggles of people throughout the third world as united with their own concerns in the United States.

In the minds of some in the audiences who viewed these performances, Ivanildo Silvino de Araújo's obvious African heritage may have disassociated him somewhat from an image of a Latin American revolutionary like Che Guevara with European features and long flowing black hair. However, to many of the generation of youth that attended this theater piece, revolutionaries came in all races. Malcolm X, the Black Panthers, Ho Chi Minh, and Nelson Mandela all symbolized resistance to the "system," nationally and internationally. For those watching the performance who knew even a little about Brazilian history and culture, seeing a person on the perch who simulated a "real" Brazilian revolutionary probably gave even more legitimacy to the performance.

The Living Theater collective did not choose to portray the rape of a female revolutionary under torture, although they surely had heard of such incidents while incarcerated in 1971 and when carrying out a campaign in the United States after the Brazil government expelled them. While imprisoned, Judith Malina became friends with a female political prisoner who had been jailed for her alleged involvement in a bombing. Malina also published her "Prison Diaries" in the local journal, O Estado de Minas, in hopes of helping the other prisoners, most of whom had been involved in armed struggle.[66] In choosing to follow a metascript that glorified the male rebel, the parrot's perch scene presents a valiant masculine figure, who, in spite of his vulnerability, resists (just as the Che resisted, in the mythic recounting of his tale) to the bitter end. While the male's body is exposed, violated, and suffers extreme pain, no comrades are turned in. The tortured person does not reveal information that betrays the revolution. In all of his vulnerability, he remains a "true" revolutionary.

The power of the scene also lies in the shocking image of the revolutionary stripped naked, his masculinity threatened by the electric currents pulsating toward his anus. The youthful protagonist, caught up in a wave of repression and outnumbered, is not only beaten and tortured but also sexually violated, if only symbolically. Recalling this scene, Malina commented on its effect on the audience: "The impact of this [scene] was very great because of two things — and culturally that is important: The relationship between the sexual taboo and the horror of the sexual taboo. That is why we called it political sado-masochism, which is the horrible meeting place of the sadistic, that is, the sexually cruel and the politically cruel."[67] This breach of the notion of the male body's impenetrability creates a scene in complete conflict with acceptable norms of appropriate treatment toward the masculine form and, as Malina noted, left the audience entirely unsettled.

The Living Theater performance, like the torture scene reenacted by Boal in *Torquemada*, offered a symbolic reconfiguration of the Brazilian body, or in this case, the male body. In these performances, it is no longer a site of sensual pleasure on sparkling sands under the radiant sun. Rather, the body becomes a recipient of sadistic, almost inexplicably violent behavior. Tanned bodies walking to the sea become prostrated and emasculated bodies shrieking out cries of pain. The tortured revolutionary, motivated by idealism and a political commitment, is treated with abject inhumanity. A new image had become fixed to the constellation of representations of Brazil that circulated in the 1970s.

## Naked Savages

While the Living Theater played, for the most part, to college crowds and in alternative theater spaces, another drama about the Brazilian political reality managed to reach a prominent and visible venue. In Christopher Hampton's show *Savages*, the British playwright dramatizes the kidnapping of a British official by Brazilian revolutionary guerrillas. Unlike *Seven Meditations*, Hampton does not reproduce the horrors of the parrot's perch on stage. Rather the script focuses on the alleged genocide of Brazilian Indians, the indifference of revolutionaries to their plight, and the complicity of the Brazilian dictatorship, missionaries, foreign companies, and international public opinion. *Savages* opened at the Royal Court, London, in 1973. After a short New York run, the play had a more publicized premier at the Mark Taper Forum of the Los Angeles Music Center in 1974, winning the Los Angeles Drama Critics Circle Award for Distinguished Playwrighting. The show briefly reopened on an Off-Off Broadway stage in early 1977. Hampton went on to write and produce many other successful plays and musicals, winning an Oscar in 1989 for his screenplay of *Dangerous Liaisons* and collaborating with Andrew Lloyd Webber in the musical *Sunset Boulevard*.

The set for *Savages* is a reconstructed Amazonian Indian village. Actors, representing indigenous people, the women bare-breasted and both sexes otherwise nude except for small *tangas* hiding their genitals, weave silently around each other in the background, carrying out everyday tasks of cooking, hunting, playing, and interacting as the main action takes place downstage. In the two-act play, the Movimento Revolucionário Brasileiro kidnaps Alan West, a would-be poet, gatherer of indigenous folk tales, and a high-level British diplomat. The revolutionaries offer his freedom in exchange for "the release of twenty-five prominent political prisoners, together with a safe conduct and facilities for flying them to Cuba."[68] Carlos Esquerdo, his captor, apologizes for the inconvenience and discusses Marxist economics and revolutionary politics with West. They pass the time playing chess. In flashback, West interacts with an anthropologist, Mark Crawford, who tells him about indigenous customs and relates the stories of the death of Indians through a government policy of integration that exposes them to diseases and to the avarice of land-grabbing Brazilians and foreigners. We also meet Major Brigg, who describes the multiple methods that the Brazilians invented to massacre the Indians over the years, and Reverend Elmer Penn, a missionary who brings them Christianity. As the drama about when and how West will be released by the revolutionaries plays out, the audience also follows the slow pacification, integration, and genocide of Brazil's native population.

At times, the script's pamphleteering language and style is not very subtle, and its symbolism (the name "West" for the British diplomat, and "Esquerdo" [left] for the revolutionary) is far too obvious. Ultimately, however, Hampton develops a nuanced political message that exempts no one from blame. The Brazilian left, the military regime, foreign missionaries, and romantic diplomats are all targets. Although guerrilla kidnapper Carlos is kind to his captor and concerned about his comfort, he is not an entirely likeable character. He makes dismissive remarks about a homosexual murdered by a death squad and then offsets the story with a detailed description of "real" horrors, namely, the rape and torture of a female political prisoner. When West queries him about the left's position on the Indians, Carlos counters with indifference, weighing their extinction against the abject poverty of the majority of the Brazilian population, as if the indigenous people were not a part of the nation. Hampton supplies the audience with exacting details of the involvement of foreign corporations in pushing the indigenous people off their land. His portrayal of the paternalistic Christian missionaries, while overdrawn, indicts their participation in the "pacification" of Brazil's original inhabitants. Throughout the production, the playwright also spells out the military regime's collaboration with the massacre of the indigenous population.

*Savages* ends in tragedy. An aircraft bombs and kills the members of the Indians' village as they are engaged in an indigenous religious ceremony. In the last scene, just as it seems that negotiations with the government have been successful and the guerrillas are preparing to release West, Carlos rushes into the guerrilla hideaway, shoots West in the chest, and flees with other revolutionaries. Police sirens sound. Projected images of newspaper clippings tell of a state funeral for the diplomat. The light comes up on the bodies of West and the dead Indians.

To guarantee that the print media was convinced that the play was based on hard facts, Gordon Davidson, who directed the Los Angeles production, organized a dramatic background briefing at the play's press opening. The director invited Niva Padilha, who was still living in Berkeley and helping to produce the *Brazilian Information Bulletin*, to an after-show discussion. Donning a ski mask to hide his identity, Niva struck a dramatic pose as he calmly answered the audience's questions about the political situation in Brazil. The anthropologist Shelton H. Davis, who had acted as a consultant to Davidson on the production, was also on hand to offer his expert knowledge about the main topic of the play. Although the director also invited the Brazilian government to send a representative, consular officials declined to appear.[69]

Theater critics were enthusiastic about the production and gave the play mostly positive reviews.[70] The *Brazilian Information Bulletin* worked closely with the director to make sure that the program for the production complemented the play's message. Its ten pages were crammed with information about the history of Brazil and its Indians. It included a detailed timeline and newspaper articles about torture, the high cost of living, foreign investment, and the Trans-Amazonian Highway. Davis wrote an impassioned denunciation of the genocide of Brazilian Indians. Desiring to move the audience to action, the program suggested that those interested in more information should contact the American Friends of Brazil, the publishers of *Brazilian Information Bulletin*; Indigena, a documentation center of the native people of the Americas; and Amnesty International.

No doubt audiences came away from the performance both educated about Brazilian politics and society and haunted by the images of the inhuman treatment of the Brazilian indigenous population. In remembering the impact of the play on public opinion, Davis, who had worked since 1971 in building international opposition to the mistreatment of the Brazilian

Indians, pointed to the fact that *Savages* came out at a time when the American Indian Movement was educating the public about the U.S. history of atrocities against the Native American population.[71] The staging of the drama's action with the picturesque Indian village as a backdrop elicits sympathy through a glimpse of rituals, dances, and other indigenous customs. However, the Indians remain part of the scenery and are portrayed as noble savages—innocent, pure, and simple, naked in their oneness with nature and corrupted by the missionary who seeks to clothe them. They are not protagonists of the drama but merely its victims. Rather than focusing on the torture of the Brazilian body (something talked about in the play but not dramatically enacted), *Savages* presents the *annihilation* of those bodies.

In the spirit of confrontational drama, at the end of the Living Theater's *Seven Meditations*, members of the collective weave through the audience asking "What can we do?" until they find someone willing to engage in a conversation about solutions to problems charted out during the performance. The director of *Savages* challenged the more conventional audience in a less direct way. *Savages* ends with human carnage and provides the ticket holder with a theater program, complete with tables, charts, and articles, to make sense of the slaughter.

It is impossible to know how many people who saw this drama took up the call to action suggested by the production's program. Certainly one could imagine that Hampton was preaching to the choir, as liberal-minded theatergoers might acknowledge the horrors of the message and then go on with their lives as usual. Hampton himself seemed quite cognizant of the limitations of theater in effecting political change: "I don't have much faith in the power of writers to change society, except in a very minimal way, in the very long run. Theater reflects society and very, very occasionally changes the way people think."[72] Yet the drama resonated beyond the Los Angeles run and another successful but brief staging in New York three years later. In an interview published in 1991, Hampton noted that *Savages* had been his best-selling play as a reading text "simply because the subject of the Indians and the rain forest is very much in people's consciousness."[73] Although *Savages* may not have moved many to act against the injustices being perpetrated in Brazil, it certainly offered another layer of information about the country to those interested in the subject. Moreover, this performance and that of the Living Theater left the clear message that something was sorely wrong in the land of tropical delights.

## CAPÍTULO X

---

## *"Quem é essa mulher?"*

Who is that woman
Who always sings that refrain?

**Miltinho and Chico Buarque, "Angélica," 1977**

Zuzu Angel dress worn at fashion show, New York City, September 1971.

Zuzu Angel had presented extensive documentation to the Brazilian Commission for the Defense of Human Rights about the disappearance of her son, yet the government-controlled entity perfunctorily archived the petition in 1972.[1] When all of the family's valiant efforts led nowhere, they resigned themselves to the possibility that Stuart had died. Yet, Zuzu still clung to the hope that her son might indeed have survived somewhere. In 1973, four separate military courts dismissed all charges that they had brought against Stuart in his absence.[2] Then, in October 1974, Zuzu discussed her son's case with Amnesty International officials in London.[3] They asked her for more documentation. "I couldn't pull back any more. I forgot the fantasy and dived into reality," she wrote in her unfinished memoirs.[4]

With renewed energy, Zuzu initiated another campaign to pressure the Brazilian military government. She wrote an impassioned letter to President Ernesto Geisel.[5] She drafted a letter to Senator John Sparkman, the chair of the U.S. Senate Foreign Relations Committee, requesting his assistance: "The American press has mentioned, even recently, numerous instances of Brazilians who have allegedly been tortured and killed for political reasons. It has also documented the Brazilian Government's persistent unwillingness to give a public accounting of their cases, despite pressures from local political and religious organizations. This is a case which, we believe, demands authoritative intervention from the U.S. Government because the democratic image of the United States in Brazil and elsewhere is seriously at stake."[6] Amnesty International secretary general Martin Ennals wrote a second letter to Senator Sparkman pointing out the case's broader significance: "Although justice still needs to be done with regard to Stuart Edgar Angel Jones, Amnesty International is equally concerned by the continuing serious violations of human rights in Brazil today, the echoes of which are heard internationally. Evidence of such violations is received by us virtually every day."[7]

In June 1975, Zuzu flew to Washington to begin a lobbying campaign. Although the military regime may have attempted to discourage her efforts by not providing information about her son, her national prominence protected her from imprisonment. Zuzu made contacts with Senator Church and visited half a dozen senators and congressional representatives, as well as State Department officials. Members of Congress sent a strongly worded letter to both Secretary of State Henry Kissinger and the Brazilian ambassador in Washington requesting information about the case. Robert Zimmerman, who worked the State Department Brazil Desk, responded in a letter to Ana Cristina about the family's inquiries: "The American Embassy in Brasília raised the question of your brother's welfare and whereabouts with the Brazilian Foreign Ministry in August. The Ministry responded that information available to date indicated that Stuart Angel Jones had not been in the custody of the Brazilian authorities. As a result of the embassy's inquiry, however, the Ministry agreed to check further with the appropriate authorities, noting matters of this type were outside the Ministry's direct competence."[8]

While State Department bureaucrats went through the motions of making inquiries, they did not provide Zuzu with a copy of a 1973 State Department telegram to Secretary of State Henry Kissinger revealing official knowledge about the her son's death. The communiqué noted, "As final chapter to the tragic case of Stuart Edgar Angel Jones, the Supreme Military Court last week in a secret session reaffirmed decision of the Air Force Tribunal in absolving Jones from his alleged contravention of National Security Act. As Department is aware, Jones was reported detained at Galeão Airport (Rio) in 1971 and subsequently murdered by Air Force Security agents." U.S. Ambassador Rountree signed the telegram.[9]

Although the State Department offered no direct assistance in clarifying the fate of Stuart, Zuzu continued to insist on the political significance of official solicitations of information. "The report requested from the State Department by the Foreign Relations Committee and by other senators and congressmen is very important because, regardless of what they find, it will be used during the Senate Foreign Relations Hearings (Humphrey Sept/75) and in the House (Fraser Jan/76) *to decide whether or not to suspend military aid to Brazil.*"[10] Indeed, as Zuzu pointed out in her memoirs, Congress had cut military aid to Chile and Korea due to hearings that offered proof of human rights violations in those countries.

Several months later, Zuzu had an opportunity once again to lobby a U.S. official. Secretary of State Henry Kissinger visited Rio de Janeiro in February 1976. In order to get around the tight security in the Sheraton Hotel, she posed as a sophisticated and elegant elderly American woman, donned hat and gloves, and delivered a dossier about her son to one of Kissinger's aides.[11] There is no indication, however, that Kissinger ever read the material or responded to her denunciation. A month later, a story appeared in the Brazilian press announcing that the Special Justice Council of the Office of the Auditor of the Navy unanimously declared the preventative detention of Stuart and twenty-three other leftists accused of "subversion."[12] It was a thinly disguised effort by the military regime to intimate that Stuart was still alive, at large, and involved in revolutionary activities.

In 1971, Zuzu had found it virtually impossible to get publicity for her case within Brazil. However, the gradual though uneven political liberalization under President Geisel permitted information about Stuart's disappearance to reach a larger audience. In 1975, historian Hélio Silva published a dossier about the case in the twentieth volume of *História da República Brasileira* that was widely circulated.[13] Two years before the Argentine Madres de la Plaza de Mayo (who were pejoratively known as the "locas" or "crazy women" of the Plaza de Mayo) gained international recognition for their courageous efforts to demand the whereabouts of missing relatives, Zuzu placed herself in the national and international arena as a relentless and visible testimony of the on-going arbitrary and authoritarian nature of the Brazilian regime. Unlike the Madres, who tied white scarves around their heads with the names of their disappeared relatives embroidered on them, Zuzu, the incarnation of lively and colorful fashion, chose to dress in black mourning garb. She also began to fear for her own life. Soon after she renewed her efforts on behalf of her son, Zuzu reported to her friends that she had been followed at night when she left her boutique and had received death threats.[14]

On April 14, 1976, Zuzu Angel was driving home from a dinner party when her car crashed. She died instantly. The official version was that she fell asleep at the wheel. Medical experts found no alcohol in her blood, but a report prepared by the Divisão de Segurança e Informações (Division of Security and Intelligence, DSI), the government's intelligence gathering agency, noted the political volatility surrounding potential accusations that someone might have assassinated the fashion designer. The report summarized interviews with friends to build the argument that she had been very tired, had had a busy day with a television crew that had come to her boutique to film her latest fashions, and had commented on her exhausted state to people at the dinner party. The report concluded that it was an accidental death; but, in view of the "probable international campaign against the Government," it mentioned the importance of "the clinical mental state of ZUZU ANGEL before her death, given the fact that there were indications in her written declarations of persecution mania and morbid fixation about the memory of her son."[15]

Attached to the DSI report was a duplicate of a letter that Zuzu had left with several trusted friends. The government's intelligence gathering services had affixed a copy of the second page of Zuzu's signed letter to President Geisel to verify her handwriting. It stated, "This document is outside the country in the hands of American relations of my martyred son. If something were to happen to me, if I turn up dead by an accident, assault or other means, it will have been the work of the same murderers of my beloved son.[16]

For eighteen years, the government's official story about Zuzu Angel's car accident was the one outlined by the Division of Security and Intelligence. Then, in 1998, the Ministry of Justice's Special Commission about the Death and Disappearance of Political Activists voted four to three that Zuzu Angel's death had not been an accident but politically motivated.[17]

In Zuzu Angel's 1968 début in *Women's Daily Wear* she is quoted as saying, "Because I have this freedom thing about fashion, designing is also for me complete happiness, handling fabric, . . . creating color combinations, . . . letting all the thoughts and ideas flow freely. It's both a mystical and a sensuous experience."[18] The shift from apparently apolitical creative fashion designer to impassioned, valiant, and suffering mother, from designing clothes for international celebrities to being ignored among official circles in Brazil, and then her untimely death in 1976, all converged to create a hero and a martyr. Zuzu Angel became the suffering mother, the Holy Mother of God, seeking the body of her crucified son, who had disappeared, snatched from his tomb, with no record even of the whereabouts of his mortal remains. Even though the Brazilian military regime prohibited any mention in the media of Zuzu Angel in the early stages of her odyssey in search of Stuart, news of her politicized fashion show, as well as her efforts to locate her son, or his body, spread among the middle-class anti-dictatorship circles.

Zuzu Angel's death anointed her, along with her son, as martyrs of the opposition to the generals. A musical ode to Zuzu entitled *Angélica*, written in 1977 by songwriter Chico Buarque, hauntingly invited the question: "Quem é essa mulher . . .?"

> Who is this woman
> Who always sings this refrain?
> I only want to rock my son
> Who lives in the darkness of the sea.[19]

Buarque had become renowned for his lyrical political prose that at times managed to circumvent censors and criticize the regime. His melodic elegy helped enshrine Zuzu among the pantheon of latter-day saints who had resisted the military regime. In the process, Zuzu re-clothed the Brazilian body and gave it new meaning as a form upon which to fashion a protest. Sensuous tropical corporality had a new content. The pleasure-seeking, exotic, and erotic Brazilian body and its coverings had become political and mournful, if only for a brief moment.[20]

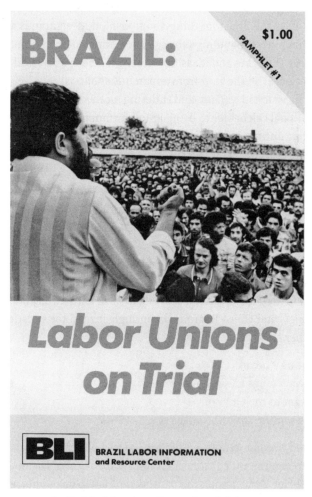

# BRAZIL:

$1.00

PAMPHLET #1

## Labor Unions on Trial

**BLI** BRAZIL LABOR INFORMATION
and Resource Center

Brazilian Labor Information and Resource Center *Bulletin*, 1981.
REPRINTED BY PERMISSION OF BRAZILIAN LABOR INFORMATION AND RESOURCE CENTER.

# 11

# THE SLOW-MOTION RETURN TO DEMOCRACY

. . . Finally, American complicity after the 1964 coup helped set in motion a decade of authoritarian rule, just as official US silence in the face of repeated repression must share the blame for the erosion of human rights. Congress should seriously question the use of tax dollars for regimes which systematically violate human rights; while American scholars, religious leaders, and journalists must see in it that [Vladimir] Herzog's death puts new life into the common struggle for justice and liberty. — **Richard Morse, Thomas Skidmore, Alfred Stepan, Stanley Stein, and Charles Wagley, letter to the editor,** *New York Review of Books*, **November 27, 1975**

One cannot minimize the impact of the military coup in Chile on September 11, 1973, on people in the United States who had gazed south and enthusiastically embraced the progressive agenda of the Allende government. The Popular Unity electoral coalition victory in 1970 had promised the possibility of a Latin American "peaceful road to socialism." Pictures of the Chilean Air Force bombing the presidential palace and the image of Salvador Allende, machine gun in hand, symbolically posed to defend his government offered a dramatic and tragic ending to this possibility. The photos of thousands detained in the National Stadium, where many were executed, symbolized the brutality of the new regime. Pinochet's dark glasses and somber poses confirmed pervasive stereotypical images of Latin American dictators. The Chilean tragedy of September 1973 immediately galvanized those activists who had been working on Latin America. They focused their attentions on the unfolding drama under the Pinochet dictatorship. New solidarity committees sprouted up across the country. The Vietnam War had engendered widespread cynicism in American youth about U.S. foreign policy. Jack Anderson's revelations in 1972 about the collusion of the Nixon administration and ITT, the multinational telecommunication giant, in disrupting the Chilean economy to bring Allende's downfall merely reinforced the distrust in White House policies abroad.[1] The fact that the Nixon administration did not denounce the new regime simply confirmed widely held suspicions among activists that the CIA had been behind Allende's overthrow.[2] Chile became a noble cause with clear characters in concise roles. A progressive democratic socialist government had attempted a peaceful road to socialism through the ballot box. The people of Chile had united, but, sadly, had been defeated. They had been cut down by an alliance of fascist generals, right-wing politicians, international capitalists, and their allies in the Pentagon, the State Department, and the White House. By February 1974, more than two hundred groups had formed across the country, and three hundred activists held a conference in Chicago to coordinate activities nationally.[3]

Those working on the *Brazilian Information Bulletin* in Berkeley and the Common Front for Latin America (COFFLA) in Washington, D.C., as well as activists in the National Council of Churches in New York and the National Conference of U.S. Bishops in Washington all agreed that they too needed to shift their energies toward the serious human rights violations taking place in Chile. For some, like Marcos Arruda and Niva Padilha, this was not merely an ideological question of international solidarity. Many of their friends and comrades in the student movement and in Ação Popular had gone into exile in Chile, and their lives were immediately endangered. In an anticommunist and xenophobic move, the Pinochet government had called on Chileans to turn in to the police any suspicious foreigners. The police and military rounded up thousands of revolutionaries, political exiles, and their families from Argentina, Bolivia, Brazil, Paraguay, Peru, and Uruguay and took them to the National Stadium or detention centers. The Chilean government simply summarily executed many of them. Floods of people crowded into foreign embassies seeking political asylum.[4] Jean Marc Von der Weid was among those Brazilians in Chile at the time, and people in the United States who had met him on his tour in 1973 were particularly concerned about his whereabouts.

Harry and Loretta Strharsky commented on the shift in activities that took place in Washington, D.C. "After the coup we were so focused on Chile for such a long time that I think that COFFLA just did Chile work . . . , and the rest tailed away gradually. There was no political split or people moving out of the area. Everyone got so totally consumed by the aftermath of the coup in Chile because it had been such a beacon of hope. It was such a great potential for a model that people wanted to see work, and it came to such a disastrous end."[5] A burst of energy gave renewed impetus to the Latin American collectives, study groups, and action committees throughout the country. New volunteers joined veteran activists in an urgency to respond to the wave of repression in Chile.

At the same time, the new Brazilian government of General Ernesto Geisel offered signs that the regime was loosening up.[6] Unlike Marcos Arruda's cautious characterizations of the Brazilian political situation proffered at the New York meeting in early September 1973, other observers predicted that Geisel would implement a series of liberal measures. Below the surface, the economic situation in Brazil was also changing, although it was not apparent in 1973, the fourth year of a record 10 percent yearly growth in the GNP. Two events, however, would push the Geisel regime toward political liberalization. The sharp rise in oil prices in 1974 began to put a damper on the dramatic expansion of the Brazilian economy. At the time, Brazil had few national oil resources to fuel growth, forcing the government to spent valuable foreign reserves on imports. This eventually meant a return to inflation, as the government borrowed money to keep the economy afloat. Simultaneously, the Movimento Democrático Brasileiro, the legal political opposition, gained electoral ground.

The November 1974 congressional elections in Brazil and the United States shifted the political balance in both countries. Still confident that the ruling generals were firmly entrenched in power and could ride to another legislative electoral victory based on the previous four years' economic performance, the Brazilian government authorized television and radio campaigning, engendering an intense public political debate. The outcome was startling. In senate races, the opposition MDB garnered 4.6 million more votes than ARENA, the government's party, and doubled its seats in the lower house. In state assembly elections, the opposition won control of the states of Paraná and Rio Grande do Sul and made significant gains in Rio de Janeiro and São Paulo. "For most political analysts, as well as for MDB members, the opposition victory was a reversal of electoral patterns and a surprise," writes the political scientist Maria Helena Moreira Alves. "The elections were generally considered to have been equivalent to a plebiscite in which voters voted *against* the government, rather than *for* the opposition."[7] Within a year, the dispersed forces that opposed the regime within Brazil would begin to coalesce.

The November 1974 electoral outcomes in the United States were even more dramatic. In the aftermath of the Watergate scandal, the resignation of President Nixon, and his subsequent pardon by President Ford, popular sentiment turned against the Republicans. Democrats made significant gains in U.S. congressional elections, winning a 2 to 1 margin in the House and sixty-one seats in the Senate. A batch of young liberal Democrats swept into Congress poised to undo the legacy of Nixon's foreign policy.

This chapter charts the shifts in activities employed by those committed to supporting human rights in Brazil in the mid- and late 1970s and into the early 1980s, as the political situation crept toward a political liberalization and, eventually, the process of democratization. As in previous years, reduced numbers of activists did not discourage ongoing efforts to leverage significant results from modest resources.

### A Washington Lobby

In 1970, Bill Wipfler, Brady Tyson, Phil Wheaton, Tom Quigley, Mary Lou Suhor, John Sinclair, and others formed the Latin American Strategy Committee (LASC) to coordinate activities on the East Coast. Though its mission was broad, its members focused considerable attention on building interest for issues related to Latin America among religious constituencies. The committee also closely followed events in Brazil. The ad-hoc group periodically met to formulate plans about how to mobilize their efforts among religious and liberal supporters. The LASC also played a crucial role in behind-the-scenes organizing for the Church committee hearings in 1971 and developed close relationships with congressional aides.[8] After the Chilean coup, the committee realized it needed a more effective sustained presence in the nation's capital. Originally, LASC envisioned setting up an office with a staff person who would collect information about congressional and administrative policy on Latin America and channel it to national religious bodies. The idea evolved into the Washington Office on Latin America (WOLA), with Joseph Eldridge as the paid staff person.

Eldridge was the ideal person for the job. A minister by vocation, he had been sent to Chile in 1970 by the United Methodist Church. "I arrived the week that Allende was elected and witnessed the tumultuous and exuberant excitement of folks who saw this as a major transformation of Chilean society. Of course, I didn't know what was going on."[9] Eldridge had grown up in Dallas, Texas, and east Tennessee and had been involved in the civil rights movement. "I became enamored by the vision of a government led by a president who went out of his way to preserve constitutional norms and operate within a framework that protected core freedoms and yet tried to bring about a profound social, political, and economic revolution." For three years he closely followed the political process in Chile, working primarily with foreign missionaries and Chilean religious activists. "We saw as our charge to alert the bodies back in the United States to encourage them to convey information [about the situation in Chile] to their constituency so that pressure could be brought on the U.S. government to stop meddling in Chile."

Then the coup occurred. On September 16, 1973, armed forces invaded and ransacked the office where Eldridge and other religious activists worked and abducted two U.S.-born Maryknoll seminarians, whom they took to the National Stadium. Although authorities eventually released and expelled the two from the country, it soon became clear to Eldridge and others that they could do little in Chile. "Our Chilean friends said, 'The biggest contribution will be in the States. Go!'" Eldridge followed their advice and returned to the United States. From Tennessee, he called Brady Tyson to seek counsel about what to do next. Eldridge had met Tyson at a religious training program before leaving for Chile. "He was a southern, radical, a populist and deeply involved in civil rights. We hit it off. I called him out of the blue and said, 'What do I do?' And Brady said, 'Here is what you do: you come to Washington. You can stay in my house and enroll in American University." Soon thereafter, the LASC asked if Eldridge could staff the newly formed Washington Office on Latin America.

With the support of Ed Snyder of the Friends Committee on National

Legislation, a liberal Quaker-based lobbying group, Eldridge began working Capitol Hill, meeting with senators and representatives but more with their aides, especially those hired by the new crop of liberal Congress people. WOLA's immediate legislative agenda was to cut off aid to the Chilean government, provide refugee status to exiles, and reverse the State Department's policy that gave backhanded, if not outright, support to military regimes.[10] Ironically, another incident of torture in Brazil ended up serving as political leverage to help consolidate WOLA's lobbying against the Pinochet regime and to legitimize the organization in Washington.

### Prayers in Prison

Fred B. Morris comes from a long line of Protestant pastors. His father, grandfather, great-grandfather, and brother were all Methodist ministers. After receiving a master's degree in theology and serving in several U.S. churches, he became a missionary in Brazil, arriving in the country in January 1964. From 1965 to 1967, he worked in different rural Methodist churches and then was assigned to a congregation in an outlying district of Rio de Janeiro. He also taught at the Methodist Seminary. After a two-year furlough in the United States, when he received a master's degree in urban sociology, he returned to Brazil in October 1970 at the invitation of the Brazilian Methodist Church to organize and direct a community center in Recife, Pernambuco, and build ecumenical relations between Protestants and Catholics. He also worked as a stringer for *Time* magazine, earning extra money by assisting the correspondent based in Rio de Janeiro, while also occasionally feeding stories to the Associated Press.[11]

While in Recife, Morris built contacts with Archbishop Hélder Câmara and other progressive Catholics and taught urban sociology.[12] The breakup of his marriage and a financial crisis in the Board of Global Ministries that forced them to recall ministers led him to request a leave of absence from religious duties.[13] He began working in a local industry while continuing as a lay volunteer in the community center, located in an impoverished neighborhood. "On September 30, 1974, as I was leaving my home in the company of a Brazilian friend, Luís Soares de Lima, we were surrounded by a dozen armed men with machine guns and .45 caliber automatics, who proceeded to carry us off at gunpoint to the headquarters of the Fourth Army."[14] He was systematically tortured for the next four days.

Two months later, he described the first moments of his harrowing seventeen-day imprisonment in testimony before the Subcommittee on

International Organizations and Movements of the House of Representatives Committee on Foreign Affairs:

> After about 15 minutes, the door of the cell was flung open, my head was again covered, my hands were handcuffed behind my back, and I was again pushed and shoved about 20 yards through various twists and turns into a small room, which seemed to be one of several interrogation rooms.
>
> On the way, I calmed myself by repeating the 23rd Psalm, affirming for myself my Christian faith that there is that part of me that they could not reach even though they were to kill me.
>
> I arrived at the torture chamber with a strong inner calm even though I could already hear Luís's voice screaming in pain.[15]

The torture stopped only because of the intervention of the American consul stationed in Recife and the assistance of the U.S. ambassador. After Morris spent eleven more days in solidarity confinement, the government expelled him from the country on orders signed by President Geisel as a person "prejudicial to the interests of Brazil."[16]

To this day, Fred Morris does not know all the reasons for which the authorities arrested him. One explanation might have been his journalistic activities. *Time* magazine had recently published a favorable article about Archbishop Hélder Câmara titled "Pastor of the Poor."[17] The piece mentioned that the prelate's associates had been arrested and tortured and that he continued to denounce the military regime abroad. While Morris was incarcerated, his interrogators insistently pressed him to discuss his involvement in writing the article, but as the Methodist minister explained in his testimony before the House committee, the *Time* reporter had not even consulted him.[18] Another reason might have been his alleged involvement in a "subversive" organization. Authorities arrested Luís Soares de Lima along with Morris and accused him of being a part of the leadership of the Communist Party of Brazil. Morris's captors demanded that he explain his relationship to Soares and what he knew about left-wing clandestine organizing in the region. Morris insisted under torture and later in sworn testimony before the House committee that he only found out Luís's real name after the military had imprisoned and tortured him.[19]

Representative Donald Fraser, a liberal Democrat from Minnesota, conducted the hearing in which Fred Morris testified, one in a series that the congressional representative held over the course of late 1973 and 1974 about human rights violations in Chile, South Korea, and other parts of the world.

The title given to the published testimony, *Torture and Oppression in Brazil*, summed up the underlying themes that antidictatorship activists in the United States had articulated over the previous five years about the Brazilian government. It also marked a clear success for their efforts.

At the hearing, Morris's testimony was clear and direct."[20] Joe Eldridge explained that activists working on Chile had brought other torture victims to Congress in order to bring home to politicians the brutality of the Pinochet regime. "It is very difficult for a Latin American to sit down and in the eight minutes that a member of Congress gives them to tick off with precision why they are there. Despite coaching, they cannot convey the message as forcefully as an American . . . Fred knew how to do it and do it very powerfully. He knew how psychologically, emotionally, and politically to make an impact, and he had a big impact in Washington."

Events in Chile had brought the issue of human rights in Latin America to Congress's attention, to a certain extent pushing aside educational efforts about ongoing repression in Brazil. Yet the July 1974 Amnesty International *Newsletter* was emphatic: "New wave of arrests, disappearances, and torture in Brazil makes mockery of 'economic miracle,' . . . These latest waves of arrests, the continuing 'disappearance' of people throughout Brazil because of their real or imagined opposition to the government, and the persistence of the brutal torture for which Brazil has become notorious in recent years."[21] In short, little had changed since AI's report in 1972. Thus, Fred Morris's case served a threefold end. He brought renewed attention to Brazil through his lobbying efforts in Washington. He offered U.S. politicians convincing testimony that activists did not exaggerate the news of torture in Latin America. It was not "communist propaganda," and military governments could even torture Methodist ministers. Finally, he helped strengthen WOLA's efforts to move Congress into legislative action. As Eldridge assessed Morris's impact: "Although bad stuff was happening in Brazil, it was very difficult for anyone to pay any attention to it because Chile dominated the discussion. Chile had the attraction. Fred clearly elevated the profile of Brazil on Capitol Hill, and also began to let people know that torture was not relegated only to Pinochet, but it was widespread throughout the hemisphere, including in the most populous, and largest and most economically powerful country."

No doubt, the fact that Morris was a stringer for *Time* magazine was one of the reasons that the weekly picked up the story of Morris's ordeal in a full-page article, "Torture Brazilian Style," in November 1974 that dramatically recounted his experience in prison.[22] The magazine also organized a whirlwind tour in order to promote the piece, starting with a ten-minute interview on the *Today Show*. Morris appeared on twenty-six other television programs and numerous national and local radio broadcasts, recounting the ordeal in Brazil and generalizing about his experience within the context of the deteriorating human rights situation in Latin America. His was a powerful narrative of a pastor retelling the story of his torture, including how he had found strength by continually reciting the Twenty-third Psalm during his seventeen-day imprisonment. It likely touched political, emotional, and religious chords among the viewing and listening audiences.

### Chile and the Bertrand Russell Tribunal

Like Fred Morris and WOLA, grassroots activists linked repression in Brazil to the deterioration of human rights in Chile and other countries of Latin America. In April 1974, the Madison, Wisconsin–based group Community Action on Latin America (CALA) organized a national conference titled "Repression and Development in Brazil and Latin America."[23] Organizers originally had planned the weekend event to focus exclusively on Brazil, but after the coup in Chile, its scope widened, and the gathering brought together many leading activists and progressive academics from around the country working on diverse areas of Latin America. In the imagination of U.S. leftists, Brazil had become folded into more generalized notions about a new wave of torture and human rights abuses sweeping the Southern Cone of Latin America. The conference served as well as an organizing tool for those trying to mobilize support for the Bertrand Russell Tribunal (described in chapter 9) that had also enlarged its mandate to examine repression in Brazil, Chile, and other Latin American countries. Tribunal organizers had composed an international jury that included three U.S. members: James Petras, a radical professor of Latin American sociology at the State University of New York, Binghamton; Benjamin Spock, the renowned pediatrician and anti–Vietnam War leader; and George Wald, a Nobel Prize winner in biology. The tribunal also invited Noam Chomsky, the linguist and radical intellectual, as an honorary member.[24] The idea of the tribunal, however, never took hold among U.S. progressive circles, in spite of valiant attempts by members of the Common Front for Latin America, the Washington–based group that led the effort in the United States.

The Russell Tribunal II on Latin America held sessions from March 30 to April 5, 1974, in Rome and received documentation of human rights violations in Brazil, Chile, Uruguay, and Bolivia. The "Provisional Verdict" summarized the human rights situation in Brazil, reiterating evidence and testimonies that had already been amply circulated in Europe and the United

States. Then, focusing on Chile, the document began, "Leaving Brazil and going on to Chile means passing from a slow process of destruction to a savage eruption of violence that has tried to accomplish in a few months what other dictatorial regimes have sought to do in the course of many years."[25] The report outlined similar human rights violations that occurred in the other three countries of the Southern Cone of Latin America and concluded "the authorities that exercise power in Brazil, Chile, Uruguay, and Bolivia to be guilty of serious, repeated, and systematic violations of human rights."[26] The overall language of the "provisional verdict" reflected the left-wing influence of the tribunal organizers, and for that reason the media might not have picked up its sessions as a viable news story. The U.S. press had portrayed the original tribunal on Vietnam in 1967 as biased and unduly anti-American, and perhaps this image continued to tarnish the validity of its proceedings or findings in the eyes of correspondents covering events in Europe at the time. Yet the tribunal's conclusion was not unlike that of the IACHR of the OAS, which had summed up a four-year-long assessment of Brazil that same month in its report to the OAS General Assembly. Both unequivocally held that the military regime had been involved in systematic gross violations of human rights.

### Death of a Journalist

By 1975, the Brazilian forces of repression had successfully eliminated the last vestiges of the guerrilla movement. Between 1972 and 1975, the army carried out a massive campaign that mobilized up to twenty thousand men in order to smash an attempt by no more than a hundred or so militants of the Communist Party of Brazil to establish a rural guerrilla movement in the Amazon region of Araguaia.[27] With the "radical" left crushed, the armed forces turned its attention to the more moderate pro-Soviet Brazilian Communist Party.[28] On October 24, 1975, agents of the DOI-CODI unit of the Second Army in São Paulo visited TV Cultura, the state-run public television station, to talk with Vladmir Herzog, the director of journalism. The plain-clothes police wanted to detain him immediately, but after a long conversation he managed to convince them that he would voluntarily appear for questioning the following morning. He dutifully showed up at eight o'clock. Twelve hours later, the police announced that he had hanged himself with a piece of cloth from the window bars of the police cell where he had been detained. A photo of the corpse intended to document his suicide showed him hanging with his legs bent and his knees almost touching the floor. No one who knew Vladimir thought that he had killed himself.[29]

When Bela Feldman-Bianco read the news about his death in the *New York Times*, she became extremely distressed. Vladimir Herzog and his wife Clarice were close friends who had just recently visited her in New York City. Raised in a left-wing Jewish family in São Paulo, Feldman-Bianco completed her degree in social sciences at the University of São Paulo in 1966. Fondly recalling her student days in the early 1960s during an interview in 2003, she reminisced, "We were a part of Jângo's [Goulart] times: the reform, everyone willing to make a revolution. Our mission was to transform Brazil . . . We had the idea that our fate was tied to those movements. Then came the 1964 coup; it was a real shock."[30] When police arrested colleagues that she knew well in 1969 and her then-husband received a fellowship to study in the United States, they decided to leave the country. Her former professor Florestan Fernandes encouraged her to contact Charles Wagley at Columbia University for help in entering the field of anthropology. Sometime in 1970, she met Ralph Della Cava and joined discreet activities against the military regime while circulating among the large number of Brazilians studying in New York. When she read the *Times* article, "Brazilian TV Man Held as Communist Is Reported Suicide," she immediately tried to call Clarice Herzog in São Paulo. "When I finally managed to talk to Clarice, she asked me, 'Please, get the word out.'" Her political commitment and the close ties to the Herzog family motivated her to take action.

In Brazil, the faked suicide mobilized broad forces against the military regime.[31] A rejuvenated student movement headed by a new generation of activists led 30,000 university students and professors in a weeklong strike. The journalists' union remained in permanent session in protest against the military's measures. Forty-two bishops signed a statement against the state's violence. In defiance of government bans on public demonstrations, less than a week after Herzog's death, 8,000 people converged on the downtown cathedral to celebrate an ecumenical service in honor of the murdered journalist. Cardinal Arns, the progressive prelate of São Paulo who had begun to assume a leadership role in the legal opposition to the dictatorship, officiated.[32] Because Herzog was Jewish, and in a show of ecumenical and oppositional unity, Rabbi Henry Sobel and Jaime Wright, a Presbyterian minister active in antidictatorship activities, joined the cardinal at the mass.[33] It was a turning point in unifying opposition to the military regime.

In New York, Feldman-Bianco, Della Cava, and others organized a flurry of activities to denounce the death of Herzog. Once again, Della Cava, through Wagley at Columbia University, solicited the support of prominent Brazilian specialists, who signed a letter to the editor of the *New York Review of Books*.[34]

Effectively, "Brazil: The Sealed Coffin" was a manifesto against the dictatorship that presented the contradictions embedded in the alleged moves toward the liberalization of the regime. "Despite the conciliatory policies of Brazil's President Ernesto Geisel over the last eighteen months and the restoration of some legal guarantees, hard-line military circles, centered chiefly but not exclusively in São Paulo, and allied to foreign and national interests, continue to exert a major role in national affairs . . . At stake in the outcome of the Herzog case, then, is whether the corporativist military faction within the Brazilian armed forces will achieve greater political control or whether efforts for a gradual return to civil liberties are still workable."[35]

Under national and international pressure, President Geisel ordered an investigation that ratified the finding that Herzog had committed suicide, even though it was clear that the police had killed him under torture. Four months later, authorities arrested Manoel Fiel Filho, a trade union activist from the São Paulo Metalworkers' Union. He also allegedly committed suicide.[36] Geisel was furious that the forces of repression in São Paulo had continued out of control and challenged his authority. He sacked the commander of the Second Army. Missteps by the torturers, combined with growing civilian opposition to the regime, had forced the president to take drastic measures.[37] The uneven process toward controlled liberalization continued.

In the early 1970s, Archbishop Hélder Câmara had played an important role in coalescing religious critics of the military regime and in building international links to supporters in the United States and Europe. Government censorship, however, had silenced his voice within Brazil.[38] By the mid-1970s, Cardinal Arns, the prelate of the largest Catholic diocese in the world, eclipsed his popularity. A revitalized student movement slowly pushed the limits of police control through localized strikes and protest actions at key universities around the country. Other sectors of civil society, such as the Brazilian Bar Association and the Brazilian Press Association, began taking a more visible stand against the military. Like the more radical sectors within the MDB, they were more actively working for democracy. Facing the possibility of another electoral defeat in the November 1976 elections, Geisel used IA-5 to take away the political rights of several outspoken congressmen and forced a law through Congress that set severe limitations on radio and television ads. Despite these restrictions on campaigning, in the November elections the MDB won control of municipal councils in the country's largest cities.[39]

At the same time, political changes in the United States opened new possibilities for activists supporting the "decompression" process in Brazil. Jimmy Carter, a one-term governor from Georgia running as a moralizing outsider, took advantage of the generalized skepticism of the electorate in the wake of the Nixon's imperial presidency to make a successful bid for the White House. Carter made several public pronouncements linking his candidacy to a policy of distancing the White House from countries that tortured their citizens.[40] After his election, Carter upgraded the mild mechanisms set up by the Ford administration to implement new human rights legislation by establishing the Bureau of Human Rights and Humanitarian Affairs under the direction of an assistant secretary of state. Carter appointed Patricia Derian, a Mississippi civil rights activist, to head the bureau. Although significantly expanding the administration's profile regarding human rights, Carter reserved the right to refrain from taking a stand against a given country when he deemed it necessary.[41]

### An Envoy Voices Regret

The election of Jimmy Carter offered Brady Tyson an unusual new opportunity. The tireless activist had maintained close links to the U.S. civil rights movement while in Washington. When Carter tapped Andrew Young, an assistant to Dr. Martin Luther King Jr. and two-term congressional representative from Georgia, to serve as the U.S. ambassador to the United Nations, Young invited Brady Tyson to join the administration and work on human rights in Latin America. His first international assignment was in Geneva. Tyson was assigned to serve as an advisor to Allard K. Lowenstein, the American delegate to the United Nations Human Rights Commission, which at the time had only "timidly approached issues of political repression in Latin America because of the resistance by countries opposed to that body being critical of their countries' internal affairs."[42] In his maiden speech before the international entity, Tyson addressed the thirty-two-nation commission during a discussion of the human rights situation in Chile. His candid remarks shocked both State Department officials and representatives of the Chilean government.

> Our delegation would be less than candid and untrue to ourselves and our people if we did not express our profoundest regrets for the role some Government officials, agencies and private groups played in the subversion of the previously democratically elected Chilean Government that was overthrown by the coup of Sept. 11, 1973. We recognize fully that the expression of regrets, however profound, cannot contribute significantly to the reduction of suffering and terror that the people of Chile have experienced in the last two years.[43]

His speech also criticized the governments of Argentina, Brazil, and Uruguay.

Tyson's "regrets" garnered worldwide news coverage and a quick disclaimer from the U.S. government. A White House spokesperson insisted that President Carter had not been consulted about the speech in advance, and the State Department described it "as a personal and unauthorized statement that did not reflect the views of the Administration."[44] The State Department immediately "invited" Tyson to "visit" Washington "to make sure he understands the ground rules." In typical candor, Brady recognized his diplomatic faux pas. "As a personal statement I do not regret what I said, but I now understand that I exceeded my instructions, for which I am very sorry." However, he still insisted that he had acted within the general "framework" of the Carter administration's concern for human rights.[45] At a news conference, President Carter commented that Tyson's statement was "inappropriate" and that the 1975 Church Commission had found no evidence directly linking the U.S. government to the overthrow of Allende. The State Department press spokesperson credited the incident to the fact that the new administration was facing many difficult issues in its first days in power.[46] Tyson's rift with the Carter administration paralleled a growing chasm between the U.S. government and the Brazilian generals that had been brewing for several years.

### A Special Relationship Revised

The amendment to the Foreign Assistance Act of 1961, drawn up on June 30, 1976 and known as 502B, marked a significant victory for human rights advocates and their allies in Congress because it denied security assistance to those countries that violated the human rights of their citizens. It also mandated that the State Department prepare an annual report for all countries receiving U.S. military aid. Suddenly the political situation in Brazil came under closer official scrutiny. Moreover, after the November elections, early efforts by the new Carter administration to void Brazil's nuclear accord with Germany chilled relations with the Geisel government. In March 1977, a crisis between the two nations erupted.[47]

Following the new provision in the Foreign Assistance Act, the State Department prepared a report on the state of human rights in Brazil. The document recognized that under the Geisel administration there had been improvements in the treatment of political prisoners and that censorship was at the lowest level in many years.[48] Amnesty International's 1977 report recorded a similar trend.[49] The Brazilian government, however, was not pleased with the report, even though the U.S. government had not yet officially released it, and President Geisel announced Brazil's refusal to accept further U.S. military assistance. In reality, as the political scientist Timothy J. Power has noted, the rejection of U.S. military assistance was symbolic, as it involved $50 million in credits to buy U.S. arms and $100,000 for training. Similar credit assistance for weapons purchases had gone unused the previous year. Moreover, the announced break with Washington did not include other long-term military agreements.[50]

Just as anticommunist nationalists had attacked senators Kennedy and Church for their pronouncements about human rights abuses in Brazil in 1970 and 1971, politicians from ARENA, the progovernment party, blasted the United States for interference in Brazil's domestic affairs. Ironically, the opposition MDB split in reaction to the Brazilian government's decision to reject further military aid. Moderate sectors backed the generals' nationalist discourse, whereas more radical congressional representatives, the auténticos, (authentics), although a minority voice, saw the report as a means of pushing their agenda for democratization. Geisel took advantage of this division to create the misleading impression that the country had closed ranks against Washington's ultimatums. Geisel's stance also served to win the backing of "hard-line" sectors of the military that had resisted his policy of a controlled and gradual political liberalization.[51] A week later, the Brazilian government announced the severance of all military agreements, including supplementary assistance packages. Since Brazil's arms industry was producing 75 percent of its own weapons, the break would have little impact on its security needs.[52] At the same time, Geisel had managed to gain support among sectors of the opposition within Congress in a nationalist move that would also eliminate any future embarrassing human rights assessments of the regime emanating from Washington. He also placed the liberal and leftist opposition in the awkward position of defending continued U.S. military aid to the country. For years, one of the underlying arguments of the left-wing criticisms of the dictatorship had been its subservience to "U.S. imperialism." The auténticos were now hard pressed to support aid from the hegemonic power to the north.[53]

### Rosalyn Carter's Four-Day Visit

In the following months, tensions between the United States and Brazil cooled down, just as mobilizations against the military regime heated up. On April 28, 1977, three youth linked to the clandestine Trotskyist organization Liga Operária (Workers' League) were arrested late at night in a working-class suburb of São Paulo distributing leaflets calling on workers to celebrate May Day as a means of opposing the dictatorship.[54] In response, student activists called for a series of demonstrations—each one pushing the limits of police restrictions—that demanded the prisoners' release. Celso Brambilla, a husky young man from a working-class family, was one of those arrested. He was particularly intransigent while on the parrot's perch and suffered accordingly. After several days of torture, he was brought to speak to one of his interrogators, who was furious with him. Celso recalled the scene: "'They want to turn you into a hero,' he shouted. I did not know what was happening, and then he pointed to a chair, where there was a copy of the Folha de São Paulo newspaper with a photograph of thousands of students marching through the streets of downtown São Paulo carrying banners demanding 'Free our prisoners.'"[55] Márcia Bassetto Paes, who was a history student at the University of São Paulo and one of the "subversives" arrested and repeatedly tortured for seven consecutive days, remembered the impact of her imprisonment on student mobilizations. "After seven days on the parrot's perch, they had to let us recuperate and gave us medical attention. At the time, the law only let the DEOPS [political police] keep political prisoners isolated from contact with the outside world for fourteen days, and so they had to give us time to get better before we could be seen by our lawyer. When we heard about the student demonstrations, we were relieved because it gave us the hope that they might release us sooner rather than later. The student protests were essential, in my opinion, for forcing the military to let us go."[56] Márcia was the last female political prisoner to be tortured in São Paulo under the dictatorship. She emphasized that the trial also took place much faster than other political cases. The court acquitted all of them, a fact that she attributed in part to the popular reaction to their arbitrary detention and treatment while in jail.

Student protests against the São Paulo arrests spread throughout the country and coincided with First Lady Rosalyn Carter's four-day stay in Brazil in June 1977. Journalists described her stop-off in Brazil, which was part of a seven-country tour of Latin America, as an attempt to mend U.S.-Brazilian relations "after their low point in early March."[57] Nonetheless, human rights ended up being the focus of her trip.[58] Fearful that student protests would spoil the official state visit, the rector of the University of Brasília shut down the campus, but a student activist managed to pass on to Terence A. Todman, the assistant secretary of state for inter-American affairs and a member of the mission, an open letter addressed to the first lady. It proclaimed, "The regime which has governed our country since 1964 may have guaranteed a measure of stability beneficial to American interests, but it has done so at the expense of freedom of speech, freedom of the press, and freedom of congregation. Arbitrary imprisonment and torture are fears that rule our lives."[59] Through intermediaries, Rosalyn Carter also received two other documents: a letter from the Women's Movement for Amnesty calling on U.S. feminists to support the human rights cause in Brazil and a report by family members relating the conditions of 129 political prisoners. The Brazilian and foreign press published the full text of all three letters, giving national and international attention to their content.

Then, in a visit to Recife, the first lady broke with her meticulously planned itinerary and invited Thomas Capuano and the Reverend Lawrence Rosebaugh, two U.S. missionaries working with the city's urban poor, to the U.S. Consulate. Police had recently arrested the religious workers, beaten them up while in jail, and, as they described it, treated them "like animals."[60] The fifteen-minute meeting, complete with photos of Roslyn Carter talking to the two men, was a signal to the Brazilian government and the opposition that the Carter administration was serious about its human rights initiatives. It also provided high-profile coverage about the human rights situation in Brazil to the U.S. public through front-page press articles and a picture of the first lady standing between the two missionaries in the garden of the U.S. consulate in Recife.[61] Nightly television news emphasized the "unexpected" meeting with the missionaries.[62] In a letter drafted by National Security Advisor Robert Pastor to Father Rosebaugh regarding his treatment while imprisoned, the White House expert on Latin America noted, "A flood of correspondence on your behalf testifies to the concern of many individual Americans for your well-being and for the importance of the work you are doing in Brazil."[63] Pastor, who had accompanied Mrs. Carter on the trip, later affirmed that the first lady had "succeeded in walking a very fine line between offending the government and encouraging the opposition."[64]

### Brazil on Broadway

The same month that Rosalyn Carter returned to the U.S. from her Latin American tour, a leading U.S. actor starred in a New York stage production with a Brazilian backdrop. The play offered a dramatic metaphor to U.S. audiences about life under an authoritarian regime. It had been six years since Zuzu Angel's one-woman fashion statement to the crème de la crème of New York's Brazilian colony. The dress designer's show had been a personal protest against the military's treatment of her son. In 1977, another representation of the Brazilian body moved to center stage to create a much more public one-woman performance. *Miss Margarida's Way*, written and directed by the Brazilian playwright Roberto Athayde and produced by Joseph Papp of the New York Shakespeare Festival, won Estelle Parson a Tony nomination and a 1978 Drama Desk Award in the category of "Unique Theatrical Experience." The play, an adaptation of Athayde's original *Apreceu a Margarida* (1973), is about an authoritarian, sexually repressive schoolteacher who incessantly disciplines her classroom—the theater audience—in a thinly disguised allusion to the Brazilian military regime.[65]

Parsons's powerhouse performance received universal accolades and rave reviews. Although not pedantically political, the drama creates the atmosphere of living under an authoritarian regime. Through two grueling acts (or eighth-grade classes) Miss Margarida lectures, badgers, bullies, and torments her audience to ensure its obedience and submission. The schoolteacher meets any public display of resistance with more shouts, demanding silence in a give-and-take with the theatergoers in which the teacher always comes out on top. The script calls for the leading lady to abuse her audience with mindless reactionary rants. Her monologue streams on endlessly without form, shifting with the moment. Her disciplining diatribes contain no apparent logic and seem as arbitrary and fluid as the plasticity of Brazil's own legal system under military rule. The rules of the game never stay the same, and proper classroom behavior seems impossible to achieve.[66]

According to Parsons, what kept the play fresh after so many performances was the unpredictability of this audience-participation piece. "You never quite know what the audience will do . . . Sometimes they throw things at me. At intermission they write rude things on the blackboard, like Miss Margarida has crabs."[67] Indeed, Miss Margarida is not a scintillating seductress enticing her pupils with sexual allure. She thunders against sex and masturbation, and, if anything, she is dry and castrating, singling out for abuse and humiliation any audience member who dares to challenge her in any way.

In an interview with a *New York Times* reporter for the revival of the play in 1990, Athayde explained, "The play reflects my own problems in school. I added my personal experiences to the dictatorship in Brazil."[68] His gendered choice of Big Brother as Big Sister is an unusual twist on the metaphoric thrust of the play. "I wanted my symbol of tyranny to be very seductive," he added. "So it came out this way: a mother underneath, a dictatorship above and a teacher in between."[69] At least one literary analyst has argued that choosing a female character to portray the authoritarian protagonists of repression in Latin America diminishes the masculine nature of those regimes.[70] Others have pointed to the fact that Miss Margarida "transgresses society's expectations of a woman as maternal and conciliatory. Instead she 'acts' as a tyrant. This would serve to heighten reactions against this 'performance' of oppression of a public . . . [that] would also be more shocked by a woman 'acting' this way than a man 'performing' in a similar manner.'"[71]

Unlike Zuzu Angel's politically imbued surprise fashion show in 1971, press releases announcing the New York debut of Miss Margarida's Way informed the public quite directly of its oppositional content. "The play . . . was closed by the Brazilian Government when it was first produced there in 1973. Officials saw it as a political allegory against the dictatorship," concluded a note announcing the first run at the Public Theater.[72] In summarizing the playwright's biography, the Playbill program noted, "Next came the first production of Miss Margarida's Way at Argentina's University of Córdoba [in 1972], then the first Brazilian production in Rio which was closed by the police five weeks later. This subsequently reopened after the necessary cuts were made and had a very successful run."[73]

Although theater critics mentioned the play's political content, they inevitably tied the play's treatment of authoritarianism to questions of authority, education, and discipline. In a review headlined "A 'Confrontation' Drama Deals with Dictatorship," Mel Gussow of the New York Times wrote, "Miss Margarida is a tyrant, a dictator, and by the playwright's description, 'a terrible monster.' Depending on one's point of view, she can be seen as a dominating mother, a powerful politician, Richard Nixon or even Adolf Hitler."[74]

Ariel Dorfman, a former Chilean exile and professor of literature, reflected on the original U.S. production in a review of Parsons's Broadway revival in 1990:

In 1977—a particularly dismal year—the spectators could identify Miss Margarida with a vast variety of favorite dictatorships, starting with Mr. Athayde's Brazil, or the sad neighboring countries of Argentina, Uruguay, Bolivia, Paraguay, or my own Chile. Other United States client dictators abounded: Somoza, the Shah, Duvalier, Marcos and the omnipresent generals in Guatemala and South Korea. In the rival camp, one could cast an eye on a genocidal Pol Pot or the beloved leader Kim Il-Sung, or in Eastern Europe, the gray Brezhnev look-alikes, patriarchal Miss Margaridas, imposing their bureaucratic socialism.[75]

Reading newspaper and magazine columns about the play, however, does not completely catch the color of the performance and its impact on the audience. One might conclude that Athayde's text and Parsons's performance served as an evening teach-in on the horrors of the Brazilian military regime. That was not the case.

In an interview some twenty-five years later about the political message that *Miss Margarida's Way* conveyed to the public, Estelle Parsons recalled that people rarely mentioned Brazil in the question-and-answer period that followed many of the show's performances. "Most of the members of the audience made references to their own experiences, either as schoolteachers or as pupils of strict teachers. They seemed to understand the play in terms of the educational system here in the United States. I really don't remember anyone ever referring to Brazil or the political situation there."[76] Brendan Gill of the *New Yorker*, however, recounted at least one after-show exchange that indicated a concern by an audience member about the play's overarching political content: "After the play was over Miss Parsons and Mr. Athayde came to the apron of the stage and volunteered to answer questions from the audience. Mr. Athayde, slender, dark-haired, trembling, and yet very sure of himself, said in answer to one question that he believed his play to be a study of ego in pursuit of power. Did that mean that the play could be read as a paradigm of the political situation in his native country of Brazil? 'I think it is something bigger than Brazil,' he said. 'Something more important than geography.'"[77]

Indeed, the *Playbill* program that accompanied the performance is quite different from the didactic informational content of the ten-page pamphlet-program distributed at presentations of *Savages* performed in an Off Off Broadway rerun of the Los Angeles production in March 1977.[78] There are no references to guerrillas, torture, repression, the massacre of the indigenous population, or the economic situation in Brazil. No history recounts the rise and the fall of the military regime. One must understand this within the context of when the production appeared on Broadway. While Athayde wrote the original version of *Miss Margarida's Way* in 1971 at the nadir of authoritarian rule, in late 1977, when it opened in New York, Brazil was edging toward political liberalization. Torture was becoming a thing of the past, employed that year only sparingly against political opponents. The political punch of using torture as an organizing tool for issues related to Brazil had lost its effectiveness, and those activists dedicated to educating the public about the military regime were beginning to focus on the implications of the democratic openings unfolding in the country.

Athayde's comment that the play transcended geography is perhaps one of the reasons for its New York success. Dorfman is correct in pointing out that audiences had a variety of examples to draw from in understanding the play, since in 1977 the discourse about dictatorships and human rights had become part of the national debate under the Carter administration. Yet life under military rule in South America was still a remote and vague notion for most theatergoers, whereas petty classroom authoritarianism was not.

### Exiles and Amnesty

By the mid-1970s, the handful of unofficial Brazilian political exiles in the United States, coupled with the growing number of graduate students on government fellowships, created a much larger grouping of Brazilian activists across the country. Those students receiving government support generally remained very circumspect and most avoided a public profile, but many still participated quietly in antidictatorship campaigns.[79] Others found alternative resources to study abroad. Clóvis Brigagão was among them. Authorities arrested Clóvis in 1971 for alleged subversive activities. In September of that year, he left the country for Mexico, where he studied at the Colégio de México with the support of a Ford Foundation fellowship. He then applied to the doctoral program in political science at the University of Chicago to study with Philippe Schmitter. Once again, the Ford Foundation gave him financial support. In Chicago, he met people working with an anti-imperialist organization known as the Chicago Area Group for the Liberation of the Americas (CAGLAS) and formed Liberation Brazil or LIBRA in order to denounce the ongoing repression in Brazil. Like the other small collectives scattered around the country working on Brazil in the early 1970s, LIBRA organized campus-oriented events at Midwestern colleges and universities. Clóvis remembers inviting Paulo Freire, the exiled educator who had just published *Pedagogy of the Oppressed*, to talk about his work and the situation in Brazil. He also helped organize a major event with Archbishop Hélder Câmara at the University of Chicago to a packed audience.[80] With the support of the Committee of Returned Volunteers, an organization of radical former Peace Corps workers, CAGLAS also produced an information booklet titled *Brazil: Who Pulls the Strings? Or: Alliance for Repression*.[81] The eighty-four-page collection of reprinted articles critical of the political, social, and economic situation in Brazil served as a useful educational tool for individuals and collectives around the country trying to inform the public about Brazil while offering a coherent critique of U.S. support for the military regime.

Since the gathering of less than a dozen Brazilians in New York City on Labor Day in 1973, Marcos Arruda, Anivaldo Padilha, and Jovelino Ramos had tried to bring together their compatriots. Between 1974 and 1977, they judiciously organized a series of discreet national meetings to coordinate work on Brazil. Clóvis remembered a gathering of thirty or so Brazilians to plan concerted activities, which was held at Princeton University. Marcos Arruda, Anivaldo Padilha, Jovelino Ramos, Rubem César Fernandes, Maria Helena Moreira Alves, Tetê Moraes, Pedro Celso Uchôa Cavalcanti, Abdias do Nascimento, and others were present.[82] Out of these meetings and other discussions arose the idea to produce a book documenting the experience of exiles as part of an effort to promote the idea of an amnesty. According to Pedro Celso Uchôa Cavalcanti, who was a political exile and professor at Washington University in St. Louis, Rubem César Fernandes initiated the idea of documenting the experience of exile. Both had fled Brazil during the 1960s and ended up studying in Poland. Pedro Celso then came to the United States to teach, and Rubem César moved to New York to complete a doctorate at Columbia. "The idea began in the year of the Portuguese Revolution in 1974, and I think that it was due in large part to the victory of the MDB in the 1974 elections," Pedro Celso recalled.[83] From New York, Rubem César got grant money from the Ford Foundation for the project, and Pedro Celso and Jovelino Ramos lent their names as editors because they had regularized their legal status in the United States. Clóvis Brigagão, Rubem César Fernandes, Valentina da Rocha Lima, and Marcos Arruda collaborated behind the scenes. Paulo Freire, Abdias do Nascimento, and Nelson Werneck Sodré, a prominent left-wing intellectual, "sponsored" the project, giving it name recognition in Brazil and among the exiles living abroad.

Although no one knows the exact number, an estimated 5,000 to 10,000 Brazilians had been exiled since 1964. The government banned some from returning. Others still faced charges of subversion while many others simply left the country fearing arrest and torture should they return. Since the nineteenth century, Brazilian governments had a long tradition of granting amnesty to regime opponents. The proposal to prepare a book to promote the idea also coincided with efforts to organize a campaign for amnesty in Brazil. Teresinha Serbini, Branca Moreira Alves, Regina Von der Weid and other relatives of exiles and political prisoners had courageously formed the Movimento Feminino pela Anistia (Feminine Movement for Amnesty) to push the government to offer some sort of reconciliation with opponents of the regime in jail or abroad.[84]

In December 1974, the U.S.-based group sent out 1,500 packets to Brazilian exiles in Latin America, Eastern and Western Europe, Africa, and Asia, requesting that respondents write fifteen to twenty pages about their experiences in exile. When people were slow to respond, a team sought out exiles throughout the world to interview. This made the project more expensive, as participants had to travel to collect people's narratives and depositions, but it also meant that the responses were more spontaneous and less formal. It also required that the organizers of the volume make decisions about whom to interview in a manner that ensured political balance and a broad range of experiences. The project coordinators ended up collecting 2,000 pages of interviews and written texts.[85] *Memórias do exílio, Brasil 1964–19??: Obra Coletiva* (Memories of Exile, Brazil 1964–19??: Collective Work) was first published in Portugal in November 1976 and a second edition came out in Brazil in September 1978, as censorship restrictions loosened and the liberalization process expanded. The open-ended date in the book's title posed the pressing question: "When will the exile experience come to a conclusion?" It also suggested that an amnesty was possible. The volume served as an important educational instrument for those in Brazil and abroad who had initiated the campaign.[86] *Memórias do exílio* offered a wide array of portraits and experiences about people of different generations, political currents, and social origins. The personal narratives humanized those living abroad and recast previous images of them as radical communists and terrorists that the military regime had projected at home and abroad. Although there was a noted gender imbalance in the book, the organizers of the first volume, along with new collaborators, corrected the absence of significant material about women in exile in a second volume, *Mémorias das mulheres no exílio* (Memories of Women in Exile) that was published in 1980 after the government had granted a political amnesty.[87]

Eight months after the first edition of *Mémorias do exílio* appeared in Portugal, the Uruguayan government abruptly revoked Leonel Brizola's permission to stay in the country, causing speculation in the press that the Brazilian government had been behind the order to end his exile in the tiny country bordering on southern Brazil. Brizola, the brother-in-law of ousted president João Goulart, was among a handful of particularly distasteful exiles from the military's point of view. Like Luís Carlos Prestes, the secretary general of the Brazilian Communist Party living in the Soviet Union, and Miguel Arraes, the former governor of Pernambuco residing in Algeria, Brizola represented the pre-1964 political currents that were anathema to the goals of the "revolution." According to Clóvis Brigagão, who later worked closely with Brizola, the former governor of the state of Rio Grande do Sul managed to get a visa to come to the United States through the intervention of Brady Tyson and Andrew Young.[88]

Although Brizola might still have been a bête noir of the military regime, over the years he had gone through a political transformation that led to an alliance with European Social Democrats. He arrived in New York City and established residency in a spacious suite in the Roosevelt Hotel. The hotel lobby suddenly became the waiting room and meeting place for exiles of all political persuasions anxious to construct a strategy to end military rule. New York was an international crossroads that facilitated Brizola's contacts with United States opponents of the military regime, as well as those living in exile in Europe. Soon after his arrival in the United States, Brizola transmitted his first radio message to Brazil in thirteen years. Brizola's fervent nationalism while governor of Rio Grande do Sul in the early 1960s and his takeover of the U.S.-owned International Telephone and Telegraph (ITT) had provoked a crisis in relations with Washington during the Kennedy administration. Nearly a decade and a half later, he expressed gratitude to the United States for offering him asylum and praised Carter's emphasis on human rights as "a message that has reached a very deep penetration among the Latin American people."[89] From New York and then later from Lisbon, Brizola worked tirelessly to pull together a broad coalition of political activists of all persuasions under his leadership in preparation for an anticipated amnesty, his return to Brazil, and a resumption of democratic rule.

At the end of 1977, from the vantage point of activists working on the East Coast, the slow and uneven liberalization policy crafted by Geisel and his chief advisor General Golbery, as well as the change in the White House, offered new opportunities. Tireless in his dedication to the cause, Ralph Della Cava continued to integrate new people into his network of those concerned about developments in Brazil. Bella Feldman-Bianco, for example, remembers that soon after the Brazilian journalist Judith Patarra arrived in New York as the *Veja* magazine correspondent, she quietly began aiding their efforts by transmitting information from Brazil about the diverse strategies the Brazilian opposition had developed to end military rule.[90] Patarra also played a key role in getting the *New York Times* to publish a feature article by Thomas M. Capuano, one of the two U.S. missionaries who had met with Rosalyn Carter in Recife that year.[91] The op-ed piece detailed his treatment in prison and was accompanied by a grim illustration depicting a man bound and gagged hanging from inside a beach umbrella while others enjoyed the sun's rays. Appearing just before the last weekend of summer vacation, it was another way of dramatizing the harsh treatment of Brazilian political prisoners and must have been a disturbing image for readers.[92]

A new host of academics working on Brazil enriched activities on the East Coast. In the New York area, activists, including Ralph Della Cava, Kenneth Erickson, Sandy Davis, organized an event at the City University of New York

(CUNY) Graduate Center titled "Return to Democracy in Brazil" to discuss the political changes taking place in the largest country in South America.[93] Maria Helena Moreira Alves, who was pursuing a Ph.D. in political science at MIT that focused on the military regime, became ever more involved in antidictatorship organizing.[94] Joan Dassin, who at the time was teaching at Amherst College and had carried out graduate research at the University of São Paulo during the worst years of political oppression, shuttled every weekend between Amherst and New York to assist in this new burst of energy around Brazil.[95] Kenneth Erickson, a historian of Brazil who at the time was teaching at Columbia, joined Della Cava in drafting a series of resolutions for an upcoming Latin American Studies Association meeting that supported the move toward democracy.[96]

The presence of Brizola in New York also served as a catalyst for rethinking how a postdictatorial regime might take shape. Clóvis Brigagão recalls having organized a meeting between Brizola and Abdias do Nascimento, the long-time Afro-Brazilian activist and intellectual, who was teaching in Buffalo. According to Brigagão, "Brizola didn't understand the black question; he thought that [racism] didn't exist in Brazil. I invited Abdias to my house and invited Zé Almino [de Alencar], Lélia Gonzalez, who was a new black leader in Brazil, [and others] . . . For hours Abdias told the story of Brazil from the blacks' and slaves' point of view. It clarified things for Brizola about the contribution of black people's labor to the development of Brazil, and it led to Abdias's being an important figure at Brizola's side when he became the governor of Rio de Janeiro [in 1982]."[97]

As 1978 began, Brazilians living in the United States and their allies were optimistic. It appeared that torture was on the decline and that progressive forces were converging in the opposition to the military regime. Student mobilizations, vocal criticisms by São Paulo business leaders about the government's economic policies, and political openings, including a reduction in censorship, presented an underlying expectation that significant change might actually take place in Brazil. They also seemed to have an ally in the White House.

### A Presidential Visit to Brazil

Not since February 1960, when Dwight D. Eisenhower visited Brazil, had a sitting U.S. president toured the country. Anticipating a political opportunity in October 1977, several months before President Carter's planned visit to Brazil, Della Cava drafted a letter to the White House that was hand delivered by Tyson. Identifying himself as the secretary for the Brazil Scholars

Group, Della Cava urged the president to arrange a meeting with Cardinal Arns during his trip. "Dom Paulo Evaristo, with whom you met last June at Notre Dame, enjoys the highest respect of each and every one of the leaders of Brazil's democratic forces—lawyers, journalists, and trade unionists." The letter continued, "Mr. President, we further believe that your meeting with Dom Paulo Evaristo . . . would hearten all those Brazilians who share your common 'faith in fundamental human rights, in the dignity and worth of the human person, in the equal rights of men and women and of nations large and small.'" The leading scholars working on Brazil, some of whom were at the nation's most prestigious universities, signed the statement.[98]

Making sure that all bases were covered, Della Cava contacted Jaime Wright, the Presbyterian minister who had been present at the ecumenical service for Vladimir Herzog in 1975. Jaime Wright's brother, Paulo Stuart Wright, had been a militant of Ação Popular. Police arrested Wright in 1973 and he "disappeared" after being tortured. Jaime Wright, who had worked closely with Cardinal Arns in human rights activities, suggested that since Arns and Carter had both received honorary doctorates at the University of Notre Dame the previous spring, the cardinal might invite the U.S. president to meet with him in Brazil. Cardinal Arns sent Carter a letter that included a list of Brazilian political prisoners who had disappeared since 1971 and expressed the hope that the two might talk during the president's visit.[99] Carter's positive response indirectly signaled a disappointment in the Brazilian government's actions, "These cases [of those who have disappeared since 1971] emphasize the importance of the rule of law, with its right of habeas corpus and due process through independent civilian courts. Such measures might not eliminate human rights violations, but they would at least show that the government was dedicated to an orderly system of justice."[100] The president's letter concluded by praising Arns, "Your work on behalf of human dignity made me proud to share the podium with you at the University of Notre Dame. I wish you the greatest success in your efforts to secure the basic rights of all human beings, to help those whose rights have been violated and to comfort their families." When Carter agreed to meet with Arns, the cardinal leaked the letter to the press to further his human rights agenda in Brazil.

Carter arrived on the eve of the anniversary of the military takeover in 1964. One high-ranking U.S. official described the president as "walking on eggshells."[101] Journalists saw in the American president's choice to frame his discussions with Geisel by initiating a dialogue that focused on broad global issues a message that Carter took the country's emergent role as an international power seriously. However, Carter did not move on his position about nuclear nonproliferation and human rights. In a press conference on March 30, Carter emphasized that he and Brazilian leaders had "sharp differences of opinion" on how to best deal with human rights issues and how specific allegations should be investigated. The *Los Angeles Times* reporter covering the visit noted, "Brazilian congressmen and journalists and finally the man on the street responded enthusiastically" to Carter's concerns about human rights and nonproliferation. "The Brazilian Congress applauded when he called for individual rights, including 'the right to criticize a government,' and again when he urged 'peaceful use of atomic power without the risk of proliferation.'"[102] Journalists also applauded at the end of Carter's press conference.

During the second of Carter's two days in Brazil in March 1978, he met with Cardinal Arns, along with a number of other opposition leaders: Cardinal Eugênio Sales of Rio de Janeiro; Raymundo Faoro, the president of the Brazilian Bar Association; Júlio Mesquita, the publisher of *O Estado de São Paulo*; José Mindlin, a prominent Paulista businessman; and Marcos Vianna, the president of a state-owned bank. During the meeting, the group discussed the human rights situation in Brazil with Carter. Wright later recalled to friends that, at the personal invitation of the U.S. president, Arns went with him to the airport at Rio, "giving him a chance for forty minutes of private conversation."[103] The meeting with the cardinal and their brief trip together sent a clear message that the White House shared the concerns of many oppositional forces.

At the time, Brazilian and foreign journalists characterized the visit as yet another sign of the gulf between the two countries that had come about because of Carter's policies. Yet a more distanced consideration of the relations between Brazil and the United States suggests that Carter had managed to patch up the tensions with the military by conducting discussions with Geisel about both nuclear proliferation and human rights within a larger framework that recognized Brazil's global importance. At the same time, the nod to opposition figures signaled that the current U.S. administration would not tolerate any backsliding regarding human rights violations in Brazil. As Timothy J. Power has argued, in the end Carter's gestures emboldened those oppositionists pushing for further political openings and perhaps even encouraged those within the Brazilian government supporting Geisel's moves toward liberalization.[104]

## Labor Mobilizations and a Growing Opposition

Less than six weeks after Carter returned to Washington, another significant actor entered the Brazilian political stage. On May 12, 1978, 3,000 workers at the Swedish Saab-Scania automobile manufacturing plant in Greater São Paulo caught their supervisors off guard when they returned from lunch and refused to start up their machines.[105] The Saab-Scania strike quickly spread to other multinational automobile plants in the industrial belt surrounding São Paulo. Soon 275,000 workers from Ford, Pirelli, Mercedes-Benz, and Fiat plants were on strike, marking the end of a decade of "labor peace." Demanding a 20 percent increase over government-controlled wage hikes, the metalworkers' unions ignored the labor courts that had declared the strike illegal. This massive strike, which challenged the military's economic and labor policies, came a year after university students had mobilized on and off campuses throughout the country. Eventually settling on a 12 percent wage increase, the strike in many ways marked the beginning of the end of military rule. Heading the movement was Luiz Inácio da Silva, popularly known as Lula, the president of the metalworkers union of São Bernardo do Campo and Diadema, who would later become the president of Brazil. He represented a new generation of labor leaders, who had not built alliances with the military regime in order to remain in control of their unions.

Six months later, the Geisel government suffered another setback. The November 1978 congressional elections proved to be, once again, a plebiscite to measure the military's popularity. A government provision promulgated in 1977, known as the April Package, modified electoral rules to favor the progovernment political party. In spite of these modifications in the law and additional restrictions implemented a month before the elections, the MDB garnered 4.3 million more votes than ARENA in the Senate races, while the progovernment party held only a slight lead in total votes in the Chamber of Deputies. In spite of the decrees of 1977 that weighted votes in favor of the military and curbed the popular support for the opposition at the ballot box, ensuring that the generals retained formal control of Congress, the military had been defeated at the polls.[106]

In one of his last gestures before leaving office, Geisel revoked the banishment order of 120 political exiles, indicating that an amnesty law was in the making under his appointed successor, João Batista Figueiredo. The former head of the military presidential staff under President Médici, and the director of the National Intelligence Service, the internal intelligence-gathering agency, under Geisel, Figueiredo assumed office in March 1979 and oversaw the "twilight" of the military government. In August 1979, he signed an Amnesty Law that freed almost all political prisoners and exiles, although a provision of the same law exonerated all those government officials who had been involved in the torture of the regime's opponents.

In an additional move to advance a liberalization project that would ensure that the military remained in control of the political system, Figueiredo championed political party reorganization. Fearing that the MDB might win a majority in Congress and in key state legislatures, thus upsetting the generals' ability to dictate Figueiredo's presidential successor, the government pushed a law through Congress that allowed politicians to form new political parties. It was a divide-and-conquer strategy directed toward splintering the legal opposition. Amnestied politicians and divergent currents within both the MDB and ARENA scrambled to gain an upper hand in the process. Luiz Inácio Lula da Silva, in alliance with sectors of the Catholic Church and left-wing oppositionists, formed the Partido dos Trabalhadores (Workers' Party, PT).[107] Leonel Brizola founded the Partido Trabalhista Democrática (Democratic Labor Party, PDT), while other politicians remained within the reformulated Partido do Movimento Democrático Brasileiro (Party of the Brazilian Democratic Movement, PMDB). Although opponents of the regime divided into different political parties, collective electoral results in November 1982 portended additional problems for the military. The electorate chose Brizola as the new governor of Rio de Janeiro, and the PMDB won the gubernatorial races in Minas Gerais and São Paulo. The opposition political parties in Congress nearly outnumbered the newly formed promilitary Partido Democrático Social (Social Democratic Party, PDS) and its allies. Since the Congress still indirectly elected the president, the 1982 electoral results suggested that the days of the dictatorship were finally numbered.

### A Labor of Love

Figueiredo's move to reorganize the political parties was also an effort to undercut the growing militancy of the labor movement and the potency of a mobilized working class backing a single opposition political party. Two more years of labor unrest followed the labor walkouts of 1978. Although the strike wave led by Lula forced foreign and Brazilian companies to begin collective bargaining with unions in the auto industry and defied the labor law's de facto no-strike provisions, the military dictatorship retaliated by taking over the São Bernardo metalworkers union that Lula had led since 1975. A military court stripped Lula and ten other strike leaders of all political and union rights and sentenced them to prison terms ranging from two to three and a half years for leading the metalworkers' work stoppage in 1980.

Inspired by the tremendous labor upsurge in Brazil between 1978 and 1980, several Brazilians living in the United States and activists interested in educating the American public about Latin America decided to do something to assist Lula and the struggling new Brazilian labor movement. With the exception of Maria Helena Moreira Alves, they had not been involved in previous U.S. campaigns, but they understood the implications of the emergent labor militancy in Brazil and organizing possibilities in the United States. Larry Wright (no relation to Jaime Wright) was a member of this cluster of activists. When he heard that Lula had been invited to Europe to build international support against the government's crackdown while his sentence was on appeal, he arranged with friends to organize a brief tour in the United States for Lula and Jacó Bittar, the head of an oil workers' union. "We thought that this was a real opportunity to help the new trade union movement in Brazil and to pull together the sectors of North American trade unions that wanted to see a more internationalist trade union policy, not fighting the Cold War, but trying to support a new and more vital trade unionism in Latin America."[108]

The meetings of Lula and Bittar with labor representatives in New York and Washington encouraged union leaders in the United States and Canada to join the international effort to overturn the harsh sentence imposed on Lula and his fellow strike leaders. To gather trade union support, Larry Wright and likeminded colleagues formed the Brazilian Labor Information and Resource Center (BLI).[109] Margaret Keck, who cofounded the center and later became a professor of political science at Johns Hopkins University, recalled how modest their initial efforts had been, although they had a surprisingly large impact. "Carol Wolverton was a tremendously important factor in our success . . . She was a professional typesetter. At a time when most organizations were putting out sloppy mimeoed material, the BLI produced really classy typeset publications, convincing unions that we were serious people . . . that we had a real infrastructural support and so on."[110] The group's first publication, Brazil: Labor Unions on Trial, recounted the story of the upsurge in militant labor activity in Brazil, profiled Lula as a representative of the new labor movement, listed multinational companies operating in Brazil, and called for international labor solidarity.

Larry Wright remembered how the Brazilian Labor Information and Resources Center managed to get such widespread backing for the campaign.

"In many ways [Brazil] was a fresh run on the CIO [Congress of Industrial Organizations] experience in this country—the birth of new industrial trade unionism on a large scale corresponding to major industrialization in part due to the military. We were not talking about a few persecuted downtrodden unionists in isolated plants. This was a major center of economic activity with major international ramifications involving all the companies that people worked for here and a mass trade union movement trying to break free both of the industrial forces and the political and military forces. It was crying out for union solidarity on an international scale."[111]

Wright reminisced, however, that the group faced the problem of how to reach out to labor leaders when none of the members of the group was actively involved in the labor movement. "We pieced together a strategy of getting several major centrist unions to sign on to give initial support, and with that we could go to others and say: 'We have got broad mainstream support. This is a bread and butter trade union issue. You have these people [in Brazil] breaking out from years of military rule trying to make a vital trade union movement. This is going to be important for people here as well, since it's all the same multinational companies and [Brazil] is a major center for multinational companies in Latin America.'"[112]

That same year, the Brazilian Labor and Information Center organized a visit to the United States by Cardinal Arns, who had given his total support to the emergent militant Brazilian labor movement. Cardinal Arns met with New York area trade unionists in an event cosponsored and hosted by the Amalgamated Clothing and Textile Workers Union. In February 1982, the BLI organized a ten-day U.S. and Canadian tour for Lula, working closely with a number of different unions, and in September 1982 the group arranged for a meeting between Cardinal Arns and trade unionists in Washington, hosted by the AFL-CIO.[113] All these activities generated support among key labor leaders who sent telegrams to the Brazilian government protesting the arbitrary sentencing of the 1980 strike leaders. In April 1982, they celebrated an important victory when Brazil's Supreme Military Tribunal in a 9 to 3 decision ruled that the government should never have tried the leadership of the 1980 strike in military courts under the harsh National Security Law. The BLI Newsletter expressed its "deep appreciation and thanks" for the "repeated waves of telegrams and other solidarity, which supported the unions through four rounds of military trials and helped force Brazil's government to finally back down."[114] The editors, however, pointed out, "While the harshest sanctions are lifted from this and similar strikes, two facts illustrate the long road ahead in the *struggle* for union freedoms: (1) Brazil's tough anti-strike laws still make most strikes illegal, and could have sent Lula and the other defendants to prison except for a two-year statue of limitation; (2) The eleven unionists remain barred for life from union office, as has been true for over 10,000 other union leaders removed by the government since 1964; this automatic ban holds even for those later judged entirely innocent of all charges against them."[115]

In 1984, a majority of the country's militant union leaders ignored government prohibitions on forming a national labor federation and founded the Central Único dos Trabalhadores (Central Workers' Organization, CUT). This new development caused the BLI to question its role as intermediaries between North American and Brazilian labor organizations. Keck recalled, "Prior to 1983, there was no official spokesperson for the Brazilian Labor movement, so you could have ad hoc voices going around saying that they were speaking on behalf of the Brazilians. After there were official people, elected people, we didn't feel comfortable speaking on behalf of the Brazilians."[116] Wright added, "The hardest part of our work was that we had no formal standing on either side of this bridge-building process. There were many ties of friendship and trust and so on. But, it was clear that as this played out, our role was going to wind up, and the CUT would take over a lot of the contacts directly. The changed international departments in this country would also want to make their own direct contacts."[117]

The efforts by the Brazil Labor Information and Resource Center reflected a transformation in many U.S. trade unions' approach to foreign policy and international solidarity in the late 1970s and early 1980s. During the same period in which the BLI gathered support for Brazil's labor leaders, trade unionists formed the National Labor Committee in Support of Democracy and Human Rights in El Salvador and the Labor Committee against Apartheid. Many of the international presidents who joined the campaign to free Lula and other Brazilian strike leaders also lent their names and support to free militant Salvadoran and South African trade unionists. They shared a common goal of working to get the AFL-CIO and other international unions to rethink worn-out Cold War perspectives and channel the resources and prestige of the labor movement in the United States toward developing new, positive relations with workers struggling for decent working conditions and a better life around the world.

During the last six months of the group's existence, Margaret Keck, Larry Wright, Maria Helena Moreira Alves, and others worked on producing information about transnational companies' involvement in Brazil. Then, as Keck put it, "There was no demise; we sort of fizzled." When asked how they assessed their efforts and if their work had been a nail in the coffin of Cold War trade unionism, Keck modestly replied, "There were a lot of nails, but yeah, it was a nail." Wright added, "One solid nail that held. We kept hammering away." He concluded, "We didn't make a revolution; they didn't make a revolution. But it was important work."[118]

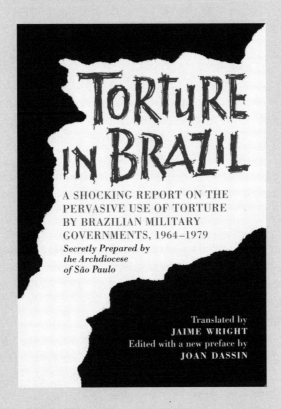

## CAPÍTULO XI

---

## "Amanhã há de ser outro dia"

Tomorrow will be another day.

**Chico Buarque, "Apesar de você," 1970**

With the passage of the Amnesty Law in 1979, political exiles slowly returned to Brazil. Some actually came back as part of a concerted campaign before the passage of the legislation to test the political climate in the country. Friends and relatives converged on the airport. Many times friends and supporters from other countries flew into a Brazilian airport with a given exiled person to ensure that the government did not arrest or harm those returning. The reception of those who had been forced out of the country became a daily ritual throughout 1979 and into 1980.

Returning opponents of the regime carried back with them the experiences of their time overseas. The uneven and at times halting process of political liberalization that Geisel and his successor Figueiredo guided and that the opposition accelerated opened new opportunities and created new spaces for rethinking a series of ways in which many Brazilians within the broadly defined anti-dictatorship movement understood their society and the possibilities embedded in the country's democratization process. Many female political dissidents found that their experiences abroad within the Brazilian exile communities and their interactions with feminists and the women's movements, especially in Europe, inspired new approaches to understanding gender roles, sexual politics, and their own activism.[1] Many female revolutionaries who lived in exile in Europe returned to Brazil and became leading figures in an emergent women's movement.[2]

In a similar fashion, Abdias do Nascimento, the long-time advocate for Afro-Brazilians, helped shaped the contours of the emergent Movimento Negro Unificado (United Black Movement), after his return from exile in Buffalo, New York. Speaking at a rally on the steps of São Paulo's Municipal Theater on July 7, 1978, Nascimento called on progressive forces to take up the challenge of confronting the racial component of the country's ongoing and severe economic and social disparities. Joining the Brizola forces in Rio de Janeiro, he ran for political office in 1982 and took a seat in the Brazilian Congress in 1983, becoming the first self-identified Afro-Brazilian member of Congress to advocate racial and human rights for this significant segment of the nation's population.[3]

Marcos Arruda, Niva Padilha, Jean Marc Von der Weid, Tetê Moraes, Maria Helena Moreira Alves, Clóvis Brigagão, Rubem César Fernandes, and many other Brazilians who had worked in assorted ways in the United States against the military regime also returned to Brazil in the 1980s, bringing with them fresh approaches to political activism. For those who had faced charges of subversion or feared renewed imprisonment, the Amnesty Law of 1979 ensured them a safe passage home. The explosion of new political parties and social movements also offered exciting possibilities within the country for social change.

At least two major issues remained unresolved in the military's gradual orchestration of a return to democratic rule. Who would choose the president and what would ultimately happen to those members of the military and police who had been involved in the gross violation of human rights? In 1983, the broadly constituted political opposition to the military regime addressed the first question through a mass-based popular campaign to demand direct presidential elections, instead of relying on the generals' imposed procedure in which the Congress chose the chief executive. The millions who mobilized on the streets throughout the country to demand direct presidential elections failed to garner sufficient political support for a constitutional change, but a subsequent split within the Partido Demócrato Social (Democratic Social Party, PDS), the military regime's political party, provided sufficient votes for Tancredo Neves, the moderate opposition leader, to gain a majority vote in Congress. Much to the country's shock and dismay, Neves's eleventh-hour illness on the eve of his presidential inauguration ended up bringing José Sarney, the military government's former ally and Neves's vice presidential running mate, to the helm. Nonetheless, the return to democracy, however uneven, had been consolidated. On the day that his successor was sworn in, Figueiredo, the fifth in the line of four-star generals who had ruled the state for twenty-one years, unceremoniously slipped out the back door of the presidential palace.

The other question related to the impunity granted to those who had tortured political prisoners over the previous fifteen years. The Amnesty Law that Figueiredo had signed guaranteed that the government would not prosecute those officials involved in these human rights violations. A group of lawyers that had defended political prisoners realized that sectors of the military and the political police might actually destroy evidence that remained in government archives in case there was a future reversal of the law. Many political prisoners had submitted detailed testimony when military courts brought them to trial, describing the torture that they had suffered after their arrests. Legal records contained a wealth of prima facie evidence to verify their claims about gross mistreatment, and the lawyers devised a plan to protect these valuable records. With financial support from the World Council of Churches, headquartered in Geneva, Reverend Jaime Wright, under the protection of Cardinal Arns, coordinated a secret operation to copy trial records and legal documents.[4] By secretly reproducing more than a million pages of legal dossiers that lawyers had submitted on behalf of political prisoners during the dark days of the dictatorship before the military regime could destroy contemporaneous testimony of torture, the opposition successively and definitively documented what so many had denounced.[5]

In 1985, the Archdiocese of São Paulo sponsored the publication of *Brasil, Nunca mais* (Brazil, Never Again), an abridged version of the seven-thousand page report that they had prepared between 1979 and 1984.[6] As a title, "Never Again" invoked other human tragedies, such as the Holocaust and genocide. It also implied the moral imperative or individual responsibility embedded in the first public petition issued in the United States denouncing torture in Brazil: "We cannot remain silent."

Relying on an international network of support that had coalesced in the preceding decade, Brazilian human rights activists organized the publication of an English version of *Brasil, Nunca Mais*. Alfred Stepan, a professor of political science at Columbia, remembers receiving a phone call from Brazil asking if he could find an editor to revise the English translation of the book. By chance, he ran into Joan Dassin, who had been active in anti-dictatorship activities in New York in the late 1970s, waiting for a bus near Columbia University. She immediately agreed to revise the translation. As luck had it, Dassin had just received a Fulbright fellowship to be in Brazil. For five months, she worked with Jaime Wright in São Paulo smoothing out the language in the English translation of a text that documents the horrific treatment of political prisoners.[7] *Torture in Brazil*, the title of the English edition of *Brazil, Nunca Mais*, evoked the fusion of the name given to the sixteen-page pamphlet *Terror in Brazil*, produced a decade and a half previously by Ralph Della Cava, Bill Wipfler, and others, and Saul Landau and Haskall Wexler's documentary *Brazil: A Report on Torture*, filmed the following year. The volume recorded the sufferings of thousands who had fought against the dictatorship. It also contained a lasting implicit message that such treatment is never acceptable.

CONCLUSIONS

## MAKING A DIFFERENCE

Picket sign
against President
Médici's visit
to the White
House, December
1971. REPRINTED
BY PERMISSION OF
THE COMMITTEE
AGAINST REPRESSION
IN BRAZIL (CARIB),
HARRY AND LORETTA
STRHARSKY.

Reasons for the use of torture can be summarized in two categories: to serve both a policing and a repressive function. In the Middle Ages, torture had served, above all, a police function and was used to extract confessions. This is still the primary reason for the use of torture in Brazilian police stations today. —**Amnesty International,** *Report on Allegations of Torture in Brazil,* **1973**

I tried to avoid it [talking about torture] because in the thinking of the left, we tried not to individualize things. We talked more about the system, the general system, the legal process, human rights in general. Systematically, in a country as individualistic as the United States, they went directly up to you and always asked: Were you tortured? How were you tortured? What do you feel? They were always very personal, and I was always forced to talk about this. —**Jean Marc Von der Weid, former political prisoner**

Mary Harding, a former Maryknoll missionary nun from a traditional Irish Catholic family, was expelled from Bolivia on January 12, 1972, for allegedly being a member of a pro-Cuban guerrilla organization. Almost immediately, she began a whirlwind speaking tour sponsored by the U.S. Committee for Justice for Latin American Political Prisoners. Although she did not share the tour organizers' political perspectives, she agreed to work with the committee because she wanted to get the word out about the situation in Bolivia. She then moved to Washington and joined Common Front for Latin America just as it was merging with the Committee against Repression in Brazil in efforts to broaden human rights activism in the nation's capital.[1]

Mary Harding remembered her first months in the United States: "I was in no·shape emotionally for the tour. I came back to the United Sates on January 14, 1972, and I started the tour April 9 and finished it near the end of May. It was grueling—seventeen major cities . . . I realized that the people wanted to hear my own personal experiences, but at each step of my own story, I tried to bring in what was happening in Bolivia or Latin America at the time." Moving from city to city, handled by people she hardly knew, going from one talk or meeting to another, she became exhausted as she coped with severe cultural shock and tried to readjust to the United States. "I think my first talk was at some place on Long Island. It was a junior college. . . . I walked into the classroom and spoke. The woman who was responsible for introducing me said she could not believe how many people were there, and it was mostly women. I had not even noticed. She said it's just this thirst that women have to learn about other women's experiences." Although many young women came to her talks, the audience in general seemed less interested in issues of gender and more curious to hear about her experience while being tortured. It provoked a deep conflict within Mary Harding, who wanted to educate people about the political situation in Latin America but kept on having to retell her personal prison story.

The reactions that Mary Harding faced on her speaking tour were similar to those of former Latin American political prisoners who had come to the United States to educate people about the situation in their home countries and to denounce U.S. government support for authoritarian regimes. Jean Marc Von der Weid remembers that on his speaking tour in 1973 people kept returning to the question of torture. In retrospect, he realized that it served a positive personal purpose. "I spoke about it so much that I became accustomed to the subject, and actually it was good because it allowed me to do some [emotional] cleansing."[2] Like Von der Weid, Niva Padilha and Marcos Arruda also tried to avoid talking about their torture when they lectured about Brazil, thinking that discussing political and social questions was the best and most effective why to reach their audiences. But they, too, found that the American public was fascinated with the topic of the tortured body and kept coming back to it. In fact, Marcos Arruda's lengthy interview in the *Washington Post* in 1971, which detailed his prison ordeal, contributed to the editor's condemnation of President Médici when he visited the White House in December of that year. Likewise, Fred Morris's incarceration and brutal treatment served as another dramatic example of Latin American dictatorships out of control and helped WOLA's lobbying effort for an end to military aid for the repressive regimes in South America. If the Brazilian government could torture a Midwestern Methodist minister for no apparent reason, what might they be doing to active opponents of the regime?

In reality, those doing political organizing about Brazil, and later those who focused on other countries in Latin America, faced a dilemma. Torture stories had real power, especially when told by a person who had lived through the nightmare experience. Quiet, calm, intelligent, and articulate speakers added drama to their stories. These were not irrational or unreasonable revolutionaries but *seemingly* middle-class idealists. They created an empathy with their audiences—including people of all political persuasions—that disarmed those who might even have disagreed with their politics. "There but for fortune, go I," must have run through the minds of those who heard their gruesome tales. Even when they attempted to avoid the subject, preferring to focus instead on sociopolitical questions of poverty, injustice, hunger, and oppression, their listeners kept returning to it.

The reluctance to emphasize their individual ordeals or the specificity of their personal contributions to the fight against the military regime was not restricted to the question of torture. After conducting interviews for this book with approximately one hundred Brazilians and Americans who had been involved directly or indirectly in campaigns against the dictatorship, I was struck by how almost each of them considered that her or his efforts had been quite modest and ultimately not essential for the cessation of the torture and the demise of the generals' rule. Yet all of them evoked a moral imperative. Once one had knowledge of what was happening to the opposition in Brazil, to remain silent was to become an accomplice. As they reached back in time to construct the memories of their activities several decades ago, their individual modesty and restraint in recalling the hundreds of small deeds that they had performed was noteworthy, especially because it repeated itself in conversations with the main protagonists of this story. In part, this humility may stem from the Christian religious roots of many activists who embraced leftist ideologies but retained a notion that one should perform good deeds without self-promotion or aggrandizement. The milieu of the progressive movements in Brazil and the United States in the 1960s and 1970s also encouraged limitless self-sacrifice for the cause, whether it was to end the war in Vietnam, fight for civil rights, topple a military dictatorship, or establish a world where equality and social justice would reign. Moreover, a notion that collective actions should override individual egos or personal sacrifice characterized a common current in the left in both the United States and Brazil. This sentiment did not prevent some former revolutionaries from creating a persona around their past militancy and using it as a springboard to journalistic, political, or literary prominence as democracy took hold in Brazil. None of the principles in this book took that route.

Most of those who had consistently worked in the United States against the Brazilian dictatorship were aware of only a small fraction of the varied activities that others had carried out in diverse campaigns against the military regime. This might explain in part why some saw their contribution more as a moral imperative than an effective political strategy. A few considered that their efforts were more annoying to the Brazilian dictatorship and politicians in the United States than successful in stopping torture or causing the regime's demise. Nonetheless, most insisted that despite the seemingly insignificant role that they had played as individuals, their concerted collective activities had made a difference. Although this conclusion might seem to be self-serving way to render a positive reading of one's life trajectory, the historical record supports this affirmation.

It is also worth mentioning that many activists who took up the cause of denouncing the Pinochet government in the 1970s or supporting the revolutionary movements in Central America in the 1980s retained only a vague notion of those who had come before them. Lisa Kokin, who joined the San Francisco Chile Solidarity Committee in the aftermath of the coup d'état in 1973, confessed that she had only a general idea of the political situation in Brazil at the time.[3] Likewise, Lorraine Thiebaud, who had been an active organizer for the San Francisco chapter of the U.S. Committee for Latin American Political Prisoners in the mid-1970s and later an activist in the Central American solidarity movement, had only a broad sense of the human rights climate in Brazil.[4] New generations of activists fought new battles, and few spent much time in the rush of events to look back to what had preceded them. On the surface, this might indicate that the series of campaigns around Brazil had little impact on those who followed and focused on other parts of Latin America. A central argument of this book, however, is that the tactics, strategies, networks, and activities employed by Tyson, Della Cava, Padilha, Arruda, and so many others directly shaped how other U.S. activists organized support or solidarity with political movements in Latin America in subsequent years. By the late 1970s, what had once been innovative had become standard practice.

It is also noteworthy that all of the Brazilians that I interviewed for this book who had passed through the United States and had worked closely with U.S. colleagues against the military dictatorship developed a new understanding of the nation to the north. They realized that their allies in academia and elsewhere were not agents of imperialism but honest liberal or left-wing humanists who wanted to respond to the atrocities committed in Brazil. Their experiences abroad, especially in the United States, reshaped their previously held unilateral and unsophisticated analyses of the nature of the United States as they returned to Brazil and became involved in social change as the country returned to democracy.

Admittedly, the numbers of Brazilian and U.S. activists numbered only in the dozens. In that regard they were the exception and even atypical in their ongoing dedication and commitment. Yet this is precisely one of the underlying arguments of this book. While few in number, they managed to mobilize many more around the issues of human rights, torture, and the process of democratization in Brazil. They also contributed to reshaping U.S. foreign policy in the later part of the century. Perhaps this book's story has not been told previously by any of those involved in these campaigns precisely because it seemed to participants that they, as individuals, each of whom was aware of only some of the many activities that took place over the years, had had little long-term impact on U.S. foreign policy. Jean Marc Von der Weid described his lobbying efforts in Washington as daunting, to say the least. "My trip to the United States was very good; it changed my life. My impression is that we were like a fly in the bakery that kept circling around the sweets, but isn't important." In the behind-the-scene discussions among the clergy who had formed the Latin American Strategy Committee to help prompt the Senate hearings conducted by Frank Church in 1971, Brady Tyson also expressed sincere doubts about the success of the "campaign on torture in Brazil." Tyson considered the effort a failure because "it didn't accomplish what it set out to do (end the torture), and the Brazilian government has learned that it can function without favorable public opinion on the international level." Other members of the Committee disagreed even then. One person argued, "Recent personal experience out in the Midwest has indicated an increased awareness (even out there!) of Brazil as a symbol of repression."[5] In hindsight, it is clear that the more optimistic voices were right.

In an interview conducted thirty years after the LASC meeting of 1971, Niva Padilha explained, "The greatest impact was that we managed to show the true image of Brazil for public opinion. Not to everyone, since we didn't have the means to do this, but at the time when you talked about Brazil, there was a certain understanding among certain segments of U.S. society about the situation in Brazil."[6] Niva went on to recall, "I tested this many times, because I traveled a lot in this period. I traveled almost everywhere in the United States. I remember that the only places that I did not go were New Orleans and Montana. . . . I even traveled to North Dakota and South Dakota." As he crisscrossed the country on planes, inevitably the person sitting next to him would ask him where he was from, and then they would begin to talk. "I would tell them that I was from Brazil, and the first thing that they would say was, 'Oh, the situation is bad there with torture and all.' When I first arrived in the United States, that had not been the case."

There are other indications that the goals of the groups organizing against the dictatorship had broader results than one might have felt at the time. Moving the *Washington Post*, the *New York Times*, and other leading mainstream political opinion makers to take clear stands against the military regime, much to the chagrin of Brazilian government officials, took time and patience to achieve. One might have expected these liberal papers to shift their editorials as Cold War mentalities melted and the Nixon administration soured public opinion against his foreign policy. The fact that even the ultraconservative *Reader's Digest* decided to offer two sides to the narrative of political developments in Brazil in 1972 offers rather convincing evidence that the campaigns to reshape the image of Brazil abroad had widespread effects. Several years later, the congressional curbs on foreign aid to countries violating their citizens' human rights and the Carter administration's emphasis on the issue brought the question to the forefront in the media and among politicians, policy makers, and the public. These politicians took up these issues in part because activists drew public attention to them. It is indeed the case that Carter had moved away from a more aggressive pro–human rights position by 1979 and that the Reagan administration overturned or undermined many if not most of the policy initiatives that had made human rights a serious foreign policy consideration. This lends some credibility to interviewees' sense that their efforts had been ephemeral at best. The political scientist Kathryn Sikkink, however, is emphatic about the long-term results of efforts like those employed by the protagonists in this book. "Human rights advocates both in government and outside, in the United States and abroad, succeeded in securing a major shift in U.S. policy and international institutions in the last quarter of the twentieth century," she insists. "Human rights issues, long seen as moral concerns inappropriate for foreign policy, have become an integral part of U.S. policy and of international and regional institutions."[7]

The contemporaneous campaigns for human rights in Eastern Europe and the then-Soviet Union in the 1970s obviously strengthened U.S. public interest in the issues raised by activists focusing on Brazil. Nonetheless, it is striking that at least in State Department and Brazilian Foreign Ministry documents, and on the editorial pages of the major dailies across the United States, few drew the connections between the issue of torture and repression in Brazil (and later in other parts of Latin America) and the question of human rights violations in the socialist bloc.

Even in the most blatantly anticommunist discourse of hardcore defenders of the Brazilian regime, there was a curious separation between the insistence that the regime's harshest measures against the "International Communist Movement" were justified and any consistent references to human rights abuses taking place in the Soviet Union or other socialist countries. Likewise, U.S. activists rarely raised parallels between the torture of political prisoners in Brazil and the incarceration of dissidents in the USSR. In part this was probably due to the fact that some left-wing supporters of the Brazilian opposition wore blinders about similar abuses taking place in countries they thought were addressing social and political problems that the Brazilian military seemed to ignore. Criticizing Cuba, China, or the Soviet Union, for some, was tantamount to treason. In general terms, it was as if there were two parallel worlds—one that concerned itself with human rights abuses in Latin America, and another in the socialist bloc. Although Amnesty International bridged these two worlds through its campaigns that adopted prisoners of conscience from the West, the socialist bloc, and the third world alike, few others working on Brazil or the rest of Latin America acknowledged these links.

Finally, the underlying organizing practices developed by clergy, academics, exiles, and activists laid out an array of approaches to influencing U.S. policy in Latin America, and those methods proved extremely fruitful as interests shifted from Brazil to Chile and Argentina, and then later Central America. Those working on issues related to Brazil certainly did not invent the approach of identifying prominent religious and intellectual figures as a means for eliciting broad public sympathy. However, the concrete connections with key individuals in mainstream Protestant denominations and sectors of the Catholic hierarchy, leaders in the civil rights movement, a wide array of experts on Latin America, and labor officials, as well as an emphasis on grassroots organizing, proved to be a successful formula for building effective human rights campaigns. Developing ongoing relations with sympathetic journalists and systematically lobbying policy makers, especially by people who had experienced firsthand the harsh brutality of the torture chamber, seems to have either created or consolidated a determination among members of the media and Congress to become consistent allies. Linking up with artistic productions that focused on Brazil also allowed activists to reach new groups of people beyond the usual student, anti–Vietnam War, and other progressive constituencies. These strategies, tactics, and diverse approaches used in activities concerning Brazil lent themselves to broader and even more successful international campaigns around Latin America and South Africa in subsequent years.

# NOTES

## Introduction

1. Amanico, *O Brasil dos gringos*, 70.
2. See Lutz and Collins, *Reading "National Geographic."* The magazine's portrayals of Brazil as the site of tropical wonders, futuristic architecture, expansive territories, and exotic Indians include Paulo A. Zahl, "Giant Insects of the Amazon," *National Geographic*, May 1959, 632–69; Hernane Tavares de Sá and Thomas J. Abercrombie, "Brasília, Metropolis Made to Order," *National Geographic*, May 1960, 704–24; Peter T. White and Winfield Parks, "Giant Brazil," *National Geographic*, September 1962, 299–353; Harald Schultz, "Brazil's Waurá Indians," *National Geographic*, January 1966, 130–52. For an example of travelogue images of Rio's Carnival, see Horace Sutton, "Bacchanal in Brazil," *Saturday Review*, March 4, 1961, 35–36, 59.
3. Page, *The Revolution That Never Was*.
4. Leacock, *Requiem for Revolution*, 118–24; Black, *United States Penetration of Brazil*, 64–69.
5. Weis, "Government News Management, Bias and Distortion."
6. Schoultz, *Human Rights and United States Policy toward Latin America*, 25.
7. *Congressional Record—Senate* (April 3, 1964): 6851–6852; (August 10, 1964): 18834–18835.
8. Smith, *Resisting Reagan*, xvi.
9. Morel, *O golpe começou em Washington*.
10. Elio Gaspari's comprehensive four-volume history of the military regime has helped to deflate the myth held by many in Brazil that there was consensus in the United States in favor of the Brazilian military dictatorship. His second volume, *A ditadura escancarada* (The Blatant Dictatorship), appeared midstream in my research for this book, and we cover similar territory (see 271–92). Gaspari offers a sweeping history of the twenty-one years of the generals' rule. My book is narrower in focus and deals with only one aspect of that story, namely, a detailed analysis of how forces emerged in the United States to challenge the Brazilian dictatorship and the U.S. administrations that backed the generals in power and how these forces helped reshape U.S. policy. Initial groundwork for this work was published as Green, "Clergy, Exiles, and Academics."
11. Schoultz, *Human Rights and United States Policy toward Latin America*, 6.
12. Forsythe, *Human Rights and World Politics*, 142. Edward L. Cleary dramatically dates the beginning of the "human rights era in Latin America" with the 1973 Chilean coup d'état but also indicates earlier organizing for Brazil (after the military assumed harsher dictatorial powers in December 1968) as critical to later efforts regarding

Chile. Cleary, *The Struggle for Human Rights in Latin America*, 1, 141–43. In an overview of U.S. human rights politics in the 1970s, Kenneth Cmiel focuses largely on the activities of Amnesty International as emblematic of the shift that took place in the mid-1970s from grassroots organizing to Washington lobbying and media campaigns. His study, however, misses the details of the origins of human rights activities as they related to Latin America and therefore emphasizes NGOs rather than less institutionalized groups studied in this book that laid the groundwork for later organizations. Cmiel, "The Emergence of Human Rights Politics in the United States."

13. Calvacante and Ramos, eds. *Mémorias do exilio*; Costa et al., eds., *Memórias das mulheres do exílio*; Rollemberg, *Exílo*; Serbin, *Secret Dialogues*, 91.
14. Keck and Sikkink, *Activists beyond Borders*, 8.
15. Fagen, "U.S. Foreign Policy and Human Rights."
16. 1973 Foreign Assistance Act, Publ. L. No. 93–189, 87 Stat. 714, 733 (1973).
17. Bertoli, Burback, Hathaway, High, and Kelly, "Human Rights," 4–11.
18. Cmiel, "The Emergence of Human Rights Politics in the United States."
19. Schoultz, correspondence with author, October 25, 2001.
20. Schoultz, *Human Rights and United States Policy toward Latin America*, 19–47.
21. Roderick J. Barman, American Historical Association, Chicago, Illinois, January 3, 2003, author's notes.

## Prólogo

1. Martinha Arruda, interview, November 2, 2004. Subsequent quotations are from this interview.
2. Bojunga, *JK*; Gomes, ed.,; Santos, *A classe media vai ao paraíso*; Maram, "Juselino Kubitschek and the Politics of Exuberance, 1956–1961."
3. Zweig, *Brazil*. Zweig and his second wife tragically committed suicide in Brazil in 1942 over despair about the developments of the war in Europe.
4. Ramos, interview, February 23, 2003. Subsequent quotations are from this interview.
5. Leonel Brizola (1922–2004) was a charismatic politician from the southern state of Rio Grande do Sul and João Goulart's brother-in-law. When Jânio Quadros renounced the presidency in August 1961, Brizola mobilized popular support and sectors of the army to force a compromise that allowed Goulart to assume the presidency, albeit with more limited powers.
6. Ridenti, *Em busca do povo brasileiro*.
7. Marcos Arruda, interview, October 4, 2002. Subsequent quotations are from this interview.
8. For more on Ação Popular, see Lima and Arantes, *História da Ação Popular da JUC ao PC do B*. Written by militants who supported the fusion of the organization with the Maoist Communist Party of Brazil, it has a sectarian tone but contains useful information about the movement's history.
9. Padilha, interview no. 2, June 12, 1998.
10. Padilha, interview no. 1, July 18, 1997.

## 1. Revolution and Counterrevolution in Brazil

1. "One Man's Cup of Coffee," *Time*, June 30, 1961, 23–31.
2. Ibid., 5.
3. Ibid., 23.
4. Ibid., 24.
5. "Establishing Relations with New Brazilian Administration," February 1, 1961, National Security Files (NSF), Brazil, January 1–February 24, 1961, box 12 A, Secret, JFK.
6. Ibid.
7. Ibid.
8. Ibid.
9. "Quadros Quits," *Time*, September 1, 1961, 26.
10. Skidmore, *Politics in Brazil*, 205–14.
11. For an outstanding analysis of the U.S. government involvement in the coup d'état and relations between the two countries in the 1960s, see Fico, *O grande irmão*.
12. "À Nação," Ato Institucional, April 9, 1964; Castelo Branco, *Os militares no poder*, 6–17.
13. Document no. 55, Sec. 4, State Department Teleconference (Secret), April 2, 1964, NSF, Brazil, Cables vol. 2, box 9, LBJ.
14. Document no. 55, Sec. 9, State Department Teleconference, April 2, 1964, NSF, Brazil, Cables vol. 2, box 9, LBJ.
15. Quoted in Beschloss, ed., *Taking Charge*, 306.
16. Morel, *O golpe começou em Washington*.
17. Gaspari, *A ditadura envergonhada*, 55.
18. Telegram, Rio de Janeiro to Washington, April 11, 1964, State Department Cables, NSF, LA Brazil, box 10, LBJ.
19. Department of State Incoming Telegram, Rio de Janeiro to Washington, April 20, 1964, State Department Cables, NSF, LA Brazil, box 10, LBJ.
20. Gordon, interview by Paige E. Mulhollan, July 10, 1969.
21. U.S. Congress, Senate Committee on Foreign Relations, *Nomination of Lincoln Gordon*, February 7, 1966, 2. Gordon's research was published as *United States Manufacturing Investment in Brazil, 1946–1960*.
22. Gordon, interview by John E. Rielly, May 30, 1964.
23. Skidmore, interview, July 28, 2005.
24. Ibid.
25. "Background Paper: Brazil," Attachment to Memorandum from L. D. Battle to Richard N. Goodwin, September 14, 1961, box 112, Brazil, Security, 1961, POF, JFK.
26. Memorandum of Conversation between President Kennedy and Senator (former President) Kubitschek of Brazil, September 15, 1961, NSF, box 12, Br. Gen. 10/61/-11/61, 1, JFK.
27. Ibid., 1. During his Latin American goodwill mission to signal Eisenhower's interest in the region, Vice President Nixon faced angry crowds and riots in Lima and Caracas.
28. Tad Szulc, "Northeast Brazil Poverty Breeds Threat of a Revolt," *New York Times*, October 31, 1960, 1.

29. Tad Szulc, "Marxists are Organizing Peasants in Brazil: Leftist League Aims at a Political Army 40 Million Strong," *New York Times*, November 1, 1960, 3. A decade later, Joseph A. Page wrote a more balanced assessment about the supposed communist threat in the Brazilian Northeast, *The Revolution That Never Was*.

30. Editorial, "The Fidelistas of Brazil," *New York Times*, November 1, 1960, 38.

31. Gordon, interview by John E. Rielly, May 30, 1964.

32. Rabe, "Dulles, Latin American and Cold War Anticommunism," 92–96.

33. Ibid., 34–36.

34. Ibid., 141–44.

35. Gordon, "The Alliance at Birth: Hopes and Fears," 73.

36. Senator John F. Kennedy, "Speech before the Hillsborough County Courthouse, Tampa, Florida" (advance release text), October 18, 1960, Speeches, JFK.

37. John F. Kennedy, "Address at a White House Reception for Members of Congress and for the Diplomatic Corps of the Latin American Republics," March 13, 1961, Speeches, JFK.

38. Rabe, *The Most Dangerous Area in the World*, 30–32.

39. http://www.peacecorps.gov/index.cfm?shell=Learn.whatispc.history.speech.

40. Senator John F. Kennedy, "Remarks at the University of Michigan Student Union Building Steps, Ann Arbor, Michigan, October 14, 1960," Presidential Speeches, JFK.

41. See Hoffman, *All You Need Is Love*.

42. Ibid., 1–38.

43. For an analysis of the Peace Corps in Brazil, see Azevedo, "Os Corpos da Paz no Brasil."

44. "Papal Program for Latin America," *Latin America Calls!* (January–February 1963): 2.

45. There are no circulations records in the publication or at the U.S. Conference of Catholic Bishops Archive in Washington. Distribution was through local parishes, especially those with missionary connections in Latin America, and each issue likely numbered in the thousands.

46. "Papal Program for Latin America."

47. Ibid.

48. Ibid., 3.

49. Quigley, interview, October 9, 2002.

50. Naftali, ed., *The Presidential Recordings, John F. Kennedy*, 18–19.

51. Dreifuss, 1964. See also Black, *United States Penetration of Brazil*.

52. Lincoln Gordon, "Castelo perdeu a batalha," interview by Roberto Garcia, *Veja*, March 9, 1977, 3–8.

53. Ibid., 5.

54. Leacock, *Requiem for Revolution*, 120–22.

55. Ibid., 135.

56. For Brazil, see especially Welch, "Labor Internationalism."

57. United States Senate, Committee on Foreign Relations, *American Institute for Free Labor Development*.

58. Agee, *Inside the Company*.

59. Romualdi, *Presidents and Peons*, 289.

60. AFL-CIO, Labor News Conference, Washington, "Text of panel broadcast on the Mutual Broadcast System, July 12, 1964," press release of July 13, 1964, 3.
61. *Diário Oficial da União*, 102, no. 113 (June 15, 1964), quoted in Alves, *State and Opposition in Military Brazil*, 48.
62. Huggins, *Political Policing*, 162–86.
63. Davis, *A Brotherhood of Arms*, 167–87.
64. Walters, *Silent Missions*, 364.
65. Ibid., 374–75.
66. Ibid., 384.
67. Gordon, *Brazil's Second Chance*, 34.
68. "What Is the Mann Doctrine?" *New York Times*, March 21, 1964, 24.
69. Gordon, *Brazil's Second Chance*, 34.
70. Simões, *Deus, pátria e família*; Starling, *Os senhores das gerais*; and Deutsch, "Christians, Homemakers, and Transgressors."
71. Rio de Janeiro to State Department, Telegram No. 48986, March 27, 1964, NSF, country file Brazil, vol. 2, 3/65, box 9, LBJ.
72. Gordon, "Novas Perspectivas das relações brasileiro-Norte-Americanas," 4.
73. Ibid., 6–9.
74. Ibid., 10.
75. Alves, *Torturas e Torturados*, 36–37.
76. "Arrested: A Big Yaw to the Left," *Life*, April 17, 1964, 38B–38C.
77. "Goulart Goes over Brink in Brazil," *Business Week*, April 4, 1964, 27.
78. Edwin D. Canham, "The Editor and the News," *Christian Science Monitor*, April 7, 1964, 9.
79. Heidenry, *Theirs Was the Kingdom*, 337.
80. Hall, "The Country that Saved Itself." A translation appeared in *Seleções*, the Brazilian version of *Reader's Digest* that had an estimated readership of 600,000. Junqueira, *Ao sul do Rio Grande*, 49; see also pp. 221–30.
81. Canning, *American Dreamers*, 128.
82. Linnell, "'Applauding the Good and Condemning the Bad.'"
83. Weis, "Government News Management, Bias and Distortion in American Press Coverage of the Brazilian Coup of 1964," 52.
84. "Hard Profound Change," *Time*, April 17, 1964, 49.
85. "Marry in Haste," *Newsweek*, April 20, 1964, 60.
86. Juan de Onis, "U.S. Envoy Urges Caution in Brazil," *New York Times*, May 6, 1964, 3.
87. Editorial, "The Brazilian Revolution," *New York Times*, May 11, 1964, 30.
88. Telegram from State Department to Rio de Janeiro, April 17, 1964, NSF, Brazil, vol. 4, Gp 2, LBJ.
89. Alves, *Torturas e Torturados*, 28.
90. Gaspari, *A ditadura envergonhada*, 150.
91. Alves, *Torturas e Torturados*, 242.
92. Ibid., 18.
93. Gaspari, *A ditadura envergonhada*, 150, n. 62.
94. See, for example, Sidney Lens, "Brazil's Police State," *The Progressive*, December 1966, 31–34; Joseph A. Page, "Close Down the Showcase," *Commonweal*, January 10, 1969,

461; Richard Shaull, "Repression Brazilian Style," *Christianity and Crisis* 29, July 21, 1969, 198–99.

95. *Congressional Record—Senate*, April 3, 1964, 6851–52.
96. *Congressional Record—Senate*, August 10, 1964, 18835.
97. *Congressional Record—House*, April 14, 1964, 7916.
98. United States Senate, *Nomination of Lincoln Gordon*, 2.
99. Phyllis R. Parker, telephone interview by author, July 27, 2005, notes. All subsequent quotations are from this interview.
100. Parker was referring to Dulles, *Unrest in Brazil*.
101. Parker, *Brazil and the Quiet Intervention*, 1964. Marcos Sá Corrêa, a Brazilian journalist, later examined the declassified documents, wrote a series of articles about the new revelations that were published in the *Jornal do Brasil*, and subsequently republished them as a book, *1964: Visto e comentado pela Casa Branca*.
102. Parker, *Brazil and the Quiet Intervention*.
103. Memorandum of Conversation with A. Johnson, R. Adams and others, March 28, 1964, NSF, Brazil, vol. 2, 3/64, box 9; Memorandum from Chase to Bundy, March 31, 1964, NSF, Brazil, vol. 2, 3/64, box 9; Joint Chiefs of Staff to USCINSO, No. 5593, No. 5594, No. 5595, "This is a Brother Sam message," March 31, 1964, NSF, Brazil, box 10; Teleconference with Ball, Johnson, Burton, Sloan, "U.S. Policy toward Brazil and other general topics," NSF, NSC Meetings, vol. 1, tab 6, April 2, 1964, LBJ.
104. Gordon, "Made in Brazil."
105. Ibid.
106. Gordon, "Brazil, 1961–1964," 68.
107. Ibid.
108. Gordon, interview, August 5, 2005.

## Capítulo I

1. Marcos Arruda, interview, October 4, 2002. Additional information about Marcos Arruda in this chapter is from this interview.
2. In 1978 J. Langguth wrote about U.S. police advisors in Latin America and their relationship to the repressive apparatuses; his account includes interviews with Jean Marc Von der Weid and Marcos Arruda in exile relating their arrest and torture. Langguth, *Hidden Terrors*.
3. In Brazil, a respectful way to address a woman older than oneself is by using the term *Dona* followed by her first name. Similarly, a man who is one's senior is given the deferential title *Dom* preceding his first name.
4. Regina Von der Weid, interview, June 30, 2006.
5. Reis and Moraes, 1968, 117–31.
6. Ramos, interview, August 24, 2006.
7. Ramos, telephone interview, February 23, 2003. Subsequent quotations are from this interview.
8. Brasil Nunca Mais, Case No. 460, Inquérito de 16/2/67, AEL.
9. Perone, *Masters of Contemporary Brazilian Song*, 2; Perrone, "Dissonance and Dissent."

## 2. The Birth of a Movement

1. Bell, "Brazilian-American Relations," 95.
2. U.S. Congress, House, *Directions for the 1970's*, 577.
3. Skidmore, *The Politics of Military Rule in Brazil*, 18–28.
4. The traditional historiography on the military regime characterizes Castelo Branco as a "moderate" and Costa e Silva as representative of the "hard-line" within the armed forces. For an insightful critique of this bipolar interpretation, see Martins Filho, *O palácio e a caserna*.
5. Gosse, *Where the Boys Are*.
6. Ibid., 117.
7. Ibid., esp. chap. 5.
8. Robert Taber, "Castro's Cuba," *Nation*, January 23, 1960, 63–71.
9. "What Is Really Happening in Cuba," *New York Times*, April 6, 1960, 33.
10. Gosse, *Where the Boys Are*, 155.
11. Ibid., 62–63.
12. "Toasts of the President and President João Goulart of Brazil at the State Luncheon in Honor of the President of Brazil," Edwin Martin Papers, box 37A, JFK.
13. "Text of Kennedy-Goulart Communique," *New York Times*, April 5, 1962, 3.
14. Davis, *A Brotherhood of Arms*, 189–94.
15. Erickson, interview, May 14, 2003.
16. Crahan, interview, May 15, 2003.
17. Hall, interview, July 20, 2003.
18. "Letter of Latin American Specialists to President Johnson on the Dominican Crisis," *New York Times*, May 23, 1965, E6.
19. Gallup, *The Gallup Poll*, 1935–1971, 1942–43.
20. McPherson, *Yankee No!*, 144.
21. These figures include Fred Goff, the son of Protestant missionaries in Colombia, the coordinator in Santo Domingo for the Commission on Free Elections in the Dominican Republic in 1966 after the U.S. invasion, and a founding member and long-time associate of the North American Congress on Latin America (NACLA); Proctor Lippencott, an election observer in the Dominican Republic and, along with Goff, one of NACLA's first two paid staff members; Richard Shaull, one of the commissioners of the Commission on Free Elections in the Dominican Republic, president of the World Student Christian Federation, a founder of NACLA, and for many years the chair of NACLA's board of directors; William L. Wipfler, an Episcopal missionary to the Dominican Republic from 1955 to 1963 who later directed the National Council of Churches' Latin American department; Harry and Loretta Strharsky, Catholic volunteers in the Dominican Republic in the mid-1960s and leading activists in the Washington-based Common Front for Latin America (COFFLA) and the Committee against Repression in Brazil (CARIB); Philip Wheaton, who served as an Episcopal missionary in the Dominican Republic and later founded the Ecumenical Program for Inter-American Communication in Action (EPICA) in Washington; and Peter Eisenberg and Michael Hall, graduate students in Brazilian history at Columbia, who mobilized against the U.S. intervention in the Dominican Republic, among others. Goff, interview, April 2, 1999. Correspondence with Goff, February 6, 2001.

Wipfler, interview, January 12, 2000. Strharsky, interview, March 31, 1999. Wheaton, interview, October 29, 1999. Correspondence with Ralph Della Cava, February 12, 2001.

22. The DEOPS (political police) taped, transcribed, and filed Tyson's remarks in their archives.

23. "Thresher Editors Baffled by Rumpus," *Citizen* (Houston, Texas), January 19, 1949, 5. Rice president W. V. Houston later wrote a letter to Brady Tyson explaining that the institution "was founded and chartered specifically for white students" and informing him that the school had "no intentions of admitting non-white students." V. W. Houston to Brady Tyson, February 14, 1949; copy in author's files. Rice University did not end its racist admission policies until 1965. Kean, "'At a Most Uncomfortable Speed,'" esp. 78–89. The Houston branch of the National Association for the Advancement of Colored People sent Tyson a congratulatory letter commending his position "on the question of Equal Educational Opportunities for Negros in Texas and the South." Lulu B. White to Brady Tyson, December 22, 1948; copy in author's files.

24. Letter from Jean and Brady Tyson, May 1966, copy in author's files.

25. Anivaldo Padilha, "Testamunho sobre Brady Tyson para João Valença," November 26, 1999; copy in author's files.

26. Erickson, interview, May 14, 2003.

27. Regional de Polícia de São José do Rio Preto, March 22, 1966, 50-Z-320–1071, AESP-DEOPS.

28. Letter, Brady and Jean Tyson, May 1966; copy in author's files.

29. Ibid.

30. Ibid.

31. The list of undergraduate and graduate students who became activists on issues related to Latin America is quite extensive. Among the people who studied at Stanford in the 1960s were Donald Bray, Ronald C. Chilcote, James Cockcroft, Peter Eisenberg, Fred Goff, Timothy Harding, Suzana Jonas, Dale Johnson, Saul Landau, and Allen Young. Chilcote, "Review," 76. At Columbia, the activists and supporters included Diana Brown, Connie Carter, Margaret Crahan, Ralph Della Cava, Kenneth Erickson, Peter Eisenberg, Michael Hall, John Lombardi, Joseph L. Love, Maxine Margolis, Stuart Schwartz, Peter Smith, Alfred Stepan, and Charles Wagley. Correspondence with Crahan, August 26, 2007; Love, interview, October 9, 2004.

32. Della Cava, *Miracle at Juazeiro*.

33. Della Cava, interview, November 26, 1999.

34. Ibid.

35. Skidmore, "Author's Preface," *Politics in Brazil*, xxv.

36. Skidmore, interview, October 12, 2002. See also an interview with Skidmore in Meihy, *A colônia Brasílianista*, 253–68. Skidmore continued his career as an expert on Brazil, producing several important histories that shaped the field of recent Brazilian history in the United States and in Brazil.

37. Crahan, interview, May 15, 2003.

38. For a history of the varied attempts to found a national organization of Latin Americanists, see Cline, "The Latin American Studies Association."

39. Peck, "Report of Activities, 1968," 3.

40. For details of Project Camelot, see Horowitz, *The Rise and Fall of Project Camelot*; Robin, *The Making of the Cold War Enemy*, 206–25; Silvert, "American Academic Ethics and Social Research Abroad, 215–36.

41. Harding, interview, March 22, 1999; Bray, interview, February 20, 2003; Chilcote, interview, April 16, 2004.

42. Cline, "The Latin American Studies Association," 64.

43. Berger, *Under Northern Eyes*; Chilcote, "Review," 73–77.

44. For a history of NACLA, see Rosen, "NACLA."

45. Tyson, "NACLA as Coalition," 4.

46. Ibid.

47. Ibid., 5.

48. Ibid.

49. NACLA *Newsletter*, March 1967, 6.

50. Goff, "February 11, 1967 Meeting," 1.

51. Rosen, "NACLA," 17.

52. NACLA encouraged activists to engage in research and investigation in order to be able to draw the links between U.S.–owned companies' operations abroad and their impact in the United States. See, for example, North American Congress on Latin America, NACLA *Research Methodology Guide*.

53. Silberstein, interview, April 27, 2002. All subsequent quotations are from this interview.

54. Returning to the United States, Young joined the anti–Vietnam War movement, was a founder of Liberation News Service (a left-wing alternative new agency), and a gay activist. He kept ties with his friends in Brazil and in the 1970s joined an international effort to protest government harassment of *Lampião da Esquina*, Brazil's first gay newspaper.

55. "Brazilian Student Union Struggles," September 4, 1964, 13; "Intellectual Plight in Brazil," September 26, 1964, 2; "Poverty Hugs Northeast Brazil," June 16, 1965, 1; "Brazilian Hotbed Kept in Cooler," June 18, 1965, 10; "Brazilian Express their Defiance in Song and Dance," July 16, 1965, 6.

56. "Morse Urges Aid Cutoff," *New York Times*, October 30, 1965, 10.

57. Editorial, "Bad Turn in Brazil," October 28, 1965, 42; Juan de Onis, "Brazil's Chief Asks Congress to Reduce Deputies by a Third," November 6, 1965, 10; Juan de Onis, "Democracy Brazilian Style," November 28, 1965, E3.

58. Hélio Jaguaribe, "Brazil's Castelo Branco Regime Opposed," letter to the editor, dated October 28, 1965. *New York Times*, November 12, 1965, 46.

59. State Department to Rio de Janeiro, Telegram No. 910, October 28, 1965, and No. 949, October 30, 1965, NSF, Latin America, Brazil, Cables, box 10, LBJ.

60. Central Intelligence Agency, "Political Developments in Brazil," No. 2341/65, October 27, 1965, NSF, Latin America, Brazil, Memos, box 10, LBJ.

61. Lincoln Gordon, "Aid Presentation on Brazil," November 4, 1965, NSF, Latin America, Brazil, Memos, box 10, LBJ.

62. U.S. Congress, Senate, *Nomination of Lincoln Gordon*.

63. *Congressional Record—Senate*, February 25, 1966, 4120.

64. Ibid., 4121.

65. Bell, "Brazilian-American Relations," 97.

66. Tuthill, "Operation Topsy."

67. Ibid., 67.

68. Rabe, *Eisenhower and Latin America*, 97.

69. Ibid., 148; Rabe, *The Most Dangerous Area in the World*, 130.

70. Johnson, *Ernest Gruening and the American Dissenting Tradition*, 223, 233–34; Gruening, *Many Battles*, 458.

## Capítulo II

1. Ventura, *1968—o ano que não terminou*.

2. Calado, *Tropicália*; Vilarino, *A MPB em movimento*; Dunn, *Brutality Garden*; Napolitano, *Seguindo a canção*.

3. Almeida and Weis, "Carro-zereo e pau-de-arara."

4. Monica Arruda, interview, November 2, 2002. Subsequent quotations are from this interview.

5. Martinha Arruda, interview, November 2, 2004. Subsequent quotations are from this interview.

6. Penna, interview, October 31, 2002.

7. A 1968 Gallup poll conducted in Brazil seems to confirm Martinha's memories of those times. "Poll Before IA-5 showed government unpopular," Telegram No. 701, Rio de Janeiro to Washington, January 27, 1969, box 1910, FRUS.

8. Marcos Arruda, "A vivência objetiva e subjetiva do trabalhador intelectual," 6.

9. Ibid., 7.

10. Ibid.

11. Alves. *State and Opposition in Military Brazil*; Skidmore, *The Politics of Military Rule in Brazil*.

12. Maria Helena Moreira Alves, interview, July 11, 2003. Subsequent quotations are from this interview.

13. Alves, *A Grain of Mustard Seed*, 49.

## 3. The World Turned Upside Down

1. See Poerner, *O Poder jovem*; Martins Filho, *Movimento estudantil e ditadura militar*; Ridenti, *O fantasma da revolução brasileira*, 115–49; Dirceu and Palmeira, *Abaixo a ditadura*; Valle, *1968*.

2. Martins Filho, *Movimento estudantil e ditadura militar*, 171–91.

3. Gorender, *Combate nas trevas*, 80–92; 103–110.

4. "Country Analysis and Strategy Paper (CASP), 7, Brazil, April 15, 1968, box 1900, FRUS.

5. Ibid., 11.

6. Ibid.

7. Ventura, *1968—o ano que não terminou*.

8. Baer and Kerstenetsky, "The Brazilian Economy."

9. Costa, "A Frente Ampla de oposição ao regime militar."

10. Gaspari, *A ditadura envergonhada*, 129.

11. "The Bishops Speak Out," *Time*, December 15, 1967, 40; "Prelate in Brazil Supports Reforms," *New York Times*, February 6, 1968, L-7.

12. "20,000 March in Rio at Youth's Funeral," *New York Times*, March 30, 1968, 3. Most Brazilian newspapers registered the number at 50,000. See, for example, "Uma grande multidão no sepultamento," *Folha de São Paulo*, March 30, 1968, section 1, back page, and "Edson Luís morreu," *Cruzeiro*, April 13, 1968, 25.

13. "Students Rap Brazil Education," *Christian Science Monitor*, April 6, 1968, 2; "Link of Violence," *Time*, April 12, 1968, 40–41; "Out of the Dungeon," *Newsweek*, April 22, 1968, 57.

14. "Army Acts in Rio to Halt Disorders," *New York Times*, April 2, 1968, 4; "Students in Brazil Get Stern Warning," *New York Times*, April 4, 1968, 3; "Police in Rio Protect Youths from Police," *New York Times*, April 5, 1968, 2; "Student Disorders Continue in Brazil," April 5, 1968, 44.

15. "São Paulo Governor Injured in Antigovernment Outbreak," *New York Times*, May 2, 1968, 18.

16. Memorandum from Richard Helms to W. Thomas Johnson Jr., September 18, 1968, Attachment No. 1, "Restless Youth" 9/68, No. 0613/68, LBJ.

17. "Restless Youth," Brazil, 1.

18. Ibid., 3–4.

19. Ibid., 9.

20. Certainly the CIA accumulated information about the student movement from sources other than those cited in dispatches sent through normal channels. A detailed reading of telegrams from the embassy consulates indicates that State Department officials had an unsophisticated understanding of the student movement's internal politics. Reports managed to identify the names of well-known public figures and leaders and offer rough characterizations of the different political groups, but there is no indication from these records that this branch of the U.S. government, at least, had any good inside sources within the student movement.

21. "Restless Youth," 10–11.

22. Gurgel, *A rebelião dos estudantes*, Brasília, 1968, 253–76.

23. Alves, *68 Mudou o mundo*, 150. See also Alves, *A Grain of Mustard Seed*, 1–25.

24. Alves, *68 Mudou o mundo*, 151.

25. Ibid.

26. James Nelson Goodsell, "Brazil Military Cracks Down," *Christian Science Monitor*, December 17, 1968, 4.

27. "Institutional Act," Telegram No. 14303, Rio de Janeiro to Washington, December 14, 1968, box 1910, FRUS.

28. "Preliminary Assessment of Brazilian Political Situation in Light of 5th Institutional Act," Telegram No. 14310, Rio de Janeiro to Washington, December 14, 1968, box 1910, FRUS.

29. Ibid.

30. "Proposed U.S. Statement on Brazilian Situation," Telegram No. 14338, Rio de Janeiro to Washington, December 15, 1968, box 1910, FRUS.

31. "Department Spokesman's Replies to Questions on Brazil," Washington to Rio de Janeiro, December 16, 1968, box 1910, FRUS.

32. "Developments in Brazil," Secret Outgoing Telegram, Washington to Brazil, December 17, 1968, box 1910, FRUS.

33. "U.S.-Brazil Relationships, Memorandum for Walt W. Rostow, White House," December 17, 1968, box 1900, FRUS.

34. "Finance Minister Forecasts Faster Progress on Economic-Financial Front: Says U.S. Aid will Continue," Telegram No. 14456, Rio de Janeiro to Washington, December 18, 1968, box 1910, FRUS. For Delfin Netto's support of IA-5, see Gaspari, A ditadura envergonhada, 336, 339.

35. "Business reactions to IA-5," Telegram 13359, Rio de Janeiro to Washington, December 21, 1968, box 1910, FRUS.

36. "Spokesman's press briefing Wednesday, December 18," Telegram from Washington to Rio de Janeiro, December 18, 1968, box 1901, FRUS.

37. Telegram No. 289961, Washington to Rio de Janeiro, December 19, 1968, box 1900, FRUS.

38. A noted exception was a series of articles by the Washington Post journalist John Goshko that described Brazil as one of eight countries in Latin American "ruled by outright military dictatorships." John M. Goshko, "Latin Arms Boomerang," Washington Post, February 4, 1968, B-1. Goshko also reported the consistent rumors that accused Vernon Walters of having "prodded his old World War II comrade, the late Marshal Humberto Castelo Branco, into leading the 1964 coup that brought Brazil under military rule." John M. Gosko, "Latins Blame the U.S. for Military Coups," Washington Post, February 5, 1968, A-1. After IA-5, the State Department followed the reflections of U.S. media closely. See, for example, "U.S. Press Reaction," Telegrams from Washington to Rio de Janeiro, December 18, 19, 20, 23, 1968, box 1910, FRUS.

39. Editorial, "Crisis in Brazil," Washington Post, December 17, 1968, A20.

40. Editorial, "Retreat in Brazil," New York Times, December 18, 1968, 46.

41. Editorial, "Backwards in Brazil," Christian Science Monitor, December 19, 1968, 16.

42. "Press Censorship," Telegram No. 14374, Rio de Janeiro to Washington, December 16, 1968, box 1910, FRUS.

43. "Brazilian Military Views of U.S. Press Reactions to Institutional Act No. 5," Telegram No. 14544, Rio de Janeiro to Washington, December 20, 1968, box 1910, FRUS. Soon after the enactment of Institutional Act No. 5, the Brazilian Foreign Ministry also ordered all of its consulates and embassies to send detailed reports about political and press reactions to the "internal political situation in Brazil." "Situação política interna no Brasil. Repercussão no Exterior," Circular No. 7831, Brasília to all Embassies, February 3, 1969," SERE 591.71, IHA.

44. "Former SNI Chief Views Crisis," Telegram 14713, Rio de Janeiro to Washington, December 28, 1968, box 1910, FRUS.

45. Editorial, "Retreat in Brazil," New York Times, December 18, 1968, 46.

46. Robert M. Levine, "Brazil's Coup," letters to the editor of New York Times, January 3, 1969, 26.

47. "Brazil to Seize 'Illicit' Holdings," New York Times, December 19, 1968, 12; "Brazil Claims Plot Forced It to Act," Washington Post, December 19, 1968, 22.

48. State Department Telegram No. 289320, Washington to Rio de Janeiro, December 18, 1968, box 1901, FRUS.

49. Serbin, *Needs of the Heart*, 144–99.

50. "2 U.S. Priests Tell of Jailing in Brazil," *New York Times*, December 29, 1968, 43.

51. "Developments in Brazil: Significance of Institutional Act (IA-5),"Telegram No. 292127, Washington to Rio de Janeiro, December 25, 1968, box 1910, FRUS.

52. "Reports Brazilian Military Confident U.S. Support," Telegram No. 2763, São Paulo to Washington, December 26,1968, box 1910, FRUS; "Military Expectation of U.S. Support," Telegram No. 14770, Rio de Janeiro to Washington, December 31, 1968, box 1910, FRUS.

53. "Assistance Policy toward Brazil," Telegram No. 3442, Rio de Janeiro to Washington, January 15, 1969, box 1900, FRUS.

54. Benjamin Welles, "Nixon Meets Diplomacy and Confusion," *New York Times*, January 24, 1969, 16.

55. Benjamin Wells, "Rockefeller Tour for Nixon Likely," *New York Times*, February 5, 1969, 1, 12.

56. Persico, *The Imperial Rockefeller*, 100.

57. "Conversation with Formin re. U.S. Assistance," Telegram 2070, Rio de Janeiro to Washington, March 19, 1969, box 1900, FRUS.

58. U.S. Congress, *United States Policies and Programs in Brazil*, 243.

59. "Brazil Moves to Prevent Violence Over Rockefeller," *New York Times*, June 9, 1969, 32; "A Good Press Ordered for Rockefeller in Brazil," *New York Times*, June 10, 1969, 4.

60. "Growing Apprehension among Students," Telegram from Rio de Janeiro to Washington, June 6, 1969, box 1901, FRUS.

61. Juan de Onis, "Rockefeller's Hosts Protect Him From the People," *New York Times*, June 22, 1969, E-5.

62. Juan de Onis, "Rockefeller Opens Parleys in Brazil," *New York Times*, June 17, 1969, 1.

63. Juan de Onis, "Rockefeller Visits Brazil's Congress," *New York Times*, June 18, 1969, 21.

64. Juan de Onis, "Pledge of Return Reported," *New York Times*, June 18, 1968, 15.

65. Juan de Onis, "Rockefeller Raises Civil Rights Issues with Brazil's Chief," *New York Times*, June 19, 1968, 1.

66. A sampling of coverage in the *Washington Post* reflects the dismal coverage of the trip in the U.S. media. A. D. Horn, "Latin Mission Seen Buying Nixon Time," May 11, 1969, A-1; A. D. Horn, "Latins Upset at Rocky's Brief Visit," May 14, 1969, A-14; "Peru Bars Visit by Rocky," May 24, 1969, A-1; "Rocky's Bogota Visit Spurs Disorders," May 28, 1969, A-1; "Quito Demonstrations Halt Rocky's Car Twice," May 30, 1969, 22; "Rockefeller Cancels Visit as Caracas Fears Riots," June 2, 1969, A-1; "Chile Is Third to Cancel Visit by Rockefeller," June 5, 1969, A-1; "Rockefeller Stumbles into Latin Whirlpool," June 15, 1969, B-2.

67. John M. Goshko, "Brazilian Regime Pulls Curtain between Rockefeller and People," *Washington Post*, June 18, 1969, 1.

68. Persico, *The Imperial Rockefeller*, 104–5.

69. Rockefeller, *The Rockefeller Report on the Americas*, 63–65; Smith, *Talons of the Eagle*, 159; Schmitz, *The United States and Right-Wing Dictatorship*, 87–93.

70. "American Protest to Governor Rockefeller against Brazilian Educational Policy," Telegram from Rio de Janeiro to Washington, May 29, 1969, box 341, FRUS.

## Capítulo III

1. "Declaration of D. Hélder Câmara regarding the murder of Padre Henrique," May 27, 1969, reprinted in American Committee for Information on Brazil, *Terror in Brazil: A Dossier*.
2. Bicudo, *Meu depoimento sobre o Esquadrão da Morte*.
3. "Notícia Sobre o Bárbaro Trucidamento do Padre Antônio Henrique Pereira da Silva Neto no Recife, a 27 de Maio de 1969," *Boletim Arquidiocesano*, órgão oficial da Arquidiocese de Olinda e Recife, no. 1 (1969): 99–100.
4. "Priest Murdered in Recife," Telegram No. 4126, Recife to Rio de Janeiro and Washington, May 28, 1969, box 3061, FRUS.
5. "Murder of Recife Priest," Telegram No. 4146, Rio de Janeiro to Washington, May 28, 1969, box 3060, FRUS.
6. *Jornal do Brasil*, May 28, 1969.
7. "Murder of Recife Priest," Telegram No. 4146.
8. Ibid.
9. See Serbin, *Secret Dialogues*.
10. "Visita do Secretário Geral da CNBB," *Boletim Arquidiocesano*, órgão oficial da Arquidiocese de Olinda e Recife, no. 1 (1969): 99.
11. "Murdered Priest in Recife," Telegram 4193, Rio de Janeiro to Washington, June 13, 1969, box 3061, FRUS 3061.
12. "Dom Hélder Criticizes Government at Mass for Murdered Priest," Airgram Recife to Washington, July 7, 1069, box 3061, FRUS.
13. Although Lens was not an expert on Brazil, he wrote a critical article against the Castelo Branco government that appeared in late 1966. Lens, "Brazil's Police State."
14. "Manifestações em Chicago," Brasília to Washington, July 3, 1969, IHA.
15. "Movimento de protesto: Piquete do Consulado," No. 20, Chicago to Washington, June 26, 1969, IHA.
16. Shamus Toomey, "Willian Hogan, Activist, Former Catholic Priest," *Chicago Sun-Times*, January 2, 2004.
17. Correspondence with David H. Finke, August 21, 2007. At the time Finke was the treasurer of the Nonviolent Training and Action Center.
18. "Student Movement Mourns a Brazilian Martyr Priest," *Latin America Calls!* 6, no. 6 (June 1969): 1.
19. Márcio Moreira Alves, "Understanding Brazil's Turbulent Church Realities," *Latin America Calls!* 6, no. 6 (June 1969): 5.
20. Darrell Rupiper, "Expelled U.S. Missioner Asks Change of Heart," *Latin America Calls!* 6, no. 6 (June 1969): 5.
21. "More Brazilian Reformers on Terrorist Death List," *Latin America Calls!* 6, no. 6 (June 1969): 4; Diego de Sales, "Rio Priests Denounce Assassination Squadron," *Latin America Calls!* 6, no. 6 (June 1969): 4.
22. "A Commitment by Every Catholic for Latin America," *Latin America Calls!* 6, no. 7 (August–September 1969): 8.
23. Bandeira, interview, July 25, 2003.

24. Piletti and Praxedes, *Dom Hélder Câmara*, 380.

25. Abernathy, interview, February 28, 2003.

26. "Joint Statement of Reverend Abernathy and Dom Hélder Camara," Recife to Washington, April 14, 1970, box 3054, FRUS. According to Reverend Abernathy's widow, Juanita, Brady Tyson organized their trip to Brazil and accompanied them to see the archbishop. Abernathy, interview.

27. "Hemispheric Solidarity Expressed through Non-violent Social Action," *Latin America Calls!* 7, no. 4 (April 1970): 7.

## 4. Defending Artistic and Academic Freedom

1. See Dunn, *Tropicália and the Emergence of a Brazilian Counterculture*.

2. Veloso, *Tropical Truth*, 263.

3. See, for example, "Gilberto Gil e Caetano no seu último show em Salvador," *Veja*, July 30, 1969, 64–65; and "Caetano e Gilberto," *Jornal do Brasil*, July 30, 1969, B-2. Other important papers such as *O Estado de São Paulo* and *O Dia* did not report the farewell concert.

4. Joseph Novitski. "Composer, Forced into Exile Sings His Farewell to Brazil," *New York Times*, July 29, 1969, 8.

5. Ibid.

6. See also Caliman, "Brazilian Art between 1968 and 1974," 49–81.

7. For an analysis of the U.S. government's participation in these cultural battles, see Berghahn, *America and the Intellectual Cold Wars in Europe*.

8. Tota, *O imperialismo sedutor*.

9. Kirby and Erera, "Historical Note," n.d.

10. "10 São Paulo Bienal, Smithsonian, M.I.T. to collaborate on U.S. Entry in Brazil Art Event; Visual Arts and New Technology to Be Combined in Unique Exhibit," press release, July 24, 1969, record unit 321, box 156, SI.

11. Caliman, "Brazilian Art between 1968 and 1974," 54.

12. Haake, interview, February 17, 2002.

13. Grace Glueck, "No Rush for Reservations," *New York Times*, July 6, 1969, D-21.

14. Ibid.

15. Gyorgy Kepes, "Memo to artists participating in the United States exhibition of the X Bienal de Sao Paulo," July 1, 1969, record unit 321, box 160, SI.

16. John Goodyear to Gyorgy Kepes, July 4, 1969, record unit 321, box 160, SI.

17. John Goodyear, telephone interview by author, notes, February 5, 2003.

18. Glueck, "No Rush for Reservations," 21.

19. "Bienal," Telegram No. 15,573, Washington to Brasília, July 11, 1969, SERE, 540.3., IHA.

20. Lois Bingham, Notes by Al Cohen USIA, July 11, 1969, record unit 321, box 160, SI.

21. Lois Bingham, Notes from call by Mr. Levitsky, State, Brazil Desk, July 11, 1969, record unit 321, box 160, SI.

22. The nine artists were Stephen Antonakos, Jack Burnham, John Goodyear, Hans Haake, Tom Lloyd, Charles Ross, Robert Smithson, Harold Tovish, and Takis Vassilakis. Most had stellar artistic careers.

23. Gyorgy Kepes, Open Letter, July 18, 1969, record unit 321, box 160, SI; Edgar J. Driscoll Jr. "MIT Pulls Out of Brazil Art Show," *Boston Globe*, July 15, 1969, 21.

24. "Bienal de São Paulo. Simpósios," Telegram No. 18022, Brasília to Washington, August 14, 1969, SERE, 540.3, IHA.

25. "X Bienal de São Paulo. Boicote," Telegram No. 16810, Brasília to Washington, July 26, 1969, SERE, 540.3, IHA.

26. Lois A. Bingham, Memorandum to Mr. Blitzer from Lois A. Bingham. Subject: Cancellation, American exhibition, X Bienal de São Paulo, July 18, 1969, record unit 321, box 160, SI.

27. U.S. Information Agency, Telegram 14325, Washington to Rio de Janeiro, August 26, 1969, record unit 321, box 160, SI.

28. William L. Jacobsen Jr., Letter to Lois Bingham, São Paulo to Washington, August 18, 1969, record unit 321, box 160, SI; Fransicso Matarazzo Sobrinho to Mario Gibson Alves Barboza, São Paulo to Washington, August 21, 1969, SERE, XB/1436, 540.3, IHA.

29. U.S. Information Agency, Incoming message from [John] Mowinckel, Rio de Janeiro to Washington, September 10, 1969, record unit 321, box 160, SI.

30. Lois A. Bingham to Francisco Matarazzo Sobrinho, Washington to São Paulo, September 19, 1969, record unit, 321, box 155, SI.

31. Frederick Tuten, "There's an Awful Bienal Down in Brazil," *New York Times*, October 12, 1969, II-25.

32. Grace Glueck, "U.S. Decides Not to Take Part in São Paulo Bienal This Year," *New York Times*, May 31, 1971, 8.

33. The U.S. Embassy prepared a detailed memo about the new decree. "GOB Prepares for School Reopening," Telegram No. 1470, Rio de Janeiro to Washington, February 26, 1969, box 341, FRUS.

34. "Patterns of Punitive Action in Universities in the North East," Memorandum of Conversation, Enclosure 1, Airgram No. A-36, Rio de Janeiro to Washington, March 25, 1969, box 341, FRUS.

35. Ibid., Enclosure 3.

36. Ibid., Enclosure 2.

37. "Brazil: Political Repression and Future Prospects," Intelligence Note, U.S. Department of State, Director of Intelligence and Research, May 16, 1969, box 1900, FRUS.

38. This characterization of Caio Prado Júnior comes from the *New York Times* letter to the editor protesting his arrest. Richard Morse, Thomas Skidmore, Stanley Stein, and Charles Wagley, letter to the editor, *New York Times*, March 8, 1970, IV-11.

39. Ibid.; Fragoso, *Advocacia da liberdade*, 93–113; and Gaspari, *A ditadura escancarada*, 229–31.

40. Associação dos Docentes da Universidade de São Paulo, *O livro negro da USP*, 38–39.

41. Telegram No. 3159, Rio de Janeiro to Washington, April, 28, 1969, box 341, FRUS.

42. ADUSP, *O livro negro da USP*, 40.

43. Schmitter, interview, December 18, 2003.

44. "Informações sobre a 'Latin American Studies Association e sobre o Senhor Philippe Schmitter," Brasília to Washington, December 10, 1969, SERE, 692.000 (20), IHA.

45. ADUSP, *O livro negro*, 49.

46. Bernardet, interview, May 23, 1994; Lobo, interview, July 29, 1999.

47. James Nelson Goodsell, "Ouster of Professors Saps Brazilian Talent," *Christian Science Monitor*, May 9, 1969, 2.

48. "Informações sobre a 'Latin American Studies Association e sobre o Senhor Philippe Schmitter," Brasília to Washington, December 10, 1969, SERE, 692.000 (20), IHA.

49. "Política interna brasileira: Telegramas de protesto de professores universitários norte-americanos," Washington to Brasília, June 4, 1969, SERE 500.236, IHA.

50. "Ex-U.S. Aide Joins Protest to Brazil," *New York Times*, June 1, 1969, 24.

51. "Ex post facto evaluation of recent professorial purge on Brazilian scientific and technological community," Airgram No. 471, Rio de Janeiro to Washington, August 14, 1969, box 341, FRUS.

52. Telegram No. 3242, Rio de Janeiro to Washington, April 30, 1969, box 341, FRUS.

53. "Summary retirement of Professors under IA-5," Telegram No. 3251, Rio de Janeiro to Washington, May 1, 1969, box 341, FRUS.

54. See Berghahn, *America and the Intellectual Cold Wars in Europe*.

55. Sorj, *A construção intelectual do Brasil contemporâneo*, 30–31.

56. Bell, interview, February 25, 2004. The following section is based on the interview with Bell. See also Keck and Sikkink, *Activists beyond Borders*, 98–101.

57. For a history of CEBRAP, including its impact on academic production in the 1970s, see Sorj, *A construção intelectual do Brasil contemporâneo*.

58. Miceli, *A desilusão americana*.

59. Miceli, "Betting on an Emerging Scientific Community," 264.

60. Della Cava, correspondence, February 23, 2004.

61. Morse et al., letter to the editor.

62. For an assessment of Caio Prado Júnior's contribution to Marxist scholarship in Brazil, as well as essays about his influence on all sectors of the Brazilian left, see D'Incao, ed., *História e ideal*.

63. Della Cava correspondence, February 23, 2004. "Organização 'Amnesty International' consulta às autoridades brasileiras," New York to Brasília, June 3, 1970, SERE, 500.000 (20), IHA.

64. Henry J. Steiner and David M. Trubek, "Brazilian Scholar, Letter to the Editor," *New York Times*, June 14, 1970, E-17.

65. "Conviction and Imprisonment of Noted Brazilian Academician," Airgram No. A-221, Rio de Janeiro to Washington, May 5, 1970, box 2133, FRUS.

66. "Well Known Intellectual Released," Airgram No. A-87, Brasília to Washington, October 8, 1971, box 2133, FRUS.

67. Pereira, "'Persecution and Farce'"; see also Pereira, *Political Injustice*.

68. Fragoso, *Advocacia da liberdade*, 112–13.

## Capítulo IV

1. Costa et al., eds., *Memórias das mulheres do exílio*.

2. Moraes, interview, July 15, 2003. Subsequent quotations are from this interview.

3. On *O Sol*, see the documentary made by Moraes, *O Sol–caminando contra o vento*.

4. Skidmore, *The Politics of Military Rule in Brazil*, 93–97; Martins Filho, *O palácio e a caserna*, 180–84.

5. "Sequestro do Embaisixador Norte Americano no Rio," September 4, 1969, Brasília to Washington, 921-22-41, IHA.

6. Gabeira, *O que é isso, campanheiro?*, 113, 129; Berquó, *O seqüestro dia a dia*. Renewed controversies about the accuracy of different accounts of the retelling of the story of the U.S. ambassador's kidnapping emerged after the release of the Brazilian feature-length movie *O que é isso, companheiro?* (Four Days in September). See Reis Filho, *Versões e ficções*.

## 5. The Campaign against Torture

1. Amnesty International, *Amnesty International 1961–62 Report*, 2.
2. Ibid., 5.
3. Amnesty International, *Annual Report, 1961–1962*, 6.
4. Amnesty International, *Annual Report, 1st June, 1966/31st May, 1967*, 9.
5. Ibid., 5.
6. Clark, "Strong Principles, Strengthening Practices," 94–104.
7. See McDonald, "The Colonels' Dictatorship," 255–315; Woodhouse, *The Rise and Fall of the Greek Colonels*. On the campaign against torture in Greece, see Amnesty International, *Torture in Greece*.
8. Post-1970 accounts of torture and repression include Márcio Moreira Alves, "Brazil: What Terror Is Like." *Nation*, March 15, 1971, 337–41; Joseph A. Page, "The Little Priest Who Stands Up to Brazil's Generals," *New York Times Magazine*, May 23, 1971, 26–27, 80–82, 84; Richard Barnet, "Letter from Rio," *Harper's Magazine*, September 20, 1972, 16, 19–20, 22. In the early 1970s, international legal scholars presented Brazil as an example par excellence of a country whose government engaged in systematic torture. See Farer, "United States Foreign Policy and the Protection of Human Rights," 626; and Shestack Cohen, "International Human Rights," 676.
9. Alves, *68: Mudou o mundo*, 173.
10. Márcio Moreira Alves, interview, October 30, 2002. Subsequent quotations from Alves in this chapter are from this interview.
11. Ibid.
12. "Chegada a Washington do ex-deputado Márcio Moreira Alves," Telegram 12616, Washington to Brasília, June 6, 1969, SERE, DSI/DAS/500, IHA.
13. Drosdoff, *Linha dura no Brasil*.
14. Skidmore, *The Politics of Military Rule in Brazil*, 105–10.
15. Joseph Novitski, "Kidnapped Envoy Is Freed Unhurt in Rio de Janeiro," *New York Times*, September 8, 1969, 1, 3; Juan de Onis, "Freed Brazilians Charger 'Tortures' by Regime," *New York Times*, September 9, 1969, 8; Georgie Anne Geyer, "Brazilian Military: Grip Grows Tighter," *Los Angeles Times*, September 7, 1969, G-1; "15 Exiled Brazilians Taste Mexico Freedom," *Los Angeles Times*, September 9, 1969, 6; "Incident on Marqui Street," *Newsweek*, September 15, 1969, 45; "Ransom for a U.S. Ambassador," *Time*, September 12, 1969, 18.
16. "Justice Minister Buzaid Denounces Torture of Political Prisoners," Airgram A-702, Rio de Janeiro to Washington, December 4, 1969, box 1239, FRUS.

17. "A violência fora da lei," *Veja*, December 3, 1969, 23.
18. "Torturas," *Veja*, December 10, 1969, 20–27.
19. Ramos, interview, February 23, 2003.
20. Rubem César, who had grown up in Niterói, across the bay from Rio de Janeiro, had known Jovelino since their childhood, as the two had grown up in Presbyterian families. Fernandes, interview, July 18, 2003.
21. Wipfler, "'Progress' in Brazil Revisited," 345.
22. Wipfler, interview, September 8, 2004.
23. American Committee for Information on Brazil, "Statement of Female Prisoners held at Ilha das Flores, Rio de Janeiro," *Terror in Brazil*, 5.
24. Wipfler, interview, September 8, 2004.
25. Oliveira, interview, July 22, 2003.
26. Pellegrino, "Prefácio," 10.
27. Moraes, interview, July 15, 2003. Subsequent quotations in this chapter are from this interview.
28. Bandeira, Antònio Rangel interview, July 23, 2003.
29. Bandeira, *Sombras do paraíso*, 125.
30. Ibid., 126.
31. Ibid.
32. Serbin, *Secret Dialogues*, 38–47; Mainwaring, *The Catholic Church and Politics in Brazil*, 79–141.
33. Alfred Friendly Jr., "Pope Given Dossier Charging Torture by Brazilian Regime," *New York Times*, January 2, 1970, 10.
34. Della Cava, "Torture in Brazil," 135.
35. Cardinal Roy's letter, February 11, 1970, Documentary Service National Catholic News Service, USCCB.
36. "Papal Talk Cheers Brazilian Prelate," *New York Times*, January 27, 1970, 9.
37. Della Cava, "Torture in Brazil," 135.
38. "Pope Deplores Brazil Torture," *Washington Post*, March 26, 1970, A-24.
39. NC News Service, "Brazil to Explain Church-State Friction to Vatican," news release, April 3, 1970, 5.
40. Della Cava, "Torture in Brazil," 141.
41. Della Cava, interview, November 26, 1999.
42. In subsequent years, Brazilian exiles set up other committees, usually with the name "The Brazilian Information Front," in Brussels, Quebec, England, Switzerland, and Sweden. Like the American Committee for Information on Brazil, these groups, as the name indicates, were coalitions of Brazilian exiles from different political tendencies that worked with solidarity supporters from their host countries with the notion that getting out information about the situation in Brazil might change conditions at home.
43. American Committee for Information on Brazil, *Terror in Brazil*, 2.
44. Brazilian Information Front, "Torture in Brazil," letter to the editor, *New York Review of Books*, February 26, 1970, 44.
45. Ibid.
46. "Letter from a Brazilian Political Prisoner," *New York Review of Books*, 44.
47. Editorial, "Oppression in Brazil," *Washington Post*, February 28, 1970, A-14.

48. Telegram No. 1345, Rio de Janeiro to Washington, March 4, 1970, box 2134, FRUS.

49. Mozart Gurgel Valente, letter to the editor, *Washington Post*, March 5, 1970, A-18.

50. Telegram No. 38640, State Department to Rio de Janeiro and Brasília, March 16, 1970, box 2134, FRUS.

51. The speechwriter was Mark Schneider, a civil rights activist, Berkeley student, and former Peace Corps volunteer in El Salvador, who had won a fellowship to work in Kennedy's office. His first assignment was to write the speech on U.S. foreign policy for the senator. Sikkink, *Mixed Signals*, 58.

52. I was unable to locate a copy of the original speech; however, the Brazilian Foreign Service (Itamaraty) translated the official release and sent a copy to Brazil. The translation is by the author and is only an approximation of the original version in English. "Discurso pronunciado pelo Senador Edward M. Kennedy na Conferencia Anual de Mansfield, Universidade de Montana, 17 de abril de 1970, annexed to "Discurso do Senhor Edward Kenedy [sic] de crítica ao regime brasileiro," Telegram No. 3092, Washington to Brasília, April 20, 1970, SERE, 604.12 (22), IHA.

53. Ibid.

54. "U.S. Presses Brazil on Torture Issues," *New York Times*, April 23, 1970, 12; Telegram No. 59960, Washington to Rio de Janeiro, April 22, 1970, box 2129, FRUS.

55. "Despacho da UPI sobre a entrevista coletiva imprensa," No. 75, Washington to Brasília, April 24, 1970, SERE, 604.12 (22), IHA.

56. "Justice Minister Buzaid Denounces Torture of Political Prisoners."

57. Letter from David M. Abshire, Assistant Secretary for Congressional Relations to Senator Peter H. Dominick, May 1, 1970, box 1293, FRUS.

58. Brazilian Embassy, Washington, *Boletim Especial*, no. 83 (May 12, 1970): 1; "Notiário da imprensa estrangeira sobre torturas no Brasil," Telegram No. 71830, Brasília to Washington, May 9, 1970, SERE, 591.71.00, IHA.

59. Editorial, "Brazil: Terror and Torture," *New York Times*, April 29, 1970, 40.

60. Wipfler, "The Price of 'Progress' in Brazil;" Bolton, "Brazilian Torture;" Brady Tyson, "Brazil Twists Thumbscrews: Brazil Junta Repression Stifles the Opposition," *Washington Post*, April 5, 1970, B1, B-5; "Death Squads," *Newsweek*, April 20, 1970, 61; Della Cava, "Torture in Brazil;" Della Cava, "Sadists in Epaulets"; Alves, "Christians, Marxists and Dictatorship in Brazil;" Lima, "Brazil's Revolution Six Years Later;" Lima, "Atrocities Charged. Brazil Loses Lutheran Assembly."

61. Hannifin, "Repression of Civil Liberties and Human Rights in Brazil."

62. "From the Parrot's Perch," *Time*, July 27, 1970, 27.

63. Gross, "Brazil: Government by Torture," 70.

64. Lincoln Gordon, "To the Editors," *Commonweal*, August 7 1970, 378.

65. Ralph Della Cava, "Reply," *Commonweal*, August 7, 1970, 398.

66. Ibid., 399.

## Capítulo V

1. *Chico Buarque vai passar*; Zappa, *Chico Buarque*, 104–9.

2. Denise Rollemberg's work on Brazilian exiles during the military regime is the definitive work on this topic. See Rollemberg, *Exílio*.

3. Hollanda, *Chico Buarque*, 128.

4. Marcos Arruda, interview, December 13, 2005.
5. Sattamini, *A Mother's Cry*.
6. Since there are no primary or secondary sources to confirm who exactly was the "first" Brazilian political exile to the United States after the coup d'état of March 31, 1964, it is quite possible that others traveled to the United States before Furtado's visit.
7. Singer, ed., *Celso Furtado*.
8. Cardoso, *A arte da política*.
9. Cardoso and Falletto, *Dependencia y desarrollo en América Latina*.
10. Cardoso, interview, March 15, 2007.
11. Schmitter, "The Persecution of Political and Social Scientists."
12. Bassetto, "Devemos rever a imagem que temos de nós mesmos"; Sevillano, "Entrevista com a Professora Emília Viotti da Costa." On the MEC-USAID controversy, see Arapiraca, *A USAID e a educação brasileira*.
13. Hall, interview, July 20, 2003.
14. Love, interview, October 9, 2004.
15. "Emília Viotti da Costa," in Costa et al., eds., *Memórias do exílio*, 390–412. The Historian Judy Bieber, in her analysis of the development of the study of Brazilian history in the United States, credits Emília Viotti da Costa as "the only female professor who has trained significant numbers of graduate students in Brazilian history." Bieber, "Brazilian History in the United States," 168.
16. For a collection of essays by her former students that reflects Emília Viotti da Costa's monumental influence on the practice of Latin American history in the United States, see Joseph, ed., *Reclaiming the Political in Latin American History*.
17. Lobo, interview, July 29, 1999.
18. Ibid.
19. Nascimento, interview, July 8, 2003.
20. See, for example, Nascimento, *Mixture or Massacre?*
21. Cavalcanti, interview, July 18, 2003.
22. Alencar, interview, July 18, 2003; Brigagão, interview, June 17, 2003; Dagnino, interview, June 2, 1999; Feldman-Bianco, interview, July 25, 2003; Fernandes, interview, July 18, 2003.
23. Stam, interview, November 20, 2002.
24. Matin-Asgari, *Iranian Student Opposition to the Shah*.
25. Stam, interview; Padilha, interview no. 1, July 18, 1997.
26. Martinha Arruda, interview, September 4, 2004.
27. Silva, "Reinventando o sonho," 245–56; Trevisan, *Devassos no paraíso*, 336–37.
28. Maria Helena Moreira Alves, interview, July 11, 2003.
29. Moraes, interview, July 15, 2003.
30. Patarra, interview, June 21, 2003.

## 6. Latin Americanists Take a Stand

1. Crahan, interview, May 15, 2003.
2. Ibid.
3. Della Cava, interview, November 26, 1999.

4. Ibid.

5. Skidmore, interview, October 12, 2002.

6. Ralph Della Cava does not recall who actually drafted the original LASA resolution on Brazil. Della Cava, correspondence, February 23, 2004. Copy in author's files.

7. Huggins, *Political Policing*.

8. *Union of Radical Latin Americanists* 1, no. 1 (1970): 2.

9. The conference offered a grand total of sixteen panels, forums, and keynote presentations. *Latin American Studies Association Newsletter* 1, no. 5 (January–February 1970): 2.

10. *Union of Radical Latin Americanists* 1, no. 1 (1970): 2.

11. A. D. Horne, "34 Groups Score Torture in Brazil," *Washington Post*, April 19, 1970, A-4.

12. "Entrevista a imprensa do ex-deputado Marcio Moreira Alves," Brazilian Embassy to Itamaray, Telegram No. 3057, April 19, 1970, SERE 591.71 (22), IHA.

13. Skidmore, interview, October 12, 2002; Márcio Moreira Alves, interview, October 30, 2002; Della Cava, correspondence, February 23, 2004.

14. "Segundo Congresso da Lasa," No. 586, April 24, 1970, Washington to Brasília, SERE 642 (22), IHA.

15. Ibid.

16. "Informações sobre 'A Latin American Studies Association' e sobre o Senhor Philippe Schmitter," December 10, 1969, Brasília to Washington, SERE, 692.00 (22), IHA.

17. "Latin American Studies Association," No. 1820, December 17, 1969 SERE, 642 (22), IHA.

18. Kottak, interview, December 8, 2003; Margolis, interview, December 16, 2003.

19. "Não Podemos Continuar Em Silencio," DEOPS, 30Z-160-7205, AESP. One cannot tell from the document which agency of the Brazilian intelligence network translated the statement or which agency retained the files. Individual records of the signers, however, are not in the DEOPS archives in São Paulo.

20. "II° Congresso da LASA," Telegram No. 298, June 1, 1970, Brasília to Washington, SERE, 642 (22), IHA.

21. "Informações sobre cidadãos norte americanos," Telegram No. 21.196, October 27, 1970, Washington to Brasília, SERE, 511.141, IHA.

22. Crahan, interview, May 15, 2003.

23. Márcio Moreira Alves, interview October 30, 2002.

24. "Gordon Tied to 1964 Coup," *Baltimore Sun*, April 23, 1970, 17.

25. This account is reconstructed from interviews with Baer and Roett and from written statements made by Baer, Roett, and Carlos Peláez soon after they had been sequestered. Roett, interview, March 5, 2004; Baer, interview, February 9, 2004. Copies of these statements in English that were found in State Department files and translations into Portuguese were also among the documents in the Brazilian Ministry of Foreign Service files.

26. Roett, interview, March 5, 2004.

27. Ibid.

28. Ibid.

29. Stanley A. Nicholson, "Letter to General Luiz França de Oliveira," Rio de Janeiro,

June 16, 1970, SERE, 500.1 (22); Memo from the Director of the Divisão de Segurança e Informações to the Secretaria de Estado das Relações Exteriores, "Incidente com nacionais americanos na Guanabara," AAA 37, June 20, 1970, IHA. English translation by the author.

30. U.S. Embassy, Brasília, Aide-Memoire, June 19, 1970, SERE, 500.1 (22), IHA; "Incidente com nacionais americanos na Guanabara," June 20, 1970, IHA.

31. "Arrest of American Researchers," Telegram No. 4132 June 15, 1970, Rio de Janeiro to Washington, box 2133, FRUS.

32. Baer interview, February 9, 2004.

33. "Arrest of American Researchers," Telegram No. 4141, June 18, 1970, Rio de Janeiro to Washington, box 2133, FRUS.

34. "Dr. Riordan Roett, Dr. Carlos Peláez, and Dr. Werner Baer," Secretaria de Segurança, CIE, Info. No. 1283, August 3, 1970, AERJ.

35. Fico, *Como eles agiam*.

36. Baer, interview, February 9, 2004.

37. Roett, interview, March 5, 2004.

38. Hahner, interview, April 18, 2004.

39. Wright, interview, March 13, 2004.

40. Skidmore, interview, October 12, 2002.

41. "Visita do Professor Thomas Skidmore ao Brasil," Telegram No. 507, Brasília to Washington, July 3, 1970, SERE, 642.64 (22) (42), IHA.

## Capitulo VI

1. Muniz, interview, April 2, 2004. Subsequent quotations are from this interview.

2. "Prisão dos subversivos," Informação No. 133, DEOPS 50D-7–1615, AESP.

3. "Viva o primeiro de maio," DEOPS 50Z-9–14905, AESP.

4. Miranda and Tibúrcio, *Dos filhos deste solo*, 528.

5. "Inquérito," May 13, 1970, DEOPS 50Z-9–14905, AESP.

6. Muniz, interview, April 2, 2004.

7. Miranda and Tibúrcio, *Dos filhos deste solo*, 528.

8. Hélio Fernandes, "Em primeira mão," *Tribuna da Imprensa*, May 5, 1970, 3.

9. Comissão de Familiares de Mortos e Desaparecidos Políticos, *Dossiê dos mortos e desaparecidos políticos a partir de 1964*, 93.

10. Miranda and Tibúrcio, *Dos filhos deste solo*, 528.

11. Brazilian Embassy, Washington, *News from Brazil*, May 8, 1970; "Notiário da imprensa estrangeira sobre torturas no Brasil," Telegram No. 71830, Brasília to Washington, May 9, 1970, SERE, 591.71.00, IHA.

12. "Relatório," August 18, 1970, DEOPS 30C-1–19935, AESP.

13. "Sindicatos denunciam violência," *Jornal do Brasil*, May 15, 1970, 3.

14. "Metalúrgicos: Assembléia geral extraordinária dos Metalúrgicos de São Paulo—Antecipação sindical," May 23, 1970, DEOPS 50B-58–1919, AESP.

## 7. Human Rights and the OAS

1. Hélio Damante, "Brazil Bishops Condemn Police Tortures," NC News Service, May 29, 1970, 1, NCNSA.
2. NC News Service, "Brazil Bishops on Torture," June 12, 1970, NCNSA.
3. International Affairs Committee of the U.S. Catholic Conference, "Statement on Brazil," May 26, 1970, Latin American Division, unprocessed files, USCCB.
4. Latin American Department, Division of Overseas Ministries, National Council of Churches of Christ in U.S.A., "Statement on Political Repression and Terror in Brazil," June 5, 1970, USCCB.
5. Subsequently, the general secretaries of the Christian Workers Federation in Paraguay, the Latin American Federation of Civil Construction Workers based in Venezuela, and Union Action from Argentina all joined the petition. "Comissão Interamericana de Direitos Humanos," Memo No. 065, February 1975, SERE, 602.60 (20), IHA.
6. Inter-American Commission on Human Rights, "Annual Report of the Inter-American Commission on Human Rights for the Year 1973," 39–40.
7. "Prisão dos subversivos," Informação No. 133, DEOPS 50-D-71615, AESP.
8. Miranda and Tibúrcio, Dos filhos deste solo, 531.
9. The internal OAS case records are not available for review to identify details about how petitioners collected the initial information to present to the IACHR. One can only assume that in the rush to put together documentation to send to Washington and with no cooperation from the Brazilian political police, those gathering information had to rely on the most accurate information at hand.
10. Comissão de Familiares de Mortos e Desaparecidos Políticos, Dossiê dos mortos e desaparecidos políticos a partir de 1964, 93; Evandro Carlos de Andrade, "A Morte de Olavo Hansen," O Estado de São Paulo, August 1, 1970, 4.
11. "Murder of São Paulo Unionist Becomes 'Cause Celebre,'" Telegram 485, São Paulo to Washington, May 21, 1970, box 1531, FRUS.
12. "Continued MDB Pressure on Olavo Hansen Case," Airgram No. 161, Brasília to Washington, August 5, 1970, box 2133, FRUS.
13. Reverend Louis M. Colonnese to Dr. Gabino Fraga, June 25, 1970, Latin American Division, unprocessed files, USCCB.
14. "Initial List of Documentation Presented to the Inter-American Commission on Human Rights of the Organization of American States," Washington, June 25, 1970, Latin American Division, unprocessed files, USCCB.
15. Wipfler, telephone interview, September 8, 2004.
16. Inter-American Commission on Human Rights, "Report on the Work Accomplished During its Twentieth Session, December 2 through 12, 1968," 15.
17. Ibid.
18. For example, when the IACHR scheduled a meeting in Santiago, Chile, in late 1971 where it would address the cases, Itamaraty officials carefully calculated when and where to send the response to the commission's requests for information so that it would arrive in Washington just before the deadline. As a result, the body could not consider the response during the meeting in Chile. "CIDH. Denúncias contra o

Brasil. 26° Período de Sessões. Santiago, 25/10/71 a 6/11/71," October 8, 1971, SERE 602.60 (20), IHA.

19. "Brazil Refuses Investigation of Torture Charges," *Washington Post*, November 22, 1970, A-13.

20. International Commission of Jurists, "Report on Police Repression and Tortures Inflicted upon Political Opponents and Prisoners in Brazil," July 22, 1970, p. 9. Copy in author's archives.

21. Ibid., 6–7.

22. Ibid., 4.

23. "Trends and Events for the Month of July," Airgram 376, August 11, 1970, Rio de Janeiro to Washington, box 1366, FRUS.

24. "Treatment of Political Prisoners in Brazil," Telegram 123958, Washington to The Hague, July 31, 1970, box 2133, FRUS.

25. Ibid.

26. "Trends and Events for the Month of July," 2.

27. Government of Brazil, "Information of the Brazilian Government to Clarify Supposed Violations of Human Rights Related in Communications Transmitted by the Inter-American Commission of Human Rights of the Organization of American States," DSI.

28. "Brazil's Image Abroad," Telegram No. 1078, São Paulo to Washington, November 11, 1970, box 1292, FRUS.

29. "Brazil Opts to Counter Poor Image Abroad," Airgram A-35, April 23, 1971, Brasília to Washington, box 1343, FRUS.

30. "Trends and Events for the Month of July," Airgram 378, Rio de Janeiro to Washington, August 11, 1970, box 1366, FRUS.

31. "Brazil Opts to Counter Poor Image Abroad."

32. Ibid.

33. "Situação interna brasileira. Repercussão na imprensa norteamericana," Telegram No. 29110, December 21, 1968, Washington to Brasília, SERE 500 (22), IHA.

34. "Police in Brazil Question Time-Life Correspondent," *New York Times*, May 20, 1971, 35; Joseph Novitski, "Head of Hemisphere Press Group Assails Brazilian Censorship," *New York Times*, December 24, 1970, 6; "Reunião da SIP em Acapulco. Comentários sobre a imprensa brasileira," Telegram No. 6873, Mexico to Brasília, March 28, 1969, SERE 691 (00). IHA; "Situação da imprensa no Brasil: Declarações do presidente do Comitê Executivo da Associação Interamerica de Imprensa," Memorandum 139, June 9, 1971 SERE 591.7 (22), IHA.

35. Leonard Greenwood, "Brazil orders Ouster of French Newsman," *Los Angeles Times* (December 25, 1970): II-5; "Trends and Events for the Month of December 1970," Airgram No. A-27, Rio de Janeiro to Washington, January 20, 1971, FRUS Box 1357.

36. "Viagem ao Brasil do redator político do 'Washington Post,' Lewis Duiguid," Telegram No. 229, Brasília to Washington, May 19, 1970, SERE 691.3 (22) (42), IHA; "Imagem do Brasil: Artigo de Daniel Griffin no 'Washington Post,'" Washington to Brasília, March 9, 1971, SERE 591.71 (22), IHA; "Joseph Novitski," Informação 1550, June 19, 1972 Ministério do Exército, CIE, SERE 691.3 (22) (42), IHA; "Imagem do Brasil: Visita do Jornalista William Carley, do 'Wall Street Journal,'" Telegram No.

17298, September 18, 1970, Washington to Brasília, SERE 500 (22), IHA; on Robert Erlander: "Situação Política Brasileira. Repercussão nos Estados Unidos," Telegram No. 28797, December 15, 1969, Washington to Brasília, SERE 500 (22), IHA.

37. "Brazil Opts to Counter Poor Image Abroad."

38. "Despesas com jornalistas estrangeiros," Telegram No. 176, May 9, 1970, SERE 303.3, IHA.

39. "Imagem do Brasil: *National Review* e jornalista Selden Rodman," Telegram No. 4286, Washington to Brasília, October 28, 1970, SERE 591.3 (22), IHA; "Visita do jornalista ao Brasil: Autorização de passagem," Telegram No. 1203, Brasília to Washington, December 3, 1970, SERE 591.3(22) (42), IHA.

40. "Imagem do Brazil: Possibilidade de inserção de artigos na 'National Review,'" Washington to Brasília, Telegram No. 19453, October 9, 1970, SERE 591.0 (22), IHA.

41. Selden Rodman, "Don't Underestimate Brazil," *National Review*, August 10, 1971, 860–63.

42. Fico, *Reinventando o otimismo*.

43. Ibid., 145.

44. D'Araújo, Soares, and Castro, *Os anos de chumbo*, 271.

45. "Almoço do Embaixador no Washington Post," Telegram No. 4963, March 7, 1969, Washington to Brasília, SERE 500 (22), IHA.

46. "Apreciação pela imprensa norte americana dos últimos fatos políticos no Brasil," Telegram No. 20454, September 10, 1969, SERE 500 (22), IHA. As the series of denunciations about torture began to flow out of Brazil in December 1969, Celso Diniz, the chargé d'affaires, wired Itamaraty about his difficulty as a diplomat stationed in the United States in influencing the *New York Times* and the *Christian Science Monitor* regarding their reporting on the topic. He pointed out that most articles appearing in the U.S. press came from correspondents living in Brazil. "Política Interna Brasileira," Telegram 28170, December 9, 1969, Washington to Brasília, SERE 500 (22), IHA.

47. "Visita do jornalista Joseph Kraft ao Brasil," Telegram No. 23811, November 21, 1970, Washington to Brasília, SERE 691.2 (22) 42, IHA.

48. "Visita do jornalista Joseph Kraft ao Brasil," Telegram No. 1246, December 11, 1970, Brasília to Washington, SERE 691.3 (22) 42, IHA.

49. Joseph Kraft, "Brazil's Big Push," *Washington Post*, December 13, 1970, B-7.

50. "Assembléia Geral Extraordinária da OEA," Itamaraty Memo 117, June 1, 1970, SERE 922.2 (00) (20), IHA.

51. "Discurso pronunciado pelo Excelentíssimo Senhor Mário Gibson Alves Barboza, Ministro de Estado das Relações Exteriores do Brasil," June 25, 1970, Organization of American States, SERE 922.2 (00) (20), IHA.

52. "O.E.A. Atos de terrorismo: Seqüestros de pessoas e extorsão conexa com esse crime," Itamaraty Memo to the President of the Republic, 141, July 1, 1970, SERE 922.2 (00) (20), IHA.

53. Ibid., 4.

54. Marilyn Berger, "Six Nations Walk Out of OAS Talks," *Washington Post*, February 2, 1971, A-1.

55. Tad Szulc, "6 Nations Stage Walkout in O.A.S," *New York Times* (February 2, 1971): 5.

56. Editorial, "The OAS Tackles Terrorism," *Washington Post* (February 3, 19781): A-16.
57. Ibid.
58. Inter-American Commission on Human Rights, "Annual Report of the Inter-American Commission on Human Rights for the Year 1973," 80.
59. Ibid., 81.
60. Editorial, "Brazil's New Chance," *New York Times*, March 23, 1974, 30.
61. Marvine Howe, "Brazil Press Faces New Curbs," *New York Times*, March 25, 1974, 9; Jack Anderson, "Press Suppression," *Washington Post*, March 18, 1974, D-11; "After Week of New Regime, Brazil Censorship Remains," *Miami Herald*, March 25, 1974.
62. Farer, *The Grand Strategy*, 77.
63. D'Araújo and Castro, eds. *Ernesto Geisel*, 223–35.
64. Inter-American Commission on Human Rights, *Ten Years of Activities*, 252–57, 261–65.
65. Farer, *The Grand Strategy*, 87–89.

## Capítulo VII

Fado (the word is translated as "destiny" or "fate") is a musical genre from Portugal characterized by mournful tunes and lyrics.

1. Padilha, interview no. 3, June 18, 1998. Subsequent quotations are from interview no. 3.
2. 50-z-9-13798, AESP.
3. Reis Filho, *Versões e ficções*. Huggins's work on twenty-three Brazilian police officers who facilitated or directly tortured and murdered "subversives" reveals how most of those involved were not sadists or fanatics, as one would suppose. Rather, the secrecy of the endeavor, occupational insularity, organizational fragmentation, and personal isolation enabled them to carry out assigned tasks. Huggins, Haritos-Fatouros, and Zimbardo, *Violence Workers*.

## 8. Congressional Questioning

1. Charles Goodell, "Report on Brazil," *Congressional Record—Senate*, June 21, 1967, 16779.
2. Ibid., 16786.
3. Charles Goodell, "Democracy in Latin America: Brazilian Retreat," *Congressional Record—Senate*, February 4, 1969, 2608.
4. Ibid., 2609.
5. Telegram No. 193, March 5, 1969, Rio de Janeiro to Washington, box 1900 FRUS.
6. Ibid.
7. Representative Otto Passman, a Democrat from Louisiana, took to the House floor to criticize the new authoritarian measures under IA-5 and called on his fellow representatives to cease aid to the country. Otto Passman, "Giveaways Do Not Solve International Problems," *Congressional Record—House*, March 13, 1969, 6437. Democrat–Farm Labor Congressman Donald Fraser from Minnesota spoke against continued U.S. aid to nations ruled by dictators—Greece, Spain, Portugal, and

Brazil—and read into the *Congressional Record* the *New York Times* article about Latin Americanists' opposition to the expulsion of academics from Brazilian universities.

8. Frank Church, "A Lament for Brazil," *Congressional Record—Senate*, August 8, 1969, 23017.

9. Asby and Gramer, *Fighting the Odds*, 269–83.

10. Juan de Onis, "End of Direct Aid to Latins Urged by Senator Church," *New York Times*, September 12, 1969, 14.

11. "Reaction to Remarks of Senator Church," Telegram No. 924, São Paulo to Washington, September 19, 1969, box 1910, FRUS.

12. "Toward a New Latin America Policy," *Congressional Record–Senate*, April 10, 1970, 11211-15.

13. "Resposta ao Senador Kennedy," *Boletim Especial* no. 75, April 29, 1970, Brazilian Embassy, Washington, D.C.

14. Letter from Dana S. Green and William L. Wipfler to Senator Frank Church, June 25, 1970, box 5, SFRC-SCLA.

15. Letter from Frank Church to Dana S. Green, July 2, 1970, box 5, SFRC-SCLA.

16. Holt, Oral History Interviews, 107–8.

17. Letter from Brady Tyson to Pat Holt, received July 25, 1970, box 5, SFRC-SCLA.

18. According to Pat Holt, Tom Dine, Senator Church's legislative assistant, told him that Church leaked Holt's memo to the press. Holt, Oral History Interviews, 250.

19. Jack Anderson, "Hart [sic] Quiz to Bare Tortures in Brazil," *Washington Post*, September 28, 1970, B-11.

20. "Hearings on Brazil," Memo of Pat M. Holt to Senator Church, September 15, 1970, box 5, SFRC-SCLA.

21. "U.S. Brazilian Relations," Telegram No. 1024, São Paulo to Washington, September 9, 1970, box 2134, FRUS.

22. "'Hearings' no Congresso Americano sobre o Brasil," Telegram No. 15974, Washington to Brasília, September 4, 1970, SERE 920 (42) (22), IHA.

23. "Imagem do Brasil nos EUA: Audiências do sub-comitê para assuntos do hemisfério ocidental do Senado," Telegram No. 1172, Washington to Brasília, January 15, 1971, SERE 591.7 (22), IHA.

24. "Some Suggestions as Guidelines for Hearings on U.S.-Brazilian Relations," Memo from Brady Tyson to Pat Holt, November 30, 1970, box 5, SFRC-SCLA.

25. Letter from Pat M. Holt to John Tuthill, January 5, 1971, box 5, SFRC-SCLA.

26. Letter from Márcio Moreira Alves to Pat Holt, March 7, 1971, box 5, SFRC-SCLA.

27. Letter from Rev. Herbert Mansfield and Sister Ann Remorino to Senator Frank Church, October 24, 1970, box 5, SFRC-SCLA.

28. Letter from Rev. Darrell Rupiper to Pat Holt, n.d., box 5, SFRC-SCLA.

29. Dockery had visited Brazil in September 1968 for the Senate Foreign Relations Committee and wrote a report noting the growing opposition to the Costa e Silva government. Robert Dockery, "Observations on the Political Situation in Brazil," Internal Memorandum, September 25, 1968, Senate Foreign Relations Committee, box 5, SFRC-SCLA.

30. Letter from Louis M. Colonnese to Pat Holt, March 4, 1971, box 5, SFRC-SCLA.

31. "Audiência da Sub-Comissão para assuntos do Hemisfério Ocidental do Senado

norte-americano: Viajem ao Brasil de Assessores do Senado," Memorandum No. 00041, March 22, 1971, SERE, 591.7 (22).

32. Mendes, interview, July 24, 2003.

33. "Church Committee Hearings," Telegram No. 7092, Washington to Rio de Janeiro, April 26, 1971, box 2134, FRUS.

34. More than twenty years later, Martha K. Huggins was still unable to gain access to some of the testimony for her analysis of the Office of Public Safety Programs. Huggins, *Political Policing*.

35. Senate, *United States Policies and Programs in Brazil*, 1.

36. Huggins, *Political Policing*, xi.

37. Ibid., 163.

38. Senate, *United States Policies and Programs in Brazil*, 160.

39. Ibid., 250.

40. Ibid., 164–66.

41. Ibid., 257.

42. "Senator Church's Statement on Brazil Hearings," Telegram No. 133689, Washington to Brasília, July 23, 1971, box 546, FRUS.

43. Telegram No. 133754, Washington to Brasília, July 23, 1971, box 546, FRUS.

44. "Relações Brasil-Estados Unidos. Entrevista colectiva do Senador Church," Memorandum No. 120, July 30, 1971, SERE, 920 (42) (22), IHA.

45. "Senator Church's Statement on Brazil Hearings," State to Brazilian Embassy, July 23, 1971, box 546, FRUS.

46. Holt, Oral History Interviews, 189.

47. *Congressional Record—House*, August 3, 1971, 29119.

48. Dellums and Halterman, *Lying Down with the Lions*, 50–92.

49. Dellums, *Congressional Record—House*, August 3, 1971, 29120.

50. Schoultz, *Human Rights and United States Policy toward Latin America*, 146.

51. *Congressional Record—House*, August 3, 1971, 29130.

52. Ibid., 29129.

53. *Congressional Record—Senate*, June 27, 1972, 22643.

54. *Congressional Record—Senate*, June 27, 1972, 22643.

55. "Allegations of Torture in Brazil," Telegram No. 116598 Washington to Brasília, June 28, 1972, box 2133, FRUS.

56. *Congressional Record—House*, August 10, 1972, 27615.

57. Ibid., 27619.

58. House Committee on Foreign Affairs, *International Protection on Human Rights*, 594–97.

59. Sikkink, *Mixed Signals*, 65–76.

60. Schoultz, *Human Rights and United States Policy*, 194–95.

61. Fraser Hearings, 187–217, 643–680, 897–912.

62. Three years later, Congress approved a similar idea, establishing the Coordinator for Human Rights and Humanitarian Affairs. The provision established a new vehicle for human rights activists, although the State Department did not significantly change its policies until 1977, when Jimmy Carter had taken over the White House. Schoultz, *Human Rights and United States Policy*, 195.

63. Ibid., 195–98.

## Capítulo VIII

1. Halstead, *Out Now*, 582–627.
2. Loretta Strharsky, December 17, 2002. Subsequent quotations are from this interview.
3. Veloso, *Tropical Truth*, 269–76.
4. Returning from Guatemala, the Melvilles penned scathing denunciations of indigenous and peasant exploitation that widely circulated in paperback editions. Melville and Melville, *Guatemala—Another Vietnam*; and *Whose Heaven, Whose Earth?* See also Berrigan, *The Trial of the Catonsville Nine*, which dramatized the trial of the nine religious and antiwar figures.
5. Sattamini, *A Mother's Cry*.

## 9. Denouncing the Dictatorship

1. Laudau, interview, February 10, 2003. Subsequent quotations by Landau are from this interview.
2. That same year, *Brazil: No Time for Tears*, a film that interviewed nine recently released political prisoners living in Chile, was also produced.
3. Soon after Marcos Arruda graduated with a degree in geology, he was blacklisted from the profession in Rio de Janeiro, and he gave up his career goals in this field. After moving to São Paulo, he decided to follow the political orientation of Ação Popular and find work in a factory.
4. Film script, *Brazil: A Report on Torture* (1971), Cinema Guild, Dove Films, 206.
5. "Filme tendenciosa sobre o Brasil. Recusa de visto: Saul Landau e Haskell Wexler," August 11, 1971, SERE, 540.612 (22), IHA.
6. In the early 1970s, NACLA West developed a close collaboration with American Friends of Brazil that produced the *Brazilian Information Bulletin*, American Friends of Guatemala, and Non-Intervention in Chile, among other Bay Area Latin American solidarity groups.
7. Immediately before the military coup d'état in Chile on September 11, 1973, the political action groups and resource centers in the United States working on Latin America included American Friends of Brazil, Berkeley; American Friends of Guatemala, Berkeley; Center for Cuban Studies, New York City; Chicago Area Group on Latin America (CAGLA); Chile-Brazil Action Group, Detroit/Ann Arbor; Committee against Repression in Brazil (CARIB), which expanded into the Common Front for Latin America (COFFLA), Washington, D.C.; Community Action on Latin America (CALA), Madison, Wis.; Committee for the Defense of Human Rights in the Dominican Republic, New York City; Cuban Resource Center, New York City; Ecumenical Program for Interamerican Communication and Action (EPICA), Washington, D.C.; Friends of Haiti, Hopewell Junction, N.Y.; Latin America Project, Cambridge, Mass.; Latin American Policy Alternative Group (LAPAG), Austin, Texas; Latin American Working Group (LAWG) of the National Council of Churches, New York City; Los Angeles Area Group for Latin America Solidarity (LAGLAS); Non-Intervention in Chile (NICH), Berkeley; North American Congress on Latin America (NACLA), Berkeley and New York City; Peru Information Committee, Los Angeles; Triconti-

nental Film Center, New York City; Union of Radical Latin Americanists (URLA), Austin; U.S. Committee for Justice to Latin American Political Prisoners (USLA), New York City; Venceremos Brigade, San Francisco. NACLA, "Keeping Up with Latin America," *Latin America and Empire Report* 6, no. 9 (November 1972): 28–31.

8. Gedick, interview, March 23, 2003.

9. Duncan, interview, April 17, 2003; Topik, interview, December 1, 2004; Rossinow, *The Politics of Authenticity*, 324.

10. Bray, interview, February 20, 2003; Harding, interview, April 22, 2003.

11. Della Cava, interview, November 23, 1999.

12. I was unable to contact the two Brazilian founders of the *Brazilian Information Bulletin*, so I have given them and others who worked on the bulletin pseudonyms.

13. Goff, interview, April 2, 1999.

14. There are no accurate figures on the numbers of Brazilians who left the country after 1964 as a result of the military dictatorship. Estimates range from 5,000 to 12,000.

15. "What Is Happening in Brazil," *Brazilian Information Bulletin*, no. 1 (February 1971): 1.

16. "The Transamazon Highway," *Brazilian Information Bulletin*, no. 1 (February 1971): 4.

17. Ibid.

18. Silberstein, interview, April 22, 2002.

19. "Brazilian Police Trained in the U.S.," *Brazilian Information Bulletin*, no. 1 (February 1971): 11.

20. Silberstein, interview, April 22, 2002.

21. Quigley, interview, October 9, 2002.

22. "Tortures Continue Unabated," *Brazilian Information Bulletin*, no. 5 (August–September 1971): 1.

23. "The Ouro Preto 15," *Brazilian Information Bulletin*, no. 5 (August–September 1971): 1.

24. Tytel, *The Living Theatre*, 274–304; Ryan, "The Living Theatre in Brazil," 21–29. Martínez, interview, June 1, 2002; George, *The Modern Brazilian Stage*, 66–69.

25. "DOPS solta 8 do Living Theater," *O Estado de Minas*, July 3, 1971, 11; "Continuaram na prisão os 13 de Living," *O Estado de Minas*, July 4, 1971, 14.

26. Malina, interview, November 21, 2002.

27. "Emergency Notice," Series IX: The Living Theater in Brazil, 1970–71, box 50, folder 06, document 1, no date, Billy Rose Collection, NYPL.

28. "Information for immediate release," Series IX: The Living Theater in Brazil, 1970–71, box 50, folder 06, document 5, no date, Billy Rose Collection, NYPL.

29. Malina, interview, November 21, 2002.

30. "American Committee for the Defense of the Living Theater," August 16, 1971, copy in author's archives.

31. Elenore Lester, "Living Theater: Jailed in Brazil." *New York Times*, August 15, 1971, sec. 2:1, 2.

32. "This Is Theater," *Newsweek*, August 16, 1971, 40.

33. "Living Theater," Series IX: The Living Theater in Brazil, 1970–71, box 50, folder 06, document 2, no date, Billy Rose Collection, NYPL; "Até prefeito de Nova Iorque pede liberdade para o Living," *O Estado de Minas*, August 26, 1970, 14.

34. "Living, o manifesto dos intelectuais a Médici," *O Estado de Minas*, August 12, 1971, 5.

35. See, for example, "'The Living' Lives: How and What It Lives By," *Berkeley Barb* 55 (November 26 to December 2, 1971), 1.

36. Strharsky, interview, December 17, 2002.
37. Quigley, interview, October 9, 2002; Dan Griffin, "The Torture of a Brazilian," *Washington Post*, September 19, 1971, 83.
38. Editorial, "Brazil and Torture," *Washington Post*, September 26, 1971, E6.
39. Strharsky, interview, December 17, 2002.
40. CARIB, *Brazil: Miracle for Whom?*, slideshow script, copy in author's files.
41. Quoted in ibid.
42. Telegram No. 198388, "Medici Visit," Ambassador Rountree from Dean, October 29, 1971, box 2130, FRUS.
43. "Visit of Brazilian President Medici," Memorandum No. 7118985, John Hugh Crimmins to the Secretary of State, November 21, 1971, box 2130, FRUS.
44. Memorandum for Mr. Henry Kissinger, subject: Press Guidance for the State Visit of President Medici, October 19, 1971, box 2130, FRUS.
45. Telegram No. 1681, "Medici Visit," Brasília to Washington, November 17, 1971, box 2130, FRUS.
46. "Médici Visit to U.S.," Telegram No. 259, November 21, 1971, Rio de Janeiro to Washington, box 2130, FRUS.
47. Ibid.
48. Ibid.
49. Telegram No. 1681, "Medici Visit," Brasília to Washington, November 17, 1971, box 2130, FRUS.
50. "Médici não fala à imprensa nos EUA," *O Estado de São Paulo*, December 3, 1971, 1.
51. Dan Griffin, "Brazil Leader to Meet with Nixon," *Washington Post*, December 6, 1971, 20.
52. Harry Strharsky, "Grass-Root Response to the Medici-Nixon State Visit," n.d., copy in author's files.
53. "Protesters Leave No Sanctuary for Médici," *Brazilian Information Bulletin*, no. 6 (February 1972): 3.
54. Nixon, *Public Papers*, 383.
55. "A visita repercutiu no Peru," *O Estado de São Paulo*, December 9, 1971; "Venezuela repele hegemonia brasileira no hemisfério," *Jornal do Brasil*, December 10, 1971; "Caracas contra," *O Estado de São Paulo*, December 10, 1971, 1; "Clarin teme resultado dos elogios ao Brasil," *O Estado de São Paulo*, December 11, 1971, 9; "Jornal argentina critica o 'exio Brasília-Washington,'" *Jornal do Brasil*, December 14, 1971.
56. Letter to General Emílio Garrastazu Médici from Clergy and Laity, December 7, 1971, copy in author's files; "Rap Brazilian Torture in Letter to General," *Brazilian Information Bulletin*, no. 6 (February 1971): 11. I was unable to find any indication in the documents of the Brazilian Foreign Ministry that President Médici actually received the letter.
57. Griffin, "Brazil Leader to Meet with Nixon."
58. "Bertrand Russell Tribunal—Investigation on Torture," *Brazilian Information Bulletin*, no. 6 (February 1972): 8.
59. "Lelio Basso's Letter to the Youth Federation of the Italian Democratic Political Parties," *Tribunale Russell Brasile 1* (February 1973): 2.
60. The student leader presented his assessment of the political situation in Brazil and

a rather optimistic evaluation of the revolutionary left in Von der Weid, *Brazil 1964 to the Present*.

61. Von der Weid, interview, November 10, 2002.
62. Seegers, "The Two Faces of Brazil," 118.
63. Ibid.
64. Ibid., 120.
65. Ibid.
66. Armbrister, "The Two Faces of Brazil," 121.
67. Padilha, interview no. 1, July 18, 1997.
68. Armbrister, "The Two Faces of Brazil," 121.
69. Ibid., 124.
70. "Indian Policy in Brazil Criticized," *San Francisco Chronicle*, May 23, 1972, quoted in *Brazilian Information Bulletin*, no. 7 (May 1972): 8.
71. Ibid.
72. "Development against the Indians," *Brazilian Information Bulletin*, no. 9 (January 1973): 8.
73. Davis, *Victims of the Miracle*, xiii–xiv.
74. Davis, interview, April 21, 2003.
75. Davis, *Victims of the Miracle*, xv.
76. Schneider, *The Political System of Brazil*; Stepan, *The Military in Politics*.
    Skidmore's analysis of the political situation in Brazil quickly became the seminal historical narrative of the country's history in the mid-twentieth century. Schneider's work on the first six seven years of the military regime offered a detailed narrative of political events based on an extensive use of secondary sources and interviews with the principal political actors. Stepan's study of the Brazilian military presented a careful analysis of the complexities and internal divisions within the armed forces and argued that it was not a unified and cohesive institution.
77. Marighella, *For the Liberation of Brazil*; Quartim, *Dictatorship and Armed Struggle in Brazil*. Carlos Marighella, a former leader in the Brazilian Communist Party who broke with the organization in 1967 to form an armed struggle organization, was assassinated by the government's repressive apparatus in November 1969. João Quartim, who had been a militant of another revolutionary organization, left Brazil for exile in Europe, where he published his analysis of the political situation in Brazil and underscored the need to organize an armed response to the generals in power.
78. To cite a sampling of these articles: "Brazil: Repression to Guerrilla Warfare," *Berkeley Tribe*, November 13, 1970, 22; "Brazil: Repression to Death," *Black Panther* July 11, 1970, 17; Ruy Marini, "Brazilian Subimperialism," *Monthly Review* 23, no. 9 (February 1972): 14–24; L. Rotcage, "Brazilian Guerrillas," *Old Mole*, July 10, 1970, 14; Andy Truskier, "Politics of Violence, Urban Guerrillas in Brazil," *Ramparts* 9, no. 4 (October 1970): 30–39; L. Perez, "Brazil: Last Days of a Dictator," *Tricontinental* 5, no. 36 (November 1970): 45–46.
79. José Yglesias, "Report from Brazil: What the Left Is Saying," *New York Times Sunday Magazine*, December 7, 1969, 52; Sanche de Gramont, "How One Pleasant, Scholarly Young Man from Brazil Became a Gun-Toting, Bombing Revolutionary," *New York Times Sunday Magazine*, November 15, 1970, 21.

80. Both Marighella's and Quartim's works circulated widely among leftists in the United States in the early 1970s. Damasceno, interview, May 6, 2003.

81. Ibid.

82. Stepan, ed., *Authoritarian Brazil*, vii.

83. Amnesty International, *Report on Allegations of Torture in Brazil*, 1.

84. Ibid., 6.

85. Ibid., 8.

86. Ibid., 24.

87. Ibid., 25.

88. Amnesty International, *Annual Report, 1972–73*, 46.

89. Amnesty International, *Annual Report, 1969–70*, 2.

90. Sattamini, *Esquecer?*, 85–87.

91. Theodor Ghercov Case, Amnesty International San Francisco #44, box 1–3, AIA Archives.

92. This estimate is based on reading all Amnesty International annual reports and internal documents of Amnesty International at the archive at the University of Colorado.

93. Clark, "Strong Principles, Strengthening Practices"; Ripp, "Transnationalism and Human Rights," 326–45.

94. Seixas, "A vida clandestina," 57–70; Projeto Brasil, *Perfil dos atingidos*, vol. 3, 70.

95. Seixas, interview, Brazil, November 13, 2002.

96. "Position Statement," and "Brazilian-American Conference, September 1–2, 1973, mimeo, copy in author's files.

## Capítulo IX

1. Archdiocese of São Paulo, *Brasil*, 239–46.

2. Gaspari, *A Ditadura Escancarada*, 470–72.

3. Comissão de Familiares de Mortos e Desaparecidos Políticos, *Dossiê dos mortos e desaparecidos políticos a partir de 1964*, 388–90; Miranda and Tibúrcio, eds., *Dos filhos deste solo*, 398–400.

4. Gorender, *Combate nas trevas*, 181–86.

5. Moraes and Ahmen, *Calvário de Sônia Angel*, 27.

6. Alex Polari, *Em busca do tesouro* (Rio de Janeiro: Editora Codecri, 1982), 170–202.

7. Padilha, interview no. 1, July 18, 1997.

## 10. Performing Opposition

1. This account is from "The Envelope," an excerpt from Joanne Pottlitzer's unpublished memoir, *Poets, Politics and Lovers*. I want to thank Joanne Pottlitzer for her generosity in sharing her writings with me for this book.

2. Boal, interview, July 18, 2003; Boal, *Hamlet and the Baker's Son*, 118–39; Quiles, "The Theatre of Augusto Boal," 242.

3. Boal, interview.

4. Ibid.; Boal, *Hamlet and the Baker's Son*, 241–43. Guarnieri and Boal, *Arena conta Zumbi*, 45–46.

5. Bader, *Brecht no Brasil*, 249–57.

6. Boal, *Hamlet and the Baker's Son*, 241–43.

7. Although the cast members of the original production of *Arena conta Zumbi* in 1965 were "white," in the New York show in 1969 there were actors and musicians of African descent in Boal's troupe. Boal, interview.

8. Pottlitzer, interview, February 15, 2003.

9. Ibid.

10. Henry Raymont, "Theater: Brazilians Offer a Legend in Bossa Nova," *New York Times*, August 19, 1969, 31.

11. Ibid.

12. "Zumbi—Fabled Black Slave 'King,'" *Daily World*, August 27, 1969, 8.

13. Pottlitzer did not recall that she or anyone from the Theater of Latin America had contacted the Brazilian government for funding. Pottlitzer, interview.

14. "Arena Conta Zumbi. Apresentação em Washington," Telegram No. 1554, Brasília to Washington, August 29, 1969, SERE, 540.611 (22), IHA.

15. Ibid.

16. "Apresentação da peça 'Arena Conta Zumbi': Autorização de saque," Telegram No. 482, New York to Brasília, September 3, 1969, SERE, 540.611 (22), IHA.

17. "Apresentação da peça 'Arena Conta Zumbi' em Nova York: Autorização de saque," Telegram No. 575, Brasília to New York, September 8, 1969, SERE, 540.611, IHA.

18. Boal, *Milagre no Brasil: Romance*, 8. The events surrounding Boal's arrest and torture are drawn from this memoir. The title, "Miracle in Brazil: Romance," is an ironic reference to the "Brazilian Economic Miracle," which Boal considered fictitious, that is, a romantic tale. It also refers to his miraculous (and therefore "romantic") survival of the ordeals of torture. Not unlike many Brazilian memoirs of the period, Boal wrote this book in a loose literary style, but the veracity of his story conforms to other versions of his arrest and imprisonment.

19. Gorender, *Combate nas trevas*, 223–32.

20. Boal, *Hamlet and the Baker's Son*, 290–91.

21. Pottlitzer, "The Envelope," 1.

22. Letter to the Editor, "Repression in Brazil," *New York Times*, April 24, 1971, 28.

23. Pottlitzer, "The Envelope," 4.

24. Letter from Senator Frank Church to Department of State, May 20, 1971, box 2133, FRUS. Although the assistant secretary for congressional relations finally responded to the senator that Boal had been released, other letters to State Department officials signed by academics remained unacknowledged. Perhaps the State Department did not want to give the impression to concerned citizens that their letter-writing efforts had any impact. "Arrest of Augusto Boal," Telegram from São Paulo to Washington, February 24, 1971, box 2133, FRUS. The consul in São Paulo noted in the telegram, "We are not acknowledging."

25. Boal, interview.

26. "Arthur Miller protesta por Augusto Boal," *Jornal do Brasil*, April 26, 1971, 39.

27. Pottlitzer, "The Envelope," 3.

28. "Situação do teatrólogo Augusto Boal," Telegram No. 489, Brasília to Washington, April 30, 1971, SERE, 540.611, IHA.

29. "Situação to teatrólogo Augusto Boal," Telegram No. 272, Brasília to Washington, July 4, 1971, SERE, 540.611, IHA.

30. Henry Raymont, "Miller and Freed Brazilian Discuss New Satire Genre," *New York Times*, June 25, 1971, 16.

31. I wish to thank Hildegard Angel and Ana Cristina Angel for providing material from the Instituto Zuzu Angel de Moda da Cidade do Rio de Janeiro archive.

32. Valli, *Eu, Zuzu Angel*, 31–32.

33. Jones, interview, June 4, 2002.

34. Fragoso, *Advocacia da liberdade*, 157–63.

35. Ibid., 150. In December 1970, the International Commission of Jurists brought denunciations of their illegal arrest before the IACHR. The Brazilian representative on the commission denied any government involvement in the sequester. See Case 1697, Inter-American Human Rights Commission of the Organization of American States, Washington College of Law, Center for Human Rights and Humanitarian Law, Washington, D.C.

36. Reproduction of letter in Valli, *Eu, Zuzu Angel*, 214.

37. "Brazilian Tortured To Death?" *Miami Herald*, August 16, 1971, 3.

38. "Stuart Edgar Angel Jones," Washington to Brasília and Rio de Janeiro, August 16, 1971, box 2133, FRUS.

39. "Further on Stuart Edgar Angel Jones," Rio de Janeiro to Washington, Telegram No. 5969, August 23, 1971, box 2133, FRUS.

40. Valli, *Eu, Zuzu Angel*, 154–55. Soon after Stuart's death, Alex Polari de Alverga managed to send news of what he had seen to Zuzu Angel. In May 1972, he also wrote a six-page letter to Zuzu Angel detailing his knowledge of Stuart's arrest, torture, and death and had it smuggled out of prison. Although Zuzu knew about the letter, she later explained that she feared receiving it because it would dash all final hopes that her son may indeed have survived somewhere. Valli, *Eu, Zuzu Angel*, 160.

41. Translation of Alex Polari's statement into English by Zuzu Angel. A copy of this translation was generously given to the author by the Instituto Zuzu Angel.

42. Eugenia Sheppard's fashion column, *Women's Daily Wear*, June 19, 1968, 10.

43. News from Bergdorf Goodman, "Zuzu Angel," press release, November 17, 1970, IZA.

44. Bernadine Morris, "Another Brazilian Designer Remembers Carmen Miranda," *Palm Beach Daily News*, November 18, 1970.

45. Maria Bonita was the lover of the Brazilian northeastern rural bandit who had become a folk myth. The *cangaceiro* hat is a leather head covering used by backland cow herders of that region.

46. News from Bergdorf Goodman, 2–3, IZA.

47. Marji Kunz, "Bare Midriffs 'in' for Spring," *Detroit Free Press*, March 23, 1971, 2B.

48. Quoted in Valli, *Eu, Zuzu Angel*, 50.

49. Jones, interview.

50. The story appeared with different titles. Dennis Redmont, "Politics and Fashion Mix," *Home News* (New Brunswick, New Jersey), September 14, 1971, 7; "Designer's Fashions Make Plea for Her Lost Son," *Montreal Star*, September 15, 1971, 90; and "Fashion Takes Political Turn," *Fort Lauderdale News and Sun Sentinel*, September 25, 1971, 2B.

51. Bill Cunningham, "Zuzu Angel, the Vivacious Brazilian Designer." *Chicago Tribune*, September 20, 1971, sec. 2, 1.

52. *Tristeza* (1966) by Haroldo Lobo and Niltinho. "Tristeza / favor vai embora / minha alma que chora / está vendo o meu fim. / Fez do meu coração / a sua moradia. / Já é demais o meu penar, / quero voltar que a vida de alegria; / quero de novo cantar. Translation by Marc Hertzman.

53. Jones, interview.

54. "Fashion Takes Political Turn."

55. Pottlitzer, interview.

56. M. Steingesser, "Brazilian Boal Tells of Playwriting in Prison," *Christian Science Monitor*, March 8, 1972, 4.

57. Pottlitzer, interview.

58. Bissett, "Victims and Violators," 28.

59. "GOB Concern over Unfavorable Criticism," Memorandum of Conversation, drafted by Steven Low, March 17 and 22, 1972, box 2134, FRUS.

60. "Seminário Político em Nova York: 'Latin American Fair of Opinion,'" Telegram No. 304, New York to Brasília, April 12, 1972, SERE, 540.611, IHA.

61. Boal, interview.

62. Tytel, *The Living Theatre*, 304–17.

63. The script to *Seven Meditations* and a detailed description of the performance at the University of North Carolina, Chapel Hill, appeared in *Fag Rag* (Boston) (Fall-Winter 1973): 13–20.

64. Malina, interview, November 21, 2002.

65. Ibid.

66. Ibid.; Tytel, *The Living Theater*, 410, n. 5; 411, n. 12.

67. Malina, interview.

68. Hampton, *Savages*, 15.

69. Davis, interview, April 21, 2003.

70. Dan Sullivan, "Skeletons in the Brazilian Closet." *Los Angeles Times*, August 17, 1974.

71. Davis, interview.

72. "Christopher Hampton's 'Savages,'" 74.

73. DiGaetani, *A Search for a Postmodern Theater*, 126.

## Capítulo X

1. Fragoso, *Advocacia da liberdade*, 159.

2. Valli, *Eu, Zuzu Angel*, 67, 188.

3. Letter from Zuzu Angel to Mr. Osting, Amnesty International, February 22, 1975. Reproduced in Valli, *Eu, Zuzu Angel*, 229.

4. Ibid., 160.

5. Ibid., 236–37.

6. Letter to the Honorable John Sparkman, Chairman, Committee on Foreign Relations, United States Senate, from Ana Cristina Angel Jones and Zuleika Angel Jones, May 28, 1975, New York. Copy in author's files.

7. Letter to Honorable John Sparkman, Chairman, Committee on Foreign Relations,

United States Senate, from Martin Ennals, Secretary General, Amnesty International, June 2, 1975, London, IZA.

8. Letter to Ana Cristina Angel Jones from Robert W. Zimmerman, Director, Office of Brazilian Affairs, October 7, 1975, IZA.

9. "Stuart Edgar Angel Jones," Telegram No. 1393, Brasília to Washington, March 14, 1973, box 2133, FRUS.

10. Valle, Eu, Zuzu Angel, 185.

11. Bruce Handler, "Brazilian Makes Plea to Kissinger," Washington Post, February 23, 1976, A20; "Kissinger viu a samba carioca," Jornal do Brasil, February 22, 1976, 5; "Na carta, a denúncia e um apelo," O Estado de São Paulo, February 24, 1976, 19.

12. "Preventiva,"O Estado de São Paulo, March 18, 1976, 24.

13. Silva, História da República Brasileira, 460–63.

14. Valli, Eu, Zuzu Angel, 196.

15. Zuzu Angel, SECOM 58808, No. 426/76/SDI/MJ, May 25, 1976, DSI.

16. Ibid.

17. Miranda and Tibúrcio, Dos filhos deste solo, 591–97.

18. Adelina Capper, "Angel Flies High," Women's Wear Daily, June 1968.

19. Miltinho and Chico Buarque de Hollanda, "Angélica": Quem é essa mulher / Que canta sempre esse estribilho / Só queria embalar meu filho / Que mora na escuridão do mar.

20. Zuzu Angel, directed by Sérgio Resende, 2006, is a film about Zuzu Angel's dramatic tale, one that reflects the ongoing power of her story.

### 11. The Slow-Motion Return to Democracy

1. Anderson, The Anderson Papers; Anderson, Peace, War, and Politics, 193–208.

2. Kornbluh, The Pinochet File.

3. Mary Harding, "Mini-Report, Chile Solidarity Conference, Chicago, March 30–31 [1974]," copy in author's files. For an account of the anti-Pinochet movement, see Van Gosse, "Unpacking the Vietnam Syndrome"; for Argentina, see Calandra, L'America della solidarietà.

4. Gabeira, O crepúsculo do macho; Rollemberg, Exílio.

5. Strharsky, interview, March 31, 1999.

6. Marvine Howe, "General Geisel is Sworn In as President of Brazil as Hopes Rise for Some Political Liberalization," New York Times, March 16, 1974, 3.

7. Alves, State and Opposition in Military Brazil, 144.

8. See, for example, "Meeting at Sen. Church's Office, 11/24/1970," "LASC Minutes—Meeting January 7, 1971," "Brady Tyson to Members of LASC, June 5, 1971," Latin American Strategy Committee, 144-1-3:15, UMCA.

9. Eldridge, interview, April 15, 2003. Subsequent quotations are from this interview.

10. Schoultz, Human Rights and United Sates Policy toward Latin America, 76–78.

11. Morris, "In the Presence of Mine Enemies."

12. Morris, "A importância da vida e ministério de Dom Hélder Câmara," 89–90.

13. Morris, "Sustained by Faith under Brazilian Torture," 57.

14. Ibid., 57–58.

15. U.S. Congress, "Torture and Oppression in Brazil," 5.

16. Morris, "Sustained by Faith," 58.

17. "Pastor of the Poor," *Time* (June 23, 1974): 61.

18. House, *Torture and Oppression in Brazil*, 24–25.

19. Ibid., 28–29.

20. Eldridge, interview.

21. Amnesty International, *Newsletter* 6, no. 7 (July 1974): 2.

22. "Torture, Brazilian Style," *Time*, November 18, 1974, 48.

23. Program of the Conference "Repression and Development in Brazil and Latin America, April 4, 5, 6," copy in author's files.

24. Common Front for Latin America, "Bertrand Russell Tribunal on Repression in Brazil, Chile, and Latin America, [1974]," copy in author's files.

25. "Russell Tribunal II on Latin America, Sentence (Provisional Verdict), Common Front for Latin America [Washington, 1974]," 6, copy in author's files.

26. Ibid., 11.

27. Moura, *Diário da guerrilha do Araguaia*; Portela, *Guerra de guerrilhas no Brazil*; Antero, Amazonas, and Silva, *Uma epoéia pela liberdade*.

28. Gaspari, *A ditadura encurralada*, 169–187.

29. Almeida Filho, *A sangue-quente*; Markun, ed., *Vlado*; Markun, *Meu querido Vlado*.

30. Feldman-Bianco, interview, July 25, 2003.

31. As the historian Kenneth P. Serbin has pointed out, the death of the student leader and Ação Libertadora Nacional militant Alexandre Vanucchi Leme at the hands of the political police in 1973 provoked a public demonstration of 3,000 students and other oppositionists at a funeral in his honor officiated by Cardinal Arns. The event took place during the Médici government and marked the largest demonstration since Institutional Act No. 5. The mobilization around Herzog's death, which occurred at a different political moment, spurred many more oppositionists. Serbin, "The Anatomy of a Death."

32. Sydow and Ferri, *Dom Paulo Evaristo Arns*, 184–206.

33. Markun, *Vlado*, 186–216.

34. Della Cava and Tyson had agreed that their names should not appear on the different petitions and statements that they initiated. Della Cava, interview, November 26, 1999.

35. Richard M. Morse, Thomas E. Skidmore, Stanley Stein, Alfred Stepan, Charles Wagley, "Brazil: The Sealed Coffin," *New York Review of Books*, November 27, 1975, 45.

36. Luppi, *Manoel Fiel Filho*.

37. D'Araújo and Castro, eds. *Ernesto Geisel*, 370–79.

38. Piletti and Praxedes, *Dom Hélder Câmara*, 386–87; Serbin, "Dom Hélder Câmara."

39. Alves, *State and Opposition in Military Brazil*, 147–48.

40. Schoutlz, *Human Rights and U.S. Policy toward Latin America*, 113.

41. Schoultz, "The Carter Administration and Human Rights in Latin America," 308.

42. Shoultz, *Human Rights and United States Policy toward Latin America*, 128–34.

43. "U.S. Official Expresses 'Regrets' for Role in Chile but Is Disavowed," *New York Times*, March 9, 1977, 1.

44. Ibid.

45. "Envoy Who Voiced "Regrets" on Chile Summoned Home," *New York Times*, March 10, 1977, 13.

46. Ibid.

47. See Power, "Brazil and the Carter Human Rights Policy." The study is partly based on an interview with the U.S. ambassador, John Crimmins, and offers insights into the U.S.-Brazilian rift.

48. U.S. Congress, *Human Rights Practices in Countries Receiving U.S. Security Assistance*, 106–8.

49. Amnesty International, *Amnesty International Report 1977*, 127–29.

50. Power, "Brazil and the Carter Human Rights Policy," 98–99.

51. Skidmore, *Politics of Military Rule*, 196.

52. Ibid., 100–109.

53. See Kinzo, *Legal Opposition Politics under Authoritarian Rule in Brazil*.

54. Zeichner, "Representing the Vanguard."

55. Brambilla, interview, July 8, 2006.

56. Paes, interview, January 25, 2008.

57. David F. Belnap, "U.S., Brazil Relations Mending," *Los Angeles Times*, June 5, 1977, 22; Susanna McBee, "Mrs. Carter Cites Hope to Improve Ties with Brazil," *Washington Post*, June 7, 1977, A-12; Joseph H. Blatchford, "U.S.-Brazilian Relations: Can the Strains be Eased," *Washington Post*, June 8, 1977, A-23.

58. Susanna McBee, "Mrs. Carter Stresses Human Rights in Brazil Visit," *Washington Post*, June 8, 1977, A-14.

59. Marlene Simons, "Mrs. Carter Arrives in Brazil Facing Toughest Test of Trip," *Los Angeles Times*, June 7, 1977, 14.

60. "Calvário no Recife," *Veja*, June 1, 1977, 22.

61. Laura Foreman, "Mrs. Carter Told by 2 Americans of Brazil Ordeal; Treated Like Animals, Missionaries Say," *New York Times*, June 9, 1977, 1; Marlene Simons, "2 Missionaries Describe Jailing to Mrs. Carter," *Los Angeles Times*, June 9, 1977, 1; Susanna McBee, "Mrs. Carter Meets Two Americans Jailed in Brazil," *Washington Post*, June 9, 1977, 1.

62. "Daily Press Summary," First Lady's Staff File, box 64, Brazil, March 29–30, Carter Library.

63. Letter from Robert A. Pastor to Father Larry Rosebaugh, National Security Council, Country File 22, box CO-13, JC.

64. Quoted in Power, "Brazil and the Carter Human Rights Policy," 119.

65. Athayde, *Apareceu a Margarida*; English version: *Miss Margarida's Way: Tragicomic Monologue for an Impetuous Woman*.

66. For a discussion of the relationship between language, power, and violence in the play, see Albuquerque, "Verbal Violence and the Pursuit of Power in *Apareceu a Margarida*," and Unruh, "Language and Power in *Miss Margarida's Way*."

67. *Cue*, July 23–August 5, 1977, 28.

68. Andrea Stevens, "Rebelling Through Poetry," *New York Times*, February 5, 1990, 5.

69. Ibid.

70. Boyle, "Re-lectura e re-presentación de una protagonista autoritaria."

71. Skar, "Engendering Violence in Roberto Athayde's *Apareceu a Margarida*, 55. See also Albuquerque, *Violent Acts*.

72. "Estelle Parsons in Brazilian Play," *New York Times*, July 18, 1977, 35.

73. *Miss Margarida's Way*, Playbill, 1977.
74. Mel Gussow, "A 'Confrontation' Drama Deals with Dictatorship.'" *New York Times*, July 24, 1977, D-4.
75. Ariel Dorfman, "Can a Dictator Tell Us Something about Ourselves?" *New York Times*, February 25, 1990, 5, 28.
76. Estelle Parsons, interview, May 20, 2003.
77. Brendan Gill, "The Divided Self," *New Yorker*, October 10, 1977, 91.
78. Clive Barnes, "Terrorism Is Drama in 'Savages,'" *New York Times*, March 1, 1977, 25.
79. Dagnino, interview, June 2, 1999.
80. Brigagão, interview, June 17, 2003.
81. Committee of Returned Volunteers, *Brazil: Who Pulls the Strings?*
82. Ibid.
83. Cavalcanti, interview, July 18, 2003.
84. Regina Von der Weid, interview, June 30, 2006; Movimento Feminino Pela Anistia e Liberdades Democráticas, *Origens e lutas*, 20–22.
85. Calvacanti and Ramos, eds., *Memórias do exílio, Brasil 1964–19??*, 10–20.
86. Ramos interview, Augusut 24, 2006; Cavalcanti, interview.
87. Costa, Moraes, Marzola, and Lima, eds. *Memórias das mulheres no exílio.*
88. Brigagão, interview.
89. Graham Hovey, "U.S. Broadcast to Brazil Appears to Add to the Strains in Relations," *New York Times*, November 7, 1977, 10.
90. Feldman-Bianco, interview, July 24, 2003; Patarra, interview, June 21, 2003.
91. Patarra, interview, June 21, 2003.
92. Thomas M. Capuano, "Scenes and Echoes of Torture in Brazil," *New York Times*, September 1, 1977, 21. Of course, it is possible that the editorial was placed in the *Times* during the last week of summer vacation as a way of diminishing the impact of the piece.
93. Della Cava, correspondence with author, March 8, 2008.
94. Maria Helena Moreira Alves, interview, July 11, 2003.
95. Dassin, interview, May 8, 2003.
96. Della Cava, correspondence.
97. Brigagão, interview.
98. The letter was signed by E. Bradford Burns, professor of history, University of California, Los Angeles; Ralph Della Cava, professor of history, City University of New York, Queens College; Richard Graham, professor of history, University of Texas at Austin; Richard Morse, professor of history, Yale University; Stuart Schwartz, professor of history, University of Minnesota; Stanley Stein, professor of history, Princeton University; Al Stepan, professor of political science, Yale University; Charles Wagley, graduate professor of anthropology, University of Florida.
99. Francis McDonagh, "Brazil's Arns Embodies Vatican II Church," *National Catholic Reporter*, July 26, 1996, 1, 5.
100. Quoted in letter from Bob Pastor to Jerry Schecter, National Security Council, March 2, 1978, Country File 22, Box 13, JC.
101. Daniel Southerland, "Carter Successful 'Walking on Eggshells' in Brazil," *Christian Science Monitor*, March 31, 1978.

102. Jack Nelson, "Carter Speaks Out on Touchy Brazil Issues," *Los Angeles Times*, March 31, 1978.

103. McDonagh, "Brazil's Arns," 5.

104. Power, "Brazil and the Carter Human Rights Policy," 172–74.

105. Green, "Liberalization on Trial," 14–15.

106. Alves, *State and Opposition*, 148–53.

107. Keck, *The Workers' Party and Democratization in Brazil*.

108. Wright, interview, April 21, 2003.

109. The founding members of the Brazil Labor Information and Resource Center were Maria Helena Moreira Alves, Roberto Codas, Margaret (Mimi) Keck, Maria Inês Lacey, Carol Wolverton, and Larry Wright. Later, Daniel Benedict, David Dyson, and Ed Gray joined.

110. Keck, interview, April 21, 2003.

111. Wright, interview.

112. Ibid.

113. Brazilian Labor Information and Resource Center, "BLI Progress Report and Plans for 1983–85," June 1983, 3, BLIRC.

114. *Brazilian Labor Information and Resource Center Newsletter*, no. 1 (May 1982): 1.

115. Ibid.

116. Ibid.

117. Wright, interview.

118. Keck, interview; Wright, interview.

## Capítulo XI

1. Brito, "Brazilian Women in Exile," 58–80.

2. Alvarez, interview, May 18, 2004; Alvarez, *Engendering Democracy in Brazil*.

3. Nascimento, interview, July 8, 2003; Hanchard, *Orpheus and Power*, 119–29.

4. Harper, *O acampamento*.

5. For a gripping account of how Wright and Arns coordinated the secret photocopying of legal dossiers documenting torture, see Weschler, *A Miracle, A Universe*, 7–79.

6. Archdiocese of São Paulo, *Brasil: Nunca mais*.

7. Cardinal Arns also insisted that copies of the extensive documentation that they had collected be stored abroad as an insurance policy against any possibility that the Brazilian materials might be destroyed. The entire archive was copied by Latin American Microfilm Project and deposited in the Center for Research Libraries in Chicago. Archdiocese of São Paulo, *Torture in Brazil*, ix–xii. Dassin, interview, May 8, 2003.

## Conclusions

1. Mary Harding, interview, April 22, 2003. Subsequent quotations are from this interview.

2. Jean Marc Von der Weid, interview, November 10, 2002.

3. Kokin, interview, April 26, 2002.

4. Thiebaud, interview, April 27, 2002.

5. General Board of Church and Society, 1444–1–3:15, UMCA.

6. Padilha, interview no. 1, July 18, 1997.

7. Sikkink, *Mixed Signals*, 208.

# BIBLIOGRAPHY

## Archives

AEL     Arquivo Edgard Leuenroth, Universidade Estudual de Campinas (UNICAMP), Campinas, Brazil

AERJ     Arquivo Público do Estado do Rio de Janeiro, Rio de Janeiro, Brazil

AESP-DEOPS     Departamento Estadual de Ordem Política e Social, Arquivo Público do Estado de São Paulo, São Paulo, Brasil

AIA     Amnesty International Archives, University of Colorado, Boulder, Colorado

BLIRC     Brazilian Labor Information and Resource Center Archive, Bethesda, Maryland

DSI     Divisão de Segurança e Informações do Ministério de Justiça, Arquivo Nacional, Rio de Janeiro, Brazil

FRUS     U.S. Department of State, *Papers Relating to the Foreign Relations of the United States*, RG 59, National Archive II, College Park, Maryland

IACHR     Inter-American Commission on Human Rights, Organization of American States

IHA     Secretária de Estado de Relações Exteriores (SERE) (Ministry of Foreign Relations), Itamaraty Historical Archives, Brasília, Brazil

IZA     Instituto Zuzu Angel de Moda da Cidade do Rio de Janeiro, Rio de Janeiro, Brazil

JC     Jimmy Carter Library, Atlanta, Georgia

JFK     John F. Kennedy Library, Boston, Massachusetts

JHU     Milton S. Eisenhower Library, Special Collections, Johns Hopkins University, Baltimore, Maryland

LBJ     Lyndon B. Johnson Library, Austin, Texas

NARA     National Archive Records Administration, Washington, D.C.

NCNSA     National Catholic News Services Archives, U.S. Conference of Catholic Bishops, Washington, D.C.

NYPL     Billy Rose Collection, New York Public Library, New York City

SFRC-SCLA     Senate Foreign Relations Committee, Senate Collection on Latin America, National Archives, Washington, D.C.

SI     Smithsonian Institution Archives, Washington, D.C.

| SWP-WHS | Socialist Workers Party Archives, Wisconsin Historical Society, Madison, Wisconsin |
|---|---|
| UMCA | General Commission on Archives and History, United Methodist Church Archives, Madison, New Jersey |
| USCCB | U.S. Conference of Catholic Bishops Archive, Washington, D.C. |

## Correspondence and Interviews

Abernathy, Juanita. Telephone interview by author, February 28, 2003. Notes.

Alencar, José Almino de. Interview by author, July 18, 2003, Rio de Janeiro. Tape recording.

Alvarez, Sonia E. Interview by author, May 18, 2004, Santa Cruz, Calif. Tape recording.

Alves, Márcio Moreira. Interview by author, October 30, 2002, Rio de Janeiro, Brazil. Tape recording.

Alves, Maria Helena Moreira. Interview by author, July 11, 2003, Rio de Janeiro, Brazil. Tape recording.

Angel Jones, Ana Cristina. Interview by author, June 4, 2002, Rio de Janeiro, Brazil. Tape recording.

Arruda, Marcos. Interview by author, October 4, 2002, Rio de Janeiro, Brazil. Tape recording.

———. Interview by author and Natan Zeichner, December 13, 2005, Providence, R.I. Mini-disc recording.

Arruda, Martinha. Interview by author, November 2, 2004, Rio de Janeiro, Brazil. Tape recording.

Arruda, Mônica. Interview by author, November 2, 2002, Rio de Janeiro, Brazil. Tape recording.

Baer, Werner. Telephone interview with author, February 9, 2004. Notes.

Bandeira, Antônio Rangel. Interview by author, July 23, 2003, Rio de Janeiro, Brazil. Tape recording.

Bandeira, Marina. Interview by author, July 25, 2003, Rio de Janeiro. Tape recording.

Bell, Peter. Telephone interview by author. February 25, 2004. Notes.

Bernardet, Jean-Claude. Interview by author, May 23, 1994, São Paulo, Brazil. Tape recording.

Black, Jan Knippers. Interview with author, December 17, 2002, Monterey, Calif. Tape recording.

Boal, Augusto. Interview by author, July 18, 2003, Rio de Janeiro, Brazil. Tape recording.

Brigagão, Clóvis. Interview by author, June 17, 2003, Rio de Janeiro. Tape recording.

Bray, Donald and Marjorie. Interview by author, February 20, 2003, Los Angeles, Calif. Tape recording.

Brambilla, Celso. Interview by author and Natan Zeichner, July 8, 2006, São Paulo. Mini-disc recording.

Cardoso, Fernando Henrique. Interview by author, March 15, 2007, Providence, R.I. Tape recording.

Cavalcanti, Pedro Celso Uchôa. Interview by author, July 18, 2003, Rio de Janeiro. Tape recording.

Chilcote, Ronald. Interview by author, April 16, 2004, Laguna Beach, Calif. Tape recording.

Crahan, Margaret (Meg). Correspondence with author, August 26, 2007.

———. Telephone interview by author, November 19, 2002. Notes.

———. Interview by author, May 15, 2003, New York City. Tape recording.

Dagnino, Evalina. Interview by author, June 2, 1999, Campinas, Brazil. Tape recording.

Damasceno, Leslie H. Interview by author, May 6, 2003, Durham, N.C. Tape recording.

Dassin, Joan. Interview by author, May 8, 2003, New York City. Tape recording.

Davis, Shelton H. Interview by author, April 21, 2003, Washington, D.C. Tape recording.

Della Cava, Ralph. Correspondence with author, February 12, 2001.

———. Correspondence with author, February 23, 2004.

———. Correspondence with author, March 8, 2009.

———. Interview by author, November 26, 1999, San Diego, Calif. Tape recording.

Duncan, Susan. Interview by author, April 17, 2003, Washington, D.C. Tape recording.

Eldridge, Joseph. Interview by author, April 15, 2003, Washington, D.C. Tape recording.

Erickson, Kenneth. Interview by author, May 14, 2003, New York City. Tape recording.

Feldman-Bianco, Bela. Interview by author, July 25, 2003, São Paulo, Brazil. Tape recording.

Fernandes, Rubem César. Interview by author, July 18, 2003, Rio de Janeiro, Brazil. Tape recording.

Finke, David H. Correspondence with author, August 21, 2007.

Gabeira, Fernando. Interview by author, July 3, 2003.

Gedick, Al. Telephone interview by author, March 23, 2003. Tape recording.

Goff, Fred. Interview by author, April 2, 1999, Oakland, Calif. Tape recording.

———. Correspondence with author, February 6, 2001.

Goodyear, John. Telephone interview by author, February 5, 2003. Notes.

Gordon, Lincoln. Interview by John E. Rielly, May 30, 1964, Kennedy Oral History Project, JFK.

———. Interview by Paige E. Mulhollan, July 10, 1969, Lyndon Baines Johnson Library Oral History Collection, LBJ.

———. Interview by author and Abigail Jones, August 5, 2005, Washington, D.C. Tape recording.

Haake, Hans. Telephone interview by author, February 17, 2002. Tape recording.

Hahner, June. Interview by author, April 18, 2004, Miami, Fla. Notes.

Hall, Michael. Interview by author, July 20, 2003, São Paulo, Brazil. Tape recording.

Harding, Mary. Interview by author, April 22, 2003, Washington, D.C. Tape recording.

Harding, Timothy. Interview by author, March 22, 1999, Santa Barbara, Calif. Tape recording.

Holt, Pat M. Oral History Interviews, November 10, 1980, Senate Historical Office, Washington, D.C., NARA.

Keck, Margaret. Interview by author, April 21, 2003, Bethesda, Md. Tape recording.

Kokin, Lisa. Interview by author, Berkeley, Calif, April 26, 2002. Tape recording.

Kottak, Betty (Isabel). Telephone interview by author, December 8, 2003. Notes.

Laudau, Saul. Interview by author, February 10, 2003, Pomona, Calif. Tape recording.

Lobo, Eulalia Maria Lahmeyer. Interview by author, July 29, 1999. Florianópolis, Santa Catarina, Brazil. Tape recording.

Love, Joseph L. Interview by author, October 9, 2004, Las Vegas, Nev. Tape recording.

Malina, Judith. Interview by author, November 21, 2002, New York City. Tape recording.

Margolis, Maxine. Interview by author, December 16, 2003, New York City. Tape recording.

Martínez, José Celso Côrrea. Interview by author, June 1, 2002, São Paulo, Brazil. Tape recording.

Mendes, Cândido. Interview by author, July 24, 2003, Rio de Janeiro, Brazil. Tape recording.

Moraes, Maria Teresa (Tetê) Porciuncula de. Interview by author, July 15, 2003, Rio de Janeiro, Brazil. Tape recording.

Muniz, Dulce. Interview by author, April 2, 2004, São Paulo, Brazil. Tape recording.

Nascimento, Abdias do. Interview by author, July 8, 2003, Rio de Janeiro, Brazil. Tape recording.

Oliveira, Miguel Darcy de. Interview by author, July 22, 2003, Rio de Janeiro, Brazil. Tape recording.

Padilha, Anivaldo. Interview by author, no. 1, July 18, 1997, São Paulo, Brazil. Tape recording.

———. Interview by author, no. 2, June 12, 1998, São Paulo, Brazil. Tape recording.

———. Interview by author, no. 3, June 18, 1998, São Paulo, Brazil. Tape recording.

———. Interview by author, no. 4, June 22, 1998, São Paulo, Brazil. Tape recording.

Paes, Márcia Bassetto. Interview by author, January 25, 2008, Providence, R.I. Notes.

Parker, Phyllis R. Telephone interview by author, July 27, 2005. Notes.

Parsons, Estelle. Telephone interview by author, May 20, 2003. Notes.

Patarra, Judith. Interview by author, June 21, 2003, São Paulo, Brazil. Tape recording.

Penna, Lina Sattamini. Interview by author, October 31, 2002, Rio de Janeiro, Brazil. Tape recording.

Pottlitzer, Joanne. Telephone interview by author, February 15, 2003. Tape recording.

Quigley, Thomas. Interview by author, October 9, 2002, Washington, D.C. Tape recording.

Ramalho, Jether. Interview by author, July 25, 2003, Rio de Janeiro, Brazil. Tape recording.

Ramos, Jovelino. Telephone interview by author, February 23, 2003. Tape recording.

———. Interview by author, August 24, 2006, Providence, R.I. Tape recording.

Roett, Riordan. Interview by author, March 5, 2004, Washington, D.C. Tape recording.

Rupiper, Darrell. Interview by author, December 12, 2002, Oakland, Calif. Tape recording.

Schmitter, Philippe C. Interview by author, December 18, 2003, San Francisco, Calif. Tape recording.

Schoultz, Lars. Correspondence with author, October 25, 2001.

Seixas, Ivan. Interview by author, November 13, 2002, São Paulo, Brazil. Tape recording.

Silberstein, Paul. Interview by author, April 27, 2002, Oakland, Calif. Tape recording.

Skidmore, Thomas E. Interview by author, October 12, 2002, Gaithersburg, Md. Tape recording.

———. Interview by author and Abigail Jones, July 28, 2005, Providence, R.I. Tape Recording.

Stam, Robert. Interview by author, November 20, 2002, New York City. Tape recording.

Strharsky, Harry and Loretta. Interview by author, December 17, 2002, Castro Valley, Calif. Tape recording.

Thiebaud, Lorraine. Interview by author, April 27, 2002, Berkeley, Calif. Tape recording.

Topik, Steven. Interview by author, December 1, 2004, Irvine, Calif. Tape recording.

Vieira, Lizst. Interview by author, June 26, 2006, Rio de Janeiro, Brazil. Tape recording.

Von der Weid, Jean Marc. Interview by author, November 10, 2002, Rio de Janeiro. Tape recording.

Von der Weid, Regina. Interview by author, June 30, 2006, Rio de Janeiro, Brazil. Tape recording.

Wheaton, Philip. Interview by author, October 29, 1999, Los Angeles, Calif. Tape recording.

Wipfler, William L. Interview by author, January 12, 2000, Buffalo, N.Y. Tape recording.

———. Telephone interview by author, September 8, 2004. Notes.

Wright, Angus. Telephone interview by author, March 13, 2004. Notes.

Wright, Larry. Interview by author, April 21, 2003, Bethesda, Md. Tape recording.


## Bulletins, Magazines, Newspapers

*América*
*Amnesty International Newsletter*
*Baltimore Sun*
*Berkeley Barb*
*Berkeley Tribe*
*Boletim Arquidiocesano, órgão oficial da Arquidiocese de Olinda e Recife, Pernambuco, Brazil.*
*Boletim Especial* (Brazilian Embassy, Washington)
*Black Panther*
*Brazilian Information Bulletin*
*Brazilian Labor Information and Resource Center Newsletter*
*Business Week*
*Chicago Tribune*
*Christian Science Monitor*
*Christian Century*
*Christianity and Crisis*
*Commonweal*
*Congressional Record, House and Senate*
*Cruzeiro* (Rio de Janeiro)
*Cue*
*Daily World*
*O Estado de São Paulo*

*Fort Lauderdale News and Sun Sentinel*
*Harper's Magazine*
*Latin America Calls!* (Washington)
*Jornal do Brasil* (Rio de Janeiro)
*Lampião da Esquina*
*Latin America & Empire Report*
*Latin American Studies Association Newsletter*
*Look*
*Monthly Review*
*Montreal Star*
NACLA *Newsletter*
*Nation*
*National Catholic Reporter*
*National Geographic*
*National Review*
*New Republic*
*New York Post*
*New York Review of Books*
*New York Times*
*New Yorker*
*News from Brazil* (Brazilian Embassy, Washington)
*Newsweek*
*Old Mole*
*Palm Beach Daily News*

Peace Corps News
Progressive
Rampart
Saturday Review
San Francisco Chronicle
Time
Tribuna da Imprensa
Tribunale Russell Brasile (Rome)
Tricontinental

Última Hora (Rio de Janeiro)
Variety
Veja
Village Voice (New York City)
Washington Post
The Worker
World Outlook
Union of Radical Latin Americanists
Women's Daily Wear

## Print Sources

Agee, Philip. *Inside the Company: CIA Diary*. New York: Bantam Books, 1976.
Albuquerque, Severino João. "Verbal Violence and the Pursuit of Power in *Apareceu a Margarida*." *Latin American Theater Review* 19, no. 2 (spring 1986): 23–29.
———. *Violent Acts: A Study of Contemporary Latin American Theater*. Detroit: Wayne State University Press, 1991.
Almeida, Maria Hermínia Tavares de, and Luiz Weis, "Carro-zero e pau-de-arara: O cotidiano da oposição de classe media ao regime militar." *História da vida privada no Brasil: Contrastes da intimidade contemporânea*, ed. Lilia Moritz Schwarcz, 319–409. São Paulo: Companhia das Letras, 1998.
Almeida Filho, Hamilton. *A sangue-quente: A morte do jornalista Vladimir Herzog*. São Paulo: Editora Alpha-Omega, 1978.
Alvarez, Sonia E. *Engendering Democracy in Brazil*. Princeton, N.J.: Princeton University Press, 1990.
Alves, Márcio Moreira. *Torturas e Torturados*, 2nd ed. Rio de Janeiro: P.N., 1967.
———. "Christians, Marxists and Dictatorship in Brazil." *Christian Century*, June 10, 1970, 723–27.
———. *A Grain of Mustard Seed: The Awakening of the Brazilian Revolution*. Garden City, N.Y.: Anchor Books, 1973.
———. *68: Mudou o mundo*. Rio de Janeiro: Editora Nova Fronteira, 1993.
Alves, Maria Helena Moreira. *State and Opposition in Military Brazil*. Austin: University of Texas Press, 1985.
Amanico, Tunico. *O Brasil dos gringos: imagens no cinema*. Niterói: Intertexto, 2000.
American Committee for Information on Brazil. *Terror in Brazil: A Dossier* (April 1970).
Amnesty International. *Amnesty International 1961–62 Report*. London: Amnesty International, 1962.
———. *International Secretariat Report, June 1, 1964 to May 31, 1965*. London: Amnesty International, 1965.
———. *Annual Report, 1st June, 1966/31st May, 1967*. London: Amnesty International, 1967.
———. *Annual Report, 1972–73*. London: Amnesty International, 1973.
———. *Report on Allegations of Torture in Brazil*. Palo Alto: West Coast Office, Amnesty International, 1973.
———. *Torture in Greece: The First Torturers' Trial 1975*. London: Amnesty International, 1977.

Anderson, Jack, with Daryl Gibson. *Peace, War, and Politics: An Eyewitness Account.* New York: Tom Doherty Association, 1999.

Anderson, Jack, with George Clifford. *The Anderson Papers.* New York: Random House, 1973.

Anderson, Jon Lee. *Che Guevara: A Revolutionary Life.* New York: Grove Press, 1997.

Antero, Luiz Carlos, João Amazonas, Aumano Silva. *Uma epoéia pela liberdade: Guerrilha do Araguaia 30 anos (1972–2002).*São Paulo: Anita Garibaldi, 2002.

Arapiraca, José de O. *A USAID e a educação brasileira: Um estudo a partir de uma abordagem crítica da teoria do capital humana.* São Paulo: Autores associados, Cortez, 1982.

Armbrister, Trevor. "The Two Faces of Brazil, II: Withered Freedom." *Readers Digest,* February 1972, 121–24.

Archdiocese of São Paulo. *Brasil: Nunca mais.* Preface by Dom Paulo Evaristo Arns. Petrópolis: Editora Vozes, 1985.

———. *Torture in Brazil.* Translated by Jaime Wright. Edited and with an introduction by Joan Dassin. 1986. Reprint, Austin: University of Texas Press, 1998.

Arruda, Marcos. "A vivência objetiva e subjetiva do trabalhador intelectual." Unpublished article.

Asby, LeRoy, and Rod Gramer. *Fighting the Odds: The Life of Senator Frank Church.* Pullman: Washington State University Press, 1994.

Associação dos Docentes da Universidade de São Paulo (ADUSP). *O livro negro da USP: O controle ideológico na universidade.* São Paulo: ADUSP, 1979.

"Atrocities Charged. Brazil Loses Lutheran Assembly." *Christianity Today,* July 3, 1970, 36.

Azevedo, Cecília. "Os Corpos da Paz no Brasil (1961–81)." Ph.D. diss., University of São Paulo, 1999.

Bader, Wolfgang. *Brecht no Brasil: Introdução e organização.* Rio de Janeiro: Paz e Terra, 1987.

Baer, Werner, and Isaac Kerstenetsky. "The Brazilian Economy." *Brazil in the Sixties,* ed. Riordan Roett, 105–45. Nashville, Tenn.: Vanderbilt University Press, 1972.

Bandeira, Antônio Rangel. *Sombras do paraíso.* Rio de Janeiro: Editora Record, 1994.

Bassetto, Sylvia. "Devemos rever a imagem que temos de nós mesmos." *Revista ADUSP* (June 1999): 15–29.

Bell, Peter D. "Brazilian-American Relations." *Brazil in the Sixties,* ed. Riordan Roett, 77–104. Nashville, Tenn.: Vanderbilt University Press, 1972.

Berger, Mark T. *Under Northern Eyes: Latin American Studies and U.S. Hegemony in the Americas, 1898–1990.* Bloomington: Indiana University Press, 1995.

Berghahn, Volker R. *America and the Intellectual Cold Wars in Europe: Sheppard Stone between Philanthropy, Academy, and Diplomacy.* Princeton, N.J.: Princeton University Press, 2001.

Berquó, Alberto. *O seqüestro dia a dia: A verdadeira história do seqüestro do embaixador americano Charles Burke Elbrick.* Rio de Janeiro: Nova Fronteira, 1997.

Berrigan, Daniel. *The Trial of the Catonsville Nine.* Boston: Beacon Press, 1970.

Bertoli, Amalia, Roger Burback, David Hathaway, Robert High, and Eugene Kelly. "Human Rights . . . 'In the Soul of Our Foreign Policy.'" *NACLA Report on the Americas* 3, no. 1 (March–April 1979): 4–11.

Beschloss, Michael R., ed. *Taking Charge: The Johnson White House Tapes, 1963–1964.* New York: Simon and Schuster, 1997.

Bicudo, Hélio. *Meu depoimento sobre o Esquadrão da Morte*. São Paulo: Pontifica Comissão de Justiça e Paz de São Paulo.

Bieber, Judy. "Brazilian History in the United States." *Envisioning Brazil: A Guide to Brazilian Studies in the United States, 1945–2003*, ed. Marshall C. Eakin and Paulo Roberto de Almeida, 162–201. Madison: University of Wisconsin Press, 2002.

Bissett, Judith L. "Victims and Violators: The Structure of Violence in *Torquemada*." *Latin American Theatre Review* 15, no.2 (spring 1982): 27–34.

Black, Jan Knippers. *United States Penetration of Brazil*. Philadelphia: University of Pennsylvania Press, 1977.

Boal, Augusto. *Milagre no Brasil: Romance*. Rio de Janeiro: Edição Civilização Brasileira, 1979.

———. *Hamlet and the Baker's Son: My Life in Theatre and Politics*. Translated by Adrian Jackson and Candida Blaker. London: Routledge, 2001.

Bojunga, Claudio. *JK: O artista do impossível*. Rio de Janeiro: Objetivo, 2001.

Bolton, Robert H. "Brazilian Torture: Specifically New Specifically Terrible." *Christian Century*, April 1, 1970, 387–88.

Boyle, Catherine M. "Re-lectura e re-presentación de una protagonista autoritaria." *Gestos* 4, no. 88 (November 1989): 172–76.

Brazil Labor Information and Resource Center. *Brazil: Labor Unions on Trial*. Brooklyn: Brazil Labor Information and Resource Center, 1981.

Brito, Angela Neves-Xavier de. "Brazilian Women in Exile: The Quest for an Identity." Translated by Charlotte Stanley. *Latin American Perspectives* 13, no. 2 (spring 1986): 58–80.

Calado, Carlos. *Tropicália: A história de uma revolução musical*. São Paulo: Editora 34, 1997.

Calandra, Benedetta. *L'America della solidarietà: L'accoglienza dei rifugiati cileni e argentine negli Stati Uniti (1973–1983)*. Roma: Edizioni Nuova Cultura, 2006.

Calirman, Claúdia. "Brazilian Art between 1968 and 1974: Art under Dictatorship." Ph.D. diss., New York University, 2004.

Calvacanti, Pedro Celso Uchôa, and Jovelino Ramos, eds. *Mémorias do exílio, Brasil 1964–197??* Lisbon: Arcádia, 1976; São Paulo: Editora e Livraria Livramento, 1978.

Canning, Peter. *American Dreamers: The Wallaces and "Reader's Digest," An Insider Story*. New York: Simon and Schuster, 1996.

Cardoso, Fernando Henrique. *A arte da política: A história que vivi*. Rio de Janeiro: Civilização Brasileira, 2006.

Cardoso, Fernando Henrique, and Enzo Falletto. *Dependencia y desarrollo en América Latina: Ensayo de interpretación sociológica*. Mexico: Siglo Veintiuno Editores, 1969.

CARIB (Committee against Repression in Brazil). *Brazil: Miracle for Whom?* Washington: CARIB, 1972.

Castelo Branco, Carlos. *Os militares no poder*. Vol. 1. 3rd ed. Rio de Janeiro: Nova Fronteira, 1976.

Chilcote, Ronald H. "Review: U.S. Hegemony and Academics in the Americas." *Latin American Perspectives* 24, no. 1 (January 1997): 73–77.

Clark, Ann Marie. "Strong Principles, Strengthening Practices: Amnesty International and Three Cases of Change in International Human Rights Standards." Ph.D. diss., University of Minnesota, 1995.

Cleary, Edward L. *The Struggle for Human Rights in Latin America*. Westport, Conn.: Praeger, 1979.

Cline, Howard F. "The Latin American Studies Association: A Summary Survey with Appendix." *Latin American Research Review* 2, no. 1 (fall 1966): 57–79.

Cmiel, Kenneth. "The Emergence of Human Rights Politics in the United States." *Journal of American History* (December 1999): 1231–50.

Comissão de Familiares de Mortos e Desaparecidos Políticos, Instituto de Estudo da Violência do Estado-IEVE, Grupo Tortura Nunca Mais-RJ e PE. *Dossiê dos mortos e desaparecidos políticos a partir de 1964*. São Paulo: Imprensa Oficial do Estado, 1996.

Committee of Returned Volunteers. *Brazil: Who Pulls the Strings? Or: Alliance for Repression*. Chicago: Committee of Returned Volunteers, [1971].

Corrêa, Marcos Sá. *1964: Visto e comentado pela Casa Branca*. Porto Alegre: L&PM, 1977.

Costa, Albertina Oliveira, et al., eds. *Memórias das mulheres no exílio*. Rio de Janeiro: Paz e Terra, 1980.

Costa, Célia Maria Leite. "A Frente Ampla de oposição ao regime militar." *João Goulart: Entre a memória e a história*, ed. Marieta de Moraes Ferreira, 177–91. Rio de Janeiro: Editora FGV, 2006.

D'Araújo, Maria Celina, and Celso Castro, eds. *Ernesto Geisel*. Rio de Janeiro: Fundação Getúlio Vargas, 1997.

D'Araújo, Maria Celina, Gláucio Ary Dillon Soares, Celso Castro, eds. *Os anos de chumbo: A memória militar sobre a repressão*. Rio de Janeiro: Relume Dumará, 1994.

Davis, Shelton H. *Victims of the Miracle: Development and the Indians of Brazil*. Cambridge: Cambridge University Press, 1977.

Davis, Sonny B. *A Brotherhood of Arms: Brazil–United States Military Relations, 1945–1977*. Niwot: University of Colorado Press, 1996.

Della Cava, Ralph. *Miracle at Juazeiro*. New York: Columbia University Press, 1970.

———. "Torture in Brazil." *Commonweal*, April 24, 1970, 1, 35–41.

———. "Reply." *Commonweal*, August 7, 1970, 378–79, 398–99.

Dellums, Ronald V., and H. Lee Halterman. *Lying Down with the Lions: A Public Life from the Streets of Oakland to the Halls of Power*. Boston: Beacon Press, 2000.

Deutsch, Sandra McGee. "Christians, Homemakers, and Transgressors: Extreme Right-Wing Women in Twentieth-Century Brazil." *Journal of Women's History* 16, no. 3 (2004): 124–37.

DiGaetani, John L. *A Search for a Postmodern Theater: Interviews with Contemporary Playwrights*. New York: Greenwood Press, 1991.

D'Incao, Maria Angela, ed. *História e ideal: Ensaios sobre Caio Prado Júnior*. São Paulo: UNESP, 1989.

Dirceu, José, and Vladimir Palmeira. *Abaixo a ditadura*. Rio de Janeiro: Garamund, 1998.

Dreifuss, René Armand. *1964: A conquista do estado, ação política, poder e golpe de classe*. Petrópolis: Vozes, 1981.

Drosdoff, Daniel. *Linha dura no Brasil: O governo Médici, 1969–74*. Translated by Norberto de Paula Lima. São Paulo: Global, 1986.

Dulles, John W. F. *Unrest in Brazil: Political-Military Crisis, 1955–1964*. Austin: University of Texas Press, 1970.

Dunn, Christopher. *Tropicália and the Emergence of a Brazilian Counterculture*. Chapel Hill: University of North Carolina Press, 2001.

"Emília Viotti da Costa." *Memórias das mulheres no exílio*, eds. Albertina de Oliveira Costa et al., 390–412. Rio de Janeiro: Paz e Terra, 1980.

Fagen, Patricia Weiss. "U.S. Foreign Policy and Human Rights: The Role of Congress." *Parliamentary Control over Foreign Policy*, ed. Antônio Cassese, 111–35. Alphen aan den Rijn, Netherlands: Sijthoff and Noordhoff, 1989.

Farer, Tom J. "United States Foreign Policy and the Protection of Human Rights: Observations and Proposals." *Virginia Journal of International Law* 14 (summer 1974): 623–46.

———. *The Grand Strategy of the United States in Latin America*. New Brunswick, N.J.: Transaction Books, 1988.

Fico, Carlos. *Reinventando o otimismo, ditadura, propaganda e imaginário social no Brasil*. Rio de Janeiro: Fundação Getúlio Vargas, 1997.

———. *Como eles agiam, os subterrânos da Ditadura Militar: Espionagem e polícia política*. Rio de Janeiro: Record, 2001.

———. *Além do golpe: Versões e controvérsias sobre 1964 e a ditadura militar*. Rio de Janeiro: Record, 2004.

———. *O grande irmão: Da Operação Brother Same aos anos de chumbo: O governo dos Estados Unidos e a ditadura militar brasileira*. Rio de Janeiro: Civilização brasileira, 2008.

Forsythe, David P. *Human Rights and World Politics*. Lincoln: University of Nebraska Press, 1983.

Fragoso, Heleno Cláudio. *Advocacia da liberdade: A defesa nos processos políticos*. Rio de Janeiro: Forense, 1984.

Gabeira, Fernando. *O que é isso, companheiro?* Rio de Janeiro: CODECRI, 1979.

———. *O crepúsculo do macho: Depoimento*. Rio de Janeiro, CODECRI, 1980.

Gallup, George Horace. *The Gallup Poll, 1935–1971*. New York: Random House, 1972.

Garfield, Seth. *Indigenous Struggle at the Heart of Brazil: State Policy, Frontier Expansion, and the Xavante Indians, 1937–1988*. Durham, N.C.: Duke University Press, 2001.

Gaspari, Elio. *A ditadura envergonhada*. São Paulo: Companhia das Letras, 2002.

———. *A ditadura escancarada*. São Paulo: Companhia das Letras, 2002.

———. *A ditadura encurralada*. São Paulo: Companhia das Letras, 2004.

George, David S. *The Modern Brazilian Stage*. Austin: University of Texas Press, 1992.

Goff, Fred. "February 11th NACLA Meeting." NACLA *Newsletter* 1, no. 2 (March 1967): 1.

Gomes, Angela de Castro, ed. *O Brasil de JK*. Rio de Janeiro: Editora da Fundação Getúlio Vargas—CPDOC, 1991.

Gordon, Lincoln. *United States Manufacturing Investment in Brazil, 1946–1960*. Boston: Division of Research, Graduate School of Business Administration, Harvard University, 1962.

———. "Novas Perspectivas das relações brasileiro-Norte-Americanas." Conferencia pronunciada pelo Embaixador Lincoln Gordon na Escola Superior de Guerra, Rio de Janeiro, May 5, 1964.

———. "To the Editors." *Commonweal*, August 7, 1970, 378–79.

———. "Made in Brazil: The 1964 Revolution." January 1977. Unpublished article.

———. "Castello perdeu a batalha." Interview with Roberto Garcia. *Veja*, March 9, 1977, 3–8.

———. "The Alliance at Birth: Hopes and Fears." *The Alliance for Progress: A Retrospective*, ed. L. Ronald Scheman, 73–79. New York: Praeger, 1988.

———. *Brazil's Second Chance: En Route toward the First World*. Supplement, Brazil, 1961–64: *The United States and the Goulart Regime*. Washington: Brookings Institute, 2003.

Gorender, Jacob. *Combate nas trevas*. 5th ed. São Paulo: Editora Ática, 1998.

Gosse, Van. *Where the Boys Are: Cuba, Cold War America and the Making of a New Left*. London: Verso, 1993.

———. "Unpacking the Vietnam Syndrome: The Coup in Chile and the Rise of Popular Anti-Interventionism." *The World the 60s Made: Politics and Culture in Recent America*, ed. Van Gosse and Richard Moser, 100–113. Philadelphia: Temple University Press, 2003.

Green, James N. "Liberalization on Trial: The Workers' Movement." NACLA: *Report on the Americas* 12, no. 3 (May–June 1979): 15–25.

———. "Clergy, Exiles, and Academics: Opposition to the Brazilian Military Dictatorship in the United States, 1964–1974." *Latin American Politics and Society* 45, no. 1 (2003): 87–117.

Gross, Leonard. "Brazil: Government By Torture," *Look*, July 14, 1970, 70–71.

Gurgel, Antônio de Pádua. *A rebelião dos estudantes, Brasília, 1968*. Brasília: Editora Universidade de Brasília, 2002.

Hall, Clarence W. "The Country That Saved Itself." *Reader's Digest*, November 1964, 135–59.

Halstead, Fred. *Out Now: A Participant's Account of the American Movement against the Vietnam War*. New York: Monad Press, 1978.

Hampton, Christopher. "Christopher Hampton's 'Savages' at the Royal Court Theater." *Theatre Quarterly* 3 (October–December 1973): 60–78.

Hanchard, Michael George. *Orpheus and Power: The Movimento Negro of Rio de Janeiro and São Paulo, Brazil, 1945–1988*. Princeton, N.J.: Princeton University Press, 1994.

Hannifin, Rieck B. "Repression of Civil Liberties and Human Rights in Brazil since the Revolution of 1964." Library of Congress Legislative Reference Service, Washington, June 26, 1970.

Harper, Charles R. *O acampamento: Ecumenical Action for Human Rights in Latin America, 1970–1990*. Geneva: World Council of Churches Publications, 2006.

Heidenry, John. *Theirs Was the Kingdom: Lila and DeWitt Wallace and the Story of the Reader's Digest*. New York: W. W. Norton, 1993.

Hoffman, Elizabeth Cobbs. *All You Need Is Love: The Peace Corps and the Spirit of the 1960s*. Cambridge, Mass.: Harvard University Press, 1998.

Hollanda, Chico Buarque. *Chico Buarque, letra e música*. São Paulo: Companhia das Letras, 1989.

Horowitz, Irving Louis. *The Rise and Fall of Project Camelot*. Cambridge, Mass.: MIT Press, 1967.

Huggins, Martha K. *Political Policing: The United States and Latin America*. Durham, N.C.: Duke University Press, 1998.

Huggins, Martha K., Mika Haritos-Fatouros, and Philip G. Zimbardo. *Violence Workers: Police Torturers and Murderers Reconstruct Brazilian Atrocities*. Berkeley: University of California Press, 2002.

Inter-American Commission on Human Rights. "Report on the Work Accomplished

During Its Twentieth Session, December 2 through 12, 1968." Washington: Organization of American States, 1969.

———. "Annual Report of the Inter-American Commission on Human Rights for the Year 1973." Washington: Organization of American States, March 5, 1974.

———. *Ten Years of Activities, 1971–1981.* Washington: Organization of American States, 1982.

Joseph, Gilbert M., ed. *Reclaiming the Political in Latin American History: Essays from the North.* Durham, N.C.: Duke University Press, 2001.

Junqueira, Mary Anne. *Ao sul do Rio Grande — imaginado a América Latina em Seleções: Oeste, wilderness e fronteira (1942–1970).* Bragança Paulista: EDUSP, 2000.

Kean, Melissa Fitzsimons. "'At a Most Uncomfortable Speed': The Desegregation of the South's Private Universities, 1945–1964." Ph.D. diss., Rice University, 2000.

Keck, Margaret E. *The Workers' Party and Democratization in Brazil.* New Haven, Conn.: Yale University Press, 1992.

Keck, Margaret E., and Kathryn Sikkink. *Activists beyond Borders: Advocacy Networks in International Politics.* Ithaca, N.Y.: Cornell University Press, 1998.

Kinzo, Maria D'Alva G. *Legal Opposition Politics under Authoritarian Rule in Brazil: The Case of the MDB, 1966–79.* New York: St. Martin's Press, 1988.

Kirby, Bruce R., and Suzanne Erera. "Historical Note." Record Unit 321, Office of Program Support, National Museum of American Art, Records 1965–1981, Smithsonian Institution Archives website, www.si.edu/archives/archives/faru0321.htm.

Kornbluh, Peter. *The Pinochet File: A Declassified Dossier on Atrocity and Accountability.* New York: New Press, 2003.

Kucinski, Bernardo. *Abertura: A história de uma crise.* São Paulo: Ed. Brasil Debates, 1982.

Kushnir, Beatriz. *Cães de guarda: Jornalistas e censores, do AI-5 à Constituição de 1988.* São Paulo: Boitempo, 2004.

Langguth, A. J. *Hidden Terrors.* New York: Pantheon Books, 1978.

Leacock, Ruth. *Requiem for Revolution: The United States and Brazil, 1961–1969.* Kent, Ohio: Kent State University Press, 1990.

Lens, Sidney. "Brazil's Police State." *The Progressive,* December 1966, 31–34.

Lima, Alceu Amoroso. "Brazil's Revolution Six Years Later." *America,* June 20, 1970, 646–49.

Lima, Haroldo, and Aldo Arantes. *História da Ação Popular da JUC ao PC do B.* São Paulo: Editora Alfa-Omega, 1984.

Lima, Mariângela Alves de. "História das idéias." *Dionysos* 24 (October 1978): 31–63.

Linnell, Greg "'Applauding the Good and Condemning the Bad': The Christian Herald and Varieties of Protestant Response to Hollywood in the 1950s." *Journal of Religion and Popular Culture* 12 (spring 2006).

Luppi, Carlos Alberto. *Manoel Fiel Filho, quem vai pagar por este crime?* São Paulo: Escrita, 1980.

Lutz, Catherine A., and Jane L. Collins. *Reading "National Geographic."* Chicago: University of Chicago Press, 1993.

Mainwaring, Scott. *The Catholic Church and Politics in Brazil, 1916–1985.* Stanford, Calif.: Stanford University Press, 1986.

Maram, Sheldon. "Juscelino Kubitschek and the Politics of Exuberance, 1956–1961." *Luso-Brazilian Review* 27, no. 1 (summer 1990): 31–45.

Marighella, Carlos. *For the Liberation of Brazil.* Middlesex, England: Penguin Books, 1971.

Markun, Paulo, ed. *Vlado: Retrato da morte de um homem e de uma época.* São Paulo: Editora Brasiliense, 1985.

———. *Meu querido Vlado.* Rio de Janeiro: Objetiva, 2005.

Martins Filho, João Roberto. *O palácio e a caserna: A dinâmica militar das crises políticas na ditadura (1964–1969).* São Carlos: Editora da UFSCar, 1995.

Matin-Asgari, Afshin. *Iranian Student Opposition to the Shah.* Costa Mesa, Calif.: Mazda Publishers, 2002.

McDonald, Robert. "The Colonels' Dictatorship, 1967–1974." *Background to Contemporary Greece,* vol. 2, ed. Mario Sarafis and Martin Eve, 255–315. London: Merlin Press, 1990.

McGowan, Chris, and Ricardo Pessanha. *The Brazilian Sound: Samba, Bossa Nova and the Popular Music of Brazil.* Philadelphia: Temple University Press, 1998.

McPherson, Alan. *Yankee No! Anti-Americanism in U.S.–Latin American Relations.* Cambridge, Mass.: Harvard University Press, 2003.

Meihy, José Carlos Sebe Bom. *A colônia Brasílianista: História oral de vida acadêmica.* São Paulo: Nova Stella, 1990.

Melville, Thomas, and Marjorie Melville. *Guatemala—Another Vietnam.* Middlesex, England: Penguin, 1971.

———. *Whose Heaven, Whose Earth?* New York: Alfred A. Knopf, 1971.

Miceli, Sérgio. *A desilusão americana: Relações acadêmicas entre Brasil e Estados Unidos.* São Paulo: Editora Sumaré; Programa Nacional do Centenário da República e Bi-Centenário da Inconfidência Mineira—MCT/CNPq, 1990.

———. "Betting on an Emerging Scientific Community: The Ford Foundation and the Social Sciences in Brazil." Translated by Alasdair G. Burman. *A Fundação Ford no Brasil,* ed. Sérgio Miceli, 271–99. São Paulo: FAPESP, Editora Sumará, 1993.

Miranda, Nilmário, and Carlos Tibúrcio. *Dos filhos deste solo: mortos e desaparecidos políticos durante a ditadura militar: a responsabilidade do Estado.* São Paulo: Editora Fundação Perseu Abramo and Boitempo Editorial, 1999.

Moraes, João Luiz de, and Azis Ahmen. *Calvário de Sônia Angel.* Rio de Janeiro: MEC, 1994.

Morel, Edmar. *O golpe começou em Washington.* Rio de Janeiro: Civilização Brasileira, 1965.

Morow, Kurt Rudolf. *Loucura nuclear (Os enganos do acordo Brasil-Alemanha).* Rio de Janeiro: Civilização brasileira, 1979.

Morris, Fred B. "In the Presence of Mine Enemies." *Ramparts,* October 1975, 57–70.

———. "Sustained by Faith under Brazilian Torture." *Christian Century,* January 22, 1975, 56–60.

———. "A importância da vida e ministério de Dom Hélder Câmara." *Hélder, o dom: Uma vida que marcou os rumos da igreja no Brasil,* ed. Zildo Rocha, 89–90. Petrópolis: Editora Vozes, 1999.

Moura, Clóvis. *Diário da guerrilha do Araguaia.* São Paulo: Editora Alfa-Omega, 1979.

Movimento Feminino Pela Anistia e Liberdades Democráticas. *Origens e lutas.* Rio de Janeiro: Imprinta Gráfica e Editora, 1990.

Naftali, Timothy, ed. *The Presidential Recordings, John F. Kennedy: The Great Crisis*, vol. 1. New York: W. W. Norton, 1997.

Napolitano, Marcos. *Seguindo a canção: Engajamento político e indústria cultural na MPB, 1959–1969*. São Paulo: Annablume, 2001.

Nascimento, Abdias do. *Mixture or massacre? Essays in the Genocide of a Black People*. Buffalo, N.Y.: Afrodiaspora, 1979.

Nixon, Richard M. *Public Papers of the President of the United States: Richard Nixon, Containing the Public Messages, Speeches, and Statements of the President*. Vol. 3, 1971. Washington: U.S. Government Printing Office, 1975.

North American Congress on Latin America (NACLA). *NACLA Research Methodology Guide*. New York: NACLA, 1970.

Padilha, Anivaldo. "Testamunho sobre Brady Tyson para João Valença." November 26, 1999. Unpublished article.

Page, Joseph A. *The Revolution That Never Was: Northeast Brazil: 1955–1964*. New York: Grossman, 1972.

Parker, Phyllis R. *Brazil and the Quiet Intervention, 1964*. Austin: University of Texas Press, 1979.

Peck, F. Taylor. *Report of Activities, 1968*. Latin American Studies Association Secretariat Publication No. 4. Washington: Latin American Studies Association, 1968.

Pellegrino, Hélio. "Prefácio." *Mário Pedrosa, Retratos do exílio*, by Carlos Eduardo de Sena Figueiredo. Rio de Janeiro: Edições Antares, 1982.

Pereira, Anthony W. "'Persecution and Farce': The Origins and Transformation of Brazil's Political Trials, 1964–79." *Latin American Research Review* 33, no.1 (1998): 43–67.

———. *Political Injustice: Authoritarianism and the Rule of Law in Brazil, Chile, and Argentina*. Pittsburgh: University of Pittsburgh Press, 2005.

Perrone, Charles A. *Masters of Contemporary Brazilian Song, MPB 1965–1985*. Austin: University of Texas Press, 1989.

———. "Dissonance and Dissent: The Musical Dramatics of Chico Buarque." *Latin American Theater Review* 22, no.2 (spring 1989):81–94.

Persico, Joseph E. *The Imperial Rockefeller: A Biography of Nelson A. Rockefeller*. New York: Simon and Schuster, 1982.

Piletti, Nelson, and Walter Praxedes. *Dom Hélder Câmara: Entre o poder e a profecia*. São Paulo: Editora Ática, 1997.

Polari, Alex. *Em busca do tesouro*. Rio de Janeiro: Editora CODECRI, 1982.

Poerner, Arthur José. *O Poder jovem: História da participação política dos estudantes brasileiros*. 2nd ed. Rio de Janeiro: Editora Civilização Brasileira, 1979.

Portela, Fernando. *Guerra de guerrilhas no Brasil: Informações novas, documentos inéditos e na íntegra*. São Paulo: Global, 1987.

Pottlitzer, Joanne. "The Envelope." "Poets, Politics and Lovers." Unpublished manuscript.

Power, Timothy J. "Brazil and the Carter Human Rights Policy, 1977–1979." Master's thesis, University of Florida, 1986.

Projeto Brasil: Nunca Mais. *Perfil dos atingidos*. Vol. 3. Petrópolis: Vozes, 1998.

Quadros, Jânio. "Brazil's New Foreign Policy." *Foreign Affairs* 40, no. 1 (October 1961): 19–27.

Quartim, João. *Dictatorship and Armed Struggle in Brazil*. London: New Left Books, 1971.

Quiles, Edgar. "The Theatre of Augusto Boal." Ph.D. diss., Michigan State University, 1981.

Rabe, Stephen G. *Eisenhower and Latin America: The Foreign Policy of Anti-Communism*. Chapel Hill: University of North Carolina Press, 1988.

———. "Dulles, Latin American and Cold War Anticommunism." *John Foster Dulles and the Diplomacy of the Cold War*, ed. Richard Immerman, 159–87. Princeton, N.J.: Princeton University Press, 1990.

———. *The Most Dangerous Area in the World: John F. Kennedy Confronts Communist Revolution in Latin America*. Chapel Hill: University of North Carolina Press, 1999.

Reis Filho, Daniel Aarão. *Versões e ficções: O seqüestro da história*. São Paulo: Editora Fundação Perseu Abramo, 1997.

Ridenti, Marcelo. *O fantasma da revolução brasileira*. São Paulo: Editora UNESP, 1993.

———. *Em busca do povo brasileiro: Artistas da revolução, do CPC à era da tv*. Rio de Janeiro: Record, 2000.

Ripp, Rudolph K. "Transnationalism and Human Rights: The Case of Amnesty International." Ph.D. diss., City University of New York, 1982.

Robin, Ron. *The Making of the Cold War Enemy: Culture and Politics in the Military-Intellectual Complex*. Princeton, N.J.: Princeton University Press, 2001.

Rocha, Zildo. *Hélder, o dom: Uma vida que marcou os rumos da Igreja no Brasil*. Petopolis: Editora Vozes, 1999.

Rockefeller, Nelson. *The Rockefeller Report on the Americas: The Official Report of a United States Presidential Mission for the Western Hemisphere*. Chicago: Quadrangle Books, 1969.

Rollemberg, Denise. *Exílio: Entre raízes e radars*. Rio de Janeiro: Record, 1999.

Romualdi, Serafino. *Presidents and Peons: Recollections of a Labor Ambassador in Latin America*. New York: Funk and Wagnall, 1967.

Rosen, Fred. "NACLA: A 35 Year Retrospective." *NACLA: Report on the Americas* 36, no. 3 (November/December 2002): 12–37.

Rossinow, Douglas. *The Politics of Authenticity: Liberalism, Christianity, and the New Left in America*. New York: Columbia University Press, 1998.

Ryan, Paul Ryder. "The Living Theatre in Brazil." *Drama Review* 15, no. 3 (1971): 21–29.

Santos, Pedro Augusto Gomes. *A classe media vai ao paraíso: JK em Manchete*. Porto Alegre: EDIPUCRGS, 2002.

Sattamini, Lina Penna. *Esquecer? Nunca mais . . . (A saga do meu filho Marcos P.S. de Arruda)*. Rio de Janeiro: OR Productor Independiente, 2000.

———. *A Mother's Cry: A Memoir of Politics, Prison, and Torture under the Brazilian Military Dictatorship*. Durham, N.C.: Duke University Press, 2010.

Schmitter, Philippe C. "The Persecution of Political and Social Scientists." *PS* 3, no. 2 (spring 1970): 123–28.

Schmitz, David F. *The United States and Right-Wing Dictatorships*. New York: Cambridge University Press, 2006.

Schneider, Ronald M. *The Political System of Brazil: Emergence of a "Modernizing" Authoritarian Regime, 1964–1970*. New York: Columbia University Press, 1971.

Schoultz, Lars. *Human Rights and United States Policy toward Latin America*. Princeton, N.J.: Princeton University Press, 1981.

————. "The Carter Administration and Human Rights in Latin America." *Human Rights and Basic Needs in the Americas*, ed. Margaret E. Crahan, 301–40. Washington: Georgetown University Press, 1982.

Seegers, Scott, and Kathleen Seegers. "The Two Faces of Brazil: I. Boom Extraordinary." *Reader's Digest*, February 1972, 118–20.

Seixas, Ivan. "A vida clandestina." *Perfis cruzados: Trajetórias e militância política no Brasil*. ed. Beatriz Kushnir, 57–70. Rio de Janeiro: Imago, 2002.

Serbin, Kenneth P. "The Anatomy of a Death: Repression, Human Rights and the Case of Alexandre Vannucchi Leme in Authoritarian Brazil." *Journal of Latin American Studies* 30, no. 1 (February 1998): 1–33.

————. *Secret Dialogues: Church-State Relations, Torture, and Social Justice in Authoritarian Brazil*. Pittsburgh: University of Pittsburgh Press, 2000.

————. "Dom Hélder Câmara: The Father of the Church of the Poor." *The Human Tradition in Modern Brazil*, ed. Peter M. Beattie, 249–66. Wilmington, Del.: Scholarly Resources, 2004.

————. *Needs of the Heart: A Social and Cultural History of Brazil's Clergy and Seminaries*. Notre Dame, Ind.: University of Notre Dame Press, 2006.

Sevillano, Daniel Cantinelli. "Entrevista com a Professora Emília Viotti da Costa." *Memória 70 anos–FFCL-FFLCH-USP*, 2002. www.fflch.usp.br/sdi/imprensa/noticia/014-2004.html (visited December 23, 2007).

Shestack, Jerome J., and Roberta Cohen. "International Human Rights: A Role for the United States." *Virginia Journal for International Law* 14 (summer 1974): 673–701.

Sikkink, Kathryn. *Mixed Signals: U.S. Human Rights Policy and Latin America*. Ithaca, N.Y.: Cornell University Press, 2004.

Silva, Cláudio Roberto da. "Reinventando o sonho: História oral de vida política e homossexualidade no Brasil contemporâneo." Master's thesis, University of São Paulo, 1999.

Silva, Hélio. *História da República Brasileira: Os governos militares, 1969–74*. São Paulo: Editora Três, 1975.

Silvert, Kalman H. "American Academic Ethics and Social Research Abroad: The Lesson of Project Camelot." *Background* 9, no. 3, Proceedings and Papers: The New Intelligence Requirements (November 1965): 215–36.

Simões, Solange de Deus. *Deus, pátria e família: As mulheres no golpe de 1964*. Petrópolis: Vozes, 1985.

Singer, Hans, ed., *Celso Furtado, 1920–2004*. Special issue. *In Focus*, United Nations Development Program, April 2005.

Skar, Stacey D. "Engendering Violence in Roberto Athayde's *Apareceu a Margarida* and Plínio Marco's *Dois perdidos numa noite suja*." *Cincinnati Romance Review* 16 (1997): 55.

Skidmore, Thomas E. *The Politics of Military Rule in Brazil, 1964–85*. New York: Oxford University Press, 1988.

————. *Politics in Brazil, 1930–1964: An Experiment in Democracy*. 2nd ed. New York: Oxford University Press, 2007.

Smith, Christian. *Resisting Reagan: The U.S. Central American Peace Movement*. Chicago: University of Chicago Press, 1996.

Smith, Peter H. *Talons of the Eagle: Dynamics of U.S.–Latin American Relations*. New York: Oxford University Press, 1996.

Sohn, Louis B., and Thomas Buergenthal. *International Protection of Human Rights*. Indianapolis: Bobbs-Merrill Company, 1973.

Sorj, Bernardo. *A construção intelectual do Brasil contemporâneo: Da resistência à ditadura ao governo* FHC. Rio de Janeiro: Jorge Zahar Editor, 2001.

Starling, Heloísa Maria Murgel. *Os senhores das gerais: Os novos inconfidentes e o golpe militar de 1964*. Petrópolis: Vozes, 1987.

Stepan, Alfred. *The Military in Politics: Changing Patterns in Brazil*. Princeton, N.J.: Princeton University Press, 1971.

———, ed. *Authoritarian Brazil: Origins, Policies, and Future*. New Haven, Conn.: Yale University Press, 1973.

———, ed. *Democratizing Brazil: Problems of Transition and Consolidation*. New York: Oxford University Press, 1989.

Sydow, Evanize, and Marilda Ferri. *Dom Paulo Evaristo Arns: Um homem amado e perseguido*. Petrópolis: Editora Vozes, 1999.

Tota, Antônio Pedro. *O imperialismo sedutor: A americanização do Brasil na época da segunda guerra*. São Paulo: Companhia das Letras, 2000.

Trevisan, João Silvério. *Devassos no paraíso*. Rio de Janeiro: Editora Record, 2004.

Tuthill, John W. "Operation Topsy." *Foreign Policy* 8 (Autumn 1972): 62–85.

Tyson, Brady. "NACLA as Coalition." *NACLA Newsletter* 1, no. 2 (March 1967): 4.

Tytel, John. *The Living Theatre: Art, Exile, and Outrage*. New York: Grove Press, 1995.

Unruh, Vicky. "Language and Power in *Miss Margarida's Way* and *The Lesson*." *Latin American Literary Review* 14, no. 27 (January–June 1986): 126–35.

U.S. Congress. House. Subcommittee on Inter-American Affairs of the Committee on Foreign Affairs. *Directions for the 1970's: Toward a Strategy of Inter-American Development*. 91st Cong., 1st sess., 1969.

———. Committee on Foreign Affairs. *International Protection on Human Rights. The Work of International Organizations and the Role of U.S. Foreign Policy: Hearings before the Subcommittee on International Organizations and Movements of the Committee on Foreign Affairs*. 93rd Cong., 1st sess., August 1; September 13, 19, 20, 27; October 3, 4, 10, 11, 16, 18, 24, 25; November 1; December 7, 1973.

———. Subcommittee on International Organizations and Movements of the Committee on Foreign Affairs. *Torture and Oppression in Brazil*. 93rd Cong., 2nd sess., December 11, 1974.

———. Committee on International Relations. *Human Rights Practices in Countries Receiving U.S. Security Assistance*. 95th Cong., 1st sess., 1977.

U.S. Congress. Senate. Committee on Foreign Relations. *Nomination of Lincoln Gordon to be Assistant Secretary of State for Inter-American Affairs*. 89th Cong., 2nd sess., February 7, 1966.

———. American Institute for Free Labor Development. Hearing with George Meany, President, AFL-CIO, 91st Cong., 1st sess., August 1, 1969.

———. Committee on Foreign Relations, Subcommittee on Western Hemisphere Affairs. *United States Policies and Programs in Brazil: Hearing before the Subcommittee on Western Hemisphere Affairs of the Committee on Foreign Relations*. 92nd Cong., 1st sess., May 4, 5, 11, 1971.

Valle, Maria Ribeiro do. *1968: O diálogo é a violência: Movimento estudantil e ditadura militar no Brasil*. Campinas: Editora da UNICAMP, 1999.

Valli, Virginia. *Eu, Zuzu Angel: Procuro meu filho*. Rio de Janeiro: Record, 1987.

Veloso, Caetano. *Tropical Truth: A Story of Music and Revolution in Brazil*. Translated by Isabel de Sena. New York: Alfred A. Knopf, 2002.

Ventura, Zuenir. *1968—o ano que não terminou: A aventura de uma geração*. Rio de Janeiro: Círculo de Livros, 1988.

Vilarino, Ramon Casas. *A MPB em movimento: Música, festivais e censura*. São Paulo: Olha d'Agua, 1989.

Von der Weid, Jean Marc. *Brazil 1964 to the Present: A Political Analysis*. Montreal: Editions Latin America, 1972.

Walters, Vernon A. *Silent Missions*. New York: Doubleday, 1978.

Weffort, Francisco. "Participação e conflito industrial: Contagem e Osasco, 1968." *Cadernos do CEBRAP*, no. 5 (1972).

Weis, W. Michael. "Government News Management, Bias and Distortion in American Press Coverage of the Brazilian Coup of 1964." *Social Science Journal* 34, no.1 (1997): 35–55.

Welch, Cliff. "Labor Internationalism: U.S. Involvement in Brazilian Unions, 1945–1965." *Latin American Research Review* 30, no. 2 (1995): 61–90.

Weschler, Lawrence. *A Miracle, a Universe: Settling Accounts with Torturers*. Chicago: University of Chicago Press, 1990.

Wipfler, William L., "The Price of 'Progress' in Brazil." *Christianity and Crisis*, March 16, 1970, 44–48.

———. "'Progress' in Brazil Revisited." *Christianity and Crisis*, October 6, 1986, 345–48.

Woll, Allen L. *The Latin Image in American Film*. Los Angeles: UCLA Latin American Center, 1977.

Woodhouse, C. M. *The Rise and Fall of the Greek Colonels*. London: Granada, 1985.

Wright, Thomas C., and Rody Oate Zúñiga. "Chilean Political Exile." *Latin American Perspectives* 34, no. 4 (July 2007): 31–49.

Zaroulis, Nancy, and Gerald Sullivan. *Who Spoke Up? American Protest against the War in Vietnam, 1963-1975*. New York: Holt, Rinehart, Winston, 1984.

Zappa, Regina. *Chico Buarque: Para todos*. Rio de Janeiro: Relume Dumará, 1999.

Zeichner, Natan. "Representing the Vanguard." *Brown Journal of History* (spring 2007): 7–23.

Zweig, Stefan. *Brazil: Land of the Future*. Translated by Andrew St. James. London: Cassell, 1942.

### Films and DVDs

*Black Orpheus*. 1958. Janus Films.

*Brazil: No Time for Tears*. 1971. Universidad de Chile; Tricontinental Films.

*Brazil: A Report on Torture*. 1971. Cinema Guild; Dove Films.

*Chico Buarque vai passar*. 2005. EMI DVD.

*O que é isso, companheiro?* (Four Days in September). 1997. Columbia Tristar.

*O Sol—caminando contra o vento*. 2006. Venver.

*Zuzu Angel*. 2006. Globo Films.

## Music

"Agora falando sério." Chico Buarque, 1969.
"Angélica." Miltinho and Chico Buarque, 1977.
"Apesar de você." Chico Buarque, 1970.
"Aquele abraço." Gilberto Gil, 1969.
"Os Argonautas." Caetano Veloso, 1969.
"Canção do subdesenvolvido." Carlos Lyra and Francisco de Assis, 1962.
"Fado tropical." Chico Buarque, Ruy Guerra, 1972–73.
"Garota de Ipanema." Music by Antônio Carlos "Tom" Jobim, lyrics by Vinicius Moraes, 1962.
"Girl from Ipanema." Lyrics by Norman Gimbel, 1964.
"London, London." Caetano Veloso, 1970.
"Opinião." Zé Keti, 1964.
"Para dizer que não falei de flores." Geraldo Vandré, 1968.
"A Rita." Chico Buarque, 1965.
"Roda viva." Chico Buarque, 1967.
"Samba de Orly." Chico Buarque, Vinicius de Moraes, Toquino.
"Tristeza." Haroldo Lobo and Niltinho, 1966.

## Musicals, Performances, Plays, and Programs

Athayde, Roberto. *Apareceu a Margarida*. Brasília: Editora Brasília, 1973.
————. *Miss Margarida's Way: Tragicomic Monologue for an Impetuous Woman*. New York: Samuel French, 1977.
*Arena conta Zumbi* Program. New York, 1969 production.
Guarnieri, Gianfranceso, and Augusto Boal, music Edu Lobo. *Arena conta Zumbi*, *Revista do Teatro* (Rio de Janeiro) 378 (November/December 1970): 31–59.
Hampton, Christopher. *Savages*. London: Samuel French, 1974.
Latin American Fair of Opinion Program. New York, 1972 production.
Living Theater. "Seven Meditations on Political Sado-Masochism." *Fag Rag* (Boston) (fall–winter 1973): 13–20.
*Miss Margarida's Way*. Playbill, 1990.

# INDEX

communism: armed struggle and, 330–31; coup of 1964 and, 4; death squads and, 108–9; domino theory and, 20–21; exile and, 343; illegality of, 35, 56, 99–100; inside U.S., 59; kidnappings and, 217; left and, 15–17; Maoist, 17; media portrayal of, 38–40; political asylum and, 170; political prisoners and, 145, 287–88; pro-Soviet, 17; repression of, 217; as scapegoat, 7, 214; U.S. foreign policy and, 23–31, 37–38, 43, 67

Communist Party of Brazil, 16–17, 35, 53, 56, 59, 86–87, 125, 134, 140, 145, 217, 327, 330, 343, 399 n. 77, 368 n. 8

Community Action on Latin America (CALA), 288, 329, 396 n. 7

companies, foreign, 3, 14, 35, 50, 82, 266, 311, 349–52; U.S., 5, 35, 38, 108, 247, 262, 266, 322, 344, 350–51, 375 n. 52

Conceição, Manoel de, xi

Congress of Cultural Freedom, 129

Congress of Industrial Organizations (CIO), 351

Conn, Harry, 32

Conselho Nacional de Mulheres (National Council of Women), 304

Constitution, Brazilian, 15, 21–22, 31, 43, 50–51, 56–58, 92, 94, 96, 98, 140–41, 148, 162, 165–66, 210, 235, 274, 281, 286, 357; Chilean, 325; U.S., 98

Coordinating Committee on Latin America, 109

corporations, U.S. multinational, 5, 35, 38, 108, 247, 262, 266, 322, 344, 350–51, 375 n. 52. See also companies, foreign

Corrêa, José Celso Martinez, 269

Correio da Manhã, 40–41, 138

Costa, Emilía Viotti da, 172–73, 387 n. 15, 387 n. 16

Costa, Octávio Pereira da, 210–11, 214–15

Costa e Silva, Artur, 57, 74, 86–89, 91–92, 95–98, 103–6, 123–25, 127–28, 140–41, 147, 207, 214, 234–36, 288, 304, 373 n. 4, 294 n. 29

Costa e Silva, Yolanda, 304

counterculture, 78, 80, 283

Country Analysis and Strategy Paper (CASP), 87, 103

Couto e Silva, Golbery do, 97, 103, 344

Crahan, Margaret, 67, 178, 181, 184–86, 374 n. 31

Crawford, Joan, 304

Croissance de Jeunes Nations, 155

Cruzeiro, O, 141

Cuban Resource Center, 257, 264, 396 n. 7

Cuban Revolution, 2, 3, 15, 20, 26, 59–62, 65, 68, 75, 87, 140, 199

cultural freedom, 117, 124, 129

Cummins Engine, 241

Cunningham, Bill, 305

Cushing, Richard Cardinal, 28–29

D'Agnino, Evelina, 174

Dassin, Joan, 345, 358

Davis, Shelton H. (Sandy), 282–83, 313, 344

Declaration of Independence, U.S., 46

Dedijer, Vladimir, 278

Delfim Netto, Antônio, 94–95

Della Cava, Ralph, 66, 133–34, 151, 156–58, 165–66, 179, 181, 186, 195, 239–40, 265, 331, 344–46, 358, 363, 374 n. 31

Dellums, Ron, 233, 248–53, 279

democracy, Brazilian: 4, 19, 22–23, 25, 36, 38, 39, 44, 47, 55, 58, 67, 73–74, 78, 88, 93, 97–98, 100–102, 105, 110, 119, 121, 140, 148, 154, 165, 179, 190, 200, 210, 213, 215–16, 221, 226, 235, 277, 279, 324, 332, 335, 340, 344–46, 356–57; Chilean, 260, 322, 333; Greek, 145, 273; Latin American, 20, 27, 37, 237, 242, 273, 321, 324; racial, 173, 295; U.S., 11, 106, 117, 162, 316; Western, 117, 273

Democrats, U.S., 64, 74, 234, 250, 324

Departamento de Ordem Política e Social (DOPS), 190–91

Departamento Estadual de Ordem Política e Social (DEOPS), 65, 199–200, 227, 336, 374 n. 22. See also police, political

Nonviolent Training and Action Center, 110

North American Congress on Latin America (NACLA), 68–70, 263–64, 373 n. 21, 375 n. 52

Novak, Kim, 304

Novitski, Joseph, 116, 212

nuclear nonproliferation, 347

nuns, 29, 146, 155, 162, 217, 257, 360–61, 394 n. 4

Nutels, Noel, 282

Oblates of the Mary Immaculate Order, 99

Ochs, Phil, 4

Oliveira, Hélio Louenço de, 126

Oliveira, Miguel Darcy de, 139, 151, 166

Oliveira, Rosiska Darcy de, 139, 151

Onis, Juan de, 72–73

Ono, Yoko, 270

Operation Bandeirante, 227–28

Operation Brother Sam, 36, 45–47

Operation Pan America, 25

Operation Topsy, 74

"Opinião," 197

O Que é isso, companheiro (Four Days in September), 229

Ordem dos Advogados do Brazil (Brazilian Bar Association; OAB), 52, 332, 347

Orfeu negro (Black Orpheus), 2, 67

Organization of American States (OAS), 26–27, 62, 101, 162, 203–10, 217–23, 247–48, 278, 330, 402 n. 35

Oswald, Lee Harvey, 187

Ouro Preto, 269

Oxford University, 282

Pacem in Terris, 16

Pacote de Abril (April Package), 348

Padillha, Anivaldo, 17, 34, 170, 175, 225–32, 268, 281, 313, 322, 341–42, 356, 361, 363–64

Paes, Márcia Bassetto, 336

Paiva, Leonel, 137

Papal Volunteers, 28, 48

Papp, Joseph, 338

Paradise Defense Fund, 269

Parker, Phyllis R., 44–46

parrot's perch, xvi, 41, 165, 170, 200, 261, 273, 307–11, 336

Parsons, Estelle, 338–40

Partido Democrático Social (PDS), 349

Partido Democrático Trabalhista (PDT), 349

Partido do Movimento Democrático Brasileiro (PMDB), 349

Partido dos Trabalhadores (PT), 349

Partido Operário Revolucionário (Trostskista), POR(T), 198–200

Partido Trabalhista Brasileiro (PTB), 3, 21

Passarinho, Jarbas, 215, 219–20

Passman, Otto, 393 n. 7

Pastor, Robert, 337

Paul VI, Pope, 109, 155, 180, 203

Peace Corps, 28, 30, 48, 68, 70, 72, 262, 351, 370 n. 43, 386 n. 51

Peace Movement, 109, 112

Peasant Leagues, 15, 25–26, 35, 61

peasants, 3, 13, 15, 25–26, 35, 37, 61, 71, 81, 155, 266, 396 n. 4

Pedagogy of the Oppressed, 321

Pedrosa, Maria Regina, 139

Pedrosa, Mario, 118, 139, 151, 153

Peláez, Carlos, 176, 187–89, 191–95, 388 n. 25

PEN International, 299

Pentagon, 3, 46, 61, 244, 256, 322

Pereira, Anthony W., 135

Pereira, Domício, 150, 202

Pereira Neto, Antônio Henrique, 108–11, 155, 203, 209

Peru Information Group, 396 n. 7

Petras, James, 181, 329

Phillips Petroleum, 241

Pinheiro, Paulo Sergio, 194

Pinochet, Augusto, 5, 222, 322–23, 326, 328, 363, 404 n. 3

Pinto, Magalães, 102–3, 235

Pirelli, 348

Pius XII, Pope, 15

Playbill, 339–40

police: Amnesty Law and, 357–58; censorship and, 339; Chilean, 322–23; communists and, 40; death squads and, 111; disappeared prisoners and, 346; false arrests and, 5; human rights groups and, 272, 337; media and, 160, 212, 219; military, 42, 165; secret, 126–27, 130; stations, 136, 298; student protests and, 52, 79–80, 89–91; torture and, 139, 149, 152; U.S. congressional hearings and, 244–47, 251; U.S. training of, 8, 32–33, 87, 161, 180–82, 267, 372 n. 1. *See also* human rights; torture

police, political, 50, 53, 81, 190; archives, 65, 199, 227–29; killing of prisoners and, 200, 204–7, 330–32; power to detain and, 336; torture and, 208–9. *See also* human rights

*Political Policing*, 32, 180, 245

political rights, 23, 56, 58, 102–3, 166, 171, 184, 234–35, 332

*Political System of Brazil*, 283

*Politics in Brazil, 1930–1964*, 283

*Politics of Military Rule in Brazil*, 82

Pol Pot, 339

Pontifical Committee for Peace and Justice, 243

Portinari, Cândido, 20

Pottlitzer, Joanne, 294–95, 299, 400 n. 1, 401 n. 13

poverty, 17, 20–21, 25–26, 28, 48, 70, 91, 111, 113, 159–60, 256, 280, 312, 361

Power, Timothy J., 335, 347

Prado, Yolanda, 133

Prado Júnior, Caio, 125–26, 133–36, 158, 178, 189, 192

"Pra não dizer que não falei das flores," 77

Prebisch, Raul, 129

Presbyterians, 15, 150, 158, 232, 331, 346, 385 n. 20

Presbyterian Theological Seminary, 15

press, Brazilian: censorship and, 104, 110, 112, 148; editorial pages, 96, 134; government news service, 211; intimidation of, 330; national press law and, 57, 206

press, international: management of, 217; National Information Service and, 149;

National Security Act and, 212; use of, 153–55, 269

press, U.S.: alternative, 284–85; editorials, 97, 156–57, 160–61; fear of, 275; Institutional act No. 5 and, 92; Johnson administration and, 3; management of, 38–40, 211–23; reliability of, 266; torture reports and, 178, 209, 299–300, 302, 306

Press Law, Brazilian, 57, 96, 206

Prestes, Luís Carlos, 343

priests, Catholic, 15–16, 28–29, 66, 81, 99, 100, 108–10, 146, 155, 159, 162, 165, 203, 217, 240, 243, 256, 262, 281; priest-workers, 15, 81

Prince, Harold, 299

Princeton University, 61, 158, 342, 407 n. 98

Project Camelot, 68, 375 n. 40

Protestant ministers, 15–16, 64, 113, 150, 231, 325–31, 346, 361

public opinion: Brazilian, 43; international, 5, 153, 159, 181, 208, 270, 282, 311, 364; U.S., 9–10, 59, 63, 95–96, 147, 185, 202, 308, 313, 364

public relations, 6, 62, 87, 210–17

public security, 33, 190

Quadros, Jânio, 3, 15, 20–21, 33, 38, 56, 61, 214, 368 n. 5

Quakers, 110, 326

Quartim, João, 283, 399 n. 77, 400 n. 80

Quigley, Tom, 195, 206, 253, 271, 324

Rabe, Steven C., 74

race, 113, 156, 173, 256, 295

Rademaker, Augusto, 147–48

Radical Caucus, 180

Ramalho, Jether Pereira, 150, 166, 202

Ramalho, Lucília, 150

Ramos, Jovelino, 15–17, 34, 52–54, 150, 170, 174–75, 341–42, 385 n. 20

Ramos, Myra, 15, 52

Rand Corporation, 240

*Reader's Digest*, 39, 380–81, 364, 371 n. 80

Reagan, Ronald, 6, 365

239–48; Foreign Relations Committee, 63, 73, 74, 135, 209, 223, 235, 239, 243, 309, 316–17, 394 n. 29; human rights and, 8, 162–63; military aid and, 248–51, 253, 273, 279; repression in Brazil and, 233–40; Subcommittee on Western Hemisphere Affairs and, 238, 274

U.S. Supreme Court, 131

Universal Declaration of Human Rights, 144, 286

Universidade Estadual de Campinas, 194

Universidade Federal de Minas Gerais, 130

Universidade Federal de Pernambuco, 125

Universidade Federal do Rio de Janeiro, 16, 50, 150, 292

University Christian Movement, 68–69

University of Brasilia, 91, 245, 336

University of California, Berkeley, 53, 71, 268, 386 n. 51

University of California, Los Angeles, 407 n. 86

University of California, Riverside, 70

University of Chicago, 126, 341

University of Córdoba, 339

University of Florida, 407 n. 98

University of Illinois, 172

University of Michigan, 27, 63

University of Montana, 162, 238

University of Notre Dame, 346

University of Paris, 171

University of São Paulo, 7, 17, 69, 126–29, 131, 133, 171–72, 198, 226, 331, 336, 345

University of South Carolina, 173

University of Texas, 44, 63, 264, 407

University of Wisconsin, Madison, 158, 278, 288, 329

USAID (U.S. Agency for International Development), 30–33, 36, 56, 86, 99, 127, 161, 172, 181, 186, 188, 234, 236, 242–46, 272

Valente, Mozart Gurgel, 161

Vanderbilt University, 186–87, 193, 241

Vandré, Geraldo, 77–79

Vargas, Getúlio, 14, 21, 51

Vatican, 28, 146, 155–56, 203–4; Vatican II, 16, 111–12

*Veja* (magazine), 137, 149, 175, 344

Veloso, Caetano, 78, 81, 116, 133, 168–69, 255, 257, 291

Venice International Art Exhibition, 117

Ventura, Zuenir, 78

*Verdade tropical*, 116

Vianna, Marcos, 347

Victory Fund, Latin American, 29

"Victory March," 51

Vietnam War, 4, 6, 11, 20, 43, 48, 58, 63, 71, 75, 83, 110, 120, 178, 187, 234, 236, 246, 254, 257, 264, 278, 322, 330, 362; opposition to, 5, 59, 66, 72, 78, 109, 193, 250, 255–56, 267, 284, 329, 366, 375 n. 54

*Village Voice*, 307

Von der Weid, Jean Marc, 51–52, 54, 79, 104, 153, 261, 278–79, 323, 356, 360–61, 364, 372 n. 2, 398 n. 60, 405 n. 31

Von der Weid, Regina, 51–52, 54, 342

Wagley, Charles, 66, 127, 156, 158, 182–83, 275, 321, 333, 374 n. 31, 382 n. 38, 407 n. 98

Wald, George, 329

*Wall Street Journal*, 212, 391 n. 36

Walters, Vernon, 33–34, 36, 45, 62, 378 n. 38

Warhol, Andy, 270

Washington Office on Latin America (WOLA), 325–26, 329

*Washington Post*, 96, 103, 139, 159–61, 181, 202, 212, 215, 219, 221, 239, 268, 271, 275–77, 308, 361, 364, 378 n. 38, 379 n. 66

Washington University, 173, 342

Watergate scandal, 254, 275, 324

Weis, Michael, 39

"We Shall Overcome," 78

Wesleyan University, 173

Wexler, Haskell, 275, 260, 262, 272, 275, 278, 358

Wheaton, Philip, 324, 373 n. 21

*White Book*, 209, 210, 217

James N. Green is a professor of history and
Brazilian studies at Brown University.

Library of Congress Cataloging-in-Publication Data
Green, James Naylor
We cannot remain silent: opposition to the Brazilian
military dictatorship in the United States / James N. Green.
p. cm. — (Radical perspectives)
Includes bibliographical references and index.
ISBN 978-0-8223-4717-0 (cloth : alk. paper)
ISBN 978-0-8223-4735-4 (pbk. : alk. paper)
1. Brazil—History—Revolution, 1964—Foreign public
opinion. 2. Brazil—Politics and government—1964–1985.
3. Dictatorship—Brazil—History—20th century.
4. United States—Relations—Brazil.
5. Brazil—Relations—United States.
I. Title. II. Series: Radical perspectives.
F2523.G74 2010
981.06′3—dc22 2010000606